WRISTWATCH AN

2014

THE CATALOG

of

PRODUCERS, PRICES, MODELS,

and

SPECIFICATIONS

BY PETER BRAUN

ABBEVILLE PRESS PUBLISHERS

New York   London

Our spirit of excellence.

www.glashuette-original.com

Senator Chronometer Regulator. Aesthetics, elegance and precision. An officially certified chronometer combined with the class display of a regulator. The dominant position is taken by the minute hand at the center, while the other hands are smaller an

Glashütte
ORIGINAL

German Watchmaking Art since *1845*.

Contents

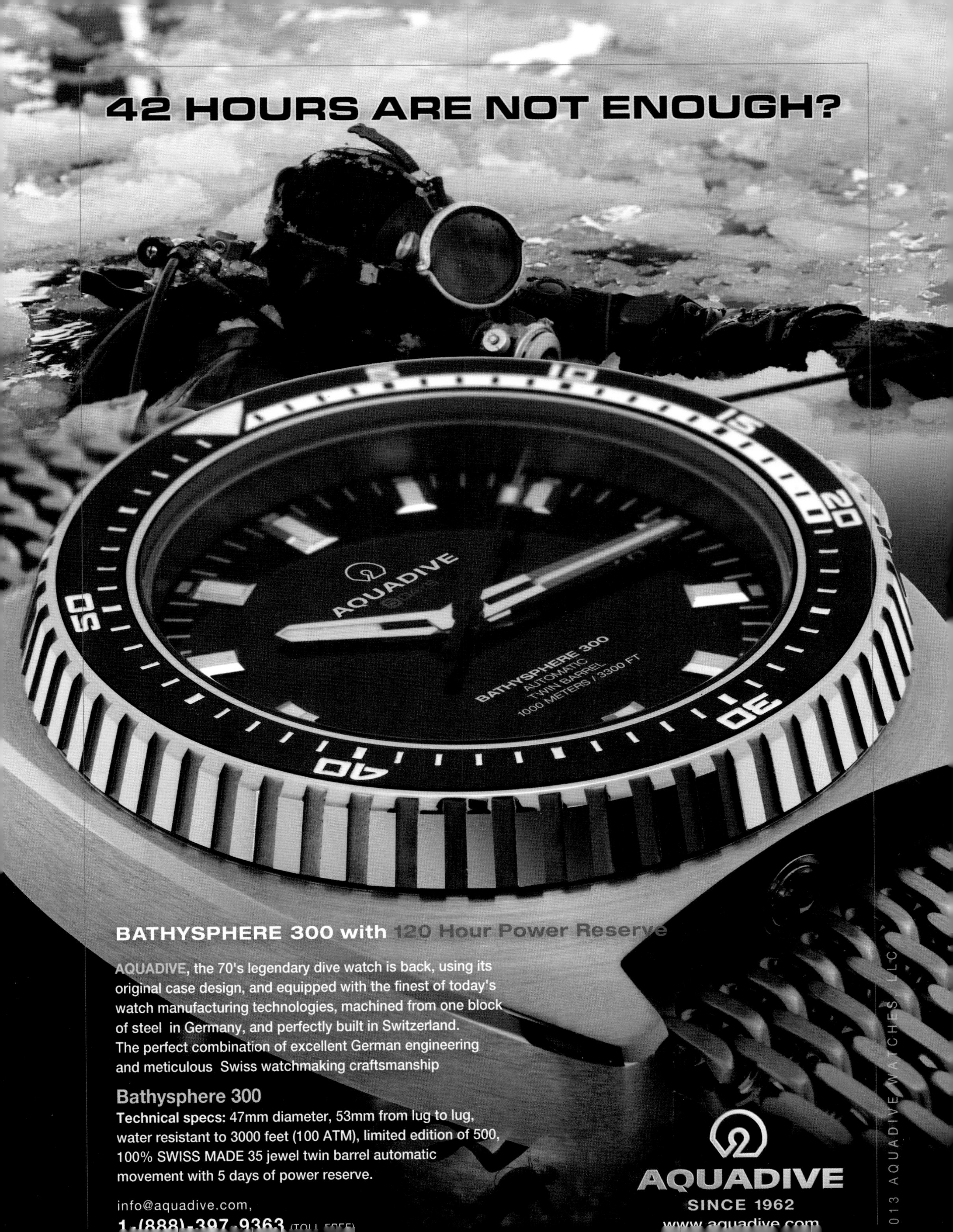

42 HOURS ARE NOT ENOUGH?

BATHYSPHERE 300 with 120 Hour Power Reserve

AQUADIVE, the 70's legendary dive watch is back, using its original case design, and equipped with the finest of today's watch manufacturing technologies, machined from one block of steel in Germany, and perfectly built in Switzerland. The perfect combination of excellent German engineering and meticulous Swiss watchmaking craftsmanship

Bathysphere 300

Technical specs: 47mm diameter, 53mm from lug to lug, water resistant to 3000 feet (100 ATM), limited edition of 500, 100% SWISS MADE 35 jewel twin barrel automatic movement with 5 days of power reserve.

info@aquadive.com,
1-(888)-397-9363 (TOLL FREE)

AQUADIVE
SINCE 1962
www.aquadive.com

RGM
WATCH COMPANY

America's Premier Watchmaker

American Made
Caliber 801 Aircraft.

RGM Watch Co.
801 W.Main Street Mount Joy, Penna 17552 USA
tel. 717-653-9799
www.RGMwatches.com

Dear Reader,

In spite of large fortunes spent on market research, the true wellspring of individual taste remains something of a mystery. First of all, it is personal and hence subject to the vagaries of upbringing and cultural and social environments. Second, it can be affected by all sorts of external factors, some controllable, like brand communication, but most uncontrollable, like the economy. This may explain why a sort of back-to-the-roots movement has been making its way through the watch industry. Rather than producing lots of stuff for idealized consumers, many brands have started looking carefully at their own lineage and putting out more organic pieces.

And why not? The industry as a whole is in good shape and can afford to evade the constraints of "target groups." That must be a relief after the somewhat obsequious enthusiasm for Chinese consumers who, over the past years, have become fairly cosmopolitan in their taste. Besides, the world is a big place, and there is still some horologically virgin territory to conquer.

So in Switzerland, where watchmaking accounts for many well-paying jobs, the brands have been focusing on their capacities, recruiting frantically, and coming up with plans and strategies to train a new generation of workers. In 2013, for the first time the number of people employed in the industry has topped the 1974 figure, that is, before the "quartz crisis."

But the sword of Damocles of the past recession still hangs, and that has led to a changing landscape. Some companies, like Cartier or Ulysse Nardin, continue to verticalize by increasing their portfolio of in-house movements. There is also the monobrand boutique phenomenon to enhance the customer experience and concentrate communication. Other brands are terminating models that have turned into dust collectors or closing doors or "streamlining" their distribution. Increasingly, groups are growing or forming for protection and synergies. And from the halls of the SIHH and GTE in January to the vast spaces of Baselworld, one hears the words "classic," "conservative," vintage," "DNA."

In terms of external communication, brands have to be careful to avoid seeming patronizing or fawning. The key may be in an observation from the past. In his *Essay On Taste*, the eighteenth-century French writer and philosopher Montesquieu tried to describe what "our soul" likes: symmetry, for one thing, "because it is spared pain, it soothes it, it cuts its work in half," and surprises for another, because the new is exciting. And, he writes elsewhere, there is the "invisible charm, a natural indefinable gracefulness that we have been forced to call a *je ne sais quoi*." For the watch brands, this translates as an exhortation to create and surprise and above all be authentic.

Watch Colors

The rest is a question of continuing to do quality work, avoiding corner-cutting, and setting the bar high. In digging

through their attics, metaphorically speaking, watchmakers have rediscovered the potential in the so-called *métiers d'art*, crafts like enameling or marquetry. Some brands still overwhelm with precious stones, while others use them as subtle spices. Across the board, though, colors have been edging out the bling. From the Tondo by de Grisogono to the Artist's Collection of Chronoswiss, passing by Baume & Mercier's collection of straps and ArtyA's phenomenal creative explosions, visual exuberance is on the rise. At times that means just a touch of red on a dusky background; at others it allows for striking objects priced in the four-digit segment, which has been gaining ground in our more austere times.

This edition of *Wristwatch Annual*, as every edition, tries to do justice to the aesthetic and technical happenings in the industry. The future comes first: Elizabeth Doerr (p. 12) gives us an expert summary of the independent scene, with such avant-garde pieces as the Type 3 from Ressence or HYT's second model. In our A-to-Z section, you will find many old friends and some new ones. Rolex's own Tudor has returned to the United States with its own fan club. Juvenia, too, is making a comeback in the Occident after spending time in Asia. And we welcome two outstanding independents, Christiaan van der Klaauw and Peter Speake-Marin, who join such brands as Christophe Claret, Urwerk, Maîtres du Temps, and MB&F. U.S. brands continue to be well represented, with new selections from Kobold, RGM, and Montana.

Our resident watchmaker Bill Yao, CEO of Mk II, is back this year to explore crowns (p. 252). Watching out for your watch is the subject of the Dos and Don'ts at the end of the book (p. 374), just before the Glossary. Mavericks and

Masters (p. 26) looks at some special pieces, such as a watch to save lives and, slipped in right before going to press, MB&F's much-anticipated Legacy Machine No. 2. Finally, there is more to fakes than just a low price (p. 22)! *Wristwatch Annual* would not be possible without the help of the contributors mentioned above and many others. My thanks, therefore, go to Peter Braun for his preparation of the German edition. Many thanks, too, to Ashley Benning for meticulously proofing the English copy, catching many errors, and keeping perfect order in hundreds of files. Please note that all prices given are subject to change. Any comments or suggestions are welcome, as they will help us improve the book next year. In the meantime, enjoy reading.

Peter Braun

Marton Radkai

The cover of this year's edition of Wristwatch Annual *sports the* Engineer Hydrocarbon Airborne *by Ball Watch. This COSC-certified chronometer was designed for rugged types. It is antimagnetic to 4,800 A/m, water-resistant to 12 atm, and shock-resistant to 5,000 Gs thanks to the patented SpringLOCK antishock system. Gaseous tritium illumination ensures permanent legibility in dark conditions, and the crown features a patented protector. The hour, minute, second, and day and date functions are driven by the automatic ETA 2836-2.*

Ball's patented SpringLOCK system.

TIME INSTRUMENTS

WW1 RÉGULATEUR Pink Gold · Limited Edition to 99 pieces
Bell & Ross Inc. +1.888.307.7887 · information@bellrossusa.com · e-Boutique: www.bellross.com

Independent Watchmaking
Elizabeth Doerr

This past year was a very good one for independent watchmakers with a number of highly provocative launches that drew the international spotlight.

Perhaps the most anticipated launch of all was that of **Vianney Halter's** new timepiece, which represented a real departure from his previous classically inclined (yet steampunk-style) work. His three-dimensional masterpiece christened Deep Space Tourbillon is more an exploration of space than an explanation of time. Arising from a deep personal need for expression, the focal point of this timepiece is a central triple-axis tourbillon that revolves at respective speeds of thirty minutes, six minutes, and forty seconds. The time (secondary to the expression of art according to Halter) is read from the peripheral scale using blued hands that follow the curvature of the highly domed sapphire crystal. The manually wound movement is barely visible below the tourbillon crossbar, further enhancing the 46 mm titanium timepiece's deliberate resemblance to the *Deep Space Nine* docking station. "I wanted to explore a new style instead of carrying on with the Futur Antérieur (Past Future), with which I had been successful with models such as the Antiqua, the Trio, and the Classic in the past," he explains. "And I decided to use the tourbillon—especially the triple axis tourbillon—as a kind of kinetic sculpture that is likely to translate the conceptual idea of the three dimensions of Euclidean space, surrounded by the fourth dimension (time)."

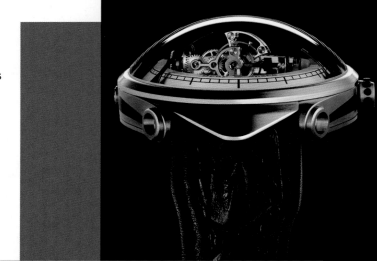

Vianney Halter's Deep Space Tourbillon, a kinetic sculpture for the wrist.

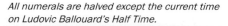

All numerals are halved except the current time on Ludovic Ballouard's Half Time.

It's Magic

Ludovic Ballouard has also had a great year. Not only was he the watchmaker behind Harry Winston's celebrated Opus XIII, but he also launched his own Half Time, which operates on a concept similar to his previous Upside Down: The numerals on the dial are cut in half (and thus illegible)—except the one showing the current hour. The illusion remains complete as the numerals (in contrast to those of the Upside Down) appear to be on one solid plane with the rest of the dial, and thus immobile. Housed in a 41 mm case of platinum or red gold, the playful Half Time is available only in a 300-piece limited edition.

The Ressence Type 3 by Benoît Mintiens uses magnets and special fluids to tell time.

Another magic timepiece was launched by **Ressence** this year: The Type 3, nicknamed Le Scaphandrier, takes the boutique brand's "platform watch" to a new level, boasting a highly curved sapphire crystal filled with a naphtha-type fluid that refracts light just like air. The result is white time indications that appear to be projected directly onto the sapphire crystal, almost like a black screen. Housed within a 44 mm titanium case with no crown and no hands, the automatic movement is physically sealed from the liquid-filled platform, and the indications are moved using magnets.

Fantastically, this was also the year **Romain Gauthier** decided to introduce his third timepiece and second movement in the powerful Logical One. The name of this watch reflects the thought process leading him to its creation. "Coming from an engineering background, it appeared strange to me to have a high-precision machine forced to run at varying power levels," he says of the standard mechanical movement's mainspring. "So I started with the premise that it would be better to have constant energy." This was achieved with a chain-and-fusée style constant force system, which compensates for the diminishing torque (and thus energy) of the mainspring as it runs down. Other elements include Gauthier's patent-pending chain links made of synthetic ruby; an ergonomic push-button winding system instead of a winding crown that transmits energy in a more logical manner; and a mainspring barrel with synthetic sapphire inserts in addition to a whole world of minute, commonsense details. Logical One is housed in a 43 mm 18-karat red gold or platinum case.

Synthetic ruby chains and a push button for winding belie the classic look of Romain Gauthier's Logical One.

Newly on the Scene

English master watchmaker **Peter Roberts,** a new figure on the independent stage, sought to create a timepiece that had been germinating inside him for decades. Back in the 1970s, an instructor at WOSTEP told him that he'd never seen a watch with more than four centrally located hands—a statement that naturally propelled Roberts to achieve it in 1972. The Grand Complication 5 is the serial result a good four decades later. Having found a cache of new-old stock Valjoux 88 movements, Roberts launched a series of forty-four pieces housed in 42 mm stainless steel and bronze and four in rose and white gold; the number

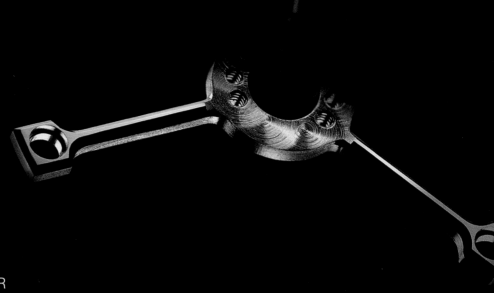

TO BREAK THE RULES, YOU MUST FIRST MASTER THEM.

IN 1986, AUDEMARS PIGUET BECAME THE FIRST WATCHMAKER TO FEATURE A TOURBILLON IN AN AUTOMATIC WRIST WATCH. TODAY THE TRADITION TOURBILLON REPETITION MINUTE IS OUR LATEST EXPRESSION OF THIS PIONEERING SPIRIT.

THE TOURBILLON COUNTERACTS THE EFFECT OF GRAVITY ON THE MOVEMENT'S MOST DELICATE COMPONENTS. THE ASSEMBLY OF ITS EXCEPTIONALLY LIGHT AND COMPLEX ELEMENTS IS A FORMIDABLE CHALLENGE THAT TAKES A MASTER WATCHMAKER THREE DAYS TO EXECUTE ENTIRELY BY HAND.

HOWEVER EVEN AT THIS MICRO SCALE, THE ARMS OF THE CAGE ARE CHAMFERED AND POLISHED. THE SPIRIT OF AUDEMARS PIGUET EXPRESSED IN EVERY DETAIL.

AUDEMARS PIGUET
Le Brassus

TRADITION
IN PINK AND WHITE GOLD.
TOURBILLON MINUTE REPEATER
AND CHRONOGRAPH.

AUDEMARS PIGUET BOUTIQUES. 646.375.0807
NEW YORK: 65 EAST 57TH STREET, NY. 888.214.6858
BAL HARBOUR: BAL HARBOUR SHOPS, FL. 866.595.9700
AUDEMARSPIGUET.COM

represents each of the four decades that have passed since Roberts made his first *concentrique*. "We had been searching for these movements for years," he reveals. The five hands emanating from the center of the dial display the time (hours, minutes, seconds), a chronograph (seconds, minutes, and hour totalizers), and a second time zone/24-hour indicator. Additionally, the watch is outfitted with a full calendar and moon phase displayed in subsidiary windows. The movement is a hand-finished, manually wound integrated chronograph with forty-six hours of power reserve.

Spero Lucem, a new brand spearheaded by Yvan Arpa (previously of Romain Jerome and currently behind ArtyA), debuted at Baselworld with an interesting, manually wound, 44 mm, red gold or titanium timepiece called La Clémence that not only includes a complicated chiming function, but also carries a rock-and-roll feel to it. And it boasts something no other watch has: a tourbillon and a new function called "crazy hands." When the time begins to chime, the hands leave their proper time-displaying positions, only to return when the chiming stops.

Out There

HYT, headed by Vincent Perriard, specializes in what it calls hydromechanical watchmaking. The debut of the H1 made quite a splash—no pun intended—at Baselworld 2012. This year, the company released the H2, which features additional elements such as retrograde hours, a minute hand that jumps across the movement's bellows

Sweep time – Peter Roberts' Grande Complication 5 manages functional central five hands.

The Spero Lucem reveals Yvan Arpa as a master of strict watchmaking as well.

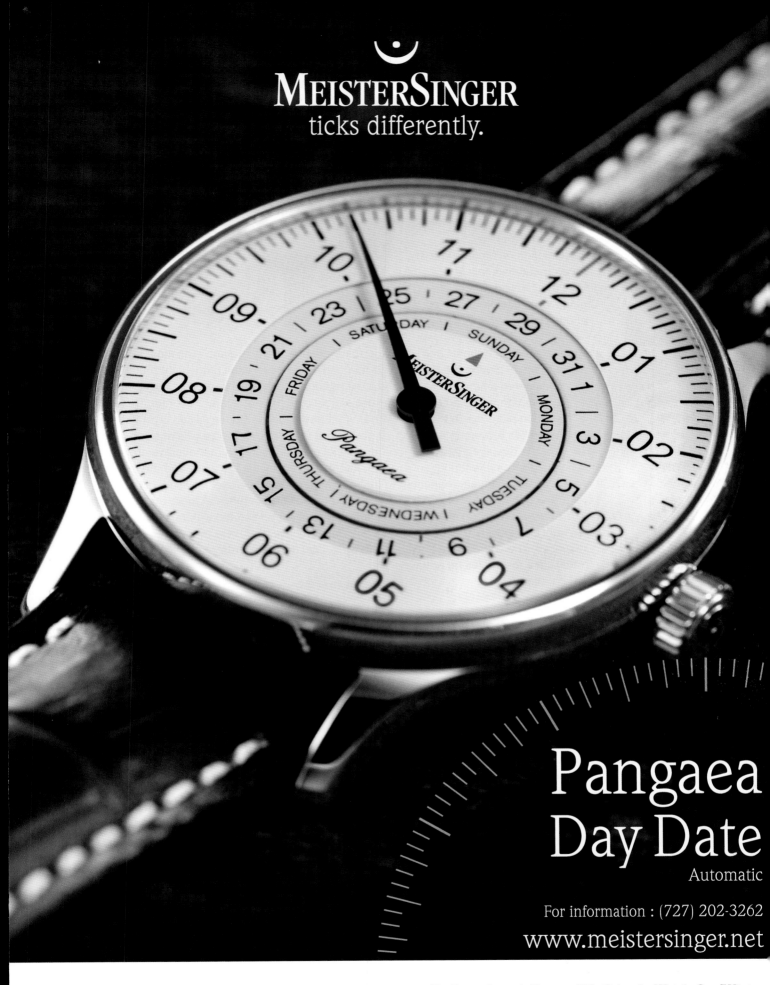

after thirty minutes, a temperature gauge for the fluid, and a crown position indicator (T, N, and W). The latter tells the user whether the crown is positioned to set the time, wind the manual movement (with an eight-day power reserve), or is simply in neutral. Titanium bridges with a black PVD coating visible within a 48.8 mm black DLC-coated, titanium case make it light to wear and contemporary to look at.

The wizards of horological hydraulics, HYT, pimp up their 2012 bestseller with fresh complications.

Russian independent watchmaker **Konstantin Chaykin,** who always comes up with stunning complications, produced the spellbinding Cinema Watch this year. It contains the first animation complication ever in a mechanical watch. The Cinema Watch commemorates photographer and inventor Eadweard Muybridge, whose serial shots of animals and humans in motion are considered a fundamental element in the invention of motion pictures. The watch uses two movements: one for the timekeeping and one for the animation, which is manually launched and depicts a small movie of a galloping horse and rider using twelve images per second. The square stainless steel case resembles an antique camera; the dial suggests a lens.

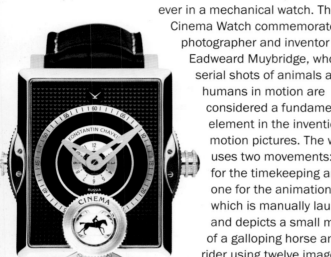

Classically Different

Andreas Strehler presented a new watch at Baselworld that carries the name Sauterelle. Astute aficionados will recognize this name from an ill-fated Chronoswiss timepiece that was announced but never launched. Indeed, Strehler had given the name—which he registered in 2008—to Chronoswiss's Gerd-Rüdiger Lang, but has now taken it back to use for this latest timepiece, which boasts constant force using a *remontoir d'égalité*. This visible satellite gear ensures that the escape wheel receives the same amount of energy once per second, resulting in a much more accurate wristwatch. The name Sauterelle (French for grasshopper) was chosen for the movements the *remontoir* makes. Strehler, by the way, also released his new Cocon wristwatch at Baselworld.

Urban Jürgensen chose Baselworld 2013 to bring out a wristwatch in honor of its own 240-year tradition of enameled dials: The Montre Observatoire Email is powered by the extraordinary P8 detent escapement caliber, which is the first detent escapement made plausible for a wristwatch. This watch's particular enamel dial has a rarely seen depth. "The effort put into this dial was nothing short of titanic," says CEO Dr. Helmut Crott. "With its handcrafted elements including our own manufacture of the transparent enamel, this slightly ivory-colored dial is

certainly unique on the market." The luminosity of the dial is founded in the absorption of the light that is reflected by the handmade dial's 18-karat gold background and the special quality of the transparent enamel. This material is manufactured in-house from a silicon crystal that is usually only utilized to created flint glass. "Flint lenses are used for special optical machines that observe orbit. Alongside the intensity of color, it is the glass and the technique used that allow us to reach this special visual dial depth." The dial is fired a full fifteen times at more than 800°C and then completely hand-painted with numerals. This high-fire *(grand feu)* process generates many rejects, making the surviving dials that much rarer and more valuable.

Andreas Strehler takes back his Sauterelle constant force mechanism.

Elizabeth Doerr is a freelance journalist specializing in watches and was senior editor of Wristwatch Annual *until the 2010 edition. She is also the author of* 12 Faces of Time, *published by TeNeues in 2010.*

CALIBER RM 030
WITH DECLUTCHABLE ROTOR

Automatic winding movement
Power reserve circa 55 hours
Declutchable and adjustable rotor geometry
Winding indicator
Date display
Free sprung balance with variable inertia
Double barrel
Baseplate, bridges and balance cock made of titanium
Torque limiting crown in titanium
Balance: Glucydur, 4 arms
Inertia moment 4.8 mg·cm², angle of lift 53°
Frequency: 28,800 vph (4 Hz)
Spline screws in grade 5 titanium for the bridges and the case
Interior flanges in carbon fiber
Baseplate and bridges in grade 5 titanium, wet sandblasted, Titalyt® treated
Barrel bridges PVD coated
Sapphire blasted and hand-drawn surfaces

Fake Time

Marton Radkai

The man who runs one of the local pizzerias down the street is proud of his watch. So proud that he keeps one sleeve rolled up at all times to show it off. It is big, with subdials and pushers, a classic tricompax build with a fashionable vintage aura. The name and logo of a moderately known brand are displayed on the dial. As he serves an espresso, I say, "Nice watch." He smiles with subdued pride. "It was not expensive," he answers and starts to undo the buckle. One glance is all it takes: "I hate to tell you, but it's a fake." By the look on his face, it's obvious he knew, but he still asks me pro forma if I really think so. The visibly ticking subsidiary second hand is the easiest giveaway. The finishing of the case is a little sloppy as well; the dial looks cheap rather than antique. It just so happens, I am carrying a copy of *Wristwatch Annual:* The watch this one is modeled after is shown inside, with an in-house, hand-wound caliber and a convenient sapphire case back opening onto a solid, Swiss-made movement. The list price is $1,700, a few bills more than the 150 Swiss francs he paid.

The *pizzaiolo* down the street is not a rare case. Yearly hundreds of thousands of counterfeit watches, many bearing famous names and usually costing five and six figures, are bought up and then worn—provided the goods arrive if sent by mail—by men and women looking for some status enhancement. Replicating industrial goods is nothing new, of course— especially luxury goods. The Federation of the Swiss Watch Industry (FH) is just one of the most active organizations trying to deal with the problem. It puts the cost in lost sales in the watch industry alone at 800 million Swiss francs annually. This might be just a drop in the bucket compared with the real cost in cash and lives that counterfeiters the world over generate by jerry-building car parts, for example, or, worse yet, drugs. But it is not just about money, according to Jean-Daniel Pasche, president of the FH: "The piracy system has become a well-oiled and illegal machine with disastrous social and financial costs," he said at the 2013 annual symposium on

The Federation of the Swiss Watch Industry hunts fakes.

A favorite of counterfeiters, Breitling sports watches.

counterfeiting, the *Journée Suisse contre la Contrefaçon*. "Our industry has managed to build a unique, worldwide reputation over four centuries, and we have to maintain customer confidence in the brands and avoid them being emptied of their value."

The industry, some might argue, has become a victim of its own success and advertising. Wearing a Rolex, a Breguet, an Hublot, or a Patek Philippe is out of sight for the average earner, so why not?

The answer to that question is first and foremost a personal and psychological issue. It is also a matter of taste and general appearance. Furthermore, it raises moral and ethical considerations that are backed by the laws governing intellectual property. Hence a vigorous sensitization campaign has begun to keep people informed of some of the dangers of buying counterfeits. It starts with the use of materials that can cause allergies, like nickel. More important, says Yves Bugmann, head of the legal department of the FH, wearing a fake Rolex (the most copied brand) or Omega means supporting some shady people. "Few buyers understand that counterfeiters are often connected to organized crime or even terrorism," he points out. "The factories are unsupervised and often use child labor as well."

Pushing Back

As a virtually unregulated global distribution channel, the Internet has greatly promoted the cause of counterfeiters. Transactions can be made with a certain amount of anonymity. So innumerable websites have sprung up offering watches for sale or at auctions, and sorting out the real pieces from gray markets (the real timepieces sold outside regular distribution channels) and the phonies is not always easy. "The consumer used to travel to the product," says Bugmann. "Today, the product is delivered to the consumer by clicks, and can be purchased anonymously."

And so the FH has been pushing back and pulling no punches in the process. The University of Applied Sciences in Bienne-Biel has developed special software to identify websites selling or auctioning brummagem timepieces. The project has resulted in thousands of sites being shut down and removal of over a million offers over the past five years, Bugmann boasts. At street level, the organization maintains a global network of investigators who track counterfeiters. It also has a program to train police forces and customs officers throughout the world to look for fakes, which are often tucked away in toys or other household items for shipping. Asia is the number one source of fake watches, with China, logically, at the top of the list since it has a native watch industry of its own providing the machines to make components.

In 2012, the industry organization seized around 1 million counterfeit Swiss watches at the country's entry points, but also in Asia, Turkey, Latin America, and the Middle East. A 2013 raid in Dubai netted 30,000 watches and a CHF 300,000 fine for the "manufacturers." The seized goods are usually crushed very graphically using a steamroller.

Tous ensemble contre le faux

Prizewinning poster by Manon Wertenbroek to support a sensitization campaign.

Destruction of counterfeit watches and luxury goods in the desert.

Caveat Emptor

Consumers also risk losing their investment, because counterfeit watches or other goods purchased abroad or on the Internet can be confiscated at the Swiss border, whether they come in a package or on a wrist. An item will then be destroyed with no recourse. In some countries, such as France or Italy, owning counterfeit goods can incur a fine.

The cost to the buyer can be very high in other ways: Increasingly, counterfeiters are manufacturing expensive replicas that can hardly be distinguished from the original without actually opening the case and looking inside. It takes an expert eye to see some small differences in

the crown, the finishing, or even the script on the dial. Unfortunately, the consumer being offered a fake watch will not, generally, have time to bring it to a watchmaker for an expert opinion.

The brands themselves are aware of the problem and have been responding in their own way. Their websites advise customers to only buy through official channels, such as boutiques or certified dealers. Most major brands like TAG Heuer, Hublot, Patek Philippe, and the hyper-luxurious Richard Mille have sophisticated electronic systems in place to identify and register owners with the company and the distributor.

Sincerest Form of Flattery

By the same token, not everyone in the industry is worried. Smaller brands, for instance, tend to fly under the counterfeiters' radar. For Parmigiani, founded in 1996, the appearance of the first fakes felt like legitimation. They litigated only once, when some quartz-run fakes of the iconic "Bugatti" model showed up at Baselworld.

Even more insulated is Yvan Arpa of ArtyA, one of the industry's more scintillating figures. Make things that are always new and you will not risk being copied. His timepieces feature a case ravaged by an electrical arc and unique dials made of diverse materials, from cut-up 50-euro bills to bullets and butterfly wings. "The guy who wants to copy my stuff will have to get up early," he says, adding provocatively, "Anyway, it's mostly Swiss brands that have grabbed my ideas."

The struggle against piracy and counterfeiting is not about to end. In fact, today just about anything can be found in a fake version, from razors to food. Perhaps we just live in the age of the fake, where appearance is all that counts in a world of rippling information that hops without any interruption from the sophomoric outrageous antics of mediagenic VIPs to intimate views of gruesome, medieval violence, all experienced in real time on various screens. Given that reality, having a genuine, beautiful piece of equipment made with passion and skill to tell the time is a very real luxury. And it does have its price.

Fake Ulysse Nardin.

Cellini Jewelers

Why do we love watches?

With two locations in the heart of New York City, Cellini continues to build upon its reputation by offering an unparalleled collection of the world's best timepieces, rare and exotic jewelry, and unsurpassed personal service.

FOR SOME, IT'S A PHYSICAL ATTRACTION to the look and feel. For others, it's an intellectual fascination with the machinery of time. Whether you appreciate a well-designed dial, a beautifully constructed movement, or both, Cellini Jewelers understands your passion. That's why its Manhattan boutiques offer one of the most extensive selections of timepieces from the world's best watchmakers.

That incredible depth is what separates Cellini, and allows it to create an unparalleled experience for aficionados. Between its stores in the Hotel Waldorf-Astoria and on Madison Avenue, Cellini has the ability to satisfy nearly every request, says Leon Adams, founder and president of Cellini. "It's rare that someone asks for a watch that we don't have," he says. "People value the immediacy of being able to find what they want, when they want it."

What the company does best, perhaps, is use the range of its collection to help someone find the right watch. "If you like a particular style—chronographs, ultra-thins, anything—we can line up different models from various brands so you can see what options are out there. Then you can judge for yourself how a watch looks and feels on your wrist."

Greubel Forsey's GMT (shown in rose gold) indicates the local hour in twenty-four different time zones simultaneously using the rotating, three-dimensional globe.

DEEP ROOTS

Over the years, Cellini earned its reputation as a place to see not only the best-known brands, but also promising independent firms. The impressive list of watchmakers that found an early home in America at Cellini includes such brands as: A. Lange & Söhne, De Bethune, DeWitt, Franck Muller, Hublot, Greubel Forsey, Jean Dunand, Ludovic Ballouard, Maîtres du Temps, Parmigiani Fleurier, Richard Mille, and Roger Dubuis. Today, Cellini is widely regarded as a leading tastemaker among collectors and watch brands alike.

It continues to stay ahead of the curve this year by showcasing the outstanding work of two gifted watchmakers, Robert Greubel and Stephen Forsey. Their firm, Greubel Forsey, is at the forefront of horological innovation, using meticulous research and development to improve timekeeping precision with original inventions, like the Tourbillon 24 Secondes and Quadruple Tourbillon. And while tourbillons are something of an obsession at Greubel Forsey, the firm proves its versatility with the GMT. Technically brilliant with aesthetics to match, the watch is instantly recognizable thanks to the globe rotating on its dial.

NATURAL BEAUTY

But even so, Cellini is known for more than just watches. It is also ranked among the finest jewelers in New York City, charming visitors from around the world for thirty-five years with its unrivaled selection, sublime quality, and impeccable service.

Whether you seek understated, overwhelming, or something in between, the extraordinary scope of its collection opens up a world of possibilities. For those who favor a particular gem, Cellini covers the full spectrum with diamonds in all shapes, sizes, and colors, as well as lush emeralds, mysterious alexandrites, lustrous South Sea and Tahitian pearls, plus Burmese rubies and Kashmir sapphires, two rare gemstones legendary for their dramatic hues.

Fancy yellow diamond rings from Cellini's extensive color diamond collection

The jewelry settings used to show off these natural wonders are equally varied and range from elegant designs made to transcend time to styles that evoke a modern point of view. You may also commission a custom jewelry creation to realize a personalized design.

Whether you desire jewelry or watches, Cellini's friendly experts will be there to offer honest advice and provide impeccable service before, during, and after a purchase.

Cellini is an authorized retailer for A. Lange & Söhne, Audemars Piguet, Backes & Strauss, Bell & Ross, Bulgari, Cartier, Chopard, De Bethune, DeWitt, Franck Muller, Girard-Perregaux, Giuliano Mazzuoli, Greubel Forsey, H. Moser & Cie., Hublot, HYT, IWC, Jaeger-LeCoultre, Jean Dunand, Ludovic Ballouard, Maîtres du Temps, Parmigiani Fleurier, Piaget, Richard Mille, Roger Dubuis, Ulysse Nardin, Vacheron Constantin, and Zenith.

Cellini's boutique on Madison Avenue was established in 1987 at the epicenter of the world's most elite shopping district.

STORE LOCATIONS

Hotel Waldorf-Astoria
301 Park Avenue at 50th Street
New York, NY 10022
212-751-9824

509 Madison Avenue at 53rd Street
New York, NY 10022
212-888-0505

CELLINI JEWELERS
800-CELLINI
www.CelliniJewelers.com

Mavericks and Masters
Marton Radkai

One of the undeniable charms of the watchmaking craft and the industry as a whole is its magnetic effect on out-of-the-box thinkers, dreamers, quasi-flimflammers, virtuosi, and brilliant amateurs alike. At the end of the day, however, whatever their creative idea, these personalities will have to come up with the investments, do the research, and sit out a long period of trial and error before seeing a product—because a watch is not a rubber duck. The common thread is passion, a gut-based emotion that keeps them plugging away for better or for worse and then, often, delivering a timepiece or an object that wows the fans.

Peter Thum, the man behind Fonderie 47, is one such personality. His talent in organizing business ventures is undisputable, and he has applied it to supporting social causes he feels are important. His road began in 2001 while working for McKinsey in Africa, where he saw firsthand the devastation caused by a lack of clean water. Being a businessman, he founded a company, Ethos Water, as a way to finance water-related projects in Africa. It was a win-win situation that was soon acquired by none other than Starbucks.

Then there was another issue that bothered him: the widespread presence of small arms and particularly the notorious AK 47 assault rifle. "Here was a problem that really prevented development dollars from having an impact," he analyzes, cool-headed. "So I thought, 'let's destroy these guns and convert them

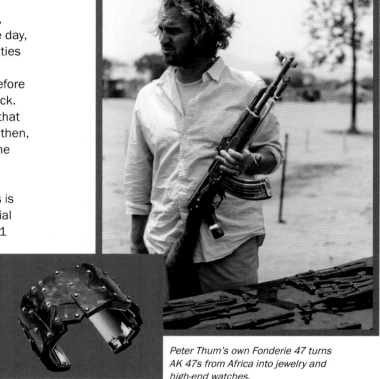

Peter Thum's own Fonderie 47 turns AK 47s from Africa into jewelry and high-end watches.

into something inspiring that makes people interested in the problem and doing something about it.'" And Fonderie 47 was born: As with the water project, which made money through water to improve water conditions, Thum decided to use the weapons' asset, steel engineering, to make jewelry. He managed to win over master jewelers Philip Crangi and James de Givenchy for the project.

The project has already helped collect and destroy 34,000 weapons in Africa's war zones, notably the Congo. So the next and most obvious step was to create a watch. As a neophyte in the watch world, Thum sought out Vallée-de-Joux-based watchmaker David Candaux and designer Adrian Glessing. Together they came up with a vision: a watch with all the bells and whistles a serious collector could desire, including an in-house movement, to be wrapped up in eighteen months.

The **Inversion Principle** was born, with a comparatively small, 42 mm case housing a manually wound timepiece with a three-dimensional dial. At the center is a calmly rotating three-minute flying tourbillon that indicates the

Revenue from the Inversion Principle, with a tourbillon and other complications, will go to destroying 1,000 firearms in Africa.

seconds on three arcs, of which only one is visible at any given time. The staccato jumping hours at 12 o'clock and retrograde minutes on the lower half of the dial do suggest the kind of motion produced when loading a rifle. The watch has a power reserve on the back and one embedded in the case band. As for the case, it comes in pink or white gold, not recycled gun materials.

"We wanted to take something industrial and mass-produced and crude and transform it into something that is rare and refined and that comes from the finest tradition of technical and creative work," says Thum. In fact, the gun itself is only subtly recalled in the watch. The frame on the dial could be construed as a sight. And through the transparent case back, on a sunburst guilloché, is a piece of blackened gun metal capping the ratchet wheel. The watches come in a limited edition of fifteen pieces in each metal, each costing $350,000. For every watch sold, Thum will organize the destruction of 1,000 weapons.

Horological Melismata

A quick acoustic scan of the watch world will reveal that minute repeaters are trending, and some brands are making a fair noise about theirs, like Ulysse Nardin with its very impressive **Stranger,** which plays a few bars of Sinatra on demand and costs $112,000. **Jacques Boegli** might just say coals to Newcastle, or maybe hairsprings to Bienne. His watches can play the opening bars of a Chopin étude, of *Für Elise,* of Vivaldi's *Four Seasons.* In fact, for a surcharge, he can customize his watches to play whatever the buyer wants.

Jacques Boegli is the spearhead of generations of watchmakers going back to one Ludwig Schwab, founder of Swiza in Moutiers, Switzerland, in 1904, a brand that went its own way and still produces clocks. Boegli joined his father François in a few ventures in the 1990s, notably manufacturing pocket watches.

This time with music: a pocket watch from Boegli's Baroque series featuring Vivaldi's Four Seasons.

Around 2003, he became enthralled with music boxes, and being a watchmaker by way of DNA, he decided to grace his watches with one by adding a second mechanical drive next to the ETA movements. "The watches were big, but by today's standards not so big," says Boegli. Instead of the wearer gazing at a tourbillon or a minute repeater, these classically simple timepieces in round, rectangular, or pocket watch cases offer a view of a

A separate movement means music can be customized as well.

little cylinder playing a metal comb. Prices for the standard versions range from $2,500 to $5,000. Having established his special brand, though, Boegli is now working on developing an integrated movement that would drive both the time and the music.

Meteorological Complications

The curious thing about the **Génie 01** is the plain fact that no one seems to have come up with the idea before. It has an altimeter and a barometer with scale adjusters and a bunch of other horological delights. The person who did dream up the concept is Vincent Dupontreué, a Frenchman from near Paris originally and one of those bohème-businessmen who bask in the thrill of doing commerce. He launched a fashion brand under his own name at twenty-two, then sold it a few years later, got an MBA, operated an art gallery in Lausanne . . . and then, in 2010, decided to create a watch brand. The USP: a watch that forecasts the weather and indicates the wearer's altitude (within limits). The name of the new brand came while he was enjoying a weekend on Lake Como in northern Italy, where a gentle wind called La Breva creates a pleasant microclimate. For the technical development, he went straight to the top: Jean-François Mojon and his company Chronode from Le Locle, specialists in ultra-complicated watches. Mojon has had his magic fingers in some outstandingly complicated timepieces, like the HYT, the Cyrus Klepcys, and the Opus X for Harry Winston.

And in fact, the Génie 01 does have some similarities to the Opus X, with its display featuring superimposed dials

Multiple levels of functionality in La Breva's Génie 01.

and indicators. To the left, at 8 o'clock, are the hours and minutes with subsidiary seconds. Along the "top" of the flange is an altimeter that ranges from minus 300 to plus 5,300 meters. The barometer is on a sapphire dial at 2 o'clock. The word "Météo" says it all: The measurements are given in old-fashioned hectopascals, or millimeters of mercury in a column, hence the mmHg legend. The barometer and the altimeter work together thanks to two aneroid cells (at 6 o'clock), a material that senses absolute pressure. A button on the crown at 4 o'clock serves to

A watch, altimeter, and barometer, by Vincent Dupontreué and Jean-François Mojon.

One of three multifunctional crowns on the Génie 01.

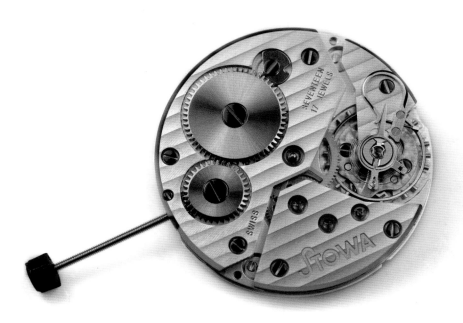

equalize atmospheric pressure inside and outside the watch. The Génie also displays power reserve (65 hours, no less, from a proprietary movement), and the bezel on the transparent case back gives the correlation between altitudes and air pressure.

The end product is a watch geek's treasure trove of buttons, pushers, meters, pointers, and engraved scales, but it does not give the feeling of being overdone or crowded. This is a well-built, fun watch for 110 deep-pocketed collectors: fifty-five will be in white gold, fifty-five in pink.

Max Out

And finally, every year, Max Büsser & Friends feeds a hungry crowd of devotees by unveiling a special timepiece after whetting their appetites for months with the promise of an even greater thrill than the previous one. Last year, the Horological Machine No. 5 revived the 1970s, with a sleek, aerodynamic look, fancy work with prisms and metal, and digital displays—the last hurrah of physical technology, one could say. With the Legacy Machines, started in 2011, MB&F began a game called "what if we were creating a watch in (pick a date)." The Legacy Machine No. 1 harked back to the late nineteenth century,

with a large balance beating away atop a vintage-looking dial. **Legacy Machine No. 2** was unveiled to a small crowd at Büsser's M.A.D. Gallery in Geneva, Switzerland, on September 3, 2013. This watch is similar in shape to No. 1, with a large convex crystal acting as a kind of display case for the happenings on the dial.

Max's "friends" in this project were none other than Kari Voutilainen and the above-mentioned Jean-François Mojon. Their idea was to take a page from the eighteenth century and a watch with two balances made by Ferdinand Berthoud (1727–1807). A lot of historic research went into the timepiece, but the modern touch is present in the two balances suspended over the dial and driving a single gear train via the raised differential at 6 o'clock. A lot of care went into making this mechanism visible, which is not the case with older watches by Berthoud and his "friends" Abraham-Louis Breguet and Aristide Janvier, who also served as inspirations. The transparent case back reveals finest finishing and the dragon-like wheelworks snaking away performing their special dance. After a while, you realize that reading the time is not really the point of this watch. But just in case, the two hands of the clock on a subdial have been blued.

Upstaging time with two balances and a visible differential.

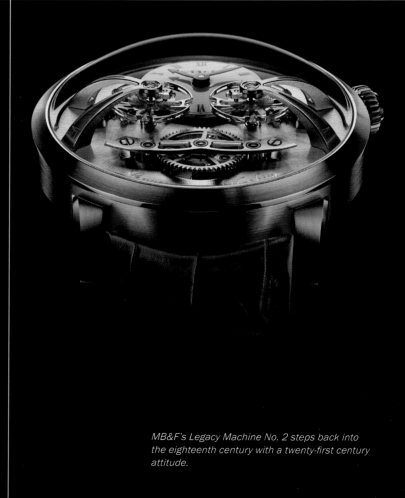

MB&F's Legacy Machine No. 2 steps back into the eighteenth century with a twenty-first century attitude.

HUBLOT

HUBLOT

Big Bang Zebra.
Chronograph in 18K red gold adorned
with baguette-cut clear topaz and black
spinels. Dial set with 8 diamonds.
Rubber and zebra coloured calf strap.
Limited edition series of 250 pieces.

Lange Uhren GmbH
Ferdinand-A.-Lange-Platz 1
D-01768 Glashütte
Germany

Tel.:
01149-35053-44-0

Fax:
01149-35053-44-5999

E-Mail:
info@lange-soehne.com

Website:
www.lange-soehne.com

Founded:
1990

Number of employees:
500 employees, almost half of whom are
watchmakers

Annual production:
not specified

U.S. distributor:
A. Lange & Söhne
645 Fifth Avenue
New York, NY 10022
800-408-8147

Most important collections/price range:
Lange 1 / $32,400 to $341,900; Saxonia
/ $18,600 to $58,400; 1815 / $22,500
to $213,000; Richard Lange / $30,300 to
$223,600; Zeitwerk / $68,900 to $117,500

A. Lange & Söhne

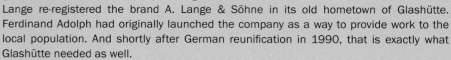

On December 7, 1990, on the exact day 145 years after the firm was founded by his great-grandfather, Ferdinand Adolph Lange, Walter Lange re-registered the brand A. Lange & Söhne in its old hometown of Glashütte. Ferdinand Adolph had originally launched the company as a way to provide work to the local population. And shortly after German reunification in 1990, that is exactly what Glashütte needed as well.

The company quickly regained its outstanding reputation as a robust innovator and manufacturer of classically beautiful watches. A. Lange & Söhne uses only mechanical, manually wound *manufacture* calibers or automatic winders finished according to the highest Glashütte standards. The movements are decorated and assembled by hand with the fine adjustment done in five positions. The typical three-quarter plate and all the structural parts of the movement are made of undecorated German silver; the balance cock is engraved freehand. The movements combine equal parts traditional elements and patented innovations, like the Lange large date, the SAX-O-MAT with an automatic "zero reset" for the seconds hand, or the patented constant force escapement (Lange 31, Lange Zeitwerk). Of the company's forty-six calibers, twenty-six are currently in production, and two-thirds of those have their own balance spring.

A. Lange & Söhne manufactures only a few watches, but they are memorable. One star is the Lange 1 Tourbillon Perpetual Calendar equipped with an automatic movement and featuring a month ring or a stop-second mechanism for extremely accurate setting. The tourbillon is visible through the transparent case back, so Lange could comply with its ideal of an uncluttered dial. As for the Grand Lange 1 "Lumen," it reveals the Lange designers as genuine artists with Superluminova.

1815 Rattrapante Perpetual Calendar

Reference number: 421.025
Movement: manually wound, Lange Caliber L101.1; ø 32.6 mm, height 9.1 mm; 43 jewels; 21,600 vph; 4 screw-mounted gold chatons; hand-engraved balance cock, screw balance, swan-neck fine adjustment; 42-hour power reserve
Functions: hours, minutes, subsidiary seconds; power reserve indicator; split-seconds chronograph; perpetual calendar with date, weekday, month, moon phase, leap year
Case: platinum, ø 41.9 mm, height 14.7 mm; sapphire crystal, transparent case back; water-resistant to 3 atm
Band: reptile skin, folding clasp; **Price:** $213,000

1815 UP/DOWN

Reference number: 234.032
Movement: manually wound, Lange Caliber L051.2; ø 30.6 mm, height 4.6 mm; 29 jewels; 21,600 vph; three-quarter, hand-engraved balance cocks, 7 screwed-mounted gold chatons, screw balance, parts finished and assembled by hand; 72-hour power reserve
Functions: hours, minutes, subsidiary seconds; power reserve indicator
Case: pink gold, ø 39 mm, height 8.9 mm; sapphire crystal, transparent case back; water-resistant to 3 atm
Band: reptile skin, buckle
Price: $27,400
Variations: yellow gold ($27,400); white gold ($28,600)

Grand Lange 1 "Lumen"

Reference number: 117.035
Movement: manually wound, Lange Caliber L095.2; ø 34.1 mm; height 4.7 mm; 42 jewels; 28,600 vph; 7 screwed-mounted gold chatons, hand-engraved balance cock, 72-hour power reserve
Functions: hours, minutes, subsidiary seconds; power reserve indicator; large date
Case: platinum, ø 40.9 mm, height 8.8 mm; sapphire crystal, transparent case back; water-resistant to 3 atm
Band: reptile skin, buckle
Remarks: translucent dial, luminescent numerals, hands, and date display
Price: $70,400, limited to 200 pieces

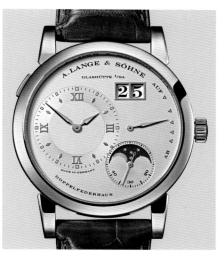

Grand Lange 1

Reference number: 117.028
Movement: manually wound, Lange Caliber L095.1; ø 34.1 mm; height 4.7 mm; 42 jewels; 21,600 vph; 7 screwed-mounted gold chatons, hand-engraved balance cock, 72-hour power reserve
Functions: hours, minutes, subsidiary seconds; power reserve indicator; large date
Case: white gold, ø 40.9 mm, height 8.8 mm; sapphire crystal, transparent case back; water-resistant to 3 atm
Band: reptile skin, buckle
Price: $40,500
Variations: yellow gold ($39,300); red gold ($39,300); platinum ($53,200); with black dial and luminous markers

Lange 1

Reference number: 101.032
Movement: manually wound, Lange Caliber L901.0; ø 30.4 mm, height 5.9 mm; 53 jewels; 21,600 vph; hand-engraved balance cock; parts finished and assembled by hand; double spring barrel, 72-hour power reserve
Functions: hours, minutes, subsidiary seconds; large date; power reserve indicator
Case: pink gold, ø 38.5 mm, height 10 mm; sapphire crystal; transparent case back; water-resistant to 3 atm
Band: reptile skin, buckle
Price: $32,400
Variations: yellow gold ($32,400); white gold ($33,600); platinum ($46,700)

Lange 1 Moonphase

Reference number: 109.032
Movement: manually wound, Lange Caliber L901.5; ø 30.4 mm, height 5.9 mm; 54 jewels; 21,600 vph; hand-engraved balance cock; 9 screw-mounted gold chatons; 72-hour power reserve
Functions: hours, minutes, subsidiary seconds; large date, moon phase; power reserve indicator
Case: pink gold, ø 38.5 mm, height 10.4 mm; sapphire crystal; transparent case back; water-resistant to 3 atm
Band: reptile skin, buckle
Price: $40,100
Variations: platinum ($54,400)

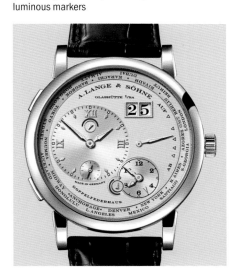

Lange 1 Timezone

Reference number: 116.039
Movement: manually wound, Lange Caliber L031.1; ø 34.1 mm, height 6.65 mm; 54 jewels; 21,600 vph; hand-engraved balance cock; 4 screw-mounted gold chatons; 72-hour power reserve; home time and zone time with day/night indicator, pusher-driven bezel with city names
Functions: hours, minutes, subsidiary seconds; second time zone; large date; power reserve indicator; day/night indicator for both time zones
Case: white gold, ø 41.9 mm, height 11 mm; sapphire crystal; transparent case back
Band: reptile skin, buckle
Price: $50,100
Variations: red gold ($47,700); platinum ($61,800)

Lange 1 Daymatic

Reference number: 320.032
Movement: automatic, Lange Caliber L021.1; ø 31.6 mm; height 6.1 mm; 67 jewels; 21,600 vph; hand-engraved balance cock, 7 screwed-mounted gold chatons, central rotor with platinum weight; 50-hour power reserve
Functions: hours, minutes, subsidiary seconds; large date; weekday (retrograde)
Case: pink gold, ø 39.5 mm, height 10.4 mm; sapphire crystal, transparent case back; water-resistant to 3 atm
Band: reptile skin, buckle
Price: $40,400
Variations: yellow gold ($40,400); platinum ($54,700)

Lange 1 Tourbillon Perpetual Calendar

Reference number: 720.025
Movement: automatic, Lange Caliber L082.1; ø 34.1 mm, height 7.8 mm; 68 jewels; 21,600 vph; 1-minute tourbillon on back; 4 gold chatons; 1 diamond endstone; hand-engraved cocks; rotor with gold weight; 50-hour power reserve
Functions: hours, minutes, subsidiary seconds; day/night indicator; perpetual calendar with large date, weekday, month, moon phase, leap year
Case: platinum, ø 41.9 mm, height 12.2 mm; sapphire crystal; exhibition case; water-resistant to 3 atm
Band: reptile skin, buckle
Price: $341,900, limited to 100 pieces

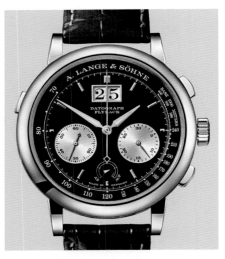

Datograph UP/DOWN

Reference number: 405.035
Movement: manually wound, Lange Caliber L951.6;
ø 30.6 mm, height 7.9 mm; 46 jewels; 18,000
vph; 4 screwed-down gold chatons; 60-hour power
reserve
Functions: hours, minutes, subsidiary seconds;
flyback chronograph with precisely jumping minute
counter; large date; power reserve indicator
Case: platinum, ø 41 mm, height 13.1 mm; sapphire
crystal; transparent case back; water-resistant to
3 atm
Band: reptile skin, buckle
Price: $87,400

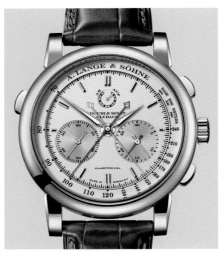

Double Split

Reference number: 404.032
Movement: manually wound, Lange Caliber L001.1;
ø 30.6 mm, height 9.5 mm; 40 jewels; 21,600 vph;
2 control wheels for chronograph's double
rattrapante function; precisely jumping minute
counter; 4 screwed-mounted gold chatons
Functions: hours, minutes; flyback chronograph;
split-second hand for second and minute counters;
power reserve indicator
Case: pink gold, ø 43.2 mm, height 15.3 mm;
sapphire crystal; transparent case back; water-
resistant to 3 atm
Band: reptile skin, buckle
Price: $120,100

Datograph Perpetual

Reference number: 410.032
Movement: manually wound, Lange Caliber L952.1;
ø 32 mm, height 8 mm; 45 jewels; 18,000 vph;
column wheel control of chronograph functions;
4 screw-mounted gold chatons
Functions: hours, minutes, subsidiary seconds;
additional 24-hour display; day/night indicator;
flyback chronograph; perpetual calendar with
month, weekday, month, moon phase, leap year
Case: pink gold, ø 41 mm, height 13.5 mm;
sapphire crystal transparent case back; water-
resistant to 3 atm
Band: reptile skin, buckle
Price: $127,700

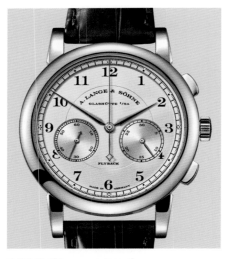

1815 Chronograph

Reference number: 402.026
Movement: manually wound, Lange Caliber L951.5;
ø 30.6 mm; height 6.1 mm; 34 jewels; 18,000 vph;
hand-engraved balance cock, 4 screw-mounted
gold chatons, 60-hour power reserve
Functions: hours, minutes, subsidiary seconds;
flyback chronograph
Case: white gold, ø 39.5 mm, height 10.8 mm;
sapphire crystal, transparent case back; water-
resistant to 3 atm
Band: reptile skin, buckle
Price: $48,200
Variations: pink gold ($47,000)

Lange Zeitwerk

Reference number: 140.029
Movement: manually wound, Lange Caliber L043.1;
ø 33.6 mm, height 9.3 mm; 66 jewels; 18,000 vph;
hand-engraved balance cock; 2 screw-mounted
gold chatons; continuous drive through constant
force escapement; 36-hour power reserve
Functions: hours and minutes (digital, jumping),
subsidiary seconds; power reserve indicator
Case: white gold, ø 41.9 mm, height 12.6 mm;
sapphire crystal; transparent case back; water-
resistant to 3 atm
Band: reptile skin, buckle
Price: $70,100
Variations: pink gold ($68,900); platinum
($83,200)

Lange Zeitwerk Striking Time

Reference number: 145.025
Movement: manually wound, Lange Caliber L043.1;
ø 33.6 mm, height 10 mm; 78 jewels; 18,000 vph;
hand-engraved balance cock; 3 screw-mounted
gold chatons; continuous drive through constant
force escapement; acoustic signal on hour and
quarter hour; 36-hour power reserve
Functions: hours and minutes (digital, jumping),
subsidiary seconds; power reserve indicator
Case: platinum, ø 44.2 mm, height 13.1
mm; sapphire crystal; transparent case back;
water-resistant to 3 atm
Band: reptile skin, buckle
Price: $117,500 platinum, limited to 100 pieces
Variations: white gold ($107,900)

Richard Lange

Reference number: 232.025
Movement: manually wound, Lange Caliber L041.2; ø 30.4 mm, height 6 mm; 27 jewels; 21,600 vph; hand-engraved balance cock; parts finished and assembled by hand; 38-hour power reserve; in-house balance spring with anchoring clip registered for patent
Functions: hours, minutes, sweep seconds
Case: platinum, ø 40.5 mm, height 10.5 mm; sapphire crystal; transparent case back; water-resistant to 3 atm
Band: reptile skin, buckle
Price: $44,600
Variations: pink gold ($30,300)

Richard Lange Tourbillon "Pour le Mérite"

Reference number: 760.025
Movement: manually wound, Lange Caliber L072.1; ø 33.6 mm, height 7.6 mm; 32 jewels including diamond endstone; 21,600 vph; chain and fusée drive; 1-minute tourbillon; hand-engraved balance cock
Functions: hours (off-center), minutes, subsidiary seconds (on tourbillon cage)
Case: platinum, ø 41.9 mm, height 12.2 mm; sapphire crystal; transparent case back; water-resistant to 3 atm
Band: reptile skin, buckle
Remarks: hour dial retracts to reveal full tourbillon once hand has passed
Price: $223,600, limited to 100 pieces
Variations: rose gold ($185,300)

Lange 31

Reference number: 130.025
Movement: manually wound, Lange Caliber L034.1; ø 37.3 mm, height 9.6 mm; 59 jewels; 21,600 vph; hand-engraved balance cock; 3 screw-mounted gold chatons; parts finished and assembled by hand; 744-hour power reserve with switch-off mechanism, double spring barrel, constant force escapement
Functions: hours, minutes, subsidiary seconds; large date; power reserve indicator
Case: platinum, ø 45.9 mm, height 15.9 mm; sapphire crystal; transparent case back; water-resistant to 3 atm
Band: reptile skin, buckle
Price: $174,900
Variations: rose gold ($140,500)

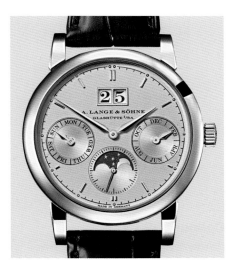

Saxonia Annual Calendar

Reference number: 330.025
Movement: automatic, Lange Caliber L085.1; SAX-O-MAT; ø 30.4 mm; height 5.4 mm; 43 jewels; 21,600 vph; hand-engraved balance cock; integrated three-quarter rotor with gold and platinum oscillating weight, reversing and reduction gears with 4 ball bearings, hand-setting mechanism with zero reset; 46-hour power reserve
Functions: hours, minutes, subsidiary seconds; full calendar with large date, weekday, month, moon phase
Case: platinum, ø 38.5 mm, height 9.8 mm; sapphire crystal, transparent case back; water-resistant to 3 atm
Band: reptile skin, buckle
Price: $58,400

Saxonia Thin

Reference number: 211.026
Movement: manually wound, Lange Caliber L093.1; ø 28 mm, height 2.9 mm; 21 jewels; 21,600 vph; hand-engraved balance cock; 3 screw-mounted gold chatons; 72-hour power reserve
Functions: hours, minutes
Case: white gold, ø 40 mm, height 5.9 mm; sapphire crystal; transparent case back; water-resistant to 3 atm
Band: reptile skin, buckle
Price: $25,100
Variations: pink gold ($23,900)

Langematik Perpetual

Reference number: 310.025
Movement: automatic, Lange Caliber L922.1; SAX-O-MAT; ø 30.4 mm; height 5.7 mm; 43 jewels; 21,600 vph; hand-engraved balance cock; rotor with gold and platinum oscillating weight; hand-setting mechanism with zero reset; main pusher for synchronous correction of all calendar functions, plus 3 individual pushers; 46-hour power reserve
Functions: hours, minutes, subsidiary seconds; additional 24-hour display; perpetual calendar with large date, weekday, month, moon phase, leap year
Case: platinum, ø 38.5 mm, height 10.2 mm; sapphire crystal, transparent case back; water-resistant to 3 atm
Band: reptile skin, buckle
Price: $91,800

Caliber L082.1

Automatic; 1-minute tourbillon with stop-second; 1-way gold rotor with platinum mass; single barrel, 50-hour power reserve
Functions: hours, minutes; subsidiary seconds; day/night; perpetual calendar, large date, weekday, month, moon phase, leap year
Diameter: 34.1 mm
Height: 7.8 mm
Jewels: 76, including 6 screwed golden chatons and 1 diamond counter-bearing
Balance: glucydur, eccentric regulating cams
Frequency: 21,600 vph
Balance spring: in-house manufacture
Shock protection: Incabloc
Remarks: three-quarter plate with untreated German silver mostly decorated and assembled by hand; hand-engraved balance and wheel cock

Caliber L951.6

Manually wound; stop-seconds mechanism, jumping minute counter; single spring barrel, 60-hour power reserve
Functions: hours, minutes, subsidiary seconds; power reserve indicator; flyback chronograph; large date
Diameter: 30.6 mm
Height: 7.9 mm
Jewels: 46
Balance: glucydur with weighted screws
Frequency: 18,000 vph
Balance spring: in-house manufacture
Shock protection: Kif
Remarks: three-quarter plate of untreated German silver, mostly decorated and assembled by hand; hand-engraved balance cock

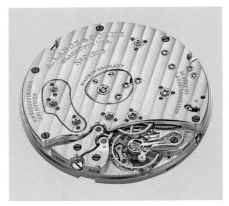

Caliber L095.1

Manually wound; stop-second system; single spring barrel, 72-hour power reserve
Functions: hours, minutes, subsidiary seconds; power reserve indicator; large date
Diameter: 34.1 mm
Height: 4.7 mm
Jewels: 42
Balance: glucydur with weighted screws
Frequency: 21,600 vph
Balance spring: in-house manufacture
Shock protection: Kif
Remarks: three-quarter plate of untreated German silver, manufactured according to highest quality criteria and mostly decorated and assembled by hand; hand-engraved balance cock

Caliber L031.1

Manually wound; stop-second system; double spring barrel, 72-hour power reserve
Functions: hours, minutes, subsidiary seconds; second time zone with city ring; large date; power reserve indicator; day/night indicator for both zones
Diameter: 34.1 mm
Height: 6.65 mm
Jewels: 54
Balance: glucydur with weighted screws
Frequency: 21,600 vph
Shock protection: Kif
Balance spring: Nivarox 1 with special terminal curve and swan-neck fine adjustment
Remarks: three-quarter plate with untreated German silver; with Glashütte ribbing; mostly assembled and decorated by hand; city ring; hand-engraved balance and wheel cock

Caliber L021.1

Manually wound; central rotor with platinum weight and shock-absorbing suspension; single spring barrel, 50-hour power reserve
Functions: hours, minutes, subsidiary seconds; large date, weekday (retrograde)
Diameter: 31.6 mm
Height: 6.1 mm
Jewels: 67
Balance: glucydur with eccentric regulating cams
Frequency: 21,600 vph
Balance spring: in-house manufacture
Shock protection: Kif
Remarks: plates and bridges of untreated German silver, manufactured according to highest quality criteria and mostly decorated and assembled by hand, hand-engraved balance cock

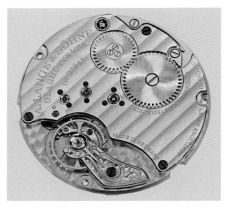

Caliber L093.1

Manually wound; single spring barrel, 72-hour power reserve
Functions: hours, minutes
Diameter: 28 mm
Height: 2.9 mm
Jewels: 21
Balance: glucydur with weighted screws
Frequency: 21,600 vph
Balance spring: in-house manufacture
Shock protection: Kif
Remarks: three-quarter plate of untreated German silver, manufactured according to highest quality criteria and mostly decorated and assembled by hand; hand-engraved balance cock

Caliber L085.1 SAX-0-MAT

Automatic; bidirectional, finely embossed three-quarter rotor of 21 kt gold and platinum, "zero reset" hand adjustment, stop-seconds mechanism; complete or individual calendar correction; single spring barrel, 46-hour power reserve

Functions: hours, minutes, subsidiary seconds; full calendar with large date, weekday, month, moon phase

Diameter: 30.4 mm

Height: 5.4 mm

Jewels: 43; **Balance:** glucydur with weighted screws

Frequency: 21,600 vph

Balance spring: Nivarox 1 with special terminal curve and swan-neck fine adjustment

Shock protection: Kif

Remarks: three-quarter plate of untreated German silver; mostly decorated and assembled by hand; hand-engraved balance cock

Caliber L922.1 SAX-0-MAT; Caliber L922.1

Manually wound; bidirectional winding, finely embossed three-quarter rotor in gold and platinum; "zero reset" hand adjustment; stop-second system; single spring barrel, 46-hour power reserve

Functions: hours, minutes, sweep seconds; additional 24-hour display; perpetual calendar with date, weekday, month, moon phase, leap year day/night indicator

Diameter: 30 mm

Height: 5.7 mm

Jewels: 43

Balance: glucydur with weighted screws

Frequency: 21,600 vph

Remarks: calendar mechanism with 48-step program disc and precision moon phase system

Caliber L043.2

Manually wound; jumping minutes; constant force escapement; patent pending on spring barrel mechanism; stop-second system; single spring barrel, 36-hour power reserve

Functions: hours and minutes (digital, jumping), subsidiary seconds; power reserve indicator

Diameter: 36 mm

Height: 10 mm

Jewels: 78

Balance: glucydur

Frequency: 18,000 vph

Balance spring: in-house manufacture

Shock protection: Incabloc

Remarks: three-quarter plate with untreated German silver; Glashütte ribbing; mostly assembled and decorated by hand; hand-engraved balance cock

Caliber L072.1

Manually wound; chain and fusée transmission; 1-minute tourbillon with patented second-stop system; single spring barrel, 36-hour power reserve

Functions: hours, minutes, subsidiary seconds; pivoting dial

Diameter: 33.6 mm

Height: 7.6 mm

Jewels: 32

Balance: glucydur with weighted screws

Frequency: 21,600 vph

Balance spring: in-house manufacture

Shock protection: Kif

Remarks: three-quarter plate of untreated German silver; chiefly decorated and assembled by hand; balance and second bridges engraved by hand; chain made of 636 individual parts, worked by hand

Caliber L001.1

Manually wound; chronometer controlled by 2 intermediate wheels; isolator mechanism; stop-second system; jumping minutes; single spring barrel, 36-hour power reserve

Functions: hours, minutes, subsidiary seconds; flyback chronograph and double rattrapante for seconds and minutes; large date

Diameter: 30.6 mm

Height: 9.45 mm

Jewels: 40

Balance: glucydur with eccentric regulating cams

Frequency: 21,600 vph

Balance spring: in-house manufacture, with balance spring fastening device

Shock protection: Incabloc

Remarks: three-quarter plate of untreated German silve; mostly decorated and assembled by hand; hand-engraved balance cock

Caliber L034.1

Manually wound, key winding with torque limiter, constant force escapement, stop-seconds mechanism; twin spring barrels, 31-day power reserve with switch-off mechanism

Functions: hours, minutes, subsidiary seconds; power reserve indicator; large date

Diameter: 37.3 mm

Height: 9.6 mm

Jewels: 62

Balance: glucydur with weighted screws

Frequency: 21,600 vph

Balance spring: Nivarox 1 with special terminal curve and swan-neck fine adjustment

Shock protection: Incabloc

Remarks: three-quarter plate of untreated German silver; mostly decorated and assembled by hand; hand-engraved balance cock; 2 mainsprings, each 1.85 m long

Alpina Watch International
Chemin de la Galaise, 8
CH-1228 Plan-les-Ouates (Geneva)
Switzerland

Tel.:
01141-22-860-87-40

Fax:
01141-22-860-04-64

E-Mail:
info@alpina-watches.com

Website:
www.alpina-watches.com

Founded:
1883

Number of employees:
100

Annual production:
10,000 watches

U.S. distributor:
Alpina Watches USA
877-61-WATCH
info@usa.alpina-watches.com

Most important collections/price range:
Extreme / from approx. $1,200; Startimer Pilot
/ from approx. $2,300; Sailing / from approx.
$1,500; Tourbillon /from approx. $50,000

Alpina

The name has a long history: The brand Alpina was introduced by the Swiss Watchmakers Corporation in 1901. Soon after, the group expanded into Germany and even opened a factory in Glashütte. For a while in the 1930s, it even merged with Gruen, one of the most important watch companies in the United States. The collaboration fell apart in 1937. After World War II, the Allied Forces decreed that the name Alpina could no longer be used in Germany, and so that branch was renamed "Dugena" for Deutsche Uhrmacher-Genossenschaft Alpina, or the German Watchmaker Cooperative Alpina.

Today, Geneva-based Alpina is no longer associated with that watchmaker cooperative of yore. Now a sister brand of Frédérique Constant, it has a decidedly modern collection enhanced with its own automatic movement—based, of course, on the caliber of its co-headquartered manufacturer. Owners Peter and Aletta Stas have built an impressive watch *manufacture* in Geneva's industrial district, Plan-les-Ouates. There, they produce about 8,000 of their own watches each year as well as reassembling other timepieces with externally manufactured movements.

Alpina, which celebrated its 120th anniversary during 2013, likes to call itself the inventor of the modern sports watch. Its iconic Block-Uhr of 1933 and the Alpina 4 of 1938, with an in-house automatic movement, set the pace of all sports watches, with a waterproof stainless steel case, an antimagnetic system, and shock absorbers. The timepieces found favor in various branches of the military, notably aviation. This past is now the future as well, as the reconstituted Alpina brand sets its sights on a modern look and on customers who engage in water and aeronautic sports.

130 Heritage Pilot Chronograph Automatic
Reference number: AL-860B4H5
Movement: automatic, AL Caliber 860 (base Sellita SW500); ø 30 mm, height 7.9 mm; 25 jewels; 28,800 vph; 42-hour power reserve
Functions: hours, minutes, subsidiary seconds; chronograph
Case: stainless steel, golden PVD coating, ø 41.5 mm, height 14 mm; sapphire crystal, transparent case back; water-resistant to 5 atm
Band: leather, buckle
Price: $3,495
Variations: white dial

130 Heritage Pilot Chronograph Automatic
Reference number: AL-860B4H6
Movement: automatic, AL Caliber 860 (base Sellita SW500); ø 30 mm, height 7.9 mm; 25 jewels; 28,800 vph; 42-hour power reserve
Functions: hours, minutes, subsidiary seconds; chronograph
Case: stainless steel, ø 41.5 mm, height 14 mm; sapphire crystal, transparent case back; water-resistant to 5 atm
Band: leather, buckle
Price: $3,250

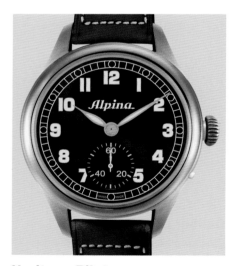

Heritage Pilot
Reference number: AL-435B4SH6
Movement: manually wound, AL Caliber 435 (base ETA 6497-2); ø 36.6 mm, height 4.5 mm; 17 jewels; 21,600 vph; 42-hour power reserve
Functions: hours, minutes, subsidiary seconds
Case: stainless steel, ø 50 mm, height 11.5 mm; sapphire crystal, transparent case back; water-resistant to 3 atm
Band: leather, buckle
Price: $1,895

Startimer Pilot Big Date

Reference number: AL-280B4S6B
Movement: quartz
Functions: hours, minutes, subsidiary seconds; large date
Case: stainless steel, ø 44 mm, height 12.4 mm; sapphire crystal, screw-in crown
Band: stainless steel, folding clasp
Price: $1,050
Variations: with leather strap ($850)

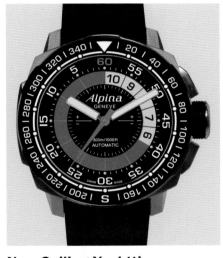

Aviation Startimer Pilot Chrono Quartz

Reference number: AL-372BGR4FBS6
Movement: quartz
Functions: hours, minutes, subsidiary seconds; chronograph; large date
Case: stainless steel, black PVD coating, ø 44 mm, height 12.5 mm; sapphire crystal; water-resistant to 10 atm
Band: nylon, buckle
Price: $1,150

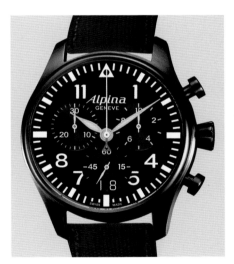

Worldtimer

Reference number: AL-718B4S6
Movement: automatic, AL Caliber 718 (base ETA 2893-1); ø 25.6 mm, height 4.1 mm; 21 jewels; 28,800 vph; 42-hour power reserve
Functions: hours, minutes, sweep seconds; world time display (second time zone); date
Case: stainless steel, ø 44 mm, height 13 mm; crown rotates inner ring with reference cities; sapphire crystal, screw-in crown; water-resistant to 10 atm
Band: leather, buckle
Price: $3,750, limited to 8,888 pieces

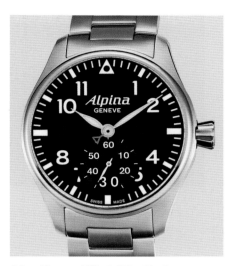

Extreme Diver 300 Chronograph Automatic

Reference number: AL-725LB4V26
Movement: automatic, AL Caliber 725 (base ETA 7750); ø 30 mm, height 7.9 mm; 25 jewels; 28,800 vph; 46-hour power reserve
Functions: hours, minutes; chronograph; date
Case: stainless steel, ø 44 mm, height 17.2 mm; unidirectional bezel with 60-minute division; sapphire crystal, transparent case back; screw-in crown; water-resistant to 30 atm
Band: rubber, buckle
Price: $2,895
Variations: with stainless steel Milanese mesh bracelet

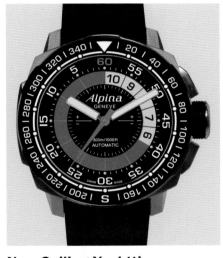

New Sailing Yachttimer

Reference number: AL-880LBG4V6
Movement: automatic, AL Caliber 880 (base Sellita SW500); ø 30 mm, height 7.9 mm; 25 jewels; 28,800 vph
Functions: hours, minutes, sweep seconds; countdown function
Case: stainless steel, ø 44 mm, height 16.7 mm; unidirectional bezel with 360 divisions; sapphire crystal, transparent case back; screw-in crown; water-resistant to 30 atm
Band: rubber, folding clasp
Price: $3,395

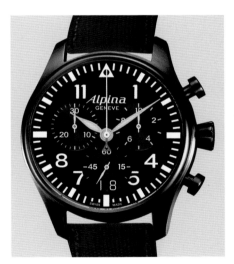

Aviation Startimer Pilot Chrono Quartz

Reference number: AL-372BFBS6
Movement: quartz
Functions: hours, minutes, subsidiary seconds; chronograph; large date
Case: stainless steel, black PVD coating; ø 44 mm, height 12.5 mm; sapphire crystal, water-resistant to 10 atm
Band: textile, buckle
Price: $1,150

Aquadive

AQUADIVE USA
1950 Oleander Street
Baton Rouge, LA 70806

Tel.:
888-397-9363

E-Mail:
info@aquadive.com

Website:
www.aquadive.com

Founded:
1962

Number of employees:
18

Annual production:
not specified

Distribution:
direct online sales

Most important collections/price range:
NOS Diver, Bathyscaphe / $1,290 to $2,990
(prices plus shipping)

According to Laver's Law, a style that shows up again at the fifty-year mark is "quaint." So much for the outward impact, maybe. But what about the intrinsic long-term personal and ephemeral value, the sometimes collective memories associated with a particular moment in our lives? Today, the very sight of a watch from times past might bring forth images of a different era, much like hearing the songs of Procol Harum or touching Naugahyde in an old Dodge Dart. Nostalgia is a powerful impulse, especially in an era like ours, which appears enamored by its own frenetic pace and refuses categorically to stop and reflect.

So the resurrection of an iconic watch of the sixties and seventies was bound to strike a positive note. In its day, the Aquadive was considered a solidly built and reliable piece of equipment seriously coveted by professional divers. It might still be around had it not been put out to pasture during the quartz revolution.

In its twenty-first century incarnation, the Aquadive bears many hallmarks of the original. The look is unmistakable: the charmingly awkward hands, the puffy cushion case, the sheer stability it exudes. In fact, some of the components, like the 200 NOS case and sapphire crystal, are leftovers from the old stock. The Swiss-made automatic movements and the gaskets, of course, are new.

Modern technologies, like DLC, and advances in CNC machining have transformed the older concepts. And to ensure reliability, the watches are assembled in Switzerland. The top of the current line is the Bathyscaphe series, machined from a block of stainless steel, and featuring new shock absorbers and an automatic helium release valve.

Bathyscaphe 100

Reference number: 1002.11.36211
Movement: automatic, ETA Caliber 2836-2;
ø 25.6 mm, height 4.6 mm; 25 jewels; 28,800 vph;
42-hour power reserve; regulated in 5 positions
Functions: hours, minutes, sweep seconds; date
Case: stainless steel, ø 43 mm, height 14 mm;
unidirectional bezel with 60-minute divisions;
antimagnetic soft iron inner case; sapphire crystal;
screw-in crown; automatic helium release valve;
water-resistant to 100 atm
Band: Isofrane, buckle
Price: $1,690, limited to 500 pieces
Variations: mesh bracelet ($1,890); gun metal
DLC-coated version ($1,890)

Bathyscaphe 300

Reference number: 3002.11.36211
Movement: automatic, ETA Caliber 2824-2;
ø 25.6 mm, height 4.6 mm; 25 jewels; 28,800 vph;
42-hour power reserve; regulated in 5 positions
Functions: hours, minutes, sweep seconds; date
Case: stainless steel, ø 47 mm, height 14 mm;
unidirectional bezel with 60-minute divisions;
sapphire crystal; screw-in crown; automatic helium
release valve; water-resistant to 300 atm
Band: Isofrane rubber, buckle
Price: $2,490

Aquadive 200 (New Old Stock)

Reference number: 200NOS.11.36211
Movement: automatic, ETA Caliber 2824-2;
ø 25.6 mm, height 4.6 mm; 25 jewels; 28,800 vph;
42-hour power reserve; regulated in 5 positions
Functions: hours, minutes, sweep seconds; date
Case: stainless steel, ø 37 mm, height 11 mm;
bidirectional bezel; NOS fiberglass crystal;
screw-in crown; water-resistant to 20 atm
Band: Isofrane, buckle
Remarks: case made from original 1962 stock
Price: $1,290
Variations: NATO strap

Aquadive Model 77 (New Old Stock)

Reference number: 771.12.365112
Movement: automatic, ETA Caliber 2836-2;
ø 25.6 mm, height 4.6 mm; 25 jewels; 28,800 vph;
42-hour power reserve; regulated in 5 positions
Functions: hours, minutes, sweep seconds; date
Case: stainless steel, 41 x 51 mm, height 16 mm;
unidirectional bezel with 60-minute divisions;
sapphire crystal; screwed-in crown; automatic
helium release valve; water-resistant to 100 atm
Band: rubber, buckle
Price: $1,290, limited to supply of old stock parts
Variations: with mesh bracelet ($1,390);
overhauled NOS Anton Schild movement ($1,390)

Bathyscaphe 100 Bronze

Reference number: 1006.13.365311
Movement: automatic, ETA Caliber 2836-2;
ø 25.6 mm, height 4.6 mm; 25 jewels; 28,800 vph;
42-hour power reserve; regulated in 5 positions
Functions: hours, minutes, sweep seconds; date
Case: German bronze alloy, ø 43 mm, height
15 mm; unidirectional bezel with 60-minute
divisions; sapphire crystal; screw-in crown;
automatic helium release valve; water-resistant to
100 atm
Band: Isofrane, buckle
Price: $1,690, limited to 100 pieces

Bathysphere 100 GMT

Reference number: 1001.13.935113
Movement: automatic, ETA Caliber 2893-2;
ø 25.6 mm, height 4.2 mm; 21 jewels; 28,800 vph;
42-hour power reserve; regulated in 5 positions
Functions: hours, minutes, sweep seconds; date,
GMT hand for 24-hour indication
Case: stainless steel case, ø 43 mm, height 15 mm;
unidirectional bezel with 60-minute divisions;
sapphire crystal; screw-in crown; automatic helium
release valve; water-resistant to 100 atm
Band: Isofrane, buckle
Price: $1,990, limited to 300 pieces
Variations: with mesh bracelet ($2,150); DLC-
coated gun metal ($2,090); 2 additional dial colors

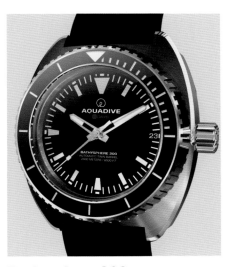

Bathysphere 300

Reference number: 2001.13.TB5D5111
Movement: automatic, custom-made Caliber TB5D;
ø 30.1 mm, height 5.9 mm; 45 jewels; 28,800 vph;
120-hour power reserve; regulated in 5 positions
Functions: hours, minutes, sweep seconds; date
Case: stainless steel, ø 42 mm, height 13 mm;
unidirectional bezel with 60-minute divisions;
sapphire crystal; screwed-in crown; automatic
helium release valve; water-resistant to 100 atm
Band: Isofrane, buckle
Price: $3,990
Variations: stainless steel link bracelet or mesh
bracelet

Bathyscaphe 300 DLC

Reference number: 3002.11.36211
Movement: automatic, ETA Caliber 2824-2;
ø 25.6 mm, height 4.6 mm; 25 jewels; 28,800 vph;
42-hour power reserve; regulated in 5 positions
Functions: hours, minutes, sweep seconds; date
Case: Diamond Like Carbon steel, ø 47 mm,
height 14 mm; unidirectional bezel with 60-minute
divisions; sapphire crystal; screw-in crown;
automatic helium release valve; water-resistant to
300 atm
Band: Isofrane rubber, buckle
Price: $2,490

AQUADIVE Model 50 Depth Gauge New Old Stock

Reference number: 1976.50
Movement: quartz, depth gauge
Functions: hours, minutes, seconds, depth gauge
Case: stainless steel, ø 47 mm, height 17 mm;
unidirectional bezel with 60-minute divisions;
mineral crystal; screw-in crown; water-resistant to
20 atm
Band: Isofrane rubber, buckle
Price: $4,490

Aristo Vollmer GmbH
Erbprinzenstr. 36
D-75175 Pforzheim
Germany

Tel.:
01149-7231-17031

Fax:
01149-7231-17033

E-Mail:
info@aristo-vollmer.de

Website:
www.aristo-vollmer.de

Founded:
1907 / 1998

Number of employees:
16

Annual production:
6,600 watches and 10,000 bracelets

Distribution:
retail

U.S. distributor:
Marc Time Imports
P.O. Box 10057
Melville, NY 11747
631-213-9112

Most important collections/price range:
Aristo watches starting at $400 up to Vollmer
watches $1,839

Aristo

"If you lie down with dogs, . . ." goes the old saying. And if you work closely with watchmakers . . . you may catch their more beneficial bug and become one yourself. That at any rate is what happened to the watch case and metal bracelet manufacturer Vollmer, Ltd, established in Pforzheim, Germany, by Ernst Vollmer in 1922. In the third generation, president Hansjörg Vollmer decided he, too, was interested in producing watches as well.

Vollmer, who studied business in Stuttgart, had the experience, but also and the connections with manufacturers in Switzerland. He also speaks French fluently, which is an asset. He acquired another maker of watch cases and watches, Aristo, and launched a series of pilot watches in 1998. The products were housed in sturdy titanium cases with bold onion crowns and secured with Vollmer's own light and comfortable titanium bracelets. Bit by bit, thanks to affordable prices and no-nonsense design—reviving some classic dials from World War II—Vollmer's watches caught hold. The collection grew with limited editions and a few chronometers.

In October 2005, Vollmer GmbH and Aristo Watches, still acting as separate brands until then, found they had enough in common to join forces for a bigger impact. Besides Vollmer and Aristo watches, they produced quartz watches, automatics, and chronographs under the brand names Messerschmitt and Aristella. The two companies operate together in Pforzheim, where they employ sixteen people. The aviator watches with hints of old military style have helped the business take off, but new design ideas are also making headway. And Vollmer continues manufacturing metal bracelets.

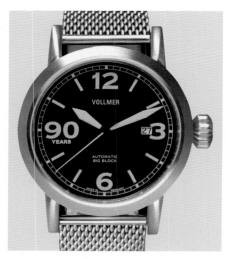

Vollmer 90 Years

Reference number: V10
Movement: automatic, ETA Caliber 2824-2; ø 25.6 mm, height 4.6 mm; 25 jewels; 28,800 vph; oversized "big block" rotor (29 mm) with tungsten oscillating mass; 42-hour power reserve
Functions: hours, minutes, sweep seconds; date
Case: stainless steel, ø 44 mm, height 11.5 mm; sapphire crystal, transparent case back; water-resistant to 5 atm
Band: stainless steel Milanese mesh, folding clasp
Remarks: limited to 90 pieces
Price: $1,299

Chronograph "Tachymeter" Flyer

Reference number: 3H129
Movement: automatic, ETA Caliber 7750; ø 30 mm, height 7.9 mm; 25 jewels; 28,800 vph; 42-hour power reserve
Functions: hours, minutes, subsidiary seconds; chronograph; weekday and date
Case: stainless steel, ø 40.5 mm, height 14.5 mm; mineral glass; transparent case back; water-resistant to 5 atm
Band: calf leather, buckle
Price: $1,390
Variations: with stainless steel Milanese mesh bracelet ($1,490)

Carbon-Watch

Reference number: 7H82
Movement: automatic, Caliber Aristomatic (base Sellita SW200); ø 25.6 mm; height 4.6 mm; 26 jewels; 28,800 vph; 38-hour power reserve
Functions: hours, minutes, sweep seconds
Case: stainless steel, ø 40 mm, height 10.6 mm; bezel with carbon insert; sapphire crystal, water-resistant to 5 atm
Band: carbon fiber, folding clasp
Price: $798
Variations: with carbon fiber link bracelet ($875); with leather strap ($675)

Armin Strom AG
Bözingenstrasse 46
CH-2502 Biel/Bienne
Switzerland

Tel.:
01141-32-343-3344

Fax:
01141-32-343-3340

E-Mail:
info@arminstrom.com

Website:
www.arminstrom.com

Founded:
2006

Number of employees:
18

Annual production:
approx. 1,000 watches

U.S. distributor:
contact Armin Strom headquarters

Most important collections/price range:
Gravity, One Week, Tourbillon, Racing, Regulator,
Skeleton / starting at $8,000

Armin Strom

For more than thirty years, Armin Strom's name was associated mainly with the art of skeletonizing. But this "grandmaster of skeletonizers" then decided to entrust his life's work to the next generation, which turned out to be the Swiss industrialist and art patron Willy Michel.

Michel had the wherewithal to expand the one-man show into a full-blown *manufacture* able to conceive, design, and produce its own mechanical movements. The endeavor attracted Claude Geisler, a very skilled designer, and Michel's own son, Serge, who became business manager. When this triumvirate joined forces, it was able to come up with a technically fascinating movement at the quaint little *manufacture* in the Biel suburb of Bözingen within a brief period of time.

The new movement went on to grow with several variants and derivatives and forms the backbone of a new collection. The acronym ARM stands for "Armin reserve de marche" (a seven-day power reserve), and AMW means "Armin manual winding" (a trimmed down manually wound movement with a single spring barrel). In sum, over the past few years, the brand has managed to gradually modernize its range of models and give itself a more contemporary profile without losing touch with its origins. The in-house movements are showing off their abilities on new, at times daring, dials. As for Strom, he still comes into the business now and then to look over shoulders and offer valuable insights from a life of watchmaking.

Manual Air

Reference number: TI11-MA.11
Movement: manually wound, Caliber AMW11; ø 36.6 mm, height 6 mm; 20 jewels; 18,000 vph; screw balance with gold weight screws, Breguet spring; 120-hour power reserve
Functions: hours, minutes, subsidiary seconds
Case: titanium, ø 43.4 mm, height 13 mm; sapphire crystal, transparent case back; water-resistant to 5 atm
Band: reptile skin, buckle
Remarks: comes with additional rubber strap
Price: $12,730
Variations: Earth, Water, and Fire

One Week Earth

Reference number: ST10-WE.40
Movement: manually wound, Caliber ARM09; ø 36.6 mm, height 6.2 mm; 34 jewels; 18,000 vph; 2 spring barrels, screw balance with gold weight screws, Breguet spring, crown wheels visible on dial side; 168-hour power reserve
Functions: hours, minutes, subsidiary seconds; power reserve indicator
Case: stainless steel with black PVD coating; ø 43.4 mm, height 13 mm; sapphire crystal, transparent case back; water-resistant to 5 atm
Band: reptile skin, buckle
Remarks: comes with extra rubber bracelet
Price: $25,360, limited to 100 pieces
Variations: Air, Water, and Fire

Gravity Water

Reference number: ST13-GW.50
Movement: automatic, Caliber AMR13; ø 36.6 mm, height 6 mm; 32 jewels; 18,000 vph; screw balance with gold weight screws, Breguet spring; visible microrotor on dial side, 120-hour power reserve
Functions: hours, minutes, subsidiary seconds
Case: stainless steel, ø 43.4 mm, height 13 mm; sapphire crystal, transparent case back; water-resistant to 5 atm
Band: reptile skin, buckle
Remarks: comes with extra rubber bracelet
Price: $14,160, limited to 100 pieces

Tourbillon Fire

Reference number: RG13-TF.90
Movement: manually wound, Caliber ATC11;
ø 36.6 mm, height 6.2 mm; 24 jewels; 18,000 vph;
1-minute tourbillon, screw balance with gold weight
screws, Breguet spring, 2 spring barrels, crown
wheels visible on dial side; 240-hour power reserve
Functions: hours, minutes, subsidiary seconds
Case: rose gold, ø 43.4 mm, height 13 mm;
sapphire crystal, transparent case back; water-
resistant to 5 atm
Band: reptile skin, double folding clasp
Remarks: comes with extra rubber bracelet
Price: $121,200, limited to 50 pieces
Variations: Air, Earth, Water

Racing Carbon

Reference number: TI12-RC.90
Movement: manually wound, Caliber ARM12;
ø 36.6 mm, height 6.2 mm; 23 jewels; 18,000 vph;
screw balance with golden screws, Breguet spring;
work plate and bridges with carbon fiber inserts;
2 spring barrels, screw balance with gold weight
screws, 168-hour power reserve
Functions: hours, minutes, subsidiary seconds
Case: titanium, ø 43.4 mm, height 13 mm; sapphire
crystal, transparent case back; water-resistant to
5 atm
Band: imitation leather, buckle
Remarks: comes with extra rubber bracelet
Price: $22,810, limited to 50 pieces

Racing One Week

Reference number: ST11-WR.90
Movement: manually wound, Caliber ARM09-MVR;
ø 36.6 mm, height 6.2 mm; 34 jewels; 18,000 vph;
plate and bridges of melted Formula 1 engine parts;
2 spring barrels, screw balance with gold weight
screws, Breguet spring, crown wheels visible on dial
side; 168-hour power reserve
Functions: hours, minutes, subsidiary seconds;
power reserve indicator
Case: stainless steel with black PVD coating;
ø 43.4 mm, height 13 mm; sapphire crystal,
transparent case back; water-resistant to 5 atm
Band: imitation leather, buckle
Remarks: comes with extra rubber bracelet
Price: $26,990, limited to 40 pieces

Caliber AMW11

Manually wound, escape wheel and pallet lever of
massive gold with hardened functional surfaces;
single spring barrel, 120-hour power reserve
Functions: hours, minutes, subsidiary seconds
Diameter: 36.6 mm
Height: 6 mm
Jewels: 20
Balance: screw balance with variable inertia
Frequency: 18,000 vph
Balance spring: Breguet spring
Shock protection: Incabloc
Remarks: fine finishing on the movement, hand-
engraved bridge

Caliber ATC11

Manually wound; 1-minute tourbillon, escape wheel
and pallet lever of massive gold with hardened
functional surfaces; double spring barrel, 240-hour
power reserve
Functions: hours, minutes, subsidiary seconds
Diameter: 36.6 mm
Height: 6.2 mm
Jewels: 24
Balance: screw balance with variable inertia
Frequency: 18,000 vph
Balance spring: Breguet spring
Shock protection: Incabloc
Remarks: fine finishing on the movement, hand-
engraved bridge

Caliber AMR13

Automatic; escape wheel and pallet lever of massive
gold with hardened functional surfaces; microrotor;
single spring barrel, 120-hour power reserve
Functions: hours, minutes, subsidiary seconds
Diameter: 36.6 mm
Height: 6 mm
Jewels: 32
Balance: screw balance with gold screws and
variable inertia
Frequency: 18,000 vph
Balance spring: Breguet spring
Shock protection: Incabloc
Remarks: fine finishing on the movement, hand-
engraved bridge

Arnold & Son
38, boulevard des Eplatures
CH-2300 La Chaux-de-Fonds
Switzerland

E-Mail:
info@arnoldandson.com

Website:
www.arnoldandson.com

Founded:
1995

Number of employees:
approx. 30

Annual production:
not specified

U.S. distributor:
Arnold & Son USA
510 W. 6th Street, Suite 309
Los Angeles, CA 90014
213-622-1133

Most important collections/price range:
UTTE, Time Pyramid, DBG, DBS, HMS, TB88,
TE8 (Tourbillon), TBR / from approx. $10,000 to
$325,000

Arnold & Son

John Arnold holds a special place among the British watchmakers of the eighteenth and nineteenth centuries because he was the first to literally organize the production of his chronometers along industrial lines. He developed his own standards and employed numerous watchmakers. During his lifetime, he is said to have manufactured around 5,000 marine chronometers which he sold at reasonable prices to the Royal Navy and the West Indies merchant fleet. Arnold chronometers were packed in the trunks of some of the greatest explorers, from John Franklin and Ernest Shackleton to Captain Cook and Dr. Livingstone.

As Arnold & Son was once synonymous with precision timekeeping on the high seas, it stands to reason, then, that the modern brand should also focus its design policies on the interplay of time and geography as well as the basic functions of navigation. Independence from The British Masters Group has meant that the venerable English chronometer brand has been reorienting itself, setting its sights on classic, elegant watchmaking. With the expertise of watch manufacturer La Joux-Perret behind it (and the expertise housed in the building behind the complex on the main road between La Chaux-de-Fonds and Le Locle), it has been able to implement a number of new ideas.

There are two main lines: The Royal Collection celebrates John Arnold's art, with luxuriously designed models that look back in time with delicate complications, tourbillons or world-time displays, or unadorned manual windings featuring the new Caliber A&S 1001 by La Joux-Perret. The Instrument Collection is dedicated to exploring the seven seas and offers a sober look reflecting old-fashioned meters. Typically, these timepieces combine two displays on a single dial: jumping seconds, for example, between the off-center displays of time and the date hand, or separate escapements driving a dual time display—left the sidereal time, right the solar time, and between the two, the difference. Perhaps the most remarkable timepiece in the collection is the skeletonized Time Pyramid with a dual power reserve, a crown between the lugs, and an overall modern look.

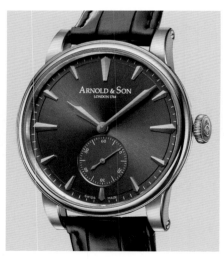

HMS1

Reference number: 1LCAP.S04A.C110A
Movement: manual winding, Arnold & Son Caliber 1101; ø 30 mm, height 2.7 mm; 21 jewels; 21,600 vph; double spring barrel, 80-hour power reserve
Functions: hours, minutes, subsidiary seconds
Case: rose gold, ø 40 mm, height 8 mm; sapphire crystal, transparent case back; water-resistant to 3 atm
Band: reptile skin, buckle
Price: $15,135
Variations: white dial ($14,960); stainless steel with black dial ($15,165); stainless steel with anthracite dial ($10,095)

TB88

Reference number: 1TBAS.S01A.C113S
Movement: manual winding, Arnold & Son Caliber 5003; ø 37.8 mm, height 5.9 mm; 32 jewels; 18,000 vph; inverted construction; escapement with jumping seconds; double barrel spring; 100-hour power reserve
Functions: hours, minutes, subsidiary seconds (jumping)
Case: stainless steel, ø 46 mm, height 12.85 mm; sapphire crystal, transparent case back; water-resistant to 3 atm
Band: reptile skin, buckle
Price: $36,550
Variations: rose gold ($53,460)

HM Perpetual Moon

Reference number: 1GLAS.B01A
Movement: manual winding, Arnold & Son Caliber 1512; ø 34 mm, height 5.35 mm; 27 jewels; 21,600 vph; astronomically accurate moon phase display; 80-hour power reserve
Functions: hours, minutes; moon phase
Case: stainless steel, ø 42 mm, height 11.43 mm; sapphire crystal, transparent case back; water-resistant to 3 atm
Band: reptile skin, buckle
Remarks: hand-engraved, golden moon
Price: $15,300
Variations: pink gold with cream dial ($27,845), pink gold with blue dial ($28,585)

TBR

Reference number: 1ARAS.S01A.C121S
Movement: automatic, Arnold & Son Caliber 6008; ø 30.4 mm, height 7.79 mm; 34 jewels; 28,800 vph; escapement with jumping seconds; 50-hour power reserve
Functions: hours and minutes (off-center), sweep seconds (jumping); date (retrograde)
Case: stainless steel, ø 44 mm, height 13.8 mm; sapphire crystal, transparent case back; water-resistant to 3 atm
Band: reptile skin, buckle
Price: $19,750
Variations: rose gold ($29,350)

DBS

Reference number: 1DSAP.W01A.C120P
Movement: manual winding, Arnold & Son Caliber 1311; ø 35 mm, height 3.9 mm; 42 jewels; 21,600 vph; 2 symmetrical independent mechanisms for parallel display each with spring barrel and escapement; 80-hour power reserve
Functions: hours, minutes, sweep seconds (solar time); hours, minutes (sidereal time); dual 24-hour display
Case: rose gold, ø 44 mm, height 9.89 mm; sapphire crystal, transparent case back; water-resistant to 3 atm
Band: reptile skin, buckle
Price: $43,095

Time Pyramid

Reference number: 1TPAR.S01A.C124A
Movement: manual winding, Arnold & Son Caliber 1615; ø 37 mm, height 4.4 mm; 27 jewels; 21,600 vph; skeletonized; pyramidal architecture; 2 spring barrels; 80-hour power reserve
Functions: hours, minutes, subsidiary seconds; double power reserve display
Case: pink gold, ø 44.6 mm, height 10.09 mm; sapphire crystal, transparent case back; water-resistant to 3 atm
Band: reptile skin, buckle
Remarks: inspired by table clocks from John and Roger Arnold
Price: $39,995

Caliber A&S5003

Manually wound; inverted movement construction; double spring barrel, 100-hour power reserve
Functions: hours, minutes, subsidiary seconds (jumping)
Diameter: 37.8 mm
Height: 5.9 mm
Jewels: 32
Balance: screw balance
Frequency: 18,000 vph
Balance spring: Breguet spring
Shock protection: Incabloc
Remarks: German-silver movement with black ruthenium coating; hand-beveled bridges and polished edges

Caliber A&S1311

Manually wound; 2 symmetrically arranged, independent mechanisms, each with its own barrel spring and escapement; 40-hour power reserve
Functions: hours, minutes, sweep seconds; hours, minutes (sidereal time); dual day/night display
Diameter: 35 mm
Height: 3.9 mm
Jewels: 42
Balance: glucydur (2x)
Frequency: 21,600 and 21,659 vph
Balance spring: flat hairspring (2)
Shock protection: Incabloc
Remarks: rhodium-coated movement; hand-beveled bridges and polished edges

Caliber A&S6008

Automatic; escapement with jumping seconds; winding rotor with ceramic ball bearings ; single barrel spring, 45 hours power reserve
Functions: hours, minutes (off-center), sweep seconds (jumping); date (retrograde),
Diameter: 30.4 mm
Height: 7.79 mm
Jewels: 34
Balance: glucydur
Frequency: 28,800 vph
Balance spring: flat hairspring
Shock protection: Incabloc
Remarks: German-silver movement with black NAC coating; hand-beveled bridges and polished edges

Luxury Artpieces SA
Route de Thonon 146
CH-1222 Vésenaz
Switzerland

Tel.:
01141-22-752-4940

Website:
www.artya.com

Founded:
2010

Number of employees:
10

Annual production:
at least 365 (one a day)

U.S. distributor:
Contact headquarters for all enquiries.

Most important collections/price range:
Son of a Gun / $4,062 to $13,521; Son of
Abstraction / $2,515 to $13,521; Son of Earth
/ $4,087 to $25,156; Son of Love / $4,087 to
$36,580; Son of Horror / $4,087 to $12,473; Son
of Sound / $5,235 to $69,430; Son of Gears /
$6,250 to $160,200

ArtyA

Shaking up the staid atmosphere of watchmaking can be achieved in many ways. The conservative approach is to make some small engineering advance and then talk loudly of tradition and innovation. Yvan Arpa, founder of ArtyA watches, takes another route and, like some Genevan Dennis the Menace, enjoys "putting his boot in the anthill," in his own words.

This refreshingly candid personality arrived at watchmaking because, after spending his *Wanderjahre* crossing Papua New Guinea on foot and practicing Thai boxing in its native land, any corporate mugginess back home did not quite cut it for him. Instead he turned the obscure brand Romain Jerome into the talk of the industry with novel material choices: rusted metal from *Titanic,* dust from the moon, and fossilized dinosaur dung (coprolite). "I looked for antimatter to gentrify common matter," he reflects, "like the rust: proof of the passage of time and the sworn enemy of watchmaking."

After leaving Romain Jerome, he founded his own company, ArtyA, where he could get his "monster" off the slab as it were, with a divine spark. Each new ArtyA case is hit with an electrical arc. "I had worked with water, rust, dust, and other elements, so this time I took fire," says Arpa. The result is different each time. Inside the cases, besides a solid Swiss-made mechanism, one finds interesting bits and pieces—from butterfly wings and cut up euros (Bye Bye Euro) to bullets (Son of a Gun). More than occasionally, a new crazy idea pops up in his head, like the Son of Sound series with a guitar-shaped case and chrono pushers designed like guitar pegs—Alice Cooper owns one, obviously. He also launched a second brand, Spero Lucem (I hope for light), a little taunt at Geneva with its Calvinistic motto *Post tenebras lux* (after the dark comes light). Arpa often uses the warty skin of toads, a pest in Australia, as straps. Killing rare animals is, he feels, "a little borderline."

ArtyA Son of Sound Gold

Reference number: SoS Gold
Movement: automatic, Artya-Woodstock by Concepto; 27 jewels; 28,800 vph; 48-hour power reserve
Functions: hours, minutes, subsidiary seconds; date; patented active "tuning pegs" system for the chronograph functions and date set; 30-minute counter
Case: pink gold, 36.62 x 52.3 mm, height 15 mm; hand-stretched pink gold strings; water-resistant to 50 atm
Band: reptile skin, buckle
Price: $69,600

ArtyA Tesla Skeleton Tourbillon

Movement: manually wound, Concepto Caliber C-8017; ø 32.6 mm, height 5.7 mm; 19 jewels; 21,600 vph; 1-minute tourbillon with openwork movement; 72-hour power reserve
Functions: hours, minutes
Case: stainless steel, ø 47 mm, height 12 mm; sapphire crystal; transparent case back; water-resistant to 5 atm
Band: cane toad, buckle
Remarks: case distressed by 1 million-volt arc giving it a unique color
Price: $125,300

ArtyA Son of a Gun Bicolor Steel/Black

Movement: automatic (Swiss-made); 25 jewels; rotor with target and bullets oscillating weight; 42-hour power reserve
Functions: hours, minutes
Case: stainless steel with PVD; ø 47 mm, height 12 mm; bezel and dial with target insert; sapphire crystal; transparent case back; water-resistant to 5 atm
Band: reptile skin, buckle
Remarks: features 5 real 6-mm Flobert rounds between dial and case
Price: $16,900

Atlantic Watch Ltd
Solothurnstrasse 44
CH-2543 Lengnau
Switzerland

Tel.:
01141-32-625-18-88

Fax:
01141-32-625-18-89

E-Mail:
info@atlantic-watch.ch

Website:
www.atlantic-watches.ch

Founded:
1888

Number of employees:
not specified

Annual production:
not specified

U.S. distributor:
USA - Online Shop
Goldstone Jewelry
6601 W. Irving Park RD
Chicago, IL 60634
info@ atlanticwatch-usa.com
www.atlanticwatch-usa.com

Most important collections/price range:
Mariner, Seacrest, Seashark, Seashore, Skipper,
Worldmaster, and many more /
$260 to $1,060

Atlantic

Atlantic, founded by Eduard Kummer in Bettlach, Switzerland in 1888, was once one of the largest manufacturers of the Roskopf pin-pallet escapement, which was at the heart of many highly popular and affordable Swiss watches during the nineteenth century. What few know is that Atlantic pioneered the waterproof watch with automatic winding and invented the date-changing "speed-switch system."

In 2013, the brand celebrated its 125th anniversary. Throughout its long history, Atlantic has followed the same principles and guidelines. As one of Switzerland's few independent watch manufacturers, it offers very attractive timepieces, in terms of both price and performance. The company treats the status "Swiss made" as both a motivation and obligation, but not as a way to pump up prices.

The company is currently headquartered in Grenchen, a town it shares with movement maker ETA, whose caliber is installed in both the quartz and the automatic movements in Atlantic's collection. These offerings include a large number of classic, elegant, and sporty watches, most of which feature a scratch-resistant sapphire crystal. Atlantic watches are waterproof up to 30 meters, and its cases are made high-grade stainless steel.

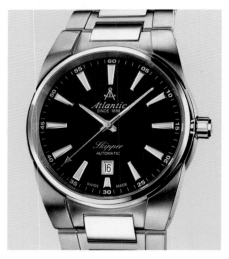

Skipper

Reference number: 83765.41.61
Movement: automatic, ETA Caliber 7751; ø 30 mm, height 10 mm; 28 jewels; 28,800 vph; 38 hours power reserve
Functions: hours, minutes, sweep seconds; date
Case: stainless steel, ø 44 mm, height 10 mm; sapphire crystal; transparent case back; water-resistant to 5 atm
Band: stainless steel, folding clasp
Price: $740
Variations: various dial colors

Worldmaster 1888

Reference number: P.03
Movement: manually wound, ETA Caliber 7751; ø 30 mm, height 10 mm; 28 jewels; 28,800 vph; 42 hours power reserve
Functions: hours, minutes, sweep seconds; date
Case: stainless steel, ø 44 mm, height 10 mm; sapphire crystal; transparent case back; water-resistant to 5 atm
Band: calf leather, folding clasp
Price: $770
Variations: various dials

Seashore

Reference number: 72765.41.25
Movement: automatic, ETA Caliber 7751; ø 30 mm, height 10 mm; 28 jewels; 28,800 vph; 42 hours power reserve
Functions: hours, minutes, sweep seconds; date
Case: stainless steel, ø 44 mm, height 10 mm; sapphire crystal; transparent case back; water-resistant to 5 atm
Band: stainless steel, folding clasp
Price: $550
Variations: various dials; with leather bracelet ($500)

AVANTGARДE

EMOTION · INNOVATION · PROVOCATION

Babylonian Hand winding. Hand engraved movement. Three levels open dial with MOP ring. Blued hands. Stainless steel. 5 ATM. 500 pcs limited Edition.

LITTLE Treasury JEWELERS

2506 New Market Lane
Gambrills, MD 21054
410-721-7100
www.littletreasury.com

ALEXANDER SHOROKHOFF

UHRENMANUFAKTUR
GERMANY

WWW.ALEXANDER-SHOROKHOFF.DE

Manufacture d'Horlogerie Audemars Piguet

Route de France 16
CH-1348 Le Brassus
Switzerland

Tel.:
01141-21-845-1400

Fax:
01141-21-845-1400

E-Mail:
info@audemarspiguet.com

Website:
www.audemarspiguet.com

Founded:
1875

Number of employees:
approx. 1,100

Annual production:
26,000 watches

U.S. distributor:
Audemars Piguet (North America) Inc.
65 East 57th Street
New York, NY 10022
212-758-8400

Most important collections/price range:
Royal Oak / from approx. $15,400

Audemars Piguet

The history of Audemars Piguet may well be one of the most engaging stories of Swiss watchmaking folklore: Ever since their school days together in the Vallée de Joux, Jules-Louis Audemars (born in 1851) and Edward-Auguste Piguet (born 1853) knew that they would follow in the footsteps of their fathers and grandfathers and become watchmakers. They were members of the same sports association, sang in the same church choir, attended the same vocational school—and both became outstandingly talented watchmakers.

The *manufacture* that was founded 135 years ago by these two is still in family hands. The company was able to make extensive investments in production facilities and new movements thanks to the ongoing success of the sporty Royal Oak collection and the profits made from selling off shares in Jaeger-LeCoultre. The Manufacture des Forges, designed according to the latest ecological and economical standards, opened in August 2009 in Le Brassus and is a key to the future of the traditional brand. The second key is no doubt the atelier Renaud et Papi, which has belonged to AP since 1992 and specializes in the most complex complications.

Something must have clicked, because general manager Philippe C. Merk steered the brand through the recession well, even crossing the CHF 550 million mark. Merk and AP parted ways in May 2012, and the company is currently under interim manager François-Henry Bennahmias, who previously handled the key Asian market.

Royal Oak Offshore Chronograph

Reference number: 26402CE.00.A002CA.01
Movement: automatic, AP Caliber 3126/3840; ø 29.92 mm, height 7.26 mm; 59 jewels, 21,600 vph; 55-hour power reserve
Functions: hours, minutes, subsidiary seconds; chronograph; date
Case: ceramic, ø 44 mm; bezel attached with 8 stainless steel screws; sapphire crystal, transparent case back; screw-in crown; water-resistant to 10 atm
Band: rubber, buckle
Price: $40,000

Royal Oak Offshore Diver

Reference number: 15707CE.00.A002CA.01
Movement: automatic, AP Caliber 3120; ø 26.6 mm, height 4.26 mm; 40 jewels, 21,600 vph; 60-hour power reserve
Functions: hours, minutes, sweep seconds; date
Case: ceramic, ø 42 mm; bezel attached with 8 stainless steel screws; crown-adjustable inner bezel with 60-minute divisions; sapphire crystal, transparent case back; screw-in crown; water-resistant to 30 atm
Band: rubber, buckle
Price: $21,800

Royal Oak Offshore Diver

Reference number: 15703ST.00.A002CA.01
Movement: automatic, AP Caliber 3120; ø 26.6 mm, height 4.25 mm; 40 jewels; 21,600 vph; entirely hand-decorated
Functions: hours, minutes, sweep seconds; date; diving timer
Case: stainless steel, ø 42 mm, bezel attached with 8 stainless steel screws; crown-adjustable inner bezel with 60-minute divisions; sapphire crystal; screwed-in crown; water-resistant to 30 atm
Band: rubber, buckle
Price: $18,900

Royal Oak Offshore

Reference number: 26170ST.OO.D101CR.02
Movement: automatic, AP Caliber 3126-3840 (base 3120); ø 29.92 mm, height 7.16 mm; 59 jewels; 21,600 vph
Functions: hours, minutes, subsidiary seconds; chronograph; date
Case: stainless steel, ø 42 mm, bezel attached with 8 stainless steel screws; sapphire crystal; screw-in crown; water-resistant to 10 atm
Band: reptile skin, folding clasp
Price: $25,700
Variations: various dial and band colors ($25,700); stainless steel with stainless steel bracelet ($27,400); titanium with titanium bracelet ($27,900)

Royal Oak Offshore Chronograph

Reference number: 26401PO.OO.A018CR.01
Movement: automatic, AP Caliber 3126/3840 (base 3120); ø 29.92 mm, height 7.26 mm; 59 jewels, 21,600 vph; entirely hand-decorated
Functions: hours, minutes, small seconds; chronograph; date
Case: platinum, ø 44 mm, height 14.45 mm; ceramic bezel attached with 8 white-gold screws; sapphire crystal, transparent case back; screw-in crown; water-resistant to 10 atm
Band: reptile skin, buckle
Price: $69,200

Lady Royal Oak Offshore

Reference number: 26048SK.ZZ.D010CA.01
Movement: automatic, AP Caliber 2385; ø 26.20 mm, height 5.5 mm; 37 jewels, 21,600 vph
Functions: hours, minutes, subsidiary seconds; chronograph; date
Case: stainless steel, ø 37 mm, height 12.2 mm; rubber-coated bezel, set with 32 diamonds, bezel attached with 8 screws; sapphire crystal, screw-in crown; water-resistant to 5 atm
Band: rubber, folding clasp
Price: $28,200

Royal Oak Offshore Grande Complication

Reference number: 26571R0.OO.A010CA.01
Movement: automatic, AP Caliber 2885; ø 31.6 mm, height 8.95 mm; 52 jewels; 19,800 vph; skeletonized; 45-hour power reserve
Functions: hours, minutes, subsidiary seconds; minute repeater; split-seconds chronograph; perpetual calendar with date, weekday, month, moon phase
Case: rose gold, ø 44 mm, black ceramic bezel attached with 8 screws; sapphire crystal, transparent case back; ceramic crown and pushers; water-resistant to 2 atm
Band: rubber, buckle
Price: $756,000, limited to 3 pieces

Royal Oak Tourbillon

Reference number: 26510OR.OO.1220OR.01
Movement: manually wound, AP Caliber 2924; ø 31.5 mm, height 4.46 mm; 25 jewels, 21,600 vph; 1-minute tourbillon, 70-hour power reserve
Functions: hours, minutes; power reserve indicator (on movement side)
Case: pink gold, ø 41 mm, bezel attached with 8 screws; sapphire crystal, transparent case back; screw-in crown; water-resistant to 5 atm
Band: pink gold, folding clasp
Price: $166,100
Variations: stainless steel with stainless steel band ($136,100)

Royal Oak

Reference number: 15450OR.OO.D002CR.01
Movement: automatic, AP Caliber 3120; ø 26.6 mm, height 4.26 mm; 60 jewels; 21,600 vph; entirely hand-decorated
Functions: hours, minutes, sweep seconds; date
Case: pink gold, ø 37 mm, height 9.8 mm; bezel attached with 8 white-gold screws; sapphire crystal, transparent case back; screw-in crown; water-resistant to 5 atm
Band: reptile skin, folding clasp
Price: $28,400
Variations: various dial colors; stainless steel with stainless steel bracelet ($16,300)

Royal Oak "Equation du Temps"

Reference number: 26603ST.OO.D002CR.01
Movement: automatic, AP Caliber 2120-2808 (base 2120); ø 28 mm, height 5.35 mm; 41 jewels; 19,800 vph
Functions: hours, minutes; equation of time, sunrise and sunset times; perpetual calendar with date, astronomical moon
Case: stainless steel, ø 42 mm, bezel attached with 8 white gold screws; sapphire crystal, screw-in crown
Band: reptile skin, folding clasp
Price: $68,700
Variations: pink gold ($84,000)

Jules Audemars Extra-Flat

Reference number: 15180BC.OO.A002CR.01
Movement: automatic, AP Caliber 2120; ø 28.4 mm, height 2.45 mm; 36 jewels; 19,800 vph
Functions: hours, minutes
Case: white gold, ø 41 mm, height 6.7 mm; sapphire crystal, transparent case back
Band: reptile skin, buckle
Price: $27,100
Variations: pink gold ($25,000)

Jules Audemars Chronograph

Reference number: 26100OR.OO.D088CR.01
Movement: automatic, AP Caliber 3124-3841 (base AP 3120); ø 29.92 mm, height 7.16 mm; 59 jewels; 21,600 vph
Functions: hours, minutes, subsidiary seconds; chronograph
Case: pink gold, ø 41 mm, height 12.7 mm; sapphire crystal, transparent case back
Band: reptile skin, folding clasp
Price: $39,800
Variations: white gold ($43,700)

Jules Audemars Full Calendar

Reference number: 26385OR.OO.A088CR.01
Movement: automatic, AP Caliber 2325/2825; ø 26.6 mm, height 4.6 mm; 40 jewels, 28,800 vph
Functions: hours, minutes; full calendar with date, weekday, moon phase
Case: pink gold, ø 39 mm, height 8.8 mm; sapphire crystal
Band: reptile skin, buckle
Price: $29,800

Millenary 4101

Reference number: 15350OR.OO.D093CR.01
Movement: automatic, AP Caliber 4101; ø 37.25 mm, height 7.46 mm; 34 jewels; 28,800 vph; inverted design with balance and escapement on dial side
Functions: hours, minutes, subsidiary seconds
Case: pink gold, ø 47 mm, height 13 mm; sapphire crystal, transparent case back
Band: reptile skin, folding clasp
Price: $39,800
Variations: stainless steel ($24,100)

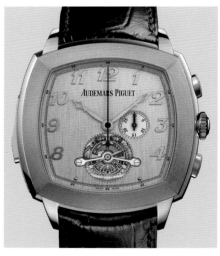

Tradition Tourbillon Minute Repeater Chronograph

Reference number: 26564IC.OO.D002CR.01
Movement: manually wound, AP Caliber 2874; ø 29.9 mm, height 7.65 mm; 38 jewels, 21,600 vph; 1-minute tourbillon; 48-hour power reserve
Functions: hours, minutes, subsidiary seconds; minute repeater; chronograph
Case: titanium, ø 47 mm; white gold bezel, crown, pushers and case back; sapphire crystal
Band: reptile skin, folding clasp
Price: $471,300, limited to 10 pieces

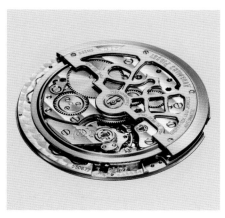

Caliber 2120

Automatic; bidirectional winding rotor; extra-flat design, lateral studs and running ring on movement for stability; single spring barrel, 40-hour power reserve
Functions: hours, minutes
Diameter: 28 mm
Height: 2.45 mm
Jewels: 36
Balance: with variable inertia
Frequency: 19,800 vph
Shock protection: Kif Elastor
Remarks: beveled and polished steel parts, perlage on plate, bridges with côtes de Genève

Caliber 2120-2808

Base caliber: 2120
Automatic; bidirectional winding rotor; extra-flat, lateral studs and running ring for stability; single spring barrel, 40-hour power reserve
Functions: hours, minutes; perpetual calendar (month, moon phase, leap year, weekday, date); equation of time, sunrise/sunset; astronomical moon
Diameter: 28 mm
Height: 5.35 mm
Jewels: 41
Balance: with variable inertia
Frequency: 19,800 vph
Shock protection: Kif Elastor
Remarks: beveled/polished parts, perlage on plate, hand-engraved rotor, côtes de Genève

Caliber 2121

Automatic; bidirectional winding rotor; extra-flat design, lateral studs and running ring on movement for stability; single spring barrel, 40-hour power reserve
Functions: hours, minutes; date
Diameter: 28 mm
Height: 3.05 mm
Jewels: 36
Balance: with variable inertia
Frequency: 19,800 vph
Shock protection: Kif Elastor
Remarks: beveled and polished steel parts, perlage on plate, bridges with côtes de Genève

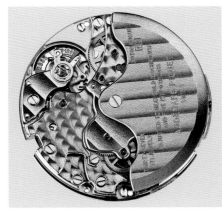

Caliber 2324-2825

Automatic; rotor with gold weight segment; single spring barrel, 40-hour power reserve
Functions: hours, minutes; date, weekday; moon phase
Diameter: 26.6 mm
Height: 4.6 mm
Jewels: 45
Balance: with variable inertia
Frequency: 28,800 vph
Shock protection: Kif Elastor
Remarks: beveled and polished steel parts, perlage on plate, bridges with côtes de Genève

Caliber 2329-2846

Automatic; rotor with gold weight segment; single spring barrel, 40-hour power reserve
Functions: hours, minutes; 24-hour display; date; power reserve indicator; day/night indicator
Diameter: 26.6 mm
Height: 4.9 mm
Jewels: 33
Balance: with adjustable inertia
Frequency: 28,800 vph
Shock protection: Kif Elastor
Remarks: beveled and polished steel parts, perlage on plate, bridges with côtes de Genève

Caliber 2385

Automatic; gold rotor; single spring barrel, 40-hour power reserve
Functions: hours, minutes, subsidiary seconds; chronograph; date
Diameter: 26.2 mm
Height: 5.5 mm
Jewels: 37
Frequency: 21,600 vph
Shock protection: Kif Elastor
Remarks: beveled and polished steel parts, perlage on plate, bridges with côtes de Genève

Caliber 2897

Automatic; hubless peripheral rotor with platinum weight turning on movement edge; column wheel control of chronograph functions; 1-minute tourbillon; simple spring barrel, 65-hour power reserve

Functions: hours, minutes, subsidiary seconds; chronograph
Diameter: 35 mm
Height: 7.75 mm
Jewels: 34
Balance: with variable inertia
Frequency: 21,600 vph
Shock protection: Kif Elastor
Remarks: beveled and guilloché steel parts, perlage on plate

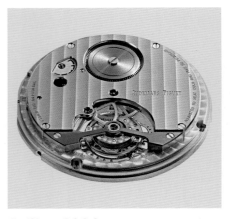

Caliber 2924

Manually wound, 1-minute tourbillon; single spring barrel, 70-hour power reserve

Functions: hours, minutes; power reserve indicator (on movement side)
Diameter: 31.5 mm
Height: 4.46 mm
Jewels: 25
Balance: screw balance
Frequency: 21,600 vph
Shock protection: Kif Elastor
Remarks: beveled and polished steel parts, perlage on plate, bridges with côtes de Genève

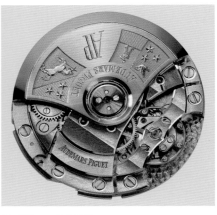

Caliber 3120

Automatic; bidirectional winding gold rotor; single spring barrel, 60-hour power reserve

Functions: hours, minutes, sweep seconds; date
Diameter: 26.6 mm
Height: 4.25 mm
Jewels: 40
Balance: with adjustable inertia
Frequency: 21,600 vph
Shock protection: Kif Elastor
Remarks: beveled and polished steel parts, perlage on plate, bridges with côtes de Genève

Caliber 3124-3841

Base caliber: 3120
Automatic; bidirectional winding gold rotor; single spring barrel, 60-hour power reserve
Functions: hours, minutes, subsidiary seconds; chronograph
Diameter: 29.94 mm
Height: 7.16 mm
Jewels: 59
Balance: with adjustable inertia
Frequency: 21,600 vph
Shock protection: Kif Elastor
Remarks: beveled and polished steel parts, perlage on plate, bridges with côtes de Genève

Caliber 3126-3840

Base caliber: 3120
Automatic; bidirectional winding gold rotor; single spring barrel, 60-hour power reserve
Functions: hours, minutes, subsidiary seconds; chronograph; date
Diameter: 29.94 mm
Height: 7.15 mm
Jewels: 59
Balance: with adjustable inertia
Frequency: 21,600 vph
Shock protection: Kif Elastor
Remarks: beveled and polished steel parts, perlage on plate, bridges with côtes de Genève

Caliber 4101

Automatic, inverted construction (escapement on dial side); bidirectional winding gold rotor with ceramic ball bearings; single spring barrel, 60-hour power reserve
Functions: hours, minutes, subsidiary seconds
Measurements: 37.25 x 32.9 mm
Height: 7.46 mm
Jewels: 34
Balance: with variable inertia
Frequency: 28,800 vph
Shock protection: Kif Elastor
Remarks: all components decorated by hand; dial side of plate with horizontal côtes de Genève, perlage on back; rhodium-plated bridges, beveled and with decorative graining

Azimuth Watch Co. Sarl
48 rue de la Gare
CH-2502 Bienne/Biel
Switzerland

Tel.:
01141-32-323-1443

Fax:
01141-32-323-1442

E-Mail:
sales@azimuthwatch.com

Website:
www.azimuthwatch.com

Founded:
2004

Number of employees:
10

Annual production:
2,000–3,000 watches

U.S. distributor:
Coast Time
800 S. Pacific Coast Highway, Suite 8-446
Redondo Beach, CA 90277
888-609-1010
www.azimuthwatchusa.com

Most important collections/price range:
SP-1 / $3,800 to $90,000; Xtreme-1 /
$2,250 to $4,000

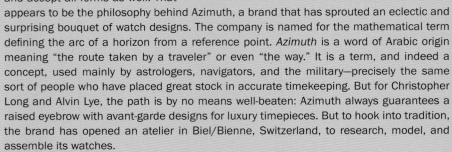

Azimuth

Creativity can take on all forms and accept all forms as well. That appears to be the philosophy behind Azimuth, a brand that has sprouted an eclectic and surprising bouquet of watch designs. The company is named for the mathematical term defining the arc of a horizon from a reference point. *Azimuth* is a word of Arabic origin meaning "the route taken by a traveler" or even "the way." It is a term, and indeed a concept, used mainly by astrologers, navigators, and the military—precisely the same sort of people who have placed great stock in accurate timekeeping. But for Christopher Long and Alvin Lye, the path is by no means well-beaten: Azimuth always guarantees a raised eyebrow with avant-garde designs for luxury timepieces. But to hook into tradition, the brand has opened an atelier in Biel/Bienne, Switzerland, to research, model, and assemble its watches.

Azimuth fans are creative thinkers themselves who appreciate the company's unusual, genuinely innovative timepieces—some known internally as "concept watches." The Mr. Roboto and the Chrono Gauge Mecha are tongue-in-cheek hyperbolic statements about the meaning of a mechanical watch. The SP-1 Mecanique Spaceship and its adventurous mix of displays, powered by a highly modified ETA Unitas 6497, feature a variety of imaginative dials. The single three-dimensional titanium hand vaguely recalls a spaceship. The secret gambler can depress the die-shaped crown of the SP-1 Roulette to send a ball zooming around the dial or play a quick game of baccarat. The SP-1 Landship or Tank Watch has made it over the top (yes, it is a World War I tank) after years of tinkering in time for commemorations of 1914. Amid all these complicated devices, the single-hand Back in Time pieces appear as mysterious as a koan.

Grande Baccarat Entry

Reference number: Grand Baccarat
Movement: automatic, modified SW 200; ø 36 mm, height 5.7 mm; 28,800 vph
Functions: hours, minutes, seconds; baccarat game activated by depressing crown
Case: stainless steel, ø 42 mm, height 15.2 mm; domed sapphire crystal; water-resistant to 3 atm
Band: calf leather, folding clasp
Price: $3,900
Variations: available in different sizes, price on request

Back In Time Silver Rose

Reference number: BIT
Movement: automatic, modified ETA/SW; ø 36 mm, height 5.7 mm
Functions: single hand, date
Case: stainless steel, ø 42 mm, height 15.2 mm; domed sapphire crystal; water-resistant to 3 atm
Band: calf leather, tang buckle
Remarks: world's first single-hand watch with counterclockwise motion
Price: $1,950

Back In Time Enamel Beige

Reference number: BIT
Movement: automatic, modified ETA/SW; ø 36 mm, height 5.7 mm
Functions: single hand, date
Case: stainless steel, ø 42 mm, height 15.2 mm; domed sapphire crystal; water-resistant to 3 atm
Band: calf leather, tang buckle
Remarks: world's first single-hand watch with counterclockwise motion
Price: $1,950

SP-1 Landship

Reference number: Landship
Movement: automatic, modified ETA; ø 32.5 mm, height 6.7 mm
Functions: wandering hour, retrograde minutes
Case: titanium, 55 x 40 mm; sapphire crystal; water-resistant to 3 atm
Band: rubber, folding clasp
Remarks: hours and minutes displayed vertically
Price: $8,400

SP-1 Spaceship Skeleton

Reference number: SP-1 SKE
Movement: automatic, modified Caliber Unitas 6497-1; ø 36.6 mm, height 4.5 mm; 18,000 vph
Functions: wandering hour, retrograde minutes
Case: titanium, 55 x 40 mm; sapphire crystal; water-resistant to 3 atm
Band: reptile skin, folding clasp
Remarks: hours and minutes displayed vertically
Price: $7,100

SP-1 Roulette

Reference number: ROU-1
Movement: automatic, modified ETA 2842-2; 33.9 x 30.9 mm, height 6.8 mm; 21,600 vph
Functions: hours, minutes, seconds; roulette activated by depressing crown
Case: stainless steel, ø 35 mm, height 15.1 mm; 55 mm lug to lug length; domed sapphire crystal; water-resistant to 5 atm
Band: leather, folding clasp
Price: $3,800, limited edition of 500 pieces

SP-1 Twin Barrel Tourbillon

Reference number: TBT-1
Movement: manual winding tourbillon; 36.3 x 32 mm, height 6.4 mm; twin barrel; 4-day power reserve
Functions: hours, minutes, seconds; specially modified twin-disc jumping hour system on 3-dimensional minute hand
Case: titanium with carbon fiber side inserts, 45 x 50 mm, height 18.3 mm; domed sapphire crystal; water-resistant to 5 atm
Band: woven black fiber, folding clasp
Price: $89,000, limited edition of 25 pieces
Variations: reptile skin strap

Mr. Roboto

Reference number: Mr. Roboto
Movement: automatic, modified ETA; ø 32.5 mm, height 6.7 mm
Functions: GMT function, regulator hour, retrograde minutes, seconds
Case: stainless steel; 43 x 50 mm; sapphire crystal; water-resistant to 5 atm
Band: rubber, tang buckle
Price: $5,200
Variations: stainless steel bracelet

Mecha-1 Chrono Gauge BMF

Reference number: CGM-1
Movement: automatic, modified Valjoux 7750; ø 30 mm, height 7.9 mm
Functions: hours, minutes, subsidiary seconds; chronograph
Case: stainless steel, 43 x 50 mm; sapphire crystal; water-resistant to 5 atm
Band: rubber, buckle
Price: $5,300
Variations: stainless steel bracelet

BALL Watch Company SA

Rue du Châtelot 21

CH-2300 La Chaux-de-Fonds

Switzerland

Tel.:

01141-32-724-53-00

Fax:

01141-32-724-53-01

E-Mail:

info@ballwatch.ch

Website:

www.ballwatch.com

Founded:

1891

Number of employees:

not specified

Annual production:

not specified

U.S. distributor:

BALL Watch USA

1131 4th Street North

St. Petersburg, FL 33701

727-896-4278

Most important collections/price range:

Engineer, Fireman, Trainmaster, Conductor /
$1,300 to $6,500

Ball Watch Co.

Engineer, Fireman, Trainmaster, Conductor...these names for the Ball Watch Co. collections trace back to the company's origins and evoke the glorious age when trains puffing smoke and steam crisscrossed America. Back then, the pocket watch was a necessity to maintain precise rail schedules. By 1893, many companies had adopted the General Railroads Timepiece Standards, which included such norms as regulation in at least five positions, precision to within thirty seconds per week, Breguet balance springs, and so on. One of the chief players in developing the standards was Webster Clay Ball. This farmboy-turned-watchmaker from Fredericktown, Ohio, decided to leave the homestead for a more lucrative occupation. He apprenticed as a watchmaker, became a salesperson for Dueber watch cases, and finally opened the Webb C. Ball Company in Cleveland. In 1891, he added the position of chief inspector of the Lake Shore Lines to his CV. When a hogshead's watch stopped resulting in an accident, Ball decided to establish quality benchmarks for watches that included antimagnetic technology, and he set up an inspection system for the timepieces.

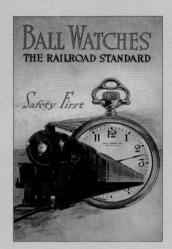

Today, Ball Watch Co. has maintained its lineage, although now producing in Switzerland. These rugged, durable watches aim to be "accurate in adverse conditions," so the company tagline says—and at a very good price. Functionality remains a top priority, so Ball will go to special lengths to work special technologies into its timepieces. Ball has also developed special oils for cold temperatures, for instance. And it is one of few brands to use tritium gas tubes to light up dials, hands, and markers. For those who need to read the time accurately in dark places—divers, pilots, commandos, hunters, etc.—this is essential.

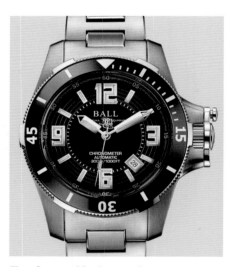

Engineer Hydrocarbon Ceramic XV

Reference number: DM2136A-SCJ-BK

Movement: automatic, ETA Caliber 2892; ø 25.6 mm, height 3.6 mm; 21 jewels; 28,800 vph; 42-hour power reserve; COSC certified chronometer

Functions: hours, minutes, sweep seconds; date

Case: stainless steel, ø 42 mm, height 13.25 mm; ceramic unidirectional bezel; antireflective sapphire crystal; crown protection system; water-resistant to 30 atm

Band: stainless steel, folding clasp and extension

Remarks: micro gas tube illumination; shock-resistant; antimagnetic

Price: $4,099

Engineer Hydrocarbon Airborne

Reference number: DM2076C-S1CAJ-BK

Movement: automatic, ETA Caliber 2836-2; ø 25.6 mm, height 5.05 mm; 25 jewels; 28,800 vph; 38-hour power reserve; COSC certified chronometer

Functions: hours, minutes, sweep seconds; day, date

Case: stainless steel, ø 42 mm, height 13.85 mm; SpringLOCK® antishock system; ceramic unidirectional bezel; antireflective sapphire crystal; crown protection system; water-resistant to 12 atm

Band: stainless steel, folding clasp and extension

Remarks: micro gas tube illumination; shock-resistant; antimagnetic

Price: $3,599

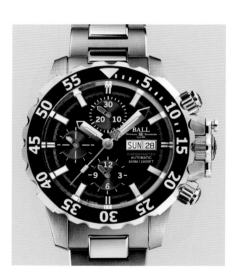

Engineer Hydrocarbon NEDU

Reference number: DC3026A-SC-BK

Movement: automatic, ETA Valjoux Caliber 7750; ø 30 mm, height 7.9 mm; 25 jewels; 28,800 vph; 42-hour power reserve; COSC certified chronometer

Functions: hours, minutes, subsidiary seconds; day, date; 12-hour chronograph operable underwater

Case: stainless steel, ø 42 mm, height 17.30 mm; patented helium system; ceramic unidirectional bezel; antireflective sapphire crystal; crown protection system; water-resistant to 60 atm

Band: titanium and stainless steel, folding clasp and extension

Remarks: micro gas tube illumination; shock-resistant; antimagnetic

Price: $4,399

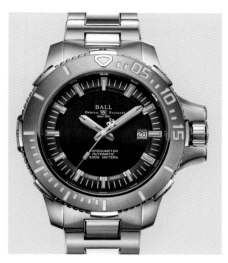

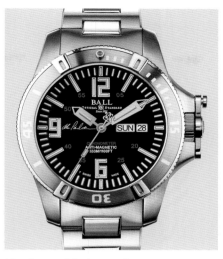

Engineer Hydrocarbon DeepQUEST

Reference number: DM3000A-SCJ-BK
Movement: automatic, ETA Caliber 2892; ø
25.6 mm, height 3.6 mm; 21 jewels; 28,800 vph;
42-hour power reserve; COSC certified chronometer
Functions: hours, minutes, sweep seconds; date
Case: titanium single-block case, ø 43 mm, height
16 mm; unidirectional bezel with patented setting
system, 5.3 mm antireflective sapphire crystal;
crown protection system; water-resistant to 300 atm
Band: titanium and stainless steel, folding clasp
and extension
Remarks: micro gas tube illumination; shock-
resistant; antimagnetic
Price: $4,099

Engineer Hydrocarbon Spacemaster Captain Poindexter

Reference number: DM2036A-S5CA-BK
Movement: automatic, ETA Caliber 2836-2;
ø 25.6 mm, height 5.05 mm; 25 jewels; 28,800 vph;
38-hour power reserve; COSC certified chronometer
Functions: hours, minutes, sweep seconds; day, date
Case: stainless steel, ø 41.5 mm, height 16.1 mm;
unidirectional bezel; antireflective sapphire crystal;
patented crown protection system; water-resistant
to 33 atm
Band: stainless steel, folding clasp and extension
Remarks: micro gas tube illumination;
shock-resistant; antimagnetic
Price: $3,699, limited to 1,000 pieces
Variation: blue dial

Engineer Hydrocarbon Black

Reference number: DM2176A-P1CAJ-BK
Movement: automatic, ETA Caliber 2892-A2;
ø 25.6 mm, height 3.6 mm; 21 jewels; 28,800 vph;
42-hour power reserve; COSC certified chronometer
Functions: hours, minutes, sweep seconds; magnified
date
Case: black DLC & titanium, ø 42 mm, height 13.25 mm;
SpringLOCK® antishock system; ceramic unidirectional
bezel; 5.3 mm antireflective sapphire crystal; patented
crown protection system; water-resistant to 30 atm
Band: rubber strap, buckle
Remarks: micro gas tube illumination; shock-resistant;
antimagnetic
Price: $3,999

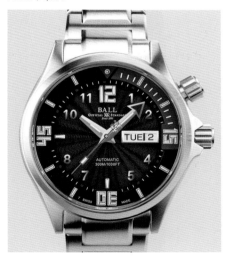

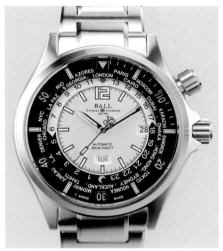

Engineer Master II Diver

Reference number: DM2020A-SA-BKGR
Movement: automatic, ETA Caliber 2836-2; ø
25.6 mm, height 5.05 mm; 25 jewels; 28,800 vph;
38-hour power reserve
Functions: hours, minutes, sweep seconds; day,
date
Case: stainless steel, ø 42 mm, height 13.3 mm;
inner bezel; antireflective sapphire crystal; screw-in
crown; water-resistant to 30 atm
Band: stainless steel, folding clasp
Remarks: micro gas tube illumination; shock-
resistant; antimagnetic
Price: $2,299
Variation: white inner bezel

Engineer Master II Diver Worldtime

Reference number: DG2022A-SA-WH
Movement: automatic, Ball Caliber 965 (base ETA
2836-2); ø 25.6 mm, height 5.05 mm; 25 jewels;
28,800 vph; 38-hour power reserve
Functions: hours, minutes, sweep seconds; day,
date; world-time display
Case: stainless steel, ø 45 mm, height 15.4 mm;
inner bezel; antireflective sapphire crystal; screw-in
crown; water-resistant to 30 atm
Band: stainless steel, folding clasp
Remarks: micro gas tube illumination; shock-
resistant; antimagnetic
Price: $2,899

Trainmaster Worldtime Chronograph

Reference number: CM2052D-LJ-BK
Movement: automatic, Ball Caliber 352 (base
ETA 7750); ø 30 mm, height 7.9 mm; 25 jewels;
28,800 vph; 42-hour power reserve
Functions: hours, minutes, subsidiary seconds; day,
date; world-time display; 12-hour chronograph
Case: stainless steel, ø 42 mm, height 13.7 mm;
antireflective sapphire crystal; screw-in crown;
sapphire crystal case back; water-resistant to 5 atm
Band: reptile skin, buckle
Remarks: micro gas tube illumination; shock-
resistant
Price: $4,149

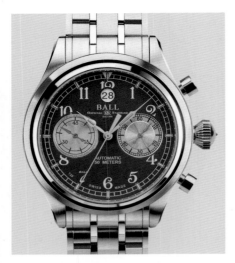

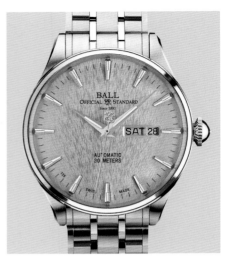

Trainmaster Cannonball

Reference number: CM1052D-S2J-GY
Movement: automatic, Ball Caliber 2050 (base ETA 2824-2); ø 25.6 mm, height 5.05 mm; 49 jewels; 28,800 vph; 38-hour power reserve
Functions: hours, minutes, subsidiary seconds; date; 45-minute double-register chronograph
Case: stainless steel, ø 43 mm, height 14.8 mm; SpringLOCK® antishock system; antireflective sapphire crystal, sapphire crystal case back; screw-in crown; water-resistant to 5 atm
Band: stainless steel, folding clasp
Remarks: micro gas tube illumination; shock-resistant
Price: $3,699

Trainmaster Cleveland Express

Reference number: NM1058D-LCJ-SL
Movement: automatic, ETA Caliber 2836-2; ø 25.6 mm, height 5.05 mm; 25 jewels; 28,800 vph; 38-hour power reserve; COSC certified chronometer
Functions: hours, minutes, sweep seconds; day, date
Case: stainless steel, ø 41 mm, height 12.5 mm; antireflective convex sapphire crystal, sapphire crystal case back; screw-in crown; water-resistant to 5 atm
Band: reptile skin, buckle or clasp
Remarks: satin dial; micro gas tube illumination; shock-resistant
Price: $2,699

Trainmaster Eternity

Reference number: NM2080D-SJ-SL
Movement: automatic, ETA Caliber 2836; ø 25.6 mm, height 5.05 mm; 25 jewels; 28,800 vph; 38-hour power reserve
Functions: hours, minutes, sweep seconds; day, date
Case: stainless steel, ø 39.5 mm, height 11.8 mm; antireflective sapphire crystal; screw-in crown; sapphire crystal case back; water-resistant to 5 atm
Band: stainless steel, folding clasp
Remarks: micro gas tube illumination; shock-resistant
Price: $2,099

Trainmaster One Hundred Twenty

Reference number: NM2888D-PG-LJ-SLGO
Movement: automatic, ETA Caliber 2892; ø 25.6 mm, height 3.6 mm; 21 jewels; 28,800 vph; 42-hour power reserve
Functions: hours, minutes, sweep seconds; date
Case: rose gold, ø 39.5 mm, height 10.5 mm; antireflective convex sapphire crystal; screw-in crown; sapphire crystal case back; water-resistant to 5 atm
Band: reptile skin, buckle
Remarks: micro gas tube illumination; shock-resistant
Price: $6,499
Variation: gray dial

Trainmaster Roman

Reference number: NM1058D-L4J-WH
Movement: automatic, ETA Caliber 2836-2; ø 25.6 mm, height 5.05 mm; 25 jewels; 28,800 vph; 38-hour power reserve
Functions: hours, minutes, sweep seconds; day, date
Case: stainless steel, ø 41 mm, height 12.55 mm; antireflective sapphire crystal; screw-in crown; sapphire crystal case back; water-resistant to 5 atm
Band: reptile skin, buckle or clasp
Remarks: micro gas tube illumination; shock-resistant
Price: $1,799
Variation: gray dial

Trainmaster First Flight

Reference number: GM1056D-L2J-BK
Movement: automatic, BALL Caliber 651 (base ETA 2892-A2); ø 25.6 mm, height 5.1 mm; 21 jewels; 28,800 vph; 42-hour power reserve
Functions: hours, minutes, sweep seconds; date; second time zone indication
Case: stainless steel, ø 41 mm, height 12.75 mm; antireflective sapphire crystal; screw-in crown; sapphire crystal case back; water-resistant to 5 atm
Band: reptile skin, buckle or clasp
Remarks: micro gas tube illumination; shock-resistant
Price: $3,499, limited to 600 pieces

Fireman Racer DLC

Reference number: NM3098C-P1J-BK
Movement: automatic, ETA Caliber 2824-2; ø
25.6 mm, height 4.6 mm; 25 jewels; 28,800 vph;
38-hour power reserve
Functions: hours, minutes, sweep seconds; date
Case: stainless steel with black DLC, ø 43 mm,
height 11.35 mm; antireflective sapphire crystal;
screw-in crown; water-resistant to 10 atm
Band: rubber, buckle
Remarks: micro gas tube illumination; shock-
resistant
Price: $1,699

BALL for BMW Classic

Reference number: NM3010D-LCFJ-SL
Movement: automatic, ETA Caliber 2892-A2;
ø 25.6 mm, height 3.6 mm; 21 jewels; 28,800 vph;
42-hour power reserve; COSC certified chronometer
Functions: hours, minutes, sweep seconds; date
Case: stainless steel, ø 40 mm, height 10.87
mm; Amortiser® antishock system; antireflective
sapphire crystal; screw-in crown; transparent case
back; water-resistant to 50 m
Band: reptile skin, folding clasp
Remarks: micro gas tube illumination; antimagnetic
Price: $3,699
Variation: black, blue, or gray dial

BALL for BMW GMT

Reference number: GM3010C-SCJ-BK
Movement: automatic, ETA Caliber 2893-2;
ø 25.6 mm, height 4.1 mm; 21 jewels; 28,800 vph;
42-hour power reserve; COSC certified chronometer
Functions: hours, minutes, sweep seconds; date;
second time zone indication
Case: stainless steel, ø 42 mm, height 12.64
mm; Amortiser® antishock system; antireflective
sapphire crystal; screw-in crown; sapphire crystal
case back; water-resistant to 10 atm
Band: stainless steel, folding clasp
Remarks: micro gas tube illumination; antimagnetic
Price: $4,399
Variation: black DLC case; black, blue, or gray dial

BALL for BMW Power Reserve

Reference number: PM3010C-P1CFJ-BK
Movement: automatic, ETA Caliber 2897;
ø 25.6 mm, height 4.85 mm; 21 jewels; 28,800 vph;
42-hour power reserve; COSC certified chronometer
Functions: hours, minutes, sweep seconds; date;
power reserve indication
Case: stainless steel with black DLC, ø 42 mm,
height 12.64 mm; Amortiser® antishock system;
antireflective sapphire crystal; screw-in crown;
sapphire crystal case back; water-resistant to 10 atm
Band: rubberized leather, folding clasp
Remarks: micro gas tube illumination; antimagnetic
Price: $4,599
Variation: stainless steel case; silver dial

BALL for BMW Chronograph

Reference number: CM3010C-P1CJ-BK
Movement: automatic, ETA Valjoux Caliber 7750;
ø 30 mm, height 7.9 mm; 25 jewels; 28,800 vph;
42-hour power reserve; COSC certified chronometer
Functions: hours, minutes, subsidiary seconds; day,
date; 12-hour chronograph
Case: stainless steel with black DLC, ø 44 mm,
height 16 mm; Amortiser® antishock system;
antireflective sapphire crystal; screw-in crown;
sapphire crystal case back; water-resistant to 10 atm
Band: rubberized leather, folding clasp
Remarks: micro gas tube illumination; antimagnetic
Price: $4,999
Variation: stainless steel case

BALL for BMW TMT

Reference number: NT3010C-P1CJ-BKF
Movement: automatic, BALL Caliber 9018 (base ETA
2892); ø 25.6 mm, height 5.1 mm; 21 jewels; 28,800
vph; 42-hour power reserve; COSC certified chronometer
Functions: hours, minutes, sweep seconds; mechanical
thermometric indication
Case: stainless steel with black DLC, ø 44 mm, height
13.25 mm; Amortiser® antishock system; antireflective
sapphire crystal; screw-in crown; sapphire crystal case
back; water-resistant to 10 atm
Band: rubberized leather, folding clasp
Remarks: micro gas tube illumination; antimagnetic
Price: $5,299, limited to 1,000 pieces
Variation: TMT Celsius scale

Baume & Mercier
chemin de la Chênaie 50
CH-1293 Bellevue
Switzerland

Tel.:
01141-022-999-5151

Fax:
01141-44-972-2086

Website:
www.baume-et-mercier.com
register on the website to contact via e-mail

Founded:
1830

Number of employees:
not specified

Annual production:
not specified

Distribution:
retail

U.S. distributor:
Baume & Mercier
Richemont North America
New York, NY 10022
800-MERCIER

Most important collections/price range:
Clifton (men) / $2,700 to $13,950; Capeland (men) / $4,350 to $19,990; Hampton (men and women) / $3,450 to $15,000; Linea (women) / $1,950 to $15,750; Classima / $1,750 to $5,950

Baume & Mercier

Baume & Mercier and its elite watchmaking peers Cartier and Piaget make up the quality timepiece nucleus in the Richemont Group's impressive portfolio. The tradition-rich brand counts among the most accessible and most affordable watches of the Genevan luxury brands. In the past decade, it has created a number of remarkable—and often copied—classics. The twelve-sided Riviera and the Catwalk have had to step off the stage, but the classic rectangular Hampton continues to evolve. In recent years, the company has worked hard to gain acceptance in the men's market for its Classima Executives line and to build on watchmaking glory of days gone by, when Baume & Mercier was celebrated as a chronograph specialist.

Though the brand has taken up residence in Geneva, most of the watches are produced in a reassembly center built a few years ago in Les Brenets near Le Locle. Individual parts are made by specialized suppliers according to the strictest of quality guidelines. Some of these manufacturers are sister companies within the Richemont Group.

Former Cartier and IWC marketing manager Alain Zimmermann took over as CEO of Baume & Mercier in 2009. The successful luxury salesman's first task was to use the opportunity of the great recession of 2008–9 to drastically streamline the retail structure, closing many doors that were seen as less profitable. He also introduced the venerable Genevan brand to modern media through Facebook and Twitter. With those tasks under control, the brand has started working on its look. The Capeland line has been retuned to late forties, with a masculine dial that is busy but not crowded. The somewhat more restrained fifties are celebrated in the new Clifton line. And for women, there is the Linea, with a large choice of pastel-colored straps to suit every mood.

Clifton

Reference number: M0A10052
Movement: automatic, Sellita Caliber SW260-1; ø 25.6 mm, height 5.6 mm; 31 jewels; 28,800 vph; decorated with côtes de Genève; 38-hour power reserve
Functions: hours, minutes, subsidiary seconds; date
Case: stainless steel, ø 41 mm, height 11.54 mm; sapphire crystal; transparent case back; water-resistant to 5 atm
Band: reptile skin, double folding clasp
Price: $2,700
Variations: with black dial ($2,700); with stainless steel band ($2,900)

Clifton 1830

Reference number: M0A10060
Movement: manually wound, La Joux-Perret Caliber 7381; ø 30.4 mm, height 2.7 mm; 21 jewels; 21,600 vph; double spring barrel; finely finished with côtes de Genève; 90-hour power reserve
Functions: hours, minutes, subsidiary seconds
Case: pink gold, ø 42 mm, height 8.85 mm; sapphire crystal; transparent case back; water-resistant to 5 atm
Band: reptile skin, buckle
Price: $13,950

Clifton Complete Calendar

Reference number: M0A10055
Movement: automatic, ETA Caliber SW300 with Dubois-Dépraz module 9000; ø 25.6 mm; 25 jewels; 28,800 vph; with côtes de Genève; 42-hour power reserve
Functions: hours, minutes, sweep seconds; annual calendar with date, weekday, month, moon phase
Case: stainless steel, ø 43 mm, height 12.25 mm; sapphire crystal; transparent case back; water-resistant to 5 atm
Band: reptile skin, double folding clasp
Price: $4,950
Variations: with blue dial ($4,950)

Hampton

Reference number: 10026
Movement: automatic, ETA Caliber 2895-1; ø 25.6 mm, height 4.35 mm; 30 jewels; 28,800 vph; 42-hour power reserve
Functions: hours, minutes, subsidiary seconds; date
Case: stainless steel, 32 x 45 mm, height 10.85 mm; sapphire crystal; water-resistant to 5 atm
Band: reptile skin, double folding clasp
Price: $3,450
Variations: various dials and bands

Hampton Lady

Reference number: 10110
Movement: quartz
Functions: hours, minutes; date
Case: stainless steel, 22 x 34.5 mm, height 9 mm; sapphire crystal; water-resistant to 5 atm
Band: calf leather, folding clasp
Price: $2,100

Hampton Lady

Reference number: 10049
Movement: quartz
Functions: hours, minutes; date
Case: stainless steel, 22 x 34.5 mm, height 9 mm; sapphire crystal; water-resistant to 5 atm
Band: stainless steel, double folding clasp
Price: $2,400

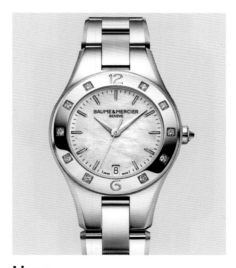

Linea Automatic

Reference number: 10114
Movement: automatic, ETA Caliber 2671; ø 17.2 mm, height 4.8 mm; 25 jewels; 28,800 vph; finely finished with côtes de Genève; 38-hour power reserve
Functions: hours, minutes, sweep seconds; date
Case: stainless steel, ø 27 mm, height 9.8 mm; bezel in rose gold; sapphire crystal; transparent case back; rose gold crown; water-resistant to 5 atm
Band: stainless steel with rose gold links, double folding clasp
Remarks: mother-of-pearl dial set with 11 diamonds
Price: $5,600

Linea

Reference number: 10071
Movement: quartz
Functions: hours, minutes, sweep seconds; date
Case: stainless steel, ø 32 mm, height 8.3 mm; bezel set with 10 diamonds; sapphire crystal; water-resistant to 5 atm
Band: stainless steel, double folding clasp
Remarks: mother-of-pearl dial
Price: $3,950

Capeland Chronograph

Reference number: 10064
Movement: automatic, ETA Caliber 7753; ø 30 mm, height 7.9 mm; 25 jewels; 28,800 vph; 42-hour power reserve
Functions: hours, minutes, subsidiary seconds; chronograph; date
Case: stainless steel, ø 44 mm, height 14.9 mm; sapphire crystal; transparent case back; water-resistant to 5 atm
Band: stainless steel, double folding clasp
Price: $4,350

Bell & Ross Ltd.
8 rue Copernic
F-75116 Paris
France

Tel.:
01133-1-73-73-93-00

Fax:
01133-1-73-73-93-01

E-Mail:
sav@bellross.com

Website:
www.bellross.com

Founded:
1992

Number of employees:
not specified

Annual production:
not specified

U.S. distributor:
Bell & Ross, Inc.
605 Lincoln Road, Suite 300
Miami Beach, FL 33139
888-307-7887; 305-672-3840 (fax)
www.bellross.com

Most important collections/price range:
Instrument BR 01 and BR 03 / approx. $3,100 to
$200,000

Bell & Ross

Known for robust, "large-print" watches with a military look, Paris-headquartered Bell & Ross develops, manufactures, assembles, and regulates its famed timepieces in a modern factory in La Chaux-de-Fonds in the Jura mountains of Switzerland. In recent years, working with outside specialists, the company has dared to design even more complicated watches such as tourbillons and wristwatches with uncommon shapes. This kind of ambitious innovation has only been possible since perfume and fashion specialist Chanel—which also maintains a successful watch line in its own right—became a significant Bell & Ross shareholder and brought the watchmaker access to the production facilities where designers Bruno Belamich and team can to create more complicated, more interesting designs for their aesthetically unusual "instrument" watches.

Belamich continues to prove his skills where technical features and artful proportions are concerned, and what sets Bell & Ross timepieces apart from those of other, more traditional professional luxury makers is their special, roguish look—a delicate balance between striking, martial, and poetic. And it is this beauty for the eye to behold that makes the company's wares popular with style-conscious "civilians" as well as with the pilots, divers, astronauts, sappers, and other hard-riding professionals drawn to Bell & Ross timepieces for their superior functionality.

BR S Officer Silver

Reference number: BRS92-SI-ST/SCR
Movement: automatic, ETA Caliber 2892-2; ø 25.6 mm, height 3.6 mm; 21 jewels; 28,800 vph; 38-hour power reserve
Functions: hours, minutes, sweep seconds; date
Case: stainless steel, 39 x 39 mm, height 10.5 mm; bezel screwed to monocoque case with 4 screws; sapphire crystal; water-resistant to 3 atm
Band: reptile skin, folding clasp
Price: $3,300

BR 01-92 Heading Indicator

Reference number: BR0192-HEADING
Movement: automatic, ETA Caliber 2892; ø 25.6 mm, height 3.6 mm; 21 jewels; 28,800 vph; 42-hour power reserve
Functions: hours, minutes, sweep seconds (disc displays)
Case: stainless steel, black PVD coating, 46 x 46 mm, height 10.5 mm; bezel screwed to monocoque case with 4 screws; sapphire crystal; screwed-in crown; water-resistant to 10 atm
Band: rubber, folding clasp
Price: $6,000

BR 01-97 Climb

Reference number: BR0197-CLIMB
Movement: automatic, ETA Caliber 2897; ø 25.6 mm, height 4.85 mm; 21 jewels; 28,800 vph; 42-hour power reserve
Functions: hours, minutes, sweep seconds; power reserve indicator; date
Case: stainless steel, black PVD-coating, 46 x 46 mm, height 10.5 mm; bezel screwed to monocoque case with 4 screws; sapphire crystal; screwed-in crown; water-resistant to 10 atm
Band: rubber, folding clasp
Price: $5,500

WW1 Régulateur Pink Gold

Reference number: BRWW1-REG-PG/SCR
Movement: automatic, Dubois Dépraz Caliber DD14070; ø 25.6 mm, height 5.2 mm; 25 jewels
Functions: hours (off-center), minutes, subsidiary seconds
Case: rose gold, ø 49 mm, height 13 mm; sapphire crystal; water-resistant to 3 atm
Band: calf leather, buckle
Price: $22,000

PW1 Heritage

Reference number: PW1
Movement: manually wound, ETA Caliber 6497; ø 36.6 mm, height 4.5 mm; 17 jewels; 21,600 vph; 38-hour power reserve
Functions: hours, minutes, subsidiary seconds
Case: stainless steel, gray PVD finish, "Barleycorn" guilloché case back, ø 49 mm; sapphire crystal; water-resistant to 3 atm
Price: $3,500

BR 03-94 Golden Heritage

Reference number: BR0394-ST-G-HE/SCA
Movement: automatic, ETA Caliber 2894-2; ø 28.6 mm, height 6.1 mm; 37 jewels; 25,200 vph; 42-hour power reserve
Functions: hours, minutes, subsidiary seconds; chronograph; date
Case: satin-brushed stainless steel, 42 x 42 mm, height 12.3 mm; bezel screwed to monocoque case with 4 screws; sapphire crystal; water-resistant to 10 atm
Band: calf leather, folding clasp
Price: $5,800

WW1 Argentium Opaline

Reference number: BRWW1-ME-AG-OP/SCR
Movement: manually wound, ETA Caliber 7001; ø 23.3 mm, height 2.5 mm; 17 jewels; 21,600 vph; 42-hour power reserve
Functions: hours, minutes, subsidiary seconds
Case: stainless steel, ø 41 mm, height 10.2 mm; sapphire crystal; water-resistant to 3 atm
Band: reptile skin, buckle
Price: $5,900

BR 03-51 GMT Carbon

Reference number: BR03-51-GMT-CA
Movement: automatic, Soprod Caliber TT651; 28.800 vph; 42-hour power reserve
Functions: hours, minutes, sweep seconds; additional 12-hour display (second time zone); large date
Case: stainless steel, black PVD coating, 42 x 42 mm, height 11 mm; sapphire crystal; water-resistant to 10 atm
Band: rubber, folding clasp
Price: $4,900

Vintage 126 Sport Heritage

Reference number: BRV126-ST-HER/SRB
Movement: automatic, ETA Caliber 2894-2; ø 28.6 mm, height 6.1 mm; 37 jewels; 28,800 vph; 42-hour power reserve
Functions: hours, minutes, subsidiary seconds; chronograph; date
Case: stainless steel, ø 41 mm, height 13.3 mm; bezel with 60-minute divisions; sapphire crystal; water-resistant to 10 atm
Band: rubber, folding clasp
Price: $4,500
Variations: with stainless steel bracelet ($4,800)

Benzinger "unique timepieces"
Dietlinger Strasse 17
D-75179 Pforzheim
Germany

Tel.:
01149-7231-464-233

Fax:
01149-7231-467-362

E-Mail:
info@jochenbenzinger.de

Website:
www.jochenbenzinger.de

Founded:
1985

Number of employees:
6

Annual production:
approx. 50 of his own watches and 100
movements for third parties

U.S. distributor:
WatchBuys
888-333-4895
www.watchbuys.com

Most important collections/price range:
from approx. $9,850 (in stainless steel)

Benzinger

Jochen Benzinger trained as a jewelry engraver and was also taught the art of guilloché by older masters from Pforzheim, which was once upon a time a hub of Germany's watch industry. In other words, he is skilled in two crafts that are no longer taught as apprenticeships in Germany today. In 1985, Benzinger took this unique know-how and started his own business. He bought an old, established guilloché atelier named Kollmar, which had an excellent reputation and, above all, a well-stocked machine park. Benzinger expanded his capacities systematically by purchasing more machines and materials from the companies going bankrupt in Pforzheim during the decline of the jewelry industry.

It has been a while since Benzinger has burnished a precious stone; at some point he found delight in decorating watches. In the 1990s, his first customers included Jörg Schauer and Martin Braun, who came to Pforzheim to have their movements decorated. Chronoswiss went so far as to release a complete edition with phenomenal guilloché and engraved works from the Benzinger atelier (the Zeitzeichen collection). In the meantime, the high quality of his work has made the rounds. Even high-end Swiss watchmakers commission him to improve their movements and components. Indeed, Benzinger's name is not always found on Benzinger's art. But it is fully present in masterpieces like the Zeitmaschine II or the Regulateur, which turn the three basic units of time into individual ballet dancers performing their pirouettes on the dial at different speeds.

Open Subscription IV

Movement: manually wound, modified ETA Caliber 6498; ø 36.6 mm, height 4.5 mm; 17 jewels; 18,000 A/h; entirely skeletonized, guillochéed, and engraved by hand; blued screws, blue platinum-coated base plate, white screw balance, skeletonized ratchet and crown wheels
Functions: hours and minutes (off-center), subsidiary seconds
Case: stainless steel, ø 42 mm, height 10.5 mm; sapphire crystal, transparent case back
Band: reptile skin, double folding clasp
Remarks: hand-guillochéed silver dial
Price: $11,900
Variations: rose or white gold (on request)

Chronograph "Time Machine"

Movement: automatic, modified ETA Caliber 7750; ø 30 mm, height 7.9 mm; 25 jewels; 28,800 vph; entirely guillochéed and engraved by hand; blue platinum-coated base plate; 42-hour power reserve
Functions: hours and minutes (off-center), subsidiary seconds; chronograph
Case: stainless steel, ø 42 mm, height 10.5 mm; sapphire crystal
Band: reptile skin, double folding clasp
Price: $13,400
Variations: rose or white gold (on request)

Regulateur Black

Movement: manually wound, modified ETA Caliber 6498; ø 36.6 mm, height 4.5 mm; 17 jewels; 18,000 vph; entirely skeletonized, guillochéed, and engraved by hand; blued screws; black PVD-coated base plate; rhodium-plated screw balance; 38-hour power reserve
Functions: hours and minutes (off-center), subsidiary seconds
Case: rose gold, ø 42 mm, height 10.5 mm; sapphire crystal, transparent case back
Band: reptile skin, double folding clasp
Remarks: 2-part hand-guillochéed silver dial
Price: on request
Variations: stainless steel ($13,500)

GRAHAM
WATCHMAKERS SINCE 1695

CHRONOFIGHTER
OVERSIZE
REF: 2CCAU.B02A

Automatic chronograph

Carbon lever

Ceramic bezel

Telemeter based on 25c

Water resistant to 100m

WWW.GRAHAM1695.COM

Blancpain

Blancpain SA
Le Rocher 12
CH-1348 Le Brassus
Switzerland

Tel.:
01141-21-796-3636

Website:
www.blancpain.com

Founded:
1735

Number of employees:
not specified

Annual production:
not specified

U.S. distributor:
Blancpain
The Swatch Group (U.S.), Inc.
1200 Harbor Boulevard
Weehawken, NJ 07087
201-271-1400

Most important collections:
L-Evolution, Villeret, Fifty Fathoms, Le Brassus /
$6,800 to $450,000

In its advertising, the Blancpain watch brand has always proudly declared that, since 1735, the company has never made quartz watches and never will. Indeed, Blancpain is Switzerland's oldest watchmaker, and by sticking to its ideals, the company was put out of business by the "quartz boom" of the 1970s.

The Blancpain brand we know today came into being in the mid-eighties, when Jean-Claude Biver and Jacques Piguet purchased the venerable name. The company was subsequently moved to the Frédéric Piguet watch factory in Le Brassus, where it quickly became largely responsible for the renaissance of the mechanical wristwatch. This success caught the attention of the Swatch Group—known at that time as SMH. In 1992, it swooped in and purchased both companies to add to its portfolio. Movement fabrication and watch production were melded to form the Blancpain Manufacture in mid-2010.

Over the past several years, Blancpain president Marc A. Hayek has put a great deal of energy into the company's technical originality. He is frank about the fact that the development of the new *manufacture* caliber harnessed most of Blancpain's creative potential, leaving little to apply to its existing collection of watches. Still, in terms of complications, Blancpain watches have always been in a class of their own. And now even more models are being introduced, watches that feature the company's own basic movement and a choice of manual or automatic winding. As far as the nurturing of Blancpain's entire collection goes, the classic Villeret line is slated to make up 40 to 50 percent of the collection, while technical gadgets (L'Evolution), sport watches (Fifty Fathoms), and ladies watches will be scaled back a bit.

Le Brassus Carrousel Répétition Minutes Chronograph Flyback

Reference number: 2358-363155B
Movement: automatic, Blancpain Caliber 2358; ø 32.8 mm, height 11.7 mm; 59 jewels; 21,600 vph; escapement system with 1-minute flying tourbillon, 1-minute carrousel
Functions: hours, minutes; minute repeater; flyback chronograph with 30-minute sweep counter
Case: pink gold, ø 45 mm, height 17.8 mm; sapphire crystal, transparent case back; water-resistant to 3 atm
Band: reptile skin, folding clasp
Remarks: enamel dial
Price: $449,600

Le Brassus Tourbillon Carrousel

Reference number: 2322-363155B
Movement: manually wound, Blancpain Caliber 2322; ø 35.3 mm, height 5.85 mm; 70 jewels; escapement system with a 1-minute flying tourbillon, a 1-minute carrousel and differential compensation; 3 spring barrels; 168-hour power reserve
Functions: hours, minutes; power reserve indicator (on case back); date
Case: pink gold, ø 44.6 mm, height 11.94 mm; sapphire crystal, transparent case back; water-resistant to 3 atm
Band: reptile skin, folding clasp
Remarks: enamel dial
Price: $319,000

Villeret Traditional Chinese Calendar

Reference number: 0888-363155B
Movement: automatic, Blancpain Caliber 3638; ø 32 mm, height 8.3 mm; 39 jewels; 28,800 vph; 3 spring barrels; 168-hour power reserve
Functions: hours, minutes; annual calendar with double hours, date, month, moon phase, zodiac, elements, celestial stems
Case: rose gold, ø 45 mm, height 15 mm; sapphire crystal, transparent case back; water-resistant to 3 atm
Band: reptile skin, folding clasp
Remarks: enamel dial
Price: $66,400
Variations: platinum, limited to 20 pieces per zodiac ($87,800)

THE GENTLEMAN EXPLORER'S WATCH

SIR RANULPH FIENNES, THE WORLD'S GREATEST LIVING EXPLORER AND KOBOLD AMBASSADOR.

KOBOLD
Embrace Adventure

Please visit www.koboldwatch.com or call 1-877-SOARWAY for more information.

Villeret Inversed Movement

Reference number: 6616-153055B
Movement: manually wound, Blancpain Caliber 152B; ø 36.1 mm, height 2.95 mm; 21 jewels; 21,600 vph; inverted design with time display on case back, bridges with black ceramic insert; 40-hour power reserve
Functions: hours, minutes
Case: white gold, ø 43 mm, height 9.5 mm; sapphire crystal, water-resistant to 3 atm
Band: reptile skin, folding clasp
Price: $38,500
Variations: white dial ($38,500); with 409 diamonds in "snow setting" ($145,600)

X Fathoms

Reference number: 5018-123064
Movement: automatic, Blancpain Caliber 9918B (base Blancpain 1315); ø 36 mm, height 13 mm; 48 jewels; 28,800 vph; 3 spring barrels, 120-hour power reserve
Functions: hours, minutes, sweep seconds; mechanical depth gauge (split scale) with display of maximum diving depth; 5-minute countdown
Case: titanium, ø 55.65 mm, height 24 mm, unidirectional bezel with 60-minute divisions; sapphire crystal, helium valve; water-resistant to 30 atm
Band: rubber, buckle
Price: $40,700

Fifty Fathoms Chronograph Flyback

Reference number: 5085FB-114063B
Movement: automatic, Blancpain Caliber F185; ø 26.2 mm, height 5.5 mm; 37 jewels; 21,600 vph
Functions: hours, minutes, subsidiary seconds; flyback chronograph; date
Case: stainless steel, ø 45 mm, height 15.5 mm; unidirectional bezel with 60-minute divisions; sapphire crystal, screw-in crown and pusher; water-resistant to 30 atm
Band: textile, folding clasp
Price: approx. $20,000

L'Evolution Tourbillon

Reference number: 8822-15B3053B
Movement: automatic, Blancpain Caliber 4225G; ø 27.6 mm, height 8.68 mm; 46 jewels; 21,600 vph; 1-minute tourbillon; 168-hour power reserve
Functions: hours, minutes; power reserve indicator on case back; large date
Case: white gold, ø 43.5 mm, height 14.9 mm; sapphire crystal, transparent case back; water-resistant to 3 atm
Band: reptile skin, folding clasp
Price: $158,400
Variations: pink gold ($158,400)

L'Evolution Carrousel Saphir Volant Une Minute

Reference number: 00222A-150053B
Movement: manually wound, Blancpain Caliber 22T; ø 32 mm; height 6.16 mm; 25 jewels, 21,600 vph; escapement system with rotating 1-minute carrousel; skeletonized
Functions: hours, minutes
Case: white gold, ø 43.5 mm, height 13.5 mm; sapphire crystal, transparent case back; water-resistant to 3 atm
Band: reptile skin, folding clasp
Remarks: movement without base plate mounted between 3 sapphire crystals
Price: $259,000, limited to 50 pieces

L'Evolution Rattrapante Chronograph

Reference number: 8886F-150352B
Movement: automatic, Blancpain Caliber 69F9; ø 32 mm, height 8.4 mm; 44 jewels; 21,600 vph; 40-hour power reserve
Functions: hours, minutes, subsidiary seconds; rattrapante chronograph; large date
Case: white gold, ø 43 mm, height 16.04 mm; carbon-fiber bezel; sapphire crystal, transparent case back; water-resistant to 30 atm
Band: textile, folding clasp
Remarks: carbon-fiber dial
Price: $55,700

1860 Edouard Heuer founded his workshop in the Swiss Jura.
1916 First mechanical stopwatch accurate to 1/100th of a second.
1963 Jack Heuer designs the Carrera Series.
2013 Carrera Automatic Chronograph Calibre 36.

Villeret Retrograde Seconds

Reference number: 6653Q-152955B
Movement: automatic, Blancpain Caliber 7663Q;
ø 27 mm, height 4.57 mm; 34 jewels; 28,800 vph;
72-hour power reserve
Functions: hours, minutes, subsidiary seconds
(retrograde); date
Case: white gold, ø 40 mm, height 10.83 mm;
sapphire crystal, transparent case back; water-
resistant to 3 atm
Band: reptile skin, folding clasp
Price: $22,500
Variations: pink gold ($22,500)

Villeret Ultra-Flat

Reference number: 6223C-152955A
Movement: automatic, Blancpain Caliber 1150; ø
26.2 mm, height 3.25 mm; 28 jewels; 21,600 vph;
2 spring barrels; 100-hour power reserve
Functions: hours, minutes, sweep seconds; date
Case: white gold, ø 38 mm, height 9.15 mm;
sapphire crystal
Band: reptile skin, buckle
Price: $17,300
Variations: pink gold ($15,500); with opaline dial or
stainless steel ($8,400), with white dial

Women Chronograph Large Date

Reference number: 3626-295458A
Movement: automatic, Blancpain Caliber 26F8G; ø
25.6 mm, height 7 mm; 44 jewels; 28,800 vph
Functions: hours and minutes (off-center);
chronograph; large date
Case: pink gold, ø 38.6 mm, height 13.1 mm; bezel
set with diamonds; sapphire crystal, crown with
diamond; water-resistant to 3 atm
Band: ostrich leather, buckle
Remarks: mother-of-pearl dial set with diamonds
Price: $43,900
Variations: stainless steel with blue mother-of-pearl
dial ($21,900)

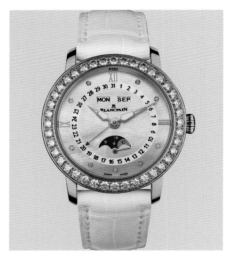

Women Full Calendar

Reference number: 3663-295455B
Movement: automatic, Blancpain Caliber 6763;
ø 27 mm, height 4.9 mm; 30 jewels; 21,600 vph
Functions: hours, minutes, subsidiary seconds;
full calendar with date, weekday, month,
moon phase
Case: pink gold, ø 35 mm, height 10.57 mm; bezel
set with diamonds; sapphire crystal, transparent
case back; water-resistant to 3 atm
Band: reptile skin, folding clasp
Remarks: mother-of-pearl dial set with 9 diamonds
Price: $28,900
Variations: stainless steel ($18,700)

Women Quantième Rétrograde

Reference number: 3653-1954L58B
Movement: automatic, Blancpain Caliber 2650RL;
ø 26.2 mm, height 5.37 mm; 32 jewels; 65-hour
power reserve
Functions: off-center hours and minutes; retrograde
calendar; moon phase
Case: white gold, ø 36 mm, height 10.75 mm, bezel
set with diamonds; sapphire crystal, water-resistant
to 3 atm
Band: ostrich leather, folding clasp
Remarks: blue mother-of-pearl dial set with diamonds
Price: $41,300
Variations: red gold with diamonds ($41,300)

Women Ultra-Thin

Reference number: 6604-294455
Movement: automatic, Blancpain Caliber
1150; ø 26.2 mm, height 3.25 mm; 28 jewels;
21,600 vph; 100-hour power reserve
Functions: hours, minutes, sweep seconds; date
Case: pink gold, ø 34 mm, height 8.46 mm; bezel
set with diamonds; sapphire crystal, water-resistant
to 3 atm
Band: reptile skin, buckle
Remarks: mother-of-pearl dial
Price: $25,600

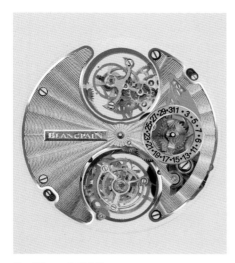

Caliber 2322

Manually wound; 2 independent escapement systems (1-minute carrousel and 1-minute tourbillon) with a differential gearbox between the two; 3 spring barrels; 168 hours power reserve
Functions: hours, minutes, date
Diameter: 35.3 mm
Height: 5.85 mm
Jewels: 70
Balance: glucydur with regulating screws (2 x)
Frequency: 21,600 vph
Remarks: hand-guillochéed bridges; very fine finishing; 379 components

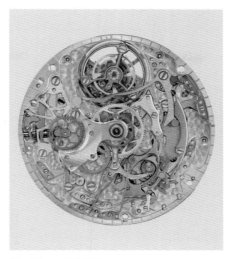

Caliber 2358

Automatic; escapement with a 1-minute carrousel; single spring barrel, 65 hours power reserve
Functions: hours, minutes, minute repeater with a cathedral gong; flyback chronograph 30-minute sweep counter
Diameter: 32.8 mm
Height: 11.7 mm
Jewels: 59
Balance: glucydur with gold regulating screws
Frequency: 28,800 vph
Balance spring: flat hairspring
Shock protection: Kif
Remarks: hand-engraved bridges and rotor; 546 components

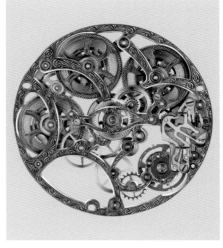

Caliber 1333SQ

Manually wound; entirely skeletonized and engraved by hand; 3 spring barrels, 192-hour power reserve
Functions: hours, minutes, sweep seconds
Diameter: 30.6 mm
Height: 4.2 mm
Jewels: 30
Balance: titanium with adjustable inertia
Frequency: 21,600 vph
Balance spring: Breguet
Shock protection: Kif

Caliber 152B

Manually wound; inverted movement structure with time display on case back, bridges with black ceramic inserts; single spring barrel, 40-hour power reserve
Functions: hours, minutes
Diameter: 35.64 mm
Height: 2.95 mm
Jewels: 21
Balance: screw balance
Frequency: 21,600 vph
Balance spring: flat hairspring
Shock protection: Kif

Caliber 69F9

Automatic; column wheel control of chronograph functions; single spring barrel, 40-hour power reserve
Functions: hours, minutes, subsidiary seconds; split-seconds chronograph with flyback function; large date
Diameter: 32 mm
Height: 8.4 mm
Jewels: 44
Balance: glucydur, with smooth rim
Frequency: 21,600 vph
Balance spring: flat hairspring
Shock protection: Kif
Remarks: 409 components

Caliber 3638

Automatic; 3 spring barrels, 168-hour power reserve
Functions: hours, minutes, complete calendar with Chinese double hours, date, month, moon phase, and Chinese zodiac, the elements, and celestial stems
Diameter: 32 mm
Height: 8.3 mm
Jewels: 39
Balance: glucydur
Frequency: 21,600 vph
Balance spring: flat hairspring
Shock protection: Kif
Remarks: 5 correctors to synchronize calendar displays

Borgward

BORGWARD
Zeitmanufaktur GmbH & Co. KG
Markgrafenstrasse 16
D-79588 Efringen-Kirchen
Germany

Tel.:
01149-7628-805-7840

Fax:
01149-7628-805-7841

E-Mail:
manufaktur@borgward.ag

Website:
www.borgward.ag

Founded:
2010

Number of employees:
3

Annual production:
approx. 350

Distribution:
Please contact Borgward directly for enquiries.

Most important collections:
P100, B2300, and B511

It is not unusual for prospective watch brand founders to search for the name of a dormant or even defunct horological company to connect their business with a glorious past. Watchmaker Jürgen Betz looked elsewhere when he launched a series of watches under the name Borgward. This former automobile concern had a reputation for outstanding quality, reliability, and durability. For connoisseurs and fans, Borgward meant technical prowess, perfect styling, and precision engineering.

Carl F. Borgward began his career as an automobile designer in 1924 when he built a small three-wheeled van. In the early 1930s, his budding company took over the Hansa-Lloyd automobile factory and went on to conquer a global market with the Lloyd, Goliath, and Borgward brands. The real Borgward legend, however, began in the 1950s with the "Goddess," the famed Isabella Coupé, whose elegant lines and state-of-the-art technology literally heralded a new era in automotive design in Germany. In 1961, the company went bankrupt due to poor management.

But the legend lives on and became the inspiration for Betz when building his Borgward watch B511. Support came from his friend Eric Borgward, grandson of Carl, who confirmed: "My grandfather would have liked it." Since the Borgward Zeitmanufaktur was founded in July 2010, it has produced three collections: the B511 limited to 511 pieces, the P100 limited to 1,890 pieces, and the B2300 limited to 1,942 pieces. They are all "made in Germany" but based on Swiss technology. At the heart of each watch is either an ETA 2824 with three hands and calendar or the famous ETA 7750 Valjoux chronograph automatic.

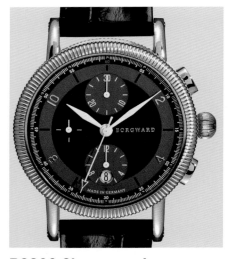

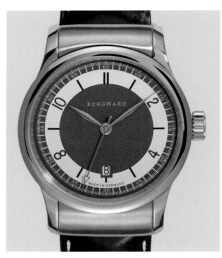

P100 Chronograph

Reference number: P100.CL.01
Movement: automatic, ETA Caliber 7750; ø 30 mm; height 7.9 mm; 25 jewels, 28,800 vph; with perlage, blackened rotor, 38-hour power reserve
Functions: hours, minutes, subsidiary seconds; chronograph; date
Case: stainless steel, ø 40 mm, height 16 mm; sapphire crystal, transparent case back; water-resistant to 5 atm
Band: calf leather, buckle
Price: $3,050
Variations: with black or silver-plated dial

B2300 Chronograph

Reference number: B2300.CL.02
Movement: automatic, ETA Caliber 7750; ø 30 mm; height 7.9 mm; 25 jewels, 28,800 vph; with perlage, blackened rotor, 38-hour power reserve
Functions: hours, minutes, subsidiary seconds; chronograph; date
Case: stainless steel, ø 44 mm, height 15 mm; sapphire crystal, transparent case back; water resistant to 5 atm
Band: calf leather, buckle
Price: $3,180

B511 Automatic

Reference number: B511.AL.04
Movement: automatic, ETA Caliber 2824-2; ø 25.6 mm; height 4.6 mm; 25 jewels, 28,800 vph; with perlage, blackened rotor, 38-hour power reserve
Functions: hours, minutes, sweep seconds; date
Case: stainless steel, ø 40.5 mm, height 12 mm; sapphire crystal, transparent case back; water-resistant to 5 atm
Band: calf leather, buckle
Remarks: limited to 511 pieces
Price: $2,460
Variations: with black or white dial

Botta Design

Botta Design develops and creates wrist-watches with a very well-defined designer look. And the company has been very strict about living up to its motto "Designed in Germany—Made in Germany." Klaus Botta chalks up his success to the long years of collaboration with German firms mostly in Pforzheim and in the Black Forest, traditional sources of components for wristwatches.

What Botta and his small team come up with falls somewhere on or around the juncture between engineering and design. Botta first studied technical physics and then industrial design before starting his own business in 1986. The company focuses on the end-to-end development of products for the audiovisual market, medical technology, furniture, and engineering, but wristwatches were a part of the portfolio right from the start. The first entry-level watch models, Botta's "Watch People," express his concept of sleek, technological design and became the hallmark of the following generations of watches—featuring one, two, or three hands.

At the company headquarters in Königstein near Frankfurt, a flexible team takes care of conceptual work, design, development, quality control, sales, and service for the watches. From the first sketches to the marketing, every aspect is directed by Klaus Botta himself. To ensure the longevity of the watches, only top-drawer materials are used—sapphire crystal, stainless steel, and titanium. The movements are Swiss ETAs or Rondas. Botta's strategy works: The company has already won 45 awards for design. The latest was from Red Dot for the Duo 24, a unique, one-hand watch with, remarkably, a second time zone.

Botta Design
Klosterstrasse 15a
D-61462 Königstein im Taunus
Germany

Tel.:
01149-6174-961-188

Fax:
01149-6174-961-189

E-Mail:
info@botta-design.de

Website:
www.botta-design.de

Founded:
1986

Number of employees:
5

Annual production:
approx. 10,000 watches

Distribution:
direct distribution only

Most important collections:
UNO one-hand series, DUO24, MONDO, TRES

UNO Automatic

Movement: automatic, ETA Caliber 2824-2; ø 25.6 mm, height 4.6 mm; 25 jewels; 28,800 vph; 38-hour power reserve
Functions: hours (each line stands for 5 minutes)
Case: stainless steel, ø 42 mm, height 9.8 mm; sapphire crystal; transparent case back; water-resistant to 3 atm
Band: calf leather, buckle
Price: $770
Variations: with black PVD coating ($825)

TRES Automatic Black Edition

Movement: automatic, ETA Caliber 2824-2; ø 25.6 mm, height 4.6 mm; 25 jewels; 28,800 vph; 42-hour power reserve
Functions: hours, minutes, sweep seconds; date
Case: stainless steel, with black PVD coating, ø 42 mm, height 9.8 mm; sapphire crystal; transparent case back; water-resistant to 3 atm
Band: calf leather, buckle, with black PVD coating
Price: $825
Variations: without PVD coating ($770)

DUO 24

Movement: quartz, Ronda Caliber 515.24H
Functions: hours (each line stands for 5 minutes); second time zone (additional 24-hour indicator, each line stands for 10 minutes)
Case: stainless steel, ø 40 mm, height 7.5 mm; sapphire crystal; water-resistant to 3 atm
Band: calf leather, buckle
Price: $290
Variations: stainless steel bracelet ($335), with rubber strap ($335)

Bovet Fleurier S.A.
109 Pont-du-Centenaire
CP183 CH-1228 Plan-les-Ouates
Switzerland

Tel.:
01141-22-731-4638

Fax:
01141-22-884-1450

E-Mail:
info@bovet.com

Website:
www.bovet.com

Founded:
1822

Number of employees:
not specified

Annual production:
2,000 watches

U.S. distributor:
Bovet LLC USA
3363 NE 163rd Street, Suite 703
North Miami Beach, FL 33160
888-909-1822

Most important collections/price range:
Pininfarina, Amadeo Fleurier, Sportster/ $18,500
to $725,250

Bovet

If any brand can claim real connections to China, it is Bovet, founded by Swiss businessman Edouard Bovet. Bovet emigrated to Canton, China in 1818 and sold four watches of his own design there. On his return to Switzerland in 1822, he set up a company for shipping his Fleurier-made watches to China. The company name, pronounced "Bo Wei" in Mandarin, became a synonym for "watch" in Asia and at one point had offices in Canton. For more than eighty years, Bovet and his successors supplied the Chinese ruling class with valuable timepieces.

In 2001, the brand was bought by entrepreneur Pascal Raffy. He ensured the company's industrial independence by acquiring several other companies as well, notably the high-end watchmaker Swiss Time Technology (STT) in Tramelan, which he renamed Dimier 1738. In addition to creating its own line of watches, this *manufacture* produces complex technical components such as tourbillons for Bovet watches. Assembly of Bovet creations takes place at the headquarters in the thirteenth-century Castle of Môtiers in Val-de-Travers not far from Fleurier.

Bovet watches have several distinctive features—undoubtedly a reason for their growing fame. The first is intricate dial work, featuring not only complex architecture, but also very fine enameling. The second is the lugs and crown at 12 o'clock, recalling Bovet's tasteful pocket watches of the nineteenth century. On some models, the wristbands are made to be easily removed so the watch can be worn on a chain or cord. Other watches convert to table clocks.

Pininfarina Cambiano Cambiano

Reference number: CHPIN010
Movement: automatic, Bovet Caliber 13BA08; ø 29.81 mm, height 14.25 mm; 28,800 vph; 48-hour power reserve
Functions: hours, minutes, subsidiary seconds; chronograph; large date
Case: stainless steel, ø 45 mm, height 15.6 mm; sapphire crystal, water-resistant to 10 atm
Band: leather, buckle
Remarks: totalizer scale of Venetian wood; flexible lugs for converting to pocket watch or table clock
Price: $32,200, limited to 80 pieces

Pininfarina Ottanta Tre Tourbillon

Reference number: TPINT001
Movement: manually wound, Bovet Caliber 16BM02AI-HSMR; ø 36.74 mm, height 13.45 mm; 21,600 vph; 1-minute tourbillon; 120-hour power reserve; reversed hand-fitting
Functions: hours (jumping), minutes (retrograde), subsidiary seconds (on tourbillon cage) on dial side; power reserve indicator; hours, minutes (off-center) on movement side
Case: pink gold, ø 44 mm, height 15.2 mm; sapphire crystal, transparent case back; water-resistant to 3 atm
Band: rubber, buckle
Remarks: flexible lugs for converting
Price: $230,000, limited to 83 pieces

Pininfarina Chronograph Cambiano

Reference number: CHPIN002
Movement: automatic, Bovet Caliber 13BA08; ø 29.81 mm, height 14.25 mm; 28,800 vph; 48-hour power reserve
Functions: hours, minutes, subsidiary seconds; chronograph; large date
Case: stainless steel with black PVD coating, ø 45 mm, height 15.6 mm; sapphire crystal, water-resistant to 10 atm
Band: rubber, buckle
Remarks: flexible lugs for converting to pocket watch or table clock
Price: $25,300

Amadeo Fleurier Tourbillon

Reference number: AIFSQ016
Movement: manually wound, Bovet Caliber 14BM02AI; ø 37.68 mm, height 11.4 mm; 21,600 vph; 1-minute tourbillon; entirely hand-engraved; double spring barrel, 168-hour power reserve
Functions: hours, minutes, subsidiary seconds; power reserve indicator; second 12-hour dial on back
Case: white gold, ø 45 mm, height 14.3 mm; sapphire crystal, transparent case back; water-resistant to 3 atm reptile skin, folding clasp
Remarks: mobile lugs for converting to pocket watch or table clock; hand-engraved dial
Price: $235,800, limited to 50 pieces
Variations: pink gold ($224,300, limited to 50 pieces)

Amadeo Fleurier Tourbillon Virtuoso

Reference number: AIVI004
Movement: manually wound, Bovet Caliber 16BM02AI-HSMR; ø 36.74, height 12.02 mm; 21,600 vph; 1-minute tourbillon; hand-engraved; 120-hour power reserve
Functions: hours, minutes (off-center) on dial side; hours (jumping), minutes (retrograde), subsidiary seconds (on tourbillon cage); power reserve indicator on movement side
Case: white gold, ø 44 mm, height 16.45 mm; sapphire crystal, transparent case back; water-resistant to 3 atm
Band: reptile skin, buckle
Price: $281,500, limited to 50 pieces

Amadeo Fleurier "Rising Star"

Reference number: AIRS002
Movement: manually wound, Bovet Caliber 16BM01AI; ø 36 mm, height 14.75 mm; 21,600 vph; 1-minute tourbillon, double spring barrel; 168-hour power reserve
Functions: hours, minutes; 2 additional 12-hour displays with world-time and day/night indicator; power reserve indicator; second 12-hour dial on movement side
Case: white gold, ø 46 mm, height 16.1 mm; sapphire crystal, transparent case back
Band: reptile skin, folding clasp
Remarks: mobile lugs for converting to pocket watch or table clock
Price: $338,000, limited to 19 pieces

Amadeo Fleurier 43

Reference number: AF43026
Movement: automatic, Bovet Caliber 11BA12; ø 25.87 mm, height 10.72 mm; 28,800 vph; pink gold rotor, 72-hour power reserve
Functions: hours, minutes, subsidiary seconds; power reserve indicator
Case: white gold, ø 43 mm, height 12.33 mm; sapphire crystal, water-resistant to 3 atm
Band: reptile skin, buckle
Remarks: mobile lugs for converting to pocket watch or table clock, with meteorite dial and limited to 39 pieces in this version
Price: $48,800

Amadeo Fleurier 42 Triple Date

Reference number: AQMP004
Movement: automatic, Bovet Caliber 11BA11; ø 25.87 mm, height 10.6 mm; 28,800 vph; pink gold rotor; 72-hour power reserve
Functions: hours, minutes; annual calendar with date, weekday, month, moon phase
Case: white gold, ø 42 mm, height 11.91 mm; sapphire crystal, water-resistant to 3 atm
Band: reptile skin, buckle
Remarks: flexible lugs for converting to pocket watch or table clock
Price: $51,800

Sportster Saguaro Chronograph

Reference number: SP0401-MA
Movement: automatic, Bovet Caliber 13BA01; ø 29.81 mm, height 14.93 mm; 28 jewels; 28,800 vph; rotor in blued stainless steel, blued screws, côtes de Genève; 42-hour power reserve
Functions: hours, minutes, subsidiary seconds; chronograph; large date
Case: stainless steel, ø 46 mm, height 17.2 mm; sapphire crystal, transparent case back; water-resistant to 30 atm
Band: rubber, folding clasp
Remarks: flexible lugs, with meteorite dial
Price: $19,800

Montres Breguet SA
CH-1344 L'Abbaye
Switzerland

Tel.:
01141-21-841-9090

Fax:
01141-21-841-9084

Website:
www.breguet.com

Founded:
1775 (Swatch Group since 1999)

Number of employees:
not specified

Annual production:
not specified

U.S. distributor:
Breguet
The Swatch Group (U.S.), Inc.
1200 Harbor Boulevard
Weehawken, NJ 07087
201-271-1400

Most important collections:
Classique, Héritage, Marine, Reine de Naples,
Type XX

Breguet

We never quite lose that attachment to the era in which we were born and grew up, nor do some brands. Abraham-Louis Breguet (1747–1823), who hailed from Switzerland, brought his craft to Paris in the *Sturm und Drang* atmosphere of the late eighteenth century. It was fertile ground for one of the most inventive watchmakers in the history of horology, and his products soon found favor with the highest levels of society.

Little has changed two centuries later. After a few years of drifting, in 1999 the brand carrying this illustrious name became the prize possession of the Swatch Group and came under the personal management of Nicolas G. Hayek, CEO. Hayek worked assiduously to restore the brand's roots, going as far as rebuilding the legendary Marie Antoinette pocket watch and contributing to the restoration of the Petit Trianon at Versailles.

Breguet is a full-fledged *manufacture,* and this has allowed it to forge ahead uncompromisingly with upscale watches and even jewelry. In modern facilities on the shores of Lake Joux, traditional craftsmanship still plays a significant role in the production of its fine watches, but at the same time, Breguet is one of the few brands to work with modern materials for its movements. This is not just a PR trick, but rather a sincere attempt to improve quality and rate precision. Many innovations have debuted at Breguet, for instance pallet levers and balance wheels made of silicon, the first Breguet hairspring with the arched terminal curve made of this glassy material, or even a mechanical high-frequency balance beating at 72,000 vph. Other innovations include the electromagnetic regulation of a minute repeater or the use of two micro-magnets to achieve contactless anchoring of a balance wheel staff.

Breguet, now under the auspices of Nicolas G. Hayek's grandson, Marc A. Hayek, continues to explore the edges of the technologically possible in watchmaking.

Classique "Chronométrie"

Reference number: 7727BR 12 9WU
Movement: manually wound, Breguet Caliber 574 DR; ø 31.6 mm, height 3.5 mm; 45 jewels, 72,000 vph; double balance spring, silicon pallet lever and escape wheel; magnetic bearing of balance pivot; 2 spring barrels, 60-hour power reserve
Functions: hours, minutes, subsidiary seconds (1/10 second display), power reserve display
Case: rose gold, ø 41 mm, height 9.65 mm; sapphire crystal, transparent case back; water-resistant to 3 atm
Band: reptile skin, folding clasp
Price: $40,000
Variations: white gold ($40,500)

Classique Tourbillon Ultra-Thin

Reference number: 5377BR 12 9WU
Movement: automatic, Breguet Caliber 581 DR; ø 36 mm, height 3 mm; 42 jewels, 28,800 vph; 1-minute tourbillon in titanium cage, silicon hairspring; hubless peripheral rotor; 90-hour power reserve
Functions: hours, minutes, subsidiary seconds (on tourbillon cage); power reserve display
Case: rose gold, ø 42 mm, height 7 mm; sapphire crystal, transparent case back; water-resistant to 3 atm
Band: reptile skin, double folding clasp
Remarks: currently thinnest automatic tourbillon movement
Price: $149,500
Variations: platinum ($163,800)

Classique Réserve de Marche

Reference number: 5277BR 12 9V6
Movement: manually wound, Breguet Caliber 515 DR; ø 34.4 mm, height 3.6 mm; 23 jewels, 28,800 vph; silicon hairspring, 96-hour power reserve
Functions: hours, minutes, subsidiary seconds; power reserve display
Case: rose gold, ø 38 mm, height 8 mm; sapphire crystal, transparent case back; water-resistant to 3 atm
Band: reptile skin, buckle
Price: $19,000
Variations: white gold ($19,500)

Classique Chronograph

Reference number: 5287BR 12 9ZV
Movement: manually wound, Breguet Caliber
533.3; ø 27 mm; height 5.57 mm; 24 jewels,
21,600 vph; Breguet spring; 48-hour power reserve
Functions: hours, minutes, subsidiary seconds;
chronograph
Case: rose gold, ø 42.5 mm, height 12.1 mm;
sapphire crystal, transparent case back; water-
resistant to 3 atm
Band: reptile skin, double folding clasp
Price: $49,700
Variations: with black dial; white gold ($50,200)

Classique Hora Mundi

Reference number: 5717PT EU 9ZU
Movement: automatic, Breguet Caliber 77F0; ø
36 mm, height 6.15 mm; 39 jewels, 28,800 vph;
silicon pallet lever, escape wheel, and hairspring
Functions: hours, minutes, sweep seconds;
world-time display (second time zone); day/night
indicator; date
Case: platinum, ø 44 mm, height 13.55 mm;
sapphire crystal, transparent case back;
water-resistant to 3 atm
Band: reptile skin, folding clasp
Price: $94,200
Variations: pink gold ($78,900), with 3 different
dials (Asia, America, Europe/Africa)

Classique Moon Phase

Reference number: 7337BA 1E 9V6
Movement: automatic, Breguet Caliber 502.3 QSE1;
ø 31 mm, height 3.8 mm; 35 jewels; 21,600 vph;
numbered and signed
Functions: hours and minutes (off-center), subsidiary
seconds; full calendar with date, weekday, moon
phase and age
Case: yellow gold, ø 39 mm, height 9.9 mm; sapphire
crystal, transparent case back; water-resistant to 3 atm
Band: reptile skin, folding clasp
Remarks: silvered, hand-guillochéed gold dial
Price: $38,800
Variations: with yellow gold bracelet ($39,900); pink
gold ($39,400); white gold ($38,800)

Classique "La Musicale"

Reference number: 7800BR AA 9Y V02
Movement: automatic, Breguet Caliber 901;
ø 38.9 mm, height 8.7 mm; 59 jewels; 28,800
vph; silicon anchor/anchor escape wheel, Breguet
balance with regulating screws; music box with
peg disc/gong strips, hand-guillochéed sonorous
liquid metal membrane, magnetic striking regulator;
45-hour power reserve
Functions: hours, minutes, sweep seconds; power
reserve display, alarm clock with music mechanism
and function display
Case: yellow gold, ø 48 mm, height 16.6 mm;
sapphire crystal, water-resistant to 3 atm
Band: reptile skin, folding clasp
Price: $89,600

Marine Ladies Chronograph

Reference number: 8827ST 5W 986
Movement: automatic, Breguet Caliber 550;
ø 23.9 mm; height 6 mm; 47 jewels, 28,800 vph;
silicon anchor and lever escapement; 45-hour
power reserve
Functions: hours, minutes, subsidiary seconds;
chronograph; date
Case: stainless steel, ø 34.6 mm, height 12.3 mm;
sapphire crystal, water-resistant to 5 atm
Band: reptile skin, folding clasp
Remarks: mother-of-pearl dial
Price: $19,500

Type XXII

Reference number: 3880BR Z2 9XV
Movement: automatic, Breguet Caliber 589F; ø
30 mm, height 8.3 mm; 27 jewels, 72,000 vph;
high-frequency silicon escapement, sweep minute
counter, 40-hour power reserve
Functions: hours, minutes, subsidiary seconds;
additional 12-hour display (second time zone);
flyback chronograph; date
Case: rose gold, ø 44 mm, height 18.05 mm;
bidirectional bezel with 60-minute divisions;
sapphire crystal, transparent case back; screw-in
crown; water-resistant to 10 atm
Band: reptile skin, folding clasp
Price: $35,500

Reine de Naples Night/Day Complication

Reference number: 8998BB 11 874 D00D
Movement: automatic, Breguet Caliber 78CS; 23 x 32 mm, height 5.8 mm; 45 jewels, 25,200 vph; silicon hairspring, 57-hour power reserve
Functions: hours, minutes; day/night indicator
Case: white gold, 32 mm x 40.5 mm, height 10.6 mm; bezel set with 143 diamonds; sapphire crystal, transparent case back; crown with a diamond; water-resistant to 3 atm
Band: satin, double folding clasp
Price: $123,900
Variations: rose gold ($122,900)

Tradition Grande Complication

Reference number: 7047BR G9 9ZU
Movement: manually wound, Breguet Caliber 569; ø 36 mm, height 10.82 mm; 43 jewels; 18,000 vph; Breguet silicon spring; torque regulator with chain and worm screw; 1-minute tourbillon, 50-hour power reserve
Functions: hours, minutes; power reserve display on case back
Case: pink gold, ø 41 mm, height 15.95 mm; sapphire crystal, transparent case back; water-resistant to 3 atm
Band: reptile skin, folding clasp
Price: $175,600
Variations: yellow gold ($174,800); platinum ($189,700)

Tradition GMT

Reference number: 7067BR G1 9W6
Movement: manually wound, Breguet Caliber 507 DRF; ø 32.8 mm; height 6.92 mm; 40 jewels; 21,600 vph; Breguet spring, silicon pallet lever and escape wheel, central barrel spring; 50-hour power reserve
Functions: hours, minutes; second time zone (additional 12-hour indicator); power reserve display
Case: rose gold, ø 40 mm, height 12.65 mm; sapphire crystal, transparent case back; water-resistant to 3 atm
Band: reptile skin, folding clasp
Price: $39,200
Variations: white gold ($40,000)

Classique Grande Complication

Reference number: 3358BB 2P 986 DD0D
Movement: manually wound, Breguet Caliber 558.1; ø 30.5 mm; height 6.02 mm; 21 jewels; 18,000 vph; self-compensating Breguet spring; 1-minute tourbillon; hand-engraved
Functions: hours, minutes (off-center), subsidiary seconds (on tourbillon cage)
Case: white gold, ø 35 mm, height 9.15 mm; bezel and lugs set with diamonds; sapphire crystal, transparent case back; water-resistant to 3 atm
Band: reptile skin, folding clasp
Price: $117,800
Variations: with blue enamel dial ($117,800); with mother-of-pearl dial ($113,500)

Classique Grande Complication

Reference number: 7637BB 12 9ZU
Movement: manually wound, Breguet Caliber 567/2; ø 28 mm; height 5.8 mm; 31 jewels, 18,000 vph; hand-decorated
Functions: hours, minutes, subsidiary seconds; additional 24-hour display (second time zone); hour, quarter-hour, and minute repeater
Case: white gold, ø 42 mm, height 12.35 mm; sapphire crystal, transparent case back; water-resistant to 3 atm
Band: reptile skin, folding clasp
Price: $237,000
Variations: pink gold ($236,400)

Classique Moon Phase

Reference number: 7787BR 12 9V6
Movement: automatic, Breguet Caliber 591 DRL; ø 26 mm, height 4.22 mm; 25 jewels; 28,800 vph; silicon hairspring, Breguet balance with 4 fine adjustment screws; hand-guillochéed golden oscillating mass
Functions: hours, minutes, sweep seconds; power reserve display, moon phase and age
Case: rose gold, ø 39 mm, height 10.2 mm; sapphire crystal, transparent case back; water-resistant to 3 atm
Band: reptile skin, buckle
Price: $29,700
Variations: with enamel dial ($29,700); white gold ($30,200)

Marine GMT

Reference number: 5857BR Z2 5ZU
Movement: automatic, Breguet Caliber 517F;
ø 26.2 mm, 28 jewels, 28,800 vph; Breguet silicon
lever escapement and hairspring; 65-hour power
reserve
Functions: hours, minutes, sweep seconds;
additional 12-hour display (second time zone); date
Case: pink gold, ø 42 mm, height 12.25 mm;
sapphire crystal, transparent case back;
water-resistant to 10 atm
Band: rubber, folding clasp
Price: $35,900
Variations: stainless steel ($26,200)

Marine Royale

Reference number: 5847BR Z2 5ZV
Movement: automatic, Breguet Caliber 519 R;
ø 27.6 mm, height 6.2 mm; 36 jewels; 28,800 vph
Functions: hours, minutes, sweep seconds; power
reserve display, alarm clock with function indicator;
date
Case: rose gold, ø 45 mm, height 17.45 mm;
unidirectional bezel with 60-minute divisions;
sapphire crystal, transparent case back; screw-in
crown; water-resistant to 30 atm
Band: rubber, folding clasp
Price: $46,300
Variations: with rose gold dial ($46,300); with rose
gold bracelet ($61,800); white gold ($42,900)

Héritage Chronograph

Reference number: 5400BB 12 9V6
Movement: automatic, Breguet Caliber 550/1;
ø 23.9 mm; height 6 mm; 47 jewels, 21,600 vph;
Breguet spring, silicon pallet lever and escape
wheel; 52-hour power reserve
Functions: hours, minutes, subsidiary seconds;
chronograph; date
Case: white gold, 35 x 42 mm, height 14.45 mm;
sapphire crystal
Band: reptile skin, folding clasp
Price: $44,100
Variations: pink gold ($43,000)

Héritage

Reference number: 8860BR 11 386
Movement: manually wound, Breguet Caliber 586L;
ø 20 mm; 38 jewels, 21,600 vph; Breguet spring,
silicon pallet lever and escape wheel; 36-hour power
reserve
Functions: hours, minutes; moon phase
Case: rose gold, 25 x 35 mm, height 9.75 mm;
sapphire crystal, water-resistant to 3 atm
Band: leather, folding clasp
Price: $28,700
Variations: with diamonds ($33,300); white gold
($29,700); white gold set with diamonds ($54,800)

Reine de Naples

Reference number: 8928BR 51 844 DD0D
Movement: automatic, Breguet Caliber 586L;
ø 20 mm; height 3.6 mm; 29 jewels; 21,600 vph
Functions: hours, minutes
Case: rose gold, 25 x 33 mm, height 8.6 mm; bezel,
lugs and flange set with 139 diamonds; sapphire
crystal, transparent case back; crown with diamond
Band: satin, folding clasp
Price: $35,100
Variations: yellow gold ($34,000); white gold
($36,100)

Reine de Naples

Reference number: 8918BR 58 864 D00D
Movement: automatic, Breguet Caliber 537/1;
ø 20 mm; height 3.6 mm; 20 jewels; 21,600 vph; hand-
guillochéed gold rotor
Functions: hours, minutes
Case: rose gold, 28.45 mm x 36.5 mm, height
10.05 mm; bezel and flange set with 117 diamonds;
sapphire crystal, transparent case back; water-resistant
to 3 atm
Band: textile, folding clasp
Remarks: pear-cut diamond at "6," mother-of-pearl dial
Price: $35,100
Variations: with rose gold bracelet ($59,700); yellow
gold ($34,000); white gold ($36,100)

Breitling
Schlachthausstrasse 2
CH-2540 Grenchen
Switzerland

Tel.:
01141-32-654-5454

Fax:
01141-32-654-5400

E-Mail:
info@breitling.com

Website:
www.breitling.com

Founded:
1884

Number of employees:
not specified

Annual production:
700,000 (estimated)

U.S. distributor:
Breitling U.S.A. Inc.
206 Danbury Road
Stamford, CT 06897
800-641-7343
www.breitling.com

Most important collections:
Navitimer Avenger, Transocean, Superocean,
Cockpit, Breitling for Bentley

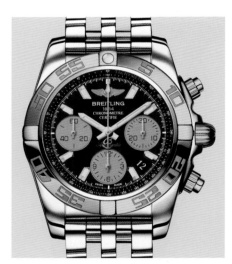

Breitling

In 1884, Léon Breitling opened his workshop in St. Imier in the Jura mountains and immediately began specializing in integrated chronographs. His business strategy was to focus consistently on instrument watches with a distinctive design. High quality standards and the rise of aviation completed the picture.

Today, Breitling's relationship with air sports and commercial and military aviation is clear from its brand identity. The watch company hosts a series of aviation days, owns an aerobatics team, and sponsors several aviation associations.

The unveiling of its own, modern chronograph movement—which, today, is used in a variety of watches in Breitling's collection—at the 2009 Basel Watch Fair was a major milestone in the company's history and also a return to its roots. Planning for the new movement began in 2004 and was kept tightly under wraps. The new design was to be "100 percent Breitling" and industrially produced in large numbers at a reasonable cost. Breitling's headquarters in Grenchen and its subsidiary Breitling Chronométrie in La Chaux-de-Fonds both boast state-of-the-art equipment. Nevertheless, the contract for the new chronograph was awarded to a small team in Geneva.

By the spring of 2005, the initial design plans were on the table. By the end of that year, the first parts of the watch were ready, and just a few months later, prototypes were available for testing. In 2006, the brand-new Caliber B01 made the COSC grade with flying colors and has enjoyed great popularity ever since. For the team of designers, the innovative centering system on the reset mechanism that requires no manual adjustment was one of the great achievements.

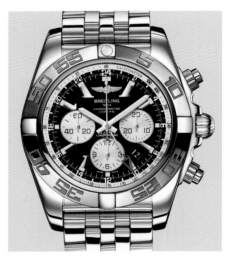

Chronomat GMT

Reference number: AB041012/BA69
Movement: automatic, Breitling Caliber 04 (base Breitling 01); ø 30 mm, height 7.4 mm; 47 jewels; 28,800 vph; column wheel control of chronograph functions; 70-hour power reserve; COSC certified chronometer
Functions: hours, minutes, subsidiary seconds; additional 24-hour display; chronograph; date
Case: stainless steel, ø 46 mm, height 17.6 mm; unidirectional bezel, 60-minute divisions; sapphire crystal; screw-in crown and pusher; water-resistant to 50 atm
Band: stainless steel, folding clasp
Price: $9,820
Variations: with calf leather tang ($8,635)

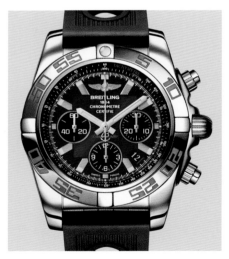

Chronomat 44

Reference number: AB011012/C789
Movement: automatic, Breitling Caliber 01; ø 30 mm, height 7.2 mm; 47 jewels; 28,800 vph; column wheel control of chronograph functions; 70-hour power reserve; COSC certified chronometer
Functions: hours, minutes, subsidiary seconds; chronograph; date
Case: stainless steel, ø 44 mm, height 17.4 mm; unidirectional bezel, 60-minute divisions; sapphire crystal; screw-in crown and pusher; water-resistant to 50 atm
Band: rubber, buckle
Price: $7,710
Variations: with stainless steel bracelet ($8,960)

Chronomat 41

Reference number: CB014012/BA53
Movement: automatic, Breitling Caliber 01; ø 30 mm, height 7.2 mm; 47 jewels; 28,800 vph; column wheel control of chronograph functions; 70-hour power reserve; COSC certified chronometer
Functions: hours, minutes, subsidiary seconds; chronograph; date
Case: stainless steel, ø 41 mm, height 16.8 mm; unidirectional bezel, 60-minute divisions; sapphire crystal; screw-in crown and pusher; water-resistant to 30 atm
Band: stainless steel with rose gold elements, folding clasp
Price: $12,800

Navitimer 01

Reference number: AB012012/BB01
Movement: automatic, Breitling Caliber 01; ø 30 mm, height 7.4 mm; 47 jewels; 28,800 vph; column wheel control of chronograph functions; 70-hour power reserve; COSC certified chronometer
Functions: hours, minutes, subsidiary seconds; chronograph; date
Case: stainless steel, ø 43 mm, height 15.4 mm; bidirectional bezel with integrated slide rule and tachymeter, sapphire crystal; water-resistant to 3 atm
Band: calf leather, tang buckle
Price: $7,715
Variations: with stainless steel bracelet ($9,020)

Navitimer World

Reference number: A2432212/B726
Movement: automatic, Breitling Caliber 24 (base ETA 7754); ø 30 mm, height 7.9 mm; 28,800 vph; COSC certified chronometer
Functions: hours, minutes, subsidiary seconds; additional 24-hour display; chronograph; date
Case: stainless steel, ø 46 mm, height 15.6 mm; bidirectional bezel with integrated slide rule, sapphire crystal; water-resistant to 3 atm
Band: stainless steel, double folding clasp
Price: $7,620
Variations: with calf leather band and buckle ($6,315) or folding clasp ($6,545)

Navitimer 1461

Reference number: A1937012/BA57
Movement: automatic, Breitling Caliber 19 (base ETA 2892-A2); ø 25.6 mm; 28,800 vph; COSC certified chronometer
Functions: hours, minutes, subsidiary seconds; chronograph; full calendar with calendar week, month, moon phase, weekday, date, leap year
Case: stainless steel, ø 46 mm, height 16.2 mm; bidirectional bezel with integrated slide rule and tachymeter, sapphire crystal; water-resistant to 3 atm
Band: stainless steel, folding clasp
Price: $10,840
Variations: reptile skin and tang buckle ($9,910), with folding clasp ($10,140)

Montbrillant 01

Reference number: AB013112/G709
Movement: automatic, Breitling Caliber 01; ø 30 mm, height 7.2 mm; 47 jewels; 28,800 A/h; column wheel control of chronograph functions; 70-hour power reserve; COSC certified chronometer
Functions: hours, minutes, subsidiary seconds; chronograph; date
Case: stainless steel, ø 40 mm, height 13.5 mm; bidirectional bezel with integrated slide rule, sapphire crystal; water-resistant to 5 atm
Band: reptile skin, tang buckle
Price: $8,030, limited to 2,000 pieces
Variations: with stainless steel bracelet ($8,960)

Transocean Chronograph Unitime

Reference number: AB0510U4/BB62
Movement: automatic, Breitling Caliber 05 (base Breitling 01); ø 30 mm, height 8.1 mm; 56 jewels; 28,800 vph; 70-hour power reserve; COSC certified chronometer
Functions: hours, minutes, subsidiary seconds; second time zone (world-time display); chronograph; date
Case: stainless steel, ø 46 mm, height 14.8 mm; crown rotates inner ring with reference city names; sapphire crystal; water-resistant to 10 atm
Band: calf leather, folding clasp
Price: $11,200

Transocean Chronograph 1461

Reference number: A1931912/G750
Movement: automatic, Breitling Caliber 19 (base ETA 2892-A2); ø 25.6 mm; 38 jewels; 28,800 vph; COSC certified chronometer
Functions: hours, minutes, subsidiary seconds; chronograph; perpetual calendar with date, weekday, weeks of year, month, moon phase, leap year
Case: stainless steel, ø 43 mm, height 15.25 mm; sapphire crystal; water-resistant to 5 atm
Band: reptile skin, buckle
Price: $9,690
Variations: with stainless steel Milanese mesh bracelet ($9,800)

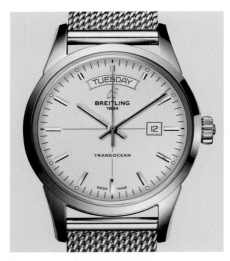

Transocean Day&Date

Reference number: A4531012/G751
Movement: automatic, Breitling Caliber 45 (base Sellita SW240); ø 29 mm, height 5.05 mm; 26 jewels; 28,800 vph; 42-hour power reserve; COSC tested chronometer
Functions: hours, minutes, sweep seconds; weekday, date
Case: stainless steel, ø 43 mm, height 12.8 mm; sapphire crystal, water-resistant to 10 atm
Band: stainless steel Milanese mesh, folding clasp
Price: $5,595
Variations: with reptile skin band tang buckle ($5,485)

Transocean Chronograph

Reference number: AB015212/BA99
Movement: automatic, Breitling Caliber 01; ø 30 mm, height 7.2 mm; 47 jewels; 28,800 vph; column wheel control of chronograph functions, 70-hour power reserve; COSC chronometer
Functions: hours, minutes, subsidiary seconds; chronograph; date
Case: stainless steel, ø 43 mm, height 14.35 mm; sapphire crystal, transparent case back; water-resistant to 10 atm
Band: stainless steel Navitimer bracelet, folding clasp
Price: $8,050
Variations: with calf leather band, tang buckle ($7,565)

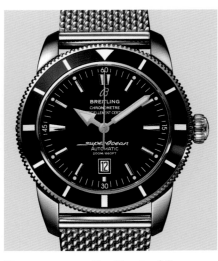

Superocean Heritage 46

Reference number: A1732024/B868
Movement: automatic, Breitling Caliber 17 (base ETA 2824-2); ø 25.6 mm, height 4.6 mm; 25 jewels; 28,800 vph; COSC certified chronometer
Functions: hours, minutes, sweep seconds; date
Case: stainless steel, ø 46 mm, height 16.4 mm; unidirectional bezel with reference markers; sapphire crystal, screw-in crown; water-resistant to 20 atm
Band: stainless steel Milanese mesh, folding clasp
Price: $4,200
Variations: with rubber band and folding clasp ($3,950)

Superocean Heritage 42

Reference number: U1732112/BA61
Movement: automatic, Breitling Caliber 17 (base ETA 2824-2); ø 25.6 mm, height 4.6 mm; 25 jewels; 28,800 vph; COSC certified chronometer
Functions: hours, minutes, sweep seconds; date
Case: stainless steel, ø 42 mm, height 12.95 mm; unidirectional bezel with pink gold insert and reference markers; sapphire crystal, screw-in crown; water-resistant to 20 atm
Band: stainless steel Milanese mesh, folding clasp
Price: $5.450
Variations: with rubber band and folding clasp ($5,200)

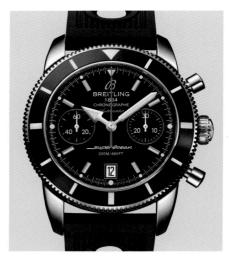

Superocean Heritage Chronograph 44

Reference number: A2337024/BB81
Movement: automatic, Breitling Caliber 23 (base ETA 7753); ø 30 mm, height 7.9 mm; 25 jewels; 28,800 vph; 42-hour power reserve; COSC certified chronometer
Functions: hours, minutes, subsidiary seconds; chronograph; date
Case: stainless steel, ø 44 mm, height 16.2 mm; unidirectional bezel with reference marker; sapphire crystal, screw-in crown; water-resistant to 20 atm
Band: rubber, folding clasp
Price: $5,750
Variations: with stainless steel Milanese mesh bracelet ($6,000)

Superocean 42

Reference number: A1736402/BA32
Movement: automatic, Breitling Caliber 17 (base ETA 2824-2); ø 25.6 mm, height 3.6 mm; 21 jewels; 28,800 vph; COSC certified chronometer
Functions: hours, minutes, sweep seconds; date
Case: stainless steel, ø 42 mm, height 15 mm; unidirectional bezel with rubber inlay and 60-minute divisions; sapphire crystal, screw-in crown; helium valve; water-resistant to 150 atm
Band: calf leather, tang buckle
Price: $3,195
Variations: stainless steel bracelet ($3,520); with rubber strap tang ($3,130)

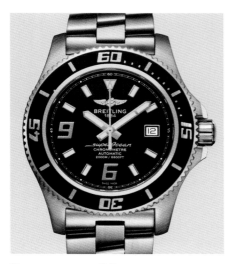

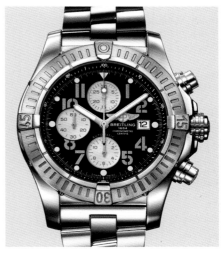

Superocean 44

Reference number: A1739102/BA78
Movement: automatic, Breitling Caliber 17 (base ETA 2824-2); ø 25.6 mm, height 4.6 mm; 25 jewels; 28,800 vph; COSC certified chronometer
Functions: hours, minutes, sweep seconds; date
Case: stainless steel, ø 44 mm, height 16.7 mm; unidirectional bezel with rubber inlay and 60-minute divisions; sapphire crystal, screw-in crown; helium valve; water-resistant to 200 atm
Band: stainless steel, folding clasp
Price: $3,890
Variations: with rubber band and buckle ($3,500); with rubber band and folding clasp ($3,800)

Superocean Chronograph

Reference number: A1334102/BA85
Movement: automatic, Breitling Caliber 13 (base ETA 7750); ø 30 mm, height 7.9 mm; 25 jewels; 28,800 vph; COSC certified chronometer
Functions: hours, minutes, subsidiary seconds; chronograph; date
Case: stainless steel, ø 44 mm, height 17.2 mm; unidirectional bezel with rubber inlay and 60-minute divisions; sapphire crystal, screw-in crown and pushers; water-resistant to 50 atm
Band: stainless steel, folding clasp
Price: $5,935
Variations: with rubber band, buckle ($5,545); with rubber band, folding clasp ($5,845)

Super Avenger

Reference number: A1337011/B973
Movement: automatic, Breitling Caliber 13 (base ETA 7750); ø 30 mm, height 7.9 mm; 25 jewels; 28,800 vph; COSC certified chronometer
Functions: hours, minutes, subsidiary seconds; chronograph; date
Case: stainless steel, ø 48.4 mm, height 18.6 mm; unidirectional bezel with 60-minute divisions; sapphire crystal, screw-in crown; water-resistant to 30 atm
Band: stainless steel, folding clasp
Price: $5,490

Bentley GMT

Reference number: A4736212/B919
Movement: automatic, Breitling Caliber 47B (base ETA 2892-A2); ø 25.6 mm, height 3.6 mm; 38 jewels; 28,800 vph; COSC certified chronometer
Functions: hours, minutes, subsidiary seconds; additional 24-hour display (second time zone); chronograph; date
Case: stainless steel, ø 49 mm, height 14.1 mm; crown rotates inner ring with reference cities; sapphire crystal, screw-in crown; water-resistant to 10 atm
Band: rubber, folding clasp
Price: $10,290
Variations: with stainless steel bracelet ($11,300)

Bentley B06

Reference number: AB061112/BC42
Movement: automatic, Breitling Caliber 06 (base Breitling 01); ø 30 mm; 47 jewels; 28,800 vph; 70-hour power reserve; chronograph with 30-second sweep minute totalizer; COSC certified chronometer
Functions: hours, minutes, subsidiary seconds; chronograph; date
Case: stainless steel, ø 49 mm; bidirectional bezel with tachymeter scale; sapphire crystal, transparent case back; screw-in crown; water-resistant to 10 atm
Band: stainless steel, folding clasp
Price: $11,770
Variations: calf leather band, tang buckle ($10,255)

Bentley Supersports Light Body

Reference number: E2736529/BA62
Movement: automatic, Breitling Caliber 27B (base ETA 2892-A2); ø 30 mm, height 7.6 mm; 38 jewels; 28,800 vph; COSC certified chronometer
Functions: hours, minutes, subsidiary seconds; additional 24-hour display (second time zone); chronograph; date
Case: titanium, ø 49 mm; crown-adjustable inner bezel with integrated slide rule; sapphire crystal, screw-in crown; water-resistant to 10 atm
Band: rubber, folding clasp
Price: $10,005, limited to 1,000 pieces

Bremont Watch Company

PO Box 4741
Henley-on-Thames
RG9 9BZ
Great Britain

Tel.:
01144-845-094-0690

Fax:
01144-870-762-0475

E-Mail:
info@bremont.com

Website:
www.bremont.com

Founded:
2002

Number of employees:
20+

Annual production:
approx. 2,400 watches

U.S. distributor:
Mike Pearson
1-855-BREMONT
michael@bremont.com

Most important collections/price range:
ALT1, MBI and MBII, Solo, U-2, BC, and limited editions / $3,900 to $30,000

Bremont

At the 2012 Olympic Games in London, stuntman Gary Connery parachuted into the stadium wearing a silvery wig and a frumpy dress that made him look suspiciously like the Queen. He was also the first to jet suit out of a helicopter. On both occasions he was wearing a Bremont watch. And so do many other adventurous types, like polar explorer Ben Saunders or free diver Sara Campbell.

Bremonts are tough stuff, created by brothers Nick and Giles English, themselves dyed-in-the-wool pilots and restorers of vintage airplanes. They began developing timepieces in 2002. The engineering vision was clear, but naming their brand required some severe brainstorming. The solution came when they remembered an adventure they had had in southern France when they were forced to land their vintage biplane in a field to avoid a storm. The farmer, himself an enthusiastic restorer of vintage engines, was more than happy to put them up. His name: Antoine Bremont.

Ever since the watches hit the market in 2007, the brand has grown by leaps and bounds. These Swiss-made timepieces reflect sobriety, functionality, history, and ruggedness. They would fit as well in an old Spitfire as on a vintage yacht. They use a sturdy in-house automatic movement, especially hardened steel, a patented shock-absorbing system, and a rotor whose cutout design recalls a flight of planes. All chronographs are COSC certified. And the brothers are not adverse to adding historic material into the watches—some World War II Spitfire parts, or wood and copper from the HMS *Victory*—to make them attractive to collectors and fans of real engines. The retro-styled 2013 Codebreaker honors the work done at Bletchley Park in World War II, particularly by the famed Enigma machine. It incorporates a bit of paper from an original punch card, pine from Hut 6 where the spy-catchers worked, and metal from the Enigma. Sales of the watch will support a fund to restore Bletchley Park.

ALTI-C/CR

Movement: automatic, Caliber BE-50AE; ø 28.04 mm, height 10.5 mm; 28 jewels; 28,800 vph; 42-hour power reserve; Bremont molded and decorated rotor; COSC certified chronometer
Functions: hours, minutes, subsidiary seconds; chronograph; date
Case: stainless steel with PVD; ø 43 mm, height 16 mm; stainless steel and flat crystal case back; sapphire crystal, water-resistant to 10 atm
Band: leather, stainless steel deployment clasp
Price: $5,900
Variations: with anthracite, black, green, or silver dial

ALT1-WT/BL

Movement: automatic, modified Caliber BE-54AE; ø 28.04 mm, height 10.5 mm; 25 jewels; 28,800 vph; Bremont molded and decorated rotor; COSC certified chronometer; 42-hour power reserve
Functions: hours, minutes, subsidiary seconds; second time zone; world-time display; chronograph; date
Case: stainless steel with PVD; ø 43 mm, height 16 mm; crown-adjustable bidirectional inner bezel; stainless steel and flat crystal case back; sapphire crystal, water-resistant to 10 atm
Band: leather, stainless steel deployment clasp
Price: $6,250
Variations: with blue, black, or white dial

ALT1-B2

Movement: automatic, modified Caliber BE-54AE; ø 28.04 mm, height 10.5 mm; 25 jewels; 28,800 vph; 42-hour power reserve; Bremont molded and skeletonized decorated DLC rotor; COSC certified chronometer
Functions: hours, minutes, subsidiary seconds; chronograph; date; 24-hour UTC hand
Case: stainless steel with DLC; ø 43 mm, height 16 mm; crown-adjustable bezel; transparent case back; sapphire crystal, water-resistant to 10 atm
Band: leather, DLC buckle with safety lock
Price: $6,395

U-2/BL

Movement: automatic, modified Caliber BE-36AE; ø 28.04 mm, height 7.5 mm; 25 jewels; 28,800 vph; 38-hour power reserve; Bremont molded and decorated rotor; COSC certified chronometer
Functions: hours, minutes, seconds; weekday, date
Case: stainless steel; ø 43 mm, height 16 mm; antimagnetic soft iron core; crown-adjustable bidirectional inner bezel; stainless steel case back with integrated flat crystal; sapphire crystal, water-resistant to 10 atm
Band: leather, buckle
Price: $5,450
Variations: NATO military strap

MBII/OR

Movement: automatic, modified Caliber BE-36AE; ø 28.04 mm, height 7.5 mm; 25 jewels; 28,800 vph; 38-hour power reserve; Bremont molded and decorated rotor; shock-absorbing mount system; COSC certified chronometer
Functions: hours, minutes, seconds; weekday, date
Case: stainless steel; ø 43 mm, height 16 mm; antimagnetic soft iron cage; crown-adjustable, bidirectional inner bezel; stainless steel case back; sapphire crystal, water-resistant to 10 atm
Band: leather with stainless steel pin buckle and NATO military strap
Price: $5,200
Variations: with orange, green, or anthracite barrel

SOLO/WH-SI

Movement: automatic, modified Caliber BE-36AE; ø 28.04 mm, height 7.5 mm; 25 jewels; 28,800 vph; 38-hour power reserve; Bremont molded and decorated rotor; COSC certified chronometer
Functions: hours, minutes, seconds; date
Case: stainless steel with PVD-coated case barrel; ø 43 mm, height 16 mm; stainless steel and crystal case back; sapphire crystal, water-resistant to 10 atm
Band: leather with stainless steel pin buckle
Price: $4,250
Variations: black dial with white or cream hands and markers

CODEBREAKER SS

Movement: automatic, modified Caliber BE-83arn; ø 28.04 mm, height 7.9 mm; 39 jewels; 28,800 vph; 46-hour power reserve; perlage and blued screws
Functions: hours, minutes; flyback chronograph, 30-minute/60-second counter; second time zone; date
Case: stainless steel; ø 43 mm, height 17 mm; transparent case back; sapphire crystal, water-resistant to 10 atm
Band: calf leather, pin buckle
Remarks: material from Bletchley Park: inner barrel with punch card limited edition number; crown with pinewood from Hut 6; hand-crafted steel rotor made
Price: $18,500, limited to 240 pieces
Variations: rose gold (limited to 50 pieces, $33,995)

S2000

Movement: automatic, modified Caliber BE-36AE; ø 28.04 mm, height 7.5 mm; 25 jewels; 28,800 vph; 38-hour power reserve; Bremont molded and decorated rotor; shock absorbers; COSC certified chronometer
Functions: hours, minutes, seconds; weekday, date
Case: stainless steel; ø 45 mm, height 16 mm; antimagnetic soft iron cage; unidirectional bezel; screwed-down case back; sapphire crystal, water-resistant to 200 atm
Band: rubber, buckle
Price: $5,900

ALT1-C/RG

Movement: automatic, Caliber BE-50AE; ø 28.04 mm, height 10.5 mm; 28 jewels; 28,800 vph; 42-hour power reserve; Bremont molded and decorated rotor; COSC certified chronometer
Functions: hours, minutes, subsidiary seconds; chronograph; date
Case: rose gold with PVD-coated inner barrel; ø 43 mm, height 16 mm; transparent case back; sapphire crystal; water-resistant to 10 atm
Band: leather, deployment clasp
Price: on request

BRM
(Bernard Richards Manufacture)
2 Impasse de L'Aubette
ZA des Aulnaies
F-95420 Magny en Vexin
France

Tel.:
01133-1-61-02-00-25

Fax:
01133-1-61-02-00-14

Website:
www.brm-manufacture.com

Founded:
2003

Number of employees:
20

Annual production:
approx. 2,000 pieces

U.S. distributor:
BRM Manufacture North America
25 Highland Park Village, Suite 100-777
Dallas, TX 75205
214-231-0144
usa@brm-manufacture.com

Most important collections/price range:
$3,000 to $150,000

BRM

Is luxury on the outside or the inside? The answer to this question can tear the veil from the hype and reveal the true craftsman. For Bernard Richards, the true sign of luxury lies in "technical skills and perfection in all stages of manufacture." The exterior of the product is of course crucial, but all of BRM's major operations for making a wristwatch—such as encasing, assembling, setting, and polishing—are performed by hand in his little garage-like factory located outside Paris in Magny-sur-Vexin.

The look: 1940s, internal combustion, axle grease, pinups, real pilots, and a can-do attitude. The inside: custom-designed components, fitting perfectly into Richards's automotive ideal. And since the beginning of 2009, BRM aficionados have been able to engage in this process to an even greater degree: When visiting the BRM website, the client can now construct his or her own V12-44-BRM model. A luxury watch that is a collaboration between the client and Richards is simply a click away.

BRM's unusual timepieces have mainly been based on the tried and trusted Valjoux 7750. But Richards has set lofty goals for himself and his young venture, for he intends to set up a true *manufacture* in his French factory. His Birotor model is thus outfitted with the Precitime, an autonomous caliber conceived and manufactured on French soil. The movement features BRM shock absorbers mounted on the conical springs of its so-called Isolastic system. Plates and bridges are crafted in Arcap, while the rotors are made of Fortale and tantalum. The twin rotors, found at 12 and 6 o'clock, are mounted on double rows of ceramic bearings that require no lubrication.

Bombers

Reference number: 45-N-US2-BN-ANJ
Movement: automatic, ETA Valjoux 7753; ø 30 mm, height 7.90 mm; 27 jewels; 28,800 vph; 42-hour power reserve; pinup girl
Functions: hours, minutes, sweep seconds
Case: brushed stainless steel with black PVD, ø 45 mm; lugs, crown; sapphire crystal; case back with bulldog or skull; water-resistant to 10 atm
Band: leather, buckle
Remarks: hands like propellers, case like plane nose
Price: $7,450
Variations: black PVD ($8,450)

BiRotor

Reference number: BRT-01
Movement: automatic, Precitime Caliber Birotor; 24 x 32 mm; 35 jewels; 28,800 vph; 45-hour power reserve; double rotors in Fortale HR and tantalum on ceramic ball bearings; patented Isolastic system with 4 shock absorbers, arcap plates, and bridges
Functions: hours, minutes, subsidiary seconds
Case: titanium with rose gold crown and strap lugs, 40 x 48 mm, height 9.9 mm; domed sapphire crystal; antireflective on both sides; domed sapphire crystal transparent case back; water-resistant to 30 m
Band: nomex, buckle
Price: $68,500

TriRotor

Movement: automatic, Precitime Caliber TriRotor; ø 48 mm; 29 jewels; 28,800 vph; 45-hour power reserve; main rotors in Fortale HR with 3 macro rotors in Fortale HR with tantalum on ceramic ball bearings; patented Isolastic system with 3 shock absorbers, arcap plates, and bridges
Functions: hours, minutes, subsidiary seconds
Case: titanium with rose gold crown and strap lugs, ø 48 mm, height 9.9 mm, domed sapphire crystal; antireflective on both sides; domed sapphire crystal transparent case back; water-resistant to 10 atm
Band: nomex, buckle
Price: $47,950
Variations: rose gold case; yellow, red, or orange hands

R50 Gulf

Movement: automatic, heavily modified ETA Caliber 2161; ø 38 mm; 35 jewels; 28,800 vph; 48-hour power reserve; patented Isolastic system with 3 shock absorbers; rotor made of Fortale HR, tantalum, and aluminum; hand-painted Gulf colors
Functions: hours, minutes, sweep seconds; power reserve indication
Case: titanium with rose gold crown and strap lugs, ø 50 mm, height 13.2 mm; sapphire crystal; antireflective on both sides; exhibition case back; water-resistant to 3 atm
Band: leather, buckle
Price: $36,500; limited to 30 pieces
Variations: rose gold ($65,000)

TR1 Tourbillon

Movement: automatic, Precitime Caliber; ø 30 mm, height 7.9 mm; 26 jewels; 28,800 vph; 46-hour power reserve; 105-second tourbillon crafted in arcap with reversed cage for visible escapement and suspended by 2 micro springs; patented Isolastic system with 4 shock absorbers; automatic assembly with ceramic ball bearings
Functions: hours, minutes, sweep seconds
Case: titanium, ø 52 mm; sapphire crystal, antireflective on both sides; transparent case back; water-resistant to 10 atm
Band: leather, buckle
Price: $145,350
Variations: ø 48 mm case ($136,150)

RG 46AB

Movement: automatic, Precitime Caliber; ø 30 mm, height 7.9 mm; 27 jewels; 28,800 vph; self-locking rotor mounted on 2 rows of ceramic ball bearings, 6 shock absorbers; suspended between 3 angled shock absorbers and vertical hydraulic cylinders; 42-hour power reserve
Functions: hours, minutes, subsidiary seconds
Case: polymer, ø 46 mm, sapphire crystal; exhibition case back; water-resistant to 10 atm
Band: technical fabric, buckle
Price: $12,950
Variations: hands and markers available in yellow, orange, red, and lime green

V6-44 SA

Movement: automatic, ETA Valjoux Caliber 2824 modified; ø 30 mm, height 7.90 mm; 27 jewels; 28,800 vph; shock absorbers connected to block; 42-hour power reserve
Functions: hours, minutes, sweep seconds; date
Case: polished stainless steel case with black PVD; lugs, crown from single titanium block; sapphire crystal, transparent case back; water-resistant to 10 atm
Band: leather, buckle
Remarks: skeletonized dial with red hands
Price: $5,600
Variations: comes without date as well

Gulf SD41

Movement: automatic, ETA Valjoux Caliber 7753; ø 30 mm, height 7.90 mm; 27 jewels; 28,800 vph; 42-hour power reserve, Gulf logo and color strip
Functions: hours, minutes, subsidiary seconds; date; chronograph
Case: grade 5 titanium, black PVD, 41 x 42 mm; sapphire crystal; transparent case back; water-resistant to 10 atm
Band: leather, buckle
Price: $10,750, limited to 200 pieces
Variations: ø 37 mm case

V12-44-MK ABL

Movement: automatic, ETA Valjoux Caliber 7753; ø 30 mm, height 7.90 mm; 27 jewels; 28,800 vph; 42-hour power reserve
Functions: hours, minutes, subsidiary seconds; date; chronograph
Case: Makrolon (polycarbonate), ø 45 mm; pushers, lugs, crown from single titanium block; sapphire crystal, exhibition case back; water-resistant to 10 atm
Band: technical fabrics for extra lightness
Remarks: lightest automatic chronograph ever made; skeleton dial with blue hands
Price: $13,450
Variations: many options with configurator

Bulgari Horlogerie SA
rue de Monruz 34
CH-2000 Neuchâtel
Switzerland

Tel.:
01141-32-722-7878

Fax:
01141-32-722-7933

E-Mail:
info@bulgari.com

Website:
www.bulgari.com

Founded:
1884 (Bulgari Horlogerie was founded in the early
1980s as Bulgari Time.)

Number of employees:
not specified

Annual production:
not specified

U.S. distributor:
Bulgari Corporation of America
625 Madison Avenue
New York, NY 10022
212-315-9700

Most important collections/price range:
Bulgari-Bulgari / from approx. $4,700 to
$30,300; Diagono / from approx. $3,200; Octo
/ from approx. $9,500 to $690,000 and above;
Daniel Roth and Gérald Genta collections

Bulgari

Although Bulgari is one of the largest jewelry manufacturers in the world, watches have always played an important role for the brand. The purchase of Daniel Roth and Gérald Genta opened new perspectives for its timepieces, thanks to specialized production facilities and the watchmaking talent in the Vallée de Joux—especially where complicated timepieces are concerned. In the meantime, the collections of the two watchmakers have been completely absorbed by the Bulgari brand and remain available as product lines.

The Bulgari family is originally from Greece, and the watches, though designed in Rome, echo classic Hellenistic architecture in many ways. They are timeless and elegant, with style elements that border on the abstract. Manufacturing is done in Switzerland. Following a move from its old location in Neuchâtel to a modern building in the industrial zone of La Chaux-de-Fonds, the company threw its energies behind its movements. It has produced, among others, the Caliber 168 automatic movement based on a Leschot design that managing director Guido Terrini calls "the tractor," because it provided the "pull" to guarantee the company's independence. This year saw the simple Octo built on the double-barreled Caliber 193.

In March 2011, luxury goods giant Louis Vuitton Moët Hennessy (LVMH) secured all the Bulgari family shares in exchange for 16.5 million LVMH shares and a say in the group's future: Paolo and Nicola Bulgari became president and vice president and acquired two seats on LVMH's board of directors. The financial backing of the mega-group bodes well as a boost for the company's continuing creativity.

Bulgari Bulgari

Reference number: BBP39WGLD
Movement: automatic, Bulgari Caliber BVL 191; ø 26.2 mm, height 3.8 mm; 26 jewels; 28,800 vph; finely finished with côtes de Genève; 42-hour power reserve
Functions: hours, minutes, sweep seconds; date
Case: rose gold, ø 39 mm; sapphire crystal; water-resistant to 3 atm
Band: reptile skin, folding clasp
Price: $19,900
Variations: stainless steel ($6,600)

Bulgari Bulgari

Reference number: BB41WSLD
Movement: automatic, Bulgari Caliber BVL 191; ø 26.2 mm, height 3.8 mm; 26 jewels; 28,800 vph; finely finished with côtes de Genève; 42-hour power reserve
Functions: hours, minutes, sweep seconds; date
Case: stainless steel, ø 41 mm; sapphire crystal; water-resistant to 5 atm
Band: reptile skin, folding clasp
Price: $6,600
Variations: rose gold ($19,900)

Bulgari Bulgari Chronograph

Reference number: BB41BSSDCH
Movement: automatic, Bulgari Caliber BVL 328 (base Zenith "El Primero"); ø 30.5 mm, height 6.62 mm; 31 jewels; 360 vph; côtes de Genève; 50-hour power reserve
Functions: hours, minutes, subsidiary seconds; chronograph; date
Case: stainless steel, ø 41 mm; sapphire crystal, screw-in crown; water-resistant to 10 atm
Band: stainless steel, folding clasp
Price: $10,200

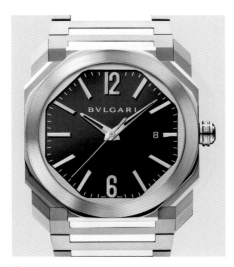

Octo

Reference number: BGO41BSSD
Movement: automatic, Bulgari Caliber BVL 193; ø 25.6 mm, height 3.7 mm; 28 jewels; 28.800 vph; double spring barrel; 50-hour power reserve
Functions: hours, minutes, sweep seconds; date
Case: stainless steel, ø 41.5 mm, height 10.55 mm; sapphire crystal, transparent case back
Band: stainless steel, folding clasp
Price: $9,550

Octo

Reference number: BGO41BSLD
Movement: automatic, Bulgari Caliber BVL 193; ø 25.6 mm, height 3.7 mm; 28 jewels; 28,800 vph; double spring barrel; 50-hour power reserve
Functions: hours, minutes, sweep seconds; date
Case: stainless steel, ø 41.5 mm, height 10.55 mm; sapphire crystal, transparent case back
Band: reptile skin, double folding clasp
Price: $8,600

Octo

Reference number: BGOP41BGLD
Movement: automatic, Bulgari Caliber BVL 193; ø 25.6 mm, height 3.7 mm; 28 jewels; 28,800 vph; double spring barrel; 50-hour power reserve
Functions: hours, minutes, sweep seconds; date
Case: rose gold, ø 41.5 mm, height 10.55 mm; sapphire crystal, transparent case back
Band: reptile skin, double folding clasp
Price: $23,900

Octo Bi-Retro Steel Ceramic

Reference number: BGO43BSCVDBR
Movement: automatic, Gérald Genta Caliber GG7722 (base GP3100); ø 25.6 mm, height 5.53 mm; 35 jewels; 28,800 vph
Functions: hours (digital, jumping), minutes (retrograde); date (retrograde)
Case: stainless steel, ø 43 mm, height 12.35 mm; ceramic bezel; sapphire crystal, transparent case back; water-resistant to 10 atm
Band: rubber, double folding clasp
Price: $18,200
Variations: rose gold ($38,100)

Octo Chronograph Quadri Rétro

Reference number: BGOP45BGLDCHQR
Movement: automatic, Gérald Genta Caliber GG7800 (base FP 1185); ø 25.66 mm, height 8.5 mm; 45 jewels; 21,600 vph
Functions: hours (digital, jumping), minutes (retrograde); chronograph with 2 retrograde totalizers; date (retrograde)
Case: rose gold, ø 45 mm, height 14.85 mm; sapphire crystal, transparent case back; water-resistant to 10 atm
Band: reptile skin, double folding clasp
Price: $60,000
Variations: white gold ($60,000)

Octo Grande Sonnerie Tourbillon

Reference number: BGOW44BGLTBGS
Movement: automatic, Gérald Genta GG31002; ø 31.5 mm, height 10.65 mm; 95 jewels; 21,600 vph; 1-minute tourbillon
Functions: hours (retrograde), hours/minutes (digital, jumping); 2 power reserve indicators; large repeater with Westminster chimes on 3 gongs
Case: white gold, ø 44 mm, height 15.76 mm; sapphire crystal, transparent case back; falcon-eye cabochon on crown; water-resistant to 3 atm
Band: reptile skin, double folding clasp
Price: on request

Magsonic Grande Sonnerie

Reference number: BGGP51GLTBGS
Movement: manually wound, Gérald Genta Caliber GG 31001; ø 31.5 mm, height 7.31 mm; 55 jewels; 21,600 vph; 1-minute tourbillon, 48-hour power reserve
Functions: hours, minutes (off-center); grande sonnerie minute repeater with Westminster chimes (4 hammers) gong; power reserve indicators
Case: rose gold, ø 51 mm, height 16.27 mm; sapphire crystal, pushers for large/small striking mechanisms and muting; water-resistant to 3 atm
Band: reptile skin, double folding clasp
Price: on request

Endurer Chronosprint

Reference number: BRE56BSVDCHS
Movement: automatic, Daniel Roth Caliber DR1306; ø 25.6 mm, height 6.1 mm; 34 jewels; 28,800 vph; single pusher for chronograph functions
Functions: hours, minutes; chronograph; large date
Case: stainless steel, 51 x 56 mm, height 14.55 mm; sapphire crystal, transparent case back; water-resistant to 10 atm
Band: rubber, buckle
Price: $16,000

Grande Lune

Reference number: BRRP46C14GLDMP
Movement: manually wound, Daniel Roth Caliber DR2300; ø 34 mm, height 2.3 mm; 32 jewels; 21,600 vph
Functions: hours, minutes, subsidiary seconds; date; moon phase
Case: rose gold, 41 x 46 mm, height 10.6 mm; sapphire crystal, transparent case back; water-resistant to 3 atm
Band: reptile skin, buckle
Price: $34,100

Papillon Voyageur

Reference number: BRRP46C14GLGMTP
Movement: automatic, Daniel Roth Caliber DR 1307; ø 25.6 mm, height 6.78 mm; 26 jewels; 28,800 vph; 45-hour power reserve
Functions: hours (digital, jumping), minutes (retrograde), subsidiary seconds (segment display with double hand); additional 24-hour indicator (second time zone)
Case: rose gold, 43 x 46 mm, height 15.2 mm; sapphire crystal, transparent case back; pusher to advance the 24-hour display; water-resistant to 3 atm
Band: reptile skin, double folding clasp
Price: $51,000

Carillon Tourbillon

Reference number: BRRP48GLTBMR
Movement: manually wound, Daniel Roth Caliber DR 3300; ø 34.6 mm, height 8.35 mm; 35 jewels; 21,600 vph; 1-minute tourbillon; double spring barrel; partially skeletonized, black finishing; 75-hour power reserve
Functions: hours, minutes; 3-hammer minute repeater
Case: rose gold, 45 x 48 mm, height 14.9 mm; sapphire crystal, transparent case back; water-resistant to 3 atm
Band: reptile skin, double folding clasp
Remarks: skeletonized dial; limited edition
Price: $257,000

Diagono Calibro 303

Reference number: DG42C6SPGLDCH
Movement: automatic, Bulgari Caliber BVL 303 (base Frédéric Piguet 1185); ø 25.6 mm, height 5.5 mm; 37 jewels; 21,600 vph; column wheel control of chronograph functions, 40-hour power reserve
Functions: hours, minutes, subsidiary seconds; chronograph; date
Case: stainless steel, ø 42 mm, height 11.7 mm; rose gold bezel; sapphire crystal, transparent case back; screw-in crown; water-resistant to 10 atm
Band: reptile skin, double folding clasp
Price: $13,900

Diagono Ceramic

Reference number: DGP42BGCVDCH
Movement: automatic, Bulgari Caliber BVL 130; ø 25.6 mm; 37 jewels; 28,800 vph; 42-hour power reserve
Functions: hours, minutes, subsidiary seconds; chronograph; date
Case: rose gold, ø 42 mm, height 12.68 mm; ceramic bezel; sapphire crystal, transparent case back; ceramic pushers and crown
Band: rubber, buckle
Price: $25,600
Variations: with white ceramic bezel

Sotirio Bulgari Tourbillon Perpetual Calendar

Reference number: SB43BPLTBPC
Movement: automatic, Bulgari Caliber BVL 465; ø 28.6 mm, height 8.3 mm; 46 jewels; 21,600 vph; 1-minute tourbillon, 2 spring barrels; fine finishing; 64-hour power reserve
Functions: hours, minutes, subsidiary seconds; perpetual calendar with date, weekday, month, day (on 4 retrograde counters)
Case: platinum, ø 43 mm, height 14.26 mm; sapphire crystal, transparent case back
Band: reptile skin, buckle
Price: $257,000, limited to 30 pieces

Il Giocatore Veneziano

Reference number: BRRW46GLGV/1
Movement: manually wound, Daniel Roth Caliber DR7300; ø 28.06 mm, height 5.8 mm; 49 jewels; 18,000 vph; 48-hour power reserve
Functions: hours, minutes; minute repeater; "shell game" animation
Case: white gold, 43 x 46 mm, height 14.1 mm; sapphire crystal; transparent case back; water-resistant to 3 atm
Band: reptile skin, double folding clasp
Remarks: hand-painted enamel dial; limited edition
Price: $505,000
Variations: various dials; rose gold ($505,000)

Commedia dell'Arte

Reference number: BGGW54GLCA/PU
Movement: manually wound, Bulgari Caliber BVL 618; ø 36 mm, height 11 mm; 91 jewels; 18,000 vph; 48-hour power reserve
Functions: hours (jumping), minutes (retrograde); automaton with 5 figures
Case: white gold, ø 54 mm, height 16.36 mm; sapphire crystal, transparent case back; water-resistant to 3 atm
Band: reptile skin, buckle
Price: price upon request, limited to 8 pieces

Tourbillon Lumière

Reference number: BRR44PLTBSK
Movement: manually wound, Gérald Genta Caliber GG 8000; ø 32.6 mm, height 7.85 mm; 19 jewels; 21,600 vph; 1-minute tourbillon; skeletonized plate and bridges of gold, 70-hour power reserve
Functions: hours, minutes; power reserve indicator on case back
Case: platinum, ø 53 mm, height 14.89 mm; sapphire crystal, transparent case back; water-resistant to 3 atm
Band: reptile skin, buckle
Price: on request
Variations: rose gold

Tourbillon Sapphire

Reference number: BGGW53GLTBSK
Movement: manually wound, Gérald Genta Caliber GG 8000; ø 32.6 mm, height 7.85 mm; 19 jewels; 21,600 vph; 1-minute tourbillon, skeletonized; 70-hour power reserve
Functions: hours, minutes
Case: white gold, ø 53 mm, height 14.89 mm; bezel set with diamonds; sapphire crystal, transparent case back; water-resistant to 3 atm
Band: reptile skin, double folding clasp
Price: $240,000, limited to 25 pieces

BWC Fabrique d'Horlogerie S.A. Bienne

Hans-Hugi-Strasse 3
CH-2502 Bienne/Biel
Switzerland

E-Mail:
info@bwc-swiss.ch

Website:
www.bwc-swiss.ch

Founded:
1924

Annual production:
not specified

Worldwide distribution:
Starck-Uhren
Manfred Starck
Schulze-Delitzsch-Strasse 29
D-75173 Pforzheim
Germany
01149-72-31-105-601 (tel.)
01149-72-31-102-533 (fax)

Most important collection/price range:
"Time zones" / $300 to $3000

BWC-Swiss

In 1924, Arthur Charlet opened the Buttes Watch Co., in his birthplace of Buttes in the canton of Neuchâtel. When he started out almost ninety years ago, Charlet produced pocket watches in all variations, and soon he was exporting his wares to neighboring Germany. In 1930, Charlet added wristwatches to his collection, though the company worked mainly with calibers like the FEF, Peseux, and FHF. In 1938, a change was made to the AS1130, a particularly robust piece of work that went into watches used by German soldiers and hence became widely known as the *Wehrmachtskaliber*.

In 1953, Charlet's son-in-law, Edwin Volkart, took over the helm of the company, and with great verve and drive—and thanks to Germany's "economic miracle" in the fifties—he managed to expand it considerably. Under his direction, BWC's workshops always kept up technologically with the times. That meant that in 1967, the company already had an electromechanical watch in its collection, followed by the first quartz digital display in 1972 and the first fully developed quartz analog watch in 1975.

Owing to a shortage of skilled watchmakers in the remote area of the Val-de-Travers and a change of ownership, in 1991 the company was forced to move its manufacturing operations to Solothurn canton and eventually to Bienne/Biel. By positioning itself in both of the important hubs of horology, Biel and Pforzheim, BWC was able to offer efficient customer service and benefit from good sales.

In 2003, Pforzheim-based watch merchant Manfred Starck became head of the traditional Swiss brand and set about developing a new marketing concept. His goal is to merge contemporary design with exceptional Swiss quality and offer all that at an affordable price.

Chicago

Reference number: 20046.50.21
Movement: manually wound, ETA Caliber 6498; ø 36.6 mm, height 4.5 mm; 17 jewels; 21,600 vph; engraved by hand and gold plated; 38-hour power reserve
Functions: hours, minutes, subsidiary seconds
Case: stainless steel, ø 42.3 mm, height 11.4 mm; sapphire crystal; transparent case back; water-resistant to 5 atm
Band: calf leather, buckle
Price: $1,359
Variations: with white dial

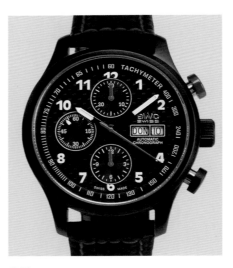

C-Type

Reference number: 20011.54.11
Movement: automatic, ETA Caliber 7750; ø 30 mm, height 7.9 mm; 25 jewels; 28,800 vph; 42-hour power reserve
Functions: hours, minutes, subsidiary seconds; chronograph; weekday, date
Case: stainless steel, with black PVD coating, ø 41.5 mm, height 15.5 mm; sapphire crystal, transparent case back; water-resistant to 5 atm
Band: calf leather, buckle
Remarks: dial of carbon fiber
Price: $1,875
Variations: polished stainless steel; with stainless steel bracelet

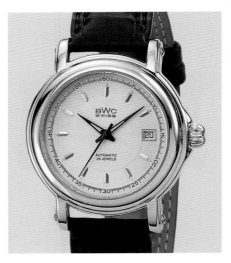

20004

Reference number: 20004.50.03
Movement: automatic, ETA Caliber 2824-2; ø 25.6 mm, height 4.6 mm; 25 jewels; 28,800 vph; 38-hour power reserve
Functions: hours, minutes, sweep seconds; date
Case: stainless steel, ø 39 mm, height 11.5 mm; sapphire crystal, transparent case back; water-resistant to 5 atm
Band: calf leather, buckle
Price: $645
Variations: various dials; with gold-plated case ($670)

Bucherer Montres SA
Langensandstrasse 27
CH-6002 Lucerne
Switzerland

Tel.:
01141-41-369-7070

Fax:
01141-41-369-7072

E-Mail:
info@carl-f-bucherer.com

Website:
www.carl-f-bucherer.com

Founded:
1919, repositioned under the name
Carl F. Bucherer in 2001

Number of employees:
approx. 100

Annual production:
approx. 15,000 watches

U.S. distributor:
Carl F. Bucherer
1805 South Metro Parkway
Dayton, OH 45459
937-291-4366
info@cfbnorthamerica.com
www.carl-f-bucherer.com

Most important collections/price range:
Patravi, Manero, and Alacria / core price segment
$5,000 to $30,000

Carl F. Bucherer

While luxury watch brand Carl F. Bucherer is still rather young, the Lucerne-based Bucherer jewelry dynasty behind it draws its vast know-how from more than ninety years of experience in the conception and design of fine wristwatches.

The summer of 2005 ushered in a new age for the watch brand: company decision makers decided to develop and manufacture an in-house mechanical movement. Together with Bucherer's longtime, Sainte-Croix-headquartered cooperative partner, Techniques Horlogères Appliquées SA (THA), an ambitious plan was hatched. When it became clear that such sophisticated construction could not be realized using outside suppliers, the next logical step was to purchase its partner's renowned atelier in the Jura mountains.

THA was integrated into the Bucherer Group, and the watch company was renamed Carl F. Bucherer Technologies SA (CFBT). At present, the Sainte-Croix operation is led by technical director Dr. Albrecht Haake, who oversees a staff of about twenty. Dr. Haake is currently focusing much of his energy on putting into place industrial structures that will allow for the further development of capacities at the workshop. "Industrialization is not a question of cost, but rather a question of quality," says Haake.

This very successful family-run business celebrated its 125th anniversary in 2013. Its birthday present to itself included a classic tourbillon and a two-tone Alacria with an in-house quartz engine. Carl F. Bucherer has also been quietly pursuing a strategy of boutique openings as a way to give its customers the right surroundings. A new store launched in Macau in March 2013, while the group opened the world's largest watch store in Paris, a favorite shopping city for travelers from Asia.

Patravi ChronoGrade

Reference number: 00.10623.08.63.01
Movement: automatic, Caliber CFB 1902; ø 30 mm, height 7.3 mm; 51 jewels; 28,800 vph; 42-hour power reserve; COSC tested chronometer
Functions: hours, minutes, subsidiary seconds; power reserve indicator; flyback chronograph with retrograde hour totalizer; full calendar with large date, month
Case: stainless steel, ø 44.6 mm, height 14.1 mm; sapphire crystal, transparent case back; screwed-in crown; water-resistant to 5 atm
Band: leather, folding clasp
Price: $10,900
Variations: rose gold ($33,900–$53,000)

Patravi TravelTec "FourX" Limited Edition

Reference number: 00.10620.22.93.01
Movement: automatic, Caliber CFB 1901; ø 28.6 mm, height 7.3 mm; 39 jewels, 28,800 vph; 42-hour power reserve
Functions: hours, minutes, subsidiary seconds; second 24-hour display (second time zone); chronograph; date
Case: pink gold, ø 46.6 mm, height 15.5 mm; ceramic bezel; pusher-activated inner bezel with 24-hour division (third time zone); sapphire crystal; screwed-in crown; water-resistant to 5 atm
Band: rubber, buckle
Price: $52,900
Variations: palladium ($52,900)

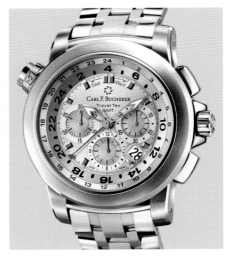

Patravi TravelTec

Reference number: 00.10620.08.63.21
Movement: automatic, Caliber CFB 1901.1; ø 28.6 mm, height 7.3 mm; 39 jewels; 28,800 vph; 42-hour power reserve; COSC tested chronometer
Functions: hours, minutes, subsidiary seconds; additional 24-hour display (second time zone); chronograph; date
Case: stainless steel, ø 46.6 mm, height 15.5 mm; pusher-activated inner bezel with 24-hour division (third time zone); sapphire crystal, screwed-in crown; water-resistant to 5 atm
Band: stainless steel, folding clasp
Price: $11,200
Variations: black dial and calf leather band ($10,900)

Patravi EvoTec Calendar

Reference number: 00.10629.08.33.01
Movement: automatic, Caliber CFB A1004;
ø 32 mm, height 6.9 mm; 33 jewels; 28,800 vph;
55-hour power reserve
Functions: hours, minutes, subsidiary seconds; full
calendar with large date, weekday, weeks of year
Case: stainless steel, ø 42.6 mm, height
12.85 mm; sapphire crystal, transparent case back;
screwed-in crown; water-resistant to 5 atm
Band: leather, folding clasp
Price: $10,300
Variations: rose gold ($31,500)

Patravi EvoTec BigDate

Reference number: 00.10625.08.33.01
Movement: automatic, Caliber CFB A1001;
ø 32 mm, height 6.3 mm; 33 jewels; 28,800 vph;
55-hour power reserve
Functions: hours, minutes, subsidiary seconds;
large date, weekday
Case: stainless steel, 43.75 x 44.5 mm, height
13.95 mm; sapphire crystal, transparent case back;
screwed-in crown; water-resistant to 5 atm
Band: leather, folding clasp
Price: $9,900

Patravi ChronoDate

Reference number: 00.10624.08.33.01
Movement: automatic, Caliber CFB 1956; ø 30 mm,
height 7.3 mm; 49 jewels; 28,800 vph; 42-hour
power reserve
Functions: hours, minutes, subsidiary seconds;
chronograph; large date
Case: stainless steel, ø 44.6 mm; sapphire crystal,
screwed-in crown; water-resistant to 5 atm
Band: leather, folding clasp
Price: $6,300

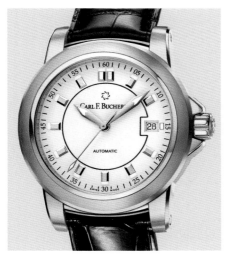

Patravi AutoDate

Reference number: 00.10617.08.23.01
Movement: automatic, Caliber CFB 1950;
ø 26.2 mm, height 4.8 mm; 26 jewels; 28,800 vph;
38-hour power reserve
Functions: hours, minutes, sweep seconds; date
Case: stainless steel, ø 38 mm, height 10.85
mm; sapphire crystal, transparent case back;
screwed-in crown; water-resistant to 5 atm
Band: reptile skin, folding clasp
Price: $3,000

Patravi T-Graph

Reference number: 00.10615.08.33.01
Movement: automatic, Caliber CFB 1960; ø 30 mm,
height 7.3 mm; 47 jewels; 28,800 vph; 42-hour
power reserve
Functions: hours, minutes, subsidiary seconds;
power reserve indicator; chronograph; large date
Case: stainless steel, 39 x 42 mm; sapphire crystal;
screwed-in crown; water-resistant to 5 atm
Band: leather, folding clasp
Price: $7,500

Patravi TravelGraph

Reference number: 00.10618.13.33.21
Movement: automatic, Caliber CFB 1901;
ø 28.6 mm, height 7.3 mm; 39 jewels; 28,800 vph;
42-hour power reserve
Functions: hours, minutes, subsidiary seconds;
additional 24-hour display (second time zone);
chronograph; date
Case: stainless steel, ø 42 mm, height 15.1 mm;
bezel with rubber insert and 24-hour divisions;
sapphire crystal, transparent case back;
screwed-in crown; water-resistant to 5 atm
Band: stainless steel, folding clasp
Price: $7,900
Variations: blue bezel

Manero PowerReserve

Reference number: 00.10912.08.13.01
Movement: automatic, Caliber CFB A1011;
ø 32 mm, height 6.3 mm; 33 jewels; 28,800 vph;
55-hour power reserve
Functions: hours, minutes, subsidiary seconds;
power reserve indicator; large date, weekday
Case: stainless steel, ø 42.5 mm, height
12.54 mm; sapphire crystal, transparent case back;
screwed-in crown; water-resistant to 5 atm
Band: leather, folding clasp
Price: $11,000

Manero Perpetual

Reference number: 00.10902.03.16.21
Movement: automatic, Caliber CFB 1955.1;
ø 26.2 mm, height 5.2 mm; 21 jewels; 28,800 vph;
42-hour power reserve; COSC tested chronometer
Functions: hours, minutes, sweep seconds;
perpetual calendar with date, weekday, month,
moon phase, leap year
Case: pink gold, ø 40 mm, height 11.5 mm;
sapphire crystal, transparent case back;
water-resistant to 3 atm
Band: pink gold, folding clasp
Price: $49,500
Variations: with reptile skin band ($33,000)

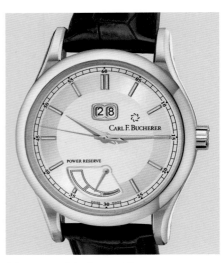

Manero BigDate Power

Reference number: 00.10905.08.13.01
Movement: automatic, Caliber CFB 1964;
ø 26.2 mm, height 5.1 mm; 28 jewels; 28,800 vph;
42-hour power reserve
Functions: hours, minutes, sweep seconds; power
reserve indicator; large date
Case: stainless steel, special alloy, ø 40 mm, height
11.5 mm; sapphire crystal, water-resistant to 3 atm
Band: calf leather, buckle
Price: $5,800
Variations: pink gold ($16,600)

Manero ChronoPerpetual

Reference number: 00.10906.08.13.01
Movement: automatic, Caliber CFB 1904; ø 30 mm,
height 7.6 mm; 49 jewels; 28,800 vph; 50-hour
power reserve
Functions: hours, minutes, sweep seconds; flyback
chronograph; perpetual calendar with month,
weekday, month, moon phase, leap year
Case: stainless steel, ø 42.6 mm, height 14.3 mm;
sapphire crystal, transparent case back; water-
resistant to 3 atm
Band: reptile skin, buckle
Price: $33,000
Variations: pink gold ($52,600)

Manero CentralChrono

Reference number: 00.10910.08.13.01
Movement: automatic, Caliber CFB 1967; ø 30 mm,
height 7.4 mm; 47 jewels; 28,800 vph; chronograph
with sweep minute totalizer, 40-hour power reserve
Functions: hours, minutes, subsidiary seconds;
additional 24-hour display; chronograph; date
Case: stainless steel, ø 42.5 mm, height
14.24 mm; sapphire crystal, transparent case back;
water-resistant to 3 atm
Band: calf leather, buckle
Price: $7,100
Variations: with stainless steel bracelet ($7,700)

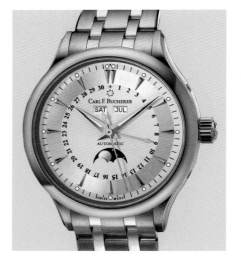

Manero MoonPhase

Reference number: 00.10909.03.13.21
Movement: automatic, Caliber CFB 1966;
ø 26.2 mm, height 5.2 mm; 21 jewels; 28,800 vph;
42-hour power reserve
Functions: hours, minutes, sweep seconds; full
calendar with date, weekday, month, moon phase
Case: pink gold, ø 38 mm, height 10.85 mm;
sapphire crystal, transparent case back;
water-resistant to 3 atm
Band: pink gold, folding clasp
Price: $27,200
Variations: with reptile skin band ($12,900)

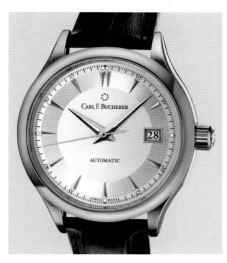

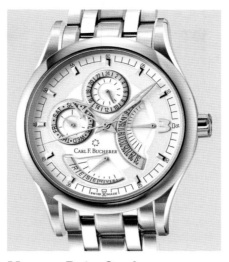

Manero AutoDate

Reference number: 00.10908.08.13.01
Movement: automatic, Caliber CFB 1965;
ø 26.2 mm, height 3.6 mm; 25 jewels; 28,800 vph;
42-hour power reserve
Functions: hours, minutes, sweep seconds; date
Case: stainless steel, ø 38 mm, height 8.75 mm;
sapphire crystal, water-resistant to 3 atm
Band: leather, buckle
Price: $2,800
Variations: pink gold ($9,000)

Manero RetroGrade

Reference number: 00.10901.08.26.21
Movement: automatic, Caliber CFB 1903;
ø 26.2 mm; height 5.1 mm; 34 jewels; 42-hour
power reserve; COSC tested chronometer
Functions: hours, minutes, sweep seconds;
additional 24-hour display (second time zone);
power reserve indicator; full calendar with date
(retrograde) and weekday
Case: stainless steel, ø 40 mm, height 11.5
mm; sapphire crystal, transparent case back;
water-resistant to 3 atm
Band: stainless steel, folding clasp
Price: $7,900
Variations: pink gold ($36,900)

Alacria Mini TwoTone

Reference number: 00.10701.07.15.21
Movement: quartz
Functions: hours, minutes
Case: stainless steel with pink gold sides;
21 x 30 mm, height 6.2 mm; bezel set with
40 brilliant-cut diamonds; sapphire crystal,
water-resistant to 3 atm
Band: stainless steel with pink gold links, folding
clasp
Price: $9,500
Variations: without diamonds ($7,000)

Adamavi

Reference number: 00.10308.03.16.01
Movement: quartz
Functions: hours, minutes
Case: pink gold, ø 26 mm, height 4.75 mm;
sapphire crystal; water-resistant to 3 atm
Band: leather, buckle
Price: $4,800

Adamavi

Reference number: 00.10307.03.13.01
Movement: automatic, ETA Caliber 2892-A2;
ø 26.2 mm, height 3.6 mm; 21 jewels; 28,800 vph;
42-hour power reserve
Functions: hours, minutes; date
Case: pink gold, ø 36 mm, height 7.2 mm; sapphire
crystal, transparent case back; water-resistant to
3 atm
Band: leather, buckle
Price: $7,500
Variations: with pink gold bracelet; with brilliant-cut
diamonds ($24,000)

Caliber CFB A1003

Automatic; bidirectional rotor, peripheral rotor
on edge of movement with spring-held support
bearings; precision fine adjustment; single spring
barrel, 55-hour power reserve
Functions: hours, minutes, subsidiary seconds
Diameter: 30 mm; **Height:** 4.3 mm
Jewels: 33
Balance: glucydur
Frequency: 21,600 vph
Balance spring: flat hairspring
Shock protection: Incabloc
Related calibers: CFB A1002 (with large date,
weekday, and power reserve indicator); CFB A1003
(with large date and weekday)

Cartier SA
boulevard James-Fazy 8
CH-1201 Geneva
Switzerland

Tel.:
01141-022-818-4321

Fax:
01141-022-310-5461

E-Mail:
info@cartier.ch

Website:
www.cartier.de

Founded:
1847

Number of employees:
approx. 1,300 (watch manufacturing)

Annual production:
not specified

U.S. distributor:
Cartier North America
653 Fifth Avenue
New York, NY 10022
800-223-4000

Most important collections:
Calibre, Santos, Rotonde de Cartier, Ballon Bleu,
Tank, Pasha

Cartier

Since the Richemont Group's founding, Cartier has played an important role in the luxury concern as its premier brand and instigator of turnover. Although it took a while for Cartier to find its footing and convince the male market of its masculinity, any concerns about Cartier's seriousness and potential are being dispelled by facts. "We aimed to become a key player in *haute horlogerie,* and we succeeded," said CEO Bernard Fornas at a July 2012 press conference at the company's main manufacturing site in La Chaux-de-Fonds. His optimism is well founded. The company is growing by leaps and bounds—a components manufacturing site that will employ 400 people is in the works.

It was Richemont Group's purchase of the Roger Dubuis *manufacture* in Geneva a few years ago that paved the way to the brand's independence and vertical integration. Cartier currently produces nineteen movements, among them the 1904, which made its debut in the Calibre model. With a diameter of 42 mm, this strikingly designed men's watch is also well positioned in the segment. The designation 1904 MC is a reference to the year in which Louis Cartier developed the first wristwatch made for men—a pilot's watch custom designed for his friend and early pioneer of aviation, Alberto Santos-Dumont.

The automatic movement is a largely unadorned, yet efficient machine, powered by twin barrels. The central rotor sits on ceramic ball bearings, and the adjustment of the conventional escapement is by excenter screw. The Cartier developers have also forged ahead with two concept watches each featuring a unique barrel spring made of microfiber able to store more energy. Yet in spite of entering the high-tech club, Cartier remains true to its classic self, coming out in 2013 with a new Tortue (a century after the first) and two breathtaking models, a mysterious hour and a double mysterious tourbillon.

Rotonde de Cartier
Double Tourbillon Mystérieux

Movement: manually wound, Cartier Caliber 9454 MC; ø 35 mm, height 5 mm; 25 jewels; 21,600 vph; double flying tourbillon integrated between 2 sapphire discs; 52-hour power reserve; Geneva Seal
Functions: hours, minutes (off-center)
Case: platinum, ø 45 mm, height 12.45 mm; sapphire crystal, transparent case back; crown with sapphire cabochon
Band: reptile skin, double folding clasp
Price: $177,000
Variations: platinum set with diamonds

Rotonde de Cartier
Mystérieuse

Movement: manually wound, Cartier Caliber 9981 MC; ø 31.9 mm; height 4.61 mm; 27 jewels; 28,800 vph; 48-hour power reserve
Functions: hours, minutes (off-center), floating hands
Case: pink gold, ø 42 mm, height 11.6 mm; sapphire crystal, transparent case back; crown with sapphire cabochon; water-resistant to 3 atm
Band: reptile skin, double folding clasp
Price: $59,000
Variations: white gold; white or pink gold set with diamonds ($63,000)

Rotonde de Cartier Quantième
Perpetual Chronograph

Movement: manually wound, Cartier Caliber 9423 MC; ø 32 mm; height 7.7 mm; 44 jewels; 28,800 vph; 48-hour power reserve
Functions: hours, minutes; chronograph; perpetual calendar with date, weekday, month
Case: pink gold, ø 42 mm, height 14.9 mm; sapphire crystal, transparent case back; crown with sapphire cabochon; water-resistant to 3 atm
Band: reptile skin, double folding clasp
Price: $74,000
Variations: white gold

Rotonde de Cartier Skeleton Flying Tourbillon

Reference number: W1580046
Movement: manually wound, Cartier Caliber 9453 MC; ø 39 mm, height 4.5 mm; 19 jewels; 21,600 vph; skeletonized with integrated Roman numerals; flying 1-minute tourbillon; Geneva Seal
Functions: hours, minutes
Case: rose gold, ø 45 mm, height 12.35 mm; sapphire crystal, transparent case back; crown with sapphire cabochon
Band: reptile skin, double folding clasp
Price: $141,000, limited to 100 pieces
Variations: white gold, limited to 100 pieces ($146,000)

Rotonde de Cartier Flying Tourbillon Minute Repeater

Reference number: W1556209
Movement: manually wound, Cartier Caliber 9402 MC; ø 33.4 mm; 45 jewels; 21,600 vph; flying 1-minute tourbillon; 50-hour power reserve; Geneva Seal
Functions: hours, minutes; minute repeater
Case: titanium, ø 45 mm, height 9.58 mm; sapphire crystal, transparent case back; crown with sapphire cabochon; water-resistant to 3 atm
Band: reptile skin, double folding clasp
Price: $330,000, limited to 50 pieces
Variations: pink gold ($350,000), limited to 50 pieces

Rotonde de Cartier Tourbillon Chronograph

Reference number: W1580007
Movement: manually wound, Cartier Kaliber 9431 MC; 26.1 x 29.9 mm, height 7.65 mm; 25 jewels; 21,600 vph; 1-minute tourbillon
Functions: hours, minutes; chronograph
Case: platinum, ø 45 mm, height 15.7 mm; sapphire crystal, transparent case back; crown with sapphire cabochon; water-resistant to 3 atm
Band: reptile skin, folding clasp
Price: $211,000, limited to 50 pieces
Variations: rose gold ($182,000)

Rotonde de Cartier Jumping Hour

Reference number: W1553851
Movement: manually wound, Cartier Caliber 9905 MC; ø 25.6 mm; height 5.1 mm; 22 jewels; 28,800 vph
Functions: hours (digital, jumping), minutes (index disc)
Case: white gold, ø 46 mm, height 11.6 mm; sapphire crystal, transparent case back; crown with sapphire cabochon
Band: reptile skin, folding clasp
Price: $41,400
Variations: pink gold ($38,600)

Rotonde de Cartier Chronographe Central

Reference number: W1555951
Movement: manually wound, Cartier Caliber 9907 MC; ø 25.6 mm; height 7.1 mm; 35 jewels; 21,600 vph; chronograph with central second and minute totalizers; 2 spring barrels
Functions: hours, minutes; chronograph
Case: rose gold, ø 42 mm, height 14.2 mm; sapphire crystal, transparent case back; crown with sapphire cabochon; water-resistant to 3 atm
Band: reptile skin, folding clasp
Price: $40,900
Variations: white gold ($43,700)

Rotonde de Cartier Annual Calendar

Reference number: W1580001
Movement: automatic, Cartier Caliber 9908 MC; ø 30 mm; height 5.9 mm; 32 jewels; 28,800 vph; 48-hour power reserve
Functions: hours, minutes; full calendar with large date, weekday, month
Case: pink gold, ø 45 mm, height 14.05 mm; sapphire crystal, crown with sapphire cabochon; water-resistant to 3 atm
Band: reptile skin, double folding clasp
Price: $41,100
Variations: white gold ($42,900)

Rotonde de Cartier Astrotourbillon

Reference number: W1556204
Movement: manually wound, Cartier Caliber 9451 MC; ø 38 mm; height 9.01 mm; 23 jewels; 21,600 vph; central flying tourbillon with eccentric balance, 60-second revolution
Functions: hours, minutes, sweep seconds (revolving tourbillon)
Case: white gold, ø 47 mm, height 15.5 mm; sapphire crystal, transparent case back; crown with sapphire cabochon; water-resistant to 3 atm
Band: reptile skin, double folding clasp
Price: $151,000
Variations: pink gold ($140,000)

Calibre de Cartier Astrotourbillon

Reference number: W7100028
Movement: manually wound, Cartier Caliber 9451 MC; ø 40.1 mm; height 9.01 mm; 23 jewels; 21,600 vph; central flying tourbillon with eccentric balance, 60-second revolution; 50-hour power reserve
Functions: hours, minutes, sweep seconds (revolving tourbillon)
Case: titanium, ø 47 mm, height 19 mm; sapphire crystal, transparent case back; water-resistant to 3 atm
Band: reptile skin, folding clasp
Price: $132,000

Calibre de Cartier Multiple Time Zone

Reference number: W7100026
Movement: automatic, Cartier Caliber 9909 MC; ø 35.1 mm; height 6.68 mm; 27 jewels; 28,800 vph; 48-hour power reserve
Functions: hours, minutes; second time zone (additional 12-hour display), day/night indicator, display of difference to local time; lateral display of reference cities
Case: white gold, ø 45 mm, height 17.4 mm; sapphire crystal; water-resistant to 3 atm
Band: reptile skin, folding clasp
Price: $57,000
Variations: rose gold ($53,500)

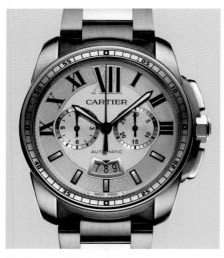

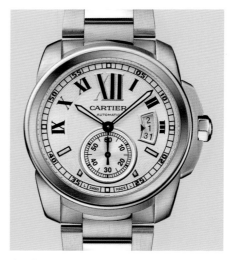

Calibre de Cartier Chronograph

Reference number: W7100045
Movement: automatic, Cartier Caliber 1904-CH MC; ø 25.6 mm; height 5.71 mm; 35 jewels; 28,800 vph; côtes de Genève; 48-hour power reserve
Functions: hours, minutes; chronograph; date
Case: stainless steel, ø 42 mm, height 12.66 mm; sapphire crystal, transparent case back; crown; water-resistant to 10 atm
Band: stainless steel, double folding clasp
Price: $11,200
Variations: pink gold with reptile skin band ($11,200)

Calibre de Cartier Perpetual Calendar

Reference number: W7100030
Movement: automatic, Cartier Caliber 9422 MC; ø 32 mm; height 5.88 mm; 33 jewels; 28,800 vph
Functions: hours, minutes; perpetual calendar with date, weekday, month, leap year
Case: white gold, ø 42 mm, height 16.5 mm; sapphire crystal; water-resistant to 3 atm
Band: reptile skin, folding clasp
Price: $71,000
Variations: rose gold ($66,500)

Calibre de Cartier

Reference number: W7100016
Movement: automatic, Cartier Caliber 1904-PS; ø 25.6 mm; height 4 mm; 27 jewels; 28,800 vph; 2 spring barrels; 48-hour power reserve
Functions: hours, minutes, subsidiary seconds; date
Case: stainless steel, ø 42 mm, height 9.64 mm; sapphire crystal, transparent case back; water-resistant to 3 atm
Band: stainless steel, folding clasp
Price: $8,050
Variations: various cases

Tortue Multifuseaux/ Multiple Time Zone

Movement: manually wound, Cartier Caliber 9914 MC; ø 35.1 mm; height 7.18 mm; 27 jewels; 28,800 vph; 48-hour power reserve
Functions: hours, minutes; world-time display (pusher-activated reference cities in lateral case window)
Case: pink gold, 45.6 x 51 mm, height 17.2 mm; mineral glass; transparent case back; crown with sapphire cabochon; water-resistant to 3 atm
Band: reptile skin, double folding clasp
Price: $43,600
Variations: white gold ($46,700); white gold set with diamonds ($46,700)

Tortue Perpetual Calendar

Reference number: W1580045
Movement: automatic, Cartier Caliber 9422 MC; ø 32 mm; height 5.88 mm; 33 jewels; 28,800 vph; 52-hour power reserve
Functions: hours, minutes; perpetual calendar with date, weekday, month, leap year
Case: pink gold, 45.6 x 51 mm, height 16.8 mm; sapphire crystal, transparent case back; crown with sapphire cabochon; water-resistant to 3 atm
Band: reptile skin, double folding clasp
Price: $63,000
Variations: white gold ($67,500)

Ballon Bleu Tourbillon

Reference number: W6920045
Movement: manually wound, Cartier Caliber 9456 MC; ø 30 mm; height 6.75 mm; 44 jewels; 21,600 vph; flying 1-minute tourbillon; 50-hour power reserve; Geneva Seal
Functions: hours (jumping, off-center), minutes; subsidiary seconds (on tourbillon cage); additional 12-hour display (second time zone)
Case: pink gold, ø 46 mm, height 13.8 mm; sapphire crystal, transparent case back; crown with sapphire cabochon; water-resistant to 3 atm
Band: reptile skin, double folding clasp
Price: $140,000, limited to 50 pieces
Variations: white gold ($151,000), limited to 50 pieces

Ballon Bleu Flying Tourbillon

Reference number: W6920021
Movement: automatic, Cartier Caliber 9452 MC; ø 24.5 mm; height 4.5 mm; 19 jewels; 21,600 vph; flying 1-minute tourbillon; Geneva Seal
Functions: hours, minutes, subsidiary seconds (on tourbillon cage)
Case: white gold, ø 46 mm, height 12.9 mm; sapphire crystal, crown with sapphire cabochon; water-resistant to 3 atm
Band: reptile skin, folding clasp
Price: $120,000
Variations: pink gold ($112,000)

Santos 100 XL Skeleton

Reference number: W2020018
Movement: manually wound, Cartier Caliber 9431 MC; 28.6 x 28.6 mm, height 3.97 mm; 20 jewels; 21,600 vph; skeletonized with integrated Roman numerals, 2 spring barrels; 72-hour power reserve
Functions: hours, minutes
Case: palladium, 46.5 x 54.9 mm, height 16.5 mm; sapphire crystal, transparent case back; water-resistant to 3 atm
Band: reptile skin, folding clasp
Price: $61,500

Santos Dumont Skeleton

Reference number: W2020033
Movement: manually wound, Cartier Caliber 9431 MC; 28.6 x 28.6 mm, height 3.97 mm; 20 jewels; 21,600 vph; skeletonized with integrated Roman numerals; 2 spring barrels; 72-hour power reserve
Functions: hours, minutes
Case: white gold, 38.7 x 47.4 mm, height 9.4 mm; sapphire crystal, transparent case back; water-resistant to 3 atm
Band: reptile skin, double folding clasp
Price: $53,500
Variations: pink gold and carbon fiber

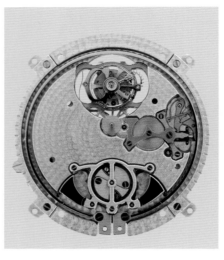

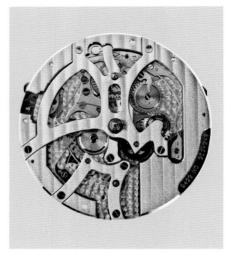

Caliber 1904-PS-MC

Automatic; bidirectional rotor system; twin spring barrels; 48-hour power reserve
Functions: hours, minutes, subsidiary seconds; date
Diameter: 25.6 mm
Height: 4 mm
Jewels: 27
Balance: screw balance
Frequency: 28,800 vph
Balance spring: flat hairspring
Remarks: 186 components; côtes de Genève finishing on bridges and rotor

Caliber 9402 MC

Manually wound; flying tourbillon with C-shaped cage; twin spring barrels, 50-hour power reserve
Functions: hours, minutes; minute, quarter-hour, and hour repeater
Diameter: 39.7 mm
Height: 9.58 mm
Jewels: 45
Balance: glucydur, screw balance
Frequency: 21,600 vph
Balance spring: flat hairspring
Remarks: 447 components; polished edges, longitudinal polishing; movements numbered individually; Geneva Seal

Caliber 9422 MC

Automatic; 52-hour power reserve
Functions: hours, minutes, subsidiary seconds; perpetual calendar with days (retrograde), month, leap year
Diameter: 32 mm
Height: 5.88 mm
Jewels: 33
Balance: screw balance
Frequency: 28,800 vph
Balance spring: flat hairspring
Remarks: 293 components; côtes de Genève finishing on bridges and rotor

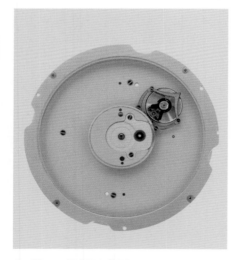

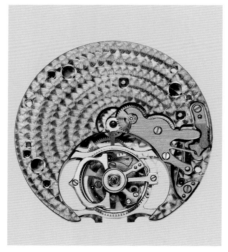

Caliber 9451 MC

Manually wound; twin spring barrels, tourbillon cage rotates around dial once a minute; 48-hour power reserve
Functions: hours, minutes, seconds marked by tourbillon cage
Diameter: 40.1 mm
Height: 9.01 mm
Jewels: 23
Balance: glucydur
Frequency: 21,600 vph
Balance spring: flat hairspring
Remarks: 187 components; movements numbered individually

Caliber 9452 MC

Manually wound; flying tourbillon with C-shaped seconds indicator; single barrel spring, 50-hour power reserve
Functions: hours, minutes, subsidiary seconds on tourbillon cage
Diameter: 24.9 mm
Height: 5.45 mm
Jewels: 19
Balance: glucydur, screw balance
Frequency: 21,600 vph
Balance spring: flat hairspring
Remarks: polished edges, longitudinal polishing; movements numbered individually; Geneva Seal

Caliber 9907 MC

Manually wound; twin spring barrels; column wheel chronograph control; vertical clutch; 50-hour power reserve
Functions: hours, minutes; chronograph with central second and minute totalizers
Diameter: 26.2 mm
Height: 7.1 mm
Jewels: 23
Balance: glucydur
Frequency: 28,800 vph
Balance spring: flat hairspring
Remarks: 227 components; movements numbered individually; bridges with côtes de Genève

Chanel

After having put the occasional jewelry watch onto the market earlier in its history, Chanel, a family-owned business headquartered in Paris, opened its own horology division in 1987, a move that gave the brand instant access to the world of watchmaking art. Chanel boasts its own studio and logistics center, both in La Chaux-de-Fonds. While the brand's first collections were still directed exclusively at its female clientele, it was actually with the rather simple and masculine J12 that Chanel finally achieved a breakthrough. Designer Jacques Helleu says he mainly designed the unpretentious ceramic watch for himself. "I wanted a timeless watch in glossy black," shares the likable eccentric. Indeed, it's not hard to imagine that the J12 will still look modern a number of years down the road—especially given the fact that the watch now comes in white and shiny, polished titanium/ceramic as well.

The J12 collection showpiece, the Rétrograde Mystérieuse, was a stroke of genius—courtesy of the innovative think tank Renaud et Papi. It propelled Chanel into the world of *haute horlogerie* in one fell swoop. And the brand has not been resting on any laurels. It has continued developing the J12, keeping the octagonal shape of Place Vendôme in Paris (home of the brand) and the famous Chanel No. 5 bottle stopper, but narrowing the bezel somewhat for a finer look.

Chanel
135, avenue Charles de Gaulle
F-92521 Neuilly-sur-Seine Cedex
France

Tel.:
01133-1-41-92-08-33

Website:
www.chanel.com

Founded:
1914

Number of employees:
not specified

Annual production:
not specified

Distribution:
retail and 200 Chanel boutiques worldwide

U.S. distributor:
Chanel Fine Jewelry and Watches
733 Madison Avenue
New York, NY 10021
800-550-0005
www.chanel.com

Most important collections:
J12, Première

J12 Noire Mate Superleggera Chronograph

Reference number: H3409
Movement: automatic, ETA Caliber 7750; ø 30 mm, height 7.9 mm; 25 jewels; 28,800 vph; 42 hours power reserve; COSC certified chronometer
Functions: hours, minutes, subsidiary seconds; chronograph; date
Case: ceramic, ø 41 mm, sapphire crystal
Band: ceramic, triple folding clasp
Price: $8,800

J12 White Phantom

Reference number: H3443
Movement: automatic, ETA Caliber 2824-2; ø 25.6 mm, height 4.6 mm; 25 jewels; 28,800 vph
Functions: hours, minutes, sweep seconds
Case: ceramic, ø 38 mm, height 13 mm; bezel in white gold with ceramic inserts; sapphire crystal; screw-in crown; water-resistant to 5 atm
Band: ceramic, triple folding clasp
Price: $5,600, limited to 2,000 pieces

J12 Jewelry

Reference number: H3384
Movement: automatic, ETA Caliber 2824-2; ø 25.6 mm, height 4.6 mm; 25 jewels; 28,800 vph
Functions: hours, minutes, sweep seconds
Case: ceramic, ø 38 mm, height 13 mm; bezel in white gold set with diamonds; sapphire crystal; screw-in crown; water-resistant to 5 atm
Band: ceramic, triple folding clasp
Remarks: dial set with 12 diamonds
Price: on request

Chopard & Cie. SA
8, rue de Veyrot
CH-1217 Meyrin (Geneva)
Switzerland

Tel.:
01141-22-719-3131

E-Mail:
info@chopard.ch

Website:
www.chopard.ch

Founded:
1860

Number of employees:
not specified

Annual production:
not specified

Distribution:
120 boutiques

U.S. distributor:
CHOPARD USA
21 East 63rd Street
New York, NY 10065
1-800-CHOPARD
www.chopard.com

Most important collections/price range:
Superfast / $9,320 to $33,190; L.U.C / $8,670 to $434,540; Imperiale / $4,390 to $617,010; Classic Racing / $4,170 to $57,130; Happy Sport / $5,120 to $287,330

Chopard

The Chopard *manufacture* was founded by Louis-Ulysse Chopard in 1860 in the tiny village of Sonvillier in the Jura mountains of Switzerland. In 1963, it was purchased by Karl Scheufele, a goldsmith from Pforzheim, Germany, and revived as a producer of fine watches and jewelry.

The past seventeen years have seen a breathtaking development, when Karl Scheufele's son, Karl-Friedrich, and his sister, Caroline, decided to create watches with in-house movements, thus restoring the old business launched by Louis-Ulysse back in the nineteenth century.

In the 1990s, literally out of nowhere, Chopard opened up its watchmaking *manufacture* in the sleepy town of Fleurier. Since 1996, the company has created no fewer than nine *manufacture* calibers, reassembled to create more than fifty watch variations ranging from the three-hand automatic to the tourbillon. The aim of Chopard's Fleurier Ebauches SA is to revive the long-standing tradition of *ébauche* production in that town.

The factory's debut caliber, the 01.03-C, is featured in its Impériale ladies watch. In 2011, Chopard produced more than 3,000 "Fleurier" watches. In 2012 came the men's version, the 01.04-C. The number of movements is scheduled to reach 15,000 by the year 2015. And the engineers are not resting on their laurels: A chronograph caliber is already in the making. The company also continues to support the Geneva Watchmaking School with special *ébauches* for the students, a demonstration of its commitment to the industry.

The original goal of Karl Scheufele can be considered achieved: With its wide range of *manufacture* watch models and over 130 boutiques worldwide, the brand enjoys firm footing in the rarified air of *haute horlogerie*.

Superfast Automatic

Reference number: 161290-5001
Movement: automatic, Chopard Manufacture Caliber 01.01-M; ø 28.8 mm, height 4.95 mm; 31 jewels; 28,800 vph; 60-hour power reserve; COSC certified chronometer
Functions: hours, minutes, sweep seconds; date
Case: rose gold, ø 41 mm, height 11.3 mm; sapphire crystal, transparent case back; screw-in crown with rubber coating; water-resistant to 10 atm
Band: rubber, folding clasp
Price: $22,280
Variations: stainless steel ($9,230)

Superfast Chronograph

Reference number: 168535-3001
Movement: automatic, Chopard Manufacture Caliber 03.05-M; ø 28.8 mm, height 7.6 mm; 45 jewels; 28,800 vph; 60-hour power reserve; COSC certified chronometer
Functions: hours, minutes, subsidiary seconds; flyback chronograph; date
Case: stainless steel, ø 45 mm, height 15.2 mm; sapphire crystal, transparent case back; screw-in crown with rubber coating; water-resistant to 10 atm
Band: rubber, folding clasp
Price: on request
Variations: rose gold ($33,190)

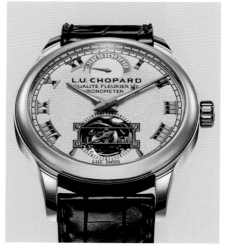

L.U.C Triple Certification Tourbillon

Reference number: 161929-5001
Movement: manually wound, L.U.C Caliber 02.13-L; ø 29.7 mm, height 6.1 mm; 33 jewels; 28,800 vph; 1-minute tourbillon, 216-hour power reserve; Geneva Seal, COSC chronometer, and Qualité Fleurier
Functions: hours, minutes, subsidiary seconds; power reserve indicator
Case: rose gold, ø 43 mm, height 11.15 mm; sapphire crystal; transparent case back; water-resistant to 5 atm
Band: reptile skin, buckle
Price: $146,270, limited to 100 pieces

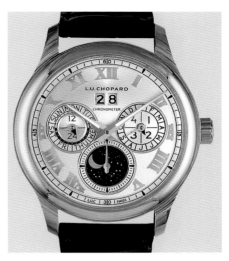

L.U.C 150 All in One

Reference number: 161925-1001
Movement: manually wound, L.U.C Caliber 4TQE;
ø 33 mm, height 11.75 mm; 42 jewels; 28,800 vph;
1-minute tourbillon; 189-hour power reserve;
Geneva Seal, COSC certified chronometer
Functions: hours, minutes, subsidiary seconds
(on tourbillon cage); day/night and power reserve
indicators; equation of time, sunrise and sunset on
movement side; perpetual calendar with large date,
weekday, month, orbital astronomic moon phase
Case: white gold, ø 46 mm, height 18.5 mm;
sapphire crystal, transparent case back; water-
resistant to 3 atm
Band: reptile skin, buckle
Price: $421,800, limited to 15 pieces

L.U.C Engine One H

Reference number: 168560-3001
Movement: manually wound, L.U.C Caliber
04.02-L; 34 x 25.9 mm, height 6.1 mm; 29 jewels;
28,800 vph; 1-minute tourbillon; 60-hour power
reserve; COSC certified chronometer
Functions: hours, minutes, subsidiary seconds;
power reserve indicator
Case: titanium, 44.5 x 35 mm, height 10.35 mm;
sapphire crystal, transparent case back; water-
resistant to 5 atm
Band: reptile skin, buckle
Price: $87,190, limited to 100 pieces

L.U.C Lunar One 2012

Reference number: 161927-5001
Movement: automatic, L.U.C Caliber 96.13-L;
ø 33 mm, height 6 mm; 32 jewels; 28,800 vph;
65-hour power reserve; Geneva Seal, COSC certified
chronometer
Functions: hours, minutes, subsidiary seconds;
perpetual calendar with large date, weekday, month,
orbital moon phase display, leap year
Case: rose gold, ø 43 mm, height 11.47 mm;
sapphire crystal, transparent case back; water-
resistant to 5 atm
Band: reptile skin, folding clasp
Price: $63,600
Variations: with diamond bezel ($98,550)

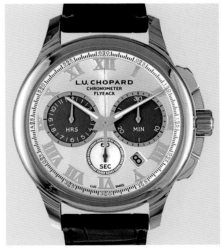

L.U.C Lunar Twin

Reference number: 161934-1001
Movement: automatic, L.U.C Caliber 96.21-L;
ø 33 mm; height 5.1 mm; 33 jewels; 28,800 vph;
bridges with côtes de Genève, 65-hour power
reserve; COSC certified chronometer
Functions: hours, minutes, subsidiary seconds;
date; moon phase
Case: white gold, ø 40 mm, height 9.97 mm;
sapphire crystal, transparent case back; water-
resistant to 3 atm
Band: reptile skin, buckle
Price: $26,550

L.U.C 1937 Classic

Reference number: 168544-3002
Movement: automatic, L.U.C Caliber 1.010; ø
28.8 mm, height 4.95 mm; 31 jewels; 28,800
vph; bridges with côtes de Genève; 60-hour power
reserve; COSC certified chronometer
Functions: hours, minutes, sweep seconds; date
Case: stainless steel, ø 42 mm, height 11.39 mm;
sapphire crystal, transparent case back; screw-in
crown; water-resistant to 10 atm
Band: reptile skin, buckle
Price: $9,230

L.U.C Chrono One

Reference number: 161928-1001
Movement: automatic, L.U.C Caliber 03.03-L;
ø 28.8 mm, height 7.6 mm; 45 jewels; 28,800 vph;
60-hour power reserve; COSC certified chronometer
Functions: hours, minutes, subsidiary seconds;
flyback chronograph; date
Case: white gold, ø 44 mm, height 14.06
mm; sapphire crystal, transparent case back;
water-resistant to 10 atm
Band: reptile skin, buckle
Price: $40,260
Variations: rose gold ($40,260)

L.U.C 8 HF

Reference number: 168554-3001
Movement: automatic, L.U.C Caliber 01.06-L;
ø 28.8 mm, height 4.95 mm; 31 jewels; 57,600 vph;
high-frequency escapement with silicone lever and
escape wheel, 60-hour power reserve; bridges with
côtes de Genève; COSC certified chronometer
Functions: hours, minutes, subsidiary seconds;
date
Case: titanium, ø 42 mm, height 11.47 mm;
sapphire crystal; water-resistant to 3 atm
Band: reptile skin, buckle
Price: $19,800, limited to 100 pieces

Classics Manufacture

Reference number: 161289-1001
Movement: automatic, L.U.C Caliber 01.04-C;
ø 28.8 mm, height 4.95 mm; 27 jewels;
28,800 vph; 60-hour power reserve
Functions: hours, minutes, subsidiary seconds;
date
Case: white gold, ø 38 mm, height 10.06 mm;
sapphire crystal, water-resistant to 3 atm
Band: reptile skin, buckle
Price: $14,740
Variations: yellow gold ($14,520); rose gold
($14,740)

Grand Prix de Monaco Historique

Reference number: 168992-3032
Movement: automatic, ETA Caliber 7750;
ø 30.4 mm, height 7.9 mm; 25 jewels; 28,800 vph;
48-hour power reserve; COSC certified chronometer
Functions: hours, minutes, subsidiary seconds;
chronograph; date
Case: titanium, ø 42.4 mm, height 14.67
mm; sapphire crystal, transparent case back;
water-resistant to 5 atm
Band: calf leather, buckle
Price: $7,540
Variations: rose gold, limited to 100 pieces
($21,040)

Classic Racing Superfast Chrono Split Second

Reference number: 168542-3001
Movement: automatic, La Joux-Perret Caliber 8721;
ø 30.4 mm, height 8.4 mm; 27 jewels; 28,800 vph;
46-hour power reserve; COSC certified chronometer
Functions: hours, minutes, subsidiary seconds;
rattrapante chronograph; date
Case: stainless steel with black DLC; ø 45 mm,
height 15.38 mm; bezel with tachymeter scale;
sapphire crystal, screw-in crown; water-resistant to
10 atm
Band: rubber, folding clasp
Price: $16,560, limited to 1,000 pieces

Mille Miglia GT XL "Speed Silver" Chrono

Reference number: 168459-3041
Movement: automatic, ETA Caliber A07.211;
ø 37.2 mm, height 7.9 mm; 25 jewels; 28,800 vph;
46-hour power reserve; COSC certified chronometer
Functions: hours, minutes, subsidiary seconds;
chronograph; date
Case: titanium, ø 44 mm, height 14.36 mm;
sapphire crystal, transparent case back; screw-in
crown; water-resistant to 10 atm
Band: calf leather, buckle
Price: $9,570, limited to 1,000 pieces

Mille Miglia 2012 GMT Chronograph

Reference number: 161288-5001
Movement: automatic, ETA Caliber 7754;
ø 30.4 mm, height 7.9 mm; 25 jewels; 28,800 vph;
48-hour power reserve; COSC certified chronometer
Functions: hours, minutes, subsidiary seconds;
additional 24-hour display (second time zone);
chronograph; date
Case: rose gold, ø 42.4 mm, height 14.87 mm;
sapphire crystal; water-resistant to 5 atm
Band: rubber, buckle
Price: $20,880
Variations: stainless steel, limited to 2,012 pieces
($6,610)

Caliber L.U.C 11 CF

Automatic; column wheel control of chronograph functions, vertical chronograph clutch, stop-second with automatic zero reset; single spring barrel, 65-hour power reserve; COSC certified chronometer
Functions: hours, minutes, subsidiary seconds; flyback chronograph; date
Diameter: 28.8 mm
Height: 7.6 mm
Jewels: 45
Balance: Variner with 4 weighted screws
Frequency: 28,800 vph
Balance spring: flat hairspring
Remarks: perlage on plate, beveled bridges with côtes de Genève, polished steel parts and screw heads

Caliber L.U.C 1.96 QP

Automatic; regulator system with micrometer screws, 22 kt gold microrotor; twin spring barrels, 65-hour power reserve; Geneva Seal; COSC certified chronometer
Functions: hours, minutes, subsidiary seconds; additional 24-hour display; perpetual calendar with large date, weekday, month, moon phase, leap year
Diameter: 33 mm
Height: 6 mm
Jewels: 32
Balance: glucydur
Frequency: 28,800 vph
Balance spring: flat hairspring, Nivarox 1
Remarks: perlage on plate, beveled bridges with côtes de Genève, polished steel parts and screw heads

Caliber L.U.C 4TQE

Manually wound; 1-minute tourbillon; 4 spring barrels, 168-hour power reserve
Functions: hours, minutes, subsidiary seconds; additional 24-hour display; power reserve indicator; perpetual calendar with large date, weekday, month, leap year; equation of time on case back, sunrise and sunset, orbital moon phase
Diameter: 33 mm
Height: 11.75 mm
Jewels: 42
Balance: glucydur
Frequency: 28,800 vph
Balance spring: flat hairspring, Nivarox 1

Caliber L.U.C 1.010

Automatic; simple barrel spring, 60-hour power reserve; COSC certified chronometer
Functions: hours, minutes, sweep seconds; date
Diameter: 28.8 mm
Height: 4.95 mm
Jewels: 31
Balance: glucydur
Frequency: 28,800 vph
Balance spring: flat hairspring, Nivarox 1

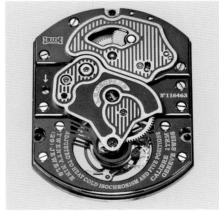

Caliber L.U.C 1TRM

Manually wound; 1-minute tourbillon; single spring barrel, 60-hour power reserve; COSC certified chronometer
Functions: hours, minutes, subsidiary seconds; power reserve indicator
Measurements: 25.9 x 34 mm
Height: 5.6 mm
Jewels: 29
Balance: glucydur
Frequency: 28,800 vph
Balance spring: flat hairspring, Nivarox 1
Remarks: special finish on movement, blackened and polished, "motor block" look

Caliber L.U.C "EHG"

Manually wound; regulator system with swan-neck fine adjustment; single spring barrel, 80-hour power reserve; Geneva Seal; COSC certified chronometer
Functions: hours, minutes, subsidiary seconds
Diameter: 43.2 mm
Height: 5.5 mm
Jewels: 20
Balance: glucydur with weighted screws
Frequency: 21,600 vph
Balance spring: flat hairspring, Nivarox 1
Remarks: reinterpretation of "training caliber" for teaching at Ecole Horlogère de Genève (EHG); bridges with côtes de Genève

Christiaan van der Klaauw Horloge Atelier b.v.
P.O. Box 87
NL-8440 AB Heerenveen
The Netherlands

Tel.:
01131-513-624-906

E-Mail:
info@klaauw.com

Website:
www.klaauw.com

Founded:
1974

Number of employees:
not specified

Annual production:
500–1,000 watches

U.S. distributor:
Kaufmann de Suisse
210 Worth Avenue
Palm Beach, FL 33480
561-832-4918

Most important collections:
astronomical watches

Christiaan van der Klaauw

Christiaan van der Klaauw was one of the earliest members of the famous AHCI, the Académie Horlogère des Créateurs Indépendents (Horological Academy of Independent Creators), in Switzerland. His main focus since 1976 has been on astronomical watches. He did not have to search long for a role model: The most obvious choice was Christiaan Huygens. The famous physicist and mathematician built the first pendulum clock. Like van der Klaauw, he too came from the Netherlands. And so did the astronomer Eise Eisinga, who set up a model of the solar system in his living room in 1774 to prove to people that the moon, the Mars, Jupiter, Mercury, and Venus would not collide with our own planet.

During his studies of microengineering, van der Klaauw worked in the world's oldest observatory (founded by J. H. Oort in 1633) and had already begun building astrolabes, planetaria, and complicated calendar watches.

The astronomical watch he completed in 1990 turned out to be his passport to the AHCI. From then on, van der Klaauw drove the watch world forward with his many elaborate creations. He also won numerous awards, most notably the Baselworld Gold Medal in 1992. In 2012, he accepted the financial and administrative assistance of a small group of Dutch watch collectors. The move was strategic, allowing him to put more time and talent into developing modern interpretations of astronomical displays and making his watches available to a greater public.

Orion

Reference number: CKOR1126
Movement: automatic, Caliber CK 1072 (with Orion module); ø 25.6 mm, height 3.6 mm; 25 jewels; 28,800 vph; planisphere turns counterclockwise 1 time per sidereal day (23 hours, 56 minutes, 4 seconds)
Functions: hours, minutes, sweep seconds; map of sky with signs of zodiac
Case: rose gold, ø 40 mm, height 13.3 mm; sapphire crystal, transparent case back
Band: reptile skin, buckle
Price: $32,500
Variations: various dials

Real Moon Joure

Reference number: CKRJ7724
Movement: automatic, Caliber CK1094 (base TT 738); ø 30 mm; height 4.35 mm; 35 jewels; 28,800 vph; hand-engraved gold rotor
Functions: hours, minutes, sweep seconds; moon phase (sculptural moon)
Case: white gold, ø 40 mm, height 14.8 mm; sapphire crystal, transparent case back
Band: reptile skin, buckle
Price: $48,900
Variations: stainless steel ($25,900); rose gold ($42,900)

Planetarium

Reference number: CKPT3344
Movement: automatic, Caliber CK1094 (base TT 738); ø 30 mm; height 4.35 mm; 35 jewels; 28,800 vph; hand-engraved gold rotor
Functions: hours, minutes, sweep seconds; orbits of Mercury, Venus, Earth, Mars, Jupiter, and Saturn; perpetual calendar with date and month
Case: stainless steel, ø 40 mm, height 14.8 mm; sapphire crystal, transparent case back; water-resistant to 5 atm
Band: reptile skin, folding clasp
Remarks: small heliocentric world planetarium
Price: $39,500
Variations: rose gold ($56,500); white gold ($62,500); platinum (price on request)

Christophe Claret

Individuals like Christophe Claret are authentic horological engineers who eat, drink, and breathe watchmaking and have developed careers based on pushing the envelope to the very edge of what's possible.

By the age of 23, the Lyon-born Claret was in Basel alongside Journe, Calabrese, and other independents, where he was spotted by the late Rolf Schnyder of Ulysse Nardin and commissioned to make a minute repeater with jacquemarts. In 1989, he opened his *manufacture,* a nineteenth-century mansion tastefully extended with a state-of-the-art machining area. Indeed, Claret embraces wholeheartedly the potential in modern tools to create the precise pieces needed to give physical expression to exceedingly complex ideas.

Over the years, Claret created complications and movements for many companies. In 2004, he came out with the Harry Winston Opus IV, a reversible moon phase with tourbillon and a minute repeater.

Twenty years after establishing his business, Claret finally launched his own complex watches: models like the DualTow, with its hours and minutes on two tracks, minute repeater, and complete view of the great ballet of arms and levers inside. Then came the Adagio, again a minute repeater, with a clear dial that manages a second time zone and large date. In 2011, Claret wowed the watch world with a humorous, on-the-wrist gambling machine telling time and playing blackjack, craps, or roulette. And 2012 saw the stunning X-TREM-1, a turbocharged DualTow with two spheres controlled by magnets hovering along the numeral tracks to tell the time. The tourbillon at the bottom is the cherry on top. The latest invention is Kantharos, named after a top-notch Thoroughbred that is still reproducing happily. The racing connection is the cathedral gong that offers an audible signal when the chronograph is activated.

Christophe Claret SA
Route du Soleil d'Or 2
CH-2400 Le Locle
Switzerland

Tel.:
01141-32-933-0000

Fax:
01141-32-933-8081

E-Mail:
info@christopheclaret.com

Website:
www.christopheclaret.com

Founded:
manufacture 1989, brand 2009

Number of employees:
100

Annual production:
not specified

Distibution:
For sales information, contact the *manufacture* directly.

Most important collections:
DualTow, Adagio, 21 Blackjack, X-TREM-1, Soprano, Kantharos, Baccara

Soprano

Reference number: MTR.TRD98.020-028
Movement: manually wound, caliber TRD98; ø 27.6 mm, height 8.45 mm; 39 jewels; 21,600 vph; single barrel; 1-minute flying tourbillon; 72-hour power reserve; parachute shock protection
Functions: hours, minutes, minute repeater
Case: white gold and anthracite PVD-coated titanium; ø 45 mm, height 15.32 mm; water-resistant to 3 atm
Band: reptile skin, white gold and titanium buckle
Remarks: 4-note minute repeater playing Westminster quarters on 4 patented gongs
Price: CHF 476,000, limited to 8 pieces

X-TREM-1

Reference number: MTR.FLY11.040-048
Movement: manually wound, Caliber FLY11; 64 jewels; 21,600 vph; twin spring barrels; flying 1-minute tourbillon; 50-hour power reserve
Functions: mysterious retrograde hours and minutes, indicated by spheres in tubes, seconds on tourbillon carriage
Case: rose gold and anthracite PVD-coated; 40.80 x 56.82 mm, height 15 mm, water-resistant to 3 atm
Band: reptile skin, folding clasp
Remarks: fast time adjustment, winding, and time-setting via levers
Price: CHF 268,000, limited to 8 pieces

Kantharos

Reference number: MTR.MBA13.902
Movement: automatic, Caliber MBA13; ø 36.6 mm, height 10.56 mm; 75 jewels; 21,600 vph; platinum oscillating mass; constant force escapement; rhodium-plated dial; 40-hour power reserve
Functions: hours, minutes; chronograph; cathedral gong
Case: white gold and anthracite PVD titanium, ø 45 mm, height 15.8 mm; water-resistant to 3 atm
Band: reptile skin, folding clasp
Remarks: monopusher chrono activates cathedral gong at start, stop, reset
Price: CHF 118,000, numbered series

Chronoswiss AG
Pilatusstr. 5
CH-6003 Lucerne
Switzerland

Tel.:
01141-41-368-0150

Fax:
01141-41-368-0159

E-Mail:
info@chronoswiss.ch

Website:
www.chronoswiss.com

Founded:
1983

Number of employees:
approx. 40

Annual production:
4,000–6,000 wristwatches

U.S. distributor:
Chiron Distribution Inc.
4858 Nancy Street
Pierrefonds, Quebec
H8Z 1Z8
Canada

Most important collections/price range:
30 models, including Kairos, Delphis, Régulateur, Sirius, Sign of the Times, Timemaster / approx. $3,900 to $60,000

Chronoswiss

Chronoswiss has been assembling its signature watches—which boast such features as coin edge bezels and onion crowns—since 1983. Chronoswiss founder Gerd-Rüdiger Lang loved to joke about having "the only Swiss watch factory in Germany" as the brand has always adhered closely to the qualities of the Swiss watch industry while still contributing a great deal to reviving mechanical watches from its facilities in Karlsfeld near Munich, with concepts and designs "made in Germany." The fact is, however, that the watches are equipped with Swiss movements and cases, as well as many other important parts. The company's financial brawn is also Swiss, ever since Eva and Oliver Ebstein bought up all Chronoswiss shares in order to ensure the brand's survival. Oliver, as a passionate watchman, is continuing the brand tradition and producing top-drawer mechanical timepieces. The spacious sun-drenched facilities in Karlsfeld are now focused on distribution and servicing.

With such developments as the *manufacture* caliber C.122—based on an old Enicar automatic movement with a patented rattrapante mechanism—and its Chronoscope chronograph, Chronoswiss has earned a solid reputation for technical prowess. The Pacific and Sirius models, additions to the classic collection, point the company in a new stylistic direction designed to help win new buyers and the attention of the international market. The year 2013 was an especially big one for the brand: Chronoswiss celebrated its thirtieth anniversary, while the best-selling Régulateur marked its twenty-fifth with a limited edition featuring jumping hours.

Régulateur 30

Reference number: CH 2811 R
Movement: automatic, Chronoswiss Caliber C.283; ø 30 mm, height 5.2 mm; 27 jewels; 28,800 vph; fine sunburst finishing, skeletonized and rhodium-plated rotor; 42-hour power reserve
Functions: hours (digital, jumping), minutes (off-center), subsidiary seconds
Case: rose gold, ø 40 mm, height 9.65 mm; sapphire crystal, transparent case back; water-resistant to 3 atm
Band: reptile skin, buckle
Remarks: sterling silver dial, limited to 130 pieces
Price: $35,550
Variations: stainless steel ($17,350); limited to 300

Régulateur

Reference number: CH 1243.1
Movement: automatic, Chronoswiss Caliber C.122 (base Enicar 165); ø 30 mm, height 5.2 mm; 30 jewels; 28,800 vph; finely finished with côtes de Genève, skeletonized rotor; 40-hour power reserve
Functions: hours (off-center), minutes, subsidiary seconds
Case: stainless steel, ø 40 mm, height 11 mm; sapphire crystal, transparent case back; water-resistant to 3 atm
Band: reptile skin, buckle
Remarks: sterling silver dial
Price: $7,000
Variations: pink gold ($17,750)

Balance Chronograph

Reference number: CH 7541 B R
Movement: automatic, Chronoswiss Caliber C.831 (base LJP 8310); ø 30 mm, height 7.9 mm; 39 jewels; 28,800 vph; finely finished with côtes de Genève, skeletonized rotor; 46-hour power reserve
Functions: hours, minutes, subsidiary seconds, (retrograde); chronograph; date (retrograde)
Case: pink gold, ø 42 mm, height 14.75 mm; sapphire crystal, transparent case back; water-resistant to 3 atm
Band: reptile skin, buckle
Price: $26,625
Variations: stainless steel ($11,875)

Grand Lunar Chronograph

Reference number: CH 7541 L R
Movement: automatic, Chronoswiss Caliber
C.755 (base ETA 7750); ø 30 mm, height 7.9 mm;
25 jewels; 28,800 vph; côtes de Genève, perlage,
skeletonized rotor; approx. 46-hour power reserve
Functions: hours, minutes, subsidiary seconds;
chronograph; date; moon phase
Case: pink gold, ø 42 mm, height 14.75 mm;
sapphire crystal, transparent case back; water-
resistant to 3 atm
Band: reptile skin, buckle
Price: $23,775
Variations: stainless steel ($8,700)

Kairolady

Reference number: CH 2041 R
Movement: automatic, Chronoswiss Caliber C.281
(base ETA 2892-A2); ø 25.6 mm, height 3.6 mm;
21 jewels; 28,800 vph; skeletonized rotor, côtes de
Genève; 42-hour power reserve
Functions: hours, minutes, sweep seconds; date
Case: pink gold, ø 36 mm, sapphire crystal,
transparent case back; water-resistant to 3 atm
Band: reptile skin, buckle
Price: $14,225
Variations: stainless steel ($5,000); stainless
steel with diamond bezel ($11,825); pink gold with
diamond bezel ($20,500)

Kairodate

Reference number: CH 3523.1
Movement: automatic, Chronoswiss Caliber
C.351; ø 25.6 mm, height 4.95 mm; 21 jewels;
28,800 vph; finely finished
Functions: hours, minutes, sweep seconds; power
reserve indicator; large date
Case: stainless steel, ø 40 mm; sapphire crystal,
transparent case back; water-resistant to 3 atm
Band: reptile skin, buckle
Price: $6,800
Variations: pink gold ($13,350)

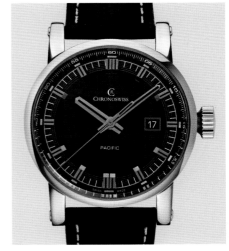

Sirius Triple Date

Reference number: CH 9343 bl
Movement: automatic, Chronoswiss Caliber C.931
(base ETA 2892-A2); ø 25.6 mm, height 5.75 mm;
21 jewels; 28,800 vph; skeletonized rotor, côtes de
Genève; 42-hour power reserve
Functions: hours, minutes, sweep seconds; full
calendar with date, weekday, month, moon phase
Case: stainless steel, ø 40 mm, height 9.9 mm;
sapphire crystal, transparent case back; water-
resistant to 3 atm
Band: reptile skin, buckle
Price: $9,025
Variations: pink gold ($21,770)

Sirius Automatic

Reference number: CH 2893
Movement: automatic, Chronoswiss Caliber C.281
(base ETA 2892-A2); ø 25.6 mm, height 3.6 mm;
21 jewels; 28,800 vph; skeletonized rotor, perlage
on plate, bridges with côtes de Genève; 42-hour
power reserve
Functions: hours, minutes, sweep seconds; date
Case: stainless steel, ø 40 mm, height 8.2 mm;
sapphire crystal, transparent case back; water-
resistant to 3 atm
Band: reptile skin, buckle
Price: $10,950
Variations: pink gold ($16,970)

Pacific

Reference number: CH 2882 R bk
Movement: automatic, Chronoswiss Caliber C.281
(base ETA 2892-A2); ø 25.6 mm, height 3.6 mm;
21 jewels; 28,800 vph; skeletonized rotor with côtes
de Genève
Functions: hours, minutes, sweep seconds; date
Case: stainless steel, ø 40 mm, height 11.25 mm;
pink gold bezel; sapphire crystal, transparent case
back; water-resistant to 10 atm
Band: leather, buckle
Price: $7,390
Variations: stainless steel ($4,190)

Pacific Chronograph

Reference number: CH 7583 B bk
Movement: automatic, Chronoswiss Caliber C.771 (base ETA 7750); ø 30 mm, height 7.9 mm; 25 jewels; 28,800 vph; skeletonized rotor, côtes de Genève; 42-hour power reserve
Functions: hours, minutes, subsidiary seconds; chronograph; date, weekday
Case: stainless steel, ø 43 mm, height 14.85 mm; sapphire crystal, transparent case back; water-resistant to 10 atm
Band: leather, buckle
Price: $6,700
Variations: with stainless steel bracelet ($6,700); DLC-coated bezel ($7,425); DLC-coated bezel and stainless steel bracelet ($7,425)

Timemaster Chronograph GMT S-Ray 007

Reference number: CHD 7535 G D/N
Movement: automatic, Chronoswiss Caliber C.754 (base La-Joux-Perret); ø 30.4 mm, height 7.9 mm; 25 jewels, 28,800 vph; skeletonized and gold-plated rotor, finished with côtes de Genève; 46-hour power reserve
Functions: hours, minutes; additional 24-hour indicator (second time zone); chronograph; date
Case: stainless steel, black DLC coating; ø 44 mm, height 16.25; with 24-hour divisions, sapphire crystal, transparent case back; water-resistant to 10 atm
Band: rubber, buckle
Price: $9,300, limited to 180 pieces

Timemaster Big Date

Reference number: CH 3535
Movement: automatic, Chronoswiss Caliber C.351 S (base LJP 3513); ø 25.6 mm, height 4.95 mm; 21 jewels; 28,800 vph; rhodium-plated and skeletonized rotor with black DLC coating, finely finished with côtes de Genève
Functions: hours, minutes, sweep seconds; power reserve indicator; large date
Case: stainless steel, black DLC coating; ø 44 mm, height 13.8 mm; bezel with 60-minute divisions, sapphire crystal, transparent case back; water-resistant to 10 atm
Band: rubber, buckle
Price: $6,475
Variations: without DLC coating ($6,700)

Artist's Collection 1

Reference number: CH 6421.1 RE2 bl
Movement: manually wound, Chronoswiss Caliber C.642 (base Unitas); ø 36.6 mm, height 4.5 mm; 17 jewels; 28,800 vph; hand-skeletonized and finely decorated; 48-hour power reserve
Functions: hours, minutes, subsidiary seconds
Case: pink gold, ø 40 mm, height 11 mm; sapphire crystal, transparent case back; water-resistant to 3 atm
Band: reptile skin, buckle
Remarks: hand-guilloché enamel dial
Price: $47,000

Artist's Collection 2

Reference number: CH 6421.1 RE2 br
Movement: manually wound, Chronoswiss Caliber C.642 (base Unitas); ø 36.6 mm, height 4.5 mm; 17 jewels; 28,800 vph; hand-skeletonized and finely decorated; 48-hour power reserve
Functions: hours, minutes, subsidiary seconds
Case: pink gold, ø 40 mm, height 11 mm; sapphire crystal, transparent case back; water-resistant to 3 atm
Band: reptile skin, buckle
Remarks: hand-guilloché enamel dial
Price: $47,000

Artist's Collection 3

Reference number: CH 6421.1 RE2 gy
Movement: manually wound, Chronoswiss Caliber C.642 (base Unitas); ø 36.6 mm, height 4.5 mm; 17 jewels; 21,600 vph; hand-skeletonized and finely decorated; 48-hour power reserve
Functions: hours, minutes, subsidiary seconds
Case: pink gold, ø 40 mm, height 11 mm; sapphire crystal, transparent case back; water-resistant to 3 atm
Band: reptile skin, buckle
Remarks: hand-guilloché enamel dial
Price: $47,000

Caliber C.111

Base caliber: Marvin 700
Manually wound; power reserve 46 hours
Functions: hours, minutes, subsidiary seconds
Diameter: 29.4 mm
Height: 3.3 mm
Jewels: 17
Balance: glucydur, 3-legged
Frequency: 21,600 vph
Balance spring: Nivarox 1
Shock protection: Incabloc
Remarks: polished pallet lever, escapement wheel and screws, bridges with côtes de Genève

Caliber C.122

Automatic; skeletonized and gold-plated rotor on ball bearings, with côtes de Genève; power reserve approx. 40 hours
Functions: hours, minutes, subsidiary seconds
Diameter: 26.8 mm
Height: 5.3 mm
Jewels: 30
Balance: glucydur, 3-legged
Frequency: 21,600 vph
Balance spring: Nivarox 1
Shock protection: Incabloc
Remarks: pallet lever, escape wheel and screws, perlage on plate, bridges with côtes de Genève; individually numbered

Caliber C.126

Automatic; E94 striking module (Dubois Dépraz), all-or-nothing strike train and 2 gongs; power reserve 35 hours
Functions: hours, minutes, subsidiary seconds; quarter hour repeater
Diameter: 28 mm
Height: 8.35 mm
Jewels: 38
Balance: glucydur, 3-legged
Frequency: 21,600 vph
Balance spring: Nivarox 1
Shock protection: Incabloc
Remarks: base plate with perlage; beveled bridges with perlage; côtes de Genève decoration; individually numbered

Caliber C.127

Automatic; calendar module with a left-side moon phase; skeletonized and gold-plated rotor on ball bearings, with côtes de Genève; power reserve 40 hours
Functions: hours, minutes, sweep seconds; perpetual calendar with months, moon phase, leap year, weekday, date
Diameter: 26.8 mm; **Height:** 8.79 mm
Jewels: 30; **Balance:** glucydur, 3-legged
Frequency: 21,600 vph
Balance spring: Nivarox 1
Shock protection: Incabloc
Remarks: polished pallet lever, escapement wheel and screws, perlage on plate, bridges with côtes de Genève; individually numbered

Caliber C.673

Base caliber: ETA 6498
Manually wound; power reserve 46 hours
Functions: hours (off-center), minutes, subsidiary seconds
Diameter: 37.2 mm
Height: 4.5 mm
Jewels: 17
Balance: glucydur screw balance with stop second
Frequency: 18,000 vph
Balance spring: Nivarox 1
Shock protection: Incabloc
Remarks: polished pallet lever, escape wheel and screws; côtes de Genève and hand perlage on bridges, balance cocks, sunburst pattern on crown and ratchet wheel; individually numbered

Caliber C.741 S

Base caliber: ETA 7750
Automatic; completely skeletonized; skeletonized and gold-plated rotor on ball bearings, with côtes de Genève; power reserve approx. 46 hours
Functions: hours, minutes, subsidiary seconds; chronograph; date
Diameter: 30 mm; **Height:** 7.9 mm; **Jewels:** 25
Balance: glucydur, 3-legged
Frequency: 28,800 vph
Balance spring: Nivarox 1
Shock protection: Incabloc
Remarks: polished pallet lever, escape wheel and screws; perlage on plate, skeletonized and beveled levers and wheels

Montres Cimier AG
Haldenstrasse 3
CH-6340 Baar
Switzerland

Tel.:
01141-41-720-2929

Fax:
01141-41-720-2925

E-Mail:
info@cimier.com

Website:
www.cimier.com

Founded:
1925

Number of employees:
not specified

Annual production:
not specified

Distribution:
specialty stores/direct sales

Most important collections/price range:
Winglet, Seven Seas / prices calculated according
to daily exchange rate; numbers listed here are
approximate.

Cimier

Like many small family-run businesses in the German-speaking region of Switzerland, at the beginning of the 1920s Joseph Lapanouse SA put its energy into the reassembly of so-called Roskopf watches, affordable timepieces "for everyman" with easily produced pin lever movements. These dated from the end of the nineteenth century, when Georg Friedrich Roskopf replaced the expensive ruby pallets in the anchor escapement with hardened steel pins and simplified movement construction via the use of simple arrows.

Cimier boomed following World War II, and in its heyday employed 500 people and produced nearly 1.5 million watches a year. It even managed to navigate the quartz crisis by manufacturing its own quartz pieces, but erroneous strategic decisions and internal conflicts forced the company to close down.

In 2003, however, the erstwhile famous crested helmet logo reappeared thanks to Martin Bärtsch, former manager of Maurice Lacroix. He worked diligently on an upgrade featuring more ambitious and complex constructions, but positioned his brand carefully in the trending under $5,000 segment. All of the new Cimier creations are designed, developed, and made in Switzerland. Cimier also launched a "Watch Academy," where customers can design their own timepieces. And Bärtsch decided to sign up ambassadors as well, like the big brands. Rather than choosing noisy VIPs in fast cars, he went for personalities like the Swiss figure skater Sarah Meier. As luck would have it, she won the European championship two weeks after becoming a "Cimierista."

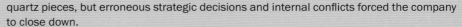

BIGMatic 16 ½'''

Reference number: 6110-SS011
Movement: automatic, Cimier Caliber BIGMatic (base ETA 6497-1); ø 37.2 mm, height 7.3 mm; 20 jewels, 28,800 vph; 53-hour power reserve
Functions: hours, minutes, subsidiary seconds
Case: stainless steel, ø 43.5 mm, height 13.95 mm; sapphire crystal; transparent case back; water-resistant to 5 atm
Band: reptile skin, folding clasp
Price: $4,530
Variations: limited edition with black PVD coating ($4,900)

Timesquare

Reference number: 5106-BP021
Movement: automatic, ETA Caliber 7750; ø 30 mm, height 7.9 mm; 25 jewels; 28,800 vph; fine finishing; 42-hour power reserve
Functions: hours, minutes, subsidiary seconds; chronograph; weekday, date
Case: stainless steel with black PVD coating; 35 x 42 mm, height 13 mm; sapphire crystal, transparent case back; water-resistant to 5 atm
Band: calf leather, folding clasp
Price: $2,690
Variations: with rubber strap ($2,690); Edoardo Molinari signature edition ($2,690)

Classics

Reference number: 2419-SS011
Movement: quartz
Functions: hours, minutes, sweep seconds; date
Case: stainless steel, ø 39 mm, height 8 mm; sapphire crystal, water-resistant to 5 atm
Band: calf leather, buckle
Price: $490
Variations: with stainless steel band ($560); women's model with smaller case and various versions

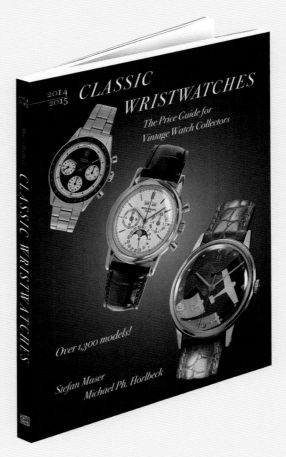

The History of Watches

Showcasing the incomparable collection of watches at the British Museum, this volume is a unique history of watches as timepieces and as works of art.

Text by David Thompson
Photographs by Saul Peckham
250 illustrations in full color
176 pages · 9⅝ × 9⅝ in.
Hardcover · $45.00
ISBN 978-0-7892-0918-4

"*The History of Watches* . . . is a colorful and enlightening tour of the superb British Museum collection of rare timepieces . . . Illustrations as precise as the inner workings of the watchworks themselves offer a dazzling display of gold repousse cases, exquisite enameling, engraving and fretwork, as well as presenting the various technical innovations and variations."
—*Copley News Service*

Classic Wristwatches 2014–2015

Classic Wristwatches contains extensive chapters on approximately 50 of the most historically interesting, sought after brands on today's secondary and auction markets. Updated and revised every two years, it contains the most current information on 1,300 vintage watches and their approximate value, including details on the movement, case, special characteristics, and estimated price of each piece.

By Stefan Muser and Michael Ph. Horlbeck
1,100 full-color illustrations
232 pages, 8¼ × 11¾ in.
Paperback · $35.00
ISBN 978-0-7892-1143-9

"If the ticking of a Rolex makes your collector's heart beat faster, then this volume is a must for you." —*ArtInvestor Magazine*

Published by ABBEVILLE PRESS
137 Varick Street, New York, NY 10013
1-800-Artbook (in U.S. only)
Also available wherever fine books are sold
Visit us at www.abbeville.com

JUVENIA
— 1860 —

Sextant

An extraordinary watch that has distinctive hands like no other.

For over 150 years, Juvenia has designed watches that respect the finest Swiss traditions. For the hands of our particular Sextant model (a tribute to the architects), we took inspiration from the tools used in architecture and design. The protractor and the ruler, a true symbol of tradition, accuracy and innovation.

Sextant
Automatic
18ct red gold

Montres Corum Sàrl
Rue du Petit-Château 1
Case postale 374
CH-2301 La Chaux-de-Fonds
Switzerland

Tel.:
01141-32-967-0670

Fax:
01141-32-967-0800

E-Mail:
info@corum-watches.ch

Website:
www.corum.ch

Founded:
1955

Number of employees:
160 worldwide

Annual production:
16,000 watches

U.S. distributor:
Montres Corum USA
14050 NW 14th Street, Suite 110
Sunrise, FL 33323
954-279-1220; 954-279-1780 (fax)
www.corum.ch

Most important collections/price range:
Admiral's Cup, Corum Bridges and Heritage,
Romvlvs and Artisan, 150 models in total / approx.
$4,100 to over $1,000,000

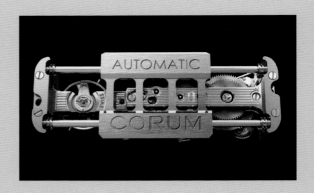

Corum

Making a name for itself since 1955, Switzerland's youngest luxury watch brand, Corum, is known for unusual—and sometimes outlandish—case and dial designs. In 1999, the company was purchased by Severin Wunderman, who had enjoyed twenty-three years of creating highly successful wristwatches for fashion giant Gucci. After a number of overly daring forays into the shimmering world of fashion watches, he led Corum back to the straight and narrow before dying of a stroke, on June 25, 2008, at the age of 69.

Together with Wunderman's son, Michael, CEO Antonio Calce turned the focus of the collection toward the brand's two "draft horses." The legendary Golden Bridge baguette movement received a complete makeover, featuring a totally new technical interpretation in modern materials and such complicated mechanisms as a flying tourbillon. The development of these extraordinary movements requires great watchmaking craftsmanship. In fact, the company has added a number of professional watchmakers to its workforce, who make good use of the new technical equipment in Corum's workshops. The product development department also underwent expansion and modernization in preparation for the development of even more innovations.

The brand's expansive policies cost money, so to secure its future, Corum was sold to China Haidian Group for over $90 million in April 2013. Calce welcomed the move not only for the financial support it will bring, but also for the access it allows to the crucial Chinese market. He was additionally named CEO of Eterna, which was purchased by the group along with Porsche Design in 2011.

Golden Bridge Automatic

Reference number: 313.165.59 0001 GLIOG
Movement: automatic, Caliber CO 313; 11.25 x 33.18 mm; 26 jewels; 28,800 vph; variable inertia balance; baguette with gold bridges and main plate; linear winding with sliding platinum weight
Functions: hours, minutes
Case: white gold, 51.8 x 37.2 mm, height 13.7 mm; sapphire crystal, transparent case back; water-resistant to 3 atm
Band: stainless steel, buckle
Remarks: lateral window on case
Price: $54,800
Variations: pink gold with pink gold bracelet ($72,400); white gold with white gold bracelet ($76,500)

Golden Bridge

Reference number: 113.165.55 0002 GLIOR
Movement: manually wound, Caliber CO113; 4.9 x 34 mm, height 3 mm; 19 jewels; 28,800 vph; baguette, gold bridges and plate, hand-engraved
Functions: hours, minutes
Case: pink gold, 34 x 51 mm, height 10.9 mm; sapphire crystal, transparent case back; water-resistant to 3 atm
Band: stainless steel, buckle
Remarks: lateral window on case; partially transparent sapphire cover
Price: $38,300
Variations: white gold ($43,100); pink gold with pink gold bracelet ($61,000); white gold with white gold bracelet ($67,500)

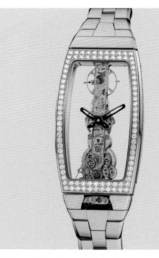

Miss Golden Bridge

Reference number: 113.102.85 V880 0000
Movement: manually wound, Caliber CO113; 4.9 x 34 mm, height 3 mm; 19 jewels; 28,800 vph; baguette movement, gold bridges and plate, hand-engraved
Functions: hours, minutes
Case: pink gold, 21 x 43 mm, height 11.24 mm; bezel set with brilliant-cut diamonds; sapphire crystal, transparent case back; water-resistant to 3 atm
Band: pink gold, double folding clasp
Remarks: lateral window on case
Price: $48,400
Variations: with reptile skin band ($33,300)

Golden Bridge Tourbillon Panoramique

Reference number: 100.160.55 OF01 0000
Movement: manually wound, Caliber CO 100; ø 29 mm; 22 jewels; 21,600 vph; flying 1-minute tourbillon; baguette movement, sapphire crystal bridges and plate; 90-hour power reserve
Functions: hours, minutes
Case: pink gold, 37.6 x 56 mm, height 12.35 mm; sapphire crystal, transparent case back; water-resistant to 3 atm
Band: reptile skin, folding clasp
Remarks: lateral window on case
Price: $185,300
Variations: white gold ($193,700)

Ti-Bridge Tourbillon

Reference number: 022.710.04 OF01 0000
Movement: manually wound, Caliber CO113; 13 x 37.8 mm; 21 jewels; 21,600 vph; baguette movement with flying tourbillon, arcap bridges and plate; twin spring barrels, 72-hour power reserve
Functions: hours, minutes
Case: titanium, 52 x 42 mm, height 12.3 mm; sapphire crystal, transparent case back; water-resistant to 3 atm
Band: reptile skin, folding clasp
Price: $65,800, limited to 50 pieces
Variations: with titanium bracelet ($66,400); pink gold ($94,500)

Ti-Bridge Power Reserve

Reference number: 107.201.05 OF81 0000
Movement: manually wound, Caliber CO113; 12.37 x 38.25 mm, height 4.4 mm; 25 jewels; 28,800 vph; baguette movement, PVD-coated titanium chassis, 72-hour power reserve
Functions: hours, minutes; power reserve indicator
Case: pink gold, 53.2 x 42.5 mm, height 13.23 mm; sapphire crystal, water-resistant to 5 atm
Band: reptile skin, double folding clasp
Price: $47,800
Variations: titanium ($19,200)

Ti-Bridge Automatic Dual Winder

Reference number: 207.201.04 OF61 0000
Movement: automatic, Caliber CO 207; 37.9 x 12.27 mm; 30 jewels; 28,800 vph; baguette movement, titanium bridges and plate; 2 winding rotors with tungsten oscillating weights coupled by a pushrod, 72-hour power reserve
Functions: hours, minutes
Case: titanium, 52 x 42 mm, height 15 mm; sapphire crystal, transparent case back; water-resistant to 3 atm
Band: leather and rubber, folding clasp
Price: $22,300
Variations: pink gold with leather strap ($51,000); with titanium bracelet ($23,000)

Ti-Bridge Lady

Reference number: 007.129.51 0009 0000
Movement: manually wound, Caliber CO 007; 37.9 x 12.27 mm, height 4.4 mm; 21 jewels; 28,800 vph; baguette movement, titanium bridges and plate; 72-hour power reserve
Functions: hours, minutes
Case: ceramic, 40.9 x 35.2 mm, height 9 mm; pink gold bezel set with 68 diamonds; sapphire crystal, transparent case back; water-resistant to 3 atm
Band: reptile skin, buckle
Price: $12,300
Variations: with white gold bezel and diamonds; without diamonds ($12,300); rose gold ($19,400)

Admiral's Cup Seafender 47 Tourbillon Chronograph

Reference number: 398.550.55 0001 AN10
Movement: automatic, Caliber CO 398; ø 36.25 mm; 28 jewels; 28,800 vph; 1-minute tourbillon; black ruthenium-coated winding rotor; 45-hour power reserve
Functions: hours, minutes; chronograph; date
Case: pink gold, ø 47 mm, height 15.72 mm; sapphire crystal, transparent case back; water-resistant to 5 atm
Band: reptile skin, buckle
Price: $88,800
Variations: aluminum ($57,600)

Admiral's Cup AC-One 45 Regatta

Reference number: 040.101.04 OF61 AN10
Movement: automatic, Caliber CO 040 (base ETA 7750 with Corum module); ø 30 mm; 25 jewels; 28,800 vph; 48-hour power reserve
Functions: hours, minutes; chronograph with adjustable regatta countdown
Case: titanium, ø 45 mm, height 15.2 mm; bezel with black PVD coating; sapphire crystal, transparent case back; water-resistant to 30 atm
Band: stainless steel, folding clasp
Price: $11,525
Variations: with titanium band ($12,100)

Admiral's Cup Legend 45 Chronograph

Reference number: 132.201.05 OF61 AN11
Movement: automatic, Caliber CO 132 (base ETA 2892-A2 with Dubois Dépraz module); ø 28.6 mm; height 6.1 mm; 39 jewels; 28,800 vph; rotor with black PVD coating; 42-hour power reserve
Functions: hours, minutes, subsidiary seconds; chronograph; date
Case: titanium, ø 45 mm, height 14.3 mm; pink gold bezel; sapphire crystal, transparent case back; water-resistant to 30 atm
Band: stainless steel, folding clasp
Price: $18,450
Variations: with titanium bezel ($9,550); with titanium bracelet ($10,150)

Admiral's Cup Seafender 48 Tides

Reference number: 277.931.06 0371 AN52
Movement: automatic, Caliber CO 277 (base ETA 2892-A2 with Dubois Dépraz module); ø 25.9 mm, height 5.2 mm; 21 jewels; 28,800 vph; COSC chronometer
Functions: hours, minutes, sweep seconds; tides display with current strength; date; moon phase
Case: titanium, ø 48 mm, height 17.35 mm; bezel of vulcanized rubber; sapphire crystal, screw-in crown; water-resistant to 30 atm
Band: rubber, buckle
Price: $9,850
Variations: pink gold with leather strap ($32,700); with titanium and rubber bracelet ($11,300)

Admiral's Cup Legend 42 Chronograph

Reference number: 984.101.20 V705 AN10
Movement: automatic, Caliber CO 984 (base ETA 2892-2); ø 28.6 mm, height 6.1 mm; 37 jewels; 28,800 vph; 42-hour power reserve; COSC chronometer
Functions: hours, minutes, subsidiary seconds; chronograph; date
Case: stainless steel, ø 42 mm, height 11.6 mm; sapphire crystal, transparent case back; water-resistant to 3 atm
Band: stainless steel, double folding clasp
Price: $6,350

Admiral's Cup Legend 42 Blue

Reference number: 395.101.30 V705 AB10
Movement: automatic, Caliber CO 395 (base ETA 2892-2); ø 25.9 mm; 27 jewels; 28,800 vph; 42-hour power reserve
Functions: hours, minutes, subsidiary seconds; date
Case: stainless steel with blue PVD coating, ø 42 mm, height 9.5 mm; sapphire crystal, transparent case back; water-resistant to 5 atm
Band: stainless steel with blue PVD coating, double folding clasp
Price: $5,800

Vintage Chargé d'Affaires

Reference number: 286.253.55 0001 BN68
Movement: manually wound, Caliber CO 286 (base historic AS 1475); ø 25.6 mm; 17 jewels; 18,000 vph; 46-hour power reserve
Functions: hours, minutes, sweep seconds; alarm
Case: pink gold, ø 39.5 mm, height 13.5 mm; sapphire crystal, water-resistant to 3 atm
Band: stainless steel, buckle
Price: $17,900, limited to 50 pieces
Variations: white gold, limited to 50 pieces ($19,800)

Cuervo y Sobrinos Habana SA

Via Carlo Maderno 54
CH-6825 Capolago
Switzerland

Tel.:
01141-91-921-2773

Fax:
01141-91-921-2775

E-Mail:
info@cuervoysobrinos.com

Website:
www.cuervosobrinos.com

Founded:
1882

Number of employees:
not specified

Annual production:
3,500 watches

U.S. distributor:
Cuervo y Sobrinos
Milestone Distribution
297 Dividend Drive, Suite B
Peachtree City, GA 30269
678-827-7900

Most important collections/price range:
Esplendidos, Prominente, Torpedo, Historiador, Robusto / $3,200 to $16,000; higher for perpetual calendars and tourbillon models

Cuervo y Sobrinos

Cuba means a lot of things to different people. Today it seems to be the last bastion of genuine retro in an age of frenzied technology. However, turn the clock back to the early twentieth century and you find that Ramón Rio y Cuervo and his sister's sons kept a watchmaking workshop and an elegant store on Quinto Avenida where they sold fine Swiss pocket watches—and more modest American models as well. With the advent of tourism from the coast of Florida, their business developed with wristwatches, whose dials Don Ramón soon had printed with Cuervo y Sobrinos—Cuervo and Nephews.

An Italian watch enthusiast and a Spanish businessman got together to resuscitate Cuervo y Sobrinos in 2002 and started manufacturing in the Italian-speaking region of Switzerland and in cooperation with various Swiss workshops. The tagline, "Latin soul, Swiss brand," says it all. These timepieces epitomize—or even romanticize—the island's heyday. The colors hint at cigar leaves and sepia photos in frames of old gold. The lines are at times elegant and sober, like the Esplendido, or radiate the ease of those who still have time on their hands, like the Prominente. Playfulness is also a Cuervo y Sobrinos quality: The Piratas have buttons shaped like the muzzle of a blunderbuss, a cannonball crown, and a porthole flange. Lately, CyS has been modernizing (the Manjuari dive watch or the Robusto Day-Date have a younger feel), and they have introduced a line of writing implements as accessories for the genuine lover of fine things and the mechanical world.

Esplendidos Solo Tiempo

Reference number: 2417.1C
Movement: automatic, ETA Caliber 2671; ø 17.5 mm, height 4.8 mm; 25 jewels; 28,800 vph; 42-hour power reserve
Functions: hours, minutes, sweep seconds
Case: stainless steel, 31 x 52 mm, height 12 mm; sapphire crystal; water-resistant to 3 atm
Band: reptile skin, folding clasp
Remarks: limited to 88 pieces
Price: $3,600
Variations: gray-black (limited to 88 pieces)

Historiador Racing Limited Edition

Reference number: 3195.1RCD13
Movement: automatic, ETA Caliber 2824-2; ø 25.6 mm, height 4.6 mm; 25 jewels; 28,800 vph; 38-hour power reserve
Functions: hours, minutes, sweep seconds; date
Case: stainless steel, ø 40 mm, height 10.4 mm; sapphire crystal; water-resistant to 3 atm
Band: calf leather, buckle
Price: $3,100

Historiador Flameante

Reference number: 3130.9FA
Movement: manually wound, ETA Caliber 7001 ("Peseux"); ø 23.3 mm, height 2.5 mm; 17 jewels; 21,600 vph; bridges with anthracite coating and côtes de Genève; 42-hour power reserve
Functions: hours, minutes, subsidiary seconds
Case: rose gold, ø 40 mm, height 6.2 mm; sapphire crystal, transparent case back; water-resistant to 3 atm
Band: reptile skin, buckle
Price: $11,500
Variations: with gray dial ($11,500)

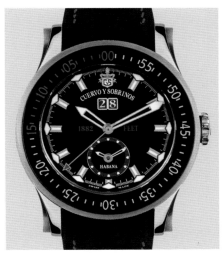

Robots Manjuari Dive Watch

Reference number: 2808.1NR
Movement: automatic, Soprod TT651, CyS2511; ø 25.6 mm, height 5.1 mm; 25 jewels; 42-hour power reserve
Functions: hours, minutes, seconds; big date; second time zone
Case: stainless steel/titanium, ø 43 mm, height 14.95 mm; titanium bezel, black rubber ring; sapphire crystal; water-resistant to 60 atm
Band: rubber, buckle
Remarks: engraving of manjuari fish on case back
Price: $6,500
Variations: with white dial

Robusto Day-Date

Reference number: 2811.1BS
Movement: automatic ETA 2834-2, CYS 2071; ø 29 mm, height 5.5 mm; 25 jewels; 42-hour power reserve
Functions: hours, minutes, seconds; date, weekday
Case: stainless steel, ø 43 mm, height 12.45 mm; sapphire crystal, transparent case back; water-resistant to 1 atm
Band: reptile skin, buckle
Price: $3,800
Variations: black, ivory, or gray dial

Prominente Solo Tiempo Date

Reference number: 1012.1AG
Movement: automatic, ETA 2892-A2 ; ø 25.6 mm, height 3.6 mm; 21 jewels, 42-hour power reserve
Functions: hours, minutes, seconds; date
Case: stainless steel, 31 x 52 mm; sapphire crystal, transparent case back; water-resistant to 3 atm
Band: reptile skin, buckle
Price: $3,900
Variations: various dials; diamond bezel and gold case ($21,000)

Torpedo Pirata Caribeno Chronograph

Reference number: 3051.5BB
Movement: automatic CYS 3061 Valjoux 7751; ø 30.4 mm, height 7.9 mm; 25 jewels; 42-hour power reserve
Functions: hours, minutes, subsidiary seconds; chronograph, 12-hour and 30-minute counters; date, weekday, month, moon phase
Case: bronze, titanium and burnished steel with DLC black coating, ø 45 mm, height 15.5 mm; sapphire crystal, transparent case back; water-resistant to 5 atm
Band: leather, titanium buckle
Price: $10,400, limited to 100 pieces
Variations: as simple date watch ($4,900)

Torpedo Pulsometro Racing Collection 2013

Reference number: 3045.1RC
Movement: automatic DP4500/base ETA 2892-A2; ø 30mm, height 7.3 mm; 49 jewels; 40-hour power reserve
Functions: hours, minutes, subsidiary seconds; chronograph, 30-minute and 12-hour counters; big date
Case: stainless steel, ø 43 mm, height 12.85; tachymeter scale on bezel; sapphire crystal; transparent back; water-resistant to 5 atm
Band: carbon-like leather strap, buckle
Remarks: rotor with "fan" decoration and CYS engraving; CYS racing logo as subsidiary second hands
Price: $6,200, limited to 100 pieces

Historiador GMT

Reference number: 3196.1C
Movement: automatic ETA 2893-1; ø 25,6 mm, height 4.10 mm; 21 jewels; 42-hour power reserve
Functions: hours, minutes, seconds; date; second time zone (24-hour display)
Case: stainless steel, ø 40 mm, height 9.9 mm; sapphire crystal, transparent case back; water-resistant to 3 atm
Band: reptile skin, buckle
Price: $3,400
Variations: with black dial

Cvstos
2, rue Albert Richard
CH-1201 Geneva
Switzerland

Tel.:
01141-22-989-1010

Fax:
01141-22-989-1019

E-Mail:
info@cvstos.com

Website:
www.cvstos.com

Founded:
2005

Number of employees:
not specified

Annual production:
not specified

U.S. distributor:
Cvstos USA, Inc.
207 W. 25th Street, 8th Floor
New York, NY 10001
212-463-8898

Most important collections/price range:
Challenge, Challenge-R, Concept-S, Evosquare,
High Fidelity / $10,000 to $315,000

Cvstos

Dials in a conventional sense are something that one can search for in vain at Cvstos (Latin for guardian); technology rules the roost at the brand, and thus these extroverted, stately timepieces show what they're made of, quite literally. The look is cultivated throughout the collection, which veers sharply from the appearance of traditional *haute horlogerie,* targeting a clientele that doesn't necessarily include elements such as *côtes de Genève,* gold, and guilloché in their watchmaking ideal. Although it may not seem so at first sight, a great deal of watchmaking know-how goes into the making of a Cvstos, and that is no surprise for a brand that is the spiritual child of Sassoun Sirmakes, son of Vartan Sirmakes, the man who led Genevan watchmaker Franck Muller to world fame. Under the tutelage of his father, the cofounder of the Watchland *manufacture* in Genthod, young Sassoun was introduced to the hands-on side of watchmaking. In 2005, fate brought him together with designer and watchmaker Antonio Terranova, who had made a name for himself in the Swiss watch industry with the timepieces he designed and produced for leading brands. Even though he had freelanced for some of the more staid brands, Terranova had the heart of an avant-gardist willing to break free of the constraints of traditional forms—he collaborated on some of the early Richard Mille pieces, for example. So a Cvstos has all the thrilling complications, but expect some technoid materials and high engineering art.

Challenge Jetliner SL

Reference number: CHJETLINERSLSTB
Movement: automatic, Cvstos Caliber 350; 21 jewels; 28,800 vph; special plasma finish, skeletonized disc; 42-hour power reserve
Functions: hours, minutes, sweep seconds; date
Case: stainless steel, 41 x 53.7 mm, height 13.35 mm; sapphire crystal; screw-in crown; transparent case back; water-resistant to 10 atm
Band: rubber, folding clasp
Price: $9,900
Variations: rose gold ($24,500)

Challenge Pilot RC Yellow

Reference number: CHPILOTNRTTBY
Movement: automatic, Cvstos Caliber 357; 25 jewels; 28,800 vph; special plasma finish; 42-hour power reserve
Functions: hours, minutes, subsidiary seconds; chronograph; date
Case: titanium with black and yellow plasma coating, 41 x 53.7 mm, height 16 mm; sapphire crystal; screw-in crown; transparent case back; water-resistant to 10 atm
Band: rubber, folding clasp
Price: $22,300
Variations: blue or red alloy with titanium ($22,300); rose gold ($34,500)

Challenge Jet Liner GT Daedalus Edition

Reference number: CHGTJETSLSTDAEDALUS
Movement: automatic, Cvstos Caliber CVS350; 25 jewels; 28,800 vph; skeletonized; black plasma and rhodium treatment; 42-hour power reserve
Functions: hours, minutes, subsidiary seconds; chronograph; date; power reserve indicator
Case: polished titanium, ø 59 x 45 mm, height 15.45 mm; titanium bezel; screw-in crown with Nitril insert; sapphire crystal; transparent case back; water-resistant to 10 atm
Remarks: titanium honeycomb dial, pierced hands
Band: rubber, folding clasp
Price: $11,700

Challenge Jet Liner Carbon

Reference number: CHJETSLCARB5NB
Movement: automatic, Cvstos Caliber CVS350; 25 jewels; 28,800 vph; skeletonized; black plasma and rhodium treatment; 42-hour power reserve
Functions: hours, minutes, sweep seconds; chronograph; date; power reserve indicator
Case: rose gold and lacquered carbon, 53.7 x 41 mm, height 13.45 mm; sapphire crystal; transparent case back; water-resistant to 10 atm
Band: carbon, carbon folding clasp
Price: $27,800

Challenge R50 Chrono High Fidelity Limited Edition

Reference number: C-R50CHF
Movement: automatic, Cvstos Caliber 577; 25 jewels; 28,800 vph; disk display for subsidiary seconds and totalizers; special finish, plasma-coated; 60-hour power reserve
Functions: hours, minutes, subsidiary seconds; chronograph; date; power reserve indicator
Case: titanium with black PVD coating, ø 50 mm, height 16 mm; pink gold bezel; sapphire crystal; transparent case back
Band: reptile skin, folding clasp
Price: $36,700, limited to 100 pieces
Variations: black steel ($31,200)

Challenge Minute Repeater Tourbillon

Reference number: CHRMTSNRTT
Movement: manually wound, Cvstos Caliber 76510; 32 jewels; 18,000 vph; flying 1-minute tourbillon; partially skeletonized; 60-hour power reserve
Functions: hours, minutes, subsidiary seconds (on tourbillon cage); hour, quarter-hour, minute repeater
Case: titanium with black plasma coating, 45 x 53.7 mm, height 16 mm; sapphire crystal; transparent case back; screw-in crown; water-resistant to 10 atm
Band: rubber, folding clasp
Price: $351,200
Variations: titanium ($333,400)

Challenge GP Black Steel

Reference number: CHCCGPNRSTBR
Movement: automatic, Cvstos Caliber 577; 25 jewels; 28,800 vph; special finish, plasma-coated, satinized, and polished; 60-hour power reserve
Functions: hours, minutes, subsidiary seconds; chronograph; date; power reserve indicator
Case: aluminum with black plasma coating, 41 x 53.7 mm, height 16 mm; sapphire crystal; transparent case back; water-resistant to 10 atm
Band: reptile skin, folding clasp
Price: $18,900, limited to 100 pieces
Variations: with large case and red, blue and yellow colors ($22,300)

CTR-S Tourbillon Chronograph

Reference number: CTR-S GT
Movement: manually wound, Cvstos Caliber 555; 48 jewels; 18,000 vph; flying 1-minute tourbillon; satinized and polished finish; partially skeletonized; 192-hour power reserve
Functions: hours and minutes (off-center), subsidiary seconds; split-seconds chronograph
Case: titanium with black plasma coating, 45 x 53.7 mm, height 16 mm; sapphire crystal; transparent case back; screwed-in crown; water-resistant to 10 atm
Band: rubber, folding clasp
Price: $277,800, limited to 5 pieces

Sea Liner

Reference number: CHSEALINERSTBL5NW
Movement: automatic, Cvstos Caliber CV350; 21 jewels; 28,800 vph; skeletonized; côtes de Genève; 42-hour power reserve
Functions: hours, minutes, sweep seconds; date (on skeletonized disc); power reserve indicator
Case: blue steel and pink gold, 53.7 x 41 mm, height 13.35 mm; sapphire crystal; transparent case back; screw-in crown with Nitril insert; water-resistant to 10 atm
Band: reptile skin, folding clasp
Remarks: teak base dial with gold/rhodium
Price: $20,000

Hasler & Co. SA
CH-2720 Tramelan
Switzerland

E-Mail:
info@davosa.com

Website:
www.davosa.com

Founded:
1861

Number of employees:
not specified

Annual production:
not specified

U.S. distributor:
D. Freemont Inc.
P.O. Box 417, 232 Karda Drive
Hollidaysburg, PA 16648
877-236-9248
david@freemontwatches.com
www.davosawatches.com

Most important collections/price range:
Argonautic, Classic, Gentleman, Pilot, Simplex,
Ternos, Titanium, Vanguard, X-Agon / $650 to
$2,600

Davosa

Davosa has come a long way from its beginnings in
1891. Back then, farmer Abel Frédéric Hasler spent
the long winter months in Tramelan, in Switzerland's
Jura mountains, making silver pocket watch cases.
Later, two of his brothers ventured out to the city of Geneva,
where they opened a watch factory. The third brother also opted
to engage with the watch industry and moved to Biel. The entire next generation of Haslers
followed the path of the previous one and went into watchmaking.
It wasn't until after World War II that brothers Paul and David Hasler dared to produce
their own timepieces.
Nevertheless, the name Hasler & Co. continued to appear on the occasional package
mailed in Switzerland or overseas. Playing the role of unassuming private-label watchmakers, the Haslers remained in the background and let their customers in Europe and
the United States run away with the show.
Finally, in 1987, the brothers developed their own line of watches under the brand name
Davosa, for which they also took on the sales and marketing roles. The brand's success
in stores and the handsome and reasonably priced array of models it produces serve as
proof that the decision to make their own watches was the right one.

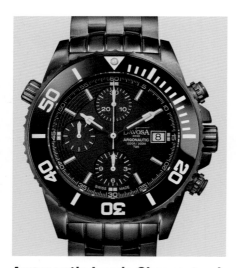

Argonautic Lumis Chronograph

Reference number: 161.508.80
Movement: automatic, ETA Caliber 7750; ø 30 mm,
height 7.9 mm; 25 jewels; 28,800 vph; 42-hour
power reserve
Functions: hours, minutes, subsidiary seconds;
chronograph; date
Case: stainless steel, with gray PVD coating, ø 42.5
mm, height 17.5 mm; unidirectional bezel with
60-minute division; sapphire crystal, screw-in crown;
helium valve; water-resistant to 30 atm
Band: stainless steel, folding clasp with safety lock
Price: $2,200
Variations: without PVD coating ($2,100); as three-
hand automatic ($900)

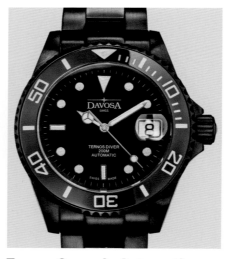

Ternos Ceramic Automatic

Reference number: 161.600.55
Movement: automatic, ETA Caliber 2824-2;
ø 25.6 mm, height 4.6 mm; 25 jewels; 28,800 vph;
38-hour power reserve
Functions: hours, minutes, sweep seconds; date
Case: stainless steel, with black PVD coating, ø
40 mm, height 12 mm; unidirectional bezel with
ceramic inlay and 60-minute divisions; sapphire
crystal, screw-in crown; helium valve; water-
resistant to 20 atm
Band: stainless steel, folding clasp with safety lock
and extension link
Price: $880
Variations: with helium valve ($920); without PVD
coating ($780)

X-Agon Automatic

Reference number: 161.493.65
Movement: automatic, ETA Caliber 2824-2;
ø 25.6 mm, height 4.6 mm; 25 jewels; 28,800 vph;
38-hour power reserve
Functions: hours, minutes, sweep seconds; date
Case: stainless steel, 33 x 47 mm, height 11.2 mm;
sapphire crystal; transparent case back; water-
resistant to 5 atm
Band: calf leather, folding clasp
Price: $728
Variations: with black or silver dial; with leather
band; with link bracelet ($848)

World Traveller Chronograph

Reference number: 161.502.55
Movement: automatic, ETA Caliber 7754; ø 30 mm, height 7.9 mm; 25 jewels; 28,800 vph; blued screws and perlage on bridges; côtes de Genève; 42-hour power reserve
Functions: hours, minutes, subsidiary seconds; second 24-hour time zone; chronograph; date
Case: stainless steel, ø 44 mm, height 15.7 mm; unidirectional bezel with 24-hour divisions; sapphire crystal; transparent case back; water-resistant to 5 atm
Band: calf leather, buckle
Price: $2,468
Variations: silvery or blue dial; automatic ($1,298)

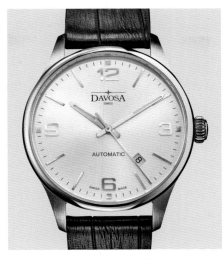

Gentleman Automatic

Reference number: 161.510.14
Movement: automatic, ETA Caliber 2892; ø 26.2 mm, height 4.85 mm; 21 jewels; 28,800 vph; 38-hour power reserve
Functions: hours, minutes, sweep seconds; date
Case: stainless steel, ø 40 mm, height 9.5 mm; sapphire crystal, transparent case back; water-resistant to 5 atm
Band: calf leather, buckle
Price: $898
Variations: with blue or black dial

Pilot Chronograph

Reference number: 161.004.56
Movement: automatic, ETA Caliber 7750; ø 30 mm, height 7.9 mm; 25 jewels; 28,800 vph; blued screws and perlage on bridges; côtes de Genève; 42-hour power reserve
Functions: hours, minutes, subsidiary seconds; chronograph; date and weekday
Case: stainless steel, ø 42 mm, height 15.6 mm; sapphire crystal; transparent case back; water-resistant to 10 atm
Band: calf leather, buckle
Price: $2,100
Variations: stainless steel bracelet; vintage model with tachymeter and telemeter display ($2,200)

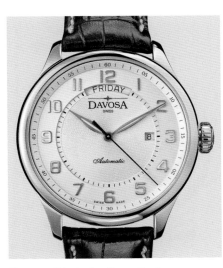

Pares Classic Day-Date

Reference number: 161.483.36
Movement: automatic, ETA Caliber 2834-2; ø 29 mm, height 5.05 mm; 25 jewels; 28,800 vph; rotor with côtes de Genève; 38-hour power reserve
Functions: hours, minutes, sweep seconds; date and weekday
Case: stainless steel, ø 44 mm, height 11.1 mm; sapphire crystal; transparent case back; water-resistant to 5 atm
Band: calf leather, buckle
Price: $748
Variations: with black dial and luminescent numerals

Black Titanium Limited Edition

Reference number: 161.506.85
Movement: automatic, ETA Caliber 7750; ø 30 mm, height 7.9 mm; 25 jewels; 28,800 vph; 42-hour power reserve
Functions: hours, minutes, subsidiary seconds; chronograph; date
Case: titanium with black PVD coating, ø 46 mm, height 15.9 mm; bezel screwed to case back with 12 screws; sapphire crystal; screw-in crown; water-resistant to 5 atm
Band: calf leather, buckle
Remarks: comes with extra rubber bracelet
Price: $2,298
Variations: without PVD coating ($2,148); with black PVD bezel ($2,200)

Titanium Automatic

Reference number: 161.491.55
Movement: automatic, ETA Caliber 2824-2; ø 25.6 mm, height 4.6 mm; 25 jewels; 28,800 vph; 38-hour power reserve
Functions: hours, minutes, sweep seconds; date
Case: titanium, ø 46 mm, height 13.9 mm; bezel with black PVD coating, held with 12 screws; sapphire crystal; screw-in crown; water-resistant to 5 atm
Band: calf leather, buckle
Remarks: with additional rubber and leather straps
Price: $998
Variations: uncoated titanium with blue or silver dial ($978); with black PVD coating ($1,048)

De Bethune

De Bethune SA
Granges Jaccard 6
CH-1454 La Chaux L'Auberson
Switzerland

Tel.:
01141-24-454-2281

Fax:
01141-24-454-2317

E-Mail:
info@debethune.ch

Website:
www.debethune.ch

Founded:
2002

Number of employees:
not specified

Annual production:
not specified

Distribution:
For all inquiries from the U.S., contact the *manufacture* directly.

De Bethune's technical director, Denis Flageollet, has more than twenty years of experience under his belt with regard to the research, conception, and successful implementation of more than 120 different, extremely prestigious timepieces—all for other firms. He and David Zanetta, a well-known consultant for a number of high-end watch brands, founded their own company in 2002, and De Bethune was born. Together, they bought what used to be the village pub and turned it into a stunning factory. The

modern CNC machinery, combined with the expertise of an experienced watchmaking team, allows Flageollet to produce prototypes in the blink of an eye and make small movement series with great dispatch. In order to become even more independent of suppliers, the little factory now also produces its own cases, dials, and hands, which guarantees a high level of excellence with regard to quality control.

Since its founding, De Bethune has developed a manually wound caliber with a power reserve of up to eight days, a self-regulating double barrel, a balance wheel in titanium and platinum that allows for an ideal inertia/mass ratio, a balance spring with a patented De Bethune end curve, and a triple "parachute" shock-absorbing system, the lightest and one of the fastest silicon/titanium tourbillons on the market.

The latest project involves research into acoustic vibrations as a power regulator. The control of the "Resonique" escapement utilizes a flying magnet that regulates the escape wheel without touching it. At a certain speed, the oscillation of the magnet reaches the vibration system's perfect frequency. This reduces to a minimum the forces that need to be overcome between the wheelworks and the oscillating system. If the mechanism speeds up or slows down, the oscillating system will correct automatically. It's a self-regulating mechanism that can keep the speed of the wheels absolutely constant.

DB 28 Skybridge

Reference number: DB28CE
Movement: manually wound, De Bethune Caliber DB 2105; ø 30 mm; 27 jewels; 28,800 vph; double spring barrel, silicon balance; 144-hour power reserve
Functions: hours, minutes; spherical moon phase
Case: titanium, 43 mm, height 12.8 mm; sapphire crystal, transparent case back
Band: reptile skin, buckle
Remarks: concave dial with golden spheres as heavenly bodies; completely sculptural moon
Price: $106,000

DB 28 Black matte

Reference number: DB28Z
Movement: manually wound, De Bethune Caliber DB 2115; ø 30 mm, height 6.85 mm; 36 jewels; 28,800 vph; double spring barrel, triply shock-protected balance with titanium hub and platinum weights; 144-hour power reserve
Functions: hours, minutes; power reserve indicator (on case back); moon phase
Case: zirconium, ø 42.6 mm, height 11.3 mm; sapphire crystal, transparent case back; screw-in crown
Band: reptile skin, buckle
Remarks: sculptural spherical moon
Price: $91,800, limited to 50 pieces

DB 25 Perpetual Calendar

Reference number: DB25QPRS1
Movement: automatic, De Bethune Caliber DB 2324 QP; ø 30 mm, height 6.81 mm; 47 jewels; 28,800 vph; double spring barrel; triply shock-protected balance with titanium hub and platinum weights
Functions: hours, minutes; perpetual calendar with date, weekday, month, moon phase
Case: rose gold, ø 44 mm, height 12.3 mm; sapphire crystal, transparent case back
Band: reptile skin, buckle
Remarks: sculptural spherical moon
Price: $136,500

de Grisogono SA
Route de St-Julien 176 bis
CH-1228 Plan-les-Ouates (Geneva)
Switzerland

Tel.:
01141-22-817-8100

Fax:
01141-22-817-8188

E-Mail:
marco@degrisogono.com

Website:
www.degrisogono.com

Founded:
1993

Number of employees:
approx. 150

Annual production:
not specified

U.S. distributor:
de Grisogono, Inc.
824 Madison Avenue, 3rd Floor
New York, NY 10065
866-DEGRISO

Most important collections/price range:
Instrumento N°Uno / starting at $32,400;
Tondo / starting at $11,300

de Grisogono

Watch connoisseurs frequently look down on jewelers who suddenly develop an interest for their trade. The brand de Grisogono had to deal with this odd prejudice when it made its debut in horology, but the critics quickly fell silent once it became obvious that the brand founder, Fawaz Gruosi, was not just producing quartz watches with lots of glitz, but was intending to grow his portfolio with a line of very high-end mechanical watches.

His jewelry pieces are renowned for showcasing precious stones of the highest quality. Gruosi applied the same standard to the manufacturing of his watches. Not only are they unusually sophisticated technically, but the actual manufacturing quality has stood the test of even the toughest experts.

Right from the start, Gruosi opted for unusual case shapes and novel ways of displaying time. He took the high road, as it were, producing, for instance, the Instrumento Doppio Tre, with a single spring barrel that drives three separate sets of hands to display three time zones, or watches with dials that open and close like camera shutters or can be turned to change the display.

For the most part, de Grisogono watches have no historical models—which is quite rare nowadays. The Meccanico dG, a large rectangular watch with a hint of 1970s chic, has an imitation digital display produced mechanically with engineering that literally reaches absurd boundaries: Twenty-three tiny multi-surface tube-like segments turn on their longitudinal axis to shape squarish numbers.

All this innovation came at a cost—exacerbated by huge setbacks from the 2009 recession. In March 2012, de Grisogono announced it had brought a number of investors on board. Ever since, it has been consolidating its existing portfolio, developing the Tondos in sharp, trendy colors and focusing on jewelry.

Meccanico dG

Reference number: DG N02
Movement: manually wound, 32,400 exclusive dG Caliber; 38.1 x 34.7 mm, height 11.05 mm; 111 jewels; 28,800 vph; 651 components
Functions: hours, minutes; second time zone (digital)
Case: titanium/rubber, 55 x 51.4 mm; height 18.85 mm; sapphire crystal; transparent case back; water-resistant to 3 atm
Band: rubber, titanium buckle
Remarks: digital time display appears in slits created by mechanically driven rollers
Price: $369,100

Occhio Ripetizione Minuti

Reference number: N01
Movement: manually wound, exclusive dG Caliber with Chr. Claret minute repeater; 37 jewels; grey finishing
Functions: hours, minutes; minute repeater with 3 cathedral gongs
Case: white gold/platinum, ø 43.6 mm, 56.4 mm length, height 17 mm; sapphire crystal
Band: reptile skin, triple folding clasp
Remarks: by activating lever, titanium slats arranged in rosette open like camera shutter to give view of repeater mechanism, whose hammers strike 3 gongs to mark hours, quarter-hours, and minutes; shutter closes at last strike
Price: $403,600

Instrumento N° Uno DF XL

Reference number: UNO DF XL 01
Movement: automatic, Caliber DF 11-96 (base Sellita SW-300 with a second time zone module); 21 jewels; 28,800 vph; 42-hour power reserve
Functions: hours, minutes; second time zone (additional 12-hour indicator); large date
Case: pink gold and matt brown PVD-coated titanium, 44 x 58 mm, height 18 mm; sapphire crystal; transparent case back; water-resistant to 5 atm
Band: reptile skin, folding clasp
Price: $32,400
Variations: various bands and dials

Grande Chrono

Reference number: Grande Chrono N01
Movement: automatic, with chronograph and large date module; ø 30 mm; 28,800 vph, 43 jewels
Functions: hours, minutes, subsidiary seconds; chronograph; large date (retrograde)
Case: rose gold, 53.6 x 47.3 mm, height 18.1 mm; sapphire crystal; transparent case back; water-resistant to 5 atm
Band: reptile skin, folding clasp
Price: $53,600
Variations: various bands and dials

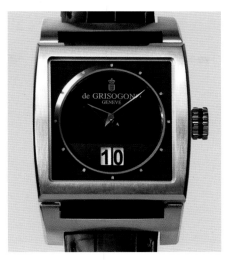

Instrumento N° Uno Big Date

Reference number: UNO BIG DATE N03
Movement: automatic with large date module; 22 jewels; 28,800 vph; 42-hour power reserve
Functions: hours, minutes; large date
Case: black PVD-coated white gold and titanium, 44 x 58 mm, height 18 mm; sapphire crystal; transparent case back; water-resistant to 5 atm
Band: reptile skin, folding clasp
Price: $33,700

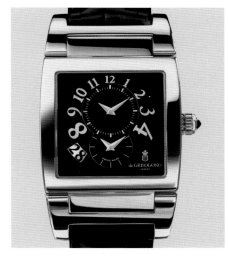

Instrumento N° Uno DF

Reference number: UNO DF 11
Movement: automatic, base ETA 2892-A2 with second time zone module; 21 jewels; 28,800 vph; 42-hour power reserve
Functions: hours, minutes; second time zone (additional 12-hour indicator); large date
Case: pink gold, 37.5 x 56.6 mm, height 15.4 mm; sapphire crystal; transparent case back; crown with black diamond cabochon; water-resistant to 3 atm
Band: reptile skin, pink gold folding clasp
Price: $39,900
Variations: various cases and dials

Tondo by Night

Reference number: TONDO BY NIGHT S07
Movement: automatic, modified Caliber SF 30-89; 24 jewels; 28,800 vph; blackened movement; inverted with winding rotor on dial side, 42-hour power reserve
Functions: hours, minutes
Case: composite (photo-luminescent fiberglass), 49 x 43 mm, height 11.65 mm; bezel set with 48 blue sapphires; sapphire crystal; water-resistant to 3 atm
Band: ray skin, folding clasp
Remarks: rotor oscillating weight set with 60 blue sapphires
Price: $13,100
Variations: various colors

Tondo by Night

Reference number: TONDO BY NIGHT S08
Movement: automatic, modified Caliber SF 30-89; 24 jewels; 28,800 vph; blackened movement; inverted with winding rotor on dial side, 42-hour power reserve
Functions: hours, minutes
Case: composite (photo-luminescent fiberglass), 49 x 43 mm, height 11.65 mm; bezel set with 48 spinel stones; sapphire crystal; water-resistant to 3 atm
Band: ray skin, folding clasp
Remarks: rotor oscillating weight set with 60 spinel stones
Price: $12,900
Variations: various colors

Tondo by Night

Reference number: TONDO BY NIGHT S09
Movement: automatic, modified Caliber SF 30-89; 24 jewels; 28,800 vph; blackened movement; inverted with winding rotor on dial side, 42-hour power reserve
Functions: hours, minutes
Case: composite (photo-luminescent fiberglass), 49 x 43 mm, height 11.65 mm; bezel set with 48 tourmalines; sapphire crystal; water-resistant to 3 atm
Band: ray skin, folding clasp
Remarks: rotor oscillating weight set with 60 tourmalines
Price: $11,300
Variations: various colors

Montres DeWitt SA

Rue du Pré-de-la-Fontaine
CH-1217 Meyrin 2
Switzerland

Tel.:
01141-22-750-9797

Fax:
01141-22-750-9799

E-Mail:
info@dewitt.ch

Website:
www.dewitt.ch

Founded:
2003

Number of employees:
70

Annual production:
over 1000 watches (estimated)

U.S. distributor:
DeWitt America
4330 NE 2nd Avenue
Miami, FL 33137
305-572-9812

Most important collections/price range:
Academia / from approx. $30,000;
Furtive / from approx. $12,000;
Classique/ from approx. $23,000;
Twenty 8 Eight / from approx. $28,000

DeWitt

It has become clear over the last few years just how fruitful and enriching it can be for the watchmaking industry when outsiders without any technical knowledge approach its challenges simply because they are curious and interested. A good example of this is DeWitt, a brand that has been highly successful with a strategy of blending traditional horology with truly unconventional ideas.

Jérôme de Witt comes from a long line of illustrious personalities reaching back on one side of his family tree to the Dutch lawyer and politician Johan de Witt, who was murdered in 1672 by supporters of the royal house of Orange-Nassau. The other side boasts Jérôme Bonaparte and German royal lines such as Sachsen-Coburg, Württemberg, and Hohenzollern.

De Witt spent a significant number of years in the construction industry, building houses and bridges all over the world. A general interest in technology and a passion for restoring vintage cars were the springboard for his ideas for original mechanical solutions for these watches. "I see myself more as a sort of conductor," says De Witt.

The team at DeWitt tirelessly experiments with new materials and has now become famous for characteristic "toothed" bezels (derived from the cam shaft of a 2CV Citroën) and special in-house dials. DeWitt's demanding founder is a man of exacting standards. He believes that this is the only way to realize his visions, such as a silicon dial made of forty-seven individual parts. The same industrial look has now softened with the new Sunday Afternoon for women, in which time is indicated on a marquetry floral pattern.

Hora Mundi

Reference number: NAC.HMI.001
Movement: automatic, DeWitt Caliber 2021; ø 26.2 mm; 46 jewels; 28,800 vph; 42-hour power reserve
Functions: hours, minutes, sweep seconds; additional 24-hour display (second time zone) with reference cities; date
Case: stainless steel, ø 43 mm, height 10.2 mm; sapphire crystal, transparent case back; water-resistant to 3 atm
Band: stainless steel with black PVD-coated elements, double folding clasp
Remarks: 10th anniversary edition
Price: $12,000, limited to 200 pieces
Variations: with rubber strap ($12,000)

Academia Mirabilis

Reference number: AC.MI.004
Movement: automatic, Caliber DW0090 (base Concepto C-2220); ø 30.4 mm, height 4.3 mm; 23 jewels; 28,800 vph; 48-hour power reserve
Functions: hours, minutes, sweep seconds
Case: titanium and blue PVD coating, ø 44 mm, height 13.25 mm; white gold and blue PVD-coated bezel; sapphire crystal; transparent case back; water-resistant to 3 atm
Band: rubber, buckle
Price: $36,000, limited to 88 pieces
Variations: titanium/pink gold with bronze-colored PVD coating ($36,000)

Tourbillon Imperial

Reference number: AC.TI.002
Movement: manually wound, DeWitt Caliber DW0082; ø 31.3 mm, height 9.55 mm; 29 jewels; 21,600 vph; 1-minute tourbillon; black-gold finish on movement, pink gold wheels, balance; 84 diamonds on lower tourbillon bridge; split-second chronograph with 2 control wheels; 50-hour power reserve
Functions: hours, minutes, subsidiary seconds; split-second chronograph; date, moon phase
Case: titanium, ø 46 mm, height 15.15 mm; sapphire crystal, transparent case back; water-resistant to 3 atm
Band: reptile skin, folding clasp
Price: $357,000, limited to 10 pieces

Dodane 1857

For pilots of all aircraft, time is not money; it is life and death. So not surprisingly, the specifications for on-board instruments put out by the world's air forces are particularly stringent. In the 1950s, the French Air Force approached several companies to produce watches that could withstand the extreme accelerations and pressure changes imposed by the new generation of jet-propelled aircraft. Pilots also needed a flyback chronograph to measure speed and distances in case of instrument failure.

One of those companies was Dodane, a small family enterprise situated in Besançon just a few miles from the Swiss border and the horologically prolific "Jurassic Arc." The company had been founded in 1857 by Alphonse Dodane on the banks of the Doubs River and produced watch components and watches. It was Alphonse's son, Alphonse Gabriel, who set the course on aviation, though. During World War I, he developed a chronograph that allowed flyers to target their payload more accurately. From then on, inventing instruments for airplanes became the main business. Among the later Dodane developments was an altimetric chronograph used by night parachutists to tell them when to pull the cord.

The Dodane range of watches is limited to the Type 21 and the Type 23, also available in quartz with many functions for sporty types. These products are authentic military—rugged, resistant, and perhaps a touch rabble-rousing. After all, they have to appeal to pilots as well as meeting the high standards of the French defense ministry.

Dodane 1857
2, Chemin des Barbizets
F-25870 Châtillon le Duc
France

Tel.:
01133-3-81-58-88-02

Fax:
01133-3-81-58-92-27

E-Mail:
info@dodane1857.com

Website:
www.Dodane1857.com

Founded:
1857

U.S. distributor:
Totally Worth It, LLC
76 Division Avenue
Summit, NJ 07901-2309
201-894-4710
info@totallyworthit.com
www.TotallyWorthIt.com

Most important collections:
Type 21 and Type 23 chronographs used by the French military

TYPE 21

Reference number: 21NLN
Movement: automatic, Caliber Dubois Dépraz 42022; ø 30 mm, height 6.8 mm; 57 jewels; 28,800 vph; 42-hour power reserve; chronometer; côtes de Genève, blued screws, cocks with perlage
Functions: hours, minutes, subsidiary seconds; date; 1/5th-second 3-hand flyback chronograph with 30-minute counter
Case: stainless steel, ø 41.5 mm, height 13.7 mm; unidirectional black anodized bezel with ratchet wheel; sapphire crystal; transparent case back; water-resistant to 10 atm
Band: reptile skin, with double folding buckle
Price: $5,750; limited to 400

TYPE 23

Reference number: 23-CF10R
Movement: automatic, Caliber Dubois Dépraz 42030; ø 30 mm, height 6.5 mm; 45 jewels; 28,800 vph
Functions: hours, minutes, sweep seconds; chronograph
Case: stainless steel, ø 42.5 mm, height 12.3 mm; sapphire crystal; transparent case back; bidirectional brushed steel bezel with ratchet wheel; sapphire crystal; transparent case back; hinged back cover for pilot ID tag; water-resistant to 10 atm
Band: reptile skin, double folding clasp
Price: $4,750
Variations: black anodized and polished steel bezel; various straps, NATO clasp

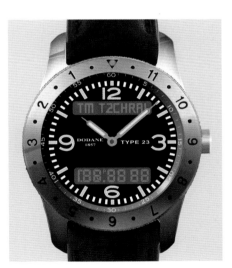

Dodane Type 23 Quartz

Reference number: 23-C7N
Movement: quartz, ETA 988.333; digital and analog display
Functions: hours, minutes, seconds; day, date, perpetual calendar; various chronograph functions (1/100th seconds); alarm; second time zone
Case: stainless steel, ø 42.5 mm, height 12.3 mm; sapphire crystal; transparent case back; bidirectional brushed steel bezel with ratchet wheel; sapphire crystal; transparent case back; water-resistant to 10 atm
Band: calf, rubber, double folding clasp
Price: $2,250

D. Dornblüth & Sohn
Westpromenade 7
D-39624 Kalbe/Milde
Germany

Tel.:
01149-39080-3206

Fax:
01149-39080-72796

E-Mail:
info@dornblueth.com

Website:
www.dornblueth.com

Founded:
1962

Number of employees:
5

Annual production:
approx. 120 watches

U.S. distributor:
Dornblüth & Sohn
WatchBuys
888-333-4895
www.watchbuys.com

Most important collections/price range:
men's wristwatches / between $3,000 and
$24,000

D. Dornblüth & Sohn

D. Dornblüth & Sohn is a two-generation team of master watchmakers. Their workshop in Kalbe, near Magdeburg in eastern Germany, turns out remarkable wristwatches with large manual winding mechanisms, three-quarter plates, screw balances, swan-neck fine adjustments, and a clever power reserve indicator.

The history of the "Dornblüth Caliber" goes back to the 1960s in the Erz mountains in East Germany. Dieter Dornblüth, the father in this father-and-son team, had sketched the first outlines for his own movement. But he only managed to complete the work in 1999 with the assistance of his son Dirk, and by that time Germany had already been reunified.

The strength of the tiny *manufacture* lies in the high level of skill that goes into producing these classical, manually wound watches in the old-fashioned way, i.e., without any CNC machines.

The 99 series is based on the reliable ETA Unitas 6497 pocket watch movement. Dirk redesigns about one-half of it by putting in a three-quarter plate and other elements. The dials are created in-house, using the 250-year-old "filled engraving" technique. They are then given a lustrous frosted layer of matte silver plating to complement the traditional *grainage* look.

The brand's fiftieth anniversary in 2012 saw the birth of a new movement entirely conceived on premises and almost entirely built there. The Q-2010 features a special Maltese cross drive that reduces linear torque between two serially positioned barrel springs. The movement now drives the latest models, like the Auf & Ab and Klassik. A specially designed lowered escape wheel minimizes position errors caused by the anchor escapement.

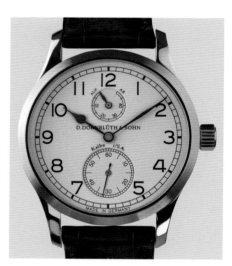

Caliber 99.5

Reference number: 99.5 (1) ST
Movement: manually wound, Dornblüth Caliber 99.5 (base ETA 6497); ø 37 mm, height 5.4 mm; 20 jewels; 18,000 vph; indirect sweep seconds driven by seconds wheel, screw balance, swan-neck fine adjustment, finely finished with côtes de Genève
Functions: hours, minutes, sweep seconds; power reserve indicator; date
Case: stainless steel, ø 42 mm, height 12.5 mm; sapphire crystal; transparent case back
Band: reptile skin, buckle
Price: $11,500
Variations: various dials; with folding clasp ($11,350)

Klassik

Reference number: Q-2010.1(GR)ST
Movement: manually wound, Dornblüth Caliber Q-2010 Classic; ø 34.3 mm, height 4.7 mm; 29 jewels; 18,000 vph; double spring barrel; driven by indirectly controlled Maltese cross spring producing almost linear torque; short anchor escapement with lower escape wheel; Breguet spring
Functions: hours, minutes, subsidiary seconds
Case: stainless steel, ø 38.5 mm, height 10 mm; sapphire crystal, transparent case back
Band: reptile skin, buckle
Price: $11,200
Variations: various dials; rose gold ($19,800)

Auf & Ab

Reference number: Q-2010.2(GR)ST
Movement: manually wound, Dornblüth Caliber Q-2010 Auf-Ab; ø 34.3 mm, height 4.7 mm; 29 jewels; 18,000 vph; double spring barrel; driven by indirectly controlled Maltese cross spring producing almost linear torque; short anchor escapement with lower escape wheel; Breguet spring
Functions: hours, minutes, subsidiary seconds; power reserve indicator
Case: stainless steel, ø 38.5 mm, height 10 mm; sapphire crystal, transparent case back
Band: reptile skin, buckle
Price: $14,000
Variations: various dials; rose gold ($23,700)

Tempting Timekeepers From Around The World

If you love the art and engineering of a fine timepiece, WristWatch Magazine is a must-read.

$49.00 (6-issues)
for a one year subscription

From the rarest masterpieces, to popular trends, **WristWatch Magazine** will fan the flames of your watch passion. Famous brands will be joined by deserving up-and-comers on the pages of **WristWatch Magazine**. Education, collecting, watch news and events from around the world will come together on our pages to sharpen your watch knowledge and immerse you in the world of micro machines that are mechanical wristwatches.

ISOCHRON Media Llc

Publishers of: **WristWatch Magazine** and **AboutTime Magazine**
Office **(203) 485-6276** • E-mail **info@isochronmedia.com**

Doxa Watches USA
5847 San Felipe, 17th Floor
Houston, TX 77057

Tel.:
877-255-5017

Fax:
866-230-2922

E-Mail:
customersupport@doxawatches.com

Website:
www.doxawatches.com

Founded:
1889

Number of employees:
48

Annual production:
not specified

Distribution:
direct sales only

Most important collections/price range:
Doxa SUB dive watch collection / $1,500 to
$3,500

Doxa

Watch aficionados who have visited the world-famous museum in Le Locle will know that the little castle in which it is housed once belonged to Georges Ducommun, the founder of Doxa. The *manufacture* was launched as a backyard operation in 1889 and originally produced pocket watches. Quality products and good salesmanship quickly put Doxa on the map, but the company's real game-changer came in 1967 with the uncompromising SUB 300, a heavy, bold diver's watch. It featured a unidirectionally rotating bezel with the official U.S. dive table engraved on it. The bright orange dial was notable for offering the best legibility under water. It also marked the beginning of a trend for colorful dials.

Doxa continued to develop successful diver's watches in the 1970s in collaboration with U.S. Divers, Spirotechnique, and Aqualung. Their popularity increased with the commercialization of diving. Thriller writer Clive Cussler, chairman and founder of the National Underwater and Marine Agency, NUMA, even chose a Doxa as gear for his action hero Dirk Pitt.

Doxa makes watches for other occasions as well. The Ultraspeed and Régulateur are just two examples combining a classic look, fine workmanship, and an affordable price. Today, the brand has also resurrected some of the older designs from the late sixties, but with improved technology, enabling divers to go down to 1,500 meters and still read the time.

SUB 300T-Graph "Sharkhunter"

Reference number: 877.10.101.10
Movement: automatic, ETA Caliber 2894-2; ø 28.6 mm, height 6.1 mm; 37 jewels; 28,800 vph; 42-hour power reserve
Functions: hours, minutes, subsidiary seconds; chronograph; date
Case: stainless steel, ø 47 mm, height 19 mm; unidirectional bezel with 60-minute divisions; sapphire crystal; screwed-in crown; water-resistant to 30 atm
Band: stainless steel, folding clasp with safety lock and extension link
Price: $2,990, limited to 250 pieces
Variations: orange dial ($2,990); rubber strap ($2,790)

SUB 1200T "Searambler"

Reference number: 872.10.021.10
Movement: automatic, ETA Caliber 2824-2; ø 25.6 mm, height 4.6 mm; 25 jewels; 28,800 vph; 42-hour power reserve
Functions: hours, minutes, sweep seconds; date
Case: stainless steel, ø 42 mm, height 14 mm; unidirectional bezel with engraved decompression scale; sapphire crystal; screwed-in crown; helium valve; water-resistant to 120 atm
Band: stainless steel, folding clasp with extension link
Remarks: new of 1969 original; with rubber strap
Price: $1,990
Variations: with Sharkhunter/black dial ($1,990); Professional/orange dial ($1,990)

SUB 4000T "Professional"

Reference number: 875.10.351.10
Movement: automatic, ETA Caliber 2897-2; ø 25.6 mm, height 4.85 mm; 21 jewels; 28,800 vph; 42-hour power reserve
Functions: hours, minutes, sweep seconds; date; power reserve indicator
Case: stainless steel, ø 47 mm, height 16 mm; unidirectional bezel with 60-minute divisions; sapphire crystal; screwed-in crown; helium valve; water-resistant to 120 atm
Band: stainless steel, folding clasp with extension link
Price: $2,590
Variations: with orange dial ($2,590); Sharkhunter/black dial ($2,590)

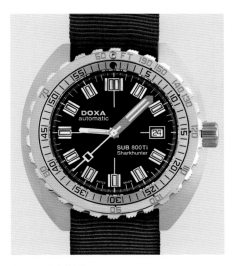

SUB 800Ti

Reference number: 880.10.101N-WH
Movement: automatic, ETA Caliber 2824-2;
ø 25.6 mm, height 4.6 mm; 25 jewels; 28,800 vph
Functions: hours, minutes, sweep seconds; date
Case: titanium, ø 44.7 mm, height 15 mm;
unidirectional bezel, with engraved decompression
table; sapphire crystal; screwed-in crown; water-
resistant to 80 atm
Band: NATO strap, folding clasp
Remarks: reissue of 1969 original, limited to 1,000
pieces; with optional titanium bracelet
Price: $2,790
Variations: Sharkhunter with black dial ($2,790);
Professional with orange hands ($2,790)

SUB MISSION 31

Reference number: 801.50.351-WH
Movement: automatic, ETA Caliber 2824-2;
ø 25.6 mm, height 4.6 mm; 25 jewels; 28,800 vph
Functions: hours, minutes, sweep seconds; date
Case: titanium, ø 44 mm, height 15 mm;
unidirectional bezel, with engraved decompression
table; sapphire crystal; screwed-in crown;
water-resistant to 100 atm
Band: BOR titanium, folding clasp with
extension link
Remarks: reissue of 1969 original, limited to 331
pieces; comes with orange NATO fabric strap
Price: $2,890
Variations: None

SUB 5000T Military Sharkhunter Black Ed.

Reference number: 880.30.101N.11
Movement: automatic, ETA Caliber 2892-2;
ø 25.6 mm, height 4.85 mm; 21 jewels; 28,800 vph
Functions: hours, minutes, sweep seconds; date
Case: stainless steel, ø 45 mm; helium valve;
unidirectional bezel, with engraved decompression
table; sapphire crystal; screwed-in crown;
water-resistant to 150 atm
Band: stainless steel, folding clasp with extension
link
Price: $2,490
Variations: Sharkhunter with orange dial ($2,490);
Caribbean with blue dial ($2,490)

SUB 750T GMT

Reference number: 850.10.351N.10
Movement: automatic, ETA Caliber 2893-2;
ø 25 6 mm, height 4.1 mm; 21 jewels; 28,800 vph
Functions: hours, minutes, sweep seconds; 24-hour
display (3 time zones); date
Case: stainless steel, ø 45 mm, height 16 mm;
unidirectional rotating bezel with engraved
decompression table (patented); sapphire crystal;
screwed-in crown; water-resistant to 75 atm
Band: stainless steel, folding clasp
Price: $2,790
Variations: Professional/orange dial ($2,790);
Sharkhunter/black dial ($2,790); Divingstar/yellow
dial ($2,790); Caribbean/blue dial ($2,790)

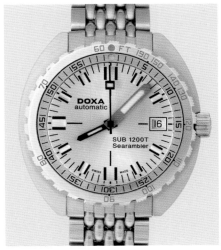

DOXA SUB 200T

Reference number: 802.10.021.10
Movement: automatic, ETA Caliber 2671;
ø 17.2 mm, height 4.8 mm; 25 jewels; 28,800 vph
Functions: hours, minutes, sweep seconds
Case: stainless steel, ø 35 mm, height 9 mm;
unidirectional bezel with engraved decompression
table (patented); sapphire crystal; screwed-in
crown; water-resistant to 20 atm
Band: stainless steel, folding clasp
Price: $1,649
Variations: as Seamaid with black dial ($1,649)

DOXA Ultraspeed Power Reserve

Reference number: 896.10.102.01US
Movement: automatic, ETA Valjoux Caliber 7750;
ø 30 mm, height 7.9 mm; 25 jewels; 28,800 vph
Functions: hours, minutes, subsidiary seconds;
date; chronograph; power reserve indicator
Case: stainless steel, ø 44 mm, height 14 mm;
sapphire crystal; sapphire crystal exhibition case
back; water-resistant to 10 atm
Band: leather, buckle
Price: $2,490

Ebel
MGI Luxury Group SA
Rue de la Paix, 113
CH-2300 La Chaux-de-Fonds
Switzerland

Tel.:
01141-32-912-3123

Fax:
01141-32-912-3124

E-Mail:
contact@ebel.com

Website:
www.ebel.com

Founded:
1911

Number of employees:
not specified

Annual production:
approx. 20,000 watches (estimated)

U.S. distributor:
Ebel USA
Movado Group Inc.
650 From Road
Paramus, NJ 07652
201-267-8000

Most important collections/price range:
Ebel Classic / approx. $1,800 to $18,500;
Brasilia / approx. $2,400 to $19,500;
Beluga / approx. $2,400 to $5,700;
1911 / approx. $4,350 to $26,500

Ebel

In 2011, Ebel celebrated its 100th anniversary with classic-design, limited edition watches. In 1911, Eugène and Alice Blum, née Levy, founded the limited partnership Fabrique Ebel, Blum & Cie. One year later, they created their first wristwatches, sold under the company's new name, Ebel, an acronym formed by the first four letters in Eugène Blum et Levy. In the 1980s, under the direction of Pierre-Alain Blum, the last representative of the founding family, Ebel became a trendsetting institution in the field of watch design.

Today, these "architects of time" strive to achieve a similar status, after two ownership changes and a drastic shift of direction caused the company to lose a little of its focus. In 2004, Ebel was bought up by the MGI Luxury Group (with a portfolio including Movado, Concord, and Coach and rights to watches sold under the labels Tommy Hilfiger, Lacoste, and Hugo Boss). The new strategy appears to be finding the perfect mix of timeless women's watches and striking men's models with sophisticated technology. So far, the strong Ebel Classic 100 collection launched by the company in 2011 fits that strategy to a tee. The series, limited to 1,911 pieces, consists of vintage designs that pick up the formal language of the 1960s. The Caliber 120 of Ebel, however, is a dyed in the wool ETA 2829-A2, while the chronograph caliber 137 ("Le Modulor"), developed in collaboration with Lemania, was sold in the meantime to Ulysse Nardin.

Ebel X-1 34 mm

Reference number: 1216157
Movement: automatic, ETA Caliber 2000-1;
ø 19.4 mm, height 3.6 mm; 20 jewels; 28,800 vph;
40-hour power reserve
Functions: hours, minutes, sweep seconds; date
Case: stainless steel, ø 34 mm, height 10.82 mm;
unidirectional rose gold bezel 60-minute divisions;
sapphire crystal, transparent case back; rose gold
crown; water-resistant to 10 atm
Band: stainless steel with rose gold elements,
folding clasp
Price: $4,900
Variations: variations with quartz movement and
without diamonds

X-1

Reference number: 1216116
Movement: quartz, ETA Caliber 955.412
Functions: hours, minutes, sweep seconds; date
Case: ceramic, ø 34 mm, height 10.77 mm; rose
gold bezel set with 48 diamonds; sapphire crystal;
bezel set with 15 diamonds; water-resistant to
10 atm
Band: ceramic with rose gold elements, folding
clasp
Remarks: dial set with 8 diamonds
Price: $7,900

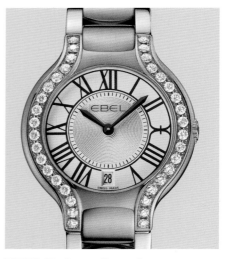

EBEL Beluga Grande

Reference number: 1216071
Movement: quartz ETA 955.112
Functions: hours, minutes
Case: stainless steel brushed/polished,
ø 36.5 mm; set with 36 diamonds; sapphire crystal;
water-resistant to 5 atm
Band: brushed/polished stainless steel,
deployment clasp
Remarks: silver-toned metallic dial with painted
Roman numerals
Price: $6,700

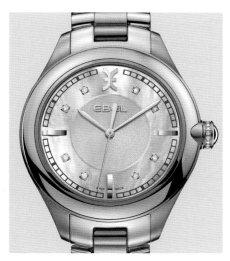

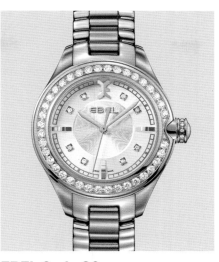

EBEL Onde 36mm

Reference number: 1216136
Movement: quartz ETA 955.102
Functions: hours, minutes, sweep seconds
Case: brushed/polished stainless steel, ø 36 mm, height 10.87 mm; diamond crown; sapphire crystal; water-resistant to 5 atm
Band: brushed/polished stainless steel, folding clasp
Remarks: white mother-of-pearl dial with diamonds
Price: $3,400

EBEL Onde 30mm

Reference number: 1216097
Movement: quartz ETA 956.102
Functions: hours, minutes, sweep seconds
Case: brushed/polished stainless steel with rose gold case, ø 30 mm; rose gold bezel set with 38 diamonds; diamond crown; sapphire crystal; water resistant to 5 atm
Band: brushed/polished stainless steel, folding clasp
Remarks: silver galvanic dial with applied indexes and 8 diamonds
Price: $7,900

Ebel 100 "Blue"

Reference number: 1216125
Movement: automatic, Caliber 120 (base ETA 2892-A2); ø 25.6 mm, height 3.6 mm; 21 jewels; 28,800 vph; 42-hour power reserve
Functions: hours, minutes, sweep seconds; date
Case: stainless steel with black PVD coating, ø 40 mm, height 10.25 mm; sapphire crystal; transparent case back; water-resistant to 5 atm
Band: reptile skin, buckle
Price: $3,200
Variations: various strap colors

Ebel 100

Reference number: 1216149
Movement: automatic, Ebel Caliber 120 (base ETA 2892-A2); ø 25.6 mm, height 3.36 mm; 21 jewels; 28,800 vph; 42-hour power reserve
Functions: hours, minutes, sweep seconds; date
Case: stainless steel, ø 40 mm, height 10.25 mm; sapphire crystal; transparent case back; water-resistant to 5 atm
Band: Milanese mesh, folding clasp
Price: $3,200
Variations: with silver-colored dial; with PVD coating

Ebel 100

Reference number: 1216152
Movement: automatic, Caliber 120 (base ETA 2892-A2); ø 25.6 mm, height 3.6 mm; 21 jewels; 28,800 vph; 42-hour power reserve
Functions: hours, minutes, sweep seconds; date
Case: stainless steel with black PVD coating, ø 40 mm, height 10.25 mm; sapphire crystal; transparent case back; water-resistant to 5 atm
Band: Milanese mesh with black PVD coating, folding clasp
Price: $3,100
Variations: various dials

Ebel 100

Reference number: 1216088
Movement: automatic, Ebel Caliber 120 (base ETA 2892-A2); ø 25.6 mm, height 3.6 mm; 21 jewels; 28,800 vph; 42-hour power reserve
Functions: hours, minutes, sweep seconds; date
Case: brushed stainless steel, ø 40 mm, height 10.25 mm; sapphire crystal; transparent case back; water-resistant to 5 atm
Band: reptile skin, buckle
Price: $2,700

Eberhard & Co.

5, rue du Manège
CH-2502 Biel/Bienne
Switzerland

Tel.:
01141-32-342-5141

Fax:
01141-32-341-0294

E-Mail:
info@eberhard-co-watches.ch

Website:
www.eberhard-co-watches.ch

Founded:
1887

Number of employees:
not specified

Annual production:
not specified

Distribution:
retail

U.S. distributor:
ABS Distributors
22600 Savi Ranch Pkwy.; Suite 274
Yorba Linda, CA 92887
www.absdist.com
714-453-1622; 714-998-0181 (fax)

Most important collections/price range:
Chrono 4; Champion V; Tazio Nuvolari; 8 Jours,
Extra Forte; Gilda / $3,000 to $25,000

Eberhard & Co.

Chronographs weren't always the main focus of the Eberhard & Co. brand. In 1887, Georges-Emile Eberhard rented a workshop in La Chaux-de-Fonds to produce a small series of pocket watches, but it was the unstoppable advancement of the automotive industry that gave the young company its inevitable direction. By the 1920s, Eberhard was producing timekeepers for the first auto races, and the chronograph specialist quickly gained an excellent reputation—on both sides of the Alps. In Italy, Eberhard & Co. functioned well

into the 1930s as the official timekeeper for all important events relating to motor sports. And the Italian air force later commissioned some split-second chronographs from the company, one of which recently was auctioned off for 56,000 euros.

Well over 100 years after its founding, Eberhard & Co. is doing well, thanks to the late Massimo Monti. In the 1990s, the Italian businessman associated the brand with the legendary racer Tazio Nuvolari. The company subsequently dedicated a chronograph collection to him and sponsored the annual Gran Premio Nuvolari oldtimer rally in his hometown of Mantua.

With the launch of its four-counter chronograph, this most Italian of Swiss watchmakers underscored its expertise and ambitions where short time/sports time measurement is concerned. Indeed, Eberhard & Co.'s Chrono 4 chronograph, featuring four little counters all in a row, has brought new life to the world of the chronograph in general. Because it is the most popular Eberhard collection, CEO Mario Peserico has continued to develop it, putting out versions with new colors and slightly altered looks.

Chrono 4 Géant Full Injection

Reference number: 31062
Movement: automatic, Eberhard Caliber EB 251-12 1/2 (base ETA 2894-2); ø 33 mm, height 7.5 mm; 53 jewels; 28,800 vph; 4 totalizers in a row
Functions: hours, minutes, subsidiary seconds; additional 24-hour display (second time zone); chronograph; date
Case: stainless steel with carbon diffusion and DLC coating; ø 46 mm, height 14.1 mm; unidirectional bezel with 60-minute divisions; sapphire crystal, screw-in crown and pushers; water-resistant to 20 atm
Band: rubber, buckle
Price: $11,500, limited to 500 pieces

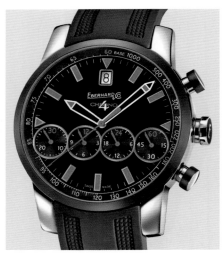

Chrono Grande Taille Colors

Reference number: 31067
Movement: automatic, Eberhard Caliber EB 251-12 1/2 (base ETA 2894-2); ø 33 mm, height 7.5 mm; 53 jewels; 28,800 vph; 4 totalizers in a row
Functions: hours, minutes, subsidiary seconds; additional 24-hour display (second time zone); chronograph; date
Case: stainless steel, ø 43 mm, height 13.32 mm; sapphire crystal, screw-in crown; water-resistant to 5 atm
Band: rubber, buckle
Price: $8,950, limited to 600 pieces
Variations: various dial designs

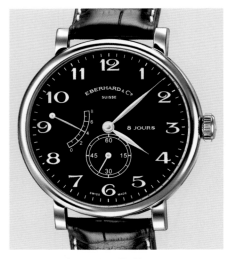

8 Jours Grande Taille

Reference number: 21027
Movement: manually wound, Eberhard Caliber EB 896 10 ½ (base ETA 7001); ø 34 mm, height 5 mm; 25 jewels; 21,600 vph; 2 winding springs; 192-hour power reserve
Functions: hours, minutes, subsidiary seconds; power reserve indicator
Case: stainless steel, ø 41 mm, height 10.85 mm; sapphire crystal, transparent case back; water-resistant to 3 atm
Band: reptile skin, buckle
Price: $5,600
Variations: with white dial

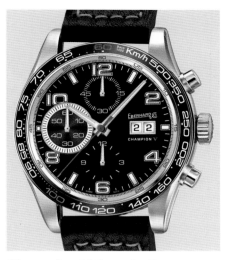

Champion V Grande Date

Reference number: 31064.2
Movement: automatic, La Joux Perret 8210;
ø 30 mm, height 8 mm; 25 jewels; 28,800 vph
Functions: hours, minutes, subsidiary seconds;
chronograph; large date
Case: stainless steel, ø 42.8 mm, height 14.45 mm;
sapphire crystal, screw-in crown; water-resistant to
5 atm
Band: calf leather, buckle
Price: $4,800

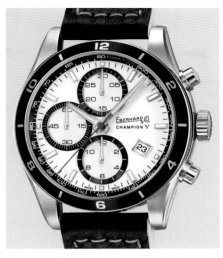

Champion V

Reference number: 31063
Movement: automatic, ETA Caliber 7750; ø 30 mm,
height 7.9 mm; 25 jewels; 28,800 vph
Functions: hours, minutes, subsidiary seconds;
chronograph; date
Case: stainless steel, ø 42.8 mm, height 14.35 mm;
sapphire crystal; screw-in crown; water-resistant to
5 atm
Band: calf leather, buckle
Price: $4,300

Extra-fort RAC 125ème Anniversaire

Reference number: 31125.2
Movement: automatic, Eberhard Caliber E/J 8150
(base ETA Caliber 7750); ø 30 mm, height 8.85
mm; 28 jewels; 28,800 vph; column wheel control
of chronograph functions
Functions: hours, minutes, subsidiary seconds;
chronograph; large date
Case: stainless steel, ø 41 mm, height 15 mm;
sapphire crystal; transparent case back; water-
resistant to 5 atm
Band: reptile skin, folding clasp
Price: $9,500, limited to 500 pieces

Tazio Nuvolari Vanderbilt Cup "Naked"

Reference number: 31068
Movement: automatic, Eberhard Caliber 131/4
(base ETA 7750); ø 30 mm, height 8.4 mm; 30
jewels; 28,800 vph; crown pusher for zero reset;
bridges with perlage, rotor with côtes de Genève;
42-hour power reserve
Functions: hours, minutes, subsidiary seconds;
chronograph
Case: stainless steel, ø 42 mm, height 13.45 mm;
sapphire crystal; water-resistant to 3 atm
Band: calf leather, buckle
Price: $7,900

Tazio Nuvolari Data

Reference number: 31066
Movement: automatic, ETA Caliber 7750; ø 30 mm,
height 7.9 mm; 25 jewels; 28,800 vph; 42-hour
power reserve
Functions: hours, minutes, chronograph; date
Case: stainless steel, ø 43 mm, height 13 mm;
sapphire crystal, screw-in crown; water-resistant to
3 atm
Band: reptile skin, buckle
Price: $5,500

Tazio Nuvolari Gold Car

Reference number: 31038.5
Movement: automatic, ETA Caliber 7750; ø 30 mm,
height 7.9 mm; 25 jewels; 28,800 vph; 42-hour
power reserve
Functions: hours, minutes; chronograph; date
Case: stainless steel, ø 43 mm, height 13 mm;
sapphire crystal, transparent case back; screw-in
crown; water-resistant to 3 atm
Band: reptile skin, buckle
Remarks: gold, stylized Alfa Romeo on the rotor
Price: $5,800

Edox & Vista SA
CH-2714 Les Genevez
Switzerland

Tel.:
01141-32-484-7010

Fax:
01141-32-484-7019

E-Mail:
info@edox.ch

Website:
www.edox.ch

Founded:
1884

Number of employees:
100

Annual production:
approx. 50,000 watches

U.S. distributor:
Edox
Gevril Group
9 Pinecrest Road
Valley Cottage, NY 10989
845-425-9882
lea@gevril.net
www.edox.ch

Most important collections/price range:
Classe Royale, Royal Lady, Les Bémonts, Les Vauberts, Grand Ocean, Class-1, WRC / approx. $750 to $4,700

Edox

Edox is interested in motion and extreme feats, and that has given its timepieces a consistently sporty look. Since the company took its place as official timekeeper of the FIA World Rally Championship, it has come out with a striking collection of timer watches with "race car" character, most recently the X-treme Pilot III. And already in the sixties, Edox had gotten more than just its feet wet in the special domain of water-resistant watches, producing the legendary Delfin and Hydrosub, which could submerge up to 500 meters. This was long before the brand became the official timekeeper of offshore yacht racing several years ago. That, too, inspired a stunning sports line. And so have car racing, bicycle racing, flying . . . and climbing up walls, since the company has associated itself with the Spider-Man film franchise.

Edox is more than 125 years old: The company started out in a tiny atelier in Biel in 1884 where owner Christian Rüefli-Flury refined ébauches. Edox was one of the first watchmakers to concentrate solely on wristwatches, a move it made in the 1920s. In 1973, Edox shares were sold to the ASUAG, a predecessor of today's Swatch Group. However, the success this partnership hoped to achieve never panned out, and in 1983, Victor Strambini, still president of the company today, bought back the shares and with them Edox's independence. Strambini subsequently relocated Edox to Les Genevez, a village in the heart of the Swiss Jura and one of the cradles of the country's watch industry. Today, the state-of-the-art factory houses 100 employees.

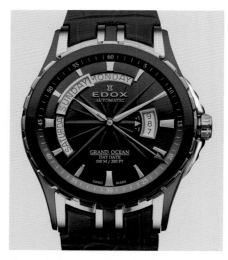

Grand Ocean Day Date Automatic

Reference number: 83006 357 B BUIN
Movement: automatic, Edox Caliber 83 (base ETA 2834-2); ø 29 mm, height 5.05 mm; 25 jewels; 28,800 vph; 42-hour power reserve
Functions: hours, minutes, sweep seconds; date and weekday
Case: stainless steel, ø 45 mm, height 12.7 mm; sapphire crystal; transparent case back; screwed-down crown; water-resistant to 10 atm
Band: reptile skin, folding clasp
Price: $3,950
Variations: with brown dial ($3,300), black dial ($3,650), or silver dial ($3,025)

Class-1 Chronoffshore Automatic

Reference number: 01115 3 NIN
Movement: automatic, Edox Caliber 011 (base ETA Valjoux 7750); ø 30 mm, height 7.9 mm; 25 jewels; 28,800 vph; 46-hour power reserve
Functions: hours, minutes, subsidiary seconds; chronograph; date and weekday
Case: stainless steel, ø 45 mm, height 17 mm; unidirectional ceramic bezel, 60-minute division, sapphire crystal; screwed-down crown; water-resistant to 50 atm
Band: rubber, folding clasp
Price: $5,300
Variations: blue dial ($5,300); black PVD ($5,775); PVD stainless steel case/bracelet ($5,775)

Chronorally Automatic

Reference number: 01110 37N PN GIN
Movement: automatic, Edox Caliber 011 (base ETA Valjoux 7750); ø 30 mm, height 7.9 mm; 25 jewels; 28,800 vph; 46-hour power reserve
Functions: hours, minutes, subsidiary seconds; chronograph; date and weekday
Case: stainless steel, ø 45 mm, height 17.5 mm; sapphire crystal; case back with rubber inlay; screwed-down crown; color anodized start-stop pusher; water-resistant to 10 atm
Band: rubber, buckle
Price: $4,225
Variations: black dial ($4,225)

Ernst Benz

Necessity is really the mother of creativity and then invention. Ernst Benz, an engineer by trade, an inventor by design, and a passionate flier, needed solid, reliable, and readable watches that could be used in the cockpits of small aircraft and gliders. Size and dial clarity were determined by the function, hence the clean look and 47 mm diameter. Reliability is guaranteed by a no-nonsense Valjoux 7750. These are the elements that save the lives of pilots. At first, Benz made what he called the Great Circle Chronograph and later the ChronoScope just for his fellow aviators. He also engineered other aviation instruments, which are now standard in many small aircraft.

In 2005, the brand was bought by the Khankins, a watchmaking family with generations of experience in complicated horology. Leonid Khankin, who has literally spent a lifetime in the hands-on side of the business, expanded both geographically and by creating new and exciting models. The ChronoScope received black PVC coating and was retooled as the ChronoDiver for those attracted to water rather than air. He was also quick to adopt ultra-hard DLC coating.

Khankin, who knows every nook and cranny of the horological world, is taking the brand places. He uses the broad dial of these distinct timepieces as a platform for adding exciting design elements. On the style side, Ernst Benz has collaborated with fashion designer John Varvatos and Food Network chef Mario Batali on a series of timepieces with distinct hands and color schemes. As for Ernst Benz, he has retired, but passion is a flame that always burns bright.

Ernst Benz
7 Route de Crassier
CH-1262 Eysins
Switzerland

E-Mail:
info@ernstbenz.com

Website:
www.ernstbenz.com

Founded:
early 1960s

Annual production:
not specified

U.S. distributor:
Ernst Benz North America
177 S. Old Woodward
Birmingham, MI 48009
248-203-2323; 248-203-6633 (fax)

Most important collections:
Great Circle, ChronoScope, ChronoLunar, ChronoRacer

ChronoRacer 47mm

Reference number: GC10100CR2-DLC
Movement: automatic, Valjoux Caliber 7750; ø 30 mm, height 7.9 mm; 25 jewels; 28,800 vph
Functions: hours, minutes, subsidiary seconds; date, day; chronograph
Case: DLC-coated stainless steel, ø 47 mm, height 16 mm; sapphire crystal; screwed-down sapphire crystal exhibition back; double O-ring sealed crown; water-resistant to 50 m
Band: reptile skin, buckle
Price: $6,500, limited to 50 pieces
Variations: black numerals, 47 mm and 44 mm ChronoSport versions

ChronoLunar DLC 47mm

Reference number: GC10311-DLC
Movement: automatic, Valjoux 7751; ø 30 mm, height 7.9 mm; 25 jewels; 28,800 vph
Functions: hours, minutes, subsidiary seconds; day, date, month, moon phase; 24-hour display; chronograph with hours, minutes, sweep seconds
Case: DLC-coated stainless steel, ø 47 mm, height 16 mm; sapphire crystal; screwed-down sapphire crystal exhibition back; double O-ring sealed crown; water-resistant to 50 m
Band: reptile skin, buckle
Price: $8,150
Variations: 44 mm case; white dial

ChronoCombat 47mm

Reference number: GC10100/CC2-DLC
Movement: automatic, Valjoux 7751; ø 30 mm, height 7.9 mm; 25 jewels; 28,800 vph
Functions: hours, minutes, subsidiary seconds; date, day; chronograph
Case: DLC-coated stainless steel, ø 47 mm, height 16 mm; sapphire crystal; screwed-down sapphire crystal exhibition back; double O-ring sealed crown; water-resistant to 50 m
Band: reptile skin, buckle
Price: $6,500, limited to 50 pieces
Variations: matching subdials, 47 mm and 44 mm ChronoSport version

Montres EPOS SA
Solothurnstrasse 44
CH-2543 Lengnau
Switzerland

Tel.:
01141-32-323-8182

Fax:
01141-32-323-6494

E-Mail:
info@epos.ch

Website:
www.epos.ch

Founded:
1925

Number of employees:
not specified

Annual production:
not specified

Distribution:
retail

U.S. distributor:
Please consult Epos directly.

Price range:
$700 to $4,000 (higher prices for special
timepieces)

Epos

This brand's roots trace back to 1925, the Vallée de Joux, and founder James Aubert. Today, its fate is in the hands of Ursula Forster, who comes from a family of watchmakers, and her husband, Tamdi Chonge, who hails from Tibet and spent many years working in the industry in Switzerland. Together with movement designer Jean Fillon—the son-in-law of the founder's nephew, Jean Aubert—they make sure that the calibers are given an exclusive touch by adding in-house complications as well as skillful decoration. And the Epos collection is impressive in its breadth, covering practically the whole spectrum of complications from simple three-hand watches, chronographs with and without flyback function, and horizontal and vertical large date displays to regulators, moon phase indicators, jumping hours, repeaters, and even tourbillons. Regardless of the complication, the look is always serene; there always seems to be space on the dial. Epos has even ventured into complicated mechanical women's watches, and its portfolio includes a number of very exciting pocket watches.

According to *Merriam-Webster's Collegiate Dictionary*, an *epos* is an "epic poem or a number of poems that treat an epic theme but are not formally united." That seems to describe rather well the strategy of this Swiss specialist in mechanical watches—if you add the word "successful." Its chances are quite good: Epos has an epic portfolio of top-notch, affordable timepieces for every taste. The brand has earned a good reputation abroad; now all it needs to do is convince the home market.

Collection Originale

Reference number: 3420
Movement: automatic, ETA Caliber 2892-A2;
ø 25.6 mm, height 3.6 mm; 21 jewels; 28,800 vph;
finely decorated; 42-hour power reserve
Functions: hours, minutes, sweep seconds; date
Case: stainless steel with rose gold-colored PVD
coating, ø 40 mm, height 7.7 mm; sapphire crystal;
transparent case back; water-resistant to 3 atm
Band: calf leather, buckle
Price: $1,300
Variations: with stainless steel bracelet ($1,450);
without PVD coating ($1,200)

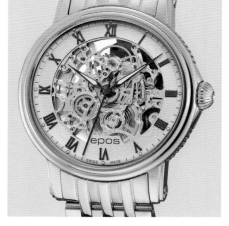

Collection Emotion

Reference number: 3390SK
Movement: automatic, ETA Caliber 2824-A2;
ø 25.6 mm, height 4.6 mm; 25 jewels; 28,800 vph;
skeletonized and hand-decorated; 38-hour power
reserve
Functions: hours, minutes, sweep seconds
Case: stainless steel, ø 41 mm, height 8 mm;
sapphire crystal; transparent case back; water-
resistant to 5 atm
Band: stainless steel, buckle
Price: $1,990

Collection Sophistiquée

Reference number: 3424SK
Movement: manually wound, ETA Caliber 6497-1;
ø 36.6 mm, height 4.5 mm; 17 jewels; 21,600 vph;
skeletonized, finely decorated, and black-coated;
38-hour power reserve
Functions: hours, minutes, subsidiary seconds
Case: stainless steel, ø 42 mm, height 10.4
mm; sapphire crystal; transparent case back;
water-resistant to 5 atm
Band: calf leather, buckle
Remarks: skeletonized dial
Price: $2,025
Variations: case with black or rose gold-colored
PVD coating ($2,085); stainless steel with uncoated
movement ($1,735)

Erwin Sattler

In 2008, for the fiftieth anniversary of their clock *manufacture,* managing directors Stephanie Sattler-Rick and Richard Müller presented something unexpected: In addition to a large pendulum clock outfitted with a perpetual calendar and an elegant table clock, the company released an impressive, limited edition of fifty of the "Trilogy" set, comprising a table clock, watch winder, and wristwatch. The wristwatch, offered only in

precious metal as part of the Trilogy, was in high demand—leading Sattler to add an unlimited stainless steel version of the wristwatch regulator to its line in 2009.

The regulator dial—including the display of seconds at 12 o'clock, hours at 6 o'clock, and a sweep minute hand—is just as much a part of Erwin Sattler's clock collection as an Invar pendulum and gold-plated gear wheels.

The dial, a miniature version of the popular Sattler wall clock regulator, features four screws and is made of solid sterling silver. The clock specialist paid a great deal of attention to the steel hands of the wristwatches. They are vaulted, hardened, and polished. Like those of their large clock cousins, the watches' hour and minute hands have steel sockets with polished grooves. The Régulateur Classica Secunda was created in conjunction with watchmaker couple Maria Kristina and Richard Habring. They turned to the tried-and-true ETA Valjoux Caliber 7750—a chronograph movement, actually—as their base, modifying it to accommodate the regulator display and adding a special technical detail: The second hand jumps in one-second increments just like its role model, one of Sattler's full-size pendulum clocks.

Erwin Sattler OHG
Grossuhrenmanufaktur
Lohenstr. 6
D-82166 Gräfelfing
Germany

Tel.:
01149-89-895-5806-0

Fax:
01149-89-895-5806-28

E-Mail:
info@erwinsattler.de

Website:
www.erwinsattler.de

Founded:
1958

Number of employees:
31

Annual production:
approx. 1,200 clocks and watches

Distribution:
direct through company in Germany

Most important collections/price range:
wristwatches, precision clocks, winders, table clocks, marine chronometers / approx. $1,000 to $200,000

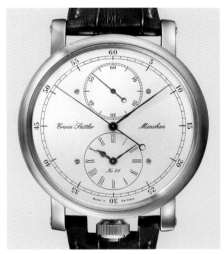

Regulateur "Classica Secunda"

Reference number: 02
Movement: automatic, Sattler Caliber ES 01 (base ETA 7750); ø 30 mm, height 7.9 mm; 28 jewels; 28,800 vph; modified to include regulator display with jumping seconds; rotor skeletonized, engraved, and guillochéed by hand; 42-hour power reserve
Functions: hours (off-center), minutes, subsidiary seconds (jumping)
Case: stainless steel, ø 44 mm, height 15 mm; sapphire crystal; water-resistant to 5 atm
Band: reptile skin, double folding clasp
Price: $10,920

Régulateur Classica Secunda Medium

Movement: manual winding, Sattler Caliber ES 02 (base Habring A09MS); ø 30 mm, height 6.25 mm; 28 jewels; 28,800 vph; modified for regulator with jumping seconds; rotor engraved and guillochéed by hand; 42-hour power reserve
Functions: hours (off-center), minutes, subsidiary seconds (jumping)
Case: stainless steel, ø 38 mm, height 12 mm; sapphire crystal; water-resistant to 5 atm
Band: reptile skin, double folding clasp
Price: $11,420

Regulateur "Classica Secunda" Medium

Movement: manually wound, Sattler Caliber ES 02 (base Habring A09MS); ø 30 mm, height 6.25 mm; 28 jewels; 28,800 vph; modified for regulator display with jumping seconds; rotor skeletonized, engraved, and guillochéed by hand
Functions: hours (off-center), minutes, subsidiary seconds (jumping)
Case: stainless steel, ø 38 mm, height 12 mm; rose gold bezel; sapphire crystal; water-resistant to 3 atm
Band: reptile skin, double folding clasp
Price: $10,170

Eterna SA
Schützenstrasse 40
CH-2540 Grenchen
Switzerland

Tel.:
01141-32-654-7211

Website:
www.eterna.com

Founded:
1856

Number of employees:
approx. 80

Annual production:
not specified

Distribution:
Contact headquarters for all enquiries.

Most important collections:
Vaughan; Madison; KonTiki; Contessa

Eterna

The brand Eterna has truly left its mark on the watchmaking industry. Founded in 1856 as Dr. Girard & Schild, the company became a *manufacture*, producing pocket watches under Urs Schild in 1870. Among its earliest claims to fame was the first wristwatch with an alarm, released in 1908, by which time the company had taken on the name Eterna. Forty years later, came the legendary Eterna-matic, featuring micro ball bearings for an automatic winding rotor. At the slightest movement of the watch, the rotor began to turn and set in motion what was another newly developed system of two ratchet wheels, which, independent of the rotational direction, lifted the mainspring over the automatic gears. Today, the five micro ball bearings used to cushion that rotor are the inspiration for Eterna's stylized pentagon-shaped logo. The invention itself is now standard in millions of watch movements.

In 2008, Eterna introduced the Spherodrive, a simple, yet brilliant technology designed to relieve tension on the spring barrel by separating the winding mechanism from the gear train. Both winding stem and spring barrel are mounted on the miniscule, ceramic orbs. And they are even used under the curved, big date display discs to ensure minimal friction. Because Eterna owes so much to this bearing technology, the company created a watch named for Welsh iron founder Philip Vaughan, inventor of the ball bearing. These watches, along with the Madison line, have a clear 1970s look that is coming into fashion again. More important, Eterna, whose original movement division became a separate company called ETA (now with the Swatch Group), has returned to building its own movements like the Caliber 39. In 1995, it was acquired by F.A. Porsche Beteiligungen GmbH and started manufacturing for Porsche Design. In 2011, International Volant Ltd., a wholly owned subsidiary of China Haidian, bought up the Porsche-owned shares in Eterna and has now put Corum CEO Antonio Calce at the helm of the traditional Swiss company to put it back on a track of serious growth.

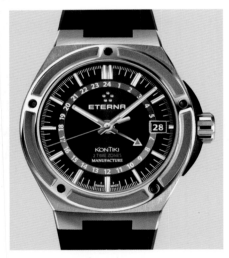

Royal KonTiki Two TimeZones

Reference number: 7740.40.41.1289
Movement: automatic, Eterna Caliber 3945A; ø 30 mm, height 5.9 mm; 28 jewels; 28,800 vph; 2 ball-bearing mounted spring barrels (Spherodrive); 68-hour power reserve
Functions: hours, minutes, sweep seconds; additional 24-hour display (second time zone); date
Case: stainless steel, ø 42 mm, height 12.3 mm; sapphire crystal, transparent case back; water-resistant to 10 atm
Band: rubber, buckle
Price: $5,600

Adventic GMT

Reference number: 7660.41.66.1273
Movement: automatic, Eterna Caliber 3843; ø 30.4 mm, height 6.1 mm; 26 jewels; 28,800 vph; ball-bearing mounted spring barrel (Spherodrive); 72-hour power reserve
Functions: hours, minutes, subsidiary seconds; second time zone (additional 24-hour display); date
Case: stainless steel, ø 44 mm, height 12.5 mm; sapphire crystal; transparent case back; water-resistant to 5 atm
Band: reptile skin, folding clasp
Price: $8,460
Variations: rose gold ($26,100)

1948 Date

Reference number: 2950.41.41.1175
Movement: automatic, ETA Caliber 2824-2; ø 25.6 mm, height 4.6 mm; 25 jewels; 28,800 vph; 38-hour power reserve
Functions: hours, minutes, sweep seconds; date
Case: stainless steel, ø 42.5 mm, height 11.7 mm; sapphire crystal; transparent case back; water-resistant to 5 atm
Band: reptile skin, folding clasp
Price: $2,140

Super KonTiki Limited Edition 1973

Reference number: 1973.41.41.1230
Movement: automatic, ETA Caliber 2824-2; ø 25.6 mm, height 4.6 mm; 25 jewels; 28,800 vph; 38-hour power reserve
Functions: hours, minutes, sweep seconds; date
Case: stainless steel, ø 44 mm, height 13.7 mm; unidirectional bezel with 60-minute divisions; sapphire crystal, screw-in crown; water-resistant to 20 atm
Band: stainless steel Milanese bracelet, folding clasp with extension link
Price: $2,460

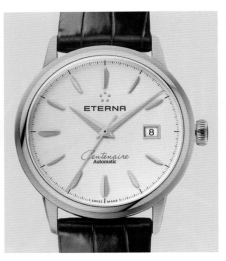

Centenaire

Reference number: 2960.69.11.1272
Movement: automatic, Sellita Caliber SW300; ø 25.6 mm, height 3.6 mm; 25 jewels; 28,800 vph; 42-hour power reserve
Functions: hours, minutes, sweep seconds; date
Case: rose gold, ø 40 mm, height 9.85 mm; sapphire crystal, water-resistant to 5 atm
Band: reptile skin, folding clasp
Price: $11,300

Vaughan Big Date

Reference number: 7630.41.61.1185
Movement: automatic, Eterna Caliber 3030; ø 30 mm, height 4.6 mm; 27 jewels; 28,800 vph
Functions: hours, minutes, sweep seconds; large date
Case: stainless steel, ø 42 mm, height 9.8 mm; sapphire crystal; transparent case back; water-resistant to 5 atm
Band: reptile skin, folding clasp
Price: $6,180
Variations: various bands and dials

Madison Eight-Days

Reference number: 7720.41.43.1228
Movement: manual winding, Eterna Caliber 3510; 26 x 32 mm, height 6.6 mm; 23 jewels; 28,800 vph; 2 ball-bearing mounted spring barrels (Spherodrive); 192-hour power reserve
Functions: hours, minutes, sweep seconds; large date; power reserve indicator
Case: stainless steel, 53.3 x 38.5 mm, height 13.25 mm; sapphire crystal; transparent case back; water-resistant to 3 atm
Band: reptile skin, folding clasp
Price: $9,500
Variations: with white or anthracite dial and leather strap

Madison Three-Hands Spherodrive

Reference number: 7712.41.41.1177
Movement: manual winding, Eterna Caliber 3505; 24 x 30 mm, height 4.1 mm; 16 jewels; 28,800 vph; ball bearing-mounted spring barrel (Spherodrive); 56-hour power reserve
Functions: hours, minutes, sweep seconds
Case: stainless steel, 34.5 x 47.4 mm, height 9.41 mm; sapphire crystal; transparent case back; water-resistant to 5 atm
Band: reptile skin, folding clasp
Price: $5,680
Variations: with black or anthracite dial

Tangaroa Three-Hands

Reference number: 2948.41.51.1261
Movement: automatic, Sellita Caliber SW200-1; ø 25.6 mm, height 4.6 mm; 26 jewels; 28,800 vph; 38-hour power reserve
Functions: hours, minutes, sweep seconds; date
Case: stainless steel, ø 42 mm, height 10.8 mm; sapphire crystal; transparent case back; water-resistant to 5 atm
Band: calf leather, buckle
Price: $1,640
Variations: various bands and dials

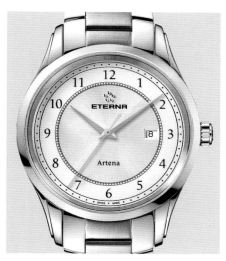

Artena Gent

Reference number: 2520.41.64.0274
Movement: quartz, ETA Caliber 955.412
Functions: hours, minutes, sweep seconds; date
Case: stainless steel, ø 40 mm, height 8.37 mm;
sapphire crystal
Band: stainless steel, folding clasp
Price: $1,120
Variations: various bands and dials

Artena Lady

Reference number: 2510.41.66.1252
Movement: automatic, ETA Caliber 956.412
Functions: hours, minutes, sweep seconds; date
Case: stainless steel, ø 34 mm, height 8.82 mm;
sapphire crystal; crown with onyx cabochons
Band: reptile skin, buckle
Price: $1,070
Variations: various bands and dials

Contessa Two-Hands

Reference number: 2410.48.67.1247
Movement: quartz, ETA Caliber 901.001
Functions: hours, minutes
Case: stainless steel, 25.75 x 40 mm, height
6.5 mm; bezel set with 46 diamonds; sapphire
crystal; water-resistant to 5 atm
Band: reptile skin, folding clasp
Remarks: dial set with 12 diamonds
Price: $5,550
Variations: various bands and dials

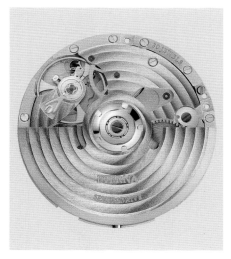

Caliber 3945A

Automatic; ball bearing mounted spring barrel and
rotor; single spring barrel, 68-hour power reserve
Functions: hours, minutes, sweep seconds;
additional 24-hour indicator (second time zone);
date
Diameter: 30 mm
Height: 5.9 mm
Jewels: 28
Balance: glucydur
Frequency: 28,800 vph
Balance spring: flat hairspring
Shock protection: Incabloc

Caliber 3843

Automatic; ball bearing mounted spring barrel and
rotor; single spring barrel; 72-hour power reserve
Functions: hours, minutes, subsidiary seconds;
second time zone (additional 24-hour display); date
Diameter: 30.4 mm
Height: 6.1 mm
Jewels: 26
Balance: glucydur
Frequency: 28,800 vph

Caliber 3510

Manually wound; 2 ball bearing mounted spring
barrels; 192-hour power reserve
Functions: hours, minutes, sweep seconds; power
reserve display
Dimensions: 27.2 x 33.2 mm
Height: 6.6 mm
Jewels: 22
Balance: glucydur
Frequency: 28,800 vph

Fortis Uhren AG
Lindenstrasse 45
CH-2540 Grenchen
Switzerland

Tel.:
01141-32-653-3361

Fax:
01141-32-652-5942

E-Mail:
info@fortis-watches.com

Website:
www.fortis-watches.com

Founded:
1912

Number of employees:
not specified

Annual production:
not specified

U.S. distributor:
Gevril Group
9 Pinecrest Road
Valley Cottage, NY 10989
845-425-9882; 845-425-9897 (fax)
www.gevrilgroup.com

Most important collections/price range:
Flieger, Official Cosmonauts, Marinemaster,
Stratoliner; Art Edition / $1,400 to $9,500

Fortis

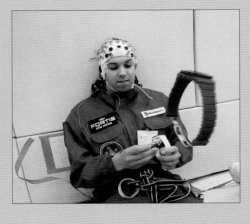

From March to September 2012, anyone visiting the Museum of Cultural History in Grenchen, Switzerland, could have enjoyed an in-depth look at one century's worth of Fortis. The exhibition was appropriately called "From Grenchen into Space." And knowing Grenchen, that is quite a step.

The 102-year history of the Fortis brand has been marked by many memorable events. The biggest milestone dates to the 1920s, when the company began the first serial production of wristwatches with automatic winding. The word *Fortis* comes from the Latin term for "strong." With its striking and sturdy watches, the brand itself has always enjoyed a reputation for reliability and consistency. But perhaps its greatest claim to fame comes from the clients it serves: These days, if you say "Fortis," the first thing that springs to mind is aeronautics and space travel. For the past seventeen years, Fortis has been collaborating with specialists from the European space agency to test how the company's first generation of space chronographs would hold up in truly extreme conditions. This resulted in approval for use aboard the Russian space station *Mir*. Since then, Fortis chronographs have become part of the official equipment of the Russian space program and, from there, on the *International Space Station*.

The competencies acquired from work in space continue to flow back into the company's traditional pilot's watches, which have long served as the role models for modern cockpit wristwatches. It's hardly astonishing that many international squadrons wear Fortis watches. Aside from such high-performance, space-traveling timepieces, Fortis also regularly enjoys creating limited edition art and design timepieces in collaboration with artists.

F-43 Flieger Day/Date

Reference number: 700.10.81 L01
Movement: automatic, Fortis Caliber F-2018 (base ETA 2836-2); ø 25.6 mm, height 5.05 mm; 26 jewels; 28,800 vph; 38-hour power reserve
Functions: hours, minutes, sweep seconds; weekday, date
Case: stainless steel, ø 43 mm, height 12.5 mm; sapphire crystal; transparent case back; water-resistant to 20 atm
Band: calf leather, buckle
Price: $2,575, limited to 2,012 pieces
Variations: with stainless steel bracelet ($3,000); with light dial and silicone band ($2,875); with chronograph ($4,025); with alarm clock ($13,975)

F-43 Flieger Chronograph Alarm GMT Certified Chronometer

Reference number: 703.10.81 LC01
Movement: automatic, Fortis Caliber F-2012 (base ETA 7750); ø 30 mm, height 7.9 mm; 39 jewels; 28,800 vph; 36-hour power reserve; COSC certified chronometer
Functions: hours, minutes, subsidiary seconds; additional 24-hour display; double power reserve display, alarm clock; chronograph; day/night indicator; date
Case: stainless steel, ø 43 mm, height 16.3 mm; sapphire crystal; water-resistant to 5 atm
Band: reptile skin, folding clasp
Price: $20,750, limited to 100 pieces
Variations: with stainless steel bracelet ($20,250)

B-42 Flieger Chronograph

Reference number: 635.10.72 Si02
Movement: automatic, ETA Caliber 7750; ø 30 mm, height 7.9 mm; 25 jewels; 28,800 vph; 42-hour power reserve
Functions: hours, minutes, subsidiary seconds; chronograph; weekday, date
Case: stainless steel, ø 42 mm, height 14.6 mm; sapphire crystal; water-resistant to 20 atm
Band: silicon, folding clasp
Price: $3,600
Variations: with leather band ($3,425); with stainless steel bracelet ($3,850); Day/Date version ($2,025); with alarm clock ($12,100)

B-42 Stratoliner Chronograph

Reference number: 665.13.19 LC01
Movement: automatic, ETA Caliber 7750; ø 30 mm, height 7.9 mm; 25 jewels; 28,800 vph; 42-hour power reserve
Functions: hours, minutes, subsidiary seconds; chronograph; weekday, date
Case: stainless steel with black PVD coating, ø 42 mm, height 15.6 mm; rose gold bezel, crown, pushers; sapphire crystal; transparent case back; water-resistant to 20 atm
Band: reptile skin, buckle
Price: $11,600, limited to 100 pieces
Variations: with rubber band ($11,000); stainless steel with black PVD coating ($6,125)

F-43 Jumping Hour Black

Reference number: 710.20.33 L01
Movement: automatic, Fortis Caliber F-2024 (base ETA 2892-2); ø 25.95 mm; 21 jewels; 28,800 vph; 42-hour power reserve
Functions: hours (digital, jumping), minutes
Case: stainless steel, ø 43 mm, height 12.5 mm; sapphire crystal; transparent case back; water-resistant to 20 atm
Band: calf leather, buckle
Price: $4,600, limited to 500 pieces
Variations: with stainless steel bracelet ($5,025); with silicone band ($4,750)

F-43 Jumping Hour

Reference number: 710.10.37 M
Movement: automatic, Fortis Caliber F-2024 (base ETA 2892-2); ø 25.95 mm; 21 jewels; 28,800 vph; 42-hour power reserve
Functions: hours (digital, jumping), minutes
Case: stainless steel, ø 43 mm, height 12.5 mm; sapphire crystal; transparent case back; water-resistant to 20 atm
Band: stainless steel, folding clasp
Price: $5,025, limited to 500 pieces
Variations: with reptile skin band ($5,500); with silicone band ($4,750)

B-47 Calculator GMT 3 Time Zones

Reference number: 669.10.31 L16
Movement: automatic, ETA Caliber 2893-2; ø 25.6 mm, height 4.1 mm; 21 jewels; 28,800 vph; 42-hour power reserve
Functions: hours, minutes, sweep seconds; additional 24-hour display (second time zone); date
Case: stainless steel, ø 47 mm, height 13.5 mm; bidirectional bezel with 24-hour divisions; crown-activated scale ring inner with 24-hour divisions; sapphire crystal; water-resistant to 20 atm
Band: calf leather, buckle
Price: $3,500, limited to 2,012 pieces
Variations: with stainless steel bracelet ($3,975)

B-47 Big Black

Reference number: 675.18.81 K
Movement: automatic, Fortis Caliber F-2016 (base ETA 2836-2); ø 25.6 mm, height 5.05 mm; 26 jewels; 28,800 vph; 42-hour power reserve
Functions: hours, minutes, sweep seconds; weekday, date
Case: stainless steel with black PVD coating, ø 47 mm, height 13.3 mm; unidirectional bezel with 60-minute divisions; sapphire crystal; water-resistant to 20 atm
Band: rubber, double folding clasp
Remarks: sapphire crystal dial
Price: $4,000, limited to 2,012 pieces

B-47 World Timer GMT

Reference number: 674.20.15 Si05
Movement: automatic, Fortis Caliber F-2022 (base ETA 2893-1); ø 25.6 mm, height 5.05 mm; 26 jewels; 28,800 vph; 42-hour power reserve
Functions: hours, minutes, sweep seconds; world-time display (second time zone); date
Case: stainless steel, ø 47 mm, height 13.3 mm; bidirectional bezel with 24 reference cities; sapphire crystal; transparent case back; water-resistant to 20 atm
Band: rubber, folding clasp
Price: $4,350, limited to 2,012 pieces
Variations: with stainless steel band ($4,875)

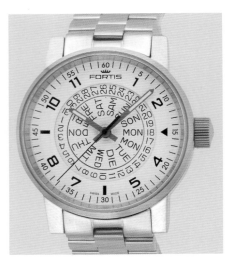

B-42 Black Mars 500 Day/Date

Reference number: 647.28.13.L13
Movement: automatic, ETA Caliber 2836-2; ø 30 mm, height 5.05 mm; 25 jewels; 28,800 vph; 38-hour power reserve
Functions: hours, minutes, sweep seconds; weekday, date
Case: titanium with black PVD coating, ø 42 mm, height 13 mm; unidirectional bezel with 60-minute divisions; sapphire crystal; water-resistant to 20 atm
Band: calf leather, buckle
Price: $3,025, limited to 2,012 pieces
Variations: with silicone band ($3,325)

Spacematic Classic White-Red

Reference number: 623.10.52 M
Movement: automatic, ETA Caliber 2836-2; ø 25.6 mm, height 5.05 mm; 25 jewels; 28,800 vph; 38-hour power reserve
Functions: hours, minutes, sweep seconds; weekday, date
Case: stainless steel, ø 40 mm, height 10.4 mm; sapphire crystal; water-resistant to 10 atm
Band: stainless steel, double folding clasp
Price: $1,975
Variations: with calf leather band ($1,575); with silicone band ($1,875)

B-42 Marinemaster Chronograph Yellow

Reference number: 671.24.14 K
Movement: automatic, ETA Caliber 7750; ø 30 mm, height 7.9 mm; 25 jewels; 28,800 vph; 42-hour power reserve
Functions: hours, minutes, subsidiary seconds; chronograph; weekday, date
Case: stainless steel, ø 42 mm, height 16 mm; unidirectional bezel with 60-minute divisions; sapphire crystal; water-resistant to 20 atm
Band: rubber, folding clasp
Price: $4,025
Variations: with calf leather band ($3,875); with stainless steel bracelet ($4,300); day/date version ($2,050)

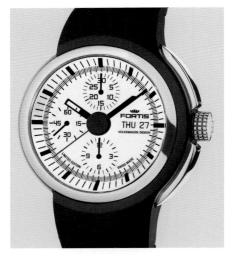

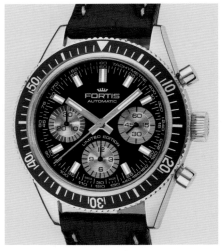

Spaceleader Chronograph by Volkswagen Design

Reference number: 661.20.32 K
Movement: automatic, ETA Caliber 7750; ø 30 mm, height 7.9 mm; 25 jewels; 28,800 vph; 42-hour power reserve
Functions: hours, minutes, subsidiary seconds; chronograph; weekday, date
Case: stainless steel, ø 43 mm, height 15.1 mm; sapphire crystal; water-resistant to 10 atm
Band: rubber, double folding clasp
Price: $5,725, limited to 2,012 pieces
Variations: with black dial ($5,725); with white silicone bracelet ($5,725)

Square Chronograph

Reference number: 667.10.71 L16
Movement: automatic, ETA Caliber 7750; ø 30 mm, height 7.9 mm; 28,800 vph; 42-hour power reserve
Functions: hours, minutes, subsidiary seconds; chronograph; weekday, date
Case: stainless steel, 38 x 38 mm, height 13.8 mm; sapphire crystal; transparent case back; water-resistant to 10 atm
Band: calf leather, buckle
Price: $4,000
Variations: with stainless steel bracelet ($4,500); with silver dial ($4,000)

Marinemaster Vintage Chrono

Reference number: 800.20.80 L01
Movement: automatic, Fortis Caliber F-2020 (base ETA 2892-A2); ø 30 mm, height 7.5 mm; 47 jewels; 28,800 vph; 42-hour power reserve
Functions: hours, minutes, subsidiary seconds; chronograph
Case: stainless steel, ø 40 mm, height 15.4 mm; unidirectional bezel with 60-minute divisions; plexiglass; transparent case back; water-resistant to 5 atm
Band: calf leather, buckle
Remarks: limited to 500 pieces; 100th anniversary edition in 1971 design
Price: $4,600

François-Paul Journe

Montres Journe SA
17 rue de l'Arquebuse
CH-1204 Geneva
Switzerland

Tel.:
01141-22-322-09-09

Fax:
01141-22-322-09-19

E-Mail:
info@fpjourne.com

Website:
www.fpjourne.com

Founded:
1999

Number of employees:
120

Annual production:
850–900 watches

U.S. distributor:
Montres Journe America
4330 NE 2nd Avenue
Miami, FL 33137
305-572-9802
phalimi@fpjourne.com

Most important collections/price range:
Souveraine and Octa
(Prices are in Swiss francs. Use daily exchange rate for calculations.)

Born in Marseilles in 1957, François-Paul Journe might have become something else had he concentrated better in school. He was kicked out and apprenticed with a watchmaking uncle in Paris instead. And he has never looked back. By the age of twenty he had made his first tourbillon and soon was producing watches for connoisseurs.

He then moved to Switzerland, where he started out with handmade creations for a limited circle of clients and developing the most creative and complicated timekeepers for other brands before taking the plunge and founding his own in the heart of Geneva.

The timepieces he basically single-handedly and certainly single-mindedly—hence his tagline *invenit et fecit*—conceives and produces are of such extreme complexity that it is no wonder that they leave his workshop in relatively small quantities. His collection is divided into two pillars: the automatic Octa line with its somewhat more readily understandable complications and the manually wound Souveraine line, which contains horological treasures that can't be found anywhere else. The latter includes a *grande sonnerie*, a minute repeater, a constant force tourbillon with deadbeat seconds, and even a timepiece containing two escapements beating in resonance—and providing chronometer-precise timekeeping. The latest piece in the series is the simpler Chronomètre Optimum.

Journe has won numerous top awards, some several times over. He particularly values the Prix de la Fondation de la Vocation Bleustein-Blanchet since it came from his peers. An Octa Calendar has also appeared on the wrist of actor Jean Dujardin playing a Russian agent in the thriller *Möbius,* a distinction not afforded to many brands.

Chronomètre à Résonance

Movement: manually wound, FP Journe Caliber 1499.3; ø 32.6 mm, height 4.2 mm; 36 jewels; 21,600 vph; unique concept with 2 escapements that mutually influence and thereby stabilize each other utilizing the resonance phenomenon; pink gold plate and bridges
Functions: hours, minutes, subsidiary seconds; second time zone; power reserve indicator
Case: platinum, ø 40 mm, height 9 mm; sapphire crystal; transparent case back
Band: reptile skin, platinum buckle
Price: $76,090
Variations: pink gold

Sonnerie Souveraine

Movement: manually wound, FP Journe Caliber 1505; ø 35.8 mm, height 7.8 mm; 42 jewels; 21,600 vph; pink gold plate and bridges; repeater chimes hours and quarter hours, automatically and on demand; on/off function; 422 components; 10 patents
Functions: hours, minutes (off-center), subsidiary seconds; grande sonnerie; power reserve indicator; chime indicator
Case: stainless steel, ø 42 mm; height 12.25 mm; sapphire crystal; screw-in crown and pusher; transparent case back
Band: reptile skin, comes with double folding clasp and stainless steel bracelet
Price: CHF 650,000 (only in Swiss francs)

Chronomètre Optimum

Movement: manually wound, FP Journe Caliber 1510; ø 34.40 mm, height 3.75 mm; 44 jewels; 21,600 vph; double barrel spring; biaxial escapement, constant force by remontoire; pink gold plate and bridges; 50-hour power reserve
Functions: hours, minutes, subsidiary seconds; deadbeat seconds on movement side; power reserve indicator
Case: pink gold, ø 40 mm, height 10.10 mm; sapphire crystal; transparent case back; water-resistant to 3 atm
Band: leather, buckle
Price: $86,960

Groupe Franck Muller Watchland SA
22, route de Malagny
CH-1294 Genthod
Switzerland

Tel.:
01141-22-959-8888

Fax:
01141-22-959-8882

E-Mail:
info@franckmuller.ch

Website:
www.franckmuller.com

Founded:
1997

Number of employees:
approx. 500 (estimated)

Annual production:
not specified

U.S. distributor:
Franck Muller USA, Inc.
207 W. 25th Street, 8th Floor
New York, NY 10001
212-463-8898
www.franckmuller.com

Most important collections:
Giga, Aeternitas, Revolution, Evolution 3-1

Franck Muller

Francesco "Franck" Muller has been considered one of the great creative minds in the industry ever since he designed and built his first tourbillon watch back in 1986. In fact, he never ceased amazing his colleagues and competition ever since, with his astounding timepieces combining complications in a new and fascinating manner.

Recently, the "master of complications" has been stepping away from the daily business of the brand, leaving space for the person who had paved young Muller's way to fame, Vartan Sirmakes. It was Sirmakes, previously a specialist in watch cases, who had contributed to the development of the double-domed, tonneau-shaped Cintrée Curvex case, with its elegant, 1920s retro look. The complications never stop either. The latest Gigatourbillons are 20 millimeters across; the Revolution series has a tourbillon that rises toward the crystal.

It was in 1997 that Muller and Sirmakes founded the Franck Muller Group Watchland, which now holds the majority interest in thirteen other companies, eight of which are watch brands. During the 2009 economic crisis, the company downsized somewhat and put all its ambitious plans for expansion on hold. Franck Muller remains the leading brand in the Watchland portfolio, but via far-reaching synergies within the group, two brands specializing in complicated movements, Pierre Kunz and Pierre-Michel Golay, play a part in the founding brand's success.

Tourbillon Rapide

Reference number: 7889 T G SQT BR
Movement: manually wound, FM Caliber 2025T; 32.2 x 38.4 mm, height 8.5 mm; 29 jewels, 21,600 vph; flying 5-second tourbillon with escapement wheel meshed on inside; fully skeletonized; 60-hour power reserve
Functions: hours, minutes
Case: white gold, 40.65 x 55.05 mm, height 13.7 mm; sapphire crystal, transparent case back
Band: reptile skin, buckle
Price: $233,400
Variations: steel ($211,200)

Giga Tourbillon

Reference number: 8889 T G SQT BR NR
Movement: manually wound, FM Caliber 2100 TS; 34.4 x 41.4 mm, height 8.5 mm; 29 jewels; 18,000 vph; flying 1-minute, 20 mm tourbillon; 4 spring barrels; fully skeletonized; 216-hour power reserve
Functions: hours, minutes; power reserve indicator
Case: rose gold, 43.7 x 59.2 mm, height 14 mm; sapphire crystal, transparent case back; water-resistant to 3 atm
Band: reptile skin, buckle
Price: $264,500
Variations: white gold

Giga Tourbillon

Reference number: 7048 T G SQT BR
Movement: manually wound, FM Caliber 2100 T RS; ø 40.5 mm; 29 jewels; 18,000 vph; flying 1-minute, 20 mm tourbillon; 4 spring barrels, 216-hour power reserve; completely skeletonized
Functions: hours, minutes; power reserve indicator
Case: white gold, ø 49 mm; sapphire crystal; transparent case back; water-resistant to 3 atm
Band: reptile skin, buckle
Price: $242,300
Variations: rose gold ($264,500)

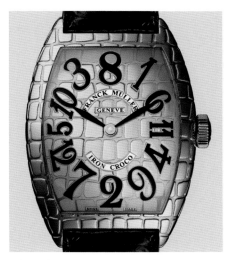

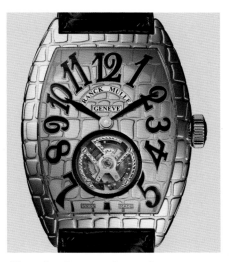

Cintrée Curvex Iron Croco Crazy Hours

Reference number: 8880 CH Iron Croco
Movement: automatic, FM Caliber 2800;
ø 25.6 mm, height 3.6 mm; 21 jewels; 28,800 vph;
hands mechanism rebuilt with "spontaneously"
jumping hour hand; finely finished with côtes de
Genève, 42-hour power reserve
Functions: hours, minutes
Case: stainless steel, structured surface; 39.6 x
55.4 mm, height 11.9 mm; sapphire crystal, water-
resistant to 3 atm
Band: reptile skin, buckle
Price: $26,200

Cintrée Curvex Iron Croco Master Banker

Reference number: 8880 MB SC DT Iron Croco
Movement: automatic, FM Caliber 2800;
ø 25.6 mm, height 3.6 mm; 21 jewels; 28,600 vph;
module for 2 additional time zones; finely finished
with côtes de Genève; 42-hour power reserve
Functions: hours, minutes, sweep seconds; 2
additional 12-hour displays (second and third time
zones)
Case: stainless steel, structured surface;
39.6 x 55.4 mm, height 11.9 mm; sapphire crystal,
water-resistant to 3 atm
Band: reptile skin, buckle
Price: $23,400

Cintrée Curvex Iron Croco Tourbillon

Reference number: 8880 T Iron Croco
Movement: automatic, FM Caliber 2001; 31.2 x
34 mm, height 5.3 mm; 21 jewels; 18,000 vph;
flying 1-minute tourbillon; rhodium-plated with
côtes de Genève; 42-hour power reserve
Functions: hours, minutes, subsidiary seconds
Case: stainless steel, structured surface; 39.6 x
55.4 mm, height 11.9 mm; sapphire crystal,
water-resistant to 3 atm
Band: reptile skin, buckle
Price: $144,500

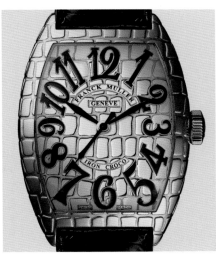

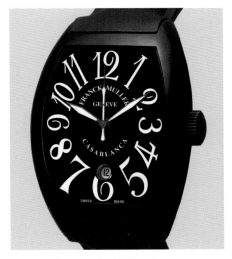

Cintrée Curvex Iron Croco

Reference number: 8880 SC Iron Croco
Movement: automatic, FM Caliber 2800;
ø 25.6 mm, height 3.6 mm; 21 jewels; 28,800 vph;
finely finished with côtes de Genève; 42-hour power
reserve
Functions: hours, minutes, sweep seconds
Case: stainless steel, structured surface; 39.6 x
55.4 mm, height 11.9 mm; sapphire crystal, water-
resistant to 3 atm
Band: reptile skin, buckle
Price: $14,800

Cintrée Curvex Black Croco Chronograph

Reference number: 8880 CC AT BLK CRO
Movement: automatic, FM Caliber 7000;
ø 30.4 mm, height 7.9 mm; 27 jewels; 28,800 vph;
finely finished with côtes de Genève
Functions: hours, minutes, subsidiary seconds;
chronograph; date
Case: stainless steel, structured surface, with black
PVD coating; 39.6 x 55.4 mm, height 11.9 mm;
sapphire crystal
Band: reptile skin, buckle
Price: $28,900
Variations: steel ($40,000)

Casablanca All Black

Reference number: 8880 CDT NR
Movement: automatic, FM Caliber 2800 (base
ETA 2892); ø 25.6 mm, height 3.6 mm; 21 jewels;
28,800 vph; finished with côtes de Genève;
platinum rotor
Functions: hours, minutes, sweep seconds; date
Case: stainless steel with black PVD coating, 39.6 x
55.4 mm, height 11.9 mm; sapphire crystal
Band: rubber, buckle
Price: $10,900

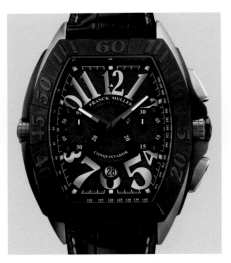

GPG Conquistador Cortez

Reference number: 10900 SC DT GPG TT TT
Movement: automatic, FM Caliber 2800;
ø 25.6 mm, height 3.6 mm; 21 jewels; 28,800 vph;
rhodium-plated; platinum rotor; bridges with côtes
de Genève, 42-hour power reserve
Functions: hours, minutes, sweep seconds; date
Case: titanium, 45 x 45 mm, height 15.25 mm;
sapphire crystal, water-resistant to 3 atm
Band: rubber, buckle
Price: $12,600
Variations: titanium with pink gold ($18,900)

Conquistador Grand Prix Chronograph

Reference number: 9900 CC GPG.TT
Movement: automatic, FM Caliber 7000; ø 30.4 mm,
height 7.9 mm; 27 jewels; 28,800 vph; with côtes de
Genève; rhodium-plated; platinum rotor
Functions: hours, minutes, subsidiary seconds;
chronograph; date
Case: titanium, 48 x 62.7 mm, height 14.6 mm;
bezel with black PVD coating and 60-minute
divisions; sapphire crystal
Band: reptile skin, buckle
Price: $23,100
Variations: titanium/ergal ($23,600);
rose gold ($30,600)

Conquistador Grand Prix Automatic

Reference number: 9900 SC GPG RG.ER
Movement: automatic, FM Caliber 800; ø 26.6 mm,
height 3.6 mm; 21 jewels; 28,800 vph; rhodium-
plated; platinum rotor; bridges with côtes de Genève
Functions: hours, minutes, sweep seconds; date
Case: titanium/red eloxed ergal; 48 x 62.7 mm,
height 14.6 mm; bezel with black PVD coating; with
60-second divisions; sapphire crystal
Band: reptile skin, buckle
Price: $12,000
Variations: with rubber strap;in titanium
($12,500); rose gold ($18,300)

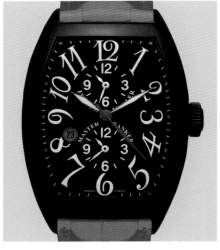

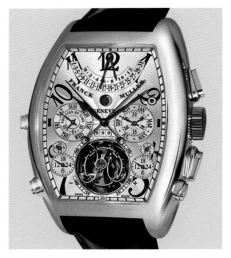

Cintrée Curvex 7 Days Power Reserve

Reference number: 8880 B S6 PR EMA
Movement: manually wound, FM Caliber 1700;
ø 31 mm, height 5 mm; 27 jewels; 18,000 vph;
double spring barrel, Breguet spring; finely finished
with côtes de Genève; 168-hour power reserve
Functions: hours, minutes, subsidiary seconds;
power reserve indicator
Case: rose gold, 39.6 x 55.4 mm, height 10.3 mm;
sapphire crystal, transparent case back; water-
resistant to 3 atm
Band: reptile skin, buckle
Price: $23,000

Cintrée Curvex Master Banker

Reference number: 7880 MB SC DT
Movement: automatic, FM Caliber 2800;
ø 25.6 mm, height 7.7 mm; 24 jewels; 28,800 vph;
module for 2 additional time zones; platinum rotor
Functions: hours, minutes, sweep seconds;
2 additional 12-hour displays (second and third
time zones); date
Case: stainless steel with black PVD coating,
35.9 x 50.3 mm, height 11.5 mm; sapphire crystal
Band: reptile skin, buckle
Price: $22,300
Variations: rose or white gold ($33,400)

Aeternitas 5

Reference number: 8888 Aeternitas 5
Movement: automatic, FM Caliber 3430; 34.4 x
41.4 mm, height 13.45 mm; 65 jewels; 18,000 vph;
flying 1-minute tourbillon; microrotor; 8-day power
reserve
Functions: hours, minutes; split-second
chronograph; perpetual secular calendar with date
(retrograde), weekday, month (retrograde), moon
phase, leap year; 2 time zones; equation of time
indicator
Case: white gold, 49.65 x 61 mm; height 19.1 mm;
sapphire crystal
Band: reptile skin, buckle
Price: $1,022,300

Advanced winding technology, for your fine watches.

AVANTI Series:
3 | 4 | 6 | 9 | 12 | 24 | 36 | 48

Frédérique Constant SA
Chemin du Champ des Filles 32
CH-1228 Plan-les-Ouates (Geneva)
Switzerland

Tel.:
01141-22-860-0440

Fax:
01141-22-860-0464

E-Mail:
info@frederique-constant.com

Website:
www.frederique-constant.com

Founded:
1988

Number of employees:
100

Annual production:
110,000 watches

U.S. distributor:
Frédérique Constant USA
877-61-WATCH; info@usa.frederique-constant.com

Most important collections/price range:
Maxime Manufacture Automatic / from approx.
$2,600; Heart Beat Manufacture / from approx.
$4,900; Delight / approx. $1,000; Lady Automatic /
from approx. $3,000; Runabout / from approx.
$1,900; Vintage Rally / from approx. $1,200; Art
Deco / approx. $995; Classics / from approx. $550;
Carrée / from approx. $900

Frédérique Constant

In a country where some brands boast centuries of existence, celebrating a seventh anniversary as a full-fledged *manufacture* might sound somewhat preposterous. On the other hand, there is no denying that Frédérique Constant has come a long way on a road of steady growth. Since 1991, the Dutch couple Peter and Aletta Stas have genuinely lived up to the tagline they use for their Swiss brand: "live your passion." The watch brand, named for Aletta's great-grandmother, Frédérique Schreiner, and Peter's great-grandfather, Constant Stas, was conceived in the late 1980s. The new company had its work cut out for it: Frédérique Constant had to compete in a watch market truly saturated with brands. After their Heart Beat *manufacture* model met with award-winning enthusiasm in 2003, the Stases decided to invest in their own watch factory, an impressive, four-floor facility with ample room for a spacious atelier, administrative offices, conference rooms, fitness area, and cafeteria, in Geneva's industrial section, Plan-les-Ouates. Frédérique Constant moved into its new home in 2006, joined shortly after by its sister brand, Alpina. The Heart Beat collection continues to make waves. The Double Heart Beat is even being used to fund charities ($50 per watch sold). But the brand is growing in other directions as well. In 2009, Frédérique Constant backed the founding of the exclusive Ateliers de Monaco. And as evidence that the Stases are genuinely interested in spreading their passion about watches, they have created a kind of sub-brand, Frédérique Constant Junior, aimed at young teenagers. These affordable watches have space for a dedication on the back. The idea is to revive the tradition of the "confirmation watch" while at the same time avoiding the propagation of "plastic rubbish," says one Stas.

Runabout Moonphase

Reference number: FC-330RM6B6
Movement: automatic, Caliber FC-330 (base Sellita SW200); ø 25.6 mm; 26 jewels; 28,800 vph; 38-hour power reserve
Functions: hours, minutes, sweep seconds; date; moon phase
Case: stainless steel, ø 43 mm, height 10.9 mm; sapphire crystal; transparent case back; water-resistant to 10 atm
Band: calf leather, folding clasp
Price: $2,650, limited to 1,888 pieces

Runabout Moonphase

Reference number: FC-330RM6B4
Movement: automatic, Caliber FC-330 (base Sellita SW200); ø 25.6 mm; 26 jewels; 28,800 vph; 38-hour power reserve
Functions: hours, minutes, sweep seconds; date; moon phase
Case: stainless steel with rose gold-colored PVD coating, ø 43 mm, height 10.9 mm; sapphire crystal; transparent case back; water-resistant to 10 atm
Band: calf leather, folding clasp
Price: $2,950, limited to 1,888 pieces

Runabout Chronograph Venice Limited Edition

Reference number: FC-392RV6B6
Movement: automatic, Caliber FC-392 (base ETA 7750); ø 30 mm, height 7.9 mm; 25 jewels; 28,800 vph; côtes de Genève; 46-hour power reserve
Functions: hours, minutes, subsidiary seconds; chronograph; date
Case: stainless steel, ø 43 mm, height 14.5 mm; sapphire crystal; transparent case back; water-resistant to 10 atm
Band: calf leather, folding clasp
Price: $3,375, limited to 1,888 pieces

Manufacture Slimline Moonphase

Reference number: FC-705S4S6
Movement: automatic, Caliber FC-705; ø 30 mm, height 6.3 mm; 26 jewels; 28,800 vph; côtes de Genève; 42-hour power reserve
Functions: hours, minutes; date; moon phase
Case: stainless steel, ø 42 mm; sapphire crystal; transparent case back; water-resistant to 3 atm
Band: calf leather, buckle
Price: $3,550

Manufacture Slimline Moonphase

Reference number: FC-705N4S6
Movement: automatic, Caliber FC705; ø 30 mm, height 6.3 mm; 26 jewels; 28,800 vph; côtes de Genève; 42-hour power reserve
Functions: hours, minutes; date; moon phase
Case: stainless steel, ø 42 mm; sapphire crystal; transparent case back; water-resistant to 3 atm
Band: calf leather, buckle
Price: $3,550

Slimline Tourbillon

Reference number: FC-980V4SZ9
Movement: automatic, FC Caliber 980; ø 30.5 mm; 33 jewels; 28,800 vph; 1-minute tourbillon; bridges with perlage and côtes de Genève; silicon escapement
Functions: hours, minutes; day/night indicator
Case: stainless steel, ø 43 mm, height 12.1 mm; sapphire crystal; transparent case back
Band: calf leather, folding clasp
Price: $39,995

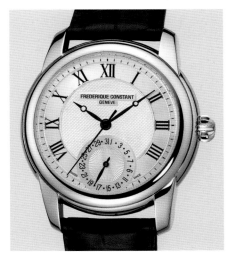

Classics Manufacture Worldtimer

Reference number: FC-718MC4H4
Movement: automatic, Caliber FC-718 (base ETA 2893-1); ø 25.6 mm, height 4.1 mm; 21 jewels; 28,800 vph; 42-hour power reserve
Functions: hours, minutes, sweep seconds; world-time display (second time zone); date
Case: stainless steel with rose gold-colored PVD coating, ø 42 mm; crown-adjustable bezel with 24-hour divisions and reference city names; sapphire crystal; transparent case back; water-resistant to 5 atm
Band: calf leather, folding clasp
Price: $4,195, limited to 1,888 pieces

Classics Manufacture Worldtimer

Reference number: FC-718WM4H4
Movement: automatic, Caliber FC-718 (base ETA 2893-1); ø 25.6 mm, height 4.1 mm; 21 jewels; 28,800 vph; 42-hour power reserve
Functions: hours, minutes, sweep seconds; world-time display (second time zone); date
Case: stainless steel with rose gold-colored PVD coating, ø 42 mm; crown-adjustable bezel with 24-hour divisions and reference city names; sapphire crystal; transparent case back; water-resistant to 5 atm
Band: calf leather, folding clasp
Price: $4,195, limited to 1,888 pieces

Classics Manufacture

Reference number: FC-710MC4H6
Movement: automatic, FC Caliber 710; ø 30 mm, height 6.3 mm; 26 jewels; 28,800 vph; côtes de Genève; 42-hour power reserve
Functions: hours, minutes, sweep seconds; date
Case: stainless steel, ø 42 mm, height 12.1 mm; sapphire crystal; transparent case back; water-resistant to 5 atm
Band: calf leather, buckle
Price: $2,595

Girard-Perregaux
136-138, rue Numa-Droz
CH-2300 La Chaux-de-Fonds
Switzerland

Tel.:
01141-32-911-3434

Fax:
01141-32-913-0343

Website:
www.girard-perregaux.com

Founded:
1791

Number of employees:
280

Annual production:
approx. 12,000 watches

U.S. distributor:
Girard-Perregaux

Tradema of America, Inc.
201 Route 17 North
Rutherford, NJ 07070
877-846-3447
www.girard-perregaux-usa.com
gpwebmaster@girard-perregaux-usa.com

Most important collections/price range:
Vintage 1945 / approx. $7,010 to $650,000;
ww.tc / $12,400 to $210,000; GP 1966 /
$13,050 to $48,500

Girard-Perregaux

When Girard-Perregaux CEO Luigi ("Gino") Macaluso died in 2010, the former minority partner of Sowind Group, PPR (Pinault, Printemps, Redoute) increased its equity stake to 51 percent. The French luxury goods holding had some excellent assets on which to rely: a magnificent, recently refurbished and modernized corporate headquarters, a strong development team—one even capable of taking on technically challenging tasks without the help of outside forces—and an excellently equipped production department.

Michele Sofisti was appointed CEO of the Sowind Group in 2011, which comprises

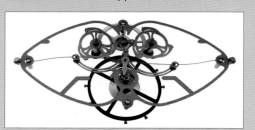

Girard-Perregaux and Jeanrichard, a research and development center, and the watch production company. Under his guidance, the company has reduced its multitude of references but continues treading the fine line between fashionable watches and technical miracles. In January 2012, the manufacturing team was reinforced with one of the most scintillating figures in horology, master watchmaker Dominique Loiseau, who had been working on a new modular movement for the brand before his unexpected passing in September 2013.

The various combinations of tourbillons and the gold bridges remain the company specialty. The elegant GP 1966 line and the very feminine Cat's Eye are still available, of course. The Vintage 45 is another standout, featuring striking rectangular and arched cases. But the most dazzling talking piece lately has undoubtedly been the Constant Escapement, a new concept that stores energy by buckling an ultra-thin silicium blade and then releasing it to the balance wheel. Like many sophisticated systems, it was born of the banal: inventor Nicolas Déhon was absentmindedly bending a train ticket one day when he was suddenly struck by an idea.

Constant Escapement

Reference number: 93500-53-131-BA6C
Movement: manually wound, GP Caliber 09100-0002; ø 39.2 mm, height 7.9 mm; 28 jewels; 21,600 vph; constant force escapement, with 2 pallet levers; pulsing silicon blade, 2 spring barrels; approx. 168-hour power reserve
Functions: hours and minutes (off-center), sweep seconds; linear power reserve indicator
Case: white gold, ø 48 mm, height 14.63 mm; sapphire crystal; transparent case back; water-resistant to 3 atm
Band: reptile skin, folding clasp
Price: $123,500

Tourbillon with Three Gold Bridges

Reference number: 99193-52-002-BA6A
Movement: automatic, GP Caliber 9600-0022; ø 31 mm, height 6.25 mm; 31 jewels; 21,600 vph; 1-minute tourbillon; platinum microrotor; 48-hour power reserve
Functions: hours, minutes, subsidiary seconds (on tourbillon cage)
Case: rose gold, ø 41 mm, height 11 mm; sapphire crystal; water-resistant to 3 atm
Band: reptile skin, folding clasp
Price: $195,500

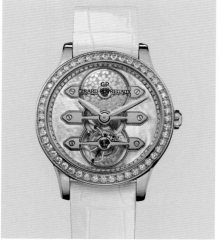

Tourbillon with Three Gold Bridges

Reference number: 99240D52A701-CK7A
Movement: automatic, GP Caliber 09600-0025; ø 30.2 mm, height 6.25 mm; 31 jewels; 21,600 vph; 1-minute tourbillon, platinum microrotor; 48-hour power reserve
Functions: hours, minutes, subsidiary seconds (on tourbillon cage)
Case: rose gold, ø 38 mm, height 11.16 mm; bezel set with 118 diamonds; sapphire crystal; water resistant to 3 atm
Band: reptile skin, folding clasp
Price: $207,500

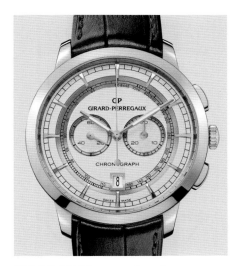

GP 1966 Chronograph

Reference number: 49529-52-131-BABA
Movement: manually wound, GP Caliber 03800-0001; ø 25.6 mm, height 5.4 mm; 31 jewels; 28,800 vph; column wheel control of chronograph functions; 56-hour power reserve
Functions: hours, minutes, subsidiary seconds; chronograph; date
Case: rose gold, ø 40 mm, height 11.25 mm; sapphire crystal; transparent case back; water-resistant to 3 atm
Band: reptile skin, folding clasp
Price: $37,400

GP 1966 Small Second

Reference number: 49543-52-131-BK6A
Movement: automatic, GP Caliber 01890-0003; ø 30 mm, height 4 mm; 28 jewels; 28,800 vph; 54-hour power reserve
Functions: hours, minutes, subsidiary seconds; date
Case: rose gold, ø 41 mm, height 10 mm; sapphire crystal; transparent case back; water-resistant to 3 atm
Band: reptile skin, buckle
Price: $16,500

GP 1966 41 mm

Reference number: 49527-53-131-BK6A
Movement: automatic, GP Caliber 4500; ø 30 mm, height 3.95 mm; 28 jewels; 28,800 vph; 54-hour power reserve
Functions: hours, minutes, sweep seconds; date
Case: white gold, ø 41 mm, height 10 mm; sapphire crystal; transparent case back; water-resistant to 3 atm
Band: reptile skin, buckle
Price: $17,000
Variations: rose gold ($16,500)

GP 1966 Annual Calendar and Equation of Time

Reference number: 49538-52-231-BK6A
Movement: automatic, GP Caliber 033MO; ø 25.6 mm, height 4.85 mm; 44 jewels; 28,800 vph; 46-hour power reserve
Functions: hours, minutes, subsidiary seconds; annual calendar with date, month, equation of time indicator
Case: rose gold, ø 40 mm, height 10.72 mm; sapphire crystal; transparent case back; water-resistant to 3 atm
Band: reptile skin, buckle
Price: $32,860
Variations: white gold ($37,300)

GP 1966 Full Calendar

Reference number: 49535-52-151-BK6A
Movement: automatic, GP Caliber 033MO; ø 26.2 mm, height 4.8 mm; 27 jewels; 28,800 vph; 46-hour power reserve
Functions: hours, minutes, sweep seconds; full calendar with date, weekday, month, moon phase
Case: rose gold, ø 40 mm, height 10.7 mm; sapphire crystal; transparent case back; water-resistant to 3 atm
Band: reptile skin, buckle
Price: $25,600
Variations: white gold ($27,400)

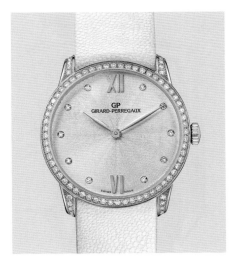

GP 1966 Lady

Reference number: 49528D52B171-IK7A
Movement: automatic, GP Caliber 03200-0005; ø 23.3 mm, height 3.2 mm; 26 jewels; 28,800 vph; 42-hour power reserve
Functions: hours, minutes
Case: rose gold, ø 30 mm, height 8.9 mm; bezel set with 80 diamonds; sapphire crystal; transparent case back; water-resistant to 3 atm
Band: ray skin, buckle
Remarks: mother-of-pearl dial set with 10 diamonds
Price: $20,300

Vintage 1945 XXL Large Date

Reference number: 25882-11-121-BB6B
Movement: automatic, GP Caliber 03300-00062;
ø 25.6 mm, height 4.9 mm; 32 jewels; 28,800 vph;
46-hour power reserve
Functions: hours, minutes, subsidiary seconds;
large date; moon phase
Case: stainless steel, 35.25 x 36.1 mm, height
11.74 mm; sapphire crystal; transparent case back;
water-resistant to 3 atm
Band: reptile skin, folding clasp
Price: $12,200

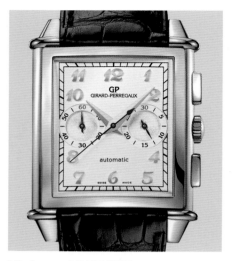

Vintage 1945 XXL Chronograph

Reference number: 25883-52-121-BB6C
Movement: automatic, GP Caliber 03300-0058;
ø 25.6 mm, height 5.5 mm; 32 jewels; 28,800 vph;
46-hour power reserve
Functions: hours, minutes, subsidiary seconds;
chronograph
Case: rose gold, 36 x 36.96 mm, height 13.09 mm;
sapphire crystal; transparent case back; water-
resistant to 3 atm
Band: reptile skin, folding clasp
Price: $32,500

Vintage 1945 Small Second

Reference number: 25880-11-221-BB6A
Movement: automatic, GP Caliber 3300-0051;
ø 26.2 mm, height 4.2 mm; 32 jewels; 28,800 vph;
48-hour power reserve
Functions: hours, minutes, subsidiary seconds
Case: stainless steel, 35.25 x 36.2 mm, height
10.83 mm; sapphire crystal; transparent case back;
water-resistant to 3 atm
Band: reptile skin, folding clasp
Price: $9,860

Vintage 1945 XXL Large Date

Reference number: 25882-52-121-BB6B
Movement: automatic, GP Caliber 03300-00062;
ø 25.6 mm, height 4.9 mm; 32 jewels; 28,800 vph;
46-hour power reserve
Functions: hours, minutes, subsidiary seconds;
large date; moon phase
Case: rose gold, 35.25 x 36.1 mm, height
11.74 mm; sapphire crystal; transparent case back;
water-resistant to 3 atm
Band: reptile skin, folding clasp
Price: $29,950

Vintage 1945 Lady

Reference number: 25860-D11A-221-CK7A
Movement: automatic, GP Caliber 02700-003;
ø 19.4 mm, height 4.2 mm; 26 jewels; 28,800 vph;
36-hour power reserve
Functions: hours, minutes; date
Case: stainless steel, 27.85 x 28.2 mm, height
10.2 mm; bezel set with 30 diamonds; sapphire
crystal; water-resistant to 3 atm
Band: reptile skin, buckle
Remarks: dial set with 2 diamonds
Price: $10,600

Vintage 1945 Lady

Reference number: 25860-D11A-121-CK7A
Movement: automatic, GP Caliber 02700-003;
ø 19.4 mm, height 4.2 mm; 26 jewels; 28,800 vph;
36-hour power reserve
Functions: hours, minutes; date
Case: stainless steel, 27.85 x 28.2 mm, height
10.2 mm; bezel set with 30 diamonds; sapphire
crystal; water-resistant to 3 atm
Band: reptile skin, buckle
Remarks: dial set with 2 diamonds
Price: $10,600

Chrono Hawk

Reference number: 49970-11-231-HD6A
Movement: automatic, GP Caliber 03300-0073;
ø 29 mm; 61 jewels; 28,800 vph; 46-hour power
reserve
Functions: hours, minutes, subsidiary seconds;
chronograph; date
Case: stainless steel, ø 44 mm, height 15.45 mm;
sapphire crystal; screw-in crown; water-resistant to
10 atm
Band: calf leather, folding clasp
Price: $13,800

Sea Hawk

Reference number: 49960-19-631-FK6A
Movement: automatic, GP Caliber 03300-0074;
ø 25.6 mm; 27 jewels; 28,800 vph; 46-hour power
reserve
Functions: hours, minutes, subsidiary seconds;
power reserve indicator; date
Case: stainless steel, ø 44 mm, height 17.1 mm;
unidirectional bezel with 60-minute divisions;
sapphire crystal; screw-in crown; water-resistant to
100 atm
Band: rubber, folding clasp
Price: $10,600

Traveller Large Date

Reference number: 49650-11-231-HBBA
Movement: automatic, GP Caliber 03300-0080;
ø 31 mm; 35 jewels; 28,800 vph; 46-hour power
reserve
Functions: hours, minutes, subsidiary seconds;
power reserve indicator; large date; moon phase
Case: stainless steel, ø 44 mm, height 12.1
mm; sapphire crystal; transparent case back;
water-resistant to 10 atm
Band: reptile skin, folding clasp
Price: $12,800

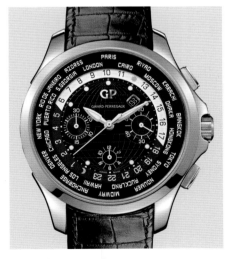

Traveller Large Date

Reference number: 49650-11-131-HBBA
Movement: automatic, GP Caliber 03300-0080;
ø 31 mm; 35 jewels; 28,800 vph; 46-hour power
reserve
Functions: hours, minutes, subsidiary seconds;
power reserve indicator; large date; moon phase
Case: stainless steel, ø 44 mm, height 12.1
mm; sapphire crystal; transparent case back;
water-resistant to 10 atm
Band: reptile skin, folding clasp
Price: $12,800

Traveller ww.tc

Reference number: 49700-11-631-BB6B
Movement: automatic, GP Caliber 03300-0084;
ø 30 mm, height 6.2 mm; 63 jewels; 28,800 vph;
46-hour power reserve
Functions: hours, minutes, subsidiary seconds;
world-time display; day/night indicator;
chronograph; date
Case: stainless steel, ø 44 mm, height 13.65 mm;
crown-adjustable inner bezel with reference city
names; sapphire crystal; transparent case back;
water-resistant to 10 atm
Band: reptile skin, folding clasp
Price: $16,000

Traveller ww.tc

Reference number: 49700-21-131-HBBB
Movement: automatic, GP Caliber 03300-0084;
ø 30 mm, height 6.2 mm; 63 jewels; 28,800 vph;
46-hour power reserve
Functions: hours, minutes, subsidiary seconds;
world-time display; day/night indicator;
chronograph; date
Case: stainless steel, ø 44 mm, height 13.65 mm;
crown-adjustable inner bezel with reference cities;
sapphire crystal; transparent case back; water-
resistant to 10 atm
Band: calf leather, folding clasp
Price: $16,000

Caliber 3200

Automatic; unidirectional rotor on ball bearings; stop-seconds; 42-hour power reserve
Functions: hours, minutes, sweep seconds or subsidiary seconds at 9 o'clock; date
Diameter: 23.3 mm
Height: 3.2 mm
Jewels: 27
Balance: glucydur
Frequency: 28,800 vph
Balance spring: flat hairspring, fine adjustment
Shock protection: Kif
Remarks: 185 components

Caliber 3300

Automatic; unidirectional rotor on ball bearings; stop-seconds; 46-hour power reserve
Functions: hours, minutes, sweep seconds or subsidiary seconds at 9 o'clock; date
Diameter: 25.6 mm
Height: 3.2 mm
Jewels: 27
Balance: glucydur
Frequency: 28,800 vph
Balance spring: flat hairspring, fine adjustment
Shock protection: Kif
Remarks: 191 components

Caliber GP3800

Manually wound; column wheel control of chronograph functions; single spring barrel, 58-hour power reserve
Functions: hours, minutes, subsidiary seconds; chronograph
Diameter: 25.6 mm
Height: 5.4 mm
Jewels: 31
Balance: Microvar with adjustable inertia
Frequency: 28,800 vph
Balance spring: flat hairspring
Shock protection: Kif
Remarks: 312 components

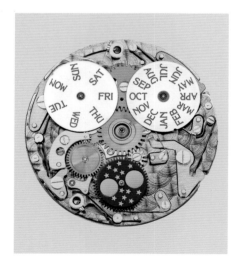

Caliber GP033M0-AL

Automatic; unidirectional rotor, stop-second system; single spring barrel, 46-hour power reserve
Functions: hours, minutes, sweep seconds; full calendar with date, weekday, month, moon phase
Diameter: 26.2 mm
Height: 4.8 mm
Jewels: 27
Balance: glucydur
Frequency: 28,800 vph
Balance spring: flat hairspring, fine adjustment
Shock protection: Kif

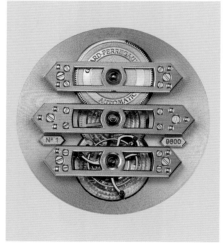

Caliber 9600

Automatic winding in both directions; 1-minute tourbillon; 48-hour power reserve
Functions: hours, minutes, small seconds (on tourbillon cage)
Diameter: 28.6 mm
Height: 6.22 mm
Jewels: 30
Frequency: 21,600 vph
Remarks: patented tourbillon construction under 3 golden bridges

Caliber GP3330-6LM00

Automatic; unidirectional rotor, stop-second system; single spring barrel, 46-hour power reserve
Functions: hours, minutes, subsidiary seconds; large date, moon phase
Measurements: 25.6 x 28.8 mm
Height: 4.9 mm
Jewels: 32
Balance: glucydur
Frequency: 28,800 vph
Balance spring: flat hairspring, fine adjustment
Shock protection: Kif

Genesis

These days, the graduating classes of watchmaking schools comprise more and more women who are passionate about precision handcrafting. Many of them have already become masters of their trade. Hamburg-based watchmaker Christine Genesis is one of these women—and her last name, the biblical term for the story of creation, can be seen as the theme of her horological activities. In addition to teaming up with designer Jorn Lund to create her own series of timelessly elegant, reliable, and affordable wristwatches in an old factory building in Hamburg's south end, Genesis, who studied at the watchmaking school of Pforzheim, also makes use of her longtime experience repairing clocks, maintaining mechanical wristwatches, and working on such larger complications as perpetual calendars. Her timepieces, however, are never overbearing. Genesis has bucked the trend toward ever larger watches and complicated dials, opting instead for uncluttered elegance, with complications subtly integrated in timepieces that are hardly ostentatious.

Genesis
Jaffestr. 6
D-21109 Hamburg
Germany

Tel.:
01149-40-414-9880-0

E-Mail:
info@genesis-uhren.de

Website:
www.genesis-uhren.de

Founded:
2005

Number of employees:
2

Annual production:
not specified

U.S. distributor:
direct sales only

Most important collections/price range:
$2,500 to $3,800
Prices may vary due to exchange
rate fluctuations.

Genesis 4

Reference number: 38.04.2
Movement: automatic, Soprod Caliber 9060 (base ETA 2892-A2); ø 25.6 mm, height 5.1 mm; 28 jewels; 28,800 vph; finely finished with perlage and côtes de Genève, engraved rotor
Functions: hours, minutes, sweep seconds; power reserve indicator; large date
Case: stainless steel, ø 38.5 mm, height 10.5 mm; sapphire crystal, transparent case back
Band: various leathers, buckle
Price: $2,980, limited to 44 pieces
Variations: light-colored dial; black DLC-coating ($3,150)

Genesis 1

Reference number: 38.01.1
Movement: automatic, Soprod Caliber 9060 (base ETA 2892-A2); ø 25.6 mm, height 5.1 mm; 26 jewels; 28,800 vph; finely finished with perlage and côtes de Genève, engraved rotor
Functions: hours, minutes, sweep seconds; power reserve indicator; weekday and date
Case: stainless steel, ø 38.5 mm, height 10.5 mm; sapphire crystal, transparent case back
Band: various leathers, buckle
Price: $2,980, limited to 44 pieces
Variations: black dial; black DLC-coating ($3,150)

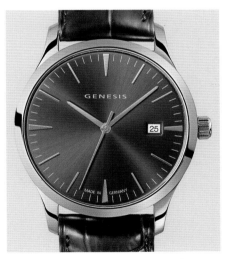

Genesis Classic

Reference number: 38.11.4
Movement: automatic, Soprod Caliber A10; ø 25.6 mm, height 3.6 mm; 25 jewels; 28,800 vph; finely finished with perlage and côtes de Genève
Functions: hours, minutes, sweep seconds; date
Case: stainless steel, ø 38.5 mm, height 9.5 mm; sapphire crystal, transparent case back
Band: various leathers, buckle
Price: $2,500, limited to 50 pieces
Variations: various dial colors

Glashütter Uhrenbetrieb GmbH
Altenberger Strasse 1
D-01768 Glashütte
Germany

Tel.:
01149-350-53-460

Fax:
01149-350-53-46-205

E-Mail:
info@glashuette-original.com

Website:
www.glashuette-original.com

Founded:
1994

Number of employees:
not specified

Annual production:
approx. 5,000 watches (estimated)

U.S. distributor:
Glashütte Original
The Swatch Group (U.S.), Inc.
1200 Harbor Boulevard
Weehawken, NJ 07087
201-271-1400

Most important collections/price range:
Senator, PanoMatic, Ladies / approx. $5,000 to
$170,000

Glashütte Original

Is there a little nostalgia creeping into the designers at Glashütte Original? Or is it just understated ecstasy for older looks? In 2012, they presented the Sixties Square Tourbillon at Baselworld, a watch definitely harkening back to an age when elegance was synonymous with simplicity. And it may be a bit of history revisited.

The Glashütte Original *manufacture* was once subsumed in the VEB Glashütter Uhrenbetriebe, a group of Glashütte watchmakers and suppliers who were collectivized as part of the former East German system. After reunification, the company took up its old moniker of Glashütte Original, and in 1995, the *manufacture* released an entirely new collection. Later, it purchased the Union Glashütte brand. In 2000, the *manufacture* was sold to the Swiss Swatch Group, which invested a sizable amount in production space expansion at Glashütte Original headquarters. All movements are designed by a team of experienced in-house engineers, while the components comprising them—with very few exceptions—such as plates, screws, pinions, wheels, levers, spring barrels, balance wheels, and tourbillon cages are manufactured in very modern production areas. These parts are lavishly finished by hand before being assembled by a group of talented watchmakers. Among the highlights of recent years was the Senator Chronometer, a large and elegant watch in a classic design. It also boasts second and minute hands that automatically jump to zero when the crown is pulled, allowing for extremely accurate time setting. And to prove that the company is not just about tradition, it has now even created a Senator-based application for smartphones.

Grande Cosmopolite Tourbillon

Reference number: 1-89-01-03-03-04
Movement: manually wound, GO Caliber 89-01; ø 39.2 mm, height 7.5 mm; 70 jewels, 2 diamond endstones; 21,600 vph; flying 1-minute tourbillon; Breguet spring, screw balance with 18 weighted screws, screw-mounted gold chatons; 72-hour power reserve
Functions: hours, minutes, subsidiary seconds (on tourbillon cage); world-time display with 37 zones, day/night indicator, power reserve indicator on back; perpetual calendar
Case: platinum, ø 48 mm, height 16 mm; sapphire crystal, transparent case back; water-resistant to 5 atm
Band: reptile skin, folding clasp
Price: on request, limited to 25 pieces

Senator Tourbillon

Reference number: 1-94-03-04-04-04
Movement: automatic, GO Caliber 94-03; ø 32.2 mm, height 7.65 mm; 50 jewels, 2 diamond endstones; 21,600 vph; flying 1-minute tourbillon; screw balance with 18 weighted screws, skeletonized rotor with gold oscillating weight; 48-hour power reserve
Functions: hours, minutes, subsidiary seconds (on tourbillon cage); date
Case: white gold, ø 42 mm, height 13.7 mm; sapphire crystal, transparent case back; water-resistant to 5 atm
Band: reptile skin, folding clasp
Price: $118,600

PanoLunarTourbillon

Reference number: 1-93-02-05-05-05
Movement: automatic, GO Caliber 93-02; ø 32.2 mm, height 7.65 mm; 48 jewels, 2 diamond endstones; 21,600 vph; flying 1-minute tourbillon; screw balance with 10 weighted screws, 8 regulation screws
Functions: hours and minutes (off-center), subsidiary seconds (on tourbillon cage); panorama date; moon phase
Case: rose gold, ø 40 mm, height 13.1 mm; sapphire crystal, transparent case back; water-resistant to 5 atm
Band: reptile skin, folding clasp
Price: $117,400
Variations: with black leather strap

PanoGraph

Reference number: 1-61-03-25-15-04
Movement: manually wound, GO Caliber 61-03;
ø-32.2 mm, height 7.2 mm; 41 jewels; 28,800 vph;
screw balance with 18 weighted screws; swan-neck
fine adjustment; hand-engraved balance bridge;
42-hour power reserve
Functions: hours, minutes, subsidiary seconds
(all off-center); flyback chronograph; 30-minute
counter; stop second; panorama date
Case: pink gold, ø 40 mm, height 13.7 mm;
sapphire crystal, transparent case back;
water-resistant to 5 atm
Band: reptile skin, folding clasp
Price: $34,500
Variations: with brown leather strap

PanoReserve

Reference number: 1-65-01-22-12-04
Movement: manually wound, GO Caliber 65-01;
ø 32.2 mm, height 6.1 mm; 48 jewels; 28,800 vph;
three-quarter plate, screw balance with 18 weighted
screws, duplex swan-neck fine adjustment, hand-
engraved balance bridge and second cock; 42-hour
power reserve
Functions: hours and minutes (off-center),
subsidiary seconds; power reserve indicator;
panorama date
Case: stainless steel, ø 40 mm, height 11.7
mm; sapphire crystal, transparent case back;
water-resistant to 5 atm
Band: reptile skin, folding clasp
Price: $11,300

PanoInverse XL

Reference number: 1-66-06-04-22-05
Movement: manually wound, GO Caliber
66-06; ø 38.3 mm, height 5.95 mm; 31 jewels;
28,800 vph; duplex swan-neck fine adjustment,
screw balance with 18 weighted screws; inverted
structure; three-quarter plate with Glashütte ribbing,
hand-engraved balance bridge; 41-hour power
reserve
Functions: hours and minutes (off-center),
subsidiary seconds; power reserve indicator
Case: stainless steel, ø 42 mm, height 12
mm; sapphire crystal, transparent case back;
water-resistant to 5 atm
Band: reptile skin, folding clasp
Price: $12,600

Senator Chronometer Regulator

Reference number: 1-58-04-04-04-04
Movement: manually wound, GO Caliber 58-04;
ø 35 mm, height 6.5 mm; 58 jewels; 28,800 vph;
Glashütte three-quarter plate, swan-neck fine
adjustment, hand-engraved balance bridge, screw
balance with 18 weighted screws; 45-hour power
reserve; DIN tested chronometer
Functions: hours (off-center), minutes, subsidiary
seconds; certified chronometer; day/night indicator
and power reserve indicator; panorama date
Case: white gold, ø 42 mm, height 12.47 mm;
sapphire crystal, transparent case back; water-
resistant to 5 atm
Band: reptile skin, folding clasp
Price: $33,300

Senator Chronometer

Reference number: 1-58-01-01-01-04
Movement: manually wound, GO Caliber 58-01;
ø 35 mm, height 6.5 mm; 58 jewels; 28,800 vph;
Glashütte three-quarter plate, second reset via
crown for precise minute setting; screw balance with
18 weighted screws, swan-neck fine adjustment;
45-hour power reserve; DIN tested chronometer
Functions: hours, minutes, subsidiary seconds;
certified chronometer; day/night and power reserve
indicator; panorama date
Case: rose gold, ø 42 mm, height 12.3 mm;
sapphire crystal, transparent case back; water-
resistant to 5 atm
Band: reptile skin, folding clasp
Price: $30,300

Senator Observer

Reference number: 100-14-05-02-05
Movement: automatic, GO Caliber 100-14;
ø 31.15 mm; height 6.5 mm; 60 jewels; 28,800 vph;
screw balance, swan-neck fine adjustment; three-
quarter plate with Glashütte ribbing, skeletonized rotor
with gold oscillating weight; 55-hour power reserve
Functions: hours, minutes, subsidiary seconds; power
reserve indicator; stop second; panorama date
Case: stainless steel, ø 44 mm, height 12 mm; sapphire
crystal, transparent case back; water-resistant to 5 atm
Band: calf leather, folding clasp
Price: $11,800
Variations: with reptile band ($11,800); with stainless
steel bracelet ($12,800)

Senator Panorama Date Moon Phase

Reference number: 100-04-32-15-04
Movement: automatic, GO Caliber 100-04; ø 31.15 mm; height 5.8 mm; 55 jewels; 28,800 vph; screw balance with 18 weighted screws, swan-neck fine adjustment; three-quarter plate with Glashütte stripe finish, skeletonized rotor with gold oscillating weight; 55-hour power reserve
Functions: hours, minutes, sweep seconds; panorama date; moon phase
Case: pink gold, ø 40 mm, height 11.52 mm; sapphire crystal, transparent case back; water-resistant to 5 atm
Band: reptile skin, folding clasp
Price: $22,800

Senator Panorama Date

Reference number: 100-03-32-42-04
Movement: automatic, GO Caliber 100-03; ø 31.15 mm, height 5.8 mm; 51 jewels; 28,800 vph; screw balance with 18 weighted screws, swan-neck fine adjustment; three-quarter plate with Glashütte stripe finish, skeletonized rotor with gold oscillating weight; 55-hour power reserve
Functions: hours, minutes, sweep seconds; panorama date
Case: stainless steel, ø 40 mm, height 11.52 mm; sapphire crystal, transparent case back; water-resistant to 5 atm
Band: reptile skin, folding clasp
Price: $9,800

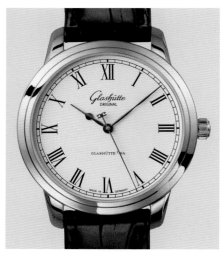

Senator Automatic

Reference number: 1-39-59-01-05-04
Movement: automatic, GO Caliber 39-59; ø 26 mm, height 4.3 mm; 25 jewels; 28,800 vph; swan-neck fine adjustment, three-quarter plate with Glashütte stripe finish, skeletonized rotor; 40-hour power reserve
Functions: hours, minutes, sweep seconds
Case: pink gold, ø 40 mm, height 9.9 mm; sapphire crystal, transparent case back; water-resistant to 5 atm
Band: reptile skin, buckle
Price: $16,000
Variations: with diamond bezel ($23,300); stainless steel ($7,000); stainless steel with diamond bezel ($14,300)

Senator Perpetual Calendar

Reference number: 100-02-25-05-04
Movement: automatic, GO Caliber 100-02; ø 31.15 mm, height 7.1 mm; 59 jewels; 28,800 vph; screw balance with 18 weighted screws, swan-neck fine adjustment; zero reset mechanism; skeletonized rotor with gold oscillating weight; 55-hour power reserve
Functions: hours, minutes, sweep seconds; perpetual calendar with panorama date, weekday, month, moon phase, leap year
Case: pink gold, ø 42 mm, height 13.6 mm; sapphire crystal, transparent case back; water-resistant to 5 atm
Band: rubber, folding clasp
Price: $36,500
Variations: stainless steel ($22,000)

Senator Diary

Reference number: 100-13-01-01-04
Movement: automatic, GO Caliber 100-13; ø 34 mm, height 8.4 mm; 86 jewels; 28,800 vph; screw balance, swan-neck fine adjustment, zero reset mechanism; three-quarter plate with Glashütte stripe finish, skeletonized rotor with gold oscillating weight; 55-hour power reserve
Functions: hours, minutes, sweep seconds; panorama date; memory function (appointment day/hour) with 80 second sonorous signal, on/off switch
Case: rose gold, ø 42 mm, height 14.4 mm; sapphire crystal, transparent case back; water-resistant to 5 atm
Band: reptile skin, folding clasp
Price: $38,000

PanoMaticCounter XL

Reference number: 1-96-01-02-02-04
Movement: automatic, GO Caliber 96-01; ø 32.2 mm, height 8.9 mm; 72 jewels; 28,800 vph; screw balance with 18 weighted screws, swan-neck fine adjustment, skeletonized rotor with gold oscillating weight; 42-hour power reserve
Functions: hours and minutes (off-center), subsidiary seconds; 2-digit counter (pusher-controlled, forward/backward); flyback chronograph; stop seconds on second dial level; panorama date
Case: stainless steel, ø 44 mm, height 16 mm; sapphire crystal, transparent case back; water-resistant to 5 atm
Band: reptile skin, folding clasp
Price: $25,100

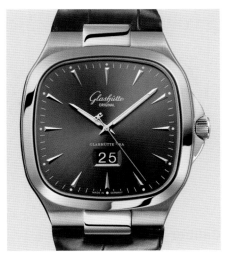

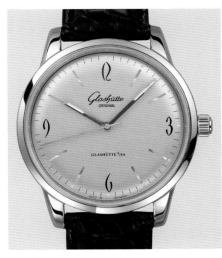

Seventies Panorama Date

Reference number: 2-39-47-12-12-04
Movement: automatic, GO Caliber 39-47;
ø 30.95 mm, height 5.9 mm; 39 jewels; 28,800
vph; swan-neck fine adjustment, three-quarter plate
with Glashütte stripe finish, skeletonized rotor with
gold oscillating weight; 40-hour power reserve
Functions: hours, minutes, sweep seconds;
panorama date
Case: stainless steel, 40 x 40 mm, sapphire
crystal, transparent case back; screw-in crown;
water-resistant to 10 atm
Band: reptile skin, folding clasp
Price: $10,100

Sixties Panorama Date

Reference number: 2-39-47-06-02-04
Movement: automatic, GO Caliber 39-47; ø 30.95
mm, height 5.9 mm; 39 jewels; 28,800 vph; swan-
neck fine adjustment, three-quarter plate with
Glashütte stripe finish, skeletonized rotor with gold
oscillating weight; 40-hour power reserve
Functions: hours, minutes, sweep seconds;
panorama date
Case: stainless steel, ø 42 mm, height 12.4 mm;
sapphire crystal, transparent case back; water-
resistant to 3 atm
Band: reptile skin, buckle
Price: $9,200
Variations: with black or silver dial ($9,200)

Sixties

Reference number: 1-39-52-01-02-04
Movement: automatic, GO Caliber 39-52; ø 26 mm,
height 4.3 mm; 25 jewels; 28,800 vph; 40-hour
power reserve
Functions: hours, minutes, sweep seconds
Case: stainless steel, ø 39 mm, height 9.4 mm;
sapphire crystal, transparent case back
Band: reptile skin, buckle
Price: $7,100
Variations: with black or blue dial ($7,100); rose
gold ($14,300)

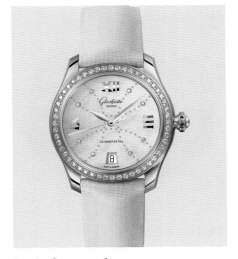

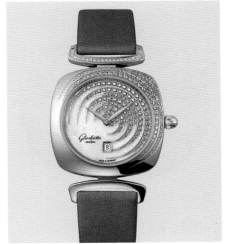

PanoMatic Luna

Reference number: 1-90-12-02-12-04
Movement: automatic, GO Caliber 90-12;
ø 32.6 mm, height 7 mm; 47 jewels; 28,800 vph;
42-hour power reserve
Functions: hours, minutes, subsidiary seconds;
panorama date; moon phase
Case: stainless steel, ø 39.4 mm, height 12 mm;
bezel set with 64 brilliant-cut diamonds; sapphire
crystal, transparent case back; water-resistant to
3 atm
Band: rubber, buckle
Price: $19,800
Variations: with reptile skin band ($19,800); with
light mother-of-pearl dial ($19,800)

Lady Serenade

Reference number: 1-39-22-12-22-44
Movement: automatic, GO Caliber 39-22; ø 26 mm,
height 4.3 mm; 25 jewels; 28,800 vph; three-quarter
plate, swan-neck fine adjustment, skeletonized rotor;
40-hour power reserve
Functions: hours, minutes, sweep seconds; date
Case: stainless steel, ø 36 mm, height 10.2 mm; bezel
set with 52 brilliant-cut diamonds; sapphire crystal,
transparent case back; water-resistant to 5 atm
Band: satin, buckle
Remarks: mother-of-pearl dial set with 8 brilliant-cut
diamonds
Price: $13,400
Variations: various straps and dials ($5,700–$22,400)

Pavonina

Reference number: 1-03-01-03-15-01
Movement: quartz
Functions: hours, minutes; date
Case: gold, 31 x 31 mm, height 7.5 mm; sapphire
crystal, water-resistant to 5 atm
Band: satin, buckle
Remarks: enamel dial with 98 diamonds; more
diamonds on strap, case, and crown
Price: $24,600
Variations: various straps and cases
($4,900–$39,600)

Caliber 39

Automatic; 40-hour power reserve
Functions: hours, minutes, sweep seconds (base caliber)
Diameter: 26.2 mm
Height: 4.3 mm
Jewels: 25
Frequency: 28,800 vph
Balance spring: flat hairspring, swan-neck fine adjustment
Shock protection: Incabloc
Related calibers: 39-55 (GMT, 40 jewels); 39-52 (automatic, 25 jewels); 39-50 (perpetual calendar, 48 jewels); 39-41/39-42 (panorama date, 44 jewels); 39-31 (chronograph, 51 jewels); 39-21/39-22 (date, 25 jewels)

Caliber 58-01

Manually wound; approx. 44-hour power reserve, second reset when crown is pulled allowing precise setting of minutes and seconds
Functions: hours (off-center), minutes (off-center), subsidiary seconds; date (retrograde); power reserve indication with planetary gear; large date
Diameter: 35 mm
Height: 6.5 mm
Jewels: 58
Balance: screw balance with 18 weighted screws
Frequency: 28,800 vph
Remarks: components finely finished, beveled edges, polished steel parts, screw-mounted gold chatons, blued screws, swan-neck fine adjustment, three-quarter plate with Glashütte ribbing, hand-engraved balance cock

Caliber 60

Manually wound; single spring barrel, 42-hour power reserve
Functions: hours, minutes, subsidiary seconds; chronograph with flyback and countdown function; acoustic signal via gong; large date
Diameter: 32.2 mm
Height: 7.2 mm
Jewels: 54
Balance: screw balance with 18 gold screws
Frequency: 28,800 vph
Balance spring: flat hairspring, swan-neck fine adjustment
Remarks: components finely finished; beveled edges, polished steel parts, screw-mounted gold chatons, blued screws, winding wheels with double sunburst decoration, bridges and cocks with Glashütte ribbing, hand-engraved balance cock

Caliber 61

Manually wound; 42-hour power reserve
Functions: hours, minutes, subsidiary seconds; chronograph with flyback function; panorama date
Diameter: 32.2 mm
Height: 7.2 mm
Jewels: 41
Balance: screw balance with 18 gold screws
Frequency: 28,800 vph
Balance spring: flat hairspring, swan-neck fine adjustment
Remarks: components finely finished, beveled edges, polished steel parts, screw-mounted gold chatons, blued screws, winding wheels with double sunburst pattern, bridges and cocks decorated with Glashütte ribbing, hand-engraved balance cock

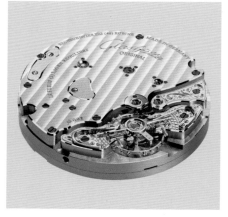

Caliber 65

Manually wound; single spring barrel, 42-hour power reserve
Functions: hours (off-center), minutes (off-center), subsidiary seconds; power reserve indication
Diameter: 32.2 mm
Height: 6.1 mm
Jewels: 48
Balance: screw balance with 18 weighted screws
Frequency: 28,800 vph
Balance spring: flat hairspring, duplex swan-neck fine adjustment (for rate and beat)
Remarks: components finely finished, beveled edges, polished steel parts, screw-mounted gold chatons, blued screws

Caliber 66

Manually wound; single barrel spring, 41-hour power reserve
Functions: hours (off-center), minutes (off-center), subsidiary seconds (off-center); power reserve indication
Diameter: 35.5 mm
Height: 5.95 mm
Jewels: 31
Balance: screw balance with 18 weighted screws
Frequency: 28,800 vph
Balance spring: flat hairspring, duplex swan-neck fine adjustment (for rate and beat)
Remarks: components finely finished, beveled edges, polished steel parts, screwed-in gold chatons, blued screws

Caliber 84-01

Manually wound; stop-second system; single spring barrel, 36-hour power reserve

Functions: hours, minutes, subsidiary seconds; quarter-hour repeater
Diameter: 43.1 mm
Height: 7.25 mm
Jewels: 44
Balance: screw balance with 18 gold weight screws
Frequency: 18,000 vph
Balance spring: Nivarox with Breguet end curve
Shock protection: Incabloc
Remarks: polished and brushed steel parts, beveled edges, blued screws, grained gold-plated three-quarter plate, hand-engraved balance cock, swan-neck fine adjustment

Caliber 90

Automatic; single spring barrel, 42-hour power reserve

Functions: hours, minutes (off-center), sweep seconds; panorama date; moon phase
Diameter: 32.6 mm
Height: 7 mm
Jewels: 41, 47, or 61
Frequency: 28,800 vph
Balance: screw balance with 18 gold screws
Balance spring: flat hairspring, duplex swan-neck fine adjustment (for rate and beat)
Shock protection: Incabloc
Remarks: components finely finished; hand-engraved balance cock; beveled edges, polished steel parts; three-quarter plate with Glashütte ribbing; off-center skeletonized rotor with 21-kt gold oscillating weight

Caliber 93-02

Automatic; flying tourbillon, single spring barrel, 48-hour power reserve

Functions: hours, minutes (off-center), subsidiary seconds (on tourbillon cage); panorama date; moon phase
Diameter: 32.2 mm
Height: 7.65 mm
Jewels: 48
Balance: screw balance with 18 weighted screws in rotating frame
Frequency: 21,600 vph
Balance spring: flat hairspring
Remarks: finely finished movement, hand-engraved balance cock, beveled edges, polished steel parts, main plate with Glashütte ribbing; oscillating, eccentric, skeletonized, 21-kt gold weight

Caliber 96-01

Automatic; twin spring barrel, 2-speed bidirectional winding via stepped reduction gear, 42-hour power reserve

Functions: hours and minutes (off-center), subsidiary seconds; 2-digit counter (pusher-controlled, forward and backward); split-seconds chronograph with flyback function; large date
Diameter: 32.2 mm; **Height:** 8.9 mm
Jewels: 72
Balance: screw balance with 18 gold weight screws
Frequency: 28,800 vph; **Shock protection:** Incabloc
Balance spring: flat hairspring, swan-neck fine adjustment
Remarks: separate wheel bridges for winding and chronograph, finely finished, beveled edges, polished steel parts, screwed-in gold chatons, blued screws, hand-engraved balance cock

Caliber 94-03

Automatic; flying tourbillon; single spring barrel, 48-hour power reserve

Functions: hours, minutes, subsidiary seconds (on tourbillon cage); panorama date
Diameter: 32.2 mm
Height: 7.65 mm
Jewels: 50
Balance: screw balance with 18 weighted screws in rotating frame
Frequency: 21,600 vph
Balance spring: flat hairspring
Remarks: finely finished movement, beveled edges, polished steel parts, main plate with Glashütte ribbing; oscillating, eccentric, skeletonized, 21-kt gold weight

Caliber 100

Automatic; skeletonized rotor; reset mechanism for second hand via button on case; 55-hour power reserve

Functions: hours, minutes, sweep seconds; panorama date
Diameter: 31.15 mm
Height: 7.1 mm
Jewels: 59
Balance: screw balance with 18 gold screws
Frequency: 28,800 vph
Balance spring: flat hairspring
Related calibers: 100-01 (power reserve display); 100-02 (perpetual calendar); 100-03 (large date); 100-04 (moon phase); 100-05 (53 weeks); 100-06 (full calendar, moon phase)

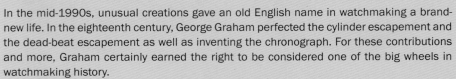

Graham
Boulevard des Eplatures 38
CH-2300 La Chaux-de-Fonds
Switzerland

Tel.:
01141-32-910-9888

Fax:
01141-32-910-9889

E-Mail:
info@graham1695.com

Website:
www.graham1695.com

Founded:
1995

Number of employees:
approx. 30

Annual production:
5,000–7,000 watches

U.S. distributor:
Graham USA
510 W. 6th Street, Suite 309
Los Angeles, CA 90014
213-622-1716

Most important collections:
Tourbillograph, Chronofighter, Silverstone,
Swordfish

Graham

In the mid-1990s, unusual creations gave an old English name in watchmaking a brand-new life. In the eighteenth century, George Graham perfected the cylinder escapement and the dead-beat escapement as well as inventing the chronograph. For these contributions and more, Graham certainly earned the right to be considered one of the big wheels in watchmaking history.

Despite his merits in the development of precision timekeeping, it was the mechanism he invented to measure short times—the chronograph—that became the trademark of his wristwatch company. To this day, the fundamental principle of the chronograph hasn't changed at all: A second set of hands can be engaged to or disengaged from the constant flow of energy of the movement. Given The British Masters' aim to honor this English inventor, it is certainly no surprise that the Graham collection includes quite a number of fascinating chronograph variations.

In 2000, the company released its Chronofighter, whose striking thumb-controlled lever mechanism—a modern twist on a function designed for WW II British fighter pilots, who couldn't activate the crown button of their flight chronographs with their thick gloves on—is a perfect example of why luxury watches are one of the male world's most beloved toys. Recently, Graham has also added comparatively conventionally designed watches to its collection. For lovers of special pieces, there are the models of the Geo.Graham series, like the Tourbillograph, created in close cooperation with the movement *manufacture* La Joux-Perret, or the boldly blue The Moon, with a stunning moon retrograde tourbillon movement.

Geo Graham "The Moon"

Reference number: 2GGAP.U01A
Movement: manually wound, Graham Caliber G 1769;
ø 32 mm, 29 jewels; 21,600 vph; flying 1-minute tourbillon; 96-hour power reserve
Functions: hours, minutes, subsidiary seconds (on tourbillon cage); moon phase
Case: rose gold, ø 46 mm; height 17 mm; bezel set with 68 diamonds; sapphire crystal; transparent case back; crown with cabochon; water-resistant to 3 atm
Band: reptile skin, buckle
Remarks: limited to 10 pieces
Price: on request

Chronofighter 1695

Reference number: 2CXAP.S03A
Movement: automatic, Graham Caliber G 1745;
ø 30 mm, height 8 mm; 25 jewels; 28,800 vph;
48-hour power reserve
Functions: hours, minutes; chronograph; date
Case: rose gold, ø 42 mm; height 15 mm; sapphire crystal; transparent case back; crown with chrono pusher and finger lever on left side; water-resistant to 5 atm
Band: reptile skin, buckle
Price: $27,990
Variations: stainless steel ($6,400)

Chronofighter Oversize Black Sahara

Reference number: 2CCAU.B02A
Movement: automatic, Graham Caliber G 1747;
ø 30 mm, height 8 mm; 25 jewels; 28,800 vph;
48-hour power reserve
Functions: hours, minutes, subsidiary seconds; chronograph; date
Case: stainless steel with black PVD coating;
ø 47 mm; height 15 mm; ceramic bezel; sapphire crystal; transparent case back; crown, pusher, and carbon finger lever on left side; water-resistant to 10 atm
Band: textile, ceramic buckle
Price: $6,900

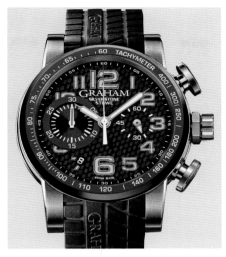

Chronofighter Oversize GMT

Reference number: 2OVGS.B26A
Movement: automatic, Graham Caliber G 1733; ø 30 mm, height 9.5 mm; 28 jewels; 28,800 vph; 48-hour power reserve
Functions: hours, minutes, subsidiary seconds; additional 24-hour display (second time zone); chronograph; large date
Case: stainless steel, ø 47 mm; height 17 mm; bezel with 24-hour divisions, sapphire crystal; transparent case back; crown and pusher with finger lever on left side; water-resistant to 10 atm
Band: reptile skin, buckle
Price: $9,980

Silverstone Stowe 44

Reference number: 2SAAC.B04A
Movement: automatic, Graham Caliber G 1702; ø 28.6 mm, height 6 mm; 59 jewels; 28,800 vph; 40-hour power reserve
Functions: hours, minutes, subsidiary seconds; chronograph; date
Case: stainless steel, ø 44 mm; height 16 mm; ceramic bezel; sapphire crystal; transparent case back; screw-in crown; water-resistant to 10 atm
Band: rubber, buckle
Price: $7,600

Silverstone Stowe GMT

Reference number: 2BLCH.B33A
Movement: automatic, Graham Caliber G 1721; ø 30.05 mm, height 8.75 mm; 28 jewels; 28,800 vph; 48-hour power reserve
Functions: hours, minutes, subsidiary seconds; additional 24-hour display (second time zone); flyback chronograph; large date
Case: stainless steel, ø 48 mm, height 16 mm; carbon bezel with 24-hour divisions, sapphire crystal; transparent case back; screw-in crown; water-resistant to 10 atm
Band: rubber, buckle
Remarks: limited to 500 pieces
Price: $9,980

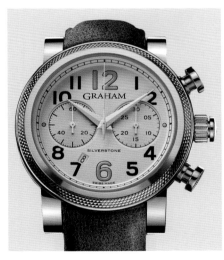

Silverstone Vintage 30

Reference number: 2BLFS.W06A
Movement: automatic, Graham Caliber G 1734; ø 30 mm, height 8.75 mm; 27 jewels; 28,800 vph; 48-hour power reserve
Functions: hours, minutes, subsidiary seconds; chronograph; date
Case: stainless steel, ø 47 mm, height 16 mm; bezel with clous de Paris decoration, sapphire crystal; transparent case back; screw-in crown; water-resistant to 10 atm
Band: calf leather, buckle
Price: $7,995
Variations: black dial ($7,995)

Prodive

Reference number: 2CDAV.U01A
Movement: automatic, Graham Caliber G 1750; ø 37 mm, 25 jewels; 28,800 vph; 48-hour power reserve
Functions: hours, minutes, subsidiary seconds; chronograph; date
Case: stainless steel, ø 45 mm, height 19 mm; unidirectional bezel with PVD coating, 60-minute divisions; sapphire crystal; crown and pusher with finger lever on left side; helium valve; water-resistant to 60 atm
Band: rubber, folding clasp
Remarks: screw-in crown with bayonet catch
Price: $13,400
Variations: with black dial and strap

Chronofighter Prodive Professional

Reference number: 2CDAV.B01A
Movement: automatic, Graham Caliber G 1750; ø 30 mm, height 8.75 mm; 28 jewels; 28,800 vph; 48-hour power reserve
Functions: hours, minutes, subsidiary seconds; chronograph; date
Case: stainless steel, ø 45 mm, height 17 mm; unidirectional bezel with PVD coating, 60-minute divisions; sapphire crystal; crown with chrono pusher and finger lever on left side; helium valve; water-resistant to 60 atm
Band: rubber, ceramic buckle
Price: $15,750, limited to 200 pieces

Greubel Forsey SA
Eplatures-Grise 16
CH-2301 La Chaux-de-Fonds
Switzerland

Tel.:
01141-32-925-4545

Fax:
01141-32-925-4500

E-Mail:
info@greubelforsey.com

Website:
www.greubelforsey.com

Founded:
2004

Number of employees:
approx. 75

Annual production:
approx. 100 watches

U.S. distributor:
Time Art Distribution
550 Fifth Avenue
New York, NY 10036
212-221-5842
info@timeartdistribution.com

Greubel Forsey

In 2004, when Alsatian Robert Greubel and Englishman Stephen Forsey presented a new movement at Baselworld, eyes snapped open: Their watch featured not one, but *two* tourbillon carriages working at a 30° incline. In their design, Forsey and Greubel not only took up the basic Abraham-Louis Breguet idea of cancelling out the deviations of the balance by the continuous rotation of the tourbillon cage, but they went further, creating a quadruple tourbillon.

Greubel Forsey's success as an independent brand, even in more difficult economic times, has been remarkable. In 2010, they moved into new facilities spread over a beautifully renovated farmhouse between Le Locle and La Chaux-de-Fonds and a brand-new modern building that seems to grow out of that horologically rich soil. After capturing an "Aiguille D'Or" for the magical Double Tourbillon 30° and the Grand Prix d'Horlogerie in Geneva, these two tourbillon specialists snatched up the top prize at the International Chronometry Competition in Le Locle for their Double Tourbillon 30°.

Greubel and Forsey continue to stun the highest-end fans with some spectacular pieces, like the Quadruple Tourbillon Secret, which shows the complex play of the tourbillons through the case back, and the Greubel Forsey GMT with the names of world cities and a huge floating globe. Nothing seems impossible to these two tourbillonists. Their first Art Piece came out in 2013, a most natural collaboration with British miniaturist Willard Wigan, who can sculpt the head of a pin. The special technical challenge for Greubel and Forsey: integrating a 20x magnifier into the watch.

GMT

Reference number: 9100 1776
Movement: manually wound, Caliber GF 05; ø 36.4 mm, height 9.8 mm; 50 jewels; 21,600 vph; 24-second tourbillon cage with variable inertia balance at 25°; 2 coaxial series-coupled barrels; 72-hour power reserve
Functions: hours, minutes, subsidiary seconds; additional 12-hour and 24-hour time zone world-time display; day/night indicator; summer/winter daylight savings time; power reserve indicator
Case: pink gold, ø 43.5 mm, height 16.14 mm; sapphire crystal; transparent case back; water-resistant to 3 atm
Band: reptile skin, folding clasp
Price: $595,000

Double Tourbillon Technique Black

Reference number: 9100 2926
Movement: manually wound, Caliber GF 02s; ø 38.4 mm; height 12.15 mm; 43 jewels; 21,600 vph; variable inertia balance; 4-minute tourbillon with inner 1-minute tourbillon inclined at 30°; 4 coaxial series-coupled spring barrels; 120-hour power reserve
Functions: hours, minutes, subsidiary seconds; 4-minute indication on large tourbillon; power reserve indicator
Case: titanium with black ADLC coating, ø 47.5 mm, height 16.84 mm; sapphire crystal, transparent back
Band: sewn rubber strap, folding clasp
Price: $545,000

Quadruple Tourbillon Secret

Reference number: 9100 0328
Movement: manually wound, Caliber GF 03j; ø 36.4 mm, height 9.85 mm; 63 jewels; 21,600 vph; variable inertia balance; 2 double tourbillon cages each with 4-minute and 30° inclined 1-minute tourbillon linked to spherical differential; 2 spring barrels; 50-hour power reserve
Functions: hours, minutes, subsidiary seconds; power reserve indicator
Case: pink gold, ø 43.5 mm, height 16.11 mm; sapphire crystal; transparent case back; water-resistant to 3 atm
Band: reptile skin, folding clasp
Remarks: 4-minute tourbillon indicator on dial
Price: $830,000, limited edition of 8 pieces

Grieb & Benzinger

Grieb & Benzinger
Schloss Dätzingen
D-71120 Grafenau
Germany

Tel.:
01149-7231-983-000

E-Mail:
georg@grieb-benzinger.de

Website:
www.grieb-benzinger.de

Founded:
2006

Number of employees:
5

Annual production:
max. 10 platinum and 20 gold watches

U.S. distributor:
Grieb & Benzinger of North America
103 Carnegie Center, Ste. 300
Princeton, NJ 08540
kraft@griebbenzinger.com

The watch brand Grieb & Benzinger combines the talents of watchmaker Hermann Grieb, engraver and guillocheur Jochen Benzinger, and designer Georg Bartkowiak. In Grieb's small workshop in one of the annex buildings of Dätzingen Castle near Stuttgart, watches are built the way they used to be, namely with a great deal of craftsmanship. Complicated and filigree one-of-a-kind pieces are produced using restored vintage pocket watch movements from the Swiss *manufactures* of the nineteenth and early twentieth century. The work, however, certainly goes well above and beyond pure restoration and often involves elaborate alterations and, of course, ornate and stunning finishing work. Specialist Benzinger contributes his talent to the guilloché decoration, engraving, and skeletonizing of the watches. He is also skilled in working with blue platinum, a precious material that, within the industry, is exclusively used by Grieb & Benzinger.

The most recent collection has the rather famous name Shades of Grey. The trio has produced a series of complex timepieces in white gold and using many different shades of rhodium to achieve their exciting exploration of a color that otherwise expresses blandness. Because a maximum of thirty watches a year hardly requires a distribution network, Grieb, Benzinger, and Bartkowiak work with their discriminating customers for the most part directly, individually, and personally.

Blue Whirlwind

Reference number: Blue Whirlwind
Movement: manually wound, base Patek Philippe Caliber R TO 27 PS; 18,000 vph; 1-minute tourbillon, fully skeletonized, engraved, and guillochéed, mysterious drive wheel for the tourbillon
Functions: hours, minutes, subsidiary seconds (on tourbillon cage); minute repeater
Case: platinum, ø 43 mm; sapphire crystal; transparent case back
Band: reptile skin, platinum buckle
Price: $850,000

Blue Danube

Reference number: Blue Danube
Movement: manually wound, base caliber by Patek Philippe; 18,000 vph; historic movement, fully skeletonized and engraved by hand, and guillochéed
Functions: hours, minutes; minute repeater; split-seconds chronograph
Case: platinum, ø 43 mm; sapphire crystal; transparent case back
Band: reptile skin, platinum buckle
Price: $450,000

Blue Danube (case back side)

Even as a basic movement, this rare, complicated pocket watch movement with a minute repeater and a split-seconds chronograph is a beauty. It was built 120 years ago. The renovated movement is an impressive example of the complex and painstaking art of guilloché, hand-skeletonizing, and modification of plates and bridges. Each of the 400 components were reworked; some were entirely rebuilt.

H. Moser & Cie.

Rundbuckstrasse 10
CH-8212 Neuhausen am Rheinfall
Switzerland

Tel.:
01141-52-674-0050

Fax:
01141-52-674-0055

E-Mail:
info@h-moser.com

Website:
www.h-moser.com

Founded:
2002

Number of employees:
70

Annual production:
approx. 1,000 watches

U.S. distributor:
H. Moser & Cie.
Milestone Distribution
297 Dividend Drive, Suite B
Peachtree City, GA 30269
678-827-7900, www.h-moser.com

Most important collections/price range:
Mayu / approx. $11,500 to $26,000; Monard /
approx. $15,000 to $25,500; Henry / approx.
$18,000 to $26,000; Perpetual 1 / approx.
$33,000 to $43,000; Perpetual Moon / approx.
$34,500 to $43,000

H. Moser & Cie.

H. Moser & Cie. is not a new name in the watch industry: In Schaffhausen between 1820 and 1824 Heinrich Moser had learned watchmaking from his father, who, like his grandfather, fulfilled the role of "city watchmaker." After his apprenticeship, Moser went to Le Locle, one of Switzerland's horological hubs in the western Jura mountains and, in 1825, founded his own company at twenty-one. Soon after, he moved to Saint Petersburg, where, at that time, ambitious watchmakers enjoyed a good market for their businesses. In 1828, H. Moser & Cie. was brought to life—a brand resuscitated in modern times by a group of investors and watch experts together with Moser's great-grandson, Roger Nicholas Balsiger.

Under the technical leadership of Dr. Jürgen Lange, H. Moser & Cie. has focused on the fundamentals. The company has made movements that contain a separate, removable escapement module supporting the pallet lever, escape wheel, and balance. The latter is fitted with the Straumann spring, made by Precision Engineering, another one of the Moser Group companies—in the case of the Henry Double Hairspring watch, of course, the balance has two Straumann springs.

This small company has considerable technical know-how, which is probably what attracted MELB Holding, owners of Hautlence. Edouard Meylan became CEO of the brand in May 2013 and aims to refresh it and maybe even lower the prices.

Monard

Reference number: 343.505-010
Movement: manually wound, Moser Caliber HMC 343; ø 34 mm, height 5.8 mm; 28 jewels; 18,000 vph; exchangeable escape with Straumann double balance spring; 168-hour power reserve
Functions: hours, minutes, sweep seconds; power reserve indicator (on movement side)
Case: white gold, ø 40.8 mm, height 10.85 mm; sapphire crystal, transparent case back
Band: reptile skin, white gold buckle
Price: $24,400
Variations: rose gold ($24,400)

Monard Date

Reference number: 342.502-002
Movement: manually wound, Moser Caliber HMC 342; ø 34 mm, height 5.8 mm; 28 jewels; 18,000 vph; exchangeable escape with Straumann double balance spring; 168-hour power reserve
Functions: hours, minutes, sweep seconds; power reserve indicator (on movement side); large date
Case: white gold, ø 40.8 mm, height 10.85 mm; sapphire crystal, transparent case back
Band: reptile skin, white gold buckle
Price: $31,000
Variations: rose gold ($31,000)

Nomad Dual Time

Reference number: 346.133-005
Movement: automatic, Moser Caliber HMC 346; ø 34 mm, height 6.5 mm; 29 jewels; 18,000 vph; exchangeable escape with Straumann double balance spring, gold oscillating mass; 72-hour power reserve
Functions: hours, minutes, subsidiary seconds; additional 12-hour display (second time zone), day/night indicator
Case: rose gold, ø 40.8 mm, height 10.97 mm; sapphire crystal, transparent case back
Band: reptile skin, rose gold buckle
Price: $36,500
Variations: platinum ($47,500)

Perpetual 1

Reference number: 341.501-022
Movement: manually wound, Moser Caliber
HMC 341; ø 34 mm, height 5.8 mm; 28 jewels;
18,000 vph; exchangeable escape with Straumann
double balance spring, "flash calendar" adjustable
forward/backward; 168-hour power reserve
Functions: hours, minutes, subsidiary seconds;
power reserve indicator; perpetual calendar with
large date, small month display in middle; leap year
display (movement side)
Case: rose gold, ø 40.8 mm, height 11.05 mm;
sapphire crystal, transparent case back
Band: reptile skin, rose gold buckle
Price: $60,000

Perpetual Moon

Reference number: 348.901-015
Movement: manually wound, Moser Caliber HMC 348;
ø 34 mm, height 5.8 mm; 26 jewels; 18,000 vph;
exchangeable escape with Straumann double balance
spring; gold pallet fork and escapement wheel; 2 spring
barrels; 168-hour power reserve
Functions: hours, minutes, sweep seconds; power
reserve indicator (on movement side); perpetual moon
phase
Case: platinum, ø 40.8 mm, height 11.05 mm; sapphire
crystal, transparent case back; water-resistant to 3 atm
Band: reptile skin, platinum folding clasp
Price: $56,700
Variations: rose gold ($41,500)

Mayu

Reference number: 321.503-021
Movement: manually wound, Moser Caliber
HMC 321; ø 32 mm, height 4.8 mm; 26 jewels;
18,000 vph; exchangeable escape with Straumann
double balance spring; hardened gold pallet fork
and escapement wheel; 72-hour power reserve
Functions: hours, minutes, subsidiary seconds;
power reserve indicator (on movement side)
Case: pink gold, ø 38.8 mm, height 9.3 mm;
sapphire crystal, transparent case back
Band: reptile skin, rose gold buckle
Price: $18,300
Variations: white gold ($18,300)

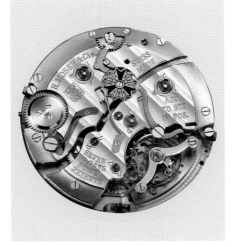

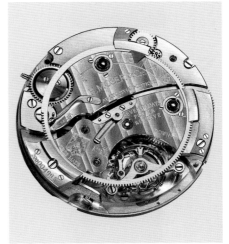

Caliber HMC 346.121

Manually wound; exchangeable escape with beveled
wheels, pallet fork, and escapement wheel of hardened
gold; double spring barrel, 72-hour power reserve
Functions: hours, minutes, subsidiary seconds; second
time zone (additional 12-hour display), a.m./p.m.
display on disc
Diameter: 34 mm
Height: 5.8 mm
Jewels: 29
Balance: glucydur with white gold screws
Frequency: 18,000 vph
Balance spring: Straumann with Breguet terminal curve
Shock protection: Incabloc
Remarks: double-pull crown mechanism for easy
switching of crown position

Caliber HMC 341

Manually wound; exchangeable escape with beveled
wheels, hardened gold pallet fork and escapement
wheel; screw mounted gold chatons; twin spring barrels,
168-hour power reserve
Functions: hours, minutes, subsidiary seconds; power
reserve indicator; perpetual calendar, perpetual calendar
with large date, small month display in middle; leap year
display (movement side)
Diameter: 34 mm; **Height:** 5.8 mm
Jewels: 28; **Balance:** glucydur with white gold screws
Frequency: 18,000 vph
Balance spring: Straumann; **Shock protection:** Incabloc
Remarks: date adjustable forward and backward;
"double-pull crown mechanism" for switching between
crown positions

Caliber HMC 348.901

Manually wound; exchangeable escape with beveled
wheels, pallet fork, and escapement wheel of hardened
gold; double spring barrel, 7-day power reserve
Functions: hours, minutes, sweep seconds; perpetual
moon phase display; power reserve indicator on case
back
Diameter: 34 mm; **Height:** 5.8 mm
Jewels: 26
Balance: glucydur with white gold weighted screws
Frequency: 18,000 vph
Balance spring: Straumann
Shock protection: Incabloc
Remarks: double-pull crown mechanism for easy
switching of crown position

Habring Uhrentechnik OG
Hauptplatz 16
A-9100 Völkermarkt
Austria

Tel.:
01143-4232-51-300

Fax:
01143-4232-51-300-4

E-Mail:
habring@aon.at

Website:
www.habring2.com; www.habring.com

Founded:
1997

Number of employees:
4

Annual production:
100 watches

U.S. distributors:
Martin Pulli (USA-East)
215-508-4610
www.martinpulli.com

Passion Fine Jewelry (USA-West)
858-794-8000
www.passionfinejewelry.com

Most important collections/price range:
Time Only / from $3,850; Jumping Second / from
$5,250; Doppel 3 / from $9,150; Chrono COS /
from $7,850

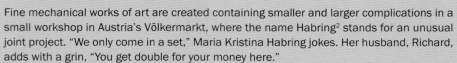

Habring²

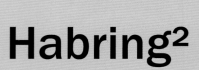

Fine mechanical works of art are created containing smaller and larger complications in a small workshop in Austria's Völkermarkt, where the name Habring² stands for an unusual joint project. "We only come in a set," Maria Kristina Habring jokes. Her husband, Richard, adds with a grin, "You get double for your money here."

In 2004, after four years of preparation, the couple's first watch labeled with their own name was finally ready: a simple, congenial three-handed watch based on a refined and unostentatiously decorated ETA pocket watch movement, the Unitas 6498-1. However, in connoisseur circles the news spread like wildfire that exceptional quality down to the smallest detail was to be found hidden behind the inconspicuous specifications.

Since then, they have put their efforts into such projects as completely revamping the Time Only, which is powered by a brand-new base movement, Caliber A09. All the little details that differentiate the movement are either especially commissioned or are made in-house. This is also the case with the components of the Seconde Foudroyante. Because the drive needs a lot of energy, the foudroyante mechanism has been given its own spring barrel. In the Caliber A07F, the eighth of a second is driven by a gear train that is directly coupled with the movement, and that without surrendering any of its reliability, power reserve, or amplitude.

For the twentieth anniversary of the IWC double chronograph, Habring² is building a limited, improved edition. The movement, based on the ETA 7750 "Valjoux," was built in 1991/1992 with an additional module level between the chronograph and the automatic winder. Richard was working as a designer at IWC back then, and so he decided to iron out some of the kinks in the mechanism. The new bridges, for example, make servicing the watch easier, and the hand-winding mechanism helps highlight the rattrapante.

Doppel 3

Reference number: Doppel 3
Movement: manually wound, Caliber A08MR-MONO; ø 30 mm, height 8.4 mm; 23 jewels; 28,800 vph; Triovis fine adjustment, 48-hour power reserve
Functions: hours, minutes, subsidiary seconds; split-seconds chronograph
Case: stainless steel, ø 42 mm, height 13 mm; sapphire crystal, transparent case back; water-resistant to 5 atm
Band: leather, buckle
Remarks: limited to 20 pieces
Price: $9,150
Variations: various dial designs

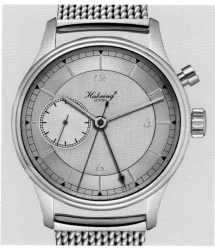

Chrono ZM

Reference number: Chrono ZM
Movement: manually wound, Caliber A08MZM-MONO; ø 30 mm, height 7 mm; 17 jewels; 28,800 vph; Triovis fine adjustment, central minute totalizer
Functions: hours, minutes, subsidiary seconds; chronograph
Case: stainless steel, ø 42 mm, height 13 mm; sapphire crystal, transparent case back; water-resistant to 5 atm
Band: stainless steel Milanese mesh, buckle
Price: $6,150

Chrono COS ZM

Reference number: Chrono COS ZM
Movement: manually wound, Caliber A08MCOSZM; ø 30 mm, height 7.0 mm; 17 jewels; 28,800 vph; Triovis fine adjustment; central minute totalizer; crown control of chronograph functions ("Crown Operation System")
Functions: hours, minutes, sweep seconds; chronograph
Case: stainless steel, ø 42 mm, height 13 mm; sapphire crystal; transparent case back; water-resistant to 5 atm
Band: calf leather, buckle
Price: $8,450
Variations: titanium ($9,850); various dial options

Chrono ZM 36 mm

Reference number: Chrono ZM 36 mm
Movement: manually wound, Caliber A08MZM-MONO; ø 30 mm, height 7 mm; 17 jewels; 28,800 vph; Triovis fine adjustment; central minute totalizer
Functions: hours, minutes, sweep seconds; chronograph
Case: stainless steel, ø 36 mm, height 12 mm; sapphire crystal, transparent case back; water-resistant to 5 atm
Band: leather, buckle
Price: $5,750

Time Date 36 mm

Reference number: Time Date 36 mm
Movement: manually wound, Caliber A09MD; ø 30 mm, height 6.25 mm; 17 jewels; 28,800 vph; Triovis fine adjustment
Functions: hours, minutes, subsidiary seconds; date
Case: stainless steel, ø 36 mm, height 12 mm; sapphire crystal, transparent case back; water-resistant to 5 atm
Band: leather, buckle
Price: $4,750
Variations: various dials

Time Only 36 mm

Reference number: Time Only
Movement: manually wound, Caliber A09M; ø 30 mm, height 6.25 mm; 17 jewels; 28,800 vph; Triovis fine adjustment
Functions: hours, minutes, subsidiary seconds
Case: stainless steel, ø 36 mm, height 12 mm; sapphire crystal, transparent case back; water-resistant to 5 atm
Band: leather, buckle
Price: $3,850
Variations: various dials

Jumping Second Pilot

Reference number: Jumping Second
Movement: manually wound, Caliber A09MS; ø 36.6 mm, height 7 mm; 20 jewels; 28,800 vph; Triovis fine adjustment
Functions: hours, minutes, dead beat seconds
Case: stainless steel, ø 42 mm, height 13 mm; sapphire crystal; transparent case back; water-resistant to 5 atm
Band: calf leather, buckle
Price: $5,250
Variations: various dials

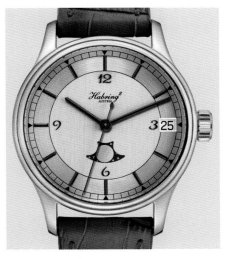

Jumping Second Moon

Reference number: Jumping Second Moon
Movement: automatic, Caliber A09SL; ø 30 mm, height 7.9 mm; 24 jewels; 28,800 vph; Triovis fine adjustment
Functions: hours, minutes, dead beat seconds; moon phase
Case: stainless steel, ø 42 mm, height 12.5 mm; sapphire crystal, transparent case back; water-resistant to 5 atm
Band: leather, buckle
Price: $7,150

Foudroyante

Reference number: Foudroyante
Movement: manually wound, Caliber A09MF; ø 30 mm, height 7 mm; 24 jewels; 28,800 vph; Triovis fine adjustment
Functions: hours, minutes, dead beat seconds, eighth of a second display (flashing second or foudroyante)
Case: stainless steel, ø 42 mm, height 13 mm; sapphire crystal, transparent case back; water-resistant to 5 atm
Band: leather, buckle
Price: $6,550
Variations: as automatic ($7,150); various dials

Hamilton International Ltd.
Längfeldweg 119
CH-2504 Biel/Bienne
Switzerland

Tel.:
01141-32-343-3860

Fax:
01141-32-343-3861

Website:
www.hamiltonwatch.com

Founded:
1892

Number of employees:
approx. 80

Annual production:
not specified

U.S. distributor:
Hamilton
The Swatch Group, Inc.
1200 Harbor Boulevard
Weehawken, NJ 07087
201-271-1400
www.hamilton-watch.com

Price range:
between approx. $500 and $2,200

Hamilton

The Hamilton Watch Co. was founded in 1892 in Lancaster, Pennsylvania and, within a very brief period, grew into one of the world's largest *manufactures*. Around the turn of the twentieth century, every second railway employee in the United States was carrying a Hamilton watch in his pocket, not only to make sure the trains were running punctually, but also to assist in coordinating them and organizing schedules. And during World War II, the American army officers' kits included a service Hamilton.

Hamilton is the sole survivor of the large U.S. watchmakers—if only as a brand within the Swiss Swatch Group. At one time, Hamilton had itself owned a piece of the Swiss watchmaking industry in the form of the Büren brand in the 1960s and 1970s. As part of a joint venture with Heuer-Leonidas, Breitling, and Dubois Dépraz, Hamilton-Büren also made a significant contribution to the development of the automatic chronograph. Just prior in its history, the tuning fork watch pioneer was all the rage when it took the new movement technology and housed it in a modern case created by renowned industrial designer Richard Arbib. The triangular Ventura hit the watch-world ground running in 1957, in what was truly a frenzy of innovation. The American spirit of freedom and belief in progress this model embodies, something evoked in Hamilton's current marketing, are taken quite seriously by its designers—even those working in Biel, Switzerland. There, they probably all have Ventura screensavers on their computers to remind them that sometimes you have to venture something to gain.

Jazzmaster Spirit of Liberty

Reference number: H32416581
Movement: automatic, Hamilton Caliber H-21 (base ETA 7750); ø 30 mm, height 7.9 mm; 25 jewels; 28,800 vph; 60-hour power reserve
Functions: hours, minutes, chronograph; date
Case: stainless steel, ø 42 mm, height 14.75 mm; sapphire crystal, transparent case back; water-resistant to 5 atm
Band: calf leather, folding clasp
Price: $1,845

Jazzmaster Auto Chrono

Reference number: H32596741
Movement: automatic, Hamilton Caliber H-21 (base ETA 7750); ø 30 mm, height 7.9 mm; 25 jewels; 28,800 vph; 42-hour power reserve
Functions: hours, minutes, subsidiary seconds; chronograph; date
Case: stainless steel, ø 42 mm, height 15.23 mm; sapphire crystal, transparent case back; water-resistant to 10 atm
Band: calf leather, folding clasp
Price: $1,795

Jazzmaster GMT

Reference number: H32605551
Movement: automatic, ETA Caliber 2893-1; ø 25.6 mm, height 4.1 mm; 21 jewels; 28,800 vph; 38-hour power reserve
Functions: hours, minutes, sweep seconds; additional 24-hour display (second time zone); date
Case: stainless steel, ø 42 mm, height 11.45 mm; bezel activated 24-hour inner ring and world-time reference cities; sapphire crystal, water-resistant to 5 atm
Band: calf leather, buckle
Price: $1,275

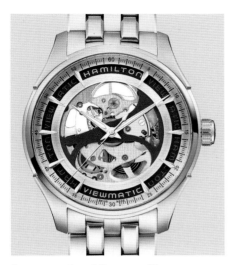

Jazzmaster Viewmatic Skeleton Gents

Reference number: H42555151
Movement: automatic, Hamilton Caliber H-20-S (base ETA 2824-2); ø 25.6 mm, height 4.6 mm; 25 jewels; 28,800 vph; skeletonized; 38-hour power reserve
Functions: hours, minutes, sweep seconds
Case: stainless steel, ø 40 mm, height 11 mm; sapphire crystal, transparent case back; water-resistant to 5 atm
Band: stainless steel, folding clasp
Price: $1,245

Jazzmaster Regulator

Reference number: H42615553
Movement: automatic, Hamilton Caliber H-12 (base ETA 2824-2); ø 25.6 mm, height 4.6 mm; 25 jewels; 28,800 vph; 38-hour power reserve
Functions: hours (off-center), minutes, subsidiary seconds
Case: stainless steel, ø 42 mm, height 13.13 mm; sapphire crystal, transparent case back; water-resistant to 5 atm
Band: calf leather, folding clasp
Price: $1,275

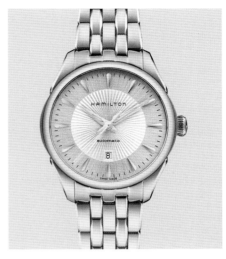

Jazzmaster Lady Auto

Reference number: H42245151
Movement: automatic, ETA Caliber 2671; ø 17.2 mm, height 4.8 mm; 25 jewels; 28,800 vph; 38-hour power reserve
Functions: hours, minutes, sweep seconds; date
Case: stainless steel with rose gold-colored PVD coating, ø 30 mm, height 10.49 mm; sapphire crystal, transparent case back; water-resistant to 5 atm
Band: stainless steel with rose gold-colored PVD coating, folding clasp
Price: $995

Khaki Pilot Pioneer Auto Chrono

Reference number: H76456435
Movement: automatic, Hamilton Caliber H-31 (base ETA 7753); ø 30 mm, height 7.9 mm; 27 jewels; 28,800 vph; 60-hour power reserve
Functions: hours, minutes, subsidiary seconds; chronograph; date
Case: stainless steel, ø 41 mm, height 16 mm; sapphire crystal, transparent case back; water-resistant to 10 atm
Band: textile, folding clasp
Price: $1,845

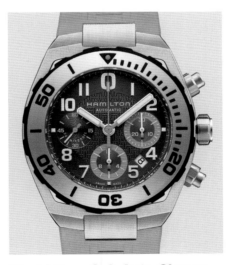

Khaki Navy Sub Auto Chrono

Reference number: H78716983
Movement: automatic, Hamilton Caliber H-31 (base ETA 7753); ø 30 mm, height 7.9 mm; 27 jewels; 28,800 vph; 60-hour power reserve
Functions: hours, minutes, subsidiary seconds; chronograph; date
Case: stainless steel, ø 43 mm, height 16.5 mm; unidirectional bezel with 60-minute divisions; sapphire crystal, screw-in crown and pushers; water-resistant to 30 atm
Band: rubber, folding clasp
Price: $1,995

Khaki Aviation Auto

Reference number: H76665835
Movement: automatic, ETA Caliber 2824-2; ø 25.6 mm, height 4.6 mm; 25 jewels; 28,800 vph; 38-hour power reserve
Functions: hours, minutes, sweep seconds; date
Case: stainless steel, ø 42 mm, height 11.5 mm; sapphire crystal, water-resistant to 5 atm
Band: calf leather, buckle
Price: $795

Hanhart AG
Hauptstrasse 17
CH-8253 Diessenhofen
Switzerland

Tel.:
01141-52-646-20-40

Fax:
01141-52-646-20-41

E-Mail:
info@hanhart.com

Website:
www.hanhart.com

Founded:
1882 in Diessenhofen, Switzerland; *manufacture* in Gütenbach, Germany

Number of employees:
35 in Gütenbach, 5 in Diessenhofen

Annual production:
approx. 150,000 stopwatches and 2,500 chronographs

U.S. distributor:
ABS Distributors
22600 Savi Ranch Parkway, Suite 274
Yorba Linda, CA 92887
714-809-0548
tony@asiragusa.com

Most important collections/price range:
ClassicTimer / from approx. $600; Pioneer / from approx. $3,800; Primus / from approx. $6,600

Hanhart

In 2012, Hanhart celebrated its 130th anniversary. But its reputation really goes back to the twenties and thirties. At the time, the brand manufactured affordable and robust stopwatches, pocket watches, and chronograph wristwatches. These core timepieces were what the fans of instrument watches wanted, and so they were thrilled as the company slowly abandoned its quartz dabbling of the eighties and reset its sights on the brand's rich and honorable tradition. A new collection was in the wings, raising expectations of great things to come. Support by the shareholding Gaydoul Group provided the financial backbone to get things moving.

The first step was to move company headquarters to the Swiss town of Diessenhofen, leaving the factory and technical offices in the Black Forest town of Gütenbach, Germany. The company's motto has thus become "German engineering, Swiss made," and its goal is expanding exports into new key markets using three solid collections: two chronographs, the Pioneer and Primus, and the ClassicTimer stopwatches.

In spite of effort and money, however, the brand has encountered some leadership difficulties. In 2012, it picked up former Carl F. Bucherer CEO Thomas Morf, who had big ideas for making Hanhart a famous brand. His ideas, apparently, did not pass muster, and in 2013 he was replaced by another old hand in the watch business, Jan Endöcs, who seems to be steering the company back to its roots. The characteristic red start/stop pusher will continue gracing the new collections and providing the color for the brand's corporate identity.

Pioneer Stealth 1882

Reference number: 735.510-001
Movement: automatic, Caliber HAN 4312 (based on Sellita SW500, modified with modules); ø 30 mm, height 7.9 mm; 34 jewels; 28,800 vph; rotor with skeletonized Hanhart logo; 42-hour power reserve
Functions: hours, minutes, subsidiary seconds; flyback chronograph
Case: stainless steel, with black DLC coating, ø 45 mm, height 16 mm; bidirectional bezel with reference marker; sapphire crystal; water-resistant to 10 atm
Band: calf leather, buckle
Price: $10,500, limited to 130 pieces
Variations: with smooth bezel ($10,300)

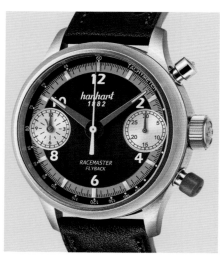

Pioneer Racemaster GTF

Reference number: 738.630-001
Movement: automatic, Caliber HAN4312 (base Sellita SW500); ø 30 mm, height 7.9 mm; 34 jewels; 28,800 vph; 42-hour power reserve
Functions: hours, minutes, subsidiary seconds; flyback chronograph
Case: stainless steel, ø 45 mm, height 16 mm; sapphire crystal, water-resistant to 10 atm
Band: calf leather, buckle
Price: $9,900

Pioneer TwinDicator

Reference number: 730.210-011
Movement: automatic, Caliber HAN 4011 (based on ETA 7750, modified with modules); ø 30 mm, height 7.9 mm; 35 jewels; 28,800 vph; rotor with skeletonized Hanhart logo; 42-hour power reserve
Functions: hours, minutes, subsidiary seconds; chronograph
Case: stainless steel, ø 45 mm, height 16 mm; sapphire crystal; water-resistant to 10 atm
Band: calf leather, buckle
Remarks: asymmetrically positioned pushers
Price: $7,750
Variations: with white dial and rotating bezel ($7,950)

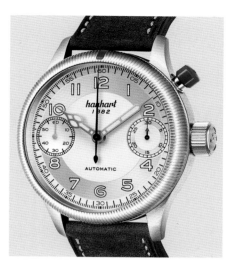

Pioneer MonoScope

Reference number: 733.220-011
Movement: automatic, Caliber HAN4212 (based on ETA 7750); ø 30 mm, 31 jewels; 28,800 vph; rebuilt for single pusher activation rotor with skeletonized brand logo, 42-hour power reserve
Functions: hours, minutes, subsidiary seconds; chronograph
Case: stainless steel, ø 45 mm, height 16 mm; bidirectional bezel with reference marker; sapphire crystal; water-resistant to 10 atm
Band: calf leather, buckle
Price: $8,100
Variations: with black dial

Pioneer MonoControl

Reference number: 732.210-6428
Movement: automatic, Caliber HAN4212 (based on ETA 7750); ø 30 mm, 31 jewels; 28,800 vph; rebuilt for single pusher activation, rotor with skeletonized brand logo, 42-hour power reserve
Functions: hours, minutes, subsidiary seconds; chronograph
Case: stainless steel, ø 45 mm, height 16 mm; sapphire crystal; water-resistant to 10 atm
Band: calf leather, buckle
Price: $8,700
Variations: with silver dial

Pioneer TachyTele

Reference number: 712.200-011
Movement: automatic, Caliber HAN3703 (based on ETA 7753); ø 30 mm, height 7.9 mm; 27 jewels; 28,800 vph; 42-hour power reserve
Functions: hours, minutes, subsidiary seconds; chronograph
Case: stainless steel, ø 40 mm, height 15 mm; bidirectional bezel with reference marker; sapphire crystal; screw-in crown; water-resistant to 10 atm
Band: calf leather, buckle
Price: $3,895
Variations: with black dial

Primus Pilot

Reference number: 740.280-012
Movement: automatic, Caliber HAN3809 (based on ETA 7750); ø 30 mm, height 7.9 mm; 28 jewels; 28,800 vph
Functions: hours, minutes, subsidiary seconds; chronograph; date
Case: stainless steel, ø 44 mm, height 15 mm; sapphire crystal; screw-in crown; transparent case back; water-resistant to 10 atm
Band: calf leather, folding clasp
Remarks: movable lugs
Price: $6,600
Variations: with silver or black dial

Primus Racer

Reference number: 741.510-102
Movement: automatic, Caliber HAN3809 (based on ETA 7750); ø 30 mm, height 7.9 mm; 28 jewels; 28,800 vph
Functions: hours, minutes, subsidiary seconds; chronograph; date
Case: stainless steel, with black DLC coating, ø 44 mm, height 15 mm; sapphire crystal; screw-in crown; transparent case back; water-resistant to 10 atm
Band: rubber, folding clasp
Remarks: movable lugs
Price: $7,950
Variations: stainless steel ($6,600)

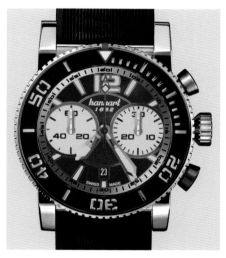

Primus Diver

Reference number: 742.270-132
Movement: automatic, Caliber HAN3809 (based on ETA 7750); ø 30 mm, height 7.9 mm; 28 jewels; 28,800 vph
Functions: hours, minutes, subsidiary seconds; chronograph; date
Case: stainless steel, ø 44 mm, height 15 mm; unidirectional bezel with 60-minute division; sapphire crystal; screw-in crown; transparent case back; water-resistant to 30 atm
Band: rubber, folding clasp
Remarks: movable lugs
Price: $6,600
Variations: with black dial

Harry Winston

Harry Winston, Inc.
718 Fifth Avenue
New York, NY 10019
800-848-3948

Website:
www.harrywinston.com

Founded:
1989

Number of employees:
not specified

Annual production:
not specified

Most important collections:
Avenue, Midnight, Premier, Ocean, Opus

Swatch Group's purchase of the luxury brand Harry Winston in early 2013 for $1 billion came as something of a surprise. But considering the upward flow of money worldwide, banking on a proven high-end luxury brand would seem obvious. On his many travels, founder Harry Winston (1896–1978) bought, recut, and set some of the twentieth century's greatest precious gems ever. He was succeeded by his son Ronald, a gifted craftsman himself with several patents in precious metals processing.

It was Ronald who added watches to the company's portfolio, inaugurating two lines: one showcasing the finest precious gems to dovetail with the company's overall focus and one containing clever, complicated timepieces. The result was the stunning Opus line launched by Harry Winston Rare Timepieces. Each of the thirteen models has been developed in conjunction with one exceptional independent watchmaker per year in very small series and containing an exclusive *manufacture* movement. The roster of artist-engineers who have participated reads like a *Who's Who* of independent watchmaking, including François-Paul Journe, Vianney Halter, Felix Baumgartner, and Greubel Forsey all the way to Denis Giguet and Emmanuel Bouchet. For the Opus XIII, the brand drew on the skills of Ludovic Ballouard. An extremely complex movement flicks fifty-nine metal pins to show the minutes and eleven triangles to show the hours. At twelve and noon, the dial cover opens to reveal the Harry Winston logo.

In May 2013, Nayla Hayek, daughter of Swatch founder Nicolas Hayek, became CEO of the brand, suggesting that Harry Winston will be staying the course in ultra-high-end watches.

Opus XIII

Reference number: OPUMHM44WW001
Movement: manually wound, Caliber HW 4101; ø 37.8 mm, height 4.95 mm; 242 jewels; 21,600 vph; 2 spring barrels; 35-hour power reserve
Functions: hours, minutes, 11 hour triangles that pivot 180° and 59 minute shafts rotating 40 degrees; HW logo at noon and midnight on dial center
Case: white gold, ø 44.25 mm, height 13.6 mm; sapphire crystal, sapphire crystal case back; water-resistant to 3 atm
Band: reptile skin, folding clasp
Remarks: concept and construction in partnership with Ludovic Ballouard; limited to 130 pieces
Price: $298,200

Histoire de Tourbillon 4

Reference number: HCOMTT47WZ001
Movement: manually wound, Caliber HW 4501; ø 40.4 mm, height 17.3 mm; 59 jewels; 21,600 vph; triple-axis tourbillon with 3 rotation speeds (45, 75, and 300 seconds); 50-hour power reserve
Functions: hours, minutes, subsidiary seconds (300 seconds indicated on tourbillon); power reserve indicator
Case: white gold, ø 47 mm, height 21.7 mm; Zalium bezel with DLC coating; sapphire crystal, sapphire crystal case back; water-resistant to 3 atm
Band: reptile skin, buckle
Remarks: limited to 20 pieces
Price: $696,600

Project Z6 Black Edition

Reference number: OCEMAL44ZZ004
Movement: manually wound, Caliber HW 1010-01; ø 34.8 mm, height 7 mm; 45 jewels; 28,800 vph; gong alarm; 72-hour power reserve
Functions: hours and minutes (off-center), subsidiary seconds; alarm with day/night and function display
Case: Zalium with black DLC coating, ø 44 mm, height 13.45 mm; sapphire crystal, water-resistant to 10 atm
Band: rubber, folding clasp
Remarks: limited to 300 pieces
Price: $48,500

Ocean Sport Chronograph Limited Edition

Reference number: OCSACH44ZZ006
Movement: automatic, Caliber HW 1018-02; ø 30 mm, height 9.7 mm; 58 jewels; 28,800 vph
Functions: hours, minutes, subsidiary seconds; chronograph; date
Case: Zalium, ø 44 mm, height 14.8 mm; unidirectional bezel with 60-minute divisions; sapphire crystal, screw-in crown; water-resistant to 20 atm
Band: rubber, folding clasp
Remarks: limited to 300 pieces
Price: $29,900

Histoire de Tourbillon 3

Reference number: HCOMTT65WZ001
Movement: manually wound, Caliber HW 1020-01; 71 jewels; 21,600 vph; dual axis tourbillon with crossed rotation axes, inner cage rotates once every 40 seconds, outer cage once every 120 seconds, additional tourbillon with single axis once every 36 seconds
Functions: hours, minutes (disc display), subsidiary seconds (120 scale); power reserve indicator
Case: white gold with Zalium, 65 x 45.9 mm, height 20.5 mm; sapphire crystal, water-resistant to 3 atm
Band: reptile skin, buckle
Remarks: limited to 20 pieces
Price: $657,200

Midnight Moon Phase

Reference number: 1 MIDQMP39WW001
Movement: quartz
Functions: hours, minutes, date, moon phase
Case: white gold, ø 39 mm, height 7.6 mm; bezel and lugs set with 91 diamonds; sapphire crystal
Band: satin, buckle
Remarks: dial set with 3 brilliant-cut diamonds and 5 gold pearls
Price: $26,700

Ocean Tourbillon Big Date

Reference number: OCEMTD45RR001
Movement: manually wound, Caliber HW4301; 28,800 vph; 1-minute tourbillon, 110-hour power reserve
Functions: hours and minutes (off-center), subsidiary seconds (on tourbillon cage); power reserve indicator (on movement side); large date
Case: rose gold, ø 45 mm, height 15 mm; sapphire crystal, transparent case back; water-resistant to 5 atm
Band: reptile skin, buckle
Remarks: limited to 25 pieces
Price: $180,200
Variations: white gold, limited to 25 pieces ($180,200)

Premier Excenter Time Zone

Reference number: PRNATZ41WW001
Movement: automatic, Caliber HW 1013-01; ø 33 mm, height 6.9 mm; 33 jewels; 28,800 vph
Functions: hours and minutes (off-center); second time zone (additional retrograde 24-hour display), day/night indicator; large date
Case: white gold, ø 41 mm, height 10.9 mm; sapphire crystal, water-resistant to 3 atm
Band: reptile skin, folding clasp
Price: $41,400
Variations: rose gold ($41,400); with silver dial ($41,400)

Ocean Sport Ladies Chrono

Reference number: OCSACH38ZZ002
Movement: automatic, ETA Caliber 2894-2/H2; ø 28.6 mm, height 6.1 mm; 37 jewels; 28,800 vph; 42-hour power reserve
Functions: hours, minutes, subsidiary seconds; chronograph; date
Case: Zalium, ø 38 mm, height 11.5 mm; bezel set with 9 brilliant-cut diamonds; unidirectional bezel with 60-minute divisions; sapphire crystal, screw-in crown; water-resistant to 20 atm
Band: rubber, folding clasp
Price: $24,500
Variations: with silver dial ($24,500)

HAUTLENCE
Rue Numa-Droz 150
CH-2300 La Chaux-de-Fonds
Switzerland

Tel.:
01141-32-924-00-62

Fax:
01141-32-924-00-64

E-Mail:
info@hautlence.com

Website:
www.hautlence.com

Founded:
2004

Number of employees:
11

Annual production:
100 watches

U.S. distributor:
Westime
132 South Rodeo Drive, Fourth Floor
Beverly Hills, CA 90212
310-205-5555
info@westime.com
www.westime.com

Hautlence

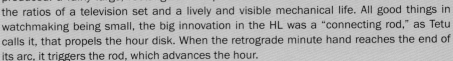

Time can be read in so many ways. Back in 2004, after spending years in the Swiss watch industry, Guillaume Tetu and Renaud de Retz decided that their idea for tracking time was new and unique. They were not watchmakers, but they knew whom to bring on board for the genesis of Hautlence, an anagram of Neuchâtel, the town where their small company is located. And soon, the first HL model was produced: a fairly large, rectangular timepiece with the ratios of a television set and a lively and visible mechanical life. All good things in watchmaking being small, the big innovation in the HL was a "connecting rod," as Tetu calls it, that propels the hour disk. When the retrograde minute hand reaches the end of its arc, it triggers the rod, which advances the hour.

Having survived the Great Recession, Hautlence persists with fewer staff and without de Retz. The watches have evolved, developing shape and character. Design and mechanics have become increasingly integrated, as inspiration from other industrial segments bears fruit. For the HLq, the movement has been reengineered for a classic round case. And instead of a tourbillon, Hautlence has found a way to have the whole escapement rotate four times a day.

In March 2012, Hautlence became the first member of the brand-new MELB Holding, headed by Georges-Henri Meylan (formerly of Audemars Piguet) and former Breguet CFO Bill Muirhead. The experience and contacts of these two horological powerhouses have energized the brand. Besides opening outlets in Dubai and Los Angeles, Hautlence has refreshed its collection with the Avant-Garde series. The stark industrial look is tempered with daubs of color, but the price is far more attractive to less-well-heeled collectors.

Avant-Garde HL RQ 03

Movement: manually wound, in-house caliber; 32 jewels; 21,600 vph; hand-beveled bridges and connecting rods; côtes de Genève; 40-hour power reserve
Functions: jumping hour, retrograde minutes; jumping date with quick corrector
Case: DLC steel, black titanium, ø 44 mm, height 12.5 mm; polished DLC steel bezel and crown; antireflective, beveled sapphire crystal; screwed-down sapphire case back; water-resistant to 3 atm
Band: reptile skin, folding buckle
Remarks: mineral glass hour disc with rhodium-treated hour markers and blue Superluminova
Price: $37,400, limited to 88 pieces
Variations: with pin buckle ($35,800)

Avant-Garde HLRS 02 Blue

Movement: manually wound, in-house caliber; 24 jewels; 21,600 vph; 40-hour power reserve
Functions: jumping hour, retrograde minutes and seconds
Case: titanium and steel, 42 x 46 mm, height 12.8 mm; polished steel bezel; silvered opaline base dial; antireflective sapphire crystal; screwed-down sapphire case back; water-resistant to 3 atm
Band: blue reptile skin, folding buckle
Remarks: transparent mineral glass hour disc with rhodium hour markers and blue Superluminova
Price: $32,100

HL2.3

Movement: automatic, in-house caliber with gear train and automatic winding system; ID HL2.3 on No. plate; 37.8 x 33.2 mm, height 12.35 mm; 18,000 vph; 92 jewels; rotating mobile bridge with oscillator; 45-hour power reserve
Functions: half-trailing hours on chain, 3-4 seconds for change, retrograde minutes
Case: black titanium (incl. crown), 50 x 42 mm, height 17.8 mm; 3D sapphire crystal; rose gold horns and case back screws; water-resistant to 3 atm
Band: reptile skin, folding buckle
Remarks: sapphire dial
Price: $192,000, limited to 28 pieces

Heritage Watch Manufactory

Precision, the watchmaker's obsession, was also the primary goal of Karsten Frässdorf, who founded a new brand of watches in September 2010 with a series of calibers boasting some fascinating technical features. At the heart of his concept was the Vivax precision balance, whose generous, 16 mm diameter makes it a lot easier to control isochronism errors in the long term.

One special mechanism to adjust the pallet lever underneath the balance allows the watchmaker to perfectly set the escapement in motion. The top of the line model, the Tensus, includes not only a wealth of different fine adjustment options, but also a special double spring barrel and a so-called "triple" escape mechanism with a double escape wheel and constant force. Frässdorf applied for five patents for these unusual details. Not surprisingly, it won the Superwatch Award at the Geneva Time Exhibition 2012.

The design of the timepieces themselves is by Eric Giroud, normally known for producing some very different time displays (for example, in the Harry Winston Opus series). For Heritage, however, he focused mainly on simplicity and symmetry to avoid overshadowing the true values of these high-precision timepieces. The Heritage Watch Manufactory is a private Swiss company backed not only by a German watchmaker, but also by German capital. It opened in Neuchâtel for both the "Swiss made" label and the proximity of suppliers and top-notch specialists.

Ever since the Tensus, the brand has proven that it is willing to move into horological realms that others have not dared to explore. The Firmamentum, for example, measures the rotation of the earth and the movement of the sun and the stars, much like navigational instruments of old. In the fall of 2012, a new CEO, Didier Decker, was brought on board with the idea of "writing a new chapter" in the still brief history of the brand. Things in watchmaking take time.

Heritage Watch Manufactory
Rue de la Treille 4
CH-2001 Neuchâtel
Switzerland

Tel.:
01141-32-724-1300

E-Mail:
info@hwm-watch.com

Website:
www.hwm-watch.com

Founded:
2010

Number of employees:
not specified

Annual production:
not specified

Distribution:
Please contact the company directly.

Most important collections/price range:
high-end mechanical wristwatches
Prices listed are based on daily exchange rate and subject to change.

Tensus

Reference number: TE-880-GRWH
Movement: manually wound, HWM Caliber 880; ø 38.3 mm, height 7 mm; 55 jewels; 18,000 vph; 5 fine adjustments (mass-regulated Vivax balance, Tenere system for balance/spring mount, Sectator fine adjustment, Sequax triple anchor escapement with double escape wheel and constant force, Pariter double spring barrel); 60-hour power reserve
Functions: hours, minutes, subsidiary seconds; power reserve indicator
Case: pink gold, ø 42.5 mm, height 13.95 mm; sapphire crystal; transparent case back; water-resistant to 5 atm
Band: reptile skin, buckle
Price: $82,750

Viator

Reference number: VI-840-STWH
Movement: manually wound, HWM Caliber 840; ø 38.3 mm, height 6.1 mm; 40 jewels; 18,000 vph; 3 fine adjustments (mass-regulated Vivax balance, Tenere system for the balance/spring mount, Sectator fine adjustment); 50-hour power reserve
Functions: hours, minutes, subsidiary seconds; second time zone (additional 12-hour display)
Case: stainless steel, ø 42.5 mm, height 13.05 mm; sapphire crystal; transparent case back; water-resistant to 5 atm
Band: reptile skin, buckle
Price: $42,550
Variations: with black dial

Firmamentum

Reference number: FI-870-STWH
Movement: manually wound, HWM Caliber 870; ø 38.9 mm, height 7.5 mm; 92 jewels; 18,000 vph; 3 fine adjustments (mass-regulated Vivax balance, Tenere system for the balance/spring mount, Sectator fine adjustment); 56-hour power reserve
Functions: hours, minutes, subsidiary seconds; second time zone; hour angle tool to observe celestial bodies with 13 hands, plus 2 displays of variable hour angle in solar or sidereal time
Case: stainless steel, ø 44.5 mm, height 15.35 mm; transparent case back; water-resistant to 5 atm
Band: reptile skin, buckle
Price: $200,500

La Montre Hermès
Erlenstrasse 31A
CH-2555 Brügg
Switzerland

Tel.:
01141-32-366-7100

Fax:
01141-32-366-7101

E-Mail:
info@montre-hermes.ch

Website:
www.hermes.ch

Founded:
1978

Number of employees:
150

Annual production:
not specified

U.S. distributor:
Hermès of Paris, Inc.
55 East 59th Street
New York, NY 10022
800-441-4488
www.hermes.com

Most important collections/price range:
Arceau, Cape Cod, Clipper, Dressage, H-Our, Kelly,
Kelly 2, Medor / $2,150 to $34,000

Hermès

This company founded in Paris in 1837 by Thierry Hermès originally specialized in the robust leather accessories that gentlemen needed for travel: chiefly headgear for horses as well as bags and suitcases. Although, over time, Hermès has largely diversified its range of products—handbags, foulards, fashion, porcelain, glass, and gold jewelry are found in its portfolio—a link has always remained to its roots. The production of watches began with the founding of Biel-based subsidiary La Montre Hermès in 1978. Here, the connection to the past is easily explained: The company's workshops in Paris were already producing straps for watches in the 1920s, thereby influencing watch fashion in a certain way.

Unlike so many other manufacturers of lifestyle products, Hermès does not have its watches simply assembled by so-called private labelers, but instead has maintained its own little watch factory in Biel since the beginning. Some interesting little complications have been produced in collaboration with external designers, such as the unusual hand movements with varying speeds or "parking options."

In 2006, Hermès invested close to 25 million Swiss francs in its movement production, securing 25 percent of the Vaucher Manufacture's stock. This didn't particularly surprise insiders, especially since Hermès has been continuously investing in and intensifying the relationship since it began working with this arm of the Sandoz empire three years ago. La Montre Hermès is directly positioned at the mouth of a grand source of first-class movements—something that is reflected in the complicated watch collection the company is now offering. By the same token, as a brand it keeps to its roots, as shown by the new Arceau Bridon series with a bridoon at 12 o'clock serving as a strap holder.

Arceau "Le Temps Suspendu"

Reference number: AR7.471.213/MHA
Movement: automatic, Hermès Caliber H1912 with module; ø 23.9 mm, height 3.7 mm; 28 jewels; 28,800 vph; hands can be parked at 12:30 and started again at current time with pusher; double spring barrel, 50-hour power reserve
Functions: hours, minutes; additional 24-hour display
Case: rose gold, ø 38 mm; bezel set with 62 diamonds; sapphire crystal
Band: reptile skin, folding clasp
Price: $41,500
Variations: without diamonds ($19,400)

Arceau "Le Temps Suspendu"

Reference number: AR7.410.220/MM76
Movement: automatic, Hermès Caliber H1912 with module; ø 23.9 mm, height 3.7 mm; 28 jewels; 28,800 vph; hands can be parked at 12:30 and started again at current time with pusher; double spring barrel; 50-hour power reserve
Functions: hours, minutes; additional 24-hour display
Case: stainless steel, ø 38 mm; sapphire crystal
Band: reptile skin, folding clasp
Price: $19,400
Variations: with diamonds ($26,500)

Arceau "Le Temps Suspendu Platine"

Reference number: AR8.965.631/MM76
Movement: automatic, modified ETA Caliber 2892; ø 26 mm, height 5.6 mm; 28,800 vph; hands can be parked and started again at current time with pusher; double spring barrel; 42-hour power reserve
Functions: hours, minutes; date (retrograde)
Case: platinum, ø 43 mm; sapphire crystal; water-resistant to 3 atm
Band: reptile skin, folding clasp
Price: $82,500

Arceau Petite Lune

Reference number: AR7.510.217/MNO
Movement: automatic, ETA Caliber 2892 with Dubois-Dépraz module; ø 26.2 mm, height 5.2 mm; 21 jewels; 28,800 vph; 42-hour power reserve
Functions: hours, minutes; date; moon phase
Case: stainless steel, ø 38 mm; sapphire crystal; water-resistant to 3 atm
Band: reptile skin, buckle
Remarks: mother-of-pearl dial
Price: $7,650
Variations: with light dial

Arceau Chrono Colors Bridon

Reference number: AR4.910.132.INA2
Movement: automatic, ETA Caliber 2894; ø 28.2 mm, height 6.1 mm; 37 jewels; 28,800 vph
Functions: hours, minutes, subsidiary seconds; chronograph; date
Case: stainless steel, ø 43 mm; sapphire crystal, transparent case back; water-resistant to 5 atm
Band: leather, folding clasp
Price: $6,500

Cape Cod GMT

Reference number: CD6.910.220/MHA
Movement: automatic, ETA Caliber 2892 with Soprod module 9351; ø 26 mm, height 3.6 mm; 25 jewels; 28,800 vph; plate and bridges with perlage, rotor with côtes de Genève; 42-hour power reserve
Functions: hours, minutes, sweep seconds; additional 12-hour display (second time zone); day/night indicator; large date
Case: stainless steel, 35.4 x 36.5 mm; sapphire crystal, transparent case back; water-resistant to 5 atm
Band: reptile skin, folding clasp with safety lock
Price: $7,500
Variations: with blue dial ($7,500)

Clipper Sport

Reference number: CP2.741.240/1C4
Movement: automatic, ETA Caliber 2892-2; ø 26 mm, height 3.6 mm; 21 jewels; 28,800 vph; 42-hour power reserve
Functions: hours, minutes, sweep seconds; date
Case: titanium, ø 41 mm; unidirectional bezel with 60-minute divisions, sapphire crystal; water-resistant to 10 atm
Band: rubber, folding clasp
Price: $4,350
Variations: various bands and dials

Clipper Sport

Reference number: CP2.741.240
Movement: automatic, ETA Caliber 2892-2; ø 26 mm, height 3.6 mm; 21 jewels, 28,800 vph; 42-hour power reserve
Functions: hours, minutes, sweep seconds; date
Case: titanium, ø 41 mm; unidirectional bezel with 60-minute divisions, sapphire crystal; water-resistant to 10 atm
Band: rubber, folding clasp
Price: $4,350
Variations: various bands and dials

Arceau H Cube

Reference number: AR8.790.320/ZBA
Movement: automatic, ETA Caliber 2892-2; ø 26 mm, height 3.7 mm; 28 jewels; 28,800 vph; 50-hour power reserve
Functions: hours, minutes
Case: white gold, ø 41 mm; sapphire crystal; water-resistant to 3 atm
Band: reptile skin, buckle
Remarks: straw marquetry dial
Price: upon request

Hublot

Hublot SA
33, chemin de la Vuarpillière
CH-1260 Nyon
Switzerland

Tel.:
01141-22-990-9900

E-Mail:
info@hublot.ch

Website:
www.hublot.com

Founded:
1980

Number of employees:
approx. 150

Annual production:
approx. 24,000 watches

U.S. distributor:
Hublot of America, Inc.
The International Building, ST-402
2455 East Sunrise Blvd.
Fort Lauderdale, FL 33304
800-536-0636

Most important collections/price range:
Big Bang / $15,000 to $35,000; King / $20,000 to $40,000; Classic / $7,000 to $15,000

Five years after the relaunch of the Hublot brand, the dream of CEO Jean-Claude Biver came true: At the beginning of 2009, the company moved to its own, 6,000-square-meter factory building in the industrial area of Nyon, ready to begin manufacturing its first in-house movement caliber. In January 2010, Hublot's longtime movement supplier, BNB Concept, declared bankruptcy. Biver acted without hesitation: He not only scooped up all the machinery in the workshop, an atelier customized to produce complicated tourbillons and repeater movements, but he also brought thirty of BNB's most talented employees on board, including head designer Mathias Buttet. The acquisition was made possible thanks to a huge cash injection by luxury holding group Louis Vuitton, Moët & Hennessy (LVMH), which Hublot joined in 2008. Apparently, at that time, the French group had dug deep into its pockets to keep Biver under contract at Hublot—so it would have been hard for them to say no to the BNB purchases. Biver, perhaps Switzerland's most astute personality in the watch business, had played his cards perfectly. Hublot quickly reached its desired *manufacture* status and earned kudos for offering safe haven to the great BNB talents. Hublot still draws on outside suppliers (ETA, Concepto, La Joux-Perret), but the in-house caliber (The HUB 1240) has launched a new era: 20,000 are expected to be generated over the medium term, for use in 70 percent of the company's chronograph models.

In 2012, Biver left the CEO position to Ricardo Guadalupe to take on chairmanship of the administrative board. But his influence is still being felt in the proliferation of the Big Bang watches Hublot produces for every mediagenic occasion. Before taking on his new duties, Biver engineered the acquisition of a high-tech company producing carbon composite. And Hublot now has its own materials research lab that can cook up all manner of fused materials for new ideas, like "Magic Gold," a sintered and molten compound of gold combined with a ceramic matrix.

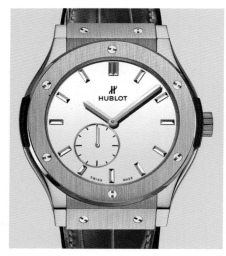

Classic Fusion Classico Ultra-Thin King Gold

Reference number: 515.OX.2210.LR
Movement: automatic, Caliber HUB 1301.4; ø 30 mm, height 2.9 mm; 21 jewels; 21,600 vph; 90-hour power reserve
Functions: hours, minutes, subsidiary seconds
Case: rose gold, ø 45 mm; bezel screwed to case back with 6 titanium screws; sapphire crystal; water-resistant to 5 atm
Band: reptile skin/rubber, folding clasp
Price: $31,400

Classic Fusion Classico Ultra-Thin King Gold

Reference number: 515.OX.1280.LR
Movement: automatic, Caliber HUB 1301.4; ø 30 mm, height 2.9 mm; 21 jewels; 21,600 vph; 90-hour power reserve
Functions: hours, minutes, subsidiary seconds
Case: rose gold, ø 45 mm; bezel screwed to case back with 6 titanium screws; sapphire crystal; water-resistant to 5 atm
Band: reptile skin/rubber, folding clasp
Price: $31,400

Classic Fusion Classico Ultra-Thin Titanium

Reference number: 515.NX.1270.LR
Movement: automatic, Caliber HUB 1301.4; ø 30 mm, height 2.9 mm; 21 jewels; 21,600 vph; 90-hour power reserve
Functions: hours, minutes, subsidiary seconds
Case: titanium, ø 45 mm; bezel screwed to case back with 6 titanium screws; sapphire crystal; water-resistant to 5 atm
Band: reptile skin/rubber, folding clasp
Price: $13,700

Classic Fusion Aerofusion Chronograph King Gold

Reference number: 525.OX.0180.LR
Movement: automatic, Hublot Caliber 1155 "Aero"; ø 30 mm, height 7.9 mm; 60 jewels; 28,800 vph; skeletonized and rhodium-plated rotor, tungsten carbide oscillating mass; 42-hour power reserve
Functions: hours, minutes, subsidiary seconds; chronograph; date
Case: pink gold, ø 45 mm; bezel screwed to case back with 6 titanium screws; sapphire crystal, transparent case back; water-resistant to 5 atm
Band: reptile skin, folding clasp
Price: $38,300

Classic Fusion Aerofusion Chronograph Titanium

Reference number: 525.NX.0170.LR
Movement: automatic, Hublot Caliber 1155 "Aero"; ø 30 mm, height 7.9 mm; 60 jewels; 28,800 vph; skeletonized and rhodium-plated rotor, tungsten carbide oscillating mass; 42-hour power reserve
Functions: hours, minutes, subsidiary seconds; chronograph; date
Case: titanium, ø 45 mm; bezel screwed to case back with 6 titanium screws; sapphire crystal, transparent case back; water-resistant to 5 atm
Band: reptile skin, folding clasp
Price: $16,400

Classic Fusion Aerofusion Chronograph Titanium Bracelet

Reference number: 525.NX.0170.NX
Movement: automatic, Hublot Caliber 1155 "Aero"; ø 30 mm, height 7.9 mm; 60 jewels; 28,800 vph; skeletonized and rhodium-plated rotor, tungsten carbide oscillating mass; 42-hour power reserve
Functions: hours, minutes, subsidiary seconds; chronograph; date
Case: titanium, ø 45 mm; bezel screwed to case back with 6 titanium screws; sapphire crystal, transparent case back; water-resistant to 5 atm
Band: titanium, folding clasp
Price: $17,700

Classic Fusion Skeleton Tourbillon All Black

Reference number: 505.CM.0140.LR
Movement: manual winding, Caliber HUB 6010.H1.1; ø 34 mm, height 4 mm; 19 jewels; 21,600 vph; 1-minute tourbillon; skeletonized; 120-hour power reserve
Functions: hours, minutes
Case: ceramic, ø 45 mm; bezel screwed to case back with 6 titanium screws; sapphire crystal, transparent case back; water-resistant to 3 atm
Band: reptile skin, folding clasp
Price: $97,700, limited to 99 pieces

Classic Fusion Classico Ultra-thin Skeleton All Black

Reference number: 515.CM.0140.LR
Movement: manual winding, Caliber HUB 1300.4; ø 28.6 mm, height 2.9 mm; 23 jewels; 21,600 vph; skeletonized; double spring barrel; 90-hour power reserve
Functions: hours, minutes, subsidiary seconds
Case: ceramic, ø 45 mm, bezel screwed to case back with 6 titanium screws; sapphire crystal, transparent case back; water-resistant to 5 atm
Band: reptile skin, folding clasp
Price: $18,300

Big Bang "Maria Riesch Limited Edition"

Reference number: 341.HX.7717.NR.MRI13
Movement: automatic, Caliber HUB 4300 (base ETA 2892-A2); ø 28.6 mm, height 6.1 mm; 37 jewels; 28,800 vph; 42-hour power reserve
Functions: hours, minutes, subsidiary seconds; chronograph; date
Case: ceramic, ø 41 mm, height 13.2 mm; bezel screwed to case back with 6 titanium screws; sapphire crystal, water-resistant to 10 atm
Band: textile and rubber, folding clasp
Remarks: dial set with 8 diamonds
Price: $16,200, limited to 50 pieces

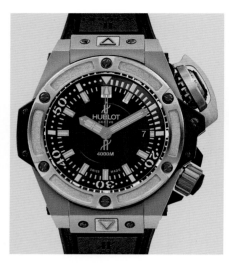

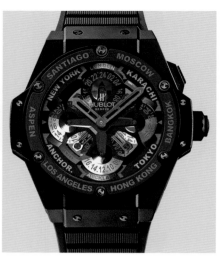

King Power Oceanographic 4000 King Gold

Reference number: 731.OX.1170.RX
Movement: automatic, Caliber HUB 1401; ø 30 mm, height 7.9 mm; 23 jewels; 28,800 vph; 42-hour power reserve
Functions: hours, minutes, sweep seconds; date
Case: pink gold, ø 48 mm; bezel screwed to case back with 6 screws; sapphire crystal, screw-in crown with protective bar; water-resistant to 400 atm
Band: rubber, buckle
Price: $46,200, limited to 200 pieces

King Power Unico Ceramic

Reference number: 701.CI.0170.RX
Movement: automatic, Caliber HUB 1240 "Unico"; ø 30 mm, height 8.05 mm; 38 jewels; 28,800 vph; black-coated plate and bridges; 72-hour power reserve
Functions: hours, minutes, subsidiary seconds; flyback chronograph; date
Case: ceramic, ø 48 mm; bezel with rubber inlays, screwed to case back with 6 titanium screws; sapphire crystal, transparent case back; water-resistant to 10 atm
Band: rubber, folding clasp
Price: $24,000

King Power Unico GMT Ceramic

Reference number: 771.CI.1170.RX
Movement: automatic, Caliber HUB 1220 "Unico"; ø 30 mm, height 8.05 mm; 38 jewels; 28,800 vph; 72-hour power reserve
Functions: hours, minutes; world-time display (second time zone)
Case: ceramic, ø 48 mm; bezel screwed to case back with 6 titanium screws; sapphire crystal, water-resistant to 10 atm
Band: rubber, folding clasp
Remarks: 4 additional local times via rotating 24-hour discs, movable in hour steps with pusher
Price: $30,900
Variations: pink gold ($48,200)

Big Bang Unico Titanium Ceramic

Reference number: 411.NM.1170.RX
Movement: automatic, Caliber HUB 1242 "Unico"; ø 30 mm, height 8.05 mm; 38 jewels; 28,800 vph; black-coated plate and bridges; 72-hour power reserve
Functions: hours, minutes, subsidiary seconds; flyback chronograph; date
Case: carbon fiber, ø 45 mm; bezel screwed to case back with 6 titanium screws; sapphire crystal, transparent case back; water-resistant to 10 atm
Band: rubber, folding clasp
Price: $21,700
Variations: various cases and dials

Big Bang Jeans

Reference number: 301.SX.2710.NR.JEANS
Movement: automatic, Caliber HUB 4100 (base ETA 2892-A2); ø 30 mm, height 8.4 mm; 27 jewels; 28,800 vph; 42-hour power reserve
Functions: hours, minutes, subsidiary seconds; chronograph; date
Case: stainless steel, ø 44 mm, height 14.6 mm; bezel screwed to case back with 6 titanium screws; sapphire crystal, transparent case back; water-resistant to 10 atm
Band: textile and rubber, folding clasp
Price: $16,000, limited to 250 pieces

Big Bang Carbon Bezel Baguette Blue Sapphires

Reference number: 301.QX.1790.HR.1901
Movement: automatic, Caliber HUB 4100 (base ETA 2892-A2); ø 30 mm, height 8.4 mm; 27 jewels; 28,800 vph; 42-hour power reserve
Functions: hours, minutes, subsidiary seconds; chronograph; date
Case: carbon fiber, ø 42 mm, height 14.9 mm; bezel set with blue sapphires; sapphire crystal, transparent case back; water-resistant to 10 atm
Band: reptile skin/rubber, folding clasp
Price: $80,300
Variations: various dials

Big Bang Ferrari Carbon Red Magic

Reference number: 401.QX.0123.VR
Movement: automatic, Caliber HUB 1241 "Unico"; ø 30 mm, height 8.05 mm; 38 jewels; 28,800 vph; black-coated plate and bridges; 72-hour power reserve
Functions: hours, minutes; flyback chronograph; date
Case: carbon fiber, ø 45.5 mm; bezel screwed to case back with 6 titanium screws; sapphire crystal, transparent case back; titanium crown and pushers; water-resistant to 10 atm
Band: reptile skin, folding clasp
Price: $32,100, limited to 1,000 pieces

Big Bang Ferrari Ceramic

Reference number: 401.CX.0123.VR
Movement: automatic, Caliber HUB 1241 "Unico"; ø 30 mm, height 8.05 mm; 38 jewels; 28,800 vph; black-coated plate and bridges; 72-hour power reserve
Functions: hours, minutes; flyback chronograph; date
Case: ceramic, ø 45.5 mm; bezel screwed to case back with 6 titanium screws; sapphire crystal, transparent case back; titanium crown and pushers; water-resistant to 10 atm
Band: reptile skin, folding clasp
Price: $29,800, limited to 1,000 pieces

Big Bang Ferrari King Gold Carbon

Reference number: 401.OQ.0123.VR
Movement: automatic, Caliber HUB 1241 "Unico"; ø 30 mm, height 8.05 mm; 38 jewels; 28,800 vph; black-coated plate and bridges; 72-hour power reserve
Functions: hours, minutes; flyback chronograph; date
Case: pink gold, ø 45.5 mm, carbon fiber bezel screwed to case back with 6 titanium screws; sapphire crystal, transparent case back; water-resistant to 10 atm
Band: reptile skin, folding clasp
Price: $43,600, limited to 500 pieces

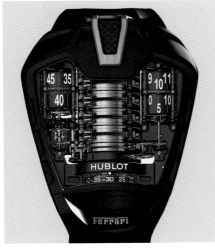

Hublot Masterpiece MP-05 "LaFerrari"

Reference number: 905.ND.0001.RX
Movement: automatic, Caliber HUB 9005.H1.6; 39.5 x 45.8 mm; 108 jewels; 21,600 vph; vertically suspended flying tourbillon; hours, minutes, seconds, power reserve indicated by black anodized aluminum cylinders; 11 spring barrels; 45-day power reserve
Functions: hours, minutes, seconds (on cylinders); power reserve indicator
Case: titanium with black aluminum coating; sapphire crystal
Band: rubber, folding clasp
Price: $345,000, limited to 50 pieces

Caliber HUB 1240

Automatic; column wheel control of chronograph functions; silicon pallet lever and escapement, removable escapement; double-pawl automatic winding (Pellaton system), winding rotor with ceramic ball bearings; simple barrel spring, 70-hour power reserve
Functions: hours, minutes, subsidiary seconds; flyback chronograph; date
Diameter: 30.4 mm; **Height:** 8.05 mm
Jewels: 36
Balance: glucydur
Frequency: 28,800 vph
Balance spring: flat hairspring with fine regulation
Shock protection: Incabloc
Remarks: 330 components

Caliber HUB1300

Manually wound; skeletonized movement, structural sections with black PVD coating; double spring barrel, 90-hour power reserve
Functions: hours, minutes, subsidiary seconds
Diameter: 28 mm
Height: 2.9 mm
Jewels: 23
Balance: glucydur
Frequency: 21,600 vph
Balance spring: flat hairspring with fine regulation
Shock protection: Incabloc
Remarks: 123 components

Itay Noy
P.O. Box 16661
Tel Aviv 61166
Israel

Tel.:
011-972-352-47-380

Fax:
011-972-352-47-381

E-Mail:
studio@itay-noy.com

Website:
www.itay-noy.com

Founded:
2000

Number of employees:
4

Annual production:
200–300 pieces

U.S. distributor:
Bareti, California
949-715-7084
info@bareti.com
www.bareti.com

Most important collections/price range:
Hyper Scape, X-ray, Duality, City Square / $2,180
to $6,240

Itay Noy

Israeli watchmaker Itay Noy started his career as a jeweler, so it comes as no surprise that his watches weigh in heavily on the form side, while the functional aspects are left to the solid technology generated by the Swiss industry. Noy focuses on his own cases and dials and makes his own straps, which are what give his timepieces such a distinct look. He reveals himself to be a pensive, philosophical storyteller who makes each timepiece a unique, encapsulated tale of sorts. The City Squares model, for example, gives the time on the backdrop of a map of the owner's favorite or native city, thus creating an intimate connection with, perhaps, a past moment. The Duality line contrasts a sober visage with a more decorative dial where the numbers shine like the rays of the sun. At Baselworld 2012, Noy showcased the "DiaLOG," a lively gaming between numbers and styles that looks, just a little, like the play between the planets and stars around us. His latest venture is a square watch run on a Technotime automatic movement with a face-like dial that changes with the movement of the hands, a reminder of how our life has become dominated by the rectangular frame of mobile gadgets. The Cityscape, square as well, represents a modern urban landscape. Seeing his work, it is no wonder he won the 2007 Andy Prize.

Itay Noy is also generous with his talent: Once a year he teaches a course in timepiece design for the Department of Jewelry and Fashion at Bezalel Academy of Art and Design Jerusalem. A glance at the imaginative works his students turn out using, for example, discarded materials suggests the beginning of a new strain of DNA.

These timepieces are quite affordable, especially considering they are made in limited and numbered editions. They are often found in museums and special exhibitions, notably the C. Bronfman Collection in New York, the Droog Design Collection in Amsterdam, and the collection of the Israel Museum in Jerusalem.

Hyper Scape

Reference number: CITYSCAPE.B
Movement: automatic, Caliber TT651-24H;
ø 26.2 mm, height 5.25 mm; 21 jewels;
28,800 vph; 42-hour power reserve
Functions: hours, minutes, sweep seconds; quick-set big date window; second time zone; 24-hour day/night indicator
Case: stainless steel, 42.4 x 42.4 mm, height 11.6 mm; sapphire crystal; transparent case back; water-resistant to 5 atm
Band: rubber or handmade leather strap, double folding clasp
Price: $5,800, limited to 99 numbered pieces
Variations: black or cream dial

Mask

Reference number: MASK01.B
Movement: automatic, Caliber TT651-24H;
ø 26.2 mm, height 5.25 mm; 21 jewels;
28,800 vph; 42-hour power reserve
Functions: hours, minutes, sweep seconds; quick-set big date window; second time zone; 24-hour day/night indicator
Case: stainless steel, 42.4 x 42.4 mm, height 11.6 mm; sapphire crystal; transparent case back; water-resistant to 5 atm
Band: rubber or handmade leather strap, double folding clasp
Price: $5,800, limited to 99 numbered pieces
Variations: black or cream dial

DiaLOG

Reference number: DiaLOG.Num
Movement: manually wound, ETA Caliber 6498-1;
ø 36.6 mm, height 4.5 mm; 17 jewels; 21,600 vph;
38-hour power reserve
Functions: hours, minutes, subsidiary seconds
Case: stainless steel, 41.6 x 44.6 mm; height 10 mm; sapphire crystal; screwed-down case back; water-resistant to 50 m
Band: dark blue handmade leather strap, double folding clasp
Price: $3,640, limited to 99 numbered pieces
Variations: aluminum ($3,900)

Netline-Skeleton

Reference number: SKEL6498
Movement: manually wound, ETA Caliber 6498-1;
ø 36.6 mm, height 4.5 mm; 17 jewels 21,600 vph,
38-hour power reserve
Functions: hours, minutes, subsidiary seconds
Case: stainless steel, 41.6 x 44.6 mm, height
10 mm; sapphire crystal; screwed-down case back;
water-resistant to 50 m
Band: handmade leather strap, double folding clasp
Price: $3,640, limited to 99 numbered pieces
Variations: with black or brown leather band

X-ray

Reference number: XRAY6498
Movement: manually wound, ETA Caliber 6498-1;
ø 36.6 mm, height 4.5 mm; 17 jewels 21,600 vph;
38-hour power reserve
Functions: hours, minutes, subsidiary seconds
Case: stainless steel, 41.6 x 44.6 mm; height 10
mm; sapphire crystal; screwed-down case back;
water-resistant to 50 m
Band: handmade leather strap, double folding clasp
Price: $3,640, limited to 99 numbered pieces
Variations: gold-plated dial ($3,900); with black or
brown leather band

City Squares–Columbus Square, New York

Reference number: CS-COL
Movement: automatic, ETA Caliber 2824-2;
ø 25.6 mm, height 4.6 mm; 25 jewels; 28,800 vph,
38-hour power reserve
Functions: hours, minutes, sweep seconds; quick-
set date window
Case: stainless steel, ø 42.4 mm, height 10
mm; sapphire crystal; screwed-down case back;
water-resistant to 50 m
Band: handmade leather strap, double folding clasp
Price: $3,640, limited to 99 numbered pieces
Variations: London, Paris, Rome, Tel Aviv,
Copenhagen

Maximalism

Reference number: MAX-DECO
Movement: automatic, ETA Caliber 2824-2;
ø 25.6 mm, height 4.6 mm; 25 jewels; 28,800 vph;
38-hour power reserve
Functions: hours, minutes, sweep seconds;
quick-set date window
Case: stainless steel, ø 42.4 mm, height 10
mm; sapphire crystal; screwed-down case back;
water-resistant to 50 m
Band: handmade leather band, double folding clasp
Price: $2,400, limited to 99 numbered pieces
Variations: with black or brown leather band

Identity-Hebrew

Reference number: ID-HEB
Movement: automatic, ETA Caliber 2824-2;
ø 25.6 mm, height 4.6 mm; 25 jewels; 28,800 vph;
38-hour power reserve
Functions: hours, minutes, sweep seconds; quick-
set date window
Case: stainless steel, ø 42.4 mm, height 10 mm;
sapphire crystal; screwed-down case back; water-
resistant to 50 m
Band: handmade leather band
Price: $2,400, limited to 99 numbered pieces
Variations: with black or brown leather strap

Duality Everyday / Holiday (double-sided watch)

Reference number: DU-EH
Movement: automatic, ETA Caliber 2804-2
(2 movements); ø 25.6 mm, height 3.35 mm;
17 jewels; 28,800 vph
Functions: hours, minutes, sweep seconds; quick-
set date window
Case: stainless steel, ø 42.4 mm, height 14.6 mm;
sapphire crystal; water-resistant to 50 m
Band: handmade leather band
Price: $3,900, limited to 99 numbered pieces
Variations: with black or brown leather band

IWC
International Watch Co.
Baumgartenstrasse 15
CH-8201 Schaffhausen
Switzerland

Tel.:
01141-52-635-6565

Fax:
01141-52-635-6501

E-Mail:
info@iwc.com

Website:
www.iwc.com

Founded:
1868

Number of employees:
approx. 750

Annual production:
Not specified

U.S. distributor:
IWC North America
645 Fifth Avenue, 5th Floor
New York, NY 10022
800-432-9330

Most important collections/price range:
Da Vinci; Pilot's; Portuguese; Ingenieur;
Aquatimer / approx. $4,000 to $260,000

IWC

It was an American who laid the cornerstone for an industrial watch factory in Schaffhausen—now modern and environmentally state-of-the-art facilities. In 1868, Florentine Ariosto Jones, watchmaker and engineer from Boston, crossed the Atlantic and came to the then low-wage country of Switzerland to open the International Watch Company Schaffhausen. Jones was not only a savvy businessperson, but also a talented designer, who had a significant influence on the development of watch movements. Soon, he gave the IWC its own seal of approval, the *Ingenieursmarke* (Engineer's Brand), a standard it still maintains today. As it always has, IWC is synonymous with excellently crafted watches that meet high technical benchmarks. Not even a large variety of owners over the past 100 years has been able to change the company's course, though it did ultimately end up in the hands of the Richemont Group in 2000.

Technical milestones from Schaffhausen include the Jones caliber, named for the IWC founder, and the pocket watch caliber 89, introduced in 1946 as the creation of then technical director Albert Pellaton. Four years later, Pellaton created the first IWC automatic movement and, with it, a company monument. Over the years, IWC has made a name for itself with its pilot's watches. The technical highlight of the present day is no doubt the Perpetual Calendar, which is programmed for 500 years.

Georges Kern, the current CEO at IWC, has pursued the further development of in-house movements, such as those found in the company's Da Vinci, Portuguese, and Ingenieur models. The watches are retro-styled, and the branding is always connected with planes or cars. IWC joined Mercedes in 2013 in putting an antique Mercedes Silver Arrow into the Klausen Race; this car won the last race there in 1934.

Ingenieur Constant-Force Tourbillon

Reference number: IW590001
Movement: manually wound, IWC Caliber 94800; ø 37.8 mm, height 7.7 mm; 43 jewels; 18,000 vph; 1-minute tourbillon, constant force escapement; 96-hour power reserve
Functions: hours, minutes, subsidiary seconds; power reserve indicator; double moon phase
Case: platinum, ø 46 mm, height 14 mm; sapphire crystal, transparent case back; water-resistant to 12 atm
Band: reptile skin, buckle
Price: $290,000

Ingenieur Perpetual Calendar Digital Date-Month

Reference number: IW379201
Movement: automatic, IWC Caliber 89802; ø 37 mm, height 9.86 mm; 51 jewels; 28,800 vph; double-pawl winding system, shockproofed rotor; 68-hour power reserve
Functions: hours, minutes, subsidiary seconds; flyback chronograph; perpetual calendar with month, (both digital); leap year
Case: titanium, ø 46 mm, height 17 mm; sapphire crystal, transparent case back; water-resistant to 12 atm
Band: rubber, buckle
Price: $49,700

Ingenieur Automatic Carbon Performance

Reference number: IW322401
Movement: automatic, IWC Caliber 80110; ø 30 mm, height 7.23 mm; 28 jewels; 28,800 vph; Pellaton winding; 44-hour power reserve
Functions: hours, minutes, sweep seconds; date
Case: carbon fiber, ø 46 mm, height 14.5 mm; sapphire crystal, screw-in crown; water-resistant to 12 atm
Band: leather/rubber, buckle
Price: $26,400, limited to 100 pieces

Ingenieur Automatic AMG Black Series Ceramic

Reference number: IW322503
Movement: automatic, IWC Caliber 80110;
ø 30 mm; height 7.23 mm; 28 jewels; 28,800 vph;
Pellaton winding; 44-hour power reserve
Functions: hours, minutes, sweep seconds; date
Case: ceramic, ø 46 mm, height 14.5 mm; sapphire
crystal, transparent case back, screw-in crown;
water-resistant to 12 atm
Band: calf leather, buckle
Price: $12,300

Ingenieur Double Chronograph Titanium

Reference number: IW386501
Movement: automatic, IWC Caliber 79420 (base
ETA 7750); ø 30 mm, height 9.5 mm; 29 jewels;
28,800 vph; 44-hour power reserve
Functions: hours, minutes, subsidiary seconds;
rattrapante chronograph; weekday, date
Case: titanium, ø 45 mm, height 16 mm; sapphire
crystal; screw-in crown; water-resistant to 12 atm
Band: rubber, buckle
Price: $12,700
Variations: with black dial ($12,700)

Ingenieur Dual Time

Reference number: IW326403
Movement: automatic, IWC Caliber 35720;
27 jewels, 28,800 vph; 42-hour power reserve
Functions: hours, minutes, sweep seconds;
additional 24-hour display (second time zone); date
Case: titanium, ø 45 mm, height 13 mm; sapphire
crystal, screw-in crown; water-resistant to 12 atm
Band: rubber, buckle
Price: $8,800

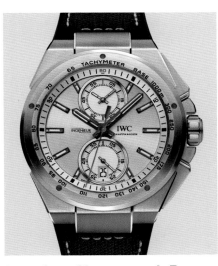

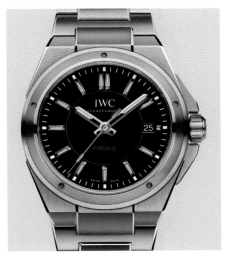

Ingenieur Chronograph Racer

Reference number: IW378507
Movement: automatic, IWC Caliber 89361; ø 30 mm,
height 7.46 mm; 38 jewels; 28,800 vph; double-pawl
automatic winding system; 68-hour power reserve
Functions: hours, minutes, subsidiary seconds;
flyback chronograph; date
Case: stainless steel, ø 45 mm, height 14.5 mm;
sapphire crystal, screw-in crown; water-resistant to
12 atm
Band: reptile skin/rubber, buckle
Price: $13,100
Variations: with ardoise dial/stainless steel
bracelet ($14,300); silver-plated dial/leather strap
($13,100); with silver-plated dial/stainless steel
bracelet ($14,300)

Ingenieur Automatic

Reference number: IW323902
Movement: automatic, IWC Caliber 30110
(base ETA 2892-A2); ø 25.6 mm, height
3.6 mm; 21 jewels; 28,800 vph; soft iron cap for
antimagnetic protection; 42-hour power reserve
Functions: hours, minutes, sweep seconds; date
Case: stainless steel, ø 40 mm, height 10 mm;
sapphire crystal, screw-in crown; water-resistant to
12 atm
Band: stainless steel, folding clasp
Price: $6,600
Variations: with silver dial with silver numerals and
silver dial with gold numerals

Ingenieur Chronograph "Silberpfeil"

Reference number: IW378505
Movement: automatic, IWC Caliber 89361;
ø 30 mm, height 7.46 mm; 38 jewels; 28,800 vph;
double-pawl automatic winding system; 68-hour
power reserve
Functions: hours, minutes, subsidiary seconds;
flyback chronograph; date
Case: stainless steel, ø 45 mm, height 14.5 mm;
sapphire crystal, transparent case back; screw-in
crown; water-resistant to 12 atm
Band: runner/leather, buckle
Price: $13,100
Variations: with brown dial ($13,100)

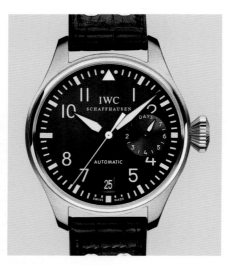

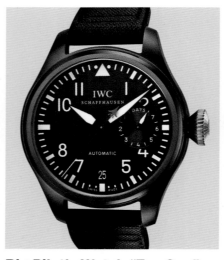

Big Pilot's Watch

Reference number: IW500901
Movement: automatic, IWC Caliber 51111;
ø 37.8 mm, height 7.53 mm; 42 jewels; 21,600 vph;
Pellaton automatic winding system; soft iron cap for
antimagnetic protection; 168-hour power reserve
Functions: hours, minutes, sweep seconds; power
reserve indicator; date
Case: stainless steel, ø 46 mm, height 16 mm;
sapphire crystal, screw-in crown; water-resistant to
6 atm
Band: reptile skin, folding clasp
Price: $15,400

Big Pilot's Watch "Top Gun"

Reference number: IW501901
Movement: automatic, IWC Caliber 51111;
ø 37.8 mm, height 7.53 mm; 42 jewels; 21,600 vph;
Pellaton automatic winding system, 168-hour power
reserve
Functions: hours, minutes, sweep seconds; power
reserve indicator; date
Case: ceramic and titanium, ø 48 mm, height
15 mm; sapphire crystal, screw-in crown;
water-resistant to 6 atm
Band: textile, buckle
Price: $18,200
Variations: "Miramar" version with anthracite dial
and green strap ($18,200)

Big Pilot's Watch "Top Gun" Miramar

Reference number: IW501902
Movement: automatic, IWC Caliber 51111; ø 37.8 mm,
height 7.53 mm; 42 jewels; 21,600 vph; Pellaton
automatic winding system, 168-hour power reserve
Functions: hours, minutes, sweep seconds; power
reserve indicator; date
Case: ceramic and titanium, ø 48 mm, height 15 mm;
sapphire crystal; screw-in crown; water-resistant to
6 atm
Band: textile, buckle
Price: $18,200
Variations: "Top Gun" version with black dial and band
($18,200)

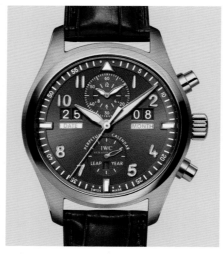

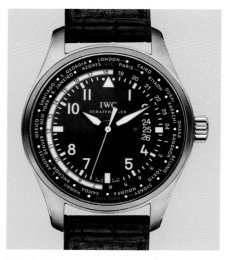

Big Pilot's Watch Perpetual Calendar "Top Gun"

Reference number: IW502902
Movement: automatic, IWC Caliber 51614;
ø 37.8 mm, height 8.75 mm; 62 jewels; 21,600 vph;
Pellaton automatic winding system, 168-hour power
reserve
Functions: hours, minutes, subsidiary seconds;
power reserve indicator; perpetual calendar with date,
weekday, month, moon phase, year display (4 digits)
Case: ceramic and titanium, ø 48 mm, height 16 mm;
sapphire crystal, screw-in crown; water-resistant to
6 atm
Band: textile, folding clasp
Price: $38,600

Ingenieur Perpetual Calendar Digital Date-Month

Reference number: IW379105
Movement: automatic, IWC Caliber 89801;
ø 37 mm, height 9.86 mm; 52 jewels; 28,800 vph;
double-pawl automatic winding system,
shockproofed rotor; 68-hour power reserve
Functions: hours, minutes, subsidiary seconds;
flyback chronograph; perpetual calendar with large
date and month (both digital), leap year
Case: pink gold, ø 46 mm, height 17.5 mm;
sapphire crystal, screw-in crown; water-resistant to
6 atm
Band: reptile skin, folding clasp
Price: $49,700

Worldtimer

Reference number: IW326201
Movement: automatic, IWC Caliber 30750 (base
ETA 2829-A2 with extra module): ø 32.9 mm, height
5.95 mm; 31 jewels; 28,800 vph; soft iron cap for
antimagnetic protection; 42-hour power reserve
Functions: hours, minutes, sweep seconds; world-
time display; date
Case: stainless steel, ø 45 mm, height 13.5 mm;
sapphire crystal, screw-in crown; water-resistant to
6 atm
Band: reptile skin, folding clasp
Price: $9,650

1888

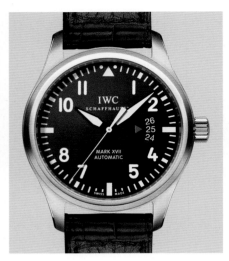

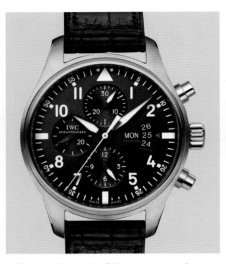

Pilot's Watch Mark XVII

Reference number: IW326501
Movement: automatic, IWC Caliber 30110
(base ETA 2892-A2); ø 25.6 mm, height
3.6 mm; 21 jewels; 28,800 vph; soft iron cap for
antimagnetic protection; 42-hour power reserve
Functions: hours, minutes, sweep seconds; date
Case: stainless steel, ø 41 mm, height 11 mm;
sapphire crystal, screw-in crown; water-resistant to
6 atm
Band: reptile skin, buckle
Price: $4,900
Variations: with stainless steel bracelet ($6,100)

Pilot's Watch Chronograph

Reference number: IW377701
Movement: automatic, IWC Caliber 79320 (base
ETA 7750); ø 30 mm, height 7.9 mm; 25 jewels;
28,800 vph; 44-hour power reserve
Functions: hours, minutes, subsidiary seconds;
chronograph; weekday, date
Case: stainless steel, ø 43 mm, height 15 mm;
sapphire crystal, screw-in crown; water-resistant to
6 atm
Band: reptile skin, buckle
Price: $5,900
Variations: with stainless steel bracelet ($7,100)

Portofino Hand-Wound
Eight Days

Reference number: IW510104
Movement: manually wound, IWC Caliber 59210;
ø 37.8 mm, height 5.8 mm; 30 jewels; 28,800 vph;
192-hour power reserve
Functions: hours, minutes, subsidiary seconds;
power reserve indicator; date
Case: pink gold, ø 45 mm, height 12 mm; sapphire
crystal, transparent case back; water-resistant to
3 atm
Band: reptile skin, buckle
Price: $10,800
Variations: stainless steel ($10,800); rose gold
($20,200)

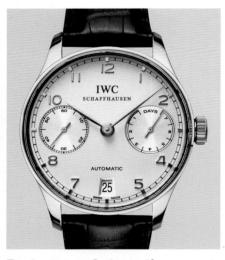

Portuguese Automatic

Reference number: IW500114
Movement: automatic, IWC Caliber 51011;
ø 37.8 mm, height 7.6 mm; 42 jewels; 21,600 vph;
Pellaton automatic winding system; 168-hour power
reserve
Functions: hours, minutes, subsidiary seconds;
date; power reserve indicator
Case: stainless steel, ø 42.3 mm, height 14
mm; sapphire crystal; transparent case back;
water-resistant to 3 atm
Band: reptile skin, folding clasp
Price: $23,700
Variations: pink gold ($21,600); white gold
($23,700); various dials

Portuguese Chronograph

Reference number: IW371480
Movement: automatic, IWC Caliber 79350 (base
ETA 7750); ø 30 mm, height 7.9 mm; 31 jewels;
28,800 vph; 44-hour power reserve
Functions: hours, minutes, subsidiary seconds;
chronograph
Case: pink gold, ø 40.9 mm, height 12.3 mm;
sapphire crystal, water-resistant to 3 atm
Band: reptile skin, buckle
Price: $7,900
Variations: various dials; stainless steel ($7,900)

Portuguese Tourbillon
Hand-Wound

Reference number: IW544705
Movement: manually wound, IWC Caliber 98900;
ø 38.2 mm; 21 jewels; 28,800 vph; 1-minute
tourbillon, three-quarter plate, Breguet spring;
54-hour power reserve
Functions: hours, minutes, subsidiary seconds
Case: rose gold, ø 43.1 mm, height 11 mm;
sapphire crystal, transparent case back; water-
resistant to 3 atm
Band: reptile skin, folding clasp
Price: $114,000, limited to 500 pieces
Variations: platinum ($136,000)

Caliber 51111

Base caliber: 5000
Automatic; double-pawl automatic winding (Pellaton system); single spring barrel, 7-day power reserve
Functions: hours, minutes, sweep seconds; date; power reserve indicator
Diameter: 37.8 mm
Height: 7.53 mm
Jewels: 44
Balance: balance with variable inertia
Frequency: 21,600 vph
Balance spring: Breguet
Shock protection: Incabloc

Caliber 51900

Base caliber: 5000
Automatic; double-pawl automatic winding (Pellaton system); flying 1-minute tourbillon; single spring barrel, 7 days power reserve
Functions: hours, minutes; date (retrograde); power reserve indicator
Diameter: 37.8 mm
Height: 8.9 mm
Jewels: 44
Balance: glucydur
Frequency: 19,800 vph
Balance spring: Breguet
Shock protection: Incabloc

Caliber 51011

Base caliber: 5000
Automatic; double-pawl automatic winding (Pellaton system); single spring barrel, 7-day power reserve
Functions: hours, minutes, subsidiary seconds; power reserve indicator
Diameter: 37.8 mm
Height: 7.6 mm
Jewels: 42
Balance: balance with variable inertia
Frequency: 21,600 vph
Balance spring: Breguet
Shock protection: Incabloc

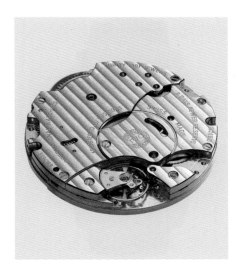

Caliber 59210

Manually wound; single spring barrel, 8-day power reserve
Functions: hours, minutes, subsidiary seconds; date; power reserve indicator
Diameter: 37.8 mm
Height: 5.8 mm
Jewels: 30
Balance: balance with variable inertia
Frequency: 28,800 vph
Balance spring: Breguet
Shock protection: Incabloc

Caliber 89361

Base caliber: 89360
Automatic; double-pawl automatic winding (Pellaton system); column wheel control of chronograph functions; single spring barrel, power reserve 68 hours
Functions: hours, minutes, subsidiary seconds; flyback chronograph; date
Diameter: 30 mm
Height: 7.46 mm
Jewels: 38
Balance: balance with variable inertia
Frequency: 28,800 vph
Balance spring: flat hairspring
Shock protection: Incabloc
Remarks: concentric chronograph counter for minutes and hours

Caliber 98295 "Jones"

Manually wound; characteristic long regulator index; single spring barrel, power reserve 46 hours
Functions: hours, minutes, subsidiary seconds
Diameter: 38.2 mm
Height: 5.3 mm
Jewels: 18
Balance: screw balance with precision adjustment cams on balance arms
Frequency: 18,000 vph
Balance spring: Breguet
Shock protection: Incabloc
Remarks: three-quarter plate of German silver, hand-engraved balance cocks

Jacob & Co. Watches
Chemin de Plein-Vent, 1
CH-1228 Arare
Switzerland

Tel.:
01141-22-310-6962

E-Mail:
geneva@jacobandco.com

Website:
www.jacobandco.com

Founded:
1986

Number of employees:
not specified

Annual production:
not specified

U.S. distributor:
Jacob & Co. Watches
48 East 57th Street
New York, NY 10022
212-888-2330
contact@jacobandco.com

Most important collections/price range:
Ghost / from $5,400; Brilliant Ladies / $12,000
to $53,500; Palatial Automatic / $19,000
to $23,500; Palatial Tourbillon / $98,000 to
$260,000; Brilliant Tourbillon / $810,000 to
$1,030,000

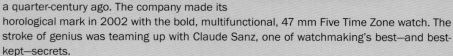

Jacob & Co.

Some watch brands manage to remain on the edge of the radar before suddenly lighting up the entire screen with pieces of bold creativity and mechanical brilliance. Such is the case with Jacob & Co., founded by Jacob Arabo over a quarter-century ago. The company made its horological mark in 2002 with the bold, multifunctional, 47 mm Five Time Zone watch. The stroke of genius was teaming up with Claude Sanz, one of watchmaking's best—and best-kept—secrets.

Sanz and Arabo share a love of gemstones and *haute horlogerie,* and given that common bond plus the explosion of illusory wealth in the first decade of the new century, the Five Time Zone line and the business itself grew rapidly. In 2007, another milestone was established when Sanz conceived the Quenttin, a maverick with a row of visible spring barrels and a 31-day power reserve with a reserve display that counts *days.*

That established the brand firmly on collectors' radar, leaving Jacob & Co. ready to find its place on the fine edge between brash, glittering time-telling objects and horological masterpieces. The recent move to Geneva is a major step in the company strategy to boost its watch manufacturing by getting closer to industry talent.

Jacob & Co. continues to surprise aficionados, be it with the ultra-steampunkish Quenttin, the high-tech Epic series, the eye-catching Brilliant Diamonds, and now the Ghost. And the company has no qualms going toe-to-toe with geekdom: The Ghost features five time zones and GPS.

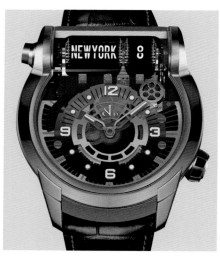

Ghost

Reference number: 300.100.11.NS.MB.4NS
Movement: exclusive digital JCDQ01 with GPS; quartz; lithium-polymer 3.7 V 80 mAh battery
Functions: multiple time zones; GPS system allowing date and time setting
Case: black PVD stainless steel, pentagon; polished and micro-blasted finishes; ø 47 mm
Band: vulcanized rubber, black PVD stainless steel deployment buckle
Price: $5,400
Variations: interchangeable bezels: rubber carbon fiber; black PVD set with diamonds; rose gold set with diamonds

Epic SF24

Reference number: 500.100.40.NS.NY.1NS
Movement: automatic, Jacob&Co Caliber JCAA02; 35.50 x 42.10 mm; height 12.20 mm; 28,800 vph; openwork dial with micro-blasted gray center; 46-hour power reserve
Functions: hours, minutes, seconds; 24-hour world-time indication
Case: rose gold, satin-finished, micro-blasted and polished finishing; ø 45 mm, height 16.4 mm; sapphire crystal
Band: reptile skin, rose gold deployment buckle
Price: $103,000
Variations: white gold ($103,000); titanium ($81,000)

Grand Baguette

Reference number: 330.800.30.BD.BD.1BD
Movement: Swiss quartz; 5 x Ronda Caliber 1042
Functions: hours, minutes, five time zones
Case: white gold, 47 mm pentagon; five crowns invisibly set with baguette diamonds; hand-engraved case back
Band: reptile skin, white gold tang buckle set with 44 baguette diamonds
Remarks: invisibly set with 767 diamonds; white gold hand-made and polished hands with blue nickel finish
Price: $1,100,000

Palatial Tourbillon, Minute Repeater

Reference number: 150.500.24.NS.OB.1NS
Movement: manually wound, Jacob&Co Caliber JCBM03; 21,600 vph; 1-minute flying tourbillon; minute repeater; titanium balance with gold timing screw; bridges with côtes de Genève, hand-polished angles, and draw-finished flanks; 100-hour power reserve
Functions: hours, minutes; minute repeater
Case: titanium, ø 43 mm; rose gold crown and lever; sapphire glass; transparent case back
Band: reptile skin, titanium tang buckle
Remarks: exclusive blue sapphire crystal dial, applied brushed treble clef
Price: $260,000

Quenttin

Reference number: 700.100.20.NS.AA.4NS
Movement: exclusive manually wound Jacob&Co Caliber JCBM04; 1-minute vertical tourbillon; height 15.35 mm; 40 jewels; 21,600 vph; 31-day power reserve; 7 spring barrels
Functions: hours, minutes; power reverse display
Case: titanium, carbon fiber inserts; 56 x 47 x 21.5 mm, curved; side window for tourbillon; sapphire glass case back
Band: rubber, titanium deployment buckle
Price: $378,000
Variations: white gold ($484,000); rose gold ($484,000); black PVD magnesium ($350,000)

Brilliant Tourbillon

Reference number: 210.543.40.BR.BR.1BR
Movement: manually wound Jacob&Co Caliber JCBM01; ø 34.10 mm, height 6 mm; 21,600 vph; 1-minute flying tourbillon; titanium balance with gold timing screw
Functions: hours, minutes; power reserve indication on back
Case: rose gold, ø 47 mm, height 14.60 mm; set with baguette rubies, crown with one rose-cut ruby and baguette rubies; sapphire crystal, transparent case back
Band: reptile skin, rose gold tang buckle set with baguette rubies
Remarks: dial with invisibly set baguette rubies
Price: $1,030,000

Palatial Automatic

Reference number: 110.300.40.NS.NA.1NS
Movement: automatic, Jacob&Co Caliber JCCM01; ø 30.40 mm, height 3.18 mm; 28,800 vph; glucydur balance wheel; côtes de Genève, circular graining, vertical satin-finish and snailing finishes, applied polished faceted hour markers; 36-hour power reserve
Functions: hours, minutes
Case: polished rose gold, 42 mm; height 6.8 mm
Band: alligator, polished rose gold tang buckle
Price: $19,000

Brilliant Collection

Reference number: 210.030.10.RD.KR.3RD
Momement: quartz, ETA, caliber 995.432
Functions: hours, minutes
Case: stainless steel set with round diamonds, ø 38 mm, height 10.75 mm; sapphire crystal
Band: satin, stainless steel buckle set with diamonds
Remarks: white mother-of-pearl dial set with diamonds and colored sapphires as hour markers
Price: $35,500

Epic X

Reference number: 550.100.20.NS.OY.4NS
Movement: manually wound exclusive caliber JCAM02; ø 34.80 mm; height 5.90 mm; 28,800 vph; 48-hour power reserve; barrel and balance vertically aligned
Functions: hours, minutes; time setting spring with 3 functions ("octopus spring"): ratchet, lever, and setting lever
Case: micro-blasted and satin-finished titanium, ø 44 mm, height 12.55 mm
Band: openwork "honeycomb" rubber, adjustable deployment clasp
Price: $27,000
Variations: black PVD stainless steel ($27,000)

Jaeger-LeCoultre

Manufacture Jaeger-LeCoultre
Rue de la Golisse, 8
CH-1347 Le Sentier
Switzerland

Tel.:
01141-21-852-0202

Fax:
01141-21-852-0505

E-Mail:
info@jaeger-lecoultre.com

Website:
www.jaeger-lecoultre.com

Founded:
1833

Number of employees:
over 1,000

Annual production:
approx. 50,000 watches

U.S. distributor:
Jaeger-LeCoultre
645 Fifth Avenue
New York, NY 10022
800-JLC-TIME
www.jaeger-lecoultre.com

Most important collection/price range:
Reverso, Rendez-Vous, Duomètre, Master, AMVOX
/ approx. $ 6000 to $130,000;
and higher for limited editions and the Grandes
Complications models

Jaeger-LeCoultre

The Jaeger-LeCoultre *manufacture* has a long and tumultuous history. In 1833, Antoine LeCoultre opened his own workshop for the production of gear wheels. Having made his fortune, he then did what many other artisans did: In 1866, he had a large house built and brought together all the craftspeople needed to produce timepieces, from the watchmakers to the turners and polishers. He outfitted the workshop with the most modern machinery of the day, all powered by a steam engine. "La Grande Maison" was the first watch *manufacture* in the Vallée de Joux.

At the start of the twentieth century, the grandson of the company founder, Jacques-David LeCoultre, built slender, complicated watches for the Paris manufacturer Edmond Jaeger. The Frenchman was so impressed with these that, after a few years of fruitful cooperation, he engineered a merger of the two companies.

In the 1970s, the *manufacture* hit hard times and was taken over by the German VDO Group (later Mannesmann). Under the leadership of Günter Blümlein, Jaeger-LeCoultre weathered the quartz crisis, and during the mechanical watch renaissance in the 1980s, the company finally recouped its status as an innovative, high-performance *manufacture*. When Mannesmann's watch division (JLC, IWC, A. Lange & Söhne) sold Jaeger-LeCoultre to the Richemont Group in 2000, words like "competence" and "capacities" were used in the sales pitch. Those qualities, plus a decade of continual expansion and growth made it a great buy. Today, Jaeger-LeCoultre boasts more than 1,000 employees, making it the largest employer in the Vallée de Joux—just as it was back in the 1860s.

Master Grande Tradition Gyrotourbillon 3 Jubilee

Reference number: 503 64 20
Movement: manually wound, JLC Caliber 176; ø 36 mm, height 11.15 mm; 82 jewels; 21,600 vph; patented spherical double-axis tourbillon with 2 different rotation speeds (24 sec/60 sec); aluminum tourbillon cage; 2 spring barrels; 48-hour power reserve
Functions: hours, minutes (off-center); day/night indicator; chronograph with jumping digital minute counter
Case: platinum, ø 43.5 mm, height 15.5 mm; sapphire crystal, transparent case back; water-resistant to 5 atm
Band: reptile skin, white gold folding clasp
Price: $499,000, limited to 75 pieces

Master Grande Tradition Tourbillon Cylindrique à Quantième Perpétuel Jubilee

Reference number: Q504 65 20
Movement: automatic, JLC Caliber 985; ø 30.7 mm, height 8.15 mm; 49 jewels; 28,800 vph; flying 1-minute tourbillon with cylindrical mainspring; 48-hour power reserve
Functions: hours, minutes, subsidiary seconds; perpetual calendar with date, weekday, month, moon phase, year display (digital, 4 digits)
Case: platinum, ø 42 mm, height 13.1 mm; sapphire crystal, transparent case back; water-resistant to 5 atm
Band: reptile skin, platinum buckle
Price: $158,000, limited to 180 pieces

Master Grande Tradition à Répétition Minutes

Reference number: 501 25 50
Movement: manually wound, JLC Caliber 947; ø 34.7 mm, height 8.95 mm; 43 jewels; 21,600 vph; fine finishing; 360 hours power reserve
Functions: hours, minutes; minute repeater; double power reserve indicator (spring and torque)
Case: rose gold, ø 44 mm, height 15.6 mm; sapphire crystal; transparent case back; water-resistant to 5 atm
Band: reptile skin, buckle
Price: $210,000

Duomètre à Chronographe

Reference number: 601 25 21
Movement: manually wound, JLC Caliber 380; ø 33.7 mm, height 6.95 mm; 47 jewels; 21,600 vph; 2 separate spring barrels, separate mechanisms for time and chronograph; chronograph functions controlled by switch on foudroyante mechanism; 50 hours power reserve
Functions: hours and minutes (off-center), sweep seconds; power reserve display, chronograph
Case: rose gold, ø 39.5 mm, height 13.6 mm; sapphire crystal, transparent case back; water-resistant to 5 atm
Band: reptile skin, buckle
Price: $47,000

Duomètre à Quantième Lunaire 40.5

Reference number: 604 25 21
Movement: manually wound, JLC Caliber 381; ø 33.7 mm, height 7.25 mm; 40 jewels; 21,600 vph; 2 spring barrels, 2 separate gear trains for watch and foudroyante mechanism; 50 hours power reserve
Functions: hours and minutes (off-center); foudroyante sixth-second counter (second foudroyante); date, moon phase and age; double power reserve display
Case: rose gold, ø 40.5 mm, height 13.07 mm; sapphire crystal; transparent case back; water-resistant to 5 atm
Band: reptile skin, buckle
Price: $36,300

Duomètre Sphérotourbillon

Reference number: 605 25 20
Movement: manually wound, JLC Caliber 382; ø 33.7 mm, height 10.45 mm; 55 jewels; 21,600 vph; 2 barrel springs, 2 separate mechanisms for watch and double-axis tourbillon, 15- or 30-second revolution; fine finishing; 50 hours power reserve per barrel spring
Functions: hours, minutes, subsidiary seconds with flyback mechanism; second time zone (additional 24-hour display); date; double power reserve display
Case: rose gold, ø 42 mm, height 14.1 mm; sapphire crystal; transparent case back; water-resistant to 5 atm
Band: reptile skin, buckle
Price: $251,000

Master Tourbillon Dualtime

Reference number: 156 25 21
Movement: automatic, JLC Caliber 978B; ø 30 mm, height 7.1 mm; 33 jewels; 28,800 vph; tourbillon; hand date (jumps from 15th to 16th of month); 48 hours power reserve
Functions: hours, minutes, subsidiary seconds; (on tourbillon cage); additional 24-hour hand (second time zone), date
Case: pink gold, ø 41.5 mm, height 12.1 mm; sapphire crystal, transparent case back; water-resistant to 5 atm
Band: reptile skin, buckle
Price: $83,000

Master Ultra Thin Tourbillon

Reference number: 132 24 10
Movement: automatic, JLC Caliber 982; ø 26 mm, height 6.4 mm; 33 jewels; 28,800 vph; 1-minute tourbillon; 48 hours power reserve
Functions: hours, minutes
Case: pink gold, ø 40 mm, height 11.3 mm; sapphire crystal; transparent case back; water-resistant to 5 atm
Band: reptile skin, buckle
Price: $70,500

Deep Sea Chronograph Cermet

Reference number: 208A570
Movement: automatic, JLC Caliber 758; ø 25.60 mm, height 6.81 mm; 47 jewels; 28,800 vph; fine hand-finishing; 65 hours power reserve
Functions: hours, minutes, subsidiary seconds; chronograph (with function display)
Case: aluminum with ceramic coating; ø 44 mm, unidirectional bezel with 60-minute divisions; sapphire crystal, water-resistant to 10 atm
Band: satin, buckle
Price: $18,000

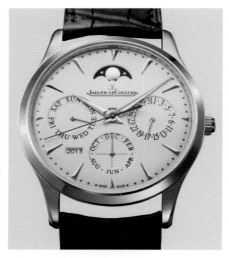

Master Ultra Thin Perpetual

Reference number: 130 35 20
Movement: automatic, JLC Caliber 868; height 4.72 mm; 46 jewels; 38 hours power reserve
Functions: hours, minutes, sweep seconds; perpetual calendar with date, weekday, month, moon phase, year display (4 digits)
Case: white gold, ø 39 mm, height 9.2 mm; sapphire crystal, transparent case back; water-resistant to 5 atm
Band: reptile skin, buckle
Price: $34,700
Variations: rose gold ($31,600)

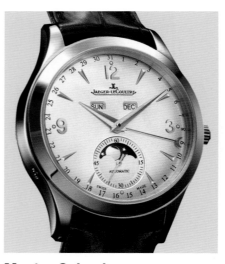

Master Calendar

Reference number: 155 25 20
Movement: automatic, JLC Caliber 866; height 5.65 mm; 32 jewels; 28,800 vph; fine hand-finishing; 43 hours power reserve
Functions: hours, minutes, subsidiary seconds; full calendar with date, weekday, month, moon phase
Case: pink gold, ø 39 mm, height 10.6 mm; sapphire crystal, transparent case back; water-resistant to 5 atm
Band: reptile skin, buckle
Price: $23,500
Variations: stainless steel with folding clasp ($10,800)

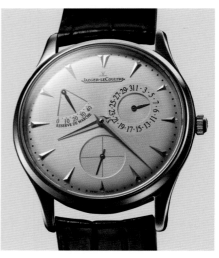

Master Ultra Thin Réserve de Marche

Reference number: 137 84 20
Movement: automatic, JLC Caliber 938; ø 26 mm, height 4.9 mm; 41 jewels; 28,800 vph; 43 hours power reserve
Functions: hours, minutes, subsidiary seconds; date; power reserve indicator
Case: stainless steel, ø 39 mm, height 9.85 mm; sapphire crystal; water-resistant to 5 atm
Band: reptile skin, buckle
Price: $9,750
Variations: rose gold ($19,400)

Master Ultra Thin Jubilee

Movement: manually wound, JLC Caliber 849; ø 26 mm, height 1.85 mm; 19 jewels; 21,600 vph; 35 hours power reserve
Functions: hours, minutes
Case: platinum, ø 39 mm, height 4.05 mm; sapphire crystal, transparent case back; water-resistant to 5 atm
Band: reptile skin, buckle
Price: $17,800, limited to 880 pieces

Master Ultra Thin 41

Reference number: Q133 25 11
Movement: automatic, JLC Caliber 898C; ø 26 mm, height 3.3 mm; 29 jewels; 28,800 vph; 43 hours power reserve
Functions: hours, minutes
Case: pink gold, ø 41 mm, height 7.48 mm; sapphire crystal; water-resistant to 5 atm
Band: reptile skin, buckle
Price: $15,200
Variations: stainless steel with folding clasp ($9,000)

Master Control

Reference number: 154 25 20
Movement: automatic, JLC Caliber 899; ø 26 mm, height 3.3 mm; 32 jewels; 28,800 vph; 43 hours power reserve
Functions: hours, minutes, sweep seconds; date
Case: rose gold, ø 39 mm, height 8.5 mm; sapphire crystal; water-resistant to 5 atm
Band: reptile skin, buckle
Price: $16,200
Variations: stainless steel ($7,200)

Master Chronograph

Reference number: 153 84 7N
Movement: automatic, JLC Caliber 751A-1
(base JLC 751); ø 26.2 mm, height 5.72 mm;
39 jewels; 28,800 vph; 2 spring barrels; 65 hours
power reserve
Functions: hours, minutes, subsidiary seconds;
chronograph; date
Case: stainless steel, ø 40 mm, height 11.7 mm;
sapphire crystal; water-resistant to 5 atm
Band: reptile skin, folding clasp
Price: $10,400
Variations: rose gold ($24,900); stainless steel in
light dial ($10,200)

Grande Reverso Ultra Thin Duoface

Reference number: Q3782520
Movement: manually wound, JLC Caliber
854/1; 17.2 x 22 mm, height 3.8 mm; 21 jewels;
21,600 vph; fine hand-finishing
Functions: hours, minutes, subsidiary seconds;
24-hour hand (second time zone), day/night
indication (on back)
Case: pink gold, sapphire crystal, transparent case
back; water-resistant to 3 atm
Band: reptile skin, buckle
Remarks: case can be turned and pivoted 180°
Price: $19,400
Variations: stainless steel ($10,400)

Grande Reverso Calendar

Reference number: 375 25 20
Movement: manually wound, JLC Caliber 843;
height 4.29 mm; 21 jewels; 21,600 vph; 45 hours
power reserve
Functions: hours, minutes; full calendar with date,
weekday, month, moon phase
Case: rose gold, 29.5 x 48.5 mm, height
10.24 mm; sapphire crystal, transparent case back;
water-resistant to 3 atm
Band: reptile skin, buckle
Remarks: case can be turned and pivoted 180°
Price: $21,900
Variations: stainless steel ($12,400)

Grande Reverso Lady Ultra Thin Duetto Duo

Reference number: 330 24 21
Movement: manually wound, JLC Caliber 864/A;
height 3.45 mm; 19 jewels; 21,600 vph; hand-
decorated
Functions: hours, minutes; additional 12-hour hand
(second time zone)
Case: pink gold, 24 x 40 mm, height 8.87 mm; bezel
set with 30 diamonds; sapphire crystal
Price: $24,300
Variations: stainless steel ($12,100); white gold set
with 153 diamonds ($47,000)

Grande Reverso Lady Ultra Thin

Reference number: 320 41 20
Movement: quartz, JLC Caliber 657
Functions: hours, minutes
Case: stainless steel, 24 x 40 mm, height 7.17 mm;
pink gold bezel; sapphire crystal
Band: stainless steel with pink gold elements,
folding clasp
Price: $10,700

Rendez-Vous Night & Day 34 mm

Reference number: 344 25 20
Movement: automatic, JLC Caliber 898A; ø 26 mm,
height 3.3 mm; 30 jewels; 28,800 vph
Functions: hours, minutes, sweep seconds; day/night
indicator
Case: pink gold, ø 34 mm, height 12.4 mm; bezel set
with 60 diamonds; sapphire crystal
Band: reptile skin, folding clasp
Price: $23,400
Variations: rose gold with rose gold bracelet
($39,000); stainless steel with reptile skin band
($14,900); stainless steel with stainless steel bracelet
($15,700)

Caliber 380

Manually wound; 2 spring barrels and 2 separate gear trains for watch and chronograph; chronograph functions controlled by switch on foudroyante mechanism

Functions: hours, minutes, sweep seconds; chronograph with foudroyante sixth-second counter (second foudroyante); double power reserve display
Diameter: 33.7 mm
Height: 6.95 mm
Jewels: 48
Balance: screw balance with weights
Frequency: 21,600 vph
Remarks: perlage on plate, bridges with côtes de Genève

Caliber 381

Manually wound; 2 spring barrels and 2 separate gear trains for watch and foudroyante mechanism; 50-hour power reserve

Functions: hours, minutes, foudroyante sixth-second counter (second foudroyante); date; moon phase and age; double power reserve indicator
Diameter: 33.7 mm
Height: 7.25 mm
Jewels: 40
Balance: screw balance with weights
Frequency: 21,600 vph
Remarks: 369 components

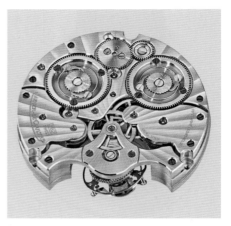

Caliber 382

Manually wound; 2 barrel springs and 2 separate mechanisms for watch and double-axis tourbillon, double-axis tourbillon with -20° tilt, 15- or 30-second revolution, pull crown to reset second hand; twin spring barrels, 50-hour power reserve

Functions: hours, minutes subsidiary seconds; second time zone (additional 24-hour display); annual calendar with date; double power reserve display
Diameter: 33.7 mm
Height: 10.45 mm
Jewels: 33
Balance: glucydur
Frequency: 21,600 vph
Balance spring: cylindrical

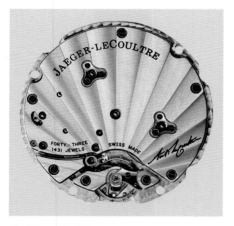

Caliber 947

Manually wound; twin spring barrels, 360-hour power reserve

Functions: hours, minutes; hour, quarter-hour, and minute repeater barrel spring torque display
Diameter: 34.7 mm
Height: 8.95 mm
Jewels: 43
Balance: screw balance
Frequency: 21,600 vph
Balance spring: flat hairspring
Shock protection: Kif
Remarks: bridges with sunburst côtes de Genève

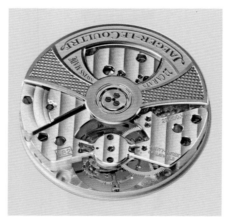

Caliber 982

Automatic; 1-minute tourbillon; full gold rotor; single spring barrel, 48-hour power reserve

Functions: hours, minutes, subsidiary seconds (on tourbillon cage)
Diameter: 30 mm
Height: 6.4 mm
Jewels: 33
Balance: glucydur with weighted screws
Frequency: 28,800 vph
Balance spring: Breguet spring
Shock protection: Kif
Remarks: perlage on plate, bridges with côtes de Genève

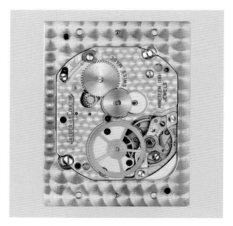

Caliber 986

Manually wound; 48-hour power reserve

Functions: hours, minutes, subsidiary seconds; 24-hour display (second time zone); date
Measurements: 22.6 x 25.6 mm
Height: 4.15 mm
Jewels: 19
Frequency: 28,800 vph
Balance spring: flat hairspring
Shock protection: Kif
Remarks: perlage on plate

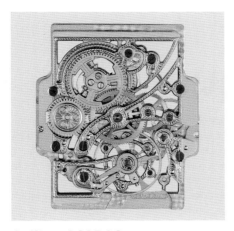

Caliber 849RSQ

Manually wound; fully skeletonized and engraved by hand; simple barrel spring, 35-hour power reserve
Functions: hours, minutes
Measurements: 20 x 23.5 mm
Height: 2.09 mm
Jewels: 19
Balance: glucydur
Frequency: 21,600 vph
Balance spring: flat spring with swan-neck fine adjustment
Shock protection: Kif
Remarks: 128 components

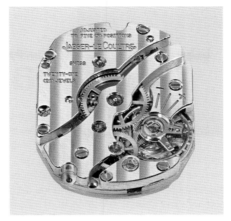

Caliber 843

Manually wound; single spring barrel, 45-hour power reserve
Functions: hours, minutes; full calendar with date, weekday, month, moon phase
Measurements: 22.6 x 25.6 mm
Height: 4.29 mm
Jewels: 21
Balance: glucydur with weighted screws
Frequency: 21,600 vph
Balance spring: flat hairspring
Shock protection: Kif

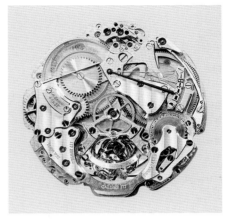

Caliber 177

Manually wound; patented spherical tourbillon; 2 spring barrels, 8-day power reserve
Functions: hours, minutes, subsidiary seconds (on tourbillon cage); perpetual calendar with date (2 retrograde hands) and month; equation of time; retrograde leap year display on back
Diameter: 36.3 mm
Height: 10.85 mm
Jewels: 77
Frequency: 21,600 vph
Remarks: 659 components, perlage on plate, bridges with côtes de Genève

Caliber 945

Manually wound; silicon pallet lever; flying tourbillon rotates with dial in 56 minutes (sidereal time, astronomical time); 48-hour power reserve
Functions: hours, minutes; 24-hour display; perpetual calendar with date and month; sky map with zodiac signs; hour, quarter-hour, and minute repeater
Diameter: 31 mm
Height: 12.62 mm
Jewels: 49
Balance: screw balance
Frequency: 28,800 vph
Balance spring: flat hairspring
Remarks: 527 components, repeater with "trébuchet" hammer for stronger strike

Caliber 978

Automatic; 1-minute tourbillon; full gold rotor; single spring barrel, 48-hour power reserve
Functions: hours, minutes, small seconds (on tourbillon cage); additional 24-hour display; hand date (jumps from 15th to 16th of month)
Diameter: 31 mm
Height: 7.05 mm
Jewels: 33
Balance: glucydur with weighted screws
Frequency: 28,800 vph
Balance spring: Breguet spring
Shock protection: Kif
Remarks: perlage on plate, bridges with côtes de Genève

Caliber 898A

Automatic; single spring barrel, 43-hour power reserve
Functions: hours, minutes, sweep seconds; day/night indicator
Diameter: 26 mm
Height: 3.3 mm
Jewels: 30
Balance: glucydur with 4 weighted screws
Frequency: 28,800 vph
Balance spring: flat hairspring
Shock protection: Kif

Montres Jaquet Droz SA
CH-2300 La Chaux-de-Fonds
Switzerland

Tel.:
01141-32-924-2888

Fax:
01141-32-924-2882

E-Mail:
info@jaquet-droz.com

Website:
www.jaquet-droz.com

Founded:
1738

Number of employees:
not specified

Annual production:
not specified

U.S. distributor:
The Swatch Group (U.S.), Inc.
1200 Harbor Boulevard
Weehawken, NJ 07086
201-271-1400
www.swatchgroup.com

Most important collections/price range:
Urban: London; Legend: Geneva; Complication:
La Chaux-de-Fonds; Majestic: Beijing; Elegance:
Paris; Les Ateliers D'Art / starting at $8,000

Jaquet Droz

Though this watch brand first gained real notice when it was bought by the Swatch Group in 2001, Jaquet Droz looks back on a long tradition. Pierre Jaquet-Droz (1721–1790) was actually supposed to be a pastor, but instead followed the call to become a mechanic and a watchmaker. In the mid-eighteenth century, he began to push the limits of micromechanics, and his enthusiasm for it quickly led him to work on watch mechanisms and more complicated movements, which he attempted to operate through purely mechanical means.

Jaquet-Droz became famous in Europe for his automatons. More than once, he had to answer to religious institutions, whose guardians of public morals suspected there might be some devil's work and witchcraft behind his mechanical children, scribes, and organists. He even designed prostheses. A small enterprise in La Chaux-de-Fonds still produces items of this applied art, proof that the name Jaquet-Droz is still alive and well in the Jura mountains. The true wealth of the Jaquet-Droz family's output, however, was shown in the stunning exhibition "Automats and Marvels" organized in Neuchâtel, La Chaux-de-Fonds, and Le Locle in 2012.

The Swatch Group has developed an aesthetically and technically sophisticated collection based on an outstanding Frédéric Piguet movement. In recent years, the classically beautiful watch dials have taken on a slightly modern look without losing any of their identity. The spirit of the maverick founder of the brand still hovers about. In fact, Jaquet Droz is a top representative in the Swatch Group's portfolio. Its CEO is Marc A. Hayek, who is also CEO of Breguet and Blancpain.

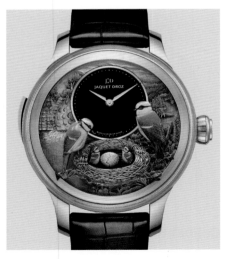

The Bird Repeater

Reference number: J031033200
Movement: manual winding, Jaquet Droz Caliber RMA88; ø 35 mm, height 8.8 mm; 69 jewels; 18,000 vph; 48-hour power reserve
Functions: hours and minutes (off-center); minute repeater
Case: pink gold, ø 47 mm, height 18.7 mm; sapphire crystal
Band: reptile skin, folding clasp
Remarks: hand-painted mother-of-pearl dial
Price: $472,500, limited to 8 pieces
Variations: white gold, limited to 8 pieces ($493,500)

Petite Heure Minute Relief Snake

Reference number: J005024273
Movement: automatic, Jaquet Droz Caliber 2653; ø 26.2 mm, height 4.47 mm; 28 jewels; 28,800 vph; double spring barrel, oscillating mass of white gold and white mother-of-pearl with hand-engraved cobra; 68-hour power reserve
Functions: hours and minutes (off-center)
Case: white gold, set with 309 diamonds; ø 41 mm, height 13.77 mm; sapphire crystal, water-resistant to 3 atm
Band: satin, buckle
Remarks: mother-of-pearl dial, snake application set with diamonds
Price: $88,200, limited to 8 pieces

Petite Heure Minute Relief Seasons

Reference number: J005024575
Movement: automatic, Jaquet Droz Caliber 2653; ø 26.2 mm, height 4.7 mm; 28 jewels; 28,800 vph; double spring barrel, oscillating mass of white gold and white mother-of-pearl, hand-engraved; 68-hour power reserve
Functions: hours and minutes (off-center)
Case: white gold, set with 272 diamonds; ø 41 mm, height 13.77 mm; sapphire crystal, water-resistant to 3 atm
Band: reptile skin, buckle
Remarks: hand-painted bird applications on mother-of-pearl dial
Price: $71,400, limited to 88 pieces

The Eclipse 39 mm

Reference number: J012613200
Movement: automatic, Jaquet Droz Caliber 6553L2; ø 27 mm, height 5.02 mm; 28 jewels; 28,800 vph; double spring barrel, white gold oscillating weight; 68-hour power reserve
Functions: hours, minutes; full calendar with date, weekday, month, moon phase
Case: pink gold, ø 39 mm, height 12.69 mm; sapphire crystal, transparent case back; water-resistant to 3 atm
Band: reptile skin, buckle
Remarks: enamel dial
Price: $27,400
Variations: white gold with diamonds ($36,500)

Perpetual Calendar Eclipse Ivory Enamel

Reference number: J030533201
Movement: automatic, Jaquet Droz Caliber 5853LR; ø 32 mm, height 6.22 mm; 34 jewels; 28,800 vph; double spring barrel, white gold oscillating mass; 68-hour power reserve
Functions: hours, minutes; perpetual calendar with retrograde date and weekday, month, moon phase, leap year
Case: pink gold, ø 43 mm, height 13.2 mm; sapphire crystal, water-resistant to 3 atm
Band: reptile skin, folding clasp
Remarks: enamel dial
Price: $54,600
Variations: with black dial ($54,600)

Grande Heure GMT

Reference number: J015233200
Movement: automatic, Jaquet Droz Caliber 5N50; ø 26.2 mm, height 4.47 mm; 28 jewels; 28,800 vph; double spring barrel; white gold oscillating mass; 68-hour power reserve
Functions: hours; additional 24-hour indicator (second time zone)
Case: pink gold, ø 43 mm, height 11.85 mm; sapphire crystal, water-resistant to 3 atm
Band: reptile skin, buckle
Remarks: enamel dial
Price: $26,400

Grande Seconde Quantième

Reference number: J007030245
Movement: automatic, Jaquet Droz Caliber 2660Q2; ø 26.2 mm, height 4.52 mm; 30 jewels; 28,800 vph; double spring barrel, heavy metal oscillating mass; 68-hour power reserve
Functions: hours and minutes (off-center), subsidiary seconds; date
Case: stainless steel, ø 43 mm, height 11.63 mm; sapphire crystal, water-resistant to 3 atm
Band: reptile skin, folding clasp
Price: $9,300
Variations: with blue, black, or brown dial

Petite Heure Minute 35 mm Blue Birds

Reference number: J005003501
Movement: automatic, Jaquet Droz Caliber 2653; ø 26.2 mm, height 4.47 mm; 28 jewels; 28,800 vph; double spring barrel, white gold oscillating mass; 68-hour power reserve
Functions: hours and minutes (off-center)
Case: pink gold; ø 35 mm, height 10.4 mm; bezel set with 232 diamonds; sapphire crystal, water-resistant to 3 atm
Band: satin, buckle
Remarks: hand-painted enamel dial
Price: $37,100, limited to 28 pieces

The Twelve Cities Aventurine

Reference number: J010110270
Movement: automatic, Jaquet Droz Caliber 5153; ø 32 mm, height 5.37 mm; 28 jewels; 28,800 vph; double spring barrel, oscillating mass of heavy metal; 68-hour power reserve
Functions: hours (digital, jumping), minutes; 12 pusher-controlled time zones with reference cities
Case: stainless steel, ø 39 mm, height 12.27 mm; sapphire crystal, water-resistant to 3 atm
Band: reptile skin, buckle
Remarks: aventurine dial
Price: $17,300

Jaermann & Stübi AG
Zürcherstrasse 91
CH-8640 Rapperswil
Switzerland

Tel.:
01141-44-213-1450

Fax:
01141-44-213-1451

E-Mail:
info@jaermann-stuebi.com

Website:
www.jaermann-stuebi.com

Founded:
2005

Number of employees:
5

Annual production:
500

U.S. After Sales Service Center:
Stoll & Co., Inc.
1801 South Metro Parkway
Dayton, OH 45459
800-786-5526; 937-434-8463 (fax)
stoll@americaswatchmaker.com
www.americaswatchmaker.com

Most important collections:
Gents' Collection, Ladies' Collection, Special
Editions

Jaermann & Stübi

Urs Jaermann and Pascal Stübi are linked by their common love of both watches and golf.
The two always wanted to conceive and build a watch together, but they never dreamed
it would turn out to be a watch for golfers. "If I were not so bad at doing arithmetic in

my head, this watch might never have
been created," Jaermann admits. "I simply
cannot concentrate on the game and my
score at the same time." The two got the
brand off the ground in 2007. In 2013, they
moved into a large new space at Baselworld
and acquired a dynamic CEO in the person
of Daniel Wechsler, who cut his teeth at
Maurice Lacroix and Porsche Design/
Eterna, among other brands.

The essential Jaermann & Stübi golf watch counts the strokes for each hole, calculates
the total score, and reconciles handicaps by means of the bezel. Its heart is the patented
golf counter complication, consisting essentially of three individual counting mechanisms
working together. The activating buttons are on the left so as not to be covered by the
golfer's glove. For their base movement, Jaermann and Stübi chose Soprod's A10 caliber.
The entire assembly is anchored inside the case with special plastic shock absorbers to
protect the filigree mechanism from the violent shocks of teeing off.
One new series has cases made from one of Seve Ballesteros's clubs, and 2013 saw the
birth of a Nick Faldo series (cases made from his irons) and a women's watch.

Faldo Series

Reference number: NF1
Movement: automatic, Soprod Caliber A10 with JS 02
module; ø 25.6 mm, height 3.6 mm; 25 jewels; 28,800
vph; held in shock absorbers with flexible winding stem;
42-hour power reserve
Functions: hours, minutes; golf counter (strokes per hole,
total strokes, handicap comparison), yard/m conversion
Case: stainless steel, ø 44 mm, height 14 mm;
bidirectional bezel with handicap factor; sapphire crystal,
transparent case back; screw-in crown, pushers; water-
resistant to 10 atm
Band: reptile skin, folding clasp
Remarks: case forged from Nick Faldo's irons
Price: $25,550

TransAtlantic

Reference number: TA3
Movement: automatic, Soprod Caliber A10 with JS
02 module; ø 25.6 mm, height 3.6 mm; 25 jewels;
28,800 vph; held in shock absorbers with flexible
winding stem; 42-hour power reserve; COSC tested
chronometer
Functions: hours, minutes, sweep seconds; golf
counter (strokes per hole, played holes, total
strokes, handicap comparison), yard/m conversion
Case: stainless steel, ø 44 mm, height 14 mm;
bidirectional bezel with handicap factor; sapphire
crystal; screw-in crown, pusher; transparent case
back; water-resistant to 10 atm
Band: rubber, folding clasp
Price: $8,250

Hole in One

Reference number: HO3
Movement: automatic, Soprod Caliber A10 with JS
02 module; ø 25.6 mm, height 3.6 mm; 25 jewels;
28,800 vph; held in shock absorbers with flexible
winding stem; 42-hour power reserve
Functions: hours, minutes, sweep seconds; golf
counter (strokes per hole, holes played, total strokes,
handicap comparison)
Case: stainless steel, ø 44 mm, height 14 mm;
bidirectional ceramic bezel with handicap factor;
sapphire crystal; transparent case back; screw-in
crown, reset pusher; water-resistant to 10 atm
Band: reptile skin, folding clasp
Price: $8,450

Jeanrichard

Daniel Jeanrichard (1665–1741) is one of the seminal figures in the art of watchmaking in the Jura region above Neuchâtel, though myth and reality may well have become a little mixed up. When he was fourteen, allegedly, a passing horse dealer noticed the filigree silver jewelry the boy had made and gave him a timepiece to repair. When he returned a few weeks later, the watch was fixed, and Daniel had caught the watchmaking bug. He ultimately moved to Le Locle, opened a small *manufacture,* taught his five sons watchmaking, and rebuilt a gear-cutting machine that had been an industrial secret in Geneva.

Jeanrichard, today, is a part of the Sowind Group, and thus has access to all the technology needed to come up with serious timepieces. For a while, though, that meant playing little sister to the more dashing Girard-Perregaux. But between the group CEO Michele Sofisti and COO Bruno Grande, a formula was devised simplifying the message through the product. The flagship 1681 series survived, and earth, air, and water are now celebrated by the Terrascope, Aeroscope, and Aquascope collections. There is nothing overly technical. The retro (as in sixties) cushion-shaped cases house a robust in-house automatic movement, and the price ceiling is around $6,000. The designers have a free hand in multiplying these models with colored dials, suggesting that the brand is on its way to serving a larger market.

Jeanrichard SA
129, rue du Progrès
CH-2300 La Chaux-de-Fonds
Switzerland

Tel.:
01141-32-911-3636

Fax:
01141-32-911-3637

Website:
www.jeanrichard.com

Founded:
1988

Number of employees:
100

Annual production:
4,000 watches

U.S. distributor:
Tradema of America, Inc.
201 Route 17 North, 8th Floor
Rutherford, NJ 07070
201-804-1904

Most important collections/price range:
1681 / approx. $4,900 to $21,400; Terrascope, Aeroscope, Aquascope / approx. $2,900 to $8,500

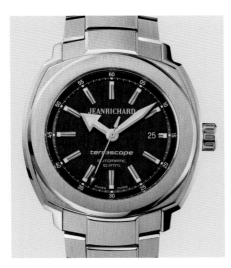

Terrascope

Reference number: 60500-11-601-11A
Movement: automatic, JR Caliber JP60 (base Sellita SW200); ø 25.6 mm, height 4.6 mm; 26 jewels; 28,800 vph; 38-hour power reserve
Functions: hours, minutes, sweep seconds; date
Case: stainless steel, ø 46 mm, height 12.6 mm; sapphire crystal, water-resistant to 10 atm
Band: stainless steel, folding clasp
Price: $3,500
Variations: with rubber or calf leather band ($2,900)

Aquascope

Reference number: 60400-11D401-FK4A
Movement: automatic, JR Caliber JP60 (base Sellita SW200); ø 25.6 mm, height 4.6 mm; 26 jewels; 28,800 vph; 38-hour power reserve
Functions: hours, minutes, sweep seconds; date
Case: stainless steel, ø 46 mm, height 13.05 mm; unidirectional bezel with 60-minute divisions; sapphire crystal, water-resistant to 30 atm
Band: rubber, folding clasp
Price: $3,200
Variations: with stainless steel bracelet ($3,800)

Aeroscope

Reference number: 60650-21G211-HDEA
Movement: automatic, JR Caliber JP66 (base Sellita SW200); ø 28.6 mm, height 6.1 mm; 43 jewels; 28,800 vph; 42-hour power reserve
Functions: hours, minutes, subsidiary seconds; chronograph; date
Case: titanium, ø 46 mm, height 12.67 mm; unidirectional bezel with 60-minute divisions; sapphire crystal, water-resistant to 10 atm
Band: calf leather, buckle
Price: $4,900
Variations: with titanium band ($5,700); with PVD coating and leather band ($5,600)

Jörg Schauer

Jörg Schauer
c/o Stowa GmbH & Co. KG
Gewerbepark 16
D-75331 Engelsbrand
Germany

Tel.:
01149-7082-9306-0

Fax:
01149-7082-9306-2

E-Mail:
info@schauer-germany.com

Website:
www.schauer-germany.com

Founded:
1990

Number of employees:
16

Annual production:
max. 500 watches and 4,000 watches for Stowa

Distribution:
direct sales; please contact the address in Germany

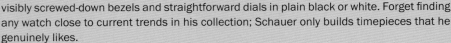

Jörg Schauer's watches attract the eye with their cool design and loving case workmanship. After all, he is a perfectionist and leaves nothing to chance. He works on every single case himself, polishing and performing his own brand of magic for as long as it takes to display his personal touch. This time-consuming process is one that Schauer believes is absolutely necessary. "I do this because I place a great deal of value on the fact that my cases are absolutely perfect," he explains. "I can do it better than anyone, and I would never let anyone else do it for me."

Schauer, a goldsmith by training, has been making watches since 1990. He began by doing one-off pieces in precious metals for collectors and then opened his business and simultaneously moved to stainless steel. His style is to produce functional, angular cases with visibly screwed-down bezels and straightforward dials in plain black or white. Forget finding any watch close to current trends in his collection; Schauer only builds timepieces that he genuinely likes.

In the meantime, purchasing a Schauer is no longer that easy—again. He has chosen a strategy of genuine quality over quantity and has reduced the number of watches he produces annually to about 500. This includes special timepieces like the One-Hand Durowe, with a movement from one of Germany's movement manufacturers, Durowe, which Schauer acquired in 2002. His production structure is a vital part of his success and includes prototyping, movement modification, finishing, case production, dial painting and printing—all done in Schauer's own workshop in Engelsbrand. Any support he needs from the outside he prefers to search out among regional specialists.

Edition 9

Reference number: Ed9
Movement: automatic, ETA Caliber 7751; ø 30 mm, height 7.9 mm; 28 jewels; 28,800 vph; decorative ribbing, blued screws, exclusive engraved Schauer rotor; 42-hour power reserve
Functions: hours, minutes, subsidiary seconds; additional 24-hour display; chronograph; full calendar with month, moon phase, weekday, date
Case: stainless steel, ø 42 mm, height 15 mm; bezel secured with 12 screws; antireflective sapphire crystal on front and back; water-resistant to 5 atm
Band: stainless steel Milanese mesh, folding clasp
Price: $4,118

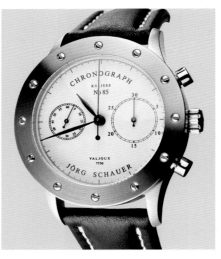

Edition 10

Reference number: Ed10
Movement: automatic, ETA Caliber 7753; ø 30 mm, height 7.9 mm; 27 jewels; 28,800 vph; finished with ornamental stripes and blued screws, exclusive engraved Schauer rotor; 42-hour power reserve
Functions: hours, minutes, subsidiary seconds; chronograph
Case: stainless steel, ø 42 mm, height 15 mm; bezel fixed with 12 screws; sapphire crystal on front and back, antireflective inside; water-resistant to 5 atm
Band: calf leather, double folding clasp
Price: $3,308
Variations: with reptile band ($3,380) with stainless steel bracelet ($3,652)

Edition 11

Reference number: Ed11
Movement: automatic, ETA Caliber 7753; ø 30 mm, height 7.9 mm; 28 jewels; 28,800 vph; decorative ribbing, blued screws, exclusive engraved Schauer rotor; 42-hour power reserve
Functions: hours, minutes, subsidiary seconds; chronograph
Case: stainless steel, ø 42 mm, height 15 mm; bezel secured with 12 screws; sapphire crystal on front and back, antireflective inside; water-resistant to 5 atm
Band: calf leather, double folding clasp
Price: $3,308
Variations: with reptile band ($3,380); with stainless steel bracelet ($3,652)

Edition 12

Reference number: Ed 12
Movement: automatic, ETA Caliber 7753; ø 30 mm, height 7.9 mm; 28 jewels; 28,800 vph; decorative ribbing, blued screws, exclusive engraved Schauer rotor; 42-hour power reserve
Functions: hours, minutes, subsidiary seconds; chronograph
Case: stainless steel, ø 41 mm, height 15 mm; bezel secured with 12 screws; sapphire crystal on front and back, antireflective inside; water-resistant to 5 atm
Band: calf leather, double folding clasp
Price: $3,552
Variations: with reptile band ($3,624); with stainless steel bracelet ($3,896)

Small Schauer One-Hand

Reference number: kleineSchauerEinzeigerschwarz
Movement: automatic, ETA Caliber 2824-2; ø 25.6 mm, height 4.6 mm; 25 jewels; 28,800 vph; German silver rotor, blued screws; 38-hour power reserve
Functions: hours (each line 5 minutes)
Case: stainless steel, ø 37 mm, height 9.15 mm; bezel fixed with 12 screws; sapphire crystal on front and back, antireflective inside; water-resistant to 5 atm
Band: calf leather, double folding clasp
Price: $1,498
Variations: with reptile band ($1,587); with stainless steel bracelet ($1,548)

Edition 14

Reference number: Ed 14
Movement: automatic, ETA Caliber 7753; ø 30 mm, height 7.9 mm; 27 jewels; 28,800 finished with ornamental stripes and blued screws, exclusive engraved Schauer rotor; 42-hour power reserve
Functions: hours, minutes, subsidiary seconds; chronograph; date
Case: stainless steel, ø 42 mm, height 15 mm; bezel fixed with 12 screws; sapphire crystal on front and back, antireflective inside; water-resistant to 5 atm
Band: calf leather, double folding clasp
Price: $3,386
Variations: with reptile band ($3,458); with stainless steel bracelet ($3,730)

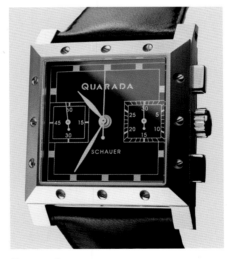

Edition 15

Reference number: Ed 15
Movement: automatic, ETA Caliber 7753; ø 30 mm, height 7.9 mm; 27 jewels; 28,800 finished with ornamental stripes and blued screws, exclusive engraved Schauer rotor; 40-hour power reserve
Functions: hours, minutes, subsidiary seconds; chronograph; date
Case: stainless steel, ø 44 mm, height 15 mm; bezel fixed with 12 screws; sapphire crystal on front and back, antireflective inside; water-resistant to 5 atm
Band: rubber, double folding clasp
Price: $3,297
Variations: with leather strap ($3,386); with stainless steel bracelet ($3,419)

Quarada

Reference number: Quarada
Movement: automatic, ETA Caliber 7753; ø 30 mm, height 7.9 mm; 27 jewels; 28,800 finished with ornamental stripes and blued screws, exclusive engraved Schauer rotor; 42-hour power reserve
Functions: hours, minutes, subsidiary seconds; chronograph
Case: stainless steel, 35 x 35 mm, height 14 mm; bezel fixed with 12 screws; sapphire crystal; water-resistant to 3 atm
Band: calf leather, double folding clasp
Price: $5,106
Variations: with reptile skin band ($5,178); with white dial

One-Hand Durowe 7440

Reference number: EinzeigerDurowe 7440
Movement: manually wound, Durowe Caliber 7440 (base ETA 6498); ø 36.6 mm, height 4.5 mm; 17 jewels; 18,000 vph; with special finish and fine regulation
Functions: hours (each line 5 minutes)
Case: stainless steel, ø 44 mm, height 12.3 mm; bezel fixed with 12 screws; sapphire crystal; water-resistant to 5 atm
Band: calf leather, double folding clasp
Price: $2,775
Variations: stainless steel bracelet ($2,808); with rubber strap ($2,686)

Juvenia Montres S.A.
Rue du Chatelot 21
CH-2304 La Chaux-de-Fonds
Switzerland

Tel.:
01141-32-925-7000

Fax:
01141-32-925-7008

E-Mail:
info@juvenia.ch

Website:
www.juvenia.ch

Founded:
1860

Number of employees:
30

Annual production:
10,000 watches

U.S. distributor:
Carat n Karat, Flushing Meadows, NY
718-888-3590; www.caratco.com
Westime, Beverly Hills, CA
310-271-0000
Hing Wa Lee, San Gabriel, CA
909-831-8888

Most important collections:
Sextant, Classic, J., Planet, specialties

Juvenia

The benefits of marketing are well illustrated by the Swiss brand Juvenia. In Hong Kong and other points east, its classic looking three-handers and two-handers are well-known. The largest Juvenia case is 41 millimeters in diameter, making these timepieces almost ideal for slimmer Asian wrists. But in the Occident, mentioning Juvenia could crease a few brows, because not many know of or remember it. Yet it is a brand whose history stretches back over 150 uninterrupted years.

It was founded in 1860 by an Alsatian watchmaker named Jacques Didisheim in the Swiss horological hub of La Chaux-de-Fonds. It became quite a powerful operation at one time, a full-fledged *manufacture* with a catalogue that served the Swiss Patent Office as a reference guide to check new filings for originality. Among its claims to fame is the smallest single lever movement ever made, which was unveiled in 1914: 9.5 by 2.5 millimeters.

The quartz crisis left Juvenia on the ropes. It reacted by cultivating the Asian markets, which turned out to be a lucrative strategy. With new stability and investments, Juvenia is now beginning to move back into Europe and the United States with a mostly staid, well-built set of timepieces. There is the Sextant, looking curiously Masonic with its protractor and compass pointer as the hour and second hand respectively. (Johnny Depp was wearing an older version in a shoot for *Esquire*.) The understated Planets fit anywhere, and the tourbillon in the specialty series is for real watch fans. Juvenia has also revived its iconic Attraction, originally released in 1951 and based on a stick movement that powers a small two-hand watch almost buried in diamonds.

Sextant

Reference number: SXA1.6.096.21
Movement: automatic, Juvenia J015; ø 25.6 mm, height 3.6 mm; 25 jewels; 28,800 vph; 42-hour power reserve
Functions: hours, minutes, sweep seconds; date
Case: red gold, ø 40 mm, height 9.35 mm; sapphire crystal; transparent case back; water-resistant to 3 atm
Band: reptile skin, buckle
Remarks: seconds hand acts as compass, minute hands as ruler; hour hand as protractor; BlackOr dial
Price: $11,000

Slimatic

Reference number: SLA1.6.536.21
Movement: automatic, Juvenia J09; ø 32.5 mm, height 4.51 mm; 26 jewels; 21,600 vph; 38-hour power reserve
Functions: hours, minutes, date
Case: pink gold, 40 mm, height 10.05 mm; sapphire crystal; screw-in crown; transparent case back; water-resistant to 3 atm
Band: reptile skin, buckle
Price: $14,200

Power Reserve

Reference number: PRA2.4.514.20
Movement: automatic, Juvenia J017; ø 25.6 mm, height 5.1 mm; 26 jewels; 28,800 vph; 42-hour power reserve
Functions: hours, minutes, sweep seconds; weekday, date; power reserve indicator
Case: stainless steel, ø 40 mm, height 10 mm; sapphire crystal; transparent case back; water-resistant to 3 atm
Band: reptile skin, folding clasp
Price: $5,100

Moon Phase

Reference number: MPA2.4.514.20
Movement: automatic, Juvenia J019; ø 25.6 mm, height 5.2 mm; 25 jewels; 28,800 vph; 42-hour power reserve
Functions: hours, minutes, sweep seconds; weekday, month, date; moon phase
Case: stainless steel, ø 40 mm, height 10 mm; sapphire crystal; transparent case back; water-resistant to 3 atm
Band: reptile skin, buckle
Price: $6,000

World Time

Reference number: WTA1.6.056.21
Movement: automatic, Juvenia J07-A; ø 34 mm, height 4.3 mm; 23 jewels; 28,800 vph; 40-hour power reserve
Functions: hours, minutes, sweep seconds; date; second time zone, day/night display; 24-hour display with reference cities and places
Case: pink gold, ø 40 mm, height 10 mm; sapphire crystal; transparent case back; water-resistant to 3 atm
Band: reptile skin, buckle
Remarks: BlackOr dial
Price: $19,100

Planet – Gents

Reference number: PLA1.4.594.04
Movement: automatic, Juvenia J026-G; ø 25.6 mm, height 3.6 mm; 25 jewels; 28,800 vph; 42-hour power reserve
Functions: hours, minutes, sweep seconds; date
Case: stainless steel, ø 40 mm, height 12.45 mm; screw-in crown; sapphire crystal; water-resistant to 10 atm
Band: stainless steel, folding clasp
Price: $3,600

Planet – Ladies

Reference number: PLB1.5.994.04
Movement: automatic, Juvenia J026-L; ø 17.2 mm, height 4.8 mm; 25 jewels; 28,800 vph; 38-hour power reserve
Functions: hours, minutes, sweep seconds; date
Case: stainless steel, ø 29 mm, height 10.35 mm; screw-in crown; sapphire crystal; bezel set with 12 diamonds; water-resistant to 10 atm
Band: stainless steel, folding clasp
Price: $4,600

Attraction

Reference number: ATT1.7.700.71
Movement: manually wound, straight Juvenia J02; height 4.17 mm; 17 jewels; 21,600 vph; 35-hour power reserve
Functions: hours, minutes
Case: pink gold, set with 426 diamonds, height 9.15 mm; transparent case back; sapphire crystal; water-resistant to 3 atm
Band: reptile skin, buckle
Price: $78,700

Tourbillon

Reference number: TBC1.6.646.21
Movement: manually wound, Juvenia J020; ø 32.8 mm, height 5.76 mm; 29 jewels; 21,600 vph; tourbillon; 56-hour power reserve
Functions: hours, minutes
Case: pink gold, ø 38 mm, height 10.85 mm; sapphire crystal; transparent case back; water-resistant to 3 atm
Band: reptile skin, buckle
Price: $77,100

Kobold Watch Company, LLC

1801 Parkway View Drive
Pittsburgh, PA 15205

Tel.:
412-722-1277

Fax:
412-722-1577

E-Mail:
info@koboldwatch.com

Website:
www.koboldwatch.com

Founded:
1998

Number of employees:
15

Annual production:
maximum 2,500 watches

Distribution:
factory-direct, select retailers

Most important collections/price range:
Soarway / $3,000 to $35,000; Old Explorers /
$2,750 to $16,500

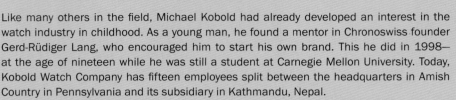

Kobold

Like many others in the field, Michael Kobold had already developed an interest in the watch industry in childhood. As a young man, he found a mentor in Chronoswiss founder Gerd-Rüdiger Lang, who encouraged him to start his own brand. This he did in 1998—at the age of nineteen while he was still a student at Carnegie Mellon University. Today, Kobold Watch Company has fifteen employees split between the headquarters in Amish Country in Pennsylvania and its subsidiary in Kathmandu, Nepal.

The latter operation is run by two former sherpas, Namgel and Thundu, who saved the lives of Michael and his wife Anita during their 2010 ascent of Mount Everest. The couple had been attempting the world's highest peak to raise money for the Navy SEAL Warrior Fund. Brand ambassador and legendary explorer Ranulph Fiennes had noticed Namgel's and Thundu's keen interest in watchmaking during a 2009 expedition. The two trained under Kobold watchmakers in Pittsburgh in 2011 and now oversee the first mechanical watch company in the Himalayas. Fiennes himself gave the keynote speech at the opening of Kobold's Nepal operation in 2012, an event that drew some 300 people, including ambassadors, the royal family, and the deputy prime minister.

The flagship piece of the new Lynx collection is a version featuring a dial made from a rock collected by Fiennes and Kobold near the summit of Everest. The Lynx is available for men and women, with or without precious stones, and is assembled in Nepal.

Back in the United States, Kobold continues to work on watches "made in America," for which the brand has developed Caliber K.2651, a strongly modified version of the vintage Förster caliber.

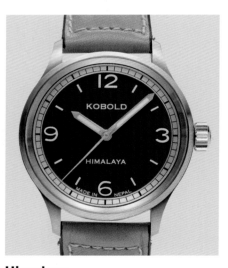

Soarway Transglobe

Reference number: KN 266853
Movement: automatic, Caliber K.793 (base ETA 2892-A2); ø 36 mm, height 4.95 mm; 26 jewels; 28,800 vph; 46-hour power reserve
Functions: hours, minutes, sweep seconds, date, second time zone with hours and minutes
Case: stainless steel, ø 44 mm, height 14.3 mm; sapphire crystal; screwed-down case back; water-resistant to 30 atm
Band: canvas, buckle
Price: $3,100

Himalaya

Reference number: KN 880121
Movement: automatic, ETA Caliber 2824-A2; ø 30.4 mm, height 10.35 mm; 25 jewels; 28,800 vph; 42-hour power reserve
Functions: hours, minutes, sweep seconds
Case: stainless steel, ø 44 mm, height 11.3 mm; antireflective sapphire crystal; screwed-down case back; water-resistant to 10 atm
Band: reptile skin, buckle
Price: $3,450
Variations: black or white dial

Himalaya 41

Reference number: KN 830854
Movement: automatic, ETA Caliber 2824-A2; ø 30.4 mm, height 10.35 mm; 25 jewels; 28,800 vph; 42-hour power reserve
Functions: hours, minutes, sweep seconds
Case: stainless steel, ø 41 mm, height 12.6 mm; antireflective sapphire crystal; screwed-down case back; water-resistant to 10 atm
Band: reptile, buckle
Price: $2,450

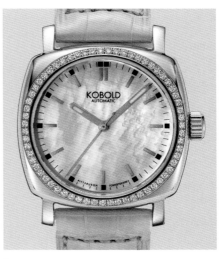

Phantom Tactical Chronograph

Reference number: KD 924451
Movement: automatic, ETA Valjoux Caliber 7750;
ø 30 mm, height 8.1 mm; 25 jewels; 28,800 vph;
46-hour power reserve; côtes de Genève, perlage,
engraved and skeletonized gold-plated rotor
Functions: hours, minutes, subsidiary seconds; date;
day; chronograph
Case: PVD-coated stainless steel, made in USA,
ø 41 mm, height 15.3 mm; unidirectional bezel
with 60-minute divisions; screw-in crown and
buttons; sapphire crystal; screwed-down case back;
water-resistant to 300 m
Band: PVD-coated stainless steel, folding clasp
Price: $5,250
Variations: titanium case with black PVD ($5,850)

Phantom Chronograph

Reference number: KD 924453
Movement: automatic, ETA Valjoux Caliber 7750;
ø 30 mm, height 8.1 mm; 25 jewels; 28,800 vph;
46-hour power reserve
Functions: hours, minutes, subsidiary seconds;
perpetual calendar, date, weekday; chronograph
Case: stainless steel, made in USA, ø 41 mm, height
15.3 mm; unidirectional bezel with 60-minute
divisions; screw-in crown and buttons; sapphire
crystal; screwed-down case back; water-resistant
to 30 atm
Band: canvas, folding clasp
Price: $4,650

Lynx

Reference number: KD 415752
Movement: automatic, ETA Caliber 2892-A2;
ø 28 mm, height 3.6 mm; 25 jewels; 28,800 vph;
46-hour power reserve
Functions: hours, minutes, sweep seconds
Case: stainless steel, ø 36 mm, height 10.2 mm;
antireflective sapphire crystal; screwed-down case
back; water-resistant to 10 atm
Band: leather, buckle
Price: $6,500
Variations: dial made from Mt. Everest summit rock

Polar Surveyor

Reference number: KD 915151
Movement: automatic, Caliber K.751 (base ETA
7750); ø 26.2 mm, height 5.3 mm; 28 jewels;
28,800 vph; 42-hour power reserve
Functions: hours, minutes, sweep seconds;
perpetual calendar, date; chronograph; day/night
indicator
Case: stainless steel, ø 41 mm, height 15.3 mm;
antireflective sapphire crystal; screwed-down case
back; screw-in crown; water-resistant to 30 atm
Band: stainless steel, folding clasp
Price: $5,500

Seal

Reference number: KD 832129
Movement: automatic, Caliber K.2651 (base
Forster 197); ø 26 mm, height 6.1 mm; 21 jewels;
18,000 vph; 46-hour power reserve
Functions: hours, minutes, sweep seconds
Case: stainless steel, made in USA; ø 44 mm,
height 17.75 mm; unidirectional bezel; soft iron
core; antireflective sapphire crystal; screwed-down
case back; screw-in crown; water-resistant to 100
atm
Band: leather, buckle
Price: $5,450

SMG-X

Reference number: KD 711121
Movement: automatic, Caliber ETA 2893-A2;
ø 26.2 mm, height 6.1 mm; 21 jewels; 28,800 vph;
40-hour power reserve
Functions: hours, minutes, sweep seconds; second
time zone; date
Case: stainless steel, made in USA; ø 43 mm,
height 12.75 mm; unidirectional bezel; soft iron
core; antireflective sapphire crystal; screwed-
down case back; screw-in crown; water-resistant to
30 atm
Band: canvas, buckle
Price: $4,450

Kudoke

Kudoke Uhren
Tannenweg 5
D-15236 Frankfurt (Oder)
Germany

Tel.:
011419-335-280-0409

E-Mail:
info@kudoke.eu

Website:
www.kudoke.eu

Founded:
2007

Number of employees:
1

Annual production:
30–50 watches

U.S. distributor:
Kudoke
WatchBuys
888-333-4895
www.watchbuys.com

Most important collections/price range:
between approx. $4,500 and $11,500

Stefan Kudoke, a watchmaker from Frankfurt/Oder, has made a name for himself as an extremely skilled and imaginative creator of timepieces. He apprenticed with two experienced watchmakers and graduated as the number one trainee in the state of Brandenburg. This earned him a stipend from a federal program promoting gifted individuals. He then moved on to one of the large *manufactures* in Glashütte, where he refined his skills in its workshop for complications and prototyping. At the age of twenty-two, with a master's diploma in his pocket, he decided to get an MBA and then devote himself to building his own company.

His guiding principle is individuality, and that is not possible to find in a serial product. So Kudoke began building unique pieces. By realizing the special wishes of customers, he manages to reflect each person's uniqueness in each watch. And he has produced some out-of-the-ordinary pieces, like the ExCentro1 and 2, whose dials are off-center and hint at a feeling for the absurd, à la Dali.

His specialties include engraving and goldsmithing. Taking a closer look at his creations, one sees that the bridges in his movements may in fact be graceful bodies, or the fine skeletonizing of a plate fragment, a world of figures and garlands. In 2012, he presented the White Flower, a watch for women, frankly romantic like a poem by Rilke and surprisingly simple. Kudoke has opened a new door in his creative processes, and his journey should be a great gift to fans of fine watchmaking.

White Flower

Movement: automatic, ETA Caliber 2824-2; ø 25.6 mm, height 4.6 mm; 25 jewels; 28,800 vph; rhodium-plated and hand-engraved rotor, 38-hour power reserve
Functions: hours, minutes, sweep seconds
Case: stainless steel, ø 38 mm, height 10 mm; sapphire crystal; transparent case back
Band: reptile skin, buckle
Remarks: silver dial with bas relief and 8 diamonds
Price: $7,750

ReKulator

Movement: manually wound, modified ETA Caliber 6498; ø 36.6 mm, height 4.5 mm; 18,000 vph; rebuilt hands as regulator; screw balance, polished pallet lever and escape wheel; engraved and skeletonized by hand
Functions: hours (off-center), minutes
Case: stainless steel, ø 42 mm, height 10.5 mm; sapphire crystal; transparent case back; water-resistant to 5 atm
Band: reptile skin, buckle
Remarks: guilloché dial
Price: $10,400

ExCentro 2

Movement: automatic, ETA Caliber 2824-2; ø 25.6 mm, height 4.6 mm; 25 jewels; 28,800 vph; partly hand-skeletonized and engraved
Functions: hours, minutes, sweep seconds; date
Case: stainless steel, ø 42 mm, height 10.5 mm; sapphire crystal; transparent case back; water-resistant to 5 atm
Band: reptile skin, buckle
Remarks: ring to hold movement engraved by hand with reliefs
Price: $6,400

Linde Werdelin

Linde Werdelin
Studio 7, 27a Pembridge Villas
London W11 3EP
United Kingdom

Tel.:
01144-207-727-6577

Fax:
01144-207-900-1722

E-Mail:
info@lindewerdelin.com

Website:
www.lindewerdelin.com

Founded:
2002

Number of employees:
20

Annual production:
500 watches

U.S. distributor:
Totally Worth It, LLC
76 Division Avenue
Summit, NJ 07901-2309
201-894-4710
info@totallyworthit.com

Most important collections/price range:
SpidoSpeed, SpidoLite, Oktopus / $10,300 to
$41,900

There are sports watches, and then there are watches for sports. Morton Linde and Jorn Werdelin, two Danes, were just teenagers when they started comparing their iconic acquisitions, like their Cartier Santos Octogonal, their Reversos, their Royal Oaks. Werdelin went on to study business; Linde became an industrial designer—the chairs in Copenhagen's park are from his drawing board.

The two men also shared a love of sports, particularly skiing. One day, when Werdelin was recovering from a severe skiing accident, the two friends dreamed up the idea of launching a sports watch. Thus Linde Werdelin was founded in 2002, and their idea gradually grew into a full-fledged concept, bold and quite literally out-of-the-box. Why confine oneself to mechanics, when electronics do some things better? A separate clip-on instrument box with a sophisticated mini-computer could be affixed to the base watch to display and log all the parameters of the activity being performed: The Reef, for divers, displays dive time, ascent rate, temperature, decompression stops, and more. For climbers, the Rock features a chronometer, altimeter, thermometer, three-point compass, incline indicator, and much more. As for the watch itself, without its IT unit, it spices up refinement with a dose of industrial ruggedness and hell-raiser edginess. So the collections were born: the Founders—the Elemental and 2-Timer—the Oktopus, and the SpidoSpeed, a three-way summit between tradition, high-tech, and style for the active and athletic with clip-ons for diving and skiing. Divers looking for the thrill and romance of a moonlit plunge now have the Oktopus II Moon, the young brand's venture into building in-house movements with unusual materials like Alloy Linde Werdelin (ALW), an ultralight metal composite combined with carbon and ceramic. The watches are manufactured in Geneva and Zurich, Switzerland.

Oktopus II Moon Gold

Reference number: OKT II.RGB.1
Movement: automatic, Concepto Caliber 2251; 28,800 vph; in-house moon phase; 42-hour power reserve
Case: rose gold and titanium DLC case with ceramic bezel, 44 x 46 mm, height 15.25 mm; 2.5-mm antireflective sapphire crystal; screwed-in DLC crown; screwed-down case back; water-resistant to 10 atm
Band: rubber, ardillon buckle
Remarks: luminous moon disk, côtes de Genève on dial
Price: $29,800, limited to 12 pieces
Variations: full titanium DLC, limited to 47 pieces ($29,800)

SpidoSpeed Black Orange

Reference number: SPS.S.BO.1
Movement: automatic, Concepto Caliber 2251; ø 30 mm, height 8.4 mm; 27 jewels; 28,800 vph; 48-hour power reserve, LW customized rotor
Functions: hours, minutes, sweep seconds; chronograph
Case: rose gold/titanium, 44 x 46 mm, height 15 mm; antireflective sapphire crystal; transparent case back; water-resistant to 10 atm
Band: calfskin, ardillon buckle
Remarks: 2-part dial with perlage base and opaline top, spiderweb engravings
Price: $21,400, limited to 100 pieces
Variations: DLC-coated stainless steel ($15,900)

SpidoLite II Tech Green

Reference number: SLTCRG II.1
Movement: automatic, LW 04 Caliber custom-made by Concepto); 28,800 vph; 42-hour power reserve
Case: carbon outer case, ALW inner case, 44 x 46 mm, height 15.25 mm; antireflective sapphire crystal; screwed-in ceramic-coated crown, transparent case back; water-resistant to 10 atm
Band: calfskin, ardillon buckle
Remarks: 33-g case Alloy Linde Werdelin "ALW," with carbon, ceramic, and new ceramic coating for titanium in fully skeletonized structure
Price: $14,800, limited to 75 pieces

Longines Watch Co.
CH-2610 St.-Imier
Switzerland

Tel.:
01141-32-942-5425

Fax:
01141-32-942-5429

E-Mail:
info@longines.com

Website:
www.longines.com

Founded:
1832

Number of employees:
worldwide approx. 560

Annual production:
not specified

U.S. distributor:
Longines
The Swatch Group (U.S.), Inc.
1200 Harbor Boulevard
Weehawken, NJ 07086
201-271-1400
www.longines.com

Most important collections/price range:
Saint-Imier, Master Collection, PrimaLuna, Sport
Collection, Heritage Collection / from approx.
$1,350 to $6,500

Longines

The Longines winged hourglass logo is the world's oldest trademark, according to the World Intellectual Property Organization (WIPO). Since its founding in 1832, the brand has manufactured somewhere in the region of 35 million watches, making it one of the genuine heavyweights of the Swiss watch world. In 1983, Nicolas G. Hayek merged the two major Swiss watch manufacturing groups ASUAG and SIHH into what would later become the Swatch Group. Longines, the leading ASUAG brand, barely missed capturing the same position in the new concern; that honor went to Omega, the SIHH frontrunner. However, from a historical and technical point of view, this brand has what it takes to be at the helm of any group. Was it not Longines that equipped polar explorer Roald Amundsen and air pioneer Charles Lindbergh with their watches? It has also been the timekeeper at many Olympic Games and, since 2007, the official timekeeper for the French Open at Roland Garros. In fact, this brand is a major sponsor at many sports events, from riding to archery.

It is not surprising then to find that this venerable Jura company also has an impressive portfolio of in-house calibers in stock, from simple manual winders to complicated chronographs. This broad technological base has benefited the company. As a genuine "one-stop shop," the brand can supply the Swatch Group with anything from cheap, thin quartz watches to heavy gold chronographs and calendars with quadruple retrograde displays. Longines does have one particular specialty, besides elegant ladies' watches and modern sports watches, in that it often has the luxury of rebuilding the classics from its own long history.

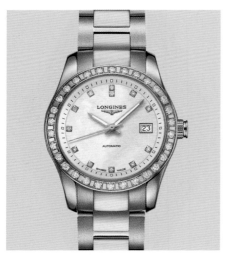

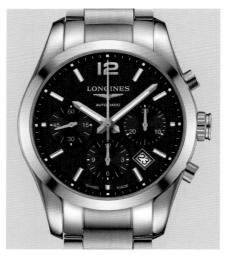

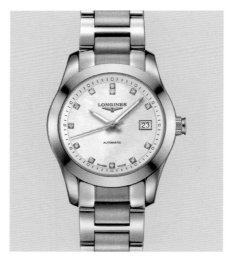

Conquest Classic

Reference number: L2.285.5.88.7
Movement: automatic, Caliber L595 (base ETA 2000-1); ø 19.4 mm, height 3.6 mm; 20 jewels; 28,800 vph; 40-hour power reserve
Functions: hours, minutes, sweep seconds; date
Case: stainless steel, ø 29.5 mm, height 9.1 mm; rose gold bezel set with 48 diamonds; sapphire crystal, transparent case back; rose gold crown and pusher; water-resistant to 5 atm
Band: stainless steel with pink gold elements, folding clasp
Remarks: mother-of-pearl dial
Price: $5,825

Conquest Classic Chronograph

Reference number: L2.786.4.56.6
Movement: automatic, Caliber L688 (base ETA A08. L01); ø 30 mm, height 7.9 mm; 27 jewels; 28,800 vph; 54-hour power reserve
Functions: hours, minutes, subsidiary seconds; chronograph; date
Case: stainless steel, ø 41 mm, height 14.2 mm; sapphire crystal, transparent case back; water-resistant to 5 atm
Band: stainless steel, folding clasp
Price: $3,175

Conquest Classic

Reference number: L2.285.4.87.6
Movement: automatic, Caliber L595 (base ETA 2000-1); ø 19.4 mm, height 3.6 mm; 20 jewels; 28,800 vph; 40-hour power reserve
Functions: hours, minutes, sweep seconds; date
Case: stainless steel, ø 29.5 mm, height 9.1 mm; sapphire crystal, transparent case back; water-resistant to 5 atm
Band: stainless steel, folding clasp
Remarks: mother-of-pearl dial set with 12 diamonds
Price: $2,400

Conquest Classic

Reference number: L2.785.4.76.6
Movement: automatic, Caliber L619 (base ETA 2892-A2); ø 25.6 mm, height 3.6 mm; 21 jewels; 28,800 vph; 42-hour power reserve
Functions: hours, minutes, sweep seconds; date
Case: stainless steel, ø 40 mm, height 10.3 mm; sapphire crystal, transparent case back; water-resistant to 5 atm
Band: stainless steel, folding clasp
Price: $2,075

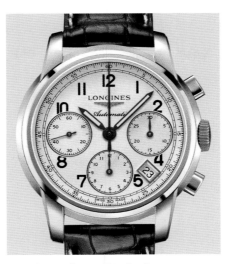

The Longines St. Imier Collection Chronograph

Reference number: L2.752.4.73.0
Movement: automatic, Caliber L688 (base ETA A08.L01); ø 30 mm, height 7.9 mm; 27 jewels; 28,800 vph; column wheel control of chronograph functions, 54-hour power reserve
Functions: hours, minutes, subsidiary seconds; chronograph; date
Case: stainless steel, ø 41 mm, height 13.94 mm; sapphire crystal, transparent case back; water-resistant to 3 atm
Band: reptile skin, folding clasp
Price: $3,225
Variations: with stainless steel bracelet ($3,275)

The Longines St. Imier Collection Chronograph

Reference number: L2.784.4.53.6
Movement: automatic, Caliber L688 (base ETA A08.L01); ø 30 mm, height 7.9 mm; 27 jewels; 28,800 vph; column wheel control of chronograph functions; 54-hour power reserve
Functions: hours, minutes, subsidiary seconds; chronograph; date
Case: stainless steel, ø 43 mm, height 14.33 mm; antireflective sapphire crystal, transparent case back; water-resistant to 3 atm
Band: stainless steel, double folding clasp
Price: $4,025

The Longines St. Imier Collection Chronograph

Reference number: L2.752.4.53.6
Movement: automatic, Caliber L688 (base ETA A08.L01); ø 30 mm, height 7.9 mm; 27 jewels; 28,800 vph; column wheel control of chronograph functions, 54-hour power reserve
Functions: hours, minutes, subsidiary seconds; chronograph; date
Case: stainless steel, ø 41 mm, height 13.94 mm; sapphire crystal, transparent case back; water-resistant to 3 atm
Band: stainless steel, double folding clasp
Price: $3,275
Variations: with leather strap ($3,225)

The Longines St. Imier Collection

Reference number: L2.763.4.72.0
Movement: automatic, Caliber L619 (base ETA 2892/-A2); ø 25.6 mm, height 3.6 mm; 21 jewels; 28,800 vph; 42-hour power reserve
Functions: hours, minutes, sweep seconds; date
Case: stainless steel, ø 38.5 mm, height 10.3 mm, sapphire crystal, transparent case back; water-resistant to 3 atm
Band: reptile skin, folding clasp
Price: $2,150

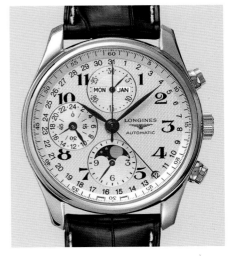

The Longines Master Collection Moon Phase

Reference number: L2.673.4.78.3
Movement: automatic, Caliber L678 (base ETA 7751); ø 30 mm, height 7.9 mm; 25 jewels; 28,800 vph; 48-hour power reserve
Functions: hours, minutes, subsidiary seconds; additional 24-hour display; chronograph; full calendar with date, weekday, month, moon phase
Case: stainless steel, ø 40 mm, height 14.24 mm; sapphire crystal, transparent case back; water-resistant to 3 atm
Band: reptile skin, folding clasp
Price: $3,050
Variations: with stainless steel bracelet ($3,150)

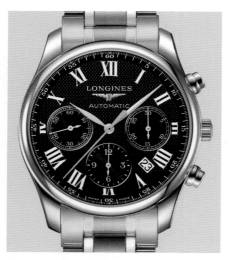

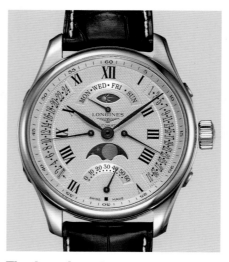

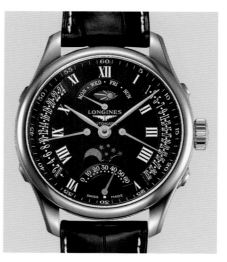

The Longines Master Collection Chronograph

Reference number: L2.759.4.51.6
Movement: automatic, Caliber L688 (base ETA A08.L01); ø 30 mm, height 7.9 mm; 27 jewels; 28,800 vph; 54-hour power reserve
Functions: hours, minutes, subsidiary seconds; chronograph; date
Case: stainless steel, ø 42 mm, height 14.2 mm; sapphire crystal, transparent case back; water-resistant to 5 atm
Band: stainless steel, folding clasp
Price: $2,950
Variations: with leather strap ($2,850)

The Longines Master Collection Retrograde Moon Phase

Reference number: L2.739.4.71.3
Movement: automatic, Caliber L707.2 (base ETA A07.L31); ø 36.6 mm, height 10 mm; 25 jewels; 28,800 vph; 46-hour power reserve
Functions: hours, minutes, subsidiary seconds (retrograde); additional 24-hour display (second time zone), retrograde; day/night indicator; full calendar with date, weekday, moon phase
Case: stainless steel, ø 44 mm, height 16.48 mm; sapphire crystal, transparent case back; water-resistant to 3 atm
Band: reptile skin, double folding clasp
Price: $3,600

The Longines Master Collection Retrograde Moon Phase

Reference number: L2.738.4.51.7
Movement: automatic, Caliber L707.2 (base ETA A07.L31); ø 36.6 mm, height 10 mm; 25 jewels; 28,800 vph; 46-hour power reserve
Functions: hours, minutes, subsidiary seconds (retrograde), additional 24-hour display (second time zone), retrograde; day/night indicator; full calendar with date, weekday, moon phase
Case: stainless steel, ø 41 mm, height 16.4 mm; sapphire crystal, transparent case back; water-resistant to 3 atm
Band: reptile skin, double folding clasp
Price: $3,600

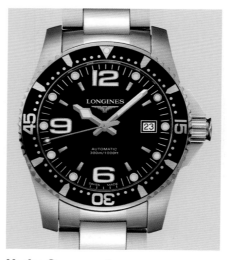

The Longines Legend Diver Watch

Reference number: L3.674.4.50.0
Movement: automatic, Caliber L633 (base ETA 2824-2); ø 25. mm, height 4.6 mm; 25 jewels; 28,800 vph; 38-hour power reserve
Functions: hours, minutes, sweep seconds; date
Case: stainless steel, ø 42 mm, height 13.55 mm; crown-adjustable inner bezel with 60-minute divisions; sapphire crystal, screw-in crown; water-resistant to 30 atm
Band: textile, buckle
Price: $2,300

HydroConquest

Reference number: L3.642.4.56.6
Movement: automatic, Caliber L633 (base ETA 2824-2); ø 25.6 mm, height 4.6 mm; 25 jewels; 28,800 vph; 38-hour power reserve
Functions: hours, minutes, sweep seconds; date
Case: stainless steel, ø 41 mm, height 11.85 mm; unidirectional bezel with aluminum inlay, 60-minute divisions; sapphire crystal, screw-in crown; water-resistant to 30 atm
Band: stainless steel, folding clasp
Price: $1,225

Hydro Conquest Chronograph

Reference number: L3.644.4.56.6
Movement: automatic, Caliber L667 (base ETA 7750); ø 30 mm, height 7.9 mm; 25 jewels; 28,800 vph; 48-hour power reserve
Functions: hours, minutes, subsidiary seconds; chronograph; date
Case: stainless steel, ø 41 mm, height 15.55 mm; unidirectional bezel with aluminum inlay, 60-minute divisions; sapphire crystal, screw-in crown; water-resistant to 30 atm
Band: stainless steel, folding clasp
Price: $1,925
Variations: with rubber strap ($1,825)

Louis Moinet

Louis Moinet (1768–1853) was a kind of renaissance personality in his time, a man of broad interests in the arts and sciences, and in horology. He was a professor at the Academy of Fine Arts in Paris and later became president of the Société Chronométrique, working with such eminent watchmakers as Breguet, Berthoud, Winnerl, Janvier, and Perrelet. Some say he even invented the balance cock, but among his certain accomplishments is an extensive two-volume treatise on horology. Moinet's timepieces were considered extremely complex, but they did find customers among the aristocracy. Following in such footsteps is hardly an easy task, but Jean-Marie Schaller and Micaela Bertolucci decided that their idiosyncratic creations were indeed imbued with the spirit of the great Frenchman. They work with a team of independent designers, watchmakers, movement specialists, and suppliers to produce the most unusual wristwatches filled with clever functions and surprising details. The Jules Verne chronographs have hinged levers, for example, and the second hand on the Tempograph changes direction every ten seconds. The new Mecanograph is a complex watch, with transparent subsidiary seconds on a split dial that boldly exhibits "rolling" côtes du Jura decoration under classic dewdrop hands.

And every limited edition has a little secret of sorts: A piece of rock that was chipped off the moon roughly 2,000 years ago by an asteroid is secured behind a discreet porthole located at 9 o'clock on the case—visible only to those who are looking for it.

Les Ateliers Louis Moinet SA
Rue du Temple 1
CH-2072 Saint-Blaise
Switzerland

Tel.:
01141-32-753-6814

E-Mail:
info@louismoinet.com

Website:
www.louismoinet.com

Founded:
1806 (refounded in 2005)

Number of employees:
not specified

Annual production:
not specified

U.S. distributor:
Louis Moinet
Milestone Distribution
297 Dividend Drive, Suite B
Peachtree City, GA 30269
678-827-7900; 678-827-7903 (fax)
info@cysusa.com

Most important collections:
Jules Verne, Tempograph, Vertalis, Geograph, Astralis

Derrick Tourbillon

Reference number: LM-14.70.03
Movement: manually wound, Louis Moinet Caliber "Derrick"; ø 32.8 mm; 19 jewels; 21,600 vph; 1-minute tourbillon; fine finishing; 72-hour power reserve
Functions: hours, minutes
Case: white gold, ø 47 mm, sapphire crystal, transparent case back
Band: reptile skin, folding clasp
Remarks: limited to 12 pieces
Price: $280,000

Chronograph "Nelson Piquet"

Reference number: LM-33.10.20
Movement: automatic, Louis Moinet Caliber LM33 (base ETA 7750); ø 30 mm, height 7.9 mm; 25 jewels; 28,800 vph; blued screws; 44-hour power reserve
Functions: hours, minutes, subsidiary seconds; chronograph
Case: stainless steel, ø 45.6 mm, height 17.1 mm; sapphire crystal, transparent case back; screw-in crown; water-resistant to 5 atm
Band: rubber, double folding clasp
Remarks: limited to 365 pieces
Price: $11,900

Jules Verne Instrument III

Reference number: LMV-30.40.55
Movement: automatic, Louis Moinet Caliber LM30 (base Concepto); ø 30 mm, height 8.4 mm; 27 jewels; 28,800 vph; monopusher for chronograph function; screw balance; finely decorated; 48-hour power reserve
Functions: hours, minutes, subsidiary seconds; chronograph with start/stop and reset display; date
Case: titanium, ø 45.5 mm, height 16.65 mm; rose gold/PVD-blackened titanium bezel; sapphire crystal; transparent case back; water-resistant to 10 atm
Band: rubber, double folding clasp
Price: $23,500, limited to 365 pieces
Variations: titanium and stainless steel ($16,900)

Louis Vuitton Malletier
2, rue du Pont Neuf
F-75034 Paris, Cedex 01
France

Tel.:
01133-1-55-80-41-40

Fax:
01133-1-55-80-41-40

Website:
www.vuitton.com

Founded:
1854

Number of employees:
not specified

Annual production:
not specified

U.S. distributor:
Louis Vuitton
1-866-VUITTON
www.louisvuitton.com

Most important collection/price range:
Tambour / starting at $3,250

Louis Vuitton

This brand's claim to quality and luxury has been governed by the philosophy that all products bearing the name Louis Vuitton must be manufactured in the company's own facilities. That is why Louis Vuitton has built its own workshop in Switzerland, whereby some synergies with the LVMH technology center in La Chaux-de-Fonds, where TAG Heuer also produces its work, could be brought to bear.

The brand is, like its brother-in-group Hublot, a kind of one-model affair. Designers in Paris created the Tambour, meaning drum or barrel (as in barrel spring), which comes in all manner of variation. The focus is on high-quality manufacturing. The cases and dials with all the details are exclusive Louis Vuitton designs, as are other components, such as the pushers and the band clasps—in other words, all that is needed to ensure a unique look. But the congenial relationship with other members of the LVMH Group does allow for some crossover. The chronograph in the Tambour line, for instance, uses the famous El Primero caliber of sister brand Zenith, and TAG Heuer is the source of valuable know-how with regard to research, development, and production.

Louis Vuitton watches are not available at the corner jewelry store, but solely through the 150 Louis Vuitton boutiques worldwide.

Tambour eVolution Chronograph GMT

Reference number: Q10520
Movement: automatic, LV Caliber 92; ø 30 mm, height 8.4 mm; 26 jewels; 28,800 vph; 42-hour power reserve
Functions: hours, minutes, subsidiary seconds; additional 12-hour display (second time zone), day/night indicator; chronograph; date
Case: stainless steel, ø 45 mm, height 15.84-mm; sapphire crystal, transparent case back; water-resistant to 10 atm
Band: stainless steel, folding clasp
Price: $11,000

Tambour Twin Chronograph

Reference number: Q102P0
Movement: automatic, LV Caliber 175; ø 37 mm, height 6.53 mm; 80 jewels; 28,800 vph; 4 barrel springs, 4 balance systems, 3 for chrono display, single pusher for 2 control wheels/4 functions; 35-hour power reserve
Functions: hours, minutes, subsidiary seconds; chronograph with 2 60-minute counters and difference indicator
Case: white gold, ø 45.5 mm, height 14.35 mm; sapphire crystal, transparent case back; water-resistant to 10 atm
Band: reptile skin, folding clasp
Price: on request

Tambour LV Cup Spin Time Regatta Chronograph

Reference number: Q102T0
Movement: automatic, LV Caliber 156; ø 35.5 mm, height 9.83 mm; 35 jewels; 28,800 vph; 48-hour power reserve
Functions: hours, minutes; chronograph with countdown function indicated by 5 jumping cubes
Case: rose gold, ø 45.5 mm, height 16 mm; sapphire crystal; water-resistant to 10 atm
Band: reptile skin, buckle
Price: on request

Tambour in Black GMT

Reference number: Q112J0
Movement: automatic, ETA Caliber 2893-2;
ø 26.2 mm, height 4.25 mm; 21 jewels;
28,800 vph; 42-hour power reserve
Functions: hours, minutes, sweep seconds;
additional 24-hour display (second time zone); date
Case: stainless steel, with black DLC coating;
ø 41.5 mm, height 12.65 mm; sapphire crystal;
water-resistant to 10 atm
Band: rubber, buckle
Price: $7,650

Tambour LV 277 Chronograph

Reference number: Q114A0
Movement: automatic, LV Caliber 277 (base Zenith
El Primero); ø 30 mm, height 6.6 mm; 31 jewels;
36,000 vph; 50-hour power reserve; COSC tested
chronometer
Functions: hours, minutes, subsidiary seconds;
chronograph; date
Case: stainless steel, ø 44 mm, height 13.25 mm;
sapphire crystal; water-resistant to 10 atm
Band: reptile skin, folding clasp
Price: $14,200

Tambour Diving II Automatic Chronograph

Reference number: Q102F0
Movement: automatic, LV Caliber 105 (base
ETA 7750); ø 30 mm, height 7.9 mm; 31 jewels;
28,800 vph
Functions: hours, minutes, subsidiary seconds;
chronograph; date
Case: stainless steel with black rubber coating,
ø 45.5 mm, unidirectional bezel with 60-minute
divisions; sapphire crystal, water-resistant to 30 atm
Band: rubber, folding clasp
Price: $11,000

Tambour LV Cup Automatic Countdown

Reference number: Q103D0
Movement: automatic, LV Caliber 138 (base
Dubois-Dépraz); ø 30 mm; 35 jewels; 28,800 vph;
42-hour power reserve
Functions: hours, minutes, sweep seconds;
countdown function, flyback system
Case: stainless steel, ø 44 mm, height 14.3 mm;
sapphire crystal; transparent case back; rubber-
covered crown and pushers; water-resistant to 10
atm
Band: reptile skin, buckle
Remarks: with additional rubber strap
Price: $11,600

Tambour Voyagez Brown Chronograph

Reference number: Q102L0
Movement: automatic, LV Caliber 172 (base
Dubois Dépraz); ø 30 mm; height 7.4 mm; 47 jewels;
28,800 vph; 42-hour power reserve
Functions: hours, minutes, subsidiary seconds;
additional 24-hour display (second time zone);
chronograph; date
Case: stainless steel, ø 44 mm, height 14.4 mm;
sapphire crystal; water-resistant to 10 atm
Band: reptile skin, buckle
Price: $8,500

Tambour Monogram Automatic

Reference number: Q13310
Movement: automatic, LV Caliber (basis ETA
2892-A2); ø 25.6 mm; height 3.6 mm; 25 jewels,
28,800 vph; 42-hour power reserve
Functions: hours, minutes, sweep seconds
Case: pink gold, ø 35 mm, height 9.96 mm; bezel
set with diamonds; sapphire crystal; water-resistant
to 5 atm
Band: reptile skin, folding clasp
Price: $26,900
Variations: stainless steel with quartz movement
(without diamonds from $2,500; with diamonds
$7,950)

Maîtres du Temps

Rue Daniel Jeanrichard 18
CP 926 CH-2301 La Chaux-de-Fonds
Switzerland

Tel.:
01141-32-911-1717

Fax:
01141-32-911-1718

E-Mail:
info@maitresdutemps.com

Website:
www.maitresdutemps.com

Founded:
2005

U.S. distributor:
Helvetia Time Inc.
100 N. Wilkes-Barre Blvd., Suite 303
Wilkes-Barre, PA 18702
570-970-8888; 570-822-4699 (fax)

Most important collections/price range:
Chapter One / from approx. CHF 474,000; Chapter
Two TCR / from approx. CHF 69,000; Chapter Three
Reveal / from approx. CHF 91,500
Prices calculated according to daily exchange rate.

Maîtres du Temps

Too many cooks can spoil the soup, but what about too many watchmakers spoiling a watch? After more than twenty-five years in the industry, Steven Holtzman decided to strike out on his own with a special concept: seeing what happens when the top people in the industry work on a piece together. The idea is not only to cross-pollinate, but also, perhaps, to compel each watchmaker to leave some room for a good colleague. Holtzman's plan, he says, "is to be actively involved in passing the craft and skills of more experienced master watchmakers to the next generation of masters."

The first timepiece was the Chapter One of 2008—inspired by a desk with some cylindrical displays dating back to pre-Scandinavian minimalism—by no means a small object, but with pleasing curves and a staggered case. Inside was a combination of tourbillon, monopusher column wheel chronograph, retrograde date, and GMT, as well as moon phase and weekday on rollers, just like the old desk. The creators of this tour de force: Peter Speake-Marin and Christophe Claret.

In 2009, Speake-Marin and Daniel Roth came up with a triple-calendar watch. The tonneau shape was back, so were the rollers, which could instantaneously switch dates. The dial: less busy, a little more staid, with large numerals. Early 2012 unveiled the Chapter Three Reveal by Kari Voutilainen and Andreas Strehler. At first glance the blue guilloché dial in a round case seems to be a radical departure from the previous two. Where are the rollers? A pusher in the crown opens up a panel in the dial to reveal them displaying a second time zone and day/night indicator. And for 2013, Chapter One has returned with a paper-thin sapphire dial that is lighter than the first edition and lets one look deep into the heart of this mechanical labyrinth.

Chapter One Round Transparence

Reference number: C1R.55.2E.60-2
Movement: Caliber SHC02.1; 51 x 31 mm; 58 jewels; crown-pusher activation of chronograph functions; correctors with integrated locking system; 21,600 vph; 1-minute tourbillon; 60-hour power reserve
Functions: hours, minutes, subsidiary seconds; chronograph; retrograde world time and date, day, and moon phase on barrels
Case: pink gold, 62 x 59 mm, height 22 mm; sapphire crystal; transparent case back
Band: reptile skin, pink gold buckle
Price: CHF 540,000 (Swiss francs only)

Chapter Two TCR

Reference number: C2R.TT0.21.120
Movement: automatic, Caliber SHC01; 45 x 32 mm, height 9 mm; 32 jewels; finished with sunburst côtes de Genève, panier guilloché, perlage and beveling; 28,800 vph; 50-hour power reserve
Functions: hours, minutes, seconds; instant triple calendar with large date, weekday, month
Case: titanium; 56 x 44 mm; height 15 mm; transparent case back with ceramic bezel; white gold crown, screws, and pushers; sapphire crystal; display-back sapphire crystals
Band: rubber, folding clasp
Price: CHF 69,000 (Swiss francs only)
Variations: titanium, black PVD with gold elements

Chapter Three Reveal

Reference number: C3R.00.00.185
Movement: manually wound, Caliber SHC03; ø 35.6 mm, height 8.2 mm; 39 jewels; twin spring barrels; Straumann balance spring with Breguet overcoil; côtes de Genève and perlage, polished screw heads; 21,600 vph; 36-hour power reserve
Functions: hours, minutes, seconds; date; moon phase; second time zone; day/night indication
Case: white gold, ø 42 mm; transparent case back; sapphire crystal; water-resistant to 3 atm
Band: reptile skin, tang buckle
Price: CHF 93,000 (Swiss francs only)
Variations: pink gold (CHF 91,500)

Marcello C.

In 1993, Marcell Kainz decided to set up his own brand of watches after spending many years working in sales and distribution for a variety of brands. For him, it was the fulfillment of a dream. The company can now look back on two decades of growth: These sporty timepieces, which come from the little town of Würselen near Aachen, have not only spread throughout Germany but also into markets worldwide.

Kainz wanted to produce quality watches, so right from the start he built up ties with well-known suppliers from Switzerland and Germany. The modern facilities in Würselen are used not only for the assembly, finishing, and regulating of the watches, but also administration, sales, and service.

Marcello C. is a low-key brand, but one that offers watch users a good choice of timepieces, from classical and colorful to three-hand watches and chronographs.

Perhaps the most successful model in the collection is the Nettuno, a 40 mm diving watch, masculine but understated. More recently, it is the elegant Diavolo designed by Kainz himself that has given the brand its unmistakable face. It has scored with the fans and comes in various special editions, with PVD coating and a pink gold bezel, and now a pilot's version.

Marcello C.
Luciastrasse 19
D-52146 Würselen
Germany

Tel.:
01149-2405-475-353

Fax:
01149-2405-475-354

E-Mail:
mail@marcelloc.de

Website:
www.marcelloc.de

Founded:
1993

Number of employees:
10

Annual production:
15,000 watches

U.S. distributor:
Marcello C Watches
1156 Lasnik Street
Erie, CO 80516
952-949-0315
www.marcelloc-watches.com

Most important collections/price range:
$900 to $3,700; special requests up to approx.
$65,000

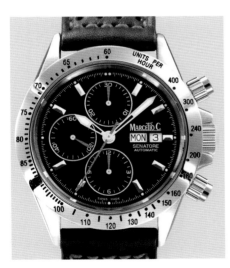

Senatore Chronograph

Reference number: 2020.2.2
Movement: automatic, ETA Caliber 7750; ø 30 mm, height 7.9 mm; 25 jewels; 28,800 vph; 42-hour power reserve
Functions: hours, minutes, subsidiary seconds; chronograph; weekday, date
Case: stainless steel, ø 42 mm, height 15.2 mm; sapphire crystal, transparent case back; screw-in crown; water-resistant to 20 atm
Band: reptile skin, folding clasp
Price: $2,298
Variations: with silver or brown dial; stainless steel band

Hydrox

Reference number: 2024.4
Movement: automatic, ETA Caliber 2824-2; ø 25.6 mm, height 4.6 mm; 25 jewels; 28,800 vph; rotor with côtes de Genève; 38-hour power reserve
Functions: hours, minutes, sweep seconds; date
Case: stainless steel, ø 43.5 mm, height 12 mm; unidirectional bezel with 60-minute divisions; sapphire crystal; screwed-in crown; water-resistant to 30 atm
Band: silicon band, folding clasp
Price: $1,698
Variations: various dial marker colors; with stainless steel bracelet ($2,098)

Diavolo Chronograph

Reference number: 2022.5.C
Movement: automatic, ETA Caliber 7750; ø 30 mm, height 7.9 mm; 25 jewels; 28,800 vph; 42-hour power reserve
Functions: hours, minutes, subsidiary seconds; chronograph; date
Case: stainless steel, ø 44 mm, height 15 mm; sapphire crystal; screw-in crown and pusher; transparent case back; water-resistant to 20 atm
Band: reptile skin, folding clasp
Price: $2,498
Variations: with stainless steel bracelet ($ 2,798); with black dial

Maurice Lacroix SA
Rüschlistrasse 6
CH-2502 Biel/Bienne
Switzerland

Tel.:
01141-44-209-1111

E-Mail:
info@mauricelacroix.com

Website:
www.mauricelacroix.com

Founded:
1975

Number of employees:
about 250 worldwide

Annual production:
approx. 90,000 watches

U.S. distributor:
DKSH Luxury & Lifestyle North America Inc.
103 Carnegie Center, Ste. 300
Princeton, NJ 08540
609-750-8800

Most important collections/price range:
Miros / $1,000 to $2,000; Les Classiques /
$1,500 to $3,500, Fiaba (ladies) / $1,500 to
3,500, Pontos / $2,500 to $5,000; Masterpiece
manufacture models / $5,000 to $30,000

Maurice Lacroix

In Maurice Lacroix headquarters in Zürich, administration offices coexist with the worldwide sales and marketing department. After all, Maurice Lacroix watches are found in sixty countries. And the brand has joined in the love for Asia by having singer/actor Dicky Cheung as a brand ambassador in 2011. The heart of the company, however, remains the production facilities in the highlands of the Jura, in Saignelégier and Montfaucon. The company built a workshop there called La Manufacture des Franches-Montagnes SA (MFM) for the production of very specific individual parts and movement components and outfitted with state-of-the-art CNC technology.

The watchmaker can thank the clever interpretations of "classic" pocket watch characteristics for its steep ascent in the 1990s. Since then, the *manufacture* has redesigned the complete collection, banning every lick of Breguet-like bliss from its watch designs. In the upper segment, *manufacture* models such as the chronograph and the retrograde variations on Unitas calibers set the tone. In the lower segment, modern "little" complications outfitted with module movements based on ETA and Sellita are the kings. The brand is mainly associated with the hypnotically turning square wheel, the "roue carrée." It picked up a red dot award in 2012 for design, as did its Masterpiece Double Rétrograde. The slow but steady tempo of Jura denizens has infected CEO Martin Bachmann and made the brand what it is: "Everything in its own time," he says, "nothing happens overnight." Increasingly, though, the brand has been straying from its staid-chic image and adopting a sporty stance. Colors have even started defusing the "dangerous" look of some models like the Pontos S, which now comes in a blue eloxed case as well.

Masterpiece
Seconde Mystérieuse

Reference number: MP6558-SS001-090
Movement: automatic, Caliber ML 215; ø 36.6 mm, 48 jewels; 18,000 vph; rhodium-plated, with côtes de Genève, 50-hour power reserve
Functions: hours and minutes (off-center), subsidiary seconds ("mysterious" time display with "floating" seconds hand)
Case: stainless steel, ø 43 mm, height 13.86 mm; sapphire crystal, transparent case back; water-resistant to 5 atm
Band: reptile skin, folding clasp
Price: $14,100

Masterpiece
Roue Carrée Seconde

Reference number: MP7158-SS001-900
Movement: manually wound, Caliber ML 156; ø 36.6 mm, height 6.15 mm; 34 jewels; 18,000 vph; 45-hour power reserve
Functions: hours, minutes, subsidiary seconds (with square wheel display); power reserve display
Case: stainless steel, ø 43 mm, height 15 mm; sapphire crystal; transparent case back; water-resistant to 5 atm
Band: reptile skin, folding clasp
Remarks: dial directly engraved on main plate, with "grand colimaçon" decoration
Price: $11,340

Masterpiece
Le Chronographe Squelette

Reference number: MP7128-SS001-300
Movement: manually wound, Caliber ML 106; ø 36.6 mm, height 6.9 mm; 22 jewels; 18,000 vph; skeletonized with black coating; 42-hour power reserve
Functions: hours, minutes, subsidiary seconds; chronograph
Case: stainless steel with black PVD coating; ø 45 mm; sapphire crystal, screw-in crown; water-resistant to 10 atm
Band: reptile skin, folding clasp
Remarks: skeletonized dial; limited to 188 pieces
Price: $16,500

Masterpiece Tradition Worldtimer

Reference number: MP6008-SS001-111
Movement: automatic, Caliber ML 164; 25 jewels;
28,800 vph; 40-hour power reserve
Functions: hours, minutes, sweep seconds;
world-time display (second time zone); day/night
indicator; date
Case: stainless steel, ø 42 mm; crown-controlled
inner ring with reference cities; sapphire crystal,
transparent case back; water-resistant to 5 atm
Band: reptile skin, folding clasp
Price: $4,800

Masterpiece Tradition 5 Hands

Reference number: MP6507-SS001-111
Movement: automatic, Caliber ML 159; 26 jewels;
28,800 vph; 38-hour power reserve
Functions: hours, minutes, sweep seconds;
weekday, date
Case: stainless steel, ø 40 mm, height 12.45 mm;
sapphire crystal, transparent case back; water-
resistant to 5 atm
Band: reptile skin, folding clasp
Price: $4,760
Variations: various bands and dials

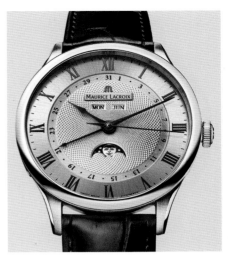

Masterpiece Tradition Phases de Lune

Reference number: MP6607-SS001-110
Movement: automatic, Caliber ML 37; 25 jewels;
28,800 vph; 38-hour power reserve
Functions: hours, minutes, sweep seconds; full
calendar with date, weekday, month, moon phase
Case: stainless steel, ø 40 mm, height 12.95
mm; sapphire crystal, transparent case back;
water-resistant to 5 atm
Band: reptile skin, folding clasp
Price: $4,980

Masterpiece Tradition Réserve de Marche

Reference number: MP6807-SS001-310
Movement: automatic, Caliber ML 113 (base ETA
2897); ø 25.6 mm, height 4.85 mm; 21 jewels;
28,800 vph; 42-hour power reserve
Functions: hours, minutes, sweep seconds; power
reserve indicator; date
Case: stainless steel, ø 40 mm, height 11.75
mm; sapphire crystal, transparent case back;
water-resistant to 5 atm
Band: reptile skin, folding clasp
Price: $3,900
Variations: various bands and dials

Masterpiece Petite Seconde

Reference number: MP6907-SS001-111
Movement: automatic, Caliber ML 158 (base ETA
2895-1); ø 25.6 mm, height 4.35 mm; 31 jewels;
28,800 vph; rhodium-plated, with côtes de Genève,
38-hour power reserve
Functions: hours, minutes, subsidiary seconds;
date
Case: stainless steel, ø 40 mm, height 11.75
mm; sapphire crystal, transparent case back;
water-resistant to 5 atm
Band: reptile skin, folding clasp
Price: $3,240
Variations: various bands and dials

Masterpiece Tradition Date

Reference number: MP6407-SS001-111
Movement: automatic, Caliber ML 155 (base Sellita
SW300); ø 25.6 mm, height 3.6 mm; 25 jewels;
28,800 vph; 38-hour power reserve
Functions: hours, minutes, sweep seconds; date
Case: stainless steel, ø 38 mm, sapphire crystal,
transparent case back; water-resistant to 5 atm
Band: reptile skin, folding clasp
Price: $2,700
Variations: various bands and dials

Pontos S Extreme Limited Edition

Reference number: PT6028-ALB01-331
Movement: automatic, Caliber ML 112 (base ETA 7750); ø 30 mm, height 7.9 mm; 25 jewels; 28,800 vph; 46-hour power reserve
Functions: hours, minutes, subsidiary seconds; chronograph; date
Case: composite material ("Powerlite"); ø 43 mm; crown-controlled inner bezel with 60-minute divisions, sapphire crystal, screw-in crown; water-resistant to 20 atm
Band: calf leather, buckle
Remarks: limited to 999 pieces
Price: $6,520
Variations: with green or blue eloxed case ($6,520)

Pontos S Extreme

Reference number: PT6028-ALB21-331
Movement: automatic, Caliber ML 112 (base ETA 7750); ø 30 mm, height 7.9 mm; 25 jewels; 28,800 vph; 46-hour power reserve
Functions: hours, minutes, subsidiary seconds; chronograph; date
Case: composite material ("Powerlite"); ø 43 mm, crown-controlled inner bezel with 60-minute divisions, sapphire crystal, screw-in crown; water-resistant to 20 atm
Band: calf leather, buckle
Price: $5,980
Variations: with blue eloxed case ($6,520)

Pontos S

Reference number: PT6008-SS001-332
Movement: automatic, Caliber ML157 (based on ETA 7753); ø 30 mm, height 7.9 mm; 25 jewels; 28,800 vph; 46-hour power reserve
Functions: hours, minutes, subsidiary seconds; chronograph; date
Case: stainless steel, ø 43 mm, height 15.5 mm; sapphire crystal, water-resistant to 20 atm
Band: textile, buckle
Price: $4,440
Variations: various bands and dials

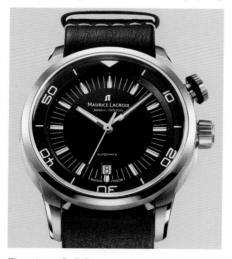

Pontos S Diver

Reference number: PT6248-SS001-330
Movement: automatic, Caliber ML 115 (base Sellita SW200); ø 25.6 mm, height 4.6 mm; 26 jewels; 28,800 vph; 38-hour power reserve
Functions: hours, minutes, sweep seconds; date
Case: stainless steel, ø 43 mm; crown-controlled inner bezel with 60-minute divisions, sapphire crystal, screw-in crown; automatic helium valve; water-resistant to 60 atm
Band: calf leather, buckle
Remarks: comes with optional textile band
Price: $3,400
Variations: with stainless steel bracelet ($3,400)

Pontos Chronographe

Reference number: PT6188-SS001-130
Movement: automatic, Caliber ML 112 (base ETA 7750); ø 30 mm, height 7.9 mm; 25 jewels; 28,800 vph; 42-hour power reserve
Functions: hours, minutes, subsidiary seconds; chronograph; date
Case: stainless steel, ø 43 mm, height 14.9 mm; sapphire crystal, transparent case back; water-resistant to 5 atm
Band: reptile skin, folding clasp
Price: $3,980
Variations: various bands and dials

Pontos Chronographe Vintage

Reference number: PT6288-SS001-130
Movement: automatic, Caliber ML 112 (base ETA 7750); ø 30 mm, height 7.9 mm; 25 jewels; 28,800 vph; 46-hour power reserve
Functions: hours, minutes, subsidiary seconds; chronograph; date
Case: stainless steel, ø 43 mm, height 14.9 mm; sapphire crystal, transparent case back; water-resistant to 5 atm
Band: calf leather, folding clasp
Price: $3,600
Variations: with dark dial

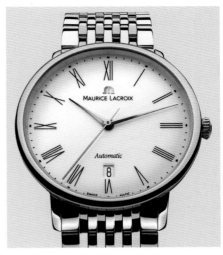

Pontos Day Date Vintage

Reference number: PT6158-SS001-331
Movement: automatic, Caliber ML 09 (base ETA 2836-2); ø 25.6 mm, height 5.05 mm; 25 jewels; 28,800 vph; 42-hour power reserve
Functions: hours, minutes, sweep seconds; weekday, date
Case: stainless steel, ø 40 mm, height 12 mm; sapphire crystal, transparent case back; water-resistant to 5 atm
Band: reptile skin, folding clasp
Price: $2,300
Variations: with light dial

Les Classiques Tradition

Reference number: LC6063-SS001-310
Movement: automatic, Caliber ML 132 (base ETA 2000); ø 19.4 mm, 20 jewels; 28,800 vph
Functions: hours, minutes, sweep seconds; date
Case: stainless steel, ø 28 mm, height 8.7 mm; sapphire crystal; transparent case back; water-resistant to 3 atm
Band: calf leather, buckle
Price: $2,660
Variations: with stainless steel bracelet ($3,320); with silver dial ($2,660); with rose gold bezel ($3,990)

Les Classiques Tradition

Reference number: LC6067-PS103-110
Movement: automatic, Caliber ML 155 (base Sellita SW300); ø 25.6 mm, height 3.6 mm; 25 jewels; 28,800 vph; 38-hour power reserve
Functions: hours, minutes, sweep seconds; date
Case: stainless steel, ø 38 mm, height 8.7 mm; rose gold bezel; sapphire crystal, transparent case back; water-resistant to 3 atm
Band: stainless steel, folding clasp
Price: $3,360
Variations: various bands and dials

Caliber ML 192

Automatic; single spring barrel, 52-hour power reserve; Qualité Fleurier
Functions: hours, minutes; power reserve indicator; full calendar with date, weekday, moon phase
Diameter: 36.6 mm
Height: 7.9 mm
Jewels: 59
Balance: glucydur
Frequency: 18,000 vph
Balance spring: Nivarox
Shock protection: Incabloc
Remarks: rhodium finish, straight-grain polished bridges, rotor with "grand colimaçon" decoration

Caliber ML 215

Manually wound; skeletonized movement; single spring barrel; 50-hour power reserve
Functions: hours and minutes (off-center), subsidiary seconds ("mysterious" display with floating double hands)
Diameter: 36.6 mm
Height: 6.3 mm
Jewels: 48
Balance: screw balance
Frequency: 18,000 vph
Balance spring: flat hairspring
Remarks: rhodium finish

Caliber ML 106

Manually wound; column wheel control of chronograph functions; single spring barrel; 42-hour power reserve
Functions: hours, minutes, subsidiary seconds; chronograph
Diameter: 36.6 mm
Height: 6.9 mm
Jewels: 22
Balance: screw balance with weights
Frequency: 18,000 vph
Balance spring: swan-neck fine adjustment
Shock protection: Kif Elastor
Remarks: eloxed movement finishing, bridges with "grand colimaçon" decoration, 2 gold chatons

MB&F

Terrasse Agrippa d'Aubigné 6
Case postale 3466
CH-1211 Geneva 3
Switzerland

Tel.:
01141-22-786-3618

Fax:
01141-22-786-3624

E-Mail:
info@mbandf.com

Website:
www.mbandf.com

Founded:
2005

Number of employees:
14

Annual production:
approx. 170 watches

U.S. distributor:
Westime Los Angeles
310-470-1388; 310-475-0628 (fax)
info@westime.com
Provident Jewelry, Florida
561-747-4449; nick@providentjewelry.com

Most important collections/price range:
Horological Machines / from $63,000; Legacy
Machines / from $92,000

MB&F

Maximilian Büsser & Friends (MB&F) goes beyond the standard notion of a brand. Perhaps calling it a tribe would be better: a tribe that aims to create unique works of horological art. At any rate, MB&F is doing something unconventional in an industry that usually takes its innovation in small doses.

After seeing the Opus projects to fruition, Max Büsser, former managing director of Harry Winston Rare Timepieces, decided that it was time to set the creators free. At MB&F he takes on the role of initiator, organizer, and coordinator. His Horological Machines, of which there are now five, are developed and realized in cooperation with highly specialized watchmakers, inventors, and designers in an "idea collective" creating unheard-of mechanical timepieces of great inventiveness, complication, and exclusivity. The composition of this collective varies as much as the shape and function of each machine. When you look at Number 4, the Thunderbolt, you find a miniature jet with two engines. The watch pays homage to all that is inside the timepiece, while the time is read by peering into the two "turbines." Number 5 ("On the Road Again") is an homage to the 1970s, when the fast and streamlined represented true strength rather than unsubtle brawn. The display in the lateral window is reflected by a prism. The "top" of the watch opens to let in light to charge the Superluminova numerals on the discs. Contrasting sharply with the modern productions is the 2011 Legacy Machine 1, an ultra-traditional timepiece with a quirky balance wheel beating away above the dial.

The spirit of Büsser is always present in each new timepiece, but it is now vented freely in the M.A.D. Gallery he opened in Geneva in 2012, where the visitor finds "mechanical art objects" that are beautiful, intriguing, technically impeccable, and sometimes perfectly useless except to entertain. They have their own muse, obviously.

Legacy Machine No.1

Reference number: LM1
Movement: manually wound, MB&F Caliber LM1; ø 37.2 mm, height 12.6 mm; 23 jewels; 18,800 vph; inverted with balance hovering over dial; finely decorated with côtes de Genève
Functions: 2 sets of hours and minutes (2 separately adjustable time zones); vertical power reserve indicator
Case: pink gold, ø 44 mm, height 16 mm; sapphire crystal; transparent case back
Band: reptile skin, buckle
Price: $92,000
Variations: white gold ($92,000)

HM3 MegaWind

Reference number: HM3 MegaWind
Movement: automatic, MB&F Caliber HM3, modified; 36 jewels; 28,800 vph; 3-part winding rotor (titanium hub, 2 gold oscillating weights)
Functions: hours (left display dome), minutes (right display dome)
Case: white gold, 47 x 50 mm, height 16 mm; sapphire crystal, transparent case back; screw-in crown; water-resistant to 3 atm
Band: reptile skin, buckle
Price: $92,000
Variations: pink gold ($92,000)

HM5 "On the Road Again"

Reference number: HM5 On the Road again
Movement: automatic, MB&F Caliber HM5, modified; 30 jewels, 28,800 vph; gold rotor; 42-hour power reserve; disc display reflected through prisms in side window
Functions: hours (digital, jumping) and minutes (digital)
Case: zirconium (stainless steel inner case); 51.5 x 49 mm, height 22.5 mm; sapphire crystal, transparent case back; water-resistant to 3 atm
Band: rubber, folding clasp
Price: $63,000

Meccaniche Veloci

The recipe almost seems too simplistic: watches and cars. With speed and exhaust fumes, the race clock ticking away . . . suddenly men become boys again. For a watch brand, choosing this aesthetic strategy is a risky game. Perhaps the trick is to be really frank about it, possibly even "in your face." Meccaniche Veloci, a young brand that was founded in 2006, has even made its name a sort of tagline: fast engineering. Its timepieces are all saturated with the techno look.

The company made its automotive theme clear right from the start: Its first watch, the Quattro Valvole, which features such auto construction elements as piston ring grooves and four embedded valve seat pockets, pushed all the right buttons with its target audience. Each year, the collection grows by a number of models, all of which build upon the original, car-inspired idea. Later designs include a watch with two valve seat pockets as the dials; clean-lined, three-hand watches; and timepieces that feature cases bejeweled with gemstones or made of special materials. Such out of the ordinary materials include sintered carbon ceramic, the stuff used in brake discs for high-performance sports cars—as well as in watch cases produced in collaboration with Italian brake manufacturer Brembo.

Meccaniche Veloci Srl.
I-36051 Olmo di Creazzo (VI)
Italy

Founded:
2006

Number of employees:
not specified

Annual production:
not specified

U.S. distributor:
Meccaniche Veloci
Gevril Group
9 Pinecrest Road
Valley Cottage, NY 10989
845-425-9882
eva@newdovergroup.com

Most important collections/price range:
Quattro Valvole / from $2,300; Due Valvole / from $1,900

Quattro Valvole 48 Classic

Reference number: W 124N177
Movement: automatic, 4 separate ETA Caliber 2671; ø 17.2 mm, height 4.8 mm; 25 jewels; 28,800 vph; 38-hour power reserve
Functions: hours and minutes (4 time zones), sweep seconds
Case: titanium, ø 48 mm, height 15.8 mm; sapphire crystal, 4 screw-in crowns; water-resistant to 100 atm
Band: rubber, buckle
Remarks: carbon fiber and ceramic composite (CCM) dial
Price: $6,725

Quattro Valvole 44 Chronograph Limited Edition

Reference number: W 123K140
Movement: automatic, ETA Caliber 7750; ø 30 mm, height 7.9 mm; 25 jewels; 28,800 vph; 42-hour power reserve
Functions: hours, minutes, subsidiary seconds; chronograph
Case: titanium, with black PVD coating, ø 44 mm, height 15.1 mm; sapphire crystal, screw-in crown; water-resistant to 10 atm
Band: rubber, buckle
Price: $5,325

Due Valvole

Reference number: W 125K019
Movement: automatic, 2 x ETA Caliber 2671; ø 17.2 mm, height 4.8 mm; 25 jewels; 28,800 vph; 38-hour power reserve
Functions: hours and minutes (2 time zones), sweep seconds; date
Case: titanium, with black PVD coating, ø 44 mm, sapphire crystal, screw-in crown; water-resistant to 10 atm
Band: rubber, buckle
Price: $8,475

MeisterSinger

MeisterSinger GmbH & Co. KG
Hafenweg 46
D-48155 Münster
Germany

Tel.:
01149-251-133-4860

E-Mail:
info@meistersinger.de

Website:
www.meistersinger.de

Founded:
2001

Number of employees:
9

Annual production:
approx. 7,000 watches

U.S. distributor:
Duber Time
1920 Dr. MLK Jr. Street North
St. Petersburg, FL 33704
727-896-4278

Most important collections/price range:
from approx. $1,200 to $7,000

"Ceci n'est pas une pipe," is how René Magritte subtitled his famous realistic rendering of a pipe. "This is not a regulator," is how one might want to subtitle the MeisterSinger Singulator. This timepiece makes use of the same typical style elements as a regulator, but with one big difference: It only has a single hand. Ever since Manfred Brassler launched his brand on the German market at the beginning of the millennium, people have had the option of reducing the day to a rhythmic succession of five-minute intervals.

Looking at these ultimately simplified dials does tempt one to classify the one-hand watch as an archetype. The single hand simply cannot be reduced any further, and the 144 minutes for 12 hours around the dial do have a normative function of sorts. But in a frenetic era, when time has become so rare, these watches do tend to slow things down a little.

"A customer once wrote me that his MeisterSinger was a symbol of leisure time for him," Brassler grins. "It measures the time in intervals of five minutes; you don't need to know what time it is any more precisely than that."

Meanwhile, Brassler has put a few three-hand watches on the market, but the hour hand remains the dominant feature on the dials. A new series geared toward women exudes its own simplicity, with just a slight breeze of color softening up the dial. Design, product planning, service, and management are all done in Münster in Germany. The watches, however, are Swiss made, with ETA and Sellita movements.

Pangaea Day Date

Reference number: PDD903
Movement: automatic, Sellita Caliber SW220-1; ø 25.6 mm, height 5.05 mm; 26 jewels; 28,800 vph; 38-hour power reserve
Functions: hours (each line stands for 5 minutes); date and weekday (disc display)
Case: stainless steel, ø 40 mm; sapphire crystal, transparent case back; water-resistant to 5 atm
Band: leather, buckle
Price: $2,825
Variations: with white or anthracite dial

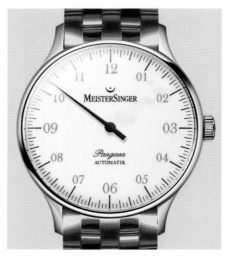

Pangaea 1Z

Reference number: PM 901
Movement: automatic, ETA Caliber 2892-2; ø 25.6 mm, height 3.6 mm; 21 jewels; 28,800 vph; finely finished with côtes de Genève; 42-hour power reserve
Functions: hours (each line stands for 5 minutes)
Case: stainless steel, ø 40 mm; height 10.1 mm; sapphire crystal, transparent case back; water-resistant to 5 atm
Band: stainless steel, folding clasp
Price: $2,675
Variations: various dials; with leather strap ($2,675)

Perigraph

Reference number: AM1007
Movement: automatic, ETA 2824-2 or Sellita SW200-1; ø 25.6 mm, height 4.6 mm; 25 or 26 jewel; 28,800 vph; with côtes de Genève; 38-hour power reserve
Functions: hours (each line stands for 5 minutes); date
Case: stainless steel, ø 43 mm; height 11 mm; sapphire crystal, transparent case back; water-resistant to 5 atm
Band: leather, buckle
Price: $2,375
Variations: various dials

Singulator

Reference number: SIM 102
Movement: manually wound, Caliber MS.0109 (base ETA 6497); ø 36.6 mm, height 5.1 mm; 17 jewels; 18,000 vph; swan-neck fine adjustment, glucydur screw balance, blued screws; skeletonized; finely finished with côtes de Genève; 46-hour power reserve
Functions: hours, minutes (off-center), subsidiary seconds
Case: stainless steel, ø 43 mm, height 13.3 mm; sapphire crystal, transparent case back; water-resistant to 5 atm
Band: reptile skin, double folding clasp
Price: $7,450
Variations: various dials

Singular

Reference number: MM 401G
Movement: automatic, ETA Caliber 7750; ø 30 mm, height 7.9 mm; 25 jewels; 28,800 vph; côtes de Genève; 42-hour power reserve
Functions: hours (each line stands for 5 minutes); chronograph (with second and minute counter)
Case: stainless steel, ø 43 mm; height 14.6 mm; sapphire crystal, transparent case back; water resistant to 5 atm
Band: leather, double folding clasp
Price: $4,475
Variations: various dials

NEO F Q

Reference number: NEFQ 903
Movement: quartz, ETA Caliber F06111
Functions: hours, (each line stands for 5 minutes); date
Case: stainless steel, ø 36 mm; height 9.7 mm; plexiglass; water-resistant to 3 atm
Band: buffalo leather, buckle
Price: $675
Variations: various dials; as 2-hand watch

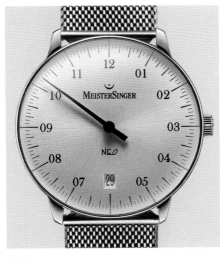

NEO

Reference number: NEF 903
Movement: automatic, ETA 2824-2 or Sellita SW200-1; ø 25.6 mm, height 4.6 mm; 25 or 26 jewel; 28,800 vph; 38-hour power reserve
Functions: hours (each line stands for 5 minutes); date
Case: stainless steel, ø 36 mm; height 9.7 mm; plexiglass; water-resistant to 3 atm
Band: stainless steel, folding clasp
Price: $1,190
Variations: various dials and bands

N° 01

Reference number: AM 3303
Movement: manually wound, ETA Caliber 2801-2; ø 35.6 mm, height 3.35 mm; 17 jewels; 28,800 vph; 42-hour power reserve
Functions: hours (each line stands for 5 minutes)
Case: stainless steel, ø 43 mm; height 11.5 mm; sapphire crystal, transparent case back; water-resistant to 5 atm
Band: leather, buckle
Price: $1,595

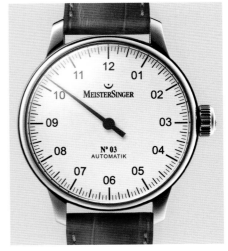

N° 03

Reference number: AM 901
Movement: automatic, ETA Caliber 2824-2 or Sellita SW200-1; ø 25.6 mm, height 4.6 mm; 25 jewels; 28,800 vph; with côtes de Genève; 38-hour power reserve
Functions: hours (each line stands for 5 minutes)
Case: stainless steel, ø 43 mm; height 11.5 mm; sapphire crystal, transparent case back; water-resistant to 5 atm
Band: leather, buckle
Price: $2,150
Variations: with 38 mm case diameter ($1,550); various dials

Milus International SA
Rue de Reuchenette 19
CH-2502 Biel/Bienne
Switzerland

Tel.:
01141-32-344-3939

Fax:
01141-32-344-3938

E-Mail:
info@milus.com

Website:
www.milus.com

Founded:
1919

Number of employees:
not specified

Annual production:
not specified

U.S. distributor:
Totally Worth It, LLC
76 Division Avenue
Summit, NJ 07901-2309
201-894-4710
info@totallyworthit.com

Most important collections/price range:
Milus Tirion Répétition Minutes TriRetrograde /
from approx. $308,000; Tirion TriRetrograde /
from approx. $9,300; Merea TriRetrograde / from
approx. $7,000; Snow Star Heritage

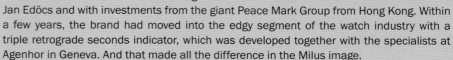

Milus

Milus was founded by Paul William Junod in Biel/ Bienne and remained in family hands until the year 2002. A new era began then with the founding of Milus International SA under the able guidance of Jan Edöcs and with investments from the giant Peace Mark Group from Hong Kong. Within a few years, the brand had moved into the edgy segment of the watch industry with a triple retrograde seconds indicator, which was developed together with the specialists at Agenhor in Geneva. And that made all the difference in the Milus image.

In the 1970s, the brand had a considerable reputation for jewelry. Now it has become a genuine and respected watchmaker producing top-drawer horological complications. The TriRetrograde function is a Milus trademark and can be found in a host of models all named after constellations (Tirion, Merea, Zetios). Fans of retrogrades will have a feast. There are watches with three separate second hands showing twenty seconds each before passing the baton to the next one or the lively "five-hand watch" or even the spectacular Tirion Répétition Minutes TriRetrograde, which also features a delicate minute repeater.

Meanwhile, the Peace Mark Group collapsed in 2008, but Milus quickly found another investor in the Chow Tai Fook Group owned by Dr. Cheng Yu-tung. In 2011, Cyril Dubois took over at the head of the company. Quietly, but surely, the brand has been expanding on several fronts with the triretrogrades in the lead. With the Apiana, Milus looks back to a time when it produced jewelry as well. The brand's Snow Star Instant Date from the 1940s was also rebuilt for vintage fans. Finally, the brand has been intensively communicating a collection of eye-catching cuff links it began launching in 2006 already featuring real rotor systems.

Tirion Répétition Minutes TriRetrograde

Reference number: TIRM600
Movement: manually wound, Milus Caliber M08-35RM module; ø 26.2 mm, height 5.2 mm; 25 jewels; 28,800 vph; 96 hours power reserve; COSC certified
Functions: hours, minutes, subsidiary triretrograde seconds; date; minute repeater
Case: pink gold, ø 46 mm, height 13.92 mm; sapphire crystal; screwed-down case back; water-resistant to 3 atm
Band: reptile skin, buckle
Remarks: blued hands, retrograde seconds displayed on three 20-second gold arcs
Price: $308,000

Merea TriRetrograde

Reference number: MER027
Movement: automatic, ETA Caliber 2892-A2 with Milus special module 3838; ø 30 mm; 37 jewels; 28,800 vph, 40 hours power reserve
Functions: hours, minutes, triple retrograde subsidiary seconds
Case: stainless steel, 35.8 x 36.8 mm, height 12.9 mm; case, crown and attachments partially set with 115 white diamonds; sapphire crystal; screwed-down case back; water-resistant to 3 atm
Band: reptile skin, buckle
Price: $12,900

Apiana Chronograph Automatic

Reference number: APIC400
Movement: automatic, ETA Caliber 2094; ø 23.3 mm; height 5.5 mm; 33 jewels; 28,800 vph; 40 hours power reserve
Functions: hours, minutes, subsidiary seconds; chronograph, 30-minute counter
Case: pink gold, 39 x 45 mm, height 12.9 mm; case and dial set with 655 white and brown diamonds; sapphire crystal; screwed-down case back; water-resistant to 3 atm
Band: galuchat, buckle
Price: $73,950

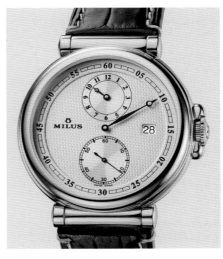

Zetios Chronograph

Reference number: ZETC027
Movement: automatic, ETA Caliber 2892 with Dubois Depraz 4500 module; ø 30 mm, height 7.5 mm; 49 jewels; 28,800 vph; 40 hours power reserve
Functions: hours, minutes, subsidiary seconds; date; chronograph; 30-minute and 12-hour counter
Case: stainless steel, ø 45 mm; sapphire crystal; screwed-down case back; water-resistant to 3 atm
Band: calf leather, buckle
Remarks: carbon dial with silver indexes, silver hands
Price: $5,350
Variations: pink gold (starting at $29,200)

Zetios Chronograph

Reference number: ZETC403
Movement: automatic, ETA Caliber 2892 with Dubois Depraz 4500 module; ø 25.6 mm, height 7.5 mm; 49 jewels; 28,800 vph; 40 hours power reserve
Functions: hours, minutes, subsidiary seconds; date; chronograph; 30-minute and 12-hour counter
Case: pink gold, ø 45 mm; sapphire crystal; screwed-down case back; water-resistant to 3 atm
Band: reptile skin, buckle
Remarks: carbon dial with gold indexes, gold hands
Price: $29,200
Variations: stainless steel (starting at $5,100)

Zetios Regulator

Reference number: ZETR400
Movement: automatic, ETA Caliber 2892-A2 with Dubois Depraz 14070 module; ø 26.2 mm, height 5.2 mm; 25 jewels; 28,800 vph; 42-hour power reserve
Functions: hours, minutes, subsidiary seconds; date
Case: pink gold, ø 42 mm; sapphire crystal; screwed-down case back; water-resistant to 3 atm
Band: reptile skin, buckle
Remarks: galvanic dial with grain de riz decoration, blued hands
Price: $23,500

Snow Star Heritage

Reference number: HKIT001
Movement: automatic, Sellita SW200; ø 25.6 mm, height 4.6 mm; 28,800 vph
Functions: hours, minutes, seconds; date
Case: stainless steel, ø 40 mm; sapphire crystal with magnifying glass at 3 o'clock; water-resistant to 3 atm
Band: calf leather, buckle
Remarks: comes with interchangeable NATO strap, compass and propeller cufflinks, and military ID tag
Price: $3,290, limited to 1,940 pieces
Variations: pink gold (limited to 99 pieces, $49,900)

Herios TriRetrograde

Reference number: HERT831 Bird of Heaven
Movement: automatic, ETA Caliber 2892-A2 with Milus special module 3838; ø 30 mm; 37 jewels; 28,800 vph, 40 hours power reserve
Functions: hours, minutes, subsidiary triretrograde seconds
Case: white gold, ø 41.7 x 42 mm; height 13.92; sapphire crystal; screwed-down case back; water-resistant to 3 atm
Band: reptile skin, buckle
Remarks: blued skeletonized hands, retrograde seconds displayed on 3 20-second arcs; partially skeletonized dial with cloisonné enamel
Price: $71,000

Milus Cufflinks

Reference number: CUF312
Movement: with an original Milus 360° rotatable rotor, white gold, ø 19 mm; set with 48 black and 16 white baguette diamonds
Case: Black Or treated white gold movement
Remarks: Milus started manufacturing cufflinks in 2006 using original movement parts
Price: $57,800
Variations: steel, pink gold, PVD-coated, rose gold and yellow gold plated (starting at $365)

Mk II

Mk II Corporation
303 W. Lancaster Ave., #283
Wayne, PA 19087

E-Mail:
info@mkiiwatches.com

Website:
www.mkiiwatches.com

Founded:
2002

Number of employees:
2

Annual production:
800 watches

Distribution:
direct sales and select retail

Most important collections/price range:
Professional series / $1,150 to $1,800; Specialist series / $799 to $1,100

If vintage and unserviceable watches had their say, they would probably be naturally attracted to Mk II for the name alone, which is a military designation for the second generation of equipment. The company, which was founded by watch enthusiast and maker Bill Yao in 2002, not only puts retired designs back into service, but also modernizes and customizes them. It's an idea whose time has come, as watch enthusiasts grow in numbers and are inheriting or finding older models.

Before the screwed-down crown, diving watches were not nearly as reliably sealed, for example. And some beautiful old pieces were made with plated brass cases or featured Bakelite components, which are either easily damaged or have aged poorly. Mk II not only substitutes proven modern materials, but also modern manufacturing techniques to ensure a better outcome.

These are material issues that the team at Mk II handles with great care. As genuine watch lovers themselves, they make sure that the final design is in the spirit of the watch itself, which still leaves a great deal of leeway given a sufficient number of parts. Vintage style and modern functionality are key. The watches are assembled by hand and subjected to a rigorous regime of testing. The components are individually inspected, the cases tested at least three times for water resistance, and at the end the whole watch is regulated in three to six positions. Looking to the future, Mk II aspires to carry its clean vintage style into the development of what it hopes will be future classics of its own.

Fulcrum (Antimagnetic)

Movement: automatic, Caliber Soprod A10; ø 26.2 mm, height 3.6 mm; 25 jewels; 28,800 vph; 42-hour power reserve; rhodium-plated; rotor with côtes de Genève
Functions: hours, minutes, sweep seconds, date
Case: stainless steel, ø 42.1 mm, height 15.1 mm; unidirectional bezel; antireflective sapphire crystal; screwed-down case back; screw-in crown; automatic helium release valve; water-resistant to 30 atm
Band: natural rubber strap
Price: $1,695
Variations: with NATO strap

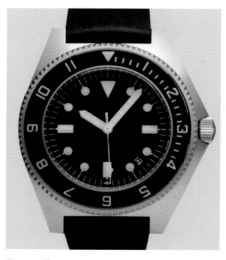

Paradive

Reference number: CD04EME011.124B01SS
Movement: automatic, Caliber ETA 2836-2; ø 26 mm, height 5.05 mm; 25 jewels; 28,800 vph; 38-hour power reserve; rhodium-plated; rotor with côtes de Genève
Functions: hours, minutes, sweep seconds, date
Case: stainless steel, ø 41.25 mm, height 15.5 mm; unidirectional steel/sapphire bezel; antireflective sapphire crystal; screwed-down case back; screw-in crown; automatic helium release valve; water-resistant to 30 atm
Band: natural rubber strap
Price: $1,650
Variations: with steel bracelet; with time elapse bezel; with no date or day/date

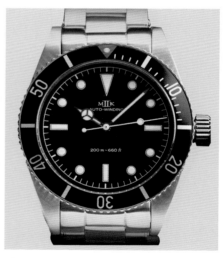

Nassau

Reference number: CD05.1R009.2NSPMWB
Movement: automatic, Caliber ETA 2836-2; ø 26 mm, height 5.05 mm; 25 jewels; 28,800 vph; 38-hour power reserve; rhodium-plated, rotor with côtes de Genève
Functions: hours, minutes, sweep seconds
Case: stainless steel; ø 39.2 mm, height 14.5 mm; unidirectional steel/aluminum bezel; domed sapphire crystal with antireflective coating; screwed down case back; screw-in crown; water resistant to 20 atm
Band: steel bracelet, folding clasp
Price: $945
Variations: with NATO strap

Montana Watch Company

Back in the nineteenth and early twentieth centuries, the American watch industry was a sizable affair, with manufacturers producing timepieces of superior craftsmanship, reliability, and simplicity, including their own movements in some instances. A century later, the Montana Watch Company in Livingston, Montana, decided to produce wristwatches that hark back to the days of old, boldly retro and therefore distinctive. Just looking at a Montana can make you hear horses galloping and banjos twanging.

The trick is in the design and the choice of materials. Think rich hand-engraved motifs, gems, and custom-designed cases. These often unique pieces are created by designer and horologist Jeffrey Nashan, who works individually with each client from concept to completion to achieve heirloom timepieces.

The traditional exterior, however, belies the state-of-the-art interior. Each case is machined in-house from a single piece of solid stock. Custom design with SolidWorks 3-D modeling CAD software and state-of-the-art CNC machines allows production of small runs in all variety of metals.

Nashan has assembled a team of master engravers well versed in every style of metal engraving, inlay, and gem setting, and one of the most highly skilled and innovative leathersmiths in the American West to produce the brand's bespoke straps. The watches featuring vignettes from John Banovich wildlife paintings using a special engraving technique are very popular. One of the latest Montana models is the Montana Travler, named for a special breed of horse—strong, with an easy gait and good personality.

Montana Watch Company
124 N. Main Street
Livingston, Montana 59047

Tel.:
406-222-8899

E-Mail:
info@montanawatch.com

Website:
www.montanawatch.com

Founded:
1998

Number of employees:
6

Annual production:
100 watches

Distribution:
direct distribution

Most important collection/price range:
Sapphire Model / starting at $2,950; Bridger Field Watch / starting at $3,200; Model 1925 / starting at $5,150; Officer's Watch / starting at $6,100; Model 1920 / starting at $3,850; Model 1930 / starting at $5,650; Highline Aviator / starting at $3,550; Miles City Pocket Watch / starting at $3,350; Montana Travler / starting at $3,750

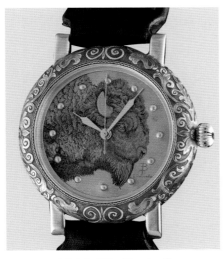

Model 1920 "Ta Tanka"

Movement: automatic, ETA Caliber 2892-A2; ø 25.6 mm, height 3.6 mm; 21 jewels; 28,800 vph
Functions: hours, minutes, sweep seconds
Case: polished sterling silver case, lugs, and yellow gold crown, ø 43 mm, height 7.5 mm; sapphire crystal; water-resistant to 3 atm
Band: tooled saddle leather, silver buckle
Remarks: custom hand-engraved dial
Price: $16,650
Variations: all custom variations available from $3,850

Sapphire

Movement: quartz, ETA 956.412; ø 20 mm, height 2.6 mm; 7 jewels
Functions: hours, minutes, sweep seconds
Case: titanium with gold overlay on engraved bezel, ø 31 mm, height 5.45 mm; gold crown; sapphire crystal; water-resistant to 3 atm
Band: reptile skin; titanium buckle with custom hand engraving
Remarks: white mother-of-pearl dial
Price: $11,650
Variations: all custom variations available from $2,950

The Montana Travler

Movement: automatic, ETA Caliber 2892-A2; ø 25.6 mm, height 3.6 mm; 21 jewels; 28,800 vph
Functions: hours, minutes, sweep seconds
Case: black oxide stainless steel, ø 46 mm, height 11.58 mm; carbon-damascus bezel; transparent case back; water-resistant to 6 atm
Band: black saddle leather; stainless oxide buckle
Remarks: black mother-of-pearl dial
Price: $5,300
Variations: all custom variations available from $3,750

Montblanc Montre SA

10, chemin des Tourelles
CH-2400 Le Locle
Switzerland

Tel.:
01141-32-933-8888

Fax:
01141-32-933-8880

E-Mail:
service@montblanc.com

Website:
www.montblanc.com

Founded:
1997 (1906 in Hamburg)

Number of employees:
worldwide approx. 3,000

Annual production:
not specified

Distribution:
retail, own boutiques

U.S. distributor:
Montblanc International
26 Main Street, Chatham, NJ 07928
908-508-2301; www.montblanc.com

Most important collections:
Star, Star Nicolas Rieussec, Star 4810,
TimeWalker, Collection Villeret

Montblanc

The fact that, in a period of fifteen years, a company once famous only for its exclusive writing implements managed to transform itself into a distinguished watch brand is one of the most impressive stories in the watch industry.

It was with great skill and cleverness that Nicolas Rieussec used the invention of the first chronograph—the "Time Writer," a device that released droplets of ink onto a rotating sheet of paper—to make a name for himself. And now, it seems, the tradition of using ink and time to create success continues: As the Richemont Group's first brand, Montblanc enjoys the exclusive use of an automatic chronograph, developed under a shroud of secrecy at the Manufacture Horlogère ValFleurier.

And it's clear that the Richemont Group places great trust in its "daughter" company, having put the little *manufacture* Minerva, which it purchased at the beginning of 2007, at the disposal of Montblanc Montre SA. Minerva is known primarily for its elegantly designed chronograph movements.

The Minerva Institute has been set up to serve as a kind of think tank for the future, a place where young watchmakers can absorb the old traditions and skills, as well as the wealth of experience and mind-set of the masters. In 2008, the Fondation Minerva began the task of financing and organizing its first nonprofit projects. In addition, it is preparing exhibitions, workshops, and industry conferences to make the competences of the institute accessible to as many people as possible.

Nicolas Rieussec Rising Hours

Reference number: 108789
Movement: automatic, Montblanc Caliber MB R220; 42 jewels; 28,800 vph; flat hairspring; column wheel control of chronograph functions using single pusher; 72-hour power reserve
Functions: hours (disc, day/night color change), minutes; chronograph; date, weekday; power reserve indicator (on movement side)
Case: pink gold, ø 43 mm, height 15.3 mm; sapphire crystal, pink gold case back; water-resistant to 3 atm
Band: reptile skin, triple folding clasp
Price: $34,700
Variations: stainless steel ($13,900); platinum $62,600 (limited to 28 pieces)

Nicolas Rieussec Chronograph Open Hometime

Reference number: 107070
Movement: manually wound, Caliber MB R210; ø 31 mm, height 8.63 mm; 40 jewels; 28,800 vph; 2 spring barrels, column wheel control of chronograph functions using single pusher; 72-hour power reserve
Functions: hours, minutes, subsidiary seconds; second time zone (additional 12-hour display); day/night indicator; chronograph; date
Case: stainless steel, ø 43 mm, height 15 mm; sapphire crystal, transparent case back; water-resistant to 3 atm
Band: reptile skin, double folding clasp
Price: $13,000

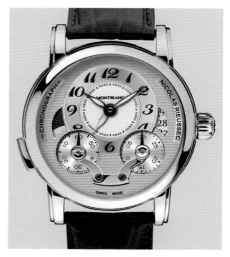

Nicolas Rieussec Chronograph Automatic

Reference number: 106487
Movement: automatic, Montblanc Caliber MB R200; ø 8.46mm, height 31 mm; 40 jewels; 28,800 vph; flat hairspring; column wheel control of chronograph functions using single pusher, 72-hour power reserve
Functions: hours, minutes, subsidiary seconds; additional 12-hour display (second time zone); chronograph; date
Case: stainless steel, ø 43 mm, height 14.8 mm; sapphire crystal, transparent case back; water-resistant to 3 atm
Band: reptile skin, double folding clasp
Price: $10,700
Variations: with dark dial ($10,700)

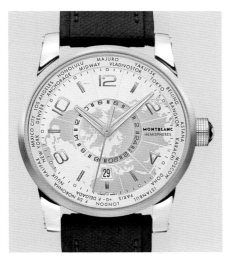

TimeWalker World-Time Southern Hemispheres

Reference number: 108956
Movement: automatic, Caliber MB 4810/412 (base ETA 2893-1); ø 25.6 mm, height 4.1 mm; 21 jewels; 28,800 vph; 42-hour power reserve
Functions: hours, minutes, sweep seconds; world-time display (second time zone); date
Case: stainless steel, ø 42 mm, height 12.05 mm; titanium bezel; sapphire crystal, transparent case back; water-resistant to 3 atm
Band: calf leather, pin buckle
Remarks: disc with 24 southern hemisphere reference cities on peripheral ring, with 24 northern hemisphere cities on case back
Price: $5,700

TimeWalker World-Time Northern Hemispheres

Reference number: 108955
Movement: automatic, Montblanc Caliber MB 4810/410 (base ETA 2893-1); ø 25.6 mm, height 4.1 mm; 21 jewels; 28,800 vph; 42-hour power reserve
Functions: hours, minutes, sweep seconds; world-time display (second time zone); date
Case: stainless steel, ø 42 mm, height 12.05 mm; titanium bezel; sapphire crystal, transparent case back; water-resistant to 3 atm
Band: stainless steel bracelet with titanium finish
Remarks: disc with 24 southern hemisphere reference cities on peripheral ring, with 24 northern hemisphere cities on case back
Price: $4,900

TimeWalker Voyager UTC

Reference number: 109137
Movement: automatic, Montblanc Caliber MB 4810/405 (base ETA 2893-2); ø 25.6 mm, height 4.1 mm; 21 jewels; 28,800 vph; 42-hour power reserve
Functions: hours, minutes, sweep seconds; additional 24-hour display (second time zone); date
Case: stainless steel, ø 42 mm, height 11 mm; titanium bezel; sapphire crystal, transparent case back; water-resistant to 3 atm
Band: calf leather, pin buckle
Price: $3,985
Variations: with reptile band ($3,860); with stainless steel bracelet ($4,100)

TimeWalker TwinFly Chronograph

Reference number: 109134
Movement: automatic, Caliber MB LL100; ø 31 mm, height 7.9 mm; 36 jewels; 28,800 vph; 72-hour power reserve; sweep minute counter
Functions: hours, minutes, subsidiary seconds; second time zone (additional 24-hour display); flyback chronograph; date
Case: stainless steel, ø 43 mm, height 15.3 mm; sapphire crystal, transparent case back; water-resistant to 3 atm
Band: reptile skin, double folding clasp
Price: $8,300
Variations: with stainless steel bracelet ($8,500)

TimeWalker TwinFly Chronograph GreyTech

Reference number: 107338
Movement: automatic, Caliber MB LL100; ø 31 mm, height 7.9 mm; 36 jewels; 28,800 vph; 72-hour power reserve; sweep minute counter
Functions: hours, minutes, subsidiary seconds; second time zone (additional 24-hour display); flyback chronograph; date
Case: titanium, ø 43 mm, height 15.3 mm; sapphire crystal, transparent case back; water-resistant to 3 atm
Band: reptile skin, buckle
Price: $15,320, limited to 888 pieces

Collection Villeret 1858 ExoTourbillon Chronographe

Reference number: 109151
Movement: manual winding, Montblanc Caliber MB M16.60; ø 38.4 mm, height 10.34 mm; 32 jewels; 18,000 vph; 4-minute tourbillon; column wheel control of chronograph functions using single pusher; 50-hour power reserve
Functions: hours (off-center), minutes, subsidiary seconds; additional 12-hour display (second time zone); day/night indicator; chronograph
Case: pink gold, ø 47 mm, height 16.67 mm; sapphire crystal, transparent case back; water-resistant to 3 atm
Band: reptile skin, pink gold buckle
Price: $251,600, limited to 8 pieces

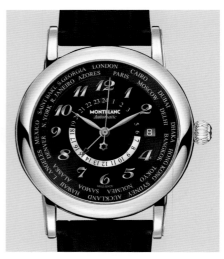

Star Classique Lady Automatic

Reference number: 107915
Movement: automatic, Montblanc Caliber MB 4810/408 (base ETA 2895-1); ø 25.6 mm, height 4.35 mm; 27 jewels; 28,800 vph; 42-hour power reserve
Functions: hours, minutes, subsidiary seconds
Case: stainless steel with rose gold elements; ø 34 mm, height 8.98 mm; sapphire crystal, transparent case back; rose gold crown; water-resistant to 3 atm
Band: stainless steel with pink gold elements, triple folding clasp
Price: $5,400
Variations: stainless steel with yellow gold caps ($5,400)

Star Quantième Complet

Reference number: 108737
Movement: automatic, Montblanc Caliber MB 4810/912 (base ETA 7751); ø 30 mm, height 7.9 mm; 25 jewels; 28,800 vph; 42-hour power reserve
Functions: hours, minutes, sweep seconds; full calendar with date, weekday, month, moon phase
Case: pink gold, ø 42 mm, height 12.17 mm; sapphire crystal, transparent case back; water-resistant to 3 atm
Band: reptile skin, pink gold buckle
Price: $17,900

Star World-Time GMT Automatic

Reference number: 106464
Movement: automatic, Caliber MB 4810/405 (base ETA 2893-1); ø 25.6 mm, height 4.1 mm; 21 jewels; 28,800 vph
Functions: hours, minutes, sweep seconds; additional 24-hour display (second time zone); date
Case: stainless steel, ø 42 mm, height 12.6 mm; sapphire crystal, transparent case back; screw-in crown; water-resistant to 3 atm
Band: reptile skin, triple folding clasp)
Price: $5,070
Variations: with stainless steel bracelet and bright dial ($5,280

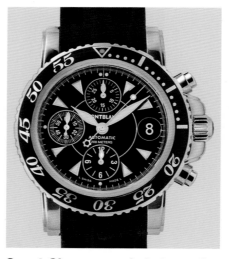

Star Chronograph Automatic

Reference number: 106466
Movement: automatic, Caliber MB 4810/501 (base ETA 7750); ø 30 mm, height 7.9 mm; 25 jewels; 28,800 vph
Functions: hours, minutes, subsidiary seconds; chronograph; weekday, date
Case: stainless steel, ø 39 mm, height 13.95 mm; sapphire crystal, transparent case back; water-resistant to 3 atm
Band: reptile skin, triple folding clasp
Price: $4,300
Variations: with dark dial ($4,300); with stainless steel bracelet ($4,500)

Sport Chronograph Automatic

Reference number: 03274
Movement: automatic, Caliber MB 4810/501 (base ETA 7750); ø 30 mm, height 7.9 mm; 25 jewels; 28,800 vph; 46-hour power reserve
Functions: hours, minutes; chronograph; date
Case: stainless steel, ø 44 mm, height 15.8 mm; unidirectional bezel with 60-minute divisions; sapphire crystal; screw-down crown and pusher; water-resistant to 20 atm
Band: black rubber, triple folding clasp
Price: $4,100

Sport DLC Chronograph Automatic

Reference number: 104279
Movement: automatic, Caliber MB 4810/501 (base ETA 7750); ø 30 mm, height 7.9 mm; 25 jewels; 28,800 vph; 46-hour power reserve
Functions: hours, minutes; chronograph; date
Case: stainless steel with black DLC coating, ø 44 mm, height 15.8 mm; unidirectional bezel with 60-minute divisions; sapphire crystal; screw-down crown and pusher; water-resistant to 20 atm
Band: reptile skin, triple folding clasp
Price: $6,105

Caliber MB M65.63

Manually wound; 1-minute tourbillon with oversized, screw balance located outside cage; single spring barrel, 45-hour power reserve
Functions: hours, minutes ("mysterious" display with 2 sapphire discs)
Diameter: 38.4 mm
Height: 10.3 mm
Jewels: 26
Balance: screw balance with weights
Frequency: 18,000 vph
Balance spring: cylindrical double balance spring
Remarks: plates and bridges of rhodium-plated German silver, partial perlage and beveled by hand

Caliber MB R200

Automatic; column wheel control using separate chronograph pushers; vertical chronograph clutch; stop-seconds; double spring barrel, 72-hour power reserve
Functions: hours, minutes, sweep seconds; additional 12-hour display; chronograph; date; power reserve indicator
Diameter: 31 mm
Height: 8.46 mm
Jewels: 40
Balance: screw balance
Frequency: 28,800 vph
Balance spring: flat hairspring
Remarks: rhodium-plated plate with perlage, bridges with côtes de Genève

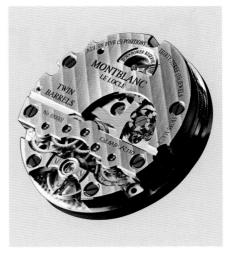

Caliber MB R110

Manually wound; column wheel control using separate chronograph pushers; vertical disc clutch; double spring barrel, 72-hour power reserve
Functions: hours, minutes, subsidiary seconds; chronograph; date; power reserve indicator on case back
Diameter: 31 mm
Height: 7.6 mm
Jewels: 33
Balance: balance with variable inertia
Frequency: 28,800 vph
Balance spring: flat hairspring
Shock protection: Incabloc
Remarks: rhodium-plated plate with perlage, bridges with côtes de Genève

Caliber MB M13.21

Manually wound; column wheel control of chronograph functions; single spring barrel, 60-hour power reserve
Functions: hours, minutes, subsidiary seconds; chronograph
Diameter: 29.5 mm
Height: 6.4 mm
Jewels: 22
Balance: screw balance with weights
Frequency: 18,000 vph
Balance spring: with Phillips end curve
Shock protection: Incabloc
Remarks: plates and bridges of rhodium-plated German silver, partial perlage and beveled by hand

Caliber MB M16.29

Manually wound; column wheel control of chronograph functions with separate pushers; single spring barrel, 55-hour power reserve
Functions: hours, minutes, subsidiary seconds; chronograph
Diameter: 38.4 mm
Height: 6.3 mm
Jewels: 22
Balance: screw balance
Frequency: 18,000 vph
Balance spring: with Phillips end curve
Remarks: rhodium-plated plate with perlage; bridges with côtes de Genève; gold-plated movement

Caliber MB LL100

Automatic; column wheel control of chronograph functions; vertical disc clutch; central minute and second counter with double flyback function; double spring barrel, 72-hour power reserve
Functions: hours, minutes, sweep seconds; additional 24-hour display; flyback chronograph; date
Diameter: 31 mm; **Height:** 7.9 mm
Jewels: 36
Balance: glucydur with variable inertia
Frequency: 28,800 vph
Balance spring: flat hairspring
Shock protection: Incabloc
Remarks: perlage on plate, bridges with côtes de Genève

Crowning Glory

Bill Yao

Function and form: the Perrelet Diamond Flower with sapphire cabochon on the crown.

Like the conductor's baton in music, the crown appears to be such an integral part of the watch, it is easy to take it for granted. In fact, the crown as we know it is of relatively recent origins. It was invented by Adrien Philippe of Patek Philippe in 1845 for use on pocket watches. Before the advent of the modern crown, time setting and winding were performed with keys, which exposed the movement to dust and moisture. Watchmakers still refer to the collection of levers, sprockets, and arms surrounding the stem of modern watches as the "keyless" works.

The earliest examples were nowhere near the crowns of today, which are the result of over a century of careful improvements designed to protect the movement from the elements, as well as to increase their own durability and longevity. But the crowns featured on wristwatches often trace their origins to designs first developed for pocket watches. The canteen-style crown used on 1940s U.S.-issued "BUSHIPS" dive watches first appeared on "travelers" pocket watches in the latter half of the nineteenth century. The system featured a kind of screw-on cap attached to the case by a little chain. It was during the same period that the screw-in crown was first developed for and used on a number of pocket watches with varying levels of commercial success. Ultimately, it was a young, dynamic brand called Rolex that popularized it as part of the iconic Rolex Oyster in 1926. The Oyster was actually a manually wound watch with a screw-in crown, which subjected this small component to a great deal of wear and tear. But the company continued doing its R&D

Detail of a standard crown with washer. (Curtesy of Esslinger.com)

and soon resolved the issue by developing the Rolex Perpetual automatic winding movement in 1931. Other watchmakers were not entirely satisfied with the idea of abandoning the manually wound watch. Panerai became the first to meet the challenge with its trademark cam-lever crown guard, patented in 1956.

Crown Types

There are two fundamental types of crowns: the dustproof or waterproof crown and the screw-in crown. The dustproof crown is commonly featured on manual winding watches and watches with minimal requirements for water resistance. This type of crown is primarily identifiable by the fact that it is pushed into its sealed position. In other words it does not mechanically attach to the case body. That being said, the dustproof crown can boast a respectable water resistance when combined with a series of gaskets. Generally speaking these crowns are not suitable for dive watches because the crown is not locked into a fixed position. Notable watches that feature a dustproof crown are the Omega Speedmaster Moonwatch, the ultrathin manually wound Piaget Altiplano, and the Seiko 5 series.

Besides the aforementioned cam-lever crown, the screw-in or screw-down crown is the standard for serious water resistance and diving watches. It gets its name from the fact that the crown will screw down onto the case body to form a secure seal against the elements. These crowns offer a respectable level of water resistance, generally between 30 and 50 meters, even when unlocked. A remarkable exception (but not something to verify at home) is the Rolex Triplock crown, a construction that has been tested to 200 meters with the crown in the open position. With the crown in its locked position this watch can resist depths that far exceed human endurance.

The screw-in crown on a vintage Soviet Komandirskie.

Diver's Delight

The screw-down crown comes in two versions: *débrayable* (declutching) and *non-débrayable* (non-declutching). If you have owned a variety of diving watches featuring automatic movements with manual winding capability, you will likely have experienced both types. The *non-débrayable* crowns continue to wind the movement as the crown is screwed down. Depending on how much torque is required to wind the movement, this can lead to "feedback" from the movement to the crown as it is screwed into its locked position. The *débrayable* crown, as the word suggests, allows the crown to disengage from the movement when it is screwed down onto the case. In this way, locking the crown onto the body is a more effortless and smooth experience.

The two types of crowns are used for different purposes. Generally speaking, the *non-débrayable* ones are chosen when a particularly robust system is required. The *débrayable* crowns are used to create a more refined feel and execution for a watch. To create a *débrayable* crown with the same robustness as a *non-débrayable* crown demands expertise in metallurgy and rigorous quality control. This is due to the tremendous friction that can build up among the parts in a *débrayable* crown. In addition, the spring that is enclosed within the crown can be subject to tremendous torsion, sometimes leading to complete failure if it was poorly manufactured.

Of course, the crowns mentioned above are only two of a great number of variations that exist for watches. Crowns are also used to rotate internal bezels, while others even incorporate a push piece to activate chronograph functions. Two of the more revolutionary developments in recent memory include Breitling's magnetic pusher system for chronographs and the Jaeger-LeCoultre compression crown. The former endows the chronograph watch with enough water resistance to allow the chronograph's use under water. The latter lets users open and close the crown quickly without having to concern themselves about cross-threading the crown/tube assembly.

Corporate identity: Hanhart's crown with the characteristic red chrono pusher.

A Word about Maintenance

The crown is one of the hardest working parts of your watch. All maintenance depends upon how much the crowns are operated or what environments they are subjected to during their lifetimes. It is safe to assume that the seals should ideally be checked annually. For screw-down crowns in particular it is important that they be checked open at a low pressure and closed at the watch's rated depth. One of the ironies of the crown is that it can be waterproof to high pressure while still being vulnerable to damaging moisture within the safety of your daily routines. The screw-down crowns' low pressure resistance essentially is what protects the watch from the normal trials of high-humidity environments.

Watchmaker Bill Yao is president of Mk II Watches in Wayne, Pennsylvania. His company specializes in customizing and modernizing retired watch designs.

The exhaust pipe–like crown on MB&F's Horological Machine No. 5.

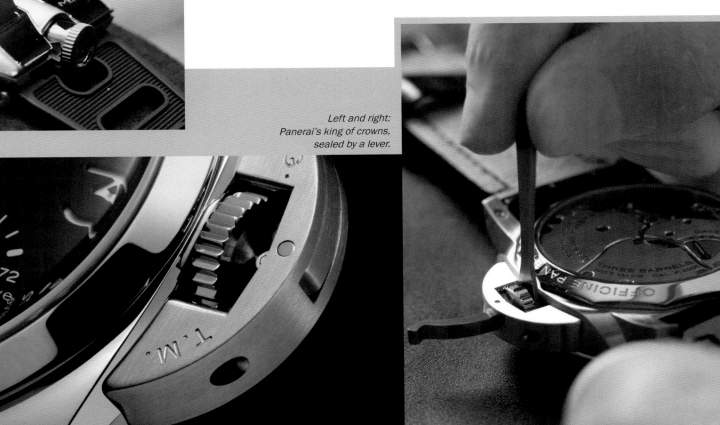

Left and right: Panerai's king of crowns, sealed by a lever.

Mühle Glashütte GmbH
Nautische Instrumente und Feinmechanik

Altenberger Strasse 35
D-01768 Glashütte
Germany

Tel.:
01149-35053-3203-0

Fax:
01149-35053-3203-136

E-Mail:
info@muehle-glashuette.de

Website:
www.muehle-glashuette.de

Founded:
first founding 1869; second founding 1993

Number of employees:
47

Annual production:
not specified

U.S. distributor:
Mühle Glashütte
Old Northeast Jewelers
1131 4th Street North
Saint Petersburg, FL 33701
800-922-4377
www.muehle-glashuette.com

Most important collections/price range:
mechanical wristwatches / approx. $1,399 to
$5,400

Mühle Glashütte

Mühle Glashütte has survived all the ups and downs of Germany's history. The firm Rob. Mühle & Sohn was founded by its namesake in 1869. At that time, the company made precision measuring instruments for the local watch industry and the German School of Watchmaking. In the early 1920s, the firm established itself as a supplier for the automobile industry, making speedometers, automobile clocks, tachometers, and other measurement instruments.

Having manufactured instruments for the military during the war, the company was not only bombarded by the Soviet air force, but was also nationalized in 1945, as it was in the eastern part of the country. After the fall of the Iron Curtain, it was reestablished as a limited liability corporation. In 2007, Thilo Mühle took over the helm from his father, Hans-Jürgen Mühle.

The company's wristwatch business was launched in 1996 and now somewhat overshadows the nautical instruments that had made the name Mühle Glashütte famous, especially among owners of luxury yachts and cruise ships. Its collection comprises mechanical wristwatches at entry-level and mid-level prices. For these, the company uses Swiss base movements that are equipped with such in-house developments as a patented "woodpecker-neck regulation" and the Mühle rotor. Chronographs are additionally fitted with the Glashütte three-quarter plate. All movement surfaces are finished in the typical Mühle style.

S.A.R. Rescue-Timer

Reference number: M1-41-03-MB
Movement: automatic, modified Sellita Caliber SW 200-1; ø 25.6 mm, height 4.6 mm; 26 jewels; 28,800 vph; woodpecker neck regulation, Mühle rotor; carefully reworked with special Mühle finish; 38-hour power reserve
Functions: hours, minutes, sweep seconds; date
Case: stainless steel, ø 42 mm, height 13.5 mm; rubber bezel; sapphire crystal, screw-in crown, water-resistant to 100 atm
Band: stainless steel, folding clasp with extension link
Price: $2,499
Variations: with rubber strap ($2,399)

S.A.R. Flieger-Chronograph

Reference number: M1-41-33-KB
Movement: automatic, Caliber MU 9408 (base ETA 7750); ø 30 mm, height 7.9 mm; 25 jewels; 28,800 vph; woodpecker neck regulation, three-quarter plate, Mühle rotor; carefully reworked with special Mühle finish; 48-hour power reserve
Functions: hours, minutes, subsidiary seconds; chronograph; date
Case: stainless steel, ø 44 mm, height 16.2 mm; bidirectional bezel with 60-minute divisions, sapphire crystal, transparent case back; screw-in crown; water-resistant to 10 atm
Band: rubber, safety folding clasp with extension
Price: $4,299
Variations: with stainless steel bracelet ($4,499)

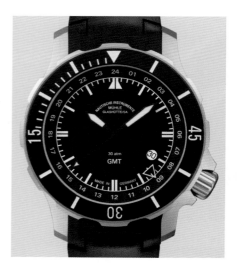

Seebataillon GMT

Reference number: M1-28-62-KB
Movement: automatic, ETA Caliber 2893-2; ø 25.6 mm, height 4.1 mm; 21 jewels; 28,800 vph; woodpecker neck regulation, Mühle rotor; carefully reworked with special Mühle finish; 42-hour power reserve
Functions: hours, minutes, sweep seconds; additional 24-hour display (second time zone); date
Case: titanium, ø 44 mm, height 12.7 mm; bidirectional bezel with 60-minute divisions; sapphire crystal, screw-in crown; water-resistant to 30 atm
Band: rubber, folding clasp
Price: $3,599

Rasmus 2000

Reference number: M1-28-82-KB
Movement: automatic, Sellita Caliber SW 200-1; ø 25.6 mm, height 4.6 mm; 26 jewels; 28,800 vph; woodpecker neck regulation, Mühle rotor; carefully reworked with special Mühle finish; 38-hour power reserve
Functions: hours, minutes, sweep seconds; date
Case: stainless steel, ø 44 mm, height 17.5 mm; unidirectional bezel with 60-minute divisions; sapphire crystal, screw-in crown; water-resistant to 200 atm
Band: rubber, folding clasp
Price: $3,499
Variations: with stainless steel bracelet ($3,599); in various colors

M 29 Classic

Reference number: M1-25-57-LB
Movement: automatic, Sellita Caliber SW 200-1; ø 25.6 mm, height 4.6 mm; 26 jewels; 28,800 vph; woodpecker neck regulation, Mühle rotor; carefully reworked with special Mühle finish; 38-hour power reserve
Functions: hours, minutes, sweep seconds; date
Case: stainless steel, ø 42.4 mm, height 11.3 mm; sapphire crystal, transparent case back; screw-in crown; water-resistant to 10 atm
Band: leather, buckle
Price: $1,899
Variations: with stainless steel bracelet ($1,999)

Antaria Chronograph

Reference number: M1-39-57-LB
Movement: automatic, Mühle Caliber MU 9408 (base ETA 7750); ø 30 mm, height 7.9 mm; 25 jewels; 28,800 vph; woodpecker neck regulation, three-quarter Glashütte plate; carefully reworked with special Mühle finish; 48-hour power reserve
Functions: hours, minutes, subsidiary seconds; chronograph; weekday, date
Case: stainless steel, ø 42 mm, height 14.2 mm; rose gold-plated bezel; sapphire crystal, transparent case back; screw-in crown; water-resistant to 5 atm
Band: leather, double folding clasp
Price: $2,499
Variations: with silver-colored dial

Teutonia II Day/Date

Reference number: M1-33-65-LB
Movement: automatic, Sellita Caliber SW 240-1; ø 29 mm, height 5.05 mm; 26 jewels; 28,800 vph; woodpecker neck regulation, Mühle rotor; carefully reworked with special Mühle finish; 38-hour power reserve
Functions: hours, minutes, sweep seconds; weekday, date
Case: stainless steel, ø 41 mm, height 11.5 mm; sapphire crystal, transparent case back; screw-in crown; water-resistant to 10 atm
Band: reptile skin, double folding clasp
Price: $2,799
Variations: with stainless steel bracelet ($2,899)

Teutonia III Hand Wound

Reference number: M1-08-01-LB
Movement: manually wound, Caliber MU 9412; ø 25.6 mm, height 3.4 mm; 18 jewels; 28,800 vph; woodpecker neck regulation, three-quarter Glashütte plate; carefully reworked with special Mühle finish; 42-hour power reserve
Functions: hours, minutes, sweep seconds; date
Case: stainless steel, ø 42 mm, height 11.2 mm; sapphire crystal, transparent case back; water-resistant to 10 atm
Band: leather, double folding clasp
Price: $2,799
Variations: with stainless steel bracelet ($2,899)

Caliber MU 9412

Manually wound, stop-seconds system; woodpecker neck regulation, regulated in 6 positions; single spring barrel, 42-hour power reserve
Functions: hours, minutes, sweep seconds; date
Diameter: 25.6 mm
Height: 3.4 mm
Jewels: 18
Balance: nickel, gold-plated
Frequency: 28,800 vph
Shock protection: Incabloc
Remarks: Glashütte three-quarter plate and typical surface finishing

Nienaber Bünde

Bahnhofstrasse 33a
D-32257 Bünde
Germany

Tel.:
01149-5223-12292

E-Mail:
info@nienaber-uhren.de

Website:
www.nienaber-uhren.de

Founded:
1984

Number of employees:
1

Annual production:
approx. 50 watches

Distribution:
Please contact Nienaber Bünde directly.

Most important collections/price range:
watches with retrograde displays / approx. $4,000
to $27,000
Prices are determined from the daily euro
exchange rate.

Rainer Nienaber

For over a quarter-century, Rainer Nienaber has manufactured, sold, and repaired watches in Bünde, Germany. Although his work has spanned large, small, simple, complicated, expensive, and inexpensive watches, they all share one trait: uniqueness. One of his particular specialties is retrograde displays, which he continually rearranges in various combinations to create new models. Nienaber uses Swiss movements; the rest is, however, "made in Germany" (cases, dials, bands). He doesn't like being called a *"manufacture,"* opting instead for the term "atelier." No one can doubt his inventiveness. He has produced watches with decimal time, a pair of watches called the Day and Night Watch (for more, visit the collections on his website). His Anterograde is designed to look like the tachometer of a classic car. Although this conceit is not that unusual in the watchmaking industry, in this case the result happens to be an unusual one-handed watch. The five-minute divisions along the dial still allow the user to read the time with considerable precision. But Nienaber has added another extraordinary feature: When the hour hand reaches the 12 o'clock mark, which is a little off-center to the left, it jumps ahead to a "0" mark to the right of center, to begin the next 12-hour period of the day. Hence the name "anterograde." This is no mean feat given the unavoidable tooth flank backlash in the display movement. However, it's not the only model in which the master retrograder has used this technique.

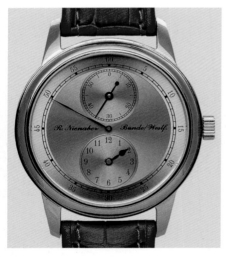

Regulator Version-1

Movement: manually wound, base ETA 6497;
ø 36.6 mm, height 4.5 mm; 17 jewels; 18,000 vph
Functions: hours (off-center), minutes, subsidiary
seconds
Case: stainless steel, ø 44 mm, height 12 mm;
sapphire crystal; transparent case back
Band: calf leather, buckle
Remarks: gold-plated brass dial
Price: $4,500
Variations: with silver dial

Retro-2

Movement: automatic, ETA Caliber 2824-2;
ø 25.6 mm, height 4.6 mm; 25 jewels; 28,800 vph
Functions: hours, minutes (both retrograde)
Case: stainless steel, ø 41 mm, height 11 mm;
yellow gold bezel; sapphire crystal; transparent case
back
Band: reptile skin, buckle
Price: $8,840
Variations: stainless steel ($8,250)

Jumping Hours 24

Movement: manually wound, Caliber AS 1130;
ø 29.5 mm, height 4.5 mm; 17 jewels; 18,000 vph
Functions: hours (digital, jumping), minutes,
subsidiary seconds
Case: stainless steel, ø 41 mm, height 10 mm;
sapphire crystal, transparent case back
Band: calf leather, buckle
Price: $5,200
Variations: steel-colored dial ($5,200)

Nivrel

In 1891, master goldsmith Friedrich Jacob Kraemer founded a jewelry and watch shop in Saarbrücken that proved to be the place to go for fine craftsmanship. Gerd Hofer joined the family business in 1956, carrying it on into the fourth generation. However, his true passion was for watchmaking. In 1993, he and his wife, Gitta, bought the rights to use the Swiss name Nivrel, a brand that had been established in 1936, and integrated production of these watches into their German-based operations.

Today, Nivrel is led by the Hofers' daughter Anja, who is keeping both lineages alive. Mechanical complications with Swiss movements of the finest technical level and finishing as well as gold watches in the high-end design segment of the industry are manufactured with close attention to detail and an advanced level of craftsmanship. In addition to classic automatic watches, the brand has introduced everything from complicated chronographs and skeletonized watches to perpetual calendars and tourbillons. The movements and all the "habillage" of the watches—case, dial, crystal, crown, etc.—are made in Switzerland. Watch design, assembly, and finishing are done in Saarbrücken.

Nivrel watches are a perfect example of how quickly a watch brand incorporating a characteristic style and immaculate quality can make a respected place for itself in the industry. Affordable prices also play a significant role in this brand's success, but they do not keep the brand from innovating. Nivrel has teamed up with the Department of Metallic Materials of Saarland University to develop a special alloy for repeater springs that is softer and does not need as much energy to press.

Nivrel Uhren
Gerd Hofer GmbH
Kossmannstrasse 3
D-66119 Saarbrücken
Germany

Tel.:
01149-681-584-6576

Fax:
01149-681-584-6584

E-Mail:
info@nivrel.com

Website:
www.nivrel.com

Founded:
1978

Number of employees:
10, plus external staff members

Annual production:
not specified

Distribution:
Please contact headquarters for enquiries.

Most important collections/price range:
mechanical watches, some with complications / approx. $600 to $45,000

Héritage Grande Automatique

Reference number: N 112.001
Movement: automatic, Soprod Caliber A10; ø 25.6 mm, height 3.6 mm; 21 jewels; 28,800 vph
Functions: hours, minutes, sweep seconds; date
Case: stainless steel, ø 40 mm, height 9 mm; sapphire crystal, transparent case back; screw-in crown; water-resistant to 5 atm
Band: reptile skin, buckle
Price: $1,800

Héritage Grand Chronographe

Reference number: N 512.001 AASDS
Movement: automatic, ETA Caliber 7750; ø 30 mm, height 7.9 mm; 25 jewels; 28,800 vph
Functions: hours, minutes, subsidiary seconds; chronograph; weekday, date
Case: stainless steel, ø 42 mm, height 13,5 mm; sapphire crystal, transparent case back; screw-in crown; water-resistant to 5 atm
Band: calf leather, buckle
Price: $2,800

Réplique Coeur de la Sarre

Reference number: N 130.001
Movement: automatic, ETA Caliber 2824-2; ø 25.6 mm, height 4.6 mm; 25 jewels; 28,800 vph; rotor with côtes de Genève, 38-hour power reserve
Functions: hours, minutes, sweep seconds
Case: stainless steel, ø 42 mm, height 12.5 mm; mineral glass; transparent case back; water-resistant to 5 atm
Band: calf leather, buckle
Price: $900

NOMOS Glashütte
Ferdinand-Adolph-Lange-Platz 2
D-01768 Glashütte
Germany

Tel.:
01149-35053-4040

Fax:
01149-35053-40480

E-Mail:
nomos@glashuette.com

Website:
www.nomos-watches.com

Founded:
1990

Number of employees:
approx. 145

Annual production:
not specified

U.S. distributor:
For the U.S. market, please contact Nomos
Glashütte directly.

Most important collections/price range:
Ahoi / $3,940 to $4,500; Tangente / $1,630 to
$3,270; Tangomat / $2,700 to $4,570; Orion /
$1,780 to $2,850; Ludwig / $1,570 to $3,500;
Tetra / $1,840 to $2,730; Club / $1,450 to
$3,320; Zürich / $3,800 to $5,760; Sundial /
$175

Nomos Glashütte

Still waters run deep, and discreet business practices at times travel far. Nomos, founded in 1990, has suddenly become a full-fledged *manufacture* with brand-new facilities and a smart policy of only so much growth as the small team gathered around the founder Roland Schwertner and his associate Uwe Ahrendt can easily absorb.

The collection is based on five or six basic models, though the number of calibers available is impressive. The origin of the manually wound movements has been the tried-and-true Peseux Caliber (ETA 7001), as evidenced by the subsidiary seconds display at 6 o'clock. In 1997, the company added a stop-seconds system; in 2001 it was time for a date mechanism; and two years later, Nomos presented a Tangente with a power reserve indicator. Then, in 2005, Nomos moved into new space in the former Glashütte train station, and Mirko Heyne designed the first automatic movement for the Tangomat. In 1989, Nomos issued a special edition of twenty times twenty Orion models with dials in various shades of gray symbolizing the Berlin Wall, which had fallen twenty years before. Then came a switchable 24-hour display, featured in the company's Tangomat GMT and Zurich World Time models. The latter, incidentally, can be traced back to the concept of the late Zurich-born designer Hannes Wettstein. The latest crazy idea is the Ahoi (as in "ship ahoy!"), a thicker swimmer's watch with an optional synthetic strap like those to carry locker keys in Germany's public swimming pools. New dials, a new movement, a series of cool accessories, and the care to stick to a perfectly identifiable look keep Nomos in the public eye—but also the understated, tongue-in-cheek publicity that can put a crack in the facade of the most serious watch collector.

Ahoi

Reference number: 550
Movement: automatic, Nomos Caliber Epsilon; ø 31 mm, height 4.3 mm; 26 jewels; 21,600 vph
Functions: hours, minutes, subsidiary seconds
Case: stainless steel, ø 40 mm, height 10.64 mm; sapphire crystal, transparent case back; screw-in crown; water-resistant to 20 atm
Band: textile, winged clasp
Price: $3,940

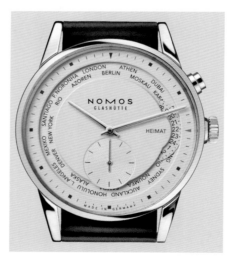

Zürich World-Timer

Reference number: 805
Movement: automatic, Nomos Caliber Xi; ø 31 mm, height 5.7 mm; 26 jewels; 21,600 vph
Functions: hours, minutes, subsidiary seconds; world time display (second time zone)
Case: stainless steel, ø 39.9 mm, height 10.85 mm; sapphire crystal; transparent case back; water-resistant to 3 atm
Band: horse leather, buckle
Price: $5,760

Orion 38 Gray

Reference number: 383
Movement: manually wound, Nomos Caliber Alpha; ø 23.3 mm, height 2.6 mm; 17 jewels; 21,600 vph
Functions: hours, minutes, subsidiary seconds
Case: stainless steel, ø 38 mm, height 8.86 mm; sapphire crystal; transparent case back; water-resistant to 3 atm
Band: horse leather, buckle
Price: $2,440

Tangente 38

Reference number: 164
Movement: manually wound, Nomos Caliber Alpha; ø 23.3 mm, height 2.6 mm; 17 jewels; 21,600 vph
Functions: hours, minutes, subsidiary seconds
Case: stainless steel, ø 37.5 mm, height 6.75 mm; sapphire crystal; transparent case back; water-resistant to 3 atm
Band: horse leather, buckle
Price: $2,140

Tangomat GMT

Reference number: 635
Movement: automatic, Nomos Caliber Xi; ø 31 mm, height 5.7 mm; 26 jewels; 21,600 vph
Functions: hours, minutes, subsidiary seconds; world-time display (second time zone)
Case: stainless steel, ø 40 mm, height 10.85 mm; sapphire crystal; transparent case back; water-resistant to 3 atm
Band: horse leather, buckle
Price: $4,570

Tangomat Date

Reference number: 602
Movement: automatic, Nomos Caliber Zeta; ø 31 mm, height 4.3 mm; 26 jewels; 21,600 vph
Functions: hours, minutes, subsidiary seconds; date
Case: stainless steel, ø 38.3 mm, height 8.3 mm; sapphire crystal; transparent case back; water-resistant to 3 atm
Band: horse leather, buckle
Price: $3,600
Variations: without date indicator; ruthenium-coated dial

Tetra Power Reserve

Reference number: 435
Movement: manually wound, Nomos Caliber Gamma (base Nomos Alpha); ø 23.3 mm, height 2.8 mm; 17 jewels; 21,600 vph; three-quarter plate; Glashütte stopwork; surfaces rhodium-plated with Glashütte ribbing
Functions: hours, minutes, subsidiary seconds; power reserve indicator
Case: stainless steel, 29.5 x 29.5 mm, height 6.3 mm; sapphire crystal; transparent case back
Band: horse leather, buckle
Price: $2,730
Variations: with dark dial without power reserve indicator (price on request)

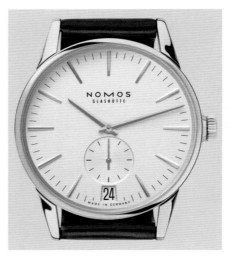

Zürich Date

Reference number: 802
Movement: automatic, Nomos Caliber Zeta; ø 31 mm, height 4.3 mm; 26 jewels; 21,600 vph
Functions: hours, minutes, subsidiary seconds; date
Case: stainless steel, ø 39.7 mm, height 9.65 mm; sapphire crystal; transparent case back; water-resistant to 3 atm
Band: horse leather, buckle
Price: $4,750

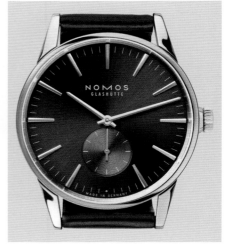

Zürich Brown-Gold

Reference number: 823
Movement: automatic, Nomos Caliber Epsilon; ø 31 mm, height 4.3 mm; 26 jewels; 21,600 vph
Functions: hours, minutes, subsidiary seconds
Case: stainless steel, ø 39.7 mm, height 9.65 mm; sapphire crystal; transparent case back; water-resistant to 3 atm
Band: horse leather, buckle
Remarks: sun ray pattern on dial
Price: $4,400

Ludwig Automatic Anthracite

Reference number: 252
Movement: automatic, Nomos Caliber Epsilon; ø 31 mm, height 4.3 mm; 26 jewels; 21,600 vph
Functions: hours, minutes, subsidiary seconds
Case: stainless steel, ø 40 mm, height 8.4 mm; sapphire crystal; transparent case back; water-resistant to 3 atm
Band: horse leather, buckle
Price: $2,910

Club Automatic

Reference number: 753
Movement: automatic, Nomos Caliber Epsilon; ø 31 mm, height 4.3 mm; 26 jewels; 21,600 vph
Functions: hours, minutes, subsidiary seconds
Case: stainless steel, ø 40 mm, height 9.73 mm; sapphire crystal; transparent case back; water-resistant to 10 atm
Band: horse leather, buckle
Price: $2,730
Variations: with stainless steel case back ($2,440)

Orion Date White

Reference number: 381
Movement: manually wound, Nomos Caliber Beta; ø 32.1 mm, height 2.8 mm; 23 jewels; 21,600 vph
Functions: hours, minutes, subsidiary seconds; date
Case: stainless steel, ø 38 mm, height 8.86 mm; sapphire crystal; transparent case back; water-resistant to 3 atm
Band: horse leather, buckle
Price: $2,850
Variations: with stainless steel case back ($2,520)

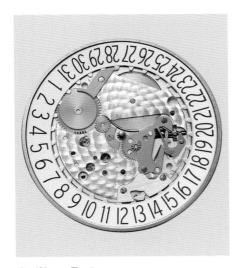

Caliber Beta

Manually wound; bidirectionally winding rotor; stop-seconds mechanism; Glashütte stopwork; single spring barrel, 42-hour power reserve
Functions: hours, minutes, subsidiary seconds; date
Diameter: 33.9 mm
Height: 2.8 mm
Jewels: 23
Balance: glucydur
Frequency: 21,600 vph
Balance spring: Nivarox with Triovis fine adjustment
Shock protection: Incabloc
Remarks: Glashütte three-quarter plate, finely finished with sunburst and côtes de Genève

Caliber Epsilon

Automatic; bidirectionally winding rotor, stop-seconds mechanism; Glashütte click; single spring barrel, 42-hour power reserve
Functions: hours, minutes, subsidiary seconds
Diameter: 31 mm
Height: 4.3 mm
Jewels: 26
Balance: glucydur
Frequency: 21,600 vph
Balance spring: Nivarox with Triovis fine adjustment
Shock protection: Incabloc
Remarks: Glashütte three-quarter plate, finely finished with blued screws, sunburst and Glashütte ribbing

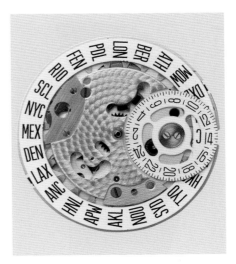

Caliber Xi

Automatic; bidirectionally winding rotor, stop-seconds mechanism; Glashütte click; single spring barrel, 42-hour power reserve
Functions: hours, minutes; subsidiary seconds; second time zone (world-time display)
Diameter: 31 mm; **Height:** 5.7 mm
Jewels: 26
Balance: glucydur
Frequency: 21,600 vph
Balance spring: Nivarox with Triovis fine adjustment
Shock protection: Incabloc
Remarks: Glashütte three-quarter plate, finely finished with blued screws, sunburst and Glashütte ribbing

Omega SA

Jakob-Stämpfli-Strasse 96
CH-2502 Biel/Bienne
Switzerland

Tel.:
01141-32-343-9211

E-Mail:
info@omegawatches.com

Website:
www.omegawatches.com

Founded:
1848

Number of employees:
not specified

Annual production:
750,000 (estimated)

U.S. distributor:
Omega
The Swatch Group (U.S.), Inc.
1200 Harbor Boulevard
Weehawken, NJ 07087
201-271-1400
www.omegawatches.com

Most important collections/price range:
Seamaster / approx. $3,900 to $138,500;
Constellation / approx. $4,500 to $50,700;
Speedmaster / approx. $4,950 to $11,900

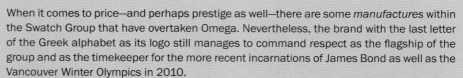

Omega

When it comes to price—and perhaps prestige as well—there are some *manufactures* within the Swatch Group that have overtaken Omega. Nevertheless, the brand with the last letter of the Greek alphabet as its logo still manages to command respect as the flagship of the group and as the timekeeper for the more recent incarnations of James Bond as well as the Vancouver Winter Olympics in 2010.

It has also played a major role in the history of the watch business in Switzerland. The brand was originally founded in 1848. In 1930, it merged with Tissot to form SIHH, which in turn merged with another watch conglomerate, ASUAG, to form the Swatch Group in 1983, of which Omega was the leading brand. In the 1990s, the brand managed to expand incrementally into the Chinese market and thus established a firm foothold in Asia. This also led to a steep growth in production numbers, putting it neck-and-neck with Rolex.

And today, Omega, whose star may have been fading, has once again put itself back in the competition with technology as the key. It has introduced the innovative coaxial escapement to several collections, notably the Constellation, Seamaster, Speedmaster, and De Ville, which has pushed the brand back into the technological frontrunners in its segment. Swatch Group subsidiary Nivarox-FAR has finally mastered the production of the difficult, oil-free parts of the system designed by the Englishman George Daniels, although the escapement continues to include lubrication as the long-term results of "dry" coaxial movements are less than satisfactory. Thus the most important plus for this escapement design remains high rate stability after careful regulation. Omega has even revived the Ladymatic, a hit in the mid-fifties, adding a silicon spring and the trademark coaxial escapement.

In July 2013, it officially unveiled a brand-new 15,000 Gauss antimagnetic movement, which, like the coaxial, will be spread throughout the brand's models in years to come. The Seamaster Aqua Terra that uses it can go into a magnetic resonance imaging machine without stopping.

Constellation Sedna LE 1952

Reference number: 123.53.38.21.02.001
Movement: automatic, Omega Caliber 8501;
ø 29 mm, height 5.5 mm; 39 jewels; 25,200 vph;
coaxial escapement, silicon balance and balance spring; 50-hour power reserve; COSC certified chronometer
Functions: hours, minutes, sweep seconds; date
Case: pink gold ("Sednagold"); ø 38 mm, height 12.52 mm; sapphire crystal, transparent case back; water-resistant to 10 atm
Band: reptile skin, folding clasp
Price: $21,400

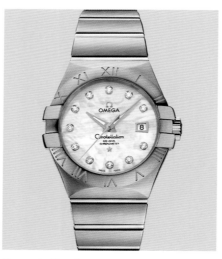

Constellation

Reference number: 123.20.31.20.55.003
Movement: automatic, Omega Caliber 8520;
ø 20 mm, height 5.3 mm; 28 jewels; 25,200 vph;
coaxial escapement, silicon balance and balance spring; 50-hour power reserve; COSC certified chronometer
Functions: hours, minutes, sweep seconds; date
Case: stainless steel with rose gold elements; ø 31 mm, height 11.87 mm; sapphire crystal; water-resistant to 10 atm
Band: stainless steel, folding clasp
Remarks: dial set with 11 diamonds
Price: $8,000
Variations: stainless steel with yellow gold elements ($8,000)

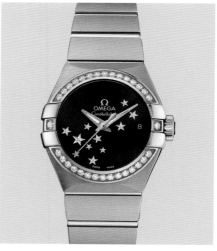

Constellation Orbis

Reference number: 123.15.27.20.03.001
Movement: automatic, Omega Caliber 8520;
ø 20 mm, height 5.3 mm; 28 jewels; 25,200 vph;
coaxial escapement, silicon balance and balance spring; 50-hour power reserve; COSC certified chronometer
Functions: hours, minutes, sweep seconds; date
Case: stainless steel, ø 27 mm, height 12.25 mm; bezel set with 32 diamonds; sapphire crystal, transparent case back; water-resistant to 10 atm
Band: stainless steel, folding clasp
Remarks: dial set with white gold stars
Price: $8,600
Variations: with 24 mm case ($5,100)

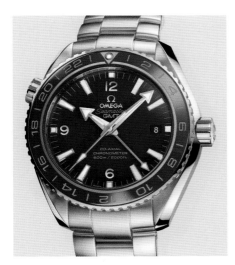

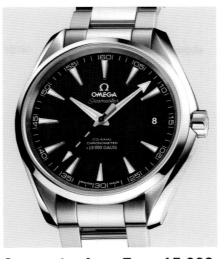

Seamaster Planet Ocean Good Planet GMT

Reference number: 232.30.44.22.03.001
Movement: automatic, Omega Caliber 8605; ø 29 mm, height 6 mm; 38 jewels; 25,200 vph; coaxial escapement, silicon balance and balance spring; 60-hour power reserve; COSC tested chronometer
Functions: hours, minutes, sweep seconds; additional 24-hour display (second time zone); date
Case: stainless steel, ø 43.5 mm, height 17.25 mm; bidirectional bezel with 24-hour divisions, sapphire crystal; screw-in crown; water-resistant to 60 atm
Band: stainless steel, folding clasp
Price: $8,100
Variations: with rubber strap ($8,000)

Seamaster Aqua Terra 15,000 Gauss

Reference number: 231.10.42.21.01.002
Movement: automatic, Omega Caliber 8500; ø 29 mm, height 5.5 mm; 39 jewels; 25,200 vph; coaxial escapement, silicon balance and balance spring; fully antimagnetic to 15,000 Gauss (1,200,000 A/m); 60-hour power reserve; COSC tested chronometer
Functions: hours, minutes, sweep seconds; date
Case: stainless steel, ø 41.5 mm, height 14.3 mm; sapphire crystal; screw-in crown; automatic helium valve; water-resistant to 15 atm
Band: stainless steel, folding clasp
Price: $6,600
Variations: with leather strap ($6,500)

Seamaster Aqua Terra Day-Date

Reference number: 231.10.42.22.03.001
Movement: automatic, Omega Caliber 8602; ø 29 mm, height 6.5 mm; 39 jewels; 25,200 vph; coaxial escapement, silicon balance and balance spring; 55-hour power reserve; COSC tested chronometer
Functions: hours, minutes, sweep seconds; weekday, date
Case: stainless steel, ø 41.5 mm, height 14.3 mm; sapphire crystal, transparent case back; screw-in crown; water-resistant to 15 atm
Band: stainless steel, folding clasp
Price: $7,800
Variations: pink gold ($35,400)

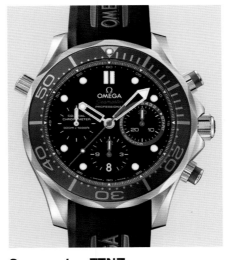

Seamaster Aqua Terra Chrono GMT

Reference number: 231.53.43.52.02.001
Movement: automatic, Omega Caliber 9615; ø 29 mm, height 6.5 mm; 39 jewels; 28,800 vph; coaxial escapement, silicon balance and balance spring; 55-hour power reserve; COSC tested chronometer
Functions: hours, minutes, subsidiary seconds; additional 24-hour display (second time zone); chronograph; date
Case: pink gold, ø 43 mm, height 16.9 mm; sapphire crystal, transparent case back; water-resistant to 15 atm
Band: reptile skin, folding clasp
Price: $27,600
Variations: stainless steel ($9,500)

Seamaster ETNZ Limited Edition

Reference number: 212.32.44.50.01.001
Movement: automatic, Omega Caliber 3330; ø 30 mm; height 7.9 mm; 31 jewels; 28,800 vph; coaxial escapement, silicon balance and balance spring; 52-hour power reserve; COSC tested chronometer
Functions: hours, minutes, sweep seconds; chronograph; date
Case: stainless steel, ø 44 mm, height 17.27 mm; unidirectional bezel with 60-minute divisions; sapphire crystal; screw-in crown; automatic helium valve; water-resistant to 30 atm
Band: rubber, folding clasp
Remarks: with extra stainless steel bracelet
Price: $6,600, limited to 2,013 pieces

Seamaster "Bullhead" Co-Axial Chronograph

Reference number: 225.12.43.50.04.001
Movement: automatic, Omega Caliber 3113; ø 27 mm; height 6.85 mm; 35 jewels; 28,800 vph; coaxial escapement, silicon balance and balance spring, 52-hour power reserve
Functions: hours, minutes, subsidiary seconds; chronograph; date
Case: stainless steel, 43 x 43 mm, height 14.85 mm; crown-adjustable inner bezel with 24-hour divisions; sapphire crystal; water-resistant to 3 atm
Band: leather, buckle
Price: $9,600
Variations: various dials

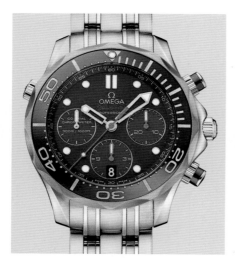

Seamaster Diver 300M
Co-Axial Chronograph

Reference number: 212.30.44.50.03.001
Movement: automatic, Omega Caliber 3330; ø 30 mm, height 7.9 mm; 31 jewels; 28,800 vph; coaxial escapement, silicon balance and balance spring; 60-hour power reserve; COSC certified chronometer
Functions: hours, minutes, subsidiary seconds; chronograph; date
Case: stainless steel, ø 44 mm, height 17.27 mm; unidirectional bezel with 60-minute divisions; sapphire crystal; screw-in crown; automatic helium valve; water-resistant to 30 atm
Band: stainless steel, folding clasp
Price: $6,000
Variations: 41.5 mm case ($6,000)

Seamaster Aqua Terra Blue Dial

Reference number: 231.10.42.21.03.001
Movement: automatic, Omega Caliber 8500; ø 29 mm, height 5.5 mm; 39 jewels; 28,800 vph; coaxial escapement, silicon balance and balance spring; 60-hour power reserve; COSC certified chronometer
Functions: hours, minutes, sweep seconds; date
Case: stainless steel, ø 41.5 mm, height 12.95 mm; sapphire crystal; water-resistant to 3 atm
Band: stainless steel, folding clasp
Price: $5,500

Speedmaster Moonwatch
"Dark Side of the Moon"

Reference number: 311.92.44.51.01.003
Movement: automatic, Omega Caliber 9300; ø 32.5 mm, height 7.6 mm; 54 jewels; 28,800 vph; coaxial escapement, silicon balance and balance spring; 60-hour power reserve; COSC certified chronometer
Functions: hours, minutes, subsidiary seconds; chronograph; date
Case: ceramic, ø 44.25 mm, height 15.79 mm; sapphire crystal, transparent case back; water-resistant to 5 atm
Band: nylon, folding clasp
Price: $12,000

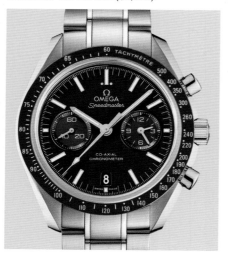

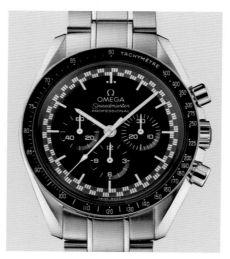

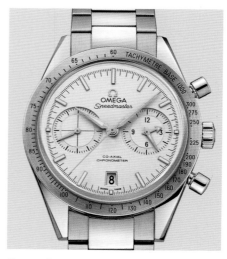

Speedmaster Moonwatch

Reference number: 311.90.44.51.03.001
Movement: automatic, Omega Caliber 9300; ø 32.5 mm, height 7.6 mm; 54 jewels; 28,800 vph; coaxial escapement, silicon balance and balance spring; 60-hour power reserve; COSC certified chronometer
Functions: hours, minutes, subsidiary seconds; chronograph; date
Case: titanium, ø 44.25 mm, height 15.82 mm; sapphire crystal; water-resistant to 10 atm
Band: titanium, folding clasp
Price: $11,400
Variations: with blue leather strap ($10,700)

Speedmaster Moonwatch

Reference number: 311.30.42.30.01.004
Movement: manually wound, Omega Caliber 1861 (base Lémania 1873); ø 27 mm, height 6.87 mm; 18 jewels; 21,600 vph; 45-hour power reserve; COSC certified chronometer
Functions: hours, minutes, subsidiary seconds; chronograph
Case: stainless steel, ø 42 mm, height 14.15 mm; sapphire crystal; water-resistant to 5 atm
Band: stainless steel, folding clasp
Price: $4,660

Speedmaster 57

Reference number: 331.10.42.51.02.002
Movement: automatic, Omega Caliber 9300; ø 32.5 mm, height 7.6 mm; 54 jewels; 28,800 vph; coaxial escapement, silicon balance and balance spring; 60-hour power reserve; COSC certified chronometer
Functions: hours, minutes, subsidiary seconds; chronograph; date
Case: stainless steel, ø 41.5 mm, height 15.82 mm; sapphire crystal; water-resistant to 10 atm
Band: stainless steel, folding clasp
Price: $9,200
Variations: various dials; with rose gold bezel and leather strap ($11,000); pink or yellow gold ($36,000)

The History of Paris in Painting

Written and edited by Georges Duby and Guy Lobrichon
350 full-color images; four gatefolds
496 pages · 11 × 17 in.
Cloth with slipcase · $235.00
ISBN 978-0-7892-1046-3

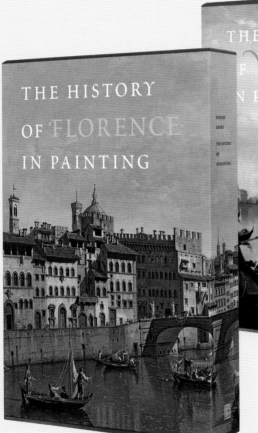

The History of Rome in Painting

Edited by Maria Teresa Caracciolo
and Roselyne de Ayala
300 full-color images; four gatefolds
496 pages · 11 × 17 in.
Cloth with slipcase · $235.00
ISBN 978-0-7892-1103-3

The History of Venice in Painting

Written and edited by Georges Duby and
Guy Lobrichon
350 full-color images; four gatefolds
496 pages · 11 × 17 in.
Cloth with slipcase · $235.00
ISBN 978-0-7892-1046-3

The History of Florence in Painting

Edited by Antonella Fenech Kroke
With contributions by Cyril Gerbron,
Stefano Calonaci and Neville Rowey
342 full-color images; four gatefolds
496 pages · 11 × 17 in.
Cloth with slipcase · $235.00
ISBN 978-0-7892-1145-3

Published by ABBEVILLE PRESS
137 Varick Street, New York, NY 10013
1-800-ARTBOOK (in U.S. only)
Also available wherever fine books are sold
Visit us at www.abbeville.com

Speedmaster 57

Reference number: 331.12.42.51.03.001
Movement: automatic, Omega Caliber 9300;
ø 32.5 mm, height 7.6 mm; 54 jewels; 28,800 vph;
coaxial escapement, silicon balance and balance
spring; 60-hour power reserve; COSC certified
chronometer
Functions: hours, minutes, subsidiary seconds;
chronograph; date
Case: stainless steel, ø 41.5 mm, height 15.82 mm;
sapphire crystal; water-resistant to 10 atm
Band: leather, folding clasp
Price: $8,900
Variations: various dials; with rose gold bezel
($11,000)

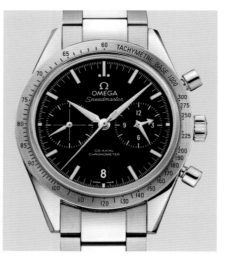

Speedmaster 57

Reference number: 331.10.42.51.01.003
Movement: automatic, Omega Caliber 9300;
ø 32.5 mm, height 7.6 mm; 54 jewels; 28,800 vph;
coaxial escapement, silicon balance and balance
spring; 60-hour power reserve; COSC certified
chronometer
Functions: hours, minutes, subsidiary seconds;
chronograph; date
Case: stainless steel, ø 41.5 mm, height 15.82 mm;
sapphire crystal; water-resistant to 3 atm
Band: stainless steel, folding clasp
Price: $9,000
Variations: various dials; with rose gold bezel
and leather strap ($11,000); pink or yellow gold
($36,000)

De Ville Ladymatic

Reference number: 425.25.34.20.55.001
Movement: automatic, Omega Caliber 8520; ø 20 mm,
height 5.3 mm; 28 jewels; 25,200 vph; coaxial
escapement, silicon balance and balance spring;
50-hour power reserve; COSC certified chronometer
Functions: hours, minutes, sweep seconds; date
Case: stainless steel with ceramic and rose gold
elements; ø 34 mm, height 11.95 mm; bezel set with
diamonds; sapphire crystal; water-resistant to 10 atm
Band: stainless steel with pink gold elements, folding
clasp
Remarks: dial set with 11 diamonds
Price: $24,600
Variations: various cases and dials

De Ville Ladymatic

Reference number: 425.27.34.20.63.001
Movement: automatic, Omega Caliber 8520;
ø 20 mm, height 5.3 mm; 28 jewels; 25,200 vph;
coaxial escapement, silicon balance and balance
spring; 50-hour power reserve; COSC certified
chronometer
Functions: hours, minutes, sweep seconds; date
Case: stainless steel with ceramic and rose gold
elements; ø 34 mm, height 11.95 mm; bezel set with
diamonds; sapphire crystal; water-resistant to 10 atm
Band: stainless steel, pink gold elements, folding clasp
Remarks: dial set with 11 diamonds
Price: $24,600

De Ville Prestige
Power Reserve

Reference number: 424.53.40.21.03.002
Movement: automatic, Omega Caliber 2627;
29 jewels, 25,200 vph; coaxial escapement,
48-hour power reserve; COSC certified chronometer
Functions: hours, minutes, subsidiary seconds;
power reserve indicator; date
Case: pink gold, ø 39.5 mm, height 10.6 mm;
sapphire crystal; water-resistant to 3 atm
Band: reptile skin, buckle
Price: $11,200
Variations: stainless steel ($4,800)

De Ville Chronograph

Reference number: 431.53.42.51.02.001
Movement: automatic, Omega Caliber 9301;
ø 32.5 mm, height 7.6 mm; 54 jewels; 25,200 vph;
coaxial escapement, silicon balance and balance
spring, 60-hour power reserve; COSC certified
chronometer
Functions: hours, minutes, subsidiary seconds;
chronograph; date
Case: pink gold, ø 42 mm, height 15.9 mm;
sapphire crystal, transparent case back;
water-resistant to 10 atm
Band: reptile skin, folding clasp
Price: $29,000
Variations: with black dial and strap

Caliber 9300

Automatic; coaxial escapement; column wheel control of chronograph functions; twin spring barrels, 60-hour power reserve; COSC certified chronometer
Functions: hours, minutes, subsidiary seconds; chronograph; date
Diameter: 32.5 mm
Height: 7.7 mm
Jewels: 54
Balance: silicon, without regulator
Frequency: 28,800 vph
Balance spring: silicon
Shock protection: Nivachoc
Remarks: base plate, bridges, and rotor with "arabesque" côtes de Genève, balance and screws blackened

Caliber 9301

Base caliber: 9300
Automatic; coaxial escapement; column wheel control of chronograph functions; twin spring barrels, 60-hour power reserve; COSC certified chronometer
Functions: hours, minutes, subsidiary seconds; chronograph; date
Diameter: 32.5 mm
Height: 7.7 mm
Jewels: 54; **Balance:** silicon, without regulator
Frequency: 28,800 vph
Balance spring: silicon
Shock protection: Nivachoc
Remarks: base plate, bridges, and rotor with "arabesque" côtes de Genève, rotor and balance bridges in pink gold, balance and screws blackened

Caliber 3313

Automatic; coaxial escapement; column wheel control of chronograph functions; single spring barrel, 52-hour power reserve; COSC certified chronometer
Functions: hours, minutes, subsidiary seconds; chronograph; date
Diameter: 27 mm
Height: 6.85 mm
Jewels: 37
Balance: without regulator
Frequency: 28,800 vph
Balance spring: freely oscillating
Remarks: perlage on plate, bridges and balance cock with côtes de Genève, gold-plated engravings; rotor hub screw of blued steel

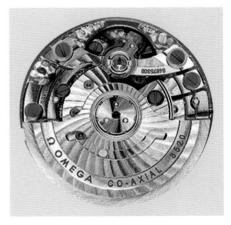

Caliber 8605

Automatic; coaxial escapement; twin spring barrels, 60-hour power reserve; COSC certified chronometer
Functions: hours, minutes, sweep seconds; second time zone (additional 24-hour indicator); date
Diameter: 29 mm
Height: 5.9 mm
Jewels: 38
Balance: silicon, without regulator
Frequency: 25,200 vph
Balance spring: silicon
Shock protection: Nivachoc
Remarks: base plate, bridges, and rotor with "arabesque" côtes de Genève, rhodium-plated, balance and screws blackened (Caliber 8615 with rotor and balance bridge in pink gold)

Caliber 8501

Base caliber: 8500
Automatic; coaxial escapement; twin spring barrels, 60-hour power reserve; COSC certified chronometer
Functions: hours, minutes, sweep seconds; date
Diameter: 29 mm
Height: 5.6 mm
Jewels: 39
Balance: silicon, without regulator
Frequency: 25,200 vph
Balance spring: silicon
Shock protection: Nivachoc
Remarks: platinum, bridges and rotor with "arabesque" côtes de Genève, rotor and balance bridges in pink gold, balance and screws blackened (base Caliber 8500 without gold finishing)

Caliber 8520

Automatic; coaxial escapement; twin spring barrels, 60-hour power reserve; COSC certified chronometer
Functions: hours, minutes sweep seconds; date
Diameter: 20 mm
Height: 5.3 mm
Jewels: 28
Balance: silicon, without regulator
Frequency: 25,200 vph
Balance spring: silicon
Shock protection: Nivachoc
Remarks: platinum, bridges and rotor with "arabesque" côtes de Genève, rhodium-plated, balance and screws blackened (Caliber 8251 with rotor and balance bridge in pink gold)

Oris SA
Ribigasse 1
CH-4434 Hölstein
Switzerland

Tel.:
01141-61-956-1111

E-Mail:
info@oris

Website:
www.oris.ch

Founded:
1904

Number of employees:
90

Annual production:
not specified

U.S. distributor:
Oris Watches USA
50 Washington Street, Suite 412
Norwalk, CT 06854
203-857-4769; 203-857-4782 (fax)

Most important collections/price range:
Diver, Big Crown, Artelier, BC3, BC4 /
approx. $1,100 to $4,000

Oris

Oris has been producing mechanical watches for over a century in the little town of Hölstein in northwestern Switzerland, near Basel. What the brand has always aimed for is quality with an advantageous price-performance ratio. This particular strategy has allowed Oris to expand in a segment being relinquished by other big-name competitors as they sought their fortune in the higher-end markets. Now as the recession dwindles, they may find their old space occupied since the past years have been marked by growing international success for Oris. Oris managing director Roland Ackermann has backed measures to really focus on caring for these models: "You cannot ignore the entry-level segment, because even younger fans of watches have a right to high quality and a strong design," he suggested in an interview.

Oris focuses on four "product worlds," each with its own distinct identity: aviation, motor sports, diving, and culture. In utilizing specific materials and functions based on these types, Oris makes certain that each will fit perfectly into the world for which it was designed. Yet the heart of every watch houses a small, high-quality "high-mech" movement identifiable by the brand's standard red rotor.

The brand's communications focus on its sharp-looking professional diver's watches. The top of the crop in 2013 was the Aquis Depth Gauge, which has no moving parts. Rather, a patented system utilizing a channel cut into the extra thick sapphire crystal cleverly applies Boyle's law to show the depth. And in spite of the uniqueness, this watch is affordable, like all Oris products.

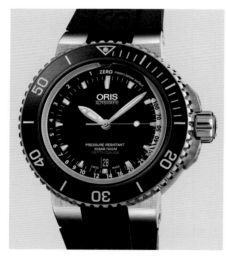

Aquis Depth Gauge

Reference number: 733 7675 4154
Movement: automatic, Oris Caliber 733 (base Sellita SW200); ø 25.6 mm, height 4.6 mm; 26 jewels; 28,800 vph; 38-hour power reserve
Functions: hours, minutes, sweep seconds; depth gauge; date
Case: stainless steel, ø 46 mm, height 15 mm; unidirectional bezel with ceramic inlay and 60-minute divisions; sapphire crystal, transparent case back; screw-in crown; water-resistant to 50 atm
Band: rubber, folding clasp
Remarks: physical depth gauge by water canal etched into crystal; additional stainless steel band
Price: $3,500

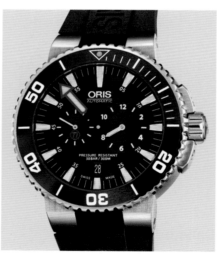

Aquis Regulator "the Master Diver"

Reference number: 749 7677 7154
Movement: automatic, Oris Caliber 749 (base Sellita SW200); ø 25.6 mm, height 5.05 mm; 28 jewels; 28,800 vph; 38-hour power reserve
Functions: hours (off-center), minutes, subsidiary seconds; date
Case: titanium, ø 43 mm, height 13.1 mm; unidirectional bezel with ceramic inlay and 60-minute divisions; sapphire crystal, screw-in crown, automatic helium valve; water-resistant to 50 atm
Band: rubber, folding clasp
Remarks: comes with additional titanium bracelet
Price: $3,150

Aquis Small Second Date

Reference number: 743 7673 4159 MB
Movement: automatic, Oris Caliber 743 (base Sellita SW220); ø 25.6 mm, height 5.5 mm; 28 jewels; 28,800 vph; 38-hour power reserve
Functions: hours, minutes, subsidiary seconds; date
Case: stainless steel, ø 46 mm, height 15.5 mm; unidirectional ceramic bezel with 60-minute divisions; sapphire crystal, screw-in crown; automatic helium valve; water-resistant to 50 atm
Band: stainless steel, folding clasp with extension link
Price: $2,450
Variations: with rubber strap ($2,250)

Aquis Titanium Chronograph

Reference number: 674 7655 7253 RS
Movement: automatic, Oris Caliber 674 (base ETA 7750); ø 30 mm, height 7.9 mm; 25 jewels; 28,800 vph; 46-hour power reserve
Functions: hours, minutes, subsidiary seconds; chronograph; date
Case: titanium, ø 46 mm, height 18.2 mm; tungsten bezel with SuperLuminova inserts, unidirectional bezel with 60-minute divisions; sapphire crystal, screw-in crown; automatic helium valve; water-resistant to 50 atm
Band: rubber, folding clasp with extension link
Price: $3,750
Variations: with titanium band ($3,900)

ProDiver Chronograph

Reference number: 774 7683 7154
Movement: automatic, Oris Caliber 774 (base ETA SW500); ø 30 mm, height 7.9 mm; 25 jewels; 28,800 vph; 48-hour power reserve
Functions: hours, minutes, subsidiary seconds; chronograph; date
Case: titanium, ø 51 mm, height 19.3 mm; unidirectional bezel with ceramic inlay and 60-minute divisions; sapphire crystal, screw-in crown; automatic helium valve; water-resistant to 100 atm
Band: rubber, folding clasp
Remarks: comes with additional titanium bracelet
Price: $4,650

ProDiver Pointer Moon

Reference number: 761 7682 7154
Movement: automatic, Oris Caliber 761 (base Sellita SW220); ø 25.6 mm, height 5.05 mm; 26 jewels; 28,800 vph; 38-hour power reserve
Functions: hours, minutes, sweep seconds; tide range display
Case: titanium, ø 49 mm, height 15.9 mm; unidirectional bezel with ceramic inlay and 60-minute divisions; sapphire crystal, water-resistant to 100 atm
Band: rubber, buckle
Remarks: comes with additional titanium bracelet
Price: $3,600

Artelier Date

Reference number: 561 7687 4051 LS
Movement: automatic, Oris Caliber 561 (base ETA 2671); ø 17.2 mm, height 4.6 mm; 25 jewels; 28,800 vph; 38-hour power reserve
Functions: hours, minutes, sweep seconds; date
Case: stainless steel, ø 31 mm, height 10.4 mm; sapphire crystal, water-resistant to 5 atm
Band: leather, folding clasp
Remarks: dial set with 12 diamonds
Price: $1,750
Variations: with stainless steel bracelet ($1,950)

Artelier Translucent Skeleton

Reference number: 734 7684 4051
Movement: automatic, Oris Caliber 733 (base Sellita SW200-1); ø 25.6 mm, height 4.6 mm; 26 jewels; 28,800 vph; 38-hour power reserve
Functions: hours, minutes, sweep seconds
Case: stainless steel, ø 40.5 mm, height 11.1 mm; sapphire crystal, transparent case back; water-resistant to 3 atm
Band: stainless steel, folding clasp
Price: $2,900
Variations: with reptile skin band ($3,000); with leather band ($2,700)

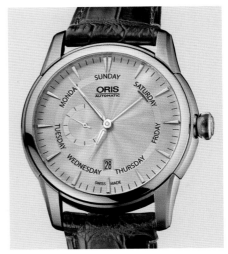

Artelier Small Second Pointer Day

Reference number: 745 7666 4051 LS
Movement: automatic, Oris Caliber 745 (base Sellita SW200); ø 25.6 mm, height 5.05 mm; 28 jewels; 28,800 vph; 38-hour power reserve
Functions: hours, minutes, subsidiary seconds; date
Case: stainless steel, ø 44 mm, height 11.3 mm; sapphire crystal, transparent case back; water-resistant to 5 atm
Band: leather, folding clasp
Price: $1,950
Variations: with stainless steel bracelet ($2,150); with alligator strap ($2,250)

Calobra Limited Edition

Reference number: 774 7661 4484
Movement: automatic, Oris Caliber 774
(base Sellita SW500); ø 30 mm, height 7.9 mm;
25 jewels; 28,800 vph; 48-hour power reserve
Functions: hours, minutes, subsidiary seconds
(linear); chronograph; date
Case: stainless steel, ø 44 mm, height 14.9 mm;
ceramic bezel; sapphire crystal, water-resistant to
10 atm
Band: leather, folding clasp
Remarks: comes with extra rubber bracelet
Price: $3,900, limited to 1,000 pieces

Tubbataha Limited Edition

Reference number: 749 7663 7185 MB
Movement: automatic, Oris Caliber 749
(base Sellita SW220); ø 25.6 mm, height 5.05 mm;
28 jewels; 28,800 vph; 38-hour power reserve
Functions: hours (off-center), minutes, subsidiary
seconds; date
Case: titanium, ø 46 mm, height 16 mm;
unidirectional bezel with ceramic inlay and
60-minute divisions; sapphire crystal, screw-in
crown; automatic helium valve; water-resistant to
50 atm
Band: titanium, folding clasp with extension link
Price: $3,000, limited to 2,000 pieces
Variations: with rubber strap ($2,800)

Royal Flying Doctor Service Limited Edition

Reference number: 735 7672 4084
Movement: automatic, Oris Caliber 735
(base Sellita SW200); ø 25.6 mm, height 5.05 mm;
26 jewels; 28,800 vph; 38-hour power reserve
Functions: hours, minutes, sweep seconds;
weekday, date
Case: stainless steel, ø 44 mm, height 12.9 mm;
crown-adjustable inner bezel with 12-hour divisions
(second time zone); sapphire crystal, transparent
case back; screw-in crown; water-resistant to 10 atm
Band: leather, buckle
Price: $1,950, limited to 2,000 pieces
Variations: with stainless steel bracelet ($2,250)

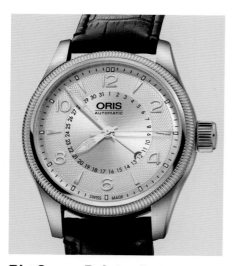

Big Crown Pointer Date

Reference number: 754 7679 4061 LS
Movement: automatic, Oris Caliber 754
(base Sellita SW200-1); ø 25.6 mm, height
5.05 mm; 26 jewels; 28,800 vph; 38-hour power
reserve
Functions: hours, minutes, sweep seconds; date
Case: stainless steel, ø 40 mm, height 11.7 mm;
sapphire crystal, screw-in crown; water-resistant to
10 atm
Band: leather, folding clasp
Price: $1,400
Variations: with stainless steel bracelet ($1,700)

Artix GT Chronograph

Reference number: 674 7661 4434 RS
Movement: automatic, modified ETA Caliber 7750;
ø 30 mm, height 7.9 mm; 25 jewels; 28,800 vph;
48-hour power reserve
Functions: hours, minutes, subsidiary seconds
(linear); chronograph; date
Case: stainless steel, ø 44 mm, height 14.9 mm;
bidirectional ceramic bezel with 60-minute
divisions; sapphire crystal, transparent case back;
screw-in crown; water-resistant to 10 atm
Band: rubber, folding clasp
Price: $3,450
Variations: with leather strap ($3,450); with
stainless steel bracelet ($3,650)

Artix GT Day Date

Reference number: 735 7662 4154 LS
Movement: automatic, Oris Caliber 735
(base Sellita SW220); ø 25.6 mm, height 5.05 mm;
26 jewels; 28,800 vph; 38-hour power reserve
Functions: hours, minutes, sweep seconds;
weekday, date
Case: stainless steel, ø 42 mm, height 12.1 mm;
bidirectional bezel with 60-minute divisions,
sapphire crystal, transparent case back;
screw-in crown; water-resistant to 10 atm
Band: leather, folding clasp
Price: $1,750
Variations: stainless steel bracelet ($1,950); with
rubber strap ($1,750)

Otium

Otium

Dirk Hillgruber
Postfach 20 16 26
D-80016 Munich
Germany

Tel.:
01149-89-688-4278

E-Mail:
dh@otium-watches.com

Website:
www.otium-watches.com

Founded:
1999

Number of employees:
not specified

Annual production:
not specified

Distribution:
For U.S. sales, please contact the company directly.

Most important collections/price range:
various models with different ways of indicating time / $1,700 to $6,600

Otium's extraordinary reputation comes care of the company founder and mastermind Dirk Hillgruber, whose dogged determination to stay away from the mainstream timepiece display forms has endured for more than ten years. Instead he has maintained the humor and daring found in Magritte's famous painting of a pipe that states "This is not a pipe." Hillgruber uses Swiss movements for his unusual ideas; otherwise he contracts with only German vendors. At the beginning, this meant mostly sophisticated systems that used moving steel balls to tell the time—if you looked closely enough. The du:z (a phonetic spelling of the French word for twelve, *douze*) watch, for instance, features a dial with a slit at each of the twelve hours, into which a ball rolls at each hour change. A disk guides the balls into the slits from inside so that they show outside. Later they go back inside, which means that a ball is in motion at all times. The last slit (clockwise) in which the whole ball can be seen indicates the correct time.

The new Deuxlateur, like the Trigulateur, displays hours and minutes only in two separate, round gauges. These are arranged like the odometers and rpm counters on the perlage-covered dashboards of 1930s race cars. And yet, the watch looks perfectly at home in the twenty-first century.

Deuxlateur

Movement: manually wound, ETA Caliber 6497-1; ø 36.6 mm, height 4.5 mm; 17 jewels; 21,600 vph; 38-hour power reserve
Functions: hours (off-center), minutes (off-center)
Case: stainless steel, ø 42 mm, height 12.1 mm; sapphire crystal, transparent case back; water-resistant to 5 atm
Band: reptile skin, buckle
Price: $5,800
Variations: with white or black dial

Flieger [du:z]

Movement: manually wound, ETA Caliber 6497-1; ø 36.6 mm, height 4.5 mm; 17 jewels; 21,600 vph; 38-hour power reserve
Functions: hours (radially mobile spheres), minutes
Case: stainless steel, ø 42 mm, height 11 mm; sapphire crystal, transparent case back; water-resistant to 5 atm
Band: reptile skin, buckle
Price: $4,360

Régulateur

Movement: manually wound, ETA Caliber 6498; ø 36.6 mm, height 4.5 mm; 17 jewels; 21,600 vph; 38-hour power reserve
Functions: hours (jumping, off-center), minutes, subsidiary seconds
Case: stainless steel, ø 42 mm, height 12.1 mm; sapphire crystal, transparent case back; water-resistant to 5 atm
Band: reptile skin, buckle
Price: $6,100
Variations: with blackened case ($6,100)

Officine Panerai
Casella Postale 17030
viale Monza, 259
20126 Milan
Italy

Tel.:
01139-02-363-138

Fax:
01139-02-363-13-297

E-Mail:
officinepanerai@panerai.com

Website:
www.panerai.com

Founded:
1860 in Florence, Italy

Number of employees:
approx. 250

Annual production:
not specified

U.S. distributor:
Panerai
645 Fifth Avenue
New York, NY 10022
877-PANERAI
www.panerai.com

Most important collections/price range:
Historic / approx. $5,000 to $35,000;
Contemporary / approx. $7,000 to $25,000;
Special Editions / approx. $5,000 to $125,000;
Specialties / approx. $20,000 to $250,000

Panerai

Officine Panerai (in English: Panerai Workshops) joined the Richemont Group in 1997. Since then, it has made an unprecedented rise from an insider niche brand to a lifestyle phenomenon. The company, founded in 1860 by Giovanni Panerai, supplied the Italian navy with precision instruments. In the 1930s, the Florentine engineers developed a series of waterproof wristwatches that could be used by commandos under especially extreme and risky conditions. After 1997, under the leadership of Angelo Bonati, the company came out with a collection of oversize wristwatches, both stylistically and technically based on these historical models.

In 2006, the Panerai headquarters was moved to Neuchâtel, Switzerland. A year later, the brand produced its first in-house *manufacture* movements (caliber family P.2000). In 2009, the new "little" Panerai *manufacture* movements (caliber family P.9000) were released. From the start, the idea behind them was to provide a competitive alternative to the base movements available until a couple of years ago.

Panerai movements are produced at the Manufacture Horlogère ValFleurier in Buttes, a facility that services other watch brands of the Richemont Group (Montblanc, for instance). The ValFleurier design office, to a certain extent the think tank of the whole concern, is located on the top floor of Panerai headquarters in Neuchâtel.

The most recent calibers round off the *manufacture*'s portfolio well. There is the P.3000, which powers such pieces as the Luminor Submersible 1950 in a retro bronze case, and the 9100/R, which has a countdown function for regattas.

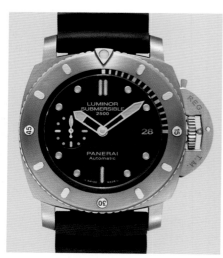

Luminor Submersible 1950 2500m 3 Days Automatic Titanio

Reference number: PAM00364
Movement: automatic, Panerai Caliber P.9000; ø 31 mm, height 7.9 mm; 28 jewels; 28,800 vph; 2 spring barrels; 72-hour power reserve
Functions: hours, minutes, subsidiary seconds; date
Case: titanium, ø 47 mm, height 20.2 mm; unidirectional bezel with 60-minute divisions; sapphire crystal; hinged-lever crown protector; water-resistant to 250 atm
Band: rubber, buckle
Remarks: with extra strap and changing tools, limited to 1,000 pieces
Price: $12,600

Luminor Submersible 1950 3 Days Automatic Ceramica

Reference number: PAM00508
Movement: automatic, Panerai Caliber P.9000; ø 31 mm, height 7.9 mm; 28 jewels; 28,800 vph; 2 spring barrels; 72-hour power reserve
Functions: hours, minutes, subsidiary seconds; date
Case: ceramic, ø 47 mm, height 16.85 mm; unidirectional bezel with 60-minute division; sapphire crystal; hinged-lever crown protector; water-resistant to 30 atm
Band: leather, buckle
Remarks: with extra strap and changing tools, limited to 1,000 pieces
Price: $17,500

Luminor Submersible 1950 3 Days Power Reserve Automatic Bronzo

Reference number: PAM00507
Movement: automatic, Panerai Caliber P.9002; ø 31 mm, height 7.9 mm; 29 jewels; 28,800 vph; 2 spring barrels; 72-hour power reserve
Functions: hours, minutes, subsidiary seconds; power reserve display; date
Case: bronze; ø 47 mm, height 17.9 mm; unidirectional bezel with 60-minute divisions; sapphire crystal, transparent case back; hinged-lever crown protector; water-resistant to 30 atm
Band: leather, buckle
Remarks: with extra strap and changing tools
Price: $13,200, limited to 1,000 pieces

Luminor Submersible 1950 Amagnetic 3 Days Automatic Titanio

Reference number: PAM00389
Movement: automatic, Panerai Caliber P.9000; ø 31 mm, height 7.9 mm; 28 jewels; 28,800 vph; 2 spring barrels; 72-hour power reserve
Functions: hours, minutes, subsidiary seconds; date
Case: titanium, ø 47 mm, height 18.3 mm; unidirectional bezel with 60-minute divisions; sapphire crystal; hinged-lever crown protector; water-resistant to 30 atm
Band: rubber, buckle
Price: $12,400

Luminor 1950 3 Days Chrono Flyback

Reference number: PAM00524
Movement: automatic, Panerai Caliber P.9100; ø 31 mm, height 8.15 mm; 37 jewels; 28,800 vph; 2 spring barrels; 72-hour power reserve
Functions: hours, minutes, subsidiary seconds; flyback chronograph; date
Case: stainless steel, ø 44 mm, height 17 mm; sapphire crystal; transparent case back; hinged-lever crown protector; water-resistant to 10 atm
Band: leather, buckle
Price: $13,000
Variations: pink gold ($32,200)

Luminor 1950 Regatta 3 Days Chrono Flyback Titanio

Reference number: PAM00526
Movement: automatic, Panerai Caliber P.9100/R; ø 31 mm; height 9.55 mm; 37 jewels; 28,800 vph; 2 spring barrels; 72-hour power reserve
Functions: hours, minutes, subsidiary seconds; flyback chronograph with preprogrammed countdown function, precise to the minute
Case: titanium, ø 47 mm, height 19.06 mm; sapphire crystal, transparent case back; hinged-lever crown protector; water-resistant to 10 atm
Band: rubber, buckle
Price: $18,800

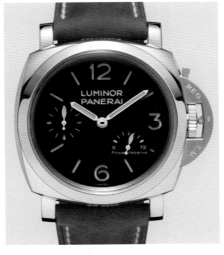

Luminor 1950 Rattrapante 8 Days Titanio

Reference number: PAM00530
Movement: manually wound, Panerai Caliber P.2006/3; ø 31 mm, height 9.6 mm; 34 jewels; 28,800 vph; column wheel control of chronograph functions, 192-hour power reserve
Functions: hours, minutes, subsidiary seconds; power reserve indicator; split-seconds chronograph
Case: titanium, ø 47 mm, height 21.2 mm; sapphire crystal, transparent case back; hinged-lever crown protector; water-resistant to 10 atm
Band: rubber, buckle
Price: $26,500

Luminor 1950 3 Days Power Reserve

Reference number: PAM00423
Movement: manually wound, Panerai Caliber P.3002; ø 37.2 mm, height 6.3 mm; 21 jewels; 21,600 vph; 2 spring barrels; 72-hour power reserve
Functions: hours, minutes, subsidiary seconds; power reserve indicator
Case: stainless steel, ø 47 mm, height 17.2 mm; sapphire crystal, transparent case back; hinged-lever crown protector; water-resistant to 10 atm
Band: leather, buckle
Price: $11,300

Luminor Marina 1950 3 Days Automatic

Reference number: PAM00523
Movement: automatic, Panerai Caliber P.9000; ø 31 mm, height 7.9 mm; 28 jewels; 28,800 vph; 2 spring barrels; 72-hour power reserve
Functions: hours, minutes, subsidiary seconds; date
Case: stainless steel, ø 42 mm, height 16.35 mm; sapphire crystal, transparent case back; hinged-lever crown protector; water-resistant to 10 atm
Band: reptile skin, buckle
Price: $7,800

Luminor 1950 8 Days GMT

Reference number: PAM00233
Movement: manually wound, Panerai Caliber P.2002; ø 31 mm, height 6.6 mm; 21 jewels; 28,800 vph; 3 spring barrels; second hand reset to zero by pulling the crown, 192-hour power reserve
Functions: hours, minutes, subsidiary seconds; second time zone (additional 24-hour display); power reserve indicator (linear); date
Case: stainless steel, ø 44 mm, height 10.5 mm; sapphire crystal, transparent case back; hinged-lever crown protector; water-resistant to 10 atm
Band: leather, buckle
Price: $14,900
Variations: rose gold ($32,200)

Radiomir 1940 3 Days

Reference number: PAM00514
Movement: manually wound, Panerai Caliber P.3000; ø 37.2 mm, height 5.4 mm; 21 jewels; 21,600 vph; 2 spring barrels; 72-hour power reserve
Functions: hours, minutes, subsidiary seconds; date
Case: stainless steel, ø 47 mm, height 13.6 mm; sapphire crystal, transparent case back; screw-in crown; water-resistant to 10 atm
Band: leather, buckle
Price: $8,900
Variations: pink gold ($26,500)

Radiomir 1940 Oro Rosso

Reference number: PAM00513
Movement: manually wound, Panerai Caliber P.999; ø 26.8 mm, height 3.4 mm; 19 jewels; 21,600 vph; 60-hour power reserve
Functions: hours, minutes, subsidiary seconds
Case: pink gold, ø 42 mm, height 11.15 mm; sapphire crystal, transparent case back; screw-in crown; water-resistant to 10 atm
Band: reptile skin, buckle
Price: $22,300
Variations: stainless steel ($7,800)

Radiomir California 3 Days

Reference number: PAM00424
Movement: manually wound, Panerai Caliber P.3000; ø 37.2 mm, height 5.3 mm; 21 jewels; 28,800 vph; 2 spring barrels; 72-hour power reserve
Functions: hours, minutes; date
Case: stainless steel, ø 47 mm, height 15.97 mm; sapphire crystal, transparent case back; screw-in crown; water-resistant to 10 atm
Band: leather, buckle
Price: $8,700

Radiomir Composite 3 Days

Reference number: PAM00504
Movement: manually wound, Panerai Caliber P.3000; ø 37.2 mm, height 5.3 mm; 21 jewels; 21,600 vph; 2 spring barrels; 72-hour power reserve
Functions: hours, minutes, subsidiary seconds
Case: composite material, ø 47 mm, height 14.2 mm; sapphire crystal, transparent case back; screw-in crown; water-resistant to 10 atm
Band: leather, buckle
Price: $10,600

Radiomir 10 Days GMT

Reference number: PAM00323
Movement: automatic, Panerai Caliber P.2003/6; ø 31 mm, height 8 mm; 25 jewels; 28,800 vph; 3 spring barrels; 240-hour power reserve
Functions: hours, minutes, subsidiary seconds; additional 12-hour display (second time zone); day/night indicator; power reserve indicator; date
Case: stainless steel, ø 47 mm, height 16.8 mm; sapphire crystal, transparent case back; screw-in crown; water-resistant to 10 atm
Band: reptile skin, buckle
Price: $14,100

Caliber P.9000

Automatic; twin serially connected spring barrels, 8-day power reserve
Functions: hours, minutes, subsidiary seconds; date
Diameter: 31 mm
Height: 7.9 mm
Jewels: 28
Balance: glucydur
Frequency: 28,800 vph
Remarks: 197 components

Caliber P.9100

Automatic; twin serially connected spring barrels, 72-hour power reserve
Functions: hours, minutes, subsidiary seconds; flyback chronograph; date
Diameter: 31.1 mm
Height: 8.15 mm
Jewels: 37
Balance: glucydur
Frequency: 28,800 vph
Balance spring: flat hairspring
Shock protection: Kif
Remarks: reset second hand to zero by pulling the crown ("zero reset"); 302 components

Caliber P.9100/R

Automatic; twin serially connected spring barrels, 72-hour power reserve
Functions: hours, minutes, subsidiary seconds; flyback chronograph with preprogrammed countdown function, precise to the minute
Diameter: 31.1 mm
Height: 9.55 mm
Jewels: 37
Balance: glucydur
Frequency: 28,800 vph
Balance spring: flat hairspring
Shock protection: Kif
Remarks: reset second hand to zero by pulling the crown ("zero reset"); 328 components

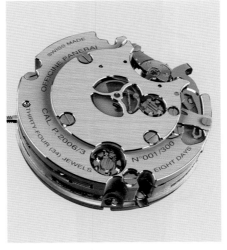

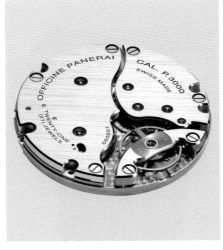

Caliber P.2003

Automatic; ball bearing-mounted rotor; 3 serially connected spring barrels; 10-day power reserve
Functions: hours, minutes, subsidiary seconds; additional 24-hour display; day/night indicator
Diameter: 31 mm
Height: 8 mm
Jewels: 25
Balance: glucydur
Frequency: 28,800 vph
Remarks: second hand zero reset function by pulling crown ("zero reset"); 281 components

Caliber P.2006

Manually wound; 2 control wheels to control the chronograph and flyback mechanism; 3 serially connected spring barrels, 192-hour power reserve
Functions: hours, minutes, subsidiary seconds; power reserve indicator; split-seconds chronograph
Diameter: 31 mm
Height: 9.6 mm
Jewels: 34
Balance: glucydur
Frequency: 28,800 vph
Balance spring: flat hairspring
Shock protection: Kif
Remarks: reset second hand to zero by pulling the crown ("zero reset")

Caliber P.3000

Manually wound; 8-day power reserve
Functions: hours, minutes
Diameter: 37.2 mm
Height: 5.3 mm
Jewels: 21
Balance: glucydur
Frequency: 21,600 vph
Remarks: 160 components

Parmigiani Fleurier SA
Rue du Temple 11
CH-2114 Fleurier
Switzerland

Tel.:
01141-32-862-6630

Fax:
01141-32-862-6631

E-Mail:
info@parmigiani.ch

Website:
www.parmigiani.ch

Founded:
1996

Number of employees:
550

Annual production:
approx. 6,000 watches

U.S. distributor:
Parmigiani Fleurier
Distribution Americas LLC
999 Brickell Avenue, Suite 740
Miami, FL 33131
305-260-7770; 305-269-7770
info@parmigiani.ch

Most important collections/price range:
Kalpa, Tonda, Pershing, Toric, Bugatti / approx.
$7,800 to $500,000 for *haute horlogerie* pieces,
no limit for unique pieces

Parmigiani

What began as the undertaking of a single man—a gifted watchmaker and reputable restorer of complicated vintage timepieces—in the small town of Fleurier in Switzerland's Val de Travers has now grown into an empire of sorts comprising several factories and more than 400 employees.

Michel Parmigiani is in fact just doing what he has done since 1975 when he began restoring vintage works. An exceptional talent, his output soon attracted the attention of the Sandoz Family Foundation, an organization established by a member of one of Switzerland's most famous families in 1964. The foundation bought 51 percent of Parmigiani Mesure et Art du Temps SA in 1996, turning what was practically a one-man show into a full-fledged and fully financed watch *manufacture*.

Four short years after the merger, three Swiss suppliers were acquired by the partners, furthering the quest for horological autonomy. Atokalpa SA in Alle (Canton of Jura) manufactures parts such as pinions, wheels, and micro components. Bruno Affolter SA in La Chaux-de-Fonds produces precious metal cases, dials, and other specialty parts. Elwin SA in Moutier specializes in turned parts. In 2003, the movement development and production department officially separated from the rest as Vaucher Manufacture, now an autonomous entity.

Parmigiani has enjoyed strong growth, notably in the United States. And having put its finger to the wind, it decided also to set its sights on Latin America, notably Brazil, where it signed a partnership with the Confederação Brasileira de Futebol. In addition to making watches and unique pieces, like his famed Islamic clock based on a lunar calendar, Parmigiani also devotes a part of the premises to restoring ancient timepieces.

Bugatti SuperSport

Reference number: PFH365-1001400-HA1442
Movement: manually wound, Parmigiani Caliber 372; 25 x 37.01mm, height 15.96 mm; 40 jewels; 21,600 vph; stacked; 2 serial spring barrels; 28,800 vph; côtes de Genève; 240-hour power reserve
Functions: hours, minutes; power reserve indicator
Case: rose gold, 36 mm x 50.7 mm, height 22.7 mm; sapphire crystal; transparent case back
Band: reptile skin, folding clasp
Remarks: case with lateral window
Price: $285,000, limited to 30 pieces

Pershing 005 CBF

Reference number: PFC528-3102500-XA3142
Movement: automatic, Parmigiani Caliber 334; ø 30 mm, height 6.81 mm; 68 jewels; 28,800 vph; 50-hour power reserve
Functions: hours, minutes, subsidiary seconds; chronograph; date
Case: titanium, ø 45 mm, height 14.2 mm; white gold, unidirectional bezel with 60-minute divisions; sapphire crystal; screw-in crown; water-resistant to 3 atm
Band: reptile skin, folding clasp
Price: $25,000
Variations: pink gold bezel

Toric Quaestor Labyrinthe

Reference number: PFH439-2004100-HA1441
Movement: manually wound, Parmigiani Caliber 357; ø 29.3 mm, height 6.55 mm; 35 jewels; 21,600 vph; 72-hour power reserve
Functions: hours, minutes, subsidiary seconds; power reserve display, minute repeater
Case: platinum, ø 46 mm, height 13.2 mm; sapphire crystal; transparent case back; crown with sapphire cabochon
Band: reptile skin, buckle
Remarks: dial of Burmese jade and gold
Price: $550,000

Transforma CBF Quator

Reference number: PFC299-1687000-XA1432-000000E
Movement: automatic, Parmigiani Caliber 339; ø 27.1 mm, height 5.5 mm; 32 jewels; 28,800 vph; double spring barrel, 50-hour power reserve
Functions: hours, minutes, sweep seconds; annual calendar with date (retrograde), weekday, month and moon phase (120 years)
Case: pink gold, ø 43 mm, height 12.8 mm; stainless steel bezel; sapphire crystal; transparent case back; water-resistant to 3 atm
Band: reptile skin, folding clasp
Remarks: kit with Transforma CBF Chronograph; movement can be table clock or pocket watch
Price: $66,500

Transforma CBF Chronograph

Reference number: PFC299-1687000-XA1432-000000E
Movement: automatic, Parmigiani Caliber 334; ø 30 mm, height 6.8 mm; 68 jewels; 28,800 vph; 50-hour power reserve
Functions: hours, minutes, subsidiary seconds; chronograph; date
Case: carbon fiber, ø 43 mm, height 12.8 mm; stainless steel bezel; sapphire crystal; screw-in crown; water-resistant to 3 atm
Band: reptile skin, folding clasp
Remarks: kit with Transforma CBF Chronograph; movement can be table clock or pocket watch
Price: $66,500

Kalpagraph

Reference number: PFC128-1001400-HA1441
Movement: automatic, Parmigiani Caliber PF334; ø 30 mm, height 6.8 mm; 68 jewels; 28,800 vph; 50-hour power reserve
Functions: hours, minutes, subsidiary seconds; chronograph; date
Case: rose gold, tonneau-shape, 44.5 x 39.2 mm; height 12.8 mm; sapphire crystal; transparent case back; water-resistant to 3 atm
Band: reptile skin, buckle
Price: $29,800
Variations: white gold ($29,800); stainless steel ($15,900)

Tonda 1950

Reference number: PFC267-1002400-HA1441
Movement: automatic, Parmigiani Caliber PF701; ø 30 mm, height 2.6 mm; 29 jewels; 21,600 vph; 42-hour power reserve
Functions: hours, minutes, subsidiary seconds
Case: rose gold, ø 39 mm, height 12.8 mm; sapphire crystal; transparent case back; water-resistant to 3 atm
Band: reptile skin, buckle
Price: $16,900
Variations: white gold ($16,900)

Tonda 1950

Reference number: PFC267-1202400-HA1241
Movement: automatic, Parmigiani Caliber PF701; ø 30 mm, height 2.6 mm; 29 jewels; 21,600 vph; 42-hour power reserve
Functions: hours, minutes, subsidiary seconds
Case: white gold, ø 39 mm, height 7.8 mm; sapphire crystal; transparent case back; water-resistant to 3 atm
Band: reptile skin, buckle
Price: $16,900
Variations: rose gold ($16,900)

Tonda 1950 Set

Reference number: PFC267-1060300-HA1421
Movement: automatic, Parmigiani Caliber PF701; ø 30 mm, height 2.6 mm; 29 jewels; 21,600 vph; 42-hour power reserve
Functions: hours, minutes, subsidiary seconds
Case: rose gold, ø 39 mm, height 7.8 mm; bezel set with diamonds; sapphire crystal; transparent case back; water-resistant to 3 atm
Band: reptile skin, buckle
Price: $21,000

Tonda 42 Hemispheres

Reference number: PFC231-1002400-HA1241
Movement: automatic, Parmigiani Caliber PF337;
ø 35.6 mm, height 5.1 mm; 38 jewels; 28,800 vph;
double spring barrel, côtes de Genève, 50-hour
power reserve
Functions: hours, minutes, subsidiary seconds;
additional 12-hour display (second time zone);
double day/night indicator; date
Case: rose gold, ø 42 mm, height 11.15 mm;
sapphire crystal; transparent case back;
water-resistant to 3 atm
Band: reptile skin, buckle
Price: $32,900
Variations: white gold ($34,700)

Tonda Centum

Reference number: PFH227-1002600-HA1441
Movement: automatic, Parmigiani Caliber PF333;
ø 27 mm, height 5.5 mm; 32 jewels; 28,800 vph;
module for perpetual calendar; double spring barrel,
50-hour power reserve
Functions: hours, minutes, sweep seconds;
perpetual calendar with retrograde date, weekday,
month, double moon phase, leap year
Case: white gold, ø 42 mm, height 11.15
mm; sapphire crystal; transparent case back;
water-resistant to 3 atm
Band: reptile skin, folding clasp
Price: $60,000
Variations: rose gold ($60,000)

Tonda Quator

Reference number: PFC272-1200200-HA1241
Movement: automatic, Parmigiani Caliber PF339;
ø 27 mm, height 5.5 mm; 32 jewels; 28,800 vph;
double spring barrel, 50-hour power reserve
Functions: hours, minutes, sweep seconds; annual
calendar with date (retrograde), weekday, month,
double moon phase
Case: rose gold, ø 40 mm, height 11.2 mm;
sapphire crystal; transparent case back;
water-resistant to 3 atm
Band: reptile skin, buckle
Price: $32,800
Variations: white gold ($32,800)

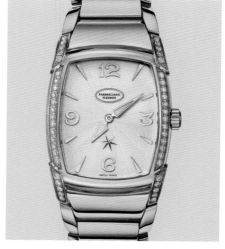

Kalparisma Agenda

Reference number: PFC123-1000700
Movement: automatic, Parmigiani Caliber PF331;
ø 25.6 mm, height 3.5 mm; 32 jewels; 28,800 vph;
2 spring barrels
Functions: hours, minutes, sweep seconds; date
Case: rose gold, 31.2 x 37.5 mm, height 8.4 mm;
sapphire crystal; transparent case back;
water-resistant to 3 atm
Band: reptile skin, buckle
Price: $18,500
Variations: set with brilliant-cut diamonds
($21,900); with rose gold bracelet ($34,500)

Kalparisma Steel

Reference number: PFC124-0020700-XA2422
Movement: automatic, Parmigiani Caliber PF331;
ø 25.6 mm, height 3.5 mm; 32 jewels; 28,800 vph;
côtes de Genève; 55-hour power reserve
Functions: hours, minutes, subsidiary seconds;
date
Case: stainless steel, 31.2 x 37.5 mm, height
8.4 mm; bezel and lugs set with 46 diamonds;
sapphire crystal; transparent case back;
water-resistant to 3 atm
Band: reptile skin, folding clasp
Price: $12,800
Variations: without diamonds ($9,800)

Kalparisma Nova

Reference number: PFC125-1020700-B10002
Movement: automatic, Parmigiani Caliber PF332; ø
25.6 mm, height 3.5 mm; 32 jewels; 28,800 vph
Functions: hours, minutes
Case: rose gold, 31.2 x 37.5 mm, height 8.4 mm;
bezel and lugs set with 46 diamonds; sapphire
crystal; transparent case back; water-resistant to
3 atm
Band: rose gold, folding clasp
Price: $34,500
Variations: with reptile skin strap ($21,900); with
reptile skin strap and no diamonds ($18,500)

Caliber PF333

Automatic; module for perpetual calendar with retrograde date and precision moon phase; double spring barrel; 55-hour power reserve
Functions: hours, minutes, sweep seconds; perpetual calendar with month, moon phase, leap year, weekday, date
Diameter: 27 mm
Height: 5.5 mm
Jewels: 32
Frequency: 28,800 vph
Balance spring: flat hairspring

Caliber PF511

Manually wound; 30-second tourbillon; skeletonized main plate and bridges; double spring barrel, 7-day power reserve
Functions: hours, minutes, sweep seconds; power reserve indicator
Diameter: 33.9 mm
Height: 5.55 mm
Jewels: 30
Frequency: 21,600 vph
Balance spring: flat hairspring

Caliber PF701

Automatic; platinum microrotor; single spring barrel, 42-hour power reserve
Functions: hours, minutes, subsidiary seconds
Diameter: 30 mm
Height: 2.6 mm
Jewels: 29
Frequency: 21,600 vph

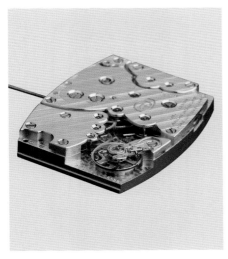

PF110

Manual winding; double spring barrel, 8-day power reserve
Functions: hours, minutes, subsidiary seconds; date; power reserve indicator
Measurements: 29.3 x 23.6 mm
Height: 4.9 mm
Jewels: 28
Frequency: 21,600 vph

Caliber PF334

Automatic; double spring barrel, 50-hour power reserve
Functions: hours, minutes, subsidiary seconds; chronograph, date
Diameter: 30.3 mm
Height: 6.8 mm
Jewels: 68
Frequency: 28,800 vph

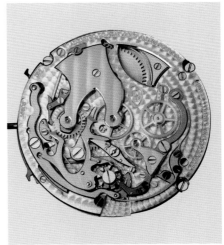

Caliber PF354

Manually wound; Dubois Dépraz chronograph module; double spring barrel, 72-hour power reserve
Functions: hours, minutes, subsidiary seconds; chronograph, power reserve indicator
Diameter: 29.9 mm
Height: 7.6 mm
Jewels: 29
Frequency: 21,600 vph

Patek Philippe president Thierry Stern with his father Philippe Stern

Patek Philippe

Patek Philippe SA
Chemin du pont-du-centenaire 141
CH-1228 Plan-les-Ouates
Switzerland

Tel.:
01141-22-884-20-20

Fax:
01141-22-884-20-40

Website:
www.patek.com

Founded:
1839

Number of employees:
approx. 2,000 (estimated)

Annual production:
approx. 45,000 watches worldwide per year

U.S. distributor:
Henri Stern Watch Agency
1 Rockefeller Center, Floor 9
New York, NY 10020
212-218-1240

Most important collections/price range:
Calatrava; Nautilus; Gondolo, Ellipse, Aquanaut /
ladies' timepieces begin at $13,000 (Twenty~4)
and men's at $20,800 (basic Calatrava)

As the last independent family-owned business in the Swiss watch industry, Patek Philippe has managed to hold on to a very special status. The company was founded by Count Norbert Antoine de Patek in 1839, and in 1845, master watchmaker Jean Adrien Philippe came on board. Literally since then, Patek Philippe has been known for creating high-quality mechanical watches, some with extremely sophisticated complications. Even among its competition, the *manufacture* enjoys the highest respect. Proof of the brand's enduring reputation, perhaps, is the almost $3 million auction price achieved at Sotheby's in June 2012 for the Yellow Gold Repeating Wristwatch.

In 1997, Patek Philippe moved into new quarters, based on the most modern standards. The facility boasts the world's largest assembly of watchmakers under one roof, and yet production figures are comparatively modest. Approximately 20,000 mechanical watches leave the *manufacture* in Plan-les-Ouates—the rest of the offerings are women's quartz watches. A small section of the building is reserved for restoring old watches using either parts from a large and valuable collection of components or rebuilding them from scratch. The company recently opened a highly industrialized second branch between La Chaux-de-Fonds and Le Locle, where case components are manufactured, cases are polished, and gemstone setting is done. Patek Philippe's main headquarters remain in Geneva, but the *manufacture* no longer has a need for that city's famed seal: All of the company's mechanical watches now feature the "Patek Philippe Seal," the criteria for which far exceed the requirements of the *Poinçon de Genève* and include specifications for the entire watch, not just the movement.

Calatrava
Reference number: 5227G
Movement: automatic, Patek Philippe Caliber 324 S C; ø 27 mm, height 3.3 mm; 29 jewels; 28,800 vph; Spiromax silicon spring
Functions: hours, minutes, sweep seconds; date
Case: white gold, ø 39 mm, height 9.24 mm; sapphire crystal; transparent case back; water-resistant to 3 atm
Band: reptile skin, buckle
Remarks: hinged case back cover
Price: $37,300 (white gold)
Variations: yellow gold ($35,400); rose gold ($37,300)

Calatrava
Reference number: 5116R
Movement: manually wound, Patek Philippe Caliber 215 PS; ø 21.9 mm, height 2.55 mm; 18 jewels; 28,800 vph
Functions: hours, minutes, subsidiary seconds
Case: rose gold, ø 36 mm, height 7.93 mm; bezel with clous de Paris; sapphire crystal; transparent case back; water-resistant to 3 atm
Band: reptile skin, buckle
Price: $28,100

Gondolo
Reference number: 5200G
Movement: manually wound, Patek Philippe Caliber 28-20 REC 8J PS IRM C J; 20 x 28 mm, height 5.05 mm; 28 jewels; 28,800 vph; 192-hour power reserve
Functions: hours, minutes, subsidiary seconds; date, weekday; power reserve indicator
Case: white gold, 32.4 x 46.9 mm, height 11.63 mm; sapphire crystal; transparent case back; water-resistant to 3 atm
Band: reptile skin, buckle
Price: $59,400

Nautilus Chronograph

Reference number: 5980/1R
Movement: automatic, Patek Philippe Caliber CH 28 520 C; ø 30 mm, height 6.63 mm; 35 jewels; 28,800 vph
Functions: hours, minutes; chronograph; date
Case: rose gold, ø 40.5 mm, height 12.2 mm; sapphire crystal; transparent case back; screw-in crown; water-resistant to 12 atm
Band: rose gold, folding clasp
Price: $91,400
Variations: stainless steel

Nautilus Chronograph

Reference number: 5980/1AR
Movement: automatic, Patek Philippe Caliber CH 28 520 C; ø 30 mm, height 6.63 mm; 35 jewels; 28,800 vph
Functions: hours, minutes; chronograph; date
Case: stainless steel, ø 40.5 mm, height 12.16 mm; rose gold bezel; sapphire crystal; transparent case back; screw-in crown; rose gold crown and pushers; water-resistant to 12 atm
Band: stainless steel with pink gold elements, folding clasp
Price: $67,000
Variations: stainless steel ($51,000)

Annual Calendar

Reference number: 5205R
Movement: automatic, Patek Philippe Caliber 324 S QA LU 24H; ø 32.6 mm, height 5.78 mm; 34 jewels; 28,800 vph; silicon pallet lever, gold rotor; 45-hour power reserve
Functions: hours, minutes, sweep seconds; additional 24-hour display (second time zone); annual calendar with date, weekday, month, moon phase
Case: rose gold, ø 40 mm; sapphire crystal; transparent case back; water-resistant to 3 atm
Band: reptile skin, buckle
Price: $49,500
Variations: white gold ($49,500)

Chronograph

Reference number: 5170G
Movement: manual winding, Patek Philippe Caliber CH 29-535 PS; ø 29.6 mm, height 5.35 mm; 33 jewels; 28,800 vph; column wheel control of chronograph; very fine finishing
Functions: hours, minutes, subsidiary seconds; chronograph
Case: white gold, ø 39.4 mm, height 10.9 mm; sapphire crystal; transparent case back; water-resistant to 3 atm
Band: reptile skin, folding clasp
Price: $87,100
Variations: yellow gold ($84,900)

Annual Calendar

Reference number: 5396/1G
Movement: automatic, Patek Philippe Caliber 324 S QA LU 24H/303; ø 33.3 mm, height 5.78 mm; 34 jewels; 28,800 vph
Functions: hours, minutes, sweep seconds; additional 24-hour display; annual calendar with date, weekday, month, moon phase
Case: white gold, ø 38.5 mm, height 11.2 mm; sapphire crystal; transparent case back; water-resistant to 3 atm
Band: white gold, folding clasp
Price: $76,900
Variations: rose gold ($76,900)

Annual Calendar

Reference number: 5146/1R
Movement: automatic, Patek Philippe Caliber 324 S IRM QA LU; ø 30 mm, height 5.32 mm; 36 jewels; 28,800 vph
Functions: hours, minutes, sweep seconds; perpetual calendar with date, weekday, month, moon phase; power reserve indicator
Case: rose gold, ø 39 mm, height 11.23 mm; sapphire crystal; transparent case back; water-resistant to 3 atm
Band: rose gold, folding clasp
Price: $71,000
Variations: yellow gold 5146/1J ($68,500); white gold 5146/1G ($71,000); platinum ($68,700)

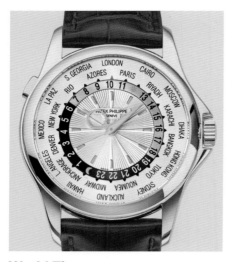

World Time

Reference number: 5130J
Movement: automatic, Patek Philippe Caliber 240 HU; ø 27.5 mm, height 3.88 mm; 33 jewels; 21,600 vph
Functions: hours, minutes; world-time display (second time zone)
Case: yellow gold, ø 39.5 mm, height 9.6 mm; pusher-activated inner ring with reference cities of 24 world time zones; sapphire crystal; transparent case back; water-resistant to 3 atm
Band: reptile skin, buckle
Price: $45,400
Variations: rose with no white gold ($47,000); platinum ($65,300)

Annual Calendar Chronograph

Reference number: 5960P
Movement: automatic, Patek Philippe Caliber CH 28 520 IRM QA 24H; ø 33 mm, height 7.68 mm; 40 jewels; 28,800 vph
Functions: hours, minutes, sweep seconds; flyback chronograph; annual calendar with date, weekday, month; power reserve indicator
Case: platinum, ø 40.5 mm, height 13.5 mm; sapphire crystal; transparent case back; water-resistant to 3 atm
Band: reptile skin, folding clasp
Price: $95,400
Variations: rose gold ($79,800)

Retrograde Perpetual Calendar

Reference number: 5160R
Movement: automatic, Patek Philippe Caliber 324 S QR; ø 28 mm, height 5.35 mm; 30 jewels; 28,800 vph
Functions: hours, minutes, sweep seconds; perpetual calendar with date, weekday, month, moon phase, leap year
Case: rose gold, ø 38 mm, height 11.8 mm; sapphire crystal; transparent case back; water-resistant to 3 atm
Band: reptile skin, folding clasp
Remarks: hinged case back cover
Price: $173,000

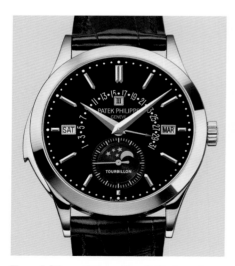

Tourbillon Perpetual Calendar Minute Repeater

Reference number: 5216P
Movement: manual winding, Patek Philippe Caliber R TO 27 PS QR; ø 28 mm, height 8.61 mm; 28 jewels; 28,800 vph; 1-minute tourbillon
Functions: hours, minutes; minute repeater; perpetual calendar with date, weekday, month, moon phase, leap year
Case: platinum, ø 39.5 mm, height 12.23 mm; sapphire crystal; transparent case back
Band: reptile skin, folding clasp
Price: CHF715,000 (only in Swiss francs)

Minute Repeater with Tourbillon

Reference number: 5539G
Movement: manual winding, Patek Philippe Caliber R TO 27 PS; ø 28 mm, height 6.58 mm; 28 jewels; 21,600 vph; 1-minute tourbillon; 48-hour power reserve
Functions: hours, minutes, subsidiary seconds; minute repeater
Case: white gold, ø 37 mm, height 11.35 mm; sapphire crystal; transparent case back
Band: reptile skin, folding clasp
Price: CHF520,000 (only in Swiss francs)

Aquanaut Luce

Reference number: 5067A
Movement: quartz
Functions: hours, minutes, sweep seconds; date
Case: stainless steel, ø 35.6 mm, height 7.7 mm; bezel set with 46 diamonds; sapphire crystal; water-resistant to 12 atm
Band: rubber, folding clasp
Price: $17,400

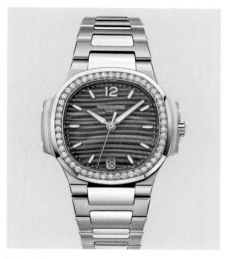

Nautilus

Reference number: 7018/1A-010
Movement: automatic, Patek Philippe Caliber 324 S C; ø 27 mm, height 3.57 mm; 29 jewels; 28,800 vph
Functions: hours, minutes, sweep seconds; date
Case: stainless steel, ø 33.6 mm, height 8.7 mm; bezel set with 50 diamonds; sapphire crystal; transparent case back; screw-in crown; water-resistant to 6 atm
Band: stainless steel, folding clasp
Price: $37,800

Nautilus

Reference number: 7010/1R
Movement: quartz
Functions: hours, minutes, sweep seconds; date
Case: rose gold, ø 32 mm, height 6.9 mm; bezel set with 46 diamonds; sapphire crystal; transparent case back; screw-in crown; water-resistant to 6 atm
Band: rose gold, folding clasp
Price: $47,600

Calatrava Travel Time

Reference number: 7134G
Movement: manual winding, Patek Philippe Caliber 215 PS FUS 24H; ø 21.9 mm, height 3.35 mm; 18 jewels; 28,800 vph; 44-hour power reserve
Functions: hours, minutes, subsidiary seconds; additional 12-hour display (second time zone), additional 24-hour display (day/night indicator)
Case: white gold, ø 35 mm, height 9.2 mm; bezel set with 112 diamonds; sapphire crystal; transparent case back; water-resistant to 3 atm
Band: reptile skin, folding clasp
Price: $44,400

World Time

Reference number: 7130R
Movement: automatic, Patek Philippe Caliber 240 HU; ø 27.5 mm, height 3.88 mm; 33 jewels; 21,600 vph
Functions: hours, minutes; world-time display (second time zone)
Case: rose gold, ø 36 mm, height 8.83 mm; bezel set with 62 diamonds; pusher-activated inner ring with reference cities of 24 world time zones; sapphire crystal; transparent case back; water-resistant to 3 atm
Band: reptile skin, buckle
Price: $54,900
Variations: white gold

Calatrava

Reference number: 7200R
Movement: automatic, Patek Philippe Caliber 240; ø 27.5 mm, height 2.53 mm; 27 jewels; 21,600 vph
Functions: hours, minutes
Case: rose gold, ø 34.6 mm, height 7.37 mm; sapphire crystal; transparent case back; water-resistant to 3 atm
Band: reptile skin, buckle
Price: $29,300

Complication

Reference number: 7121J
Movement: manual winding, Patek Philippe Caliber 215 PS LU; ø 21.9 mm, height 3 mm; 18 jewels; 28,800 vph
Functions: hours, minutes, subsidiary seconds; moon phase
Case: yellow gold, ø 33 mm, height 8.35 mm; bezel set with 66 diamonds; sapphire crystal; transparent case back; screw-in crown; water-resistant to 3 atm
Band: reptile skin, buckle (set with 32 diamonds)
Remarks: mother-of-pearl dial
Price: $36,700

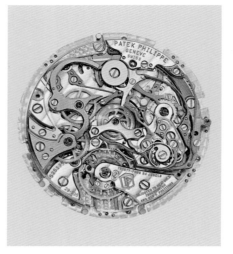

Caliber CHR 29-535 PS

Manually wound, column wheel control of chronograph functions; precisely jumping 30-minute totalizer; single spring barrel, 65 hours power reserve

Functions: hours, minutes, subsidiary seconds; chronograph

Diameter: 29.6 mm; **Height:** 5.35 mm

Jewels: 33

Balance: Gyromax, 4-armed, with 4 regulating weights; **Frequency:** 28,800 vph

Balance spring: Breguet

Shock protection: Incabloc

Remarks: 269 individual components; 6 detail solutions with patent pending

Caliber CHR 29-535 PS Q

Manually wound; 2 column wheels to control chronograph functions, split-second hand mechanism with isolator; single barrel spring, 65 hours power reserve

Functions: hours, minutes, subsidiary seconds; day/night indicator; split-second chronograph; perpetual calendar with date, weekday, month, moon phase, leap year

Diameter: 32 mm; **Height:** 8.7 mm; **Jewels:** 34

Balance: Gyromax, 4-armed, with 4 regulating weights; **Frequency:** 28,800 vph

Balance spring: Breguet

Remarks: 496 components, 182 alone for perpetual calendar and 42 for split-seconds mechanism with isolator

Caliber CHR 27-525 PS

Ultra-flat mechanical movement with manual winding, 48 hours power reserve; double column wheel control of chronograph functions with crown pusher (start-stop-reset) and separate split-seconds hand pusher

Functions: hours, minutes, subsidiary seconds; split-seconds chronograph

Diameter: 27.3 mm; **Height:** 5.25 mm

Jewels: 27

Balance: Gyromax, 2-armed, with 8 regulating weights; **Frequency:** 21,600 vph

Balance spring: Breguet

Shock protection: Kif

Remarks: 252 individual components; outstandingly high-quality finishing

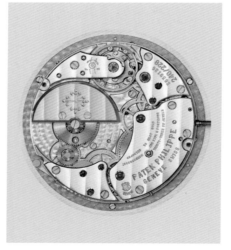

Caliber 28-20 REC 8J PS IRM C J

Manually wound; double spring barrel; 192-hour power reserve

Functions: hours, minutes, subsidiary seconds; power reserve indicator; weekday, date

Measurements: 20 x 28 mm

Height: 5.05 mm

Jewels: 28

Balance: Gyromax

Frequency: 28,800 vph

Balance spring: Spiromax silicon spring

Caliber 240 HU

Automatic; unidirectional winding off-center ball-bearing rotor in 22 kt gold; 48 hours power reserve

Functions: hours, minutes, world time (24 time zone display)

Diameter: 27.5 mm

Height: 3.88 mm

Jewels: 33

Balance: Gyromax

Frequency: 21,600 vph

Remarks: 239 individual parts

Caliber 240 PS IRM C LU

Automatic; unidirectional winding off-center ball-bearing rotor in 22 kt gold; 48 hours power reserve

Functions: hours, minutes, subsidiary seconds; date; power reserve display; moon phase

Diameter: 31 mm

Height: 3.98 mm

Jewels: 29

Balance: Gyromax

Frequency: 21,600 vph

Remarks: 265 individual parts

Caliber 315 S QA LU

Automatic; central rotor in 21 kt gold; 48 hours power reserve
Functions: hours, minutes, sweep seconds; calendar with date, day, month (programmed for 1 year), moon phase
Diameter: 30 mm
Height: 5.22 mm
Jewels: 36
Balance: Gyromax
Frequency: 21,600 vph
Remarks: 328 individual parts

Caliber 315 SC

Automatic; central rotor in 21 kt gold; 48 hours power reserve
Functions: hours, minutes, sweep seconds; date
Diameter: 27 mm
Height: 3.22 mm
Jewels: 29
Balance: Gyromax
Frequency: 21,600 vph
Remarks: 213 individual parts

Caliber 215

Manually wound; 44 hours power reserve
Functions: hours, minutes, subsidiary seconds
Diameter: 21.9 mm (9 3/4''')
Height: 2.55 mm
Jewels: 18 (escape wheel with endstone)
Balance: Gyromax with 8 masselotte regulating weights
Frequency: 28,800 vph
Balance spring: flat hairspring
Shock protection: Kif
Remarks: base plate with perlage, beveled bridges with côtes de Genève, 130 individual parts

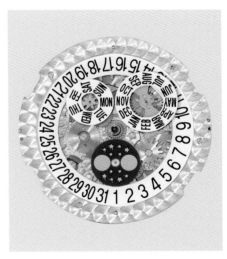

Caliber 315 S IRM QA LU

Automatic; central rotor in 21 kt gold; 48 hours power reserve
Functions: hours, minutes, sweep seconds, calendar with date, day, month (programmed for 1 year), moon phase; power reserve display
Diameter: 30 mm
Height: 5.22 mm
Jewels: 36
Balance: Gyromax
Frequency: 21,600 vph
Remarks: 355 individual parts

Caliber 324 S IRM QA LU

Automatic; central rotor in 21 kt gold; 45 hours power reserve
Functions: hours, minutes, sweep seconds; calendar with date, day, month (programmed for 1 year), moon phase; power reserve display
Diameter: 32 mm
Height: 5.3 mm
Jewels: 36
Balance: Gyromax
Frequency: 28,800 vph
Balance spring: Spiromax (silicon)
Remarks: silicon escape wheel; 355 individual parts

Caliber 324 S QA LU 24H/303

Automatic; central rotor in 21 kt gold; 45 hours power reserve
Functions: hours, minutes, sweep seconds; calendar with date, day, month (programmed for 1 year), moon phase; 24-hour display
Diameter: 32.6 mm
Height: 5.78 mm
Jewels: 34
Balance: Gyromax
Frequency: 28,800 vph
Balance spring: Spiromax (silicon)
Remarks: silicon escape wheel; 347 individual parts

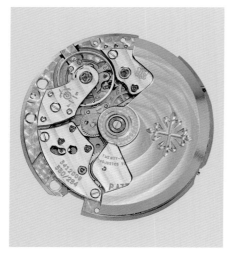

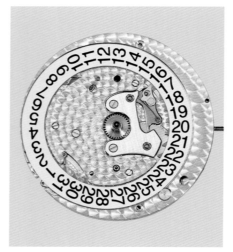

Caliber 330 SC

Automatic; central rotor in 21 kt gold; 48-hour power reserve
Functions: hours, minutes, sweep seconds; date
Diameter: 27 mm
Height: 3.5 mm
Jewels: 29
Balance: Gyromax
Frequency: 21,600 vph
Balance spring: Breguet
Remarks: 217 individual parts

Caliber CH 28-520 C

Automatic; column-wheel control of chronograph functions; central rotor in 21 kt gold; 55-hour power reserve
Functions: hours, minutes, sweep seconds; chronograph with combined hour and minute counter; date
Diameter: 30 mm
Height: 6.63 mm
Jewels: 35
Balance: Gyromax
Frequency: 28,800 vph
Balance spring: Breguet
Remarks: 327 individual parts

Caliber CH 28-520 IRM QA 24H

Automatic; column-wheel control of chronograph functions; central rotor in 21 kt gold; 55-hour power reserve
Functions: hours, minutes, sweep seconds; chronograph with combined hour and minute counter; calendar with date, day, month (programmed for 1 year), moon phase; day/night indication; power reserve display
Diameter: 33 mm
Height: 7.68 mm
Jewels: 40
Balance: Gyromax
Frequency: 28,800 vph
Balance spring: Breguet
Remarks: 456 individual parts

Caliber RTO 27 QR SID LU CL

Manually wound; minute repeater; striking mechanism with 2 cathedral gongs, release mechanism integrated in watch movement; 48-hour power reserve; COSC certified chronometer
Functions: hours, minutes; perpetual calendar with date (retrograde), day, month, moon phase; leap year (front), sidereal time, celestial map with moon phase and moon age (on back)
Diameter: 38 mm
Height: 12.61 mm
Jewels: 55
Balance: Gyromax
Frequency: 21,600 vph
Remarks: 686 individual parts

Caliber RTO 27 PS

Manually wound; 1-minute tourbillon; 48-hour power reserve; COSC certified chronometer
Functions: hours, minutes, subsidiary seconds, minute repeater
Diameter: 28 mm
Height: 6.58 mm
Jewels: 28
Balance: Gyromax
Frequency: 21,600 vph
Balance spring: Breguet
Remarks: 336 individual parts

Caliber TO 28 REC 10JPS IRM

Manually wound; 1-minute tourbillon; twin spring barrels; 240-hour power reserve (10 days); COSC certified chronometer
Functions: hours, minutes, subsidiary seconds; power reserve display
Measurements: 28 x 20 mm
Height: 6.3 mm
Jewels: 29
Balance: Gyromax
Frequency: 21,600 vph
Remarks: 231 individual parts

Paul Gerber

Watchmaker Paul Gerber has already developed mechanisms and complications, including calendar movements, alarms, and tourbillons, for numerous renowned watchmakers over the decades. Time and again, this genial watchmaker has astonished the horological world with outrageously complicated mechanisms, which he somehow manages to create by fitting hundreds of additional tiny parts into filigree movements of watches that seem to offer not one iota of extra room. Gerber is the one who designed the complicated calendar mechanism for the otherwise minimalist MIH watch conceived by Ludwig Oechslin, curator of the International Museum of Horology (MIH) in La Chaux-de-Fonds and himself a watchmaker.

When his daily work for others lets up, Gerber gets around to building watches bearing his own name with such marvelous features as a retrograde second hand in an elegant thin case and a synchronously, unidirectional rotor system with miniature oscillating weights for his self-winding Retro Twin model. Gerber's works are all limited editions.

After designing a tonneau-shaped manually wound wristwatch with a three-dimensional moon phase display, Gerber created a simple, three-hand watch with an automatic movement conceived and produced completely in-house. It features a 100-hour power reserve and is wound by three synchronically turning gold rotors. The large date can be set backward and forward. Gerber also offers the triple rotor and large date features in a watch with an ETA movement and lightweight titanium case as a classic pilot watch design or in a version with a more modern dial (the Synchron model). The Model 41 has an optional complication that switches the second hand from sweep to dead-beat motion by way of a pusher at 2 o'clock.

Paul Gerber
Uhren-Konstruktionen
Bockhornstrasse 69
CH-8047 Zürich
Switzerland

Tel.:
01141-44-401-4569

Fax:
01141-44-401-1448

E-Mail:
info@gerber-uhren.ch

Website:
www.gerber-uhren.ch

Founded:
1976

Number of employees:
2

Annual production:
over 100 watches

U.S. distributor:
Paul Gerber – Intro Swiss
7615 Estate Circle
Niwot, CO 80503
303-652-1520
introswiss@q.com

Most important collections/price range:
mechanical watches / from approx. $5,200 to $70,000; tourbillon desk clocks / from approx. $50,000 to $80,000

Retro Twin

Reference number: 156
Movement: automatic, Gerber Caliber 15 (base ETA 7001); ø 28 mm, height 5.2 mm; 27 jewels; 21,600 vph; automatic winding with 2 synchronously rotating platinum rotors
Functions: hours, minutes, subsidiary seconds (retrograde)
Case: rose gold, ø 36 mm, height 10.8 mm; sapphire crystal; transparent case back; water-resistant to 3 atm
Band: reptile skin, buckle
Price: $17,600
Variations: yellow or white gold ($17,600); with platinum rotors set with brilliants ($21,011)

Modell 41

Reference number: 416.3
Movement: automatic, Gerber Caliber 41; ø 35 mm, height 7.2 mm; 30 jewels; 21,600 vph; 2 spring barrels, 100-hour power reserve; automatic winding with 3 synchronously rotating platinum rotors
Functions: hours, minutes, sweep seconds; date
Case: stainless steel, ø 42 mm, height 13.5 mm; sapphire crystal; transparent case back; water-resistant to 3 atm
Band: calf leather, double folding clasp
Price: $20,500
Variations: with white dial ($20,500); second hand switches between sweep and deadbeat motion ($24,540)

Modell 42

Reference number: 420 DaN
Movement: automatic, Gerber Caliber 42 (base ETA 2824); ø 36 mm, height 6.1 mm; 25 jewels; 28,800 vph; automatic winding with 3 synchronously rotating gold rotors
Functions: hours, minutes, sweep seconds; day/night indication; date
Case: titanium, ø 42 mm, height 12 mm; sapphire crystal; transparent case back; screw-in crown; water-resistant to 10 atm
Band: calf leather, buckle
Price: $5,200
Variations: with pilot's / Synchron dial ($5,200); as Caliber42 pilot's / Synchron 24-hour ($6,250)

Perrelet SA
Rue Bubenberg 7
CH-2502 Biel/Bienne
Switzerland

Tel.:
01141-32-346-2626

Fax:
01141-32-346-2647

E-Mail:
perrelet@perrelet.com

Website:
www.perrelet.com

Founded:
1995

Number of employees:
12

Annual production:
5,500–6,000 watches

U.S. distributor:
H5 Group, Corp.
3230 West Commercial Blvd., Suite 160
Fort Lauderdale, FL 33309

Most important collections/price range:
Turbine, Turbine XL, Turbine XS, Seacraft, Skeleton
Chronograph / $3,100 to $19,250

Perrelet

The Perrelet story will sound familiar to anyone who has read about Swiss watchmaking: Abraham-Louis Perrelet (1729–1826) was the son of a middle-class farmer from Le Locle who developed an interest in watchmaking early on in life. He was the first watchmaker in Le Locle to work on cylinder and duplex escapements, and there is a persistent rumor that he was responsible for a repeater that could be heard echoing in the mountains.

Many watchmakers later to become famous were at one time Perrelet's apprentices, and some historians even suggest that Abraham-Louis Breguet was in this illustrious group. Suffice to say, Perrelet invented a great deal, including the "perpetual" watch from around 1770, a pocket watch that wound itself utilizing the motion of the wearer.

The brand has kept up with the times, combining modern design with solid technique. One of its outstanding models is the Turbine, which includes an element of wit and has made quite a splash, in particular in the U.S. market. The "turbo" appearance of the Turbine is achieved using Perrelet's own double rotor caliber, the P-331 (which is still something of a mystery to the watch world), which also powers the Diamond Flower and Double Rotor models. Images behind the turbine fan, which is not used as a rotor, appear to come alive, so the company has had some fun with an erotic edition, a poker edition, a "toxic" edition, and a Swiss edition, which reveals the iconic white cross of the national flag. For a while, it looked as if Perrelet were going to branch out into more traditional watches. But the times demand adherence to DNA apparently.

Turbine Helvetia

Reference number: A4037/1
Movement: automatic, P-331 in-house caliber; ø 31.60 mm, height 3.85 mm; 25 jewels; 28,800 vph; 40-hour power reserve; exclusive patented Perrelet double rotor; second Perrelet rotor acts as "turbine" on dial side
Functions: hours, minutes, sweep seconds
Case: stainless steel with DLC coating, ø 44 mm, height 13 mm; sapphire crystal; antireflective sapphire crystal; transparent case back; water-resistant to 5 atm
Band: reptile skin, folding clasp
Price: $6,250

Turbine Diver

Reference number: A1066/3
Movement: automatic, P-331 in-house caliber; ø 31.60 mm, height 3.85 mm; 25 jewels; 28,800 vph; 40-hour power reserve; exclusive patented Perrelet double rotor; second Perrelet rotor acts as "turbine" on dial side
Functions: hours, minutes, sweep seconds
Case: stainless steel, ø 47.5 mm, height 14.82 mm; sapphire crystal; transparent case back; water-resistant to 30 atm
Band: blue rubber strap, pin buckle
Price: $6,500

Peripheral Double Rotor

Reference number: A1061/1
Movement: automatic, P-341 in-house caliber; ø 34.80 mm, height 3.85 mm; 25 jewels; 28,800 vph; 40-hour power reserve; exclusive patented Perrelet double rotor
Functions: hours, minutes, seconds; date at 6:00
Case: stainless steel, ø 42 mm, height 13.15 mm; sapphire crystal; screwed-down sapphire crystal case back; water-resistant to 5 atm
Band: reptile skin, folding clasp
Price: $4,550

Turbine Chrono

Reference number: A1074/2
Movement: automatic, Perrelet Caliber P-361;
28,800 vph; 42-hour power reserve
Functions: hours, minutes; sweep chronograph
hand, 60-minute counter on central sapphire disk;
date
Case: stainless steel with DLC coating, ø 47 mm,
height 16 mm; bezel with tachymeter scale; sapphire
crystal; screwed-down sapphire crystal case back;
water-resistant to 5 atm
Band: rubber, buckle
Price: $7,850

Turbine Black & Gold

Reference number: A8080/1
Movement: automatic, Perrelet Caliber P-331;
28,800 vph; 40-hour power reserve; exclusive
patented Perrelet double rotor; second Perrelet rotor
acts as "turbine" on dial side
Functions: hours, minutes, sweep seconds
Case: pink gold, steel bezel and back with DLC
coating, ø 44 mm, height 13 mm; sapphire crystal;
transparent case back; water-resistant to 5 atm
Remarks: 12 black turbine blades produce flashing
by turning over gold subdial
Band: reptile skin, DLC-treated folding clasp
Price: $19,250, limited to 77 pieces

Turbine XS

Reference number: A2045/1
Movement: automatic, Perrelet Caliber P-181
(base ETA 2892 with Perrelet module); ø 31.6 mm,
height 4.75 mm; 21 jewels; 28,800 vph; 42-hour
power reserve; exclusive patented Perrelet double
rotor; second Perrelet rotor acts as "turbine" on dial
side
Functions: hours, minutes, sweep seconds
Case: stainless steel with DLC coating, ø 41 mm,
height 12.85 mm; sapphire crystal; bezel, lugs, and
dial with 358 diamonds; transparent case back;
water-resistant to 5 atm
Band: satin, folding clasp
Price: $18,350

Chronograph Skeleton

Reference number: A1056/1
Movement: automatic, Perrelet Caliber P-291;
ø 30.4 mm, height 8.1 mm; 25 jewels; 28,800 vph;
46-hour power reserve; open-worked exclusively
decorated Perrelet rotor
Functions: hours, minutes, subsidiary seconds;
chronograph sweep seconds; 30-minute counter at
12; subsidiary date; dual time zone
Case: stainless steel/steel bezel and back with
DLC coating, ø 43.5 mm, height 14.9 mm; sapphire
crystal; screwed-down sapphire crystal case back;
water-resistant to 10 atm
Band: rubber, folding clasp
Price: $7,200

New Diamond Flower

Reference number: A 3032/C
Movement: automatic, Perrelet Caliber P-181;
ø 31.6 mm, height 4.75 mm; 21 jewels; 28,800 vph;
42-hour power reserve; exclusive patented Perrelet
double rotor; second rotor in center of dial
Functions: hours, minutes, sweep seconds
Case: pink gold, ø 36.5 mm, height 12.3 mm;
sapphire crystal; transparent case back; water-
resistant to 5 atm
Band: rubber, folding clasp
Remarks: dial set with 24 diamonds
Price: $16,450

Double Rotor Classic

Reference number: A1006/8
Movement: automatic, Perrelet Caliber P-181;
ø 31.6 mm, height 4.75 mm; 21 jewels; 28,800 vph;
42-hour power reserve; open-worked exclusively
decorated Perrelet rotor
Functions: hours, minutes, sweep seconds; date
Case: stainless steel, ø 40 mm, height 11 mm;
sapphire crystal; screwed-down sapphire crystal
case back; water-resistant to 5 atm
Band: reptile skin, folding clasp
Price: $3,950

Piaget SA
CH-1228 Plan-les-Ouates
Switzerland

E-Mail:
info@piaget.com

Website:
www.piaget.com

Founded:
1874

Number of employees:
900

Annual production:
watches not specified; plus about 20,000
movements for Richemont Group

U.S. distributor:
Piaget North America
645 5th Avenue, 5th Floor
New York, NY 10022
212-909-4362; 212-909-4332 (fax)
www.piaget.com

Most important collections/price range:
Altiplano / between approx. $13,500 and
$22,000

Piaget

One of the oldest watch manufacturers
in Switzerland, Piaget began making watch
movements in the secluded Jura village of
La Côte-aux-Fées in 1874. For decades, those
movements were delivered to other watch brands.
The *manufacture* itself, strangely enough, remained
in the background. Until the middle of its fifth decade in business, Piaget provided
movements to almost every renowned Swiss watchmaker. It wasn't until the 1940s that
the Piaget family began to offer complete watches under their own name.

Even today, Piaget, which long ago moved the business side of things to Geneva, still
makes its watch movements at its main facility high in the Jura mountains. Among its
specialties in the 1960s were the ultra-thin calibers 9P and 12P (automatic), which were
2 mm and 2.3 mm thin, respectively. The production of movements for other brands
has been largely discontinued. Only associated brands within the Richemont Group are
occasionally supplied with special movements.

Because the brand came a little late in the day to the manufacturing of its own timepieces,
the watch *manufacture* often got less attention than it deserved. That might be changing,
albeit slowly. The brand's strategy has been to focus stubbornly on outstandingly thin
movements, which lend its watches the kind of understated elegance that is the hallmark
of the new post-recession times. Even high-tech watch fans have been impressed by the
minute repeater on the new Emperador. The Limelight's case, with the playfully dynamic
single lug on each side, testifies to the creative acumen at Piaget. Besides, in the natural
fashion cycle, the sixties are due for a revival.

Emperador Coussin
Minute Repetition XL

Reference number: G0A38019
Movement: automatic, Piaget Caliber 1290P; 34.9 x
34.9 mm, height 4.8 mm; 44 jewels; 21,600 vph;
partially skeletonized, platinum microrotor; 40-hour
power reserve; Geneva Seal
Functions: hours, minutes; minute repeater
Case: rose gold, ø 48 mm, height 9.4 mm; sapphire
crystal, transparent case back; water-resistant to
3 atm
Band: reptile skin, folding clasp
Remarks: world's thinnest automatic movement
currently
Price: on request

Emperador Coussin XL
Tourbillon

Reference number: G0A36040
Movement: automatic, Piaget Caliber 1270P;
ø 34.9 mm, height 5.5 mm; 35 jewels; 21,600
vph; flying 1-minute tourbillon; dial-side white gold
microrotor; 40-hour power reserve; Geneva Seal
Functions: hours and minutes (off-center),
subsidiary seconds (on tourbillon cage); power
reserve indicator on case back
Case: white gold, ø 46.5 mm, height 10.4 mm;
sapphire crystal; water-resistant to 3 atm
Band: reptile skin, folding clasp
Price: on request
Variations: rose gold

Emperador Coussin

Reference number: G0A36016
Movement: automatic, Piaget Caliber 850P;
ø 26.8 mm, height 4 mm; 30 jewels; 21,600 vph;
85-hour power reserve; Geneva Seal
Functions: hours, minutes, subsidiary seconds;
second time zone (additional 12-hour display); date
Case: white gold, ø 42 mm, height 8.9 mm;
sapphire crystal; transparent case back; water-
resistant to 3 atm
Band: reptile skin, folding clasp
Price: $29,000
Variations: pink gold ($28,000); white gold set with
diamonds ($60,000); pink gold set with diamonds
($59,000)

Gouverneur Moonphase Tourbillon

Reference number: G0A37114
Movement: manually wound, Piaget Caliber 642P; 22.4 x 28.6 mm, height 4 mm; 21,600 vph; flying 1-minute tourbillon; 40-hour power reserve; Geneva Seal
Functions: hours, minutes, small seconds (on tourbillon cage); moon phase
Case: rose gold, ø 43 mm, height 9.2 mm; sapphire crystal; transparent case back; water-resistant to 3 atm
Band: reptile skin, folding clasp
Price: on request
Variations: white gold with diamonds

Gouverneur Two Counters Chronograph

Reference number: G0A37112
Movement: automatic, Piaget Caliber 882P; ø 27 mm, height 5.6 mm; 28,800 vph; 50-hour power reserve; Geneva Seal
Functions: hours, minutes; flyback chronograph; date; second time zone
Case: rose gold, ø 43 mm, height 10.4 mm; sapphire crystal; transparent case back; water-resistant to 3 atm
Band: reptile skin, folding clasp
Price: $37,000
Variations: white gold with diamonds

Gouverneur

Reference number: G0A37110
Movement: automatic, Piaget Caliber 800P; ø 26.8 mm, height 4 mm; 25 jewels; 21,600 vph; twin spring barrels; 85-hour power reserve; Geneva Seal
Functions: hours, minutes, sweep seconds; date
Case: rose gold, ø 43 mm, height 9 mm; sapphire crystal; transparent case back; water-resistant to 3 atm
Band: reptile skin, buckle
Price: $26,000
Variations: white gold with diamonds

Polo Fortyfive Chronograph

Reference number: G0A37004
Movement: automatic, Piaget Caliber 880P; ø 27 mm, height 5.6 mm; 35 jewels; 28,800 vph; 50-hour power reserve; Geneva Seal
Functions: hours, minutes, subsidiary seconds; additional 24-hour display (second time zone); flyback chronograph; date
Case: stainless steel and titanium, with black DLC coating; ø 45 mm, height 12.3 mm; sapphire crystal, transparent case back; water-resistant to 10 atm
Band: rubber with black titanium elements, double folding clasp
Price: $21,000

Polo Fortyfive Chronograph

Reference number: G0A34002
Movement: automatic, Piaget Caliber 880P; ø 27 mm, height 5.6 mm; 35 jewels; 28,800 vph; 50-hour power reserve; Geneva Seal
Functions: hours, minutes, subsidiary seconds; additional 24-hour display (second time zone); flyback chronograph; date
Case: titanium and stainless steel, ø 45 mm, height 12.3 mm; sapphire crystal, transparent case back; water-resistant to 10 atm
Band: rubber and stainless steel, folding clasp
Price: $18,900

Polo Ladies Strap

Reference number: G0A38013
Movement: quartz, Piaget Caliber 690P; ø 18.4 mm, height 2.25 mm
Case: pink gold, ø 38 mm, height 9.7 mm; bezel set with 50 diamonds; sapphire crystal; water-resistant to 3 atm
Band: reptile skin, buckle
Remarks: dial set with 386 diamonds
Price: $68,000

Altiplano Date

Reference number: GOA38131
Movement: automatic, Piaget Caliber 1205P;
ø 29.9 mm, height 3 mm; 27 jewels; 21,600 vph;
rose gold microrotor, côtes de Genève; 44-hour
power reserve
Functions: hours, minutes, subsidiary seconds;
date
Case: rose gold, ø 40 mm, height 6.36 mm;
sapphire crystal, transparent case back
Band: reptile skin, buckle
Price: $25,000
Variations: white gold ($26,000)

Altiplano Skeleton

Reference number: GOA38125
Movement: automatic, Piaget Caliber 1200D;
ø 31.9 mm, height 2.4 mm; 26 jewels; 21,600 vph;
blackened platinum microrotor; fully skeletonized,
set with 259 diamonds and 11 black sapphire
cabochons; 44-hour power reserve; Geneva Seal
Functions: hours, minutes
Case: white gold/platinum, case set with 346
brilliants; ø 40 mm, height 6.1 mm; bezel set with
40 emeralds; sapphire crystal, transparent case
back; water-resistant to 3 atm
Band: reptile skin, double folding clasp set with 24
diamonds
Price: on request

Altiplano Skeleton

Reference number: GOA37132
Movement: automatic, Piaget Caliber 1200S;
ø 31.9 mm, height 2.4 mm; 26 jewels; 21,600 vph;
black platinum microrotor; fully skeletonized;
44-hour power reserve; Geneva Seal
Functions: hours, minutes
Case: white gold/platinum, ø 38 mm, height
5.34 mm; sapphire crystal; transparent case back;
water-resistant to 3 atm
Band: reptile skin, buckle
Price: $60,000

Altiplano

Reference number: GOA37126
Movement: automatic, Piaget Caliber 1208P;
ø 29.9 mm, height 2.35 mm; 27 jewels; 21,600 vph;
44-hour power reserve; Geneva Seal
Functions: hours, minutes, subsidiary seconds
Case: white gold, ø 43 mm, height 5.25 mm;
sapphire crystal; transparent case back;
water-resistant to 2 atm
Band: reptile skin, buckle
Price: $24,000
Variations: rose gold ($24,000); white or rose gold
set with diamonds

Altiplano

Reference number: GOA33112
Movement: manually wound, Piaget Caliber 838P;
ø 26.8 mm, height 2.5 mm; 19 jewels; 21,600 vph;
60-hour power reserve; Geneva Seal
Functions: hours, minutes, subsidiary seconds
Case: white gold, ø 40 mm, height 6.6 mm;
sapphire crystal, transparent case back; water-
resistant to 3 atm
Band: reptile skin, buckle
Price: $20,000
Variations: rose gold ($19,000); white or rose gold
set with diamonds

Limelight Gala

Reference number: GOA38160
Movement: quartz, Piaget Caliber 690P;
ø 18.4 mm, height 2.25 mm
Functions: hours, minutes
Case: white gold, ø 32 mm, height 7.4 mm; bezel set
with 62 diamonds; sapphire crystal; water-resistant
to 3 atm
Band: satin, folding clasp set with diamonds
Price: $35,000

Caliber 1270P

Automatic; flying 1-minute tourbillon with titanium cage; platinum microrotor visible through dial; single spring barrel; 44-hour power reserve; Geneva Seal
Functions: hours, minutes, subsidiary seconds (on tourbillon cage at "1")
Measurements: 34.9 x 34.9 mm
Height: 5.5 mm
Jewels: 35
Balance: glucydur
Frequency: 21,600 vph

Caliber 1208P

Automatic; 42-hour power reserve
Functions: hours, minutes, subsidiary seconds
Diameter: 29.9 mm
Height: 2.35 mm
Jewels: 27
Balance: glucydur
Frequency: 21,600 vph
Balance spring: flat hairspring
Shock protection: Incabloc
Remarks: world's thinnest automatic movement currently produced

Caliber 838P

Manually wound; stop-seconds; Geneva Seal; 62-hour power reserve
Functions: hours, minutes, subsidiary seconds
Diameter: 26.8 mm
Height: 2.7 mm
Jewels: 19
Balance: glucydur with weighted screws
Frequency: 21,600 vph
Balance spring: flat hairspring with fine adjustment over regulator
Shock protection: Incabloc

Caliber 882P

Automatic; stop-seconds, full gold rotor; single spring barrel, 50-hour power reserve; Geneva Seal
Functions: hours, minutes, subsidiary seconds; second time zone (additional 24-hour display); flyback chronograph; date
Diameter: 27 mm
Height: 5.6 mm
Jewels: 33
Balance: glucydur with weighted screws
Frequency: 21,600 vph
Balance spring: flat hairspring with fine adjustment regulator
Shock protection: Kif

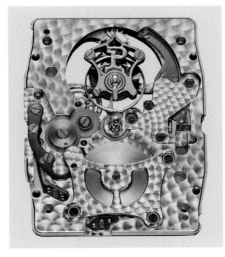

Caliber 642P

Manually wound; flying 1-minute tourbillon with titanium cage; platinum microrotor visible on dial; single spring barrel; 40-hour power reserve; Geneva Seal
Functions: hours, minutes, subsidiary seconds (on tourbillon cage); moon phase
Measurements: 22.4 x 28.6 mm
Height: 4 mm
Jewels: 23
Balance: glucydur
Frequency: 21,600 vph

Caliber 1200S

Automatic; platinum microrotor; single spring barrel; 44-hour power reserve; Geneva Seal
Functions: hours, minutes
Diameter: 31.9 mm
Height: 2.4 mm
Jewels: 26
Balance: glucydur
Frequency: 21,600 vph
Balance spring: flat hairspring
Remarks: fully skeletonized movement

Porsche Design Timepieces

c/o Eterna SA
Schützengasse 46
CH-2540 Grenchen
Switzerland

Tel.:
01141-32-654-7211

Fax:
01141-32-654-7212

E-Mail:
info@porsche-design.com

Website:
www.porsche-design.com

Founded:
1972

Number of employees:
not specified

Annual production:
not specified

U.S. distributor:
Chartpak, Inc.
19683 Boca Greens Drive
Boca Raton, FL 33498
561-470-6925
www.porsche-design.com

Most important collections:
Dashboard, Indicator, Worldtimer, Heritage

Porsche Design

Since 1976, the Schaffhausen-based brand IWC had been producing watches under the name Porsche Design through a license agreement with the design firm F.A. Porsche. But when the Porsche family purchased the watch brand Eterna in 1995, a new era began—for both Eterna and Porsche Design. When the IWC license expired in 1998, Eterna almost seamlessly took over manufacturing responsibilities for the designer brand. Thus the two watch brands have been produced in the Grenchen facility ever since.

Although Porsche Design benefits from Eterna's manufacturing expertise, the traditional Swiss watch brand also receives very welcome support when developing its own new models from the design office founded by Professor Ferdinand Alexander Porsche in 1972—the fountainhead of numerous objects used daily beyond just watches. The Professor—a title bestowed by the Austrian government—who died in April 2012, created a string of classic objects at his "Studio," but sports car fans will always remember him for the Porsche 911. The brand is proud not only of its unusual designs, but also of its use of light metals: It was the first to apply titanium in watch cases, for instance. And it also constructed a watch with an integrated compass.

Eterna and Porsche Design were sold to the Chinese company International Volant Ltd., a 100-percent subsidiary of China Haidian. This concern operates two of the largest watch companies in the People's Republic as well as a chain of stores. It also has import rights for various Japanese watch brands. In 2013, it purchased Corum, whose CEO, Antonio Calce, is also slated to lead Eterna and, presumably, Porsche Design.

P'6752 World Traveller

Reference number: 6752.10.44.1300
Movement: automatic, ETA Caliber 3945A; ø 30 mm, height 5.9 mm; 28 jewels; 28,800 vph; 2 spring barrels on ball bearings (Spherodrive); 68-hour power reserve
Functions: hours, minutes, sweep seconds; additional 24-hour display (second time zone); date
Case: titanium, ø 42 mm, height 14.8 mm; sapphire crystal, water-resistant to 5 atm
Band: rubber, folding clasp
Price: $7,290

6'510 Heritage Black Chronograph

Reference number: 6510.43.41.0272
Movement: automatic, ETA Caliber 7750; ø 30 mm, height 7.9 mm; 25 jewels; 28,800 vph; personalized rotor; 48-hour power reserve
Functions: hours, minutes, subsidiary seconds; chronograph; date, weekday
Case: stainless steel with black PVD coating, ø 44 mm, height 14.5 mm; sapphire crystal; screw-in crown
Band: stainless steel with black PVD coating, folding clasp
Price: $7,130

P'6520 Compass

Reference number: 6520.13.41.0270
Movement: automatic, Sellita Caliber SW 300; ø 25.6 mm, height 3.6 mm; 25 jewels; 28,800 vph
Functions: hours, minutes, sweep seconds; date
Case: titanium, with black PVD coating, ø 42 mm, height 14.6 mm; sapphire crystal; water-resistant to 5 atm
Band: titanium with black PVD coating, folding clasp
Remarks: compass in lower section, case back with mirror
Price: $7,440, limited to 911 pieces

P'6530 Titanium Chronograph

Reference number: 6530.11.41.1219
Movement: automatic, ETA caliber 7750; ø 30 mm, height 7.9 mm; 25 jewels; 28,800 vph; personalized rotor, COSC certified chronograph; 43-hour power reserve
Functions: hours, minutes, subsidiary seconds; chronograph; date, weekday
Case: titanium, integrated pushers, ø 44 mm, height 14.3 mm; sapphire crystal; water-resistant to 6 atm
Band: titanium, folding clasp
Price: $6,240, limited to 911 pieces

P'6780 Diver

Reference number: 6780.45.43.1218
Movement: automatic, ETA Caliber 2892-A2; ø 25.6 mm, height 3.6 mm; 21 jewels; 28,800 vph
Functions: hours, minutes, sweep seconds; date
Case: stainless steel movement container in titanium frame, opened activating lateral buttons, ø 46.8 mm, height 17.05 mm; inner 60-minute bezel activated by crown, sapphire crystal; waterproof to 100 atm
Band: rubber, folding clasp with diving extension
Price: $11,130
Variations: stainless steel and titanium with PVD coating ($12,250)

P'6910 Indicator

Reference number: 6910.12.41.1149
Movement: automatic, Eterna Caliber 6036; ø 36.4 mm, height 11.80 mm; 101 jewels; 28,800 vph; digital chronograph display; 4 spring barrels
Functions: hours, minutes, subsidiary seconds, chronograph; power reserve display with 2 concentric circles
Case: titanium with black PVD coating, ø 49 mm, height 19.9 mm; bezel affixed with 4 special screws; sapphire crystal; water-resistant to 5 atm
Band: rubber, buckle
Price: $187,500
Variations: titanium without PVD coating ($187,500)

P'6620 Dashboard

Reference number: 6620.11.46.1268
Movement: automatic, ETA caliber 7753; ø 30 mm, height 7.9 mm; 27 jewels; 28,800 vph; personalized rotor
Functions: hours, minutes, subsidiary seconds; chronograph; date
Case: titanium, ø 44 mm, height 14.5 mm; sapphire crystal; transparent case back; screw-in crown; water-resistant to 10 atm
Band: titanium, with folding clasp
Price: $6,190
Variations: with black PVD coating ($6,810)

P'6360 Flat Six Automatic Chronograph

Reference number: 6360.43.04.0275
Movement: automatic, ETA Caliber 7750; ø 30 mm, height 7.9 mm; 25 jewels; 28,800 vph; personalized rotor, 43-hour power reserve
Functions: hours, minutes, subsidiary seconds; chronograph; date and weekday
Case: stainless steel with black PVD coating, ø 44 mm, height 15 mm; sapphire crystal; screw-in crown; transparent case back; water-resistant to 12 atm
Band: PVD-coated stainless steel, folding clasp
Price: $6,180
Variations: various dials and bands between ($5,110 and $7,790)

P'6351 Flat Six Lady

Reference number: 6351.47.64.1256
Movement: automatic, Sellita Caliber SW200; ø 25.6 mm, height 4.6 mm; 26 jewels; 28,800 vph; 38-hour power reserve
Functions: hours, minutes, sweep seconds; date
Case: stainless steel, ø 40 mm, height 11.25 mm; rose gold bezel; sapphire crystal, transparent case back; screw-in crown; with rose plating
Band: rubber, buckle
Price: $9,990

Rado Uhren AG
Bielstrasse 45
CH-2543 Lengnau
Switzerland

Tel.:
01141-32-655-6111

Fax:
01141-32-655-6112

E-Mail:
info@rado.com

Website:
www.rado.com

Founded:
1957

Number of employees:
approx. 470

Annual production:
not specified

U.S. distributor:
Rado
The Swatch Group (U.S.), Inc.
1200 Harbor Boulevard
Weehawken, NJ 07086
201-271-1400

Most important collections/price range:
Centrix / from approx. $900; Diamaster / from
approx. $1,350; D-Star / from approx. $1,700;
Integral / from approx. $2,000; Sintra / from
approx. $3,000; True / from approx. $1,400;
Hyperchrome from approx: $1,600

Rado

Rado is a relatively young brand, especially for a Swiss one. The company, which grew out of the Schlup clockwork factory, launched its first watches in 1957, but it achieved international fame only five years later, in 1962, when it surprised the world with a revolutionary invention. Rado's oval DiaStar was the first truly scratch-resistant watch ever, sporting a case made of the impervious alloy hardmetal. In 1985, its parent company, the Swatch Group, decided to put Rado's know-how and extensive experience in developing materials to good use, and from then on the brand intensified its research activities at its home in Lengnau, Switzerland, and continued to produce only watches with extremely hard cases. A record of sorts was even set in 2004, when they managed to create a 10,000-Vickers material, which is as hard as natural diamonds.

Within the Swatch Group, Rado was the most successful individual brand in the upper price segment for a long time. But at some point, the brand's image became a little blurred, and it began suffering from the almost unbridgeable gap that had suddenly opened up between its jeweled watches and high-tech line. However, the pioneering spirit of the brand's ceramic researchers and engineers has won out. The company already holds more than thirty patents arising from research and production of new case materials. Nowadays, the cases begin as powders, already premixed with binding agents and additives to later achieve the desired color. They are then pressed into molds and fired. The final touch is polishing with diamond powder to make the outside of Rado timepieces even more robust and scratchproof. And the techno inside is reflected in an unabashed techno look outside.

D-Star Automatic Chronograph Rattrapante Limited Edition

Reference number: R15192152
Movement: automatic, ETA Caliber 7770; ø 30 mm, 29 jewels; 28,800 vph; finely decorated; 48-hour power reserve
Functions: hours, minutes, subsidiary seconds; split-seconds chronograph
Case: ceramic, 45.4 x 48.6 mm, height 14.7 mm; sapphire crystal, transparent case back; water-resistant to 10 atm
Band: ceramic, double folding clasp
Remarks: limited to 250 pieces
Price: $6,000

HyperChrome Court Collection

Reference number: R32525179
Movement: automatic, ETA Caliber 2894-2; ø 28.6 mm, height 6.2 mm; 37 jewels; 28,800 vph; finely decorated; 42-hour power reserve
Functions: hours, minutes, subsidiary seconds; chronograph; date
Case: ceramic, 45 x 51 mm, height 13 mm; sapphire crystal, transparent case back; stainless steel crown with rubber insert; water-resistant to 10 atm
Band: rubber, folding clasp
Price: $4,300

Diamaster

Reference number: R14066152
Movement: quartz, ETA Caliber E64.111
Functions: hours, minutes, sweep seconds; date
Case: ceramic, ø 40 mm, height 8.4 mm; sapphire crystal
Band: ceramic, double folding clasp
Price: $2,600

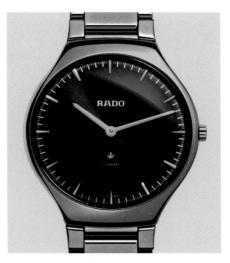

Diamaster Chronograph

Reference number: R14090192
Movement: automatic, ETA Caliber 2894-2;
ø 28.6 mm, height 6.2 mm; 37 jewels; 28,800 vph;
finely decorated; 42-hour power reserve
Functions: hours, minutes, subsidiary seconds;
chronograph; date
Case: ceramic, ø 45 mm, height 12.6 mm; sapphire
crystal, transparent case back; water-resistant to
10 atm
Band: ceramic, double folding clasp
Price: $4,700

True Thinline

Reference number: R27972162
Movement: automatic, ETA Caliber 2824-2;
ø 25.6 mm, height 4.6 mm; 25 jewels; 28,800 vph;
38-hour power reserve
Functions: hours, minutes, sweep seconds
Case: ceramic, ø 40 mm, height 7.8 mm; sapphire
crystal
Band: ceramic, folding clasp
Price: $2,500

D-Star Automatic Chronograph XXL

Reference number: R15198152
Movement: automatic, Rado Caliber RC1 (base
ETA A05.H31); ø 30 mm, 25 jewels; 28,800 vph;
60-hour power reserve
Functions: hours, minutes, subsidiary seconds;
chronograph; date
Case: ceramic, 45.4 x 48.6 mm, height 14.7 mm;
sapphire crystal, transparent case back; water-
resistant to 10 atm
Band: Plasma ceramic, folding clasp
Price: $4,000

Centrix

Reference number: R30953152
Movement: automatic, ETA Caliber 2824-2;
ø 25.6 mm, height 4.6 mm; 25 jewels; 28,800 vph;
38-hour power reserve
Functions: hours, minutes, sweep seconds; date
Case: stainless steel with rose gold-colored PVD
coating, ø 38 mm, height 9.7 mm; sapphire crystal,
transparent case back; water-resistant to 3 atm
Band: ceramic with stainless steel elements, folding
clasp
Price: $1,600

HyperChrome UTC

Reference number: R32165152
Movement: automatic, ETA Caliber 2893-2;
ø 25.6 mm, height 4.1 mm; 21 jewels; 28,800 vph;
42-hour power reserve
Functions: hours, minutes, sweep seconds;
additional 24-hour display (second time zone); date
Case: ceramic, 42 x 48.4 mm, height 10.8 mm;
sapphire crystal, transparent case back; water-
resistant to 10 atm
Band: ceramic, folding clasp
Price: $3,450

HyperChrome Glam Slam

Reference number: R32483012
Movement: automatic, ETA Caliber 2681;
ø 25.6 mm, height 4.6 mm; 25 jewels; 28,800 vph;
38-hour power reserve; finely decorated
Functions: hours, minutes, sweep seconds; date
Case: ceramic, ø 36 mm, height 10.4 mm; bezel
and case sides set with diamonds; sapphire crystal,
transparent case back; water-resistant to 5 atm
Band: ceramic, folding clasp
Price: $9,900

RGM Watch Company
801 W. Main Street
Mount Joy, PA 17552

Tel.:
717-653-9799

Fax:
717-653-9770

E-Mail:
RGMdesigns@aol.com

Website:
www.rgmwatches.com

Founded:
1992

Number of employees:
12

Annual production:
200-300 watches

Distribution:
RGM deals directly with customers.

Most important collections/price range:
Pennsylvania Series (completely made in the U.S.)
/ $2,500 to $125,000 range

RGM

If there is any part of the United States that can somehow be considered its "watch valley," it may be the state of Pennsylvania. And one of the big players there is no doubt Roland Murphy, founder of RGM. Murphy, born in Maryland, went through the watchmaker's drill, studying at the Bowman Technical School, then in Switzerland, and finally working with Swatch before launching his own business in 1992.

His first series, Signature, paid homage to local horological genius. It was powered by vintage pocket watch movements developed by Hamilton, a company that also hails from PA. His second big project was the Caliber 801, the first "high-grade mechanical movement made in series in America since Hamilton stopped production of the 992 B in 1969," Murphy grins. The next goal was to manufacture an all-American-made watch, which turned out to be the Pennsylvania Tourbillon.

And so, model by model, Murphy continues to expand his "Made in U.S.A." portfolio. In 2012, the twentieth anniversary of the brand, RGM went retro with the 801Aircraft, using an in-house movement in a watch recalling Elgin and Hamilton aircraft clocks. And the current pinnacle is the brand-new Caliber "20," which revives an old invention once in favor for railroad watches like the Illinois Bunn Special and the Hamilton 950. The motor barrel is a complex but robust system in which the watch is wound by the barrel and the barrel arbor then drives the gear train. Less friction and wear and a slimmer chance of damage to the watch if the mainspring breaks are the two main advantages. And for the real engineering enthusiasts, it is a movement with a unique look.

Caliber 20

Reference number: Caliber 20
Movement: manual winding, RGM motor barrel movement; 19 jewels; 18,000 vph; perlage and côtes de Genève
Functions: hours, minutes, subsidiary seconds on disk; moon phase
Case: stainless steel, 42 x 38.5 mm, height 9.7 mm; hands of blued steel; sapphire crystal; transparent case back
Band: reptile skin, buckle
Price: $27,500
Variations: rose gold ($42,500)

Pennsylvania Tourbillon

Reference number: MM2
Movement: manual winding, American-made; 19 jewels; 18,000 vph; German silver and rose gold finish with perlage and côtes de Genève
Functions: hours, minutes; 1-minute tourbillon
Case: stainless steel, ø 43.5 mm, height 13.5 mm; blued-steel minute and hour hands; guilloché dial; sapphire crystal; transparent case back
Band: reptile skin, buckle
Price: $95,000
Variations: rose gold ($95,000); platinum ($125,000)

Chronograph

Reference number: 400
Movement: automatic, RGM-modified Valgranges; 25 jewels; 28,800 vph; rhodium markers and hands with Superluminova
Functions: hours, minutes; date; chronograph; 30-minute and 12-hour counters
Case: brushed and polished stainless steel, ø 42 mm, height 15.3 mm
Band: reptile skin, buckle
Price: $3,500
Variations: various dials and hands; with ostrich or carbon fiber band

Professional Diver

Reference number: 300
Movement: automatic, modified ETA Caliber 2892;
ø 25.6 mm, height 3.6 mm; 21 jewels; 28,800 vph;
bridges and plates with perlage and côtes de
Genève
Functions: hours, minutes, sweep seconds; date
Case: brushed stainless steel, ø 43.5 mm,
height 17 mm; sapphire crystal (5 mm thick);
unidirectional bezel with 60-minute divisions (240
clicks); screwed-down case back; screwed-in crown;
water-resistant to more than 70 atm
Band: rubber strap, buckle
Price: $3,700, limited to 50 pieces
Variations: with stainless steel bracelet ($4,450)

Pennsylvania Series 801

Reference number: PS 801 ES
Movement: manually wound, RGM Caliber 801;
ø 37 mm; 19 jewels; lever escapement; screw
balance; U.S. components: bridges, main plate,
settings, 7-tooth winding click; circular côtes de
Genève, silver guilloché; partially skeletonized dial
Functions: hours, minutes, subsidiary seconds
Case: stainless steel, ø 43.3 mm, height 12.3 mm;
sapphire crystal; sapphire crystal transparent case
back; water-resistant to 5 atm
Band: reptile or ostrich skin, folding clasp
Price: $9,700
Variations: rose gold ($22,500); white gold
($24,500)

Pennsylvania Series

Reference number: PS 801 E
Movement: manually wound, RGM Caliber 801;
ø 37 mm; 19 jewels; lever escapement; screw
balance; U.S. components: bridges, main plate,
settings, 7-tooth winding click; circular côtes de
Genève, silver guilloché
Functions: hours, minutes, subsidiary seconds
Case: stainless steel, ø 43.3 mm, height 12.3 mm;
sapphire crystal; transparent case back; water-
resistant to 5 atm
Band: reptile or ostrich skin, folding clasp
Price: $9,700
Variations: rose gold ($22,500); white gold
($24,500)

Pilot Professional

Reference number: 151 PW
Movement: automatic, RGM/ETA Caliber 2892-A2;
ø 25.6 mm; 21 jewels; 28,800 vph; rhodium finish
with perlage and côtes de Genève
Functions: hours, minutes, sweep seconds; date;
optional no date
Case: brushed or polished stainless steel,
ø 38.5 mm, height 9.9 mm; sapphire crystal;
transparent case back
Band: rubber or reptile skin, buckle
Remarks: date at 3 o'clock, 6 o'clock, or no date
Price: $2,750
Variations: brushed stainless steel ($2,750);
titanium ($3,900); stainless steel bracelet

801 A

Reference number: 254
Movement: RGM-made 801; ø 37 mm; 19 jewels;
18,000 vph; bridges and plates finished with
perlage and côtes de Genève
Functions: hours, minutes, subsidiary seconds
Case: brushed stainless steel, ø 42 mm, height
10.5 mm; antireflective sapphire crystal;
transparent case back
Band: leather, buckle
Price: $6,900
Variations: 12-hour, 24-hour, 60-minute dials
available; with stainless steel bracelet ($7,650)

Vintage

Reference number: 250
Movement: automatic, modified ETA Valgranges
Caliber A07.111; ø 36.6 mm, height 7.9 mm;
25 jewels; 28,800 vph; bridges and plates finished
with perlage and côtes de Genève
Functions: hours, minutes, sweep seconds; date
Case: stainless steel, ø 42 mm, height
15 mm; sapphire crystal; exhibition case back;
water-resistant to 5 atm; brushed silver dial
Band: reptile skin, buckle
Price: $3,500
Variations: with folding clasp; special request
guilloché patterns for custom dials available

Richard Mille

Richard Mille Watches
c/o Horométrie SA
11, rue du Jura
CH-2345 Les Breuleux
Switzerland

Tel.:
01141-32-959-4353

Fax:
01141-32-959-4354

E-Mail:
info@richardmille.ch

Website:
www.richardmille.com

Founded:
2000

Number of employees:
not specified

Annual production:
over 2,600 watches

U.S. distributor:
Richard Mille Americas
132 South Rodeo Drive, 4th Floor
Beverly Hills, CA 90212
310-205-5555

Spain's hottest tennis star, Rafael Nadal, has been confident enough to wear a fully functional mechanical timepiece weighing less than 20 grams including the strap. That equals three quarters and a dime, but the watch, utilizing special materials, retails for over half a million dollars. It's a Richard Mille, of course. Now Jamaican sprinter Yohan Blake gets to put on a super-light, ultra-high-tech timepiece, one that will make no difference to his 9.69-second record sprint, in spite of featuring a tourbillon.

Mille never stops delivering the wow to the watch world with what he calls his "race cars for the wrist." His timepieces are usually built of exotic high-tech materials borrowed from automobile racing or even space travel. Mille is not an engineer by profession, but rather a marketing expert who earned his first paychecks in the watch division of the French defense, automobile, and aerospace concern Matra in the early 1980s. This was a time of fundamental changes in technology, and the European watch industry was being confronted with gigantic challenges.

"I have no historical relationship with watchmaking whatsoever," says Mille, "and so I have no obligations either. The mechanics of my watches are geared towards technical feasibility." In the 1990s, Mille had to go to the expert workshop of Audemars Piguet Renaud & Papi (APRP) in Le Locle to find a group of watchmakers and engineers who would take on the Mille challenge. Audemars Piguet even succumbed to the temptation of testing those scandalous innovations—materials, technologies, functions—in a Richard Mille watch before daring to use them in its own collections (Tradition d'Excellence). Since 2007, Audemars Piguet has also become a shareholder in Richard Mille, and so the three firms are now closely bound. The assembly of the watches is done in the Franches-Montagnes region in the Jura, where Richard Mille opened the firm Horométrie.

RM036 G-Force

Reference number: RM 036
Movement: manually wound, Richard Mille Caliber RM 036; 32.2 x 32.9 mm, height 4.97 mm; 26 jewels; 21,600 vph; 1-minute tourbillon, function switch for winding, hand setting, rapid setting; 70-hour power reserve
Functions: hours, minutes, subsidiary seconds; g-force meter
Case: titanium, 42.7 x 50 mm, height 16.15 mm; sapphire crystal, transparent case back; water-resistant to 5 atm
Band: rubber, folding clasp
Remarks: mechanical g-force meter to 8 g
Price: $490,000, limited to 15 pieces

RM 27-01 Nadal

Reference number: RM 27-01
Movement: manually wound, Richard Mille Caliber 27-0121; 27.2 x 21.72 mm, height mm, weight 3.5 g; 19 jewels; 21,600 vph; 1-minute tourbillon; suspended in case on cable with pulleys, tensioners at 3 and 9 o'clock; 45-hour power reserve
Functions: hours, minutes
Case: carbon fiber, 45.98 x 38.9 mm, height 10.05 mm; sapphire crystal; water-resistant to 3 atm
Band: textile, buckle
Remarks: monoblock case, weight including movement under 20 grams
Price: $690,000, limited to 50 pieces

Tourbillon RM 56-01 Sapphire

Reference number: RM 56-01
Movement: manually wound, Caliber RM 56-01; 30.9 x 33.2 mm, height 5.36 mm; 28 jewels; 21,600 vph; 1-minute tourbillon; function selector; skeletonized in titanium and sapphire crystal; double spring barrel, 70-hour power reserve
Functions: hours, minutes, subsidiary seconds; power reserve and spring barrel torque display
Case: sapphire crystal; 42.7 x 50.5 mm, height 19.25 mm; sapphire crystal, transparent case back; water-resistant to 3 atm
Band: "Aerospace nano," transparent, buckle
Price: $1,850,000, limited to 5 pieces

Tourbillon Worldtimer Jean Todt

Reference number: RM 58-01
Movement: automatic, Richard Mille Caliber RM58-01; ø 39.15 mm; height 8.54 mm; 41 jewels; 21,600 vph; titanium mainplate; 1-minute tourbillon; 2 spring barrels; 240-hour power reserve
Functions: hours, minutes; world-time display (second time zone); power reserve indicator
Case: titanium, pink gold, ø 50 mm, height 15.35 mm; unidirectional bezel to set second time zone (indicated by reference city); sapphire crystal, transparent case back; water-resistant to 3 atm
Band: rubber, folding clasp
Price: $620,000, limited to 35 pieces

Tourbillon Yohan Blake

Reference number: RM 59-01
Movement: manually wound, Richard Mille Caliber RM59-01; 28.7 x 30.5 mm, height 5.2 mm; 19 jewels; 21,600 vph; 1-minute tourbillon; bridges of green eloxized anticorodal aluminum; 48-hour power reserve
Functions: hours, minutes
Case: composite with carbon fibers; 42.7 x 50.24 mm, height 15.84 mm; sapphire crystal, transparent case back; water-resistant to 3 atm
Band: rubber, folding clasp
Remarks: homage to Jamaican sprinter Yohan Blake
Price: $620,000, limited to 50 pieces

RM 031 High Performance

Reference number: RM 031
Movement: manually wound, Caliber RM 031; ø 36 mm, height 6.35 mm; 26 jewels; 36,000 vph; AP chronometer balance; mechanism bridge of arcap, double spring barrel, selection button for winding (W= winding), null (N), hand setting (H = hands); 50-hour power reserve
Functions: hours, minutes, subsidiary seconds
Case: platinum, ø 50 mm, height 13.9 mm; sapphire crystal, transparent case back
Band: rubber, folding clasp
Price: $990,000, limited to 10 pieces

Tourbillon Flyback Chronograph "Aviation"

Reference number: RM 039
Movement: manually wound, Caliber RM 039; ø 38.95 mm, height 7.95 mm; 58 jewels; 21,600 vph; 1-minute tourbillon, selection button for winding (W= winding), null (N), hands (H), fast adjustment (S = speed), 70-hour power reserve
Functions: hours, minutes; power reserve & function display; flyback chronograph; weekday, date
Case: titanium, ø 50 mm, height 19.4 mm; bidirectional bezel with 60-minute divisions/ conversion tables; sapphire crystal, transparent case back
Band: rubber, folding clasp
Price: on request

RM 055 Bubba Watson

Reference number: RM 037
Movement: manually wound, Caliber RMUL230; 25 x 28.45 mm, height 3.15 mm; 24 jewels; 28,800 vph; skeletonized titanium; weight 4.3 grams; 2 spring barrels; 55-hour power reserve
Functions: hours, minutes, sweep seconds
Case: titanium with rubber layer; 42.7 x 49.9 mm, height 13 mm; ATZ (aluminum oxide) bezel; sapphire crystal, transparent case back; water-resistant to 3 atm
Band: rubber, folding clasp
Price: $105,000

RM 037 Automatic

Reference number: RM 037
Movement: automatic, Caliber CRMA1; 22.9 x 28 mm, height 4.82 mm; 25 jewels; 28,800 vph; function selector; skeletonized; winding rotor with variable geometry; 50-hour power reserve
Functions: hours, minutes; large date
Case: titanium, 34.4 x 52.2 mm, height 12.5 mm; sapphire crystal; transparent case back
Band: rubber, folding clasp
Price: $80,000
Variations: pink gold ($95,000); white gold ($100,000)

Manufacture Roger Dubuis

2, rue André-De-Garrini - CP 149
CH-1217 Meyrin 2 (Geneva)
Switzerland

Tel.:
01141-22-783-2828

Fax:
01141-22-783-2882

E-Mail:
info@rogerdubuis.com

Website:
www.rogerdubuis.com

Founded:
1995

Number of employees:
not specified

Annual production:
over 5,000 watches (estimated)

U.S. distributor:
Roger Dubuis N.A.
645 Fifth Avenue
New York, NY 10022
888-RDUBUIS
info@rogerdubuis.com

Most important collections:
Excalibur, La Monégasque, Pulsion, Velvet

Roger Dubuis

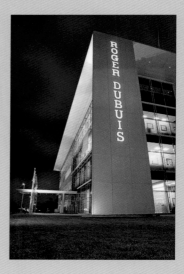

Roger Dubuis, a *manufacture* fully committed to luxury and *"très haute horlogerie,"* was taken over by the Richemont Group in the late fall of 2007. The centerpiece of the deal was without a doubt the company's state-of-the-art workshops, where the finest movement components are made—parts that, because of their quality and geographical origins, bear the coveted Seal of Geneva. These credentials are interesting to other brands in the Richemont Group as well, especially to Cartier, which gets its new skeletonized movements from the Roger Dubuis *manufacture*.

This Geneva-based company was founded in 1995 as SOGEM SA (Société Genevoise des Montres) by name-giver Roger Dubuis and financier Carlos Dias. These two exceptional men created a complete collection of unusual watches in no time flat—timepieces with unheard-of dimensions and incomparable complications. The meteoric development of this *manufacture* and the incredible frequency of its new introductions—even technical ones—continue to astound the traditional, rather conservative watch industry. Today, Roger Dubuis develops all of its own movements, currently numbering more than thirty different mechanical calibers. In addition, it produces just about all of its individual components in-house, from base plates to escapements and balance springs. With this heavy-duty technological know-how in its quiver, the brand has been able to build some remarkable movements, like the massive RD101, with four balance springs and all manner of differentials and gear works to drive the Excalibur Quatuor, the equivalent in horology to a monster truck.

Excalibur Quatuor

Reference number: RDDBEX0367
Movement: manually wound, Roger Dubuis Caliber RD101; ø 37.9 mm; height 10.6 mm; 113 jewels; 28,800 vph; 4 coupled escapement systems each with 4-Hz frequency; power transmission/synchronization via 3 satellite differentials; 40-hour power reserve; Geneva Seal
Functions: hours, minutes; power reserve indicator
Case: pink gold, ø 48 mm; sapphire crystal, transparent case back; water-resistant to 3 atm
Band: reptile skin, folding clasp
Price: $422,000, limited to 88 pieces

Excalibur Quatuor in Silicon

Reference number: RDDBEX0408
Movement: manually wound, Roger Dubuis Caliber RD101; ø 37.9 mm; height 10.06 mm; 113 jewels; 28,800 vph; 4 coupled escapement systems each with 4-Hz frequency; power transmission/synchronization via 3 satellite differentials; 40-hour power reserve; Geneva Seal
Functions: hours, minutes; power reserve indicator
Case: silicon, ø 48 mm; sapphire crystal, transparent case back; water-resistant to 3 atm
Band: reptile skin, folding clasp
Remarks: first watch case of silicon
Price: on request, limited to 3 pieces

Excalibur Table Ronde

Reference number: RDDBEX0398
Movement: automatic, Roger Dubuis Caliber RD821; ø25.93 mm, height 3.43 mm; 33 jewels; 28,800 vph; 48-hour power reserve; Geneva Seal
Functions: hours, minutes
Case: pink gold, ø 45 mm; sapphire crystal, water-resistant to 5 atm
Band: reptile skin, folding clasp
Remarks: enamel dial with 12 knights sculpted of pink gold
Price: $161,000

Excalibur Double Tourbillon Skeleton Limited Edition

Reference number: RDDBEX0397
Movement: manually wound, Roger Dubuis Caliber RD01SQ; ø 37.8 mm; height 7.67 mm; 28 jewels; 21,600 vph; flying double tourbillon with compensation differential; skeletonized; galvanic blackening, beveling, perlage; 48-hour power reserve; Geneva Seal
Functions: hours, minutes
Case: pink gold, ø 45 mm; ceramic bezel; sapphire crystal, transparent case back; water-resistant to 5 atm
Band: reptile skin, folding clasp
Price: $318,000, limited to 188 pieces

Excalibur Double Tourbillon Skeleton

Reference number: RDDBEX0395
Movement: manually wound, Caliber RD 01SQ; ø 37.8 mm; height 7.67 mm; 28 jewels; 21,600 vph; flying double tourbillon with differential; skeleton design; galvanic blackening, beveling, perlage; 48-hour power reserve; Geneva Seal
Functions: hours, minutes
Case: pink gold with black coating; ø 45 mm, sapphire crystal, transparent case back; water-resistant to 5 atm
Band: reptile skin, folding clasp
Price: $291,000

Excalibur 42 Skeleton Tourbillon

Reference number: RDDBEX0392
Movement: automatic, Roger Dubuis Caliber RD505SQ; ø 33.8 mm, height 5.7 mm; 19 jewels; 21,600 vph; flying 1-minute tourbillon; skeletonized; 60-hour power reserve; Geneva Seal
Functions: hours, minutes
Case: pink gold, ø 42 mm; sapphire crystal, transparent case back; water-resistant to 3 atm
Band: reptile skin, folding clasp
Price: $153,500
Variations: white gold ($164,500)

Excalibur 42 Chronograph

Reference number: RDDBEX0390
Movement: automatic, Roger Dubuis Caliber RD681; ø 30.6 mm, height 6.3 mm; 44 jewels; 28,800 vph; microrotor, column wheel control of chronograph functions, 52-hour power reserve; Geneva Seal
Functions: hours, minutes, subsidiary seconds; chronograph
Case: pink gold, ø 42 mm; sapphire crystal, transparent case back; water-resistant to 3 atm
Band: reptile skin, folding clasp
Price: $43,100
Variations: stainless steel ($31,200)

Excalibur 42 Chronograph

Reference number: RDDBEX0400
Movement: automatic, Roger Dubuis Caliber RD681; ø 30.6 mm, height 6.3 mm; 44 jewels; 28,800 vph; microrotor, column wheel control of chronograph functions, 52-hour power reserve; Geneva Seal
Functions: hours, minutes, subsidiary seconds; chronograph
Case: stainless steel, ø 42 mm; sapphire crystal, transparent case back; water-resistant to 3 atm
Band: stainless steel, folding clasp
Price: $26,700
Variations: pink gold on strap ($30,000)

Excalibur 42 Automatic

Reference number: RDDBEX0386
Movement: automatic, Roger Dubuis Caliber RD640; ø 31.1 mm, height 9.5 mm; 35 jewels; 28,800 vph; microrotor, 52-hour power reserve; Geneva Seal
Functions: hours, minutes, subsidiary seconds; date
Case: pink gold, ø 42 mm; sapphire crystal, transparent case back; water-resistant to 3 atm
Band: pink gold, folding clasp
Price: $54,400
Variations: stainless steel ($20,500)

Excalibur 42 Automatic

Reference number: RDDBEX0354
Movement: automatic, Roger Dubuis Caliber RD620; ø 31.1 mm, height 4.5 mm; 35 jewels; 28,800 vph; microrotor, 52-hour power reserve; Geneva Seal, COSC certified chronometer
Functions: hours, minutes, subsidiary seconds
Case: stainless steel, ø 42 mm; sapphire crystal, transparent case back; water-resistant to 3 atm
Band: reptile skin, folding clasp
Price: $26,700
Variations: with dark dial; red gold ($43,100)

La Monegasque

Reference number: RDDBMG001
Movement: automatic, Caliber RD 821; ø 25.93 mm, height 3.43 mm; 33 jewels; 28,800 vph; COSC certified chronometer; Geneva Seal
Functions: hours, minutes, subsidiary seconds
Case: stainless steel, ø 42 mm; sapphire crystal; water-resistant to 5 atm
Band: reptile skin, folding clasp
Price: $16,000
Variations: gold ($27,400)

La Monegasque Chronograph

Reference number: RDDBMG0004
Movement: automatic, Caliber RD 680; ø 30.6 mm, height 6.3 mm; 42 jewels; 28,800 vph; microrotor, column wheel control of chronograph functions; COSC certified chronometer; Geneva Seal
Functions: hours, minutes, subsidiary seconds; chronograph
Case: pink gold, ø 44 mm; pink gold bezel with inserts of black-coated titanium; sapphire crystal; water-resistant to 5 atm
Band: reptile skin, folding clasp
Price: $40,700
Variations: stainless steel ($26,300)

Excalibur Lady

Reference number: RDDBEX0378
Movement: automatic, Caliber RD 821; ø 25.93 mm, height 3.43 mm; 33 jewels; 28,800 vph; COSC certified chronometer; 48-hour power reserve; Geneva Seal
Functions: hours, minutes, subsidiary seconds
Case: stainless steel, ø 36 mm; bezel set with diamonds; sapphire crystal; bezel set with 48 diamonds; water-resistant to 3 atm
Band: reptile skin, folding clasp
Price: $27,400

Excalibur Lady

Reference number: RDDBEX0380
Movement: automatic, Caliber RD 821; ø 25.93 mm, height 3.43 mm; 33 jewels; 28,800 vph; 48-hour power reserve; Geneva Seal
Functions: hours, minutes, subsidiary seconds
Case: rose gold, ø 36 mm; bezel set with 48 diamonds; sapphire crystal, water-resistant to 3 atm
Band: rose gold, folding clasp
Price: $47,200
Variations: stainless steel ($22,200)

Velvet

Reference number: RDDBVE0007
Movement: automatic, Caliber RD821; ø 25.93 mm, height 3.43 mm; 33 jewels; 28,800 vph; 48-hour power reserve; Geneva Seal
Functions: hours, minutes
Case: white gold, ø 36 mm; bezel set with diamonds; sapphire crystal, water-resistant to 3 atm
Band: satin, folding clasp set with diamonds
Price: $37,300
Variations: pink gold ($37,300)

Caliber RD 01SQ

Manually wound; 2 flying tourbillons with differential; skeletonized movement
Functions: hours, minutes
Diameter: 37.8 mm
Height: 7.67 mm
Jewels: 28
Frequency: 21,600 vph
Remarks: galvanic blackening and beveling of frame parts, perlage, Geneva Seal, 319 components

Caliber RD 101

Manually wound; 4 radially mounted and inclined lever escapements, synchronized with 3 balancing differentials; planetary gears for winding and power reserve; skeletonized movement; double spring barrel, 40-hour power reserve; Geneva Seal
Functions: hours, minutes; power reserve indicator
Diameter: 37.9 mm
Height: 10.6 mm
Jewels: 113
Balance: glucydur (4x)
Frequency: 28,800 vph (4x)
Balance spring: flat hairspring
Remarks: galvanic blackening and beveling of frame parts, perlage, 590 components

Caliber RD 505SQ

Manually wound; flying tourbillon; skeletonized movement; single spring barrel; 60-hour power reserve; Geneva Seal, COSC certified chronometer
Functions: hours, minutes
Diameter: 33.8 mm
Height: 5.7 mm
Jewels: 19
Balance: screw balance
Frequency: 21,600 vph
Remarks: galvanic blackening and beveling of frame parts, perlage, 319 components

Caliber RD 640

Automatic; microrotor; single spring barrel, 52-hour power reserve; Geneva Seal
Functions: hours, minutes, subsidiary seconds; date
Diameter: 31.1 mm
Height: 4.5 mm
Jewels: 35
Balance: glucydur, with a smooth rim
Frequency: 28,800 vph
Balance spring: flat hairspring
Shock protection: Incabloc
Remarks: finely finished with côtes de Genève, 198 components

Caliber RD 681

Automatic; column wheel control of chronograph functions, microrotor; single spring barrel, 52-hour power reserve; Geneva Seal
Functions: hours, minutes, subsidiary seconds; chronograph
Diameter: 30.6 mm
Height: 6.3 mm
Jewels: 44
Balance: glucydur
Frequency: 28,800 vph
Balance spring: flat hairspring
Remarks: finely worked with côtes de Genève, 280 components

Caliber RD 821

Automatic; single barrel spring, 48-hour power reserve; Geneva Seal, COSC certified chronometer
Functions: hours, minutes, subsidiary seconds
Diameter: 25.95 mm
Height: 3.43 mm
Jewels: 33
Frequency: 28,800 vph
Remarks: finely finished with côtes de Genève, 168 components

Rolex

Rolex SA
Rue François-Dussaud 3
CH-1211 Geneva 26
Switzerland

Website:
www.rolex.com

Founded:
1908

Number of employees:
over 2,000 (estimated)

Annual production:
approx. 1,000,000 watches (estimated)

U.S. distributor:
Rolex Watch U.S.A., Inc.
Rolex Building
665 Fifth Avenue
New York, NY 10022-5358
212-758-7700; 212-980-2166 (fax)
www.rolex.com

Essentially, the Rolex formula for success has always been "what you see is what you get"—and plenty of it. For over a century now, the company has made wristwatch history without a need for *grandes complications,* perpetual calendars, tourbillons, or exotic materials. And its output in sheer quantity is phenomenal, at not quite a million watches per year. But make no mistake about it: The quality of these timepieces is legendary. For as long as anyone can remember, this brand has held the top spot in the COSC's statistics, and year after year Rolex delivers just about half of all of the official institute's successfully tested mechanical chronometer movements. The brand has also pioneered several fundamental innovations: Rolex founder Hans Wilsdorf invented the hermetically sealed Oyster case in the 1920s, which he later outfitted with a screwed-in crown and an automatic movement wound by rotor. Shock protection, water resistance, the antimagnetic Parachrom hairspring and automatic winding are some of the virtues that make wearing a Rolex timepiece much more comfortable and reliable. Because Wilsdorf patented his inventions for thirty years, Rolex had a head start on the competition.

Rolex watches and movements were produced for a long time in two different companies at two different sites. Only in 2004 did the Geneva-based Rolex buy and integrate the Rolex movement factory in Biel. Then, in 2008, for its 100th birthday, the company built itself three gigantic new buildings with loads of steel and dark glass in the industrial suburb of Plan-les-Ouates. Curiously, in Geneva, the latest Rolex creation is a modern cable-stayed bridge named for the company founder to replace an older structure over the Arve River. This gift to the city was inaugurated at the end of August 2012.

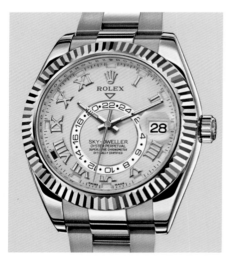

Sky-Dweller

Reference number: 326939
Movement: automatic, Rolex Caliber 9001; ø 33 mm, height 8 mm; 40 jewels; 28,800 vph; Parachrom Breguet spring; glucydur balance with microstella regulating screws; 72-hour power reserve; COSC certified chronometer
Functions: hours, minutes, sweep seconds; second time zone (additional 24-hour indicator); annual calendar with date and month
Case: white gold, ø 42 mm, height 14.1 mm; bidirectional bezel to control functions; sapphire crystal; screw-in crown; water-resistant to 10 atm
Band: Oyster white gold, folding clasp with extension
Price: $48,850

Sky-Dweller

Reference number: 326135
Movement: automatic, Rolex Caliber 9001; ø 33 mm, height 8 mm; 40 jewels; 28,800 vph; Parachrom Breguet spring; glucydur balance with microstella regulating screws; 72-hour power reserve; COSC certified chronometer
Functions: hours, minutes, sweep seconds; second time zone (additional 24-hour indicator); annual calendar with date and month
Case: rose gold, ø 42 mm, height 14.1 mm; bidirectional bezel to control functions; sapphire crystal; screw-in crown; water-resistant to 10 atm
Band: reptile skin, folding clasp
Price: $39,550

Oyster Perpetual Explorer II

Reference number: 216570
Movement: automatic, Rolex Caliber 3187 (base Rolex 3135); ø 28.5 mm, height 6.4 mm; 31 jewels; 28,800 vph; Parachrom Breguet spring; Paraflex shock absorber; COSC certified chronometer
Functions: hours, minutes, sweep seconds; additional 24-hour display; date
Case: stainless steel, ø 42 mm, height 12.3 mm; bezel with 24-hour division; sapphire crystal; screw-in crown; water-resistant to 10 atm
Band: Oysterlock stainless steel, safety folding clasp
Price: $8,100
Variations: various dials

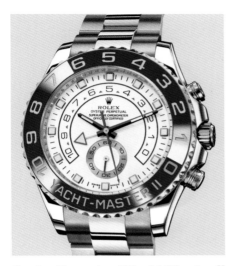

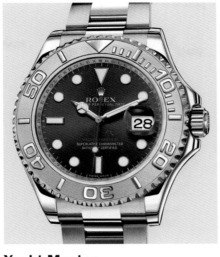

Oyster Perpetual Yacht-Master II

Reference number: 116681
Movement: automatic, Rolex Caliber 4160 (base Caliber 4130); ø 31.2 mm, height 8.05 mm; 42 jewels; Parachrom Breguet spring, 72-hour power reserve; COSC certified chronometer
Functions: hours, minutes, subsidiary seconds; programmable regatta countdown with memory
Case: stainless steel, ø 44 mm, height 13.8 mm; bidirectional rose gold bezel, ceramic inserts; sapphire crystal, screw-in crown; water-resistant to 10 atm
Band: Oysterlock stainless steel and rose gold, folding clasp with flip-lock and extension link
Price: $25,150
Variations: white ($48,150) or yellow ($43,550) gold

Yacht Master

Reference number: 116622
Movement: automatic, Rolex Caliber 3135; ø 28.5 mm, height 6 mm; 31 jewels; 28,800 vph; Parachrom Breguet spring; glucydur balance with microstella regulating screws; COSC certified chronometer
Functions: hours, minutes, sweep seconds; date
Case: stainless steel, ø 40 mm, height 11.7 mm; bidirectional platinum bezel with 60-minute divisions; sapphire crystal; screw-in crown; water-resistant to 10 atm
Band: Oysterlock stainless steel, folding clasp with flip-lock and extension link
Price: $11,550
Variations: with platinum dial ($12,350)

Oyster Perpetual Yacht-Master II

Reference number: 116681
Movement: automatic, Rolex Caliber 4161 (base Rolex 4160); ø 31.2 mm, height 8.05 mm; 42 jewels; 28,800 vph; Parachrom Breguet spring; 72-hour power reserve; COSC certified chronometer
Functions: hours, minutes, subsidiary seconds; programmable regatta countdown with memory
Case: stainless steel, ø 44 mm, height 13.8 mm; bidirectional bezel with ceramic inlay; sapphire crystal; screw-in crown; water-resistant to 10 atm
Band: Oysterlock stainless steel, folding clasp with flip-lock and extension link
Price: $18,750

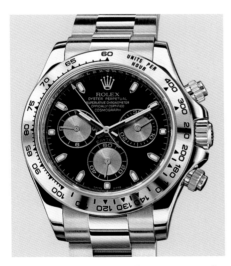

Oyster Perpetual Cosmograph Daytona

Reference number: 116505
Movement: automatic, Rolex Caliber 4130; ø 30.5 mm, height 6.5 mm; 44 jewels; 28,800 vph; Parachrom Breguet spring; COSC certified chronometer
Functions: hours, minutes, subsidiary seconds; chronograph
Case: rose gold, ø 40 mm, height 12.8 mm; sapphire crystal; screw-in crown and pusher; water-resistant to 10 atm
Band: Oyster rose gold, folding clasp with flip-lock and extension link
Price: $37,450
Variations: various dials; stainless steel ($12,000)

Oyster Perpetual Cosmograph Daytona

Reference number: 116515LN
Movement: automatic, Rolex Caliber 4130; ø 30.5 mm, height 6.5 mm; 44 jewels; 28,800 vph; Parachrom Breguet spring; COSC certified chronometer
Functions: hours, minutes, subsidiary seconds; chronograph
Case: Everose gold, ø 40 mm, height 12.1 mm; ceramic bezel, tachymeter scale; sapphire crystal; screw-in crown and pusher; water-resistant to 10 atm
Band: reptile skin, Everose gold Oysterlock safety folding clasp
Price: $28,800
Variations: various dials

Oyster Perpetual Cosmograph Daytona

Reference number: 116506
Movement: automatic, Rolex Caliber 4130; ø 30.5 mm, height 6.5 mm; 44 jewels; 28,800 vph; Parachrom Breguet spring; COSC certified chronometer
Functions: hours, minutes, subsidiary seconds; chronograph
Case: platinum, ø 40 mm; ceramic bezel; sapphire crystal, screw-in crown and pushers; water-resistant to 10 atm
Band: Oysterlock platinum, folding clasp with flip-lock and extension link
Price: $75,000

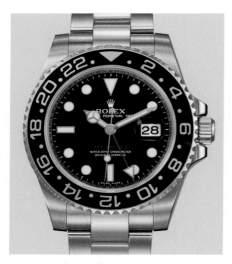

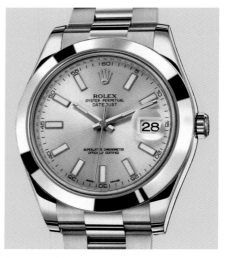

Oyster Perpetual GMT Master II

Reference number: 116713LN
Movement: automatic, Rolex Caliber 3186 (base Caliber 3135); ø 28.5 mm, height 6.4 mm; 31 jewels; 28,800 vph; COSC certified chronometer
Functions: hours, minutes, sweep seconds; second time zone (additional 24-hour indicator); date
Case: stainless steel, ø 40 mm, height 12.1 mm; bidirectional yellow gold bezel with ceramic inlay, with 24-hour division; sapphire crystal; screwed-in crown; water-resistant to 10 atm
Band: Oysterlock stainless steel and yellow gold, folding clasp with flip-lock and extension link
Price: $13,000
Variations: stainless steel ($8,450); yellow gold ($33,250)

Oyster Perpetual Submariner Date

Movement: automatic, Rolex Caliber 3135; ø 28.5 mm, height 6 mm; 31 jewels; 28,800 vph; Parachrom Breguet spring; glucydur balance with microstella regulating screws; COSC certified chronometer
Functions: hours, minutes, sweep seconds; date
Case: white gold, ø 40 mm, height 12.5 mm; unidirectional bezel with ceramic inlay; 60-minute division; sapphire crystal; screw-in crown; water-resistant to 30 atm
Band: Oysterlock stainless steel, folding clasp with flip-lock
Price: $8,550
Variations: with yellow gold bezel ($13,400); yellow gold ($34,250); white gold ($36,850)

Oyster Perpetual Datejust II

Reference number: 116300
Movement: automatic, Rolex Caliber 3136 (base Caliber 3135); ø 30.97 mm, height 6.47 mm; 31 jewels; 28,800 vph; Parachrom Breguet spring; Paraflex shock absorber; COSC certified chronometer
Functions: hours, minutes, sweep seconds; date
Case: stainless steel, ø 41 mm, height 12.2 mm; sapphire crystal; screw-in crown; water-resistant to 10 atm
Band: Oyster stainless steel, folding clasp
Price: $7,150
Variations: various dials

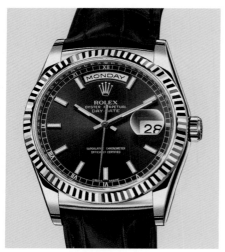

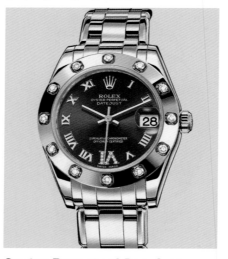

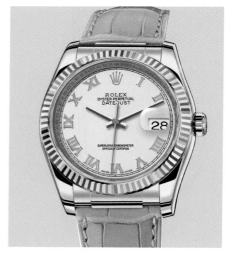

Oyster Perpetual Day-Date

Reference number: 118139
Movement: automatic, Rolex Caliber 3155 (base Caliber 3135); ø 28.5 mm; height 6.45 mm; 31 jewels; 28,800 vph; glucydur balance with microstella regulating screws; COSC certified chronometer
Functions: hours, minutes, sweep seconds; date, weekday
Case: white gold, ø 36 mm; sapphire crystal; screw-in crown; water-resistant to 10 atm
Band: reptile skin, folding clasp
Price: $22,150
Variations: various dials and straps

Oyster Perpetual Datejust Special Edition

Reference number: 81315
Movement: automatic, Rolex Caliber 2235 (base Caliber 2230); ø 20 mm; height 5.95 mm; 31 jewels; 28,800 vph; COSC certified chronometer
Functions: hours, minutes, sweep seconds; date
Case: rose gold, ø 34 mm, height 10.7 mm; bezel set with 12 diamonds; sapphire crystal, screw-in crown; water-resistant to 10 atm
Band: Pearlmaster rose gold folding clasp
Remarks: dial set with 11 diamonds at 6 o'clock
Price: $38,500
Variations: various dials; yellow gold ($34,550); white gold ($36,950)

Oyster Perpetual Datejust

Reference number: 116135
Movement: automatic, Rolex Caliber 3135; ø 28.5 mm, height 6 mm; 31 jewels, 28,800 vph; glucydur balance with microstella regulating screws; COSC certified chronometer
Functions: hours, minutes, sweep seconds; date
Case: rose gold, ø 36 mm, height 11.6 mm; sapphire crystal, screw-in crown; water-resistant to 10 atm
Band: reptile skin, folding clasp
Price: $21,600
Variations: various bracelets and dials

Oyster Perpetual Datejust Lady

Reference number: 178384
Movement: automatic, Rolex Caliber 2235 (base Caliber 2230); ø 2 mm; height 5.95 mm; 31 jewels; 28,800 vph; COSC certified chronometer
Functions: hours, minutes, sweep seconds; date
Case: stainless steel, ø 31 mm, height 10.5 mm; white gold bezel set with 46 diamonds; sapphire crystal, screw-in crown; water-resistant to 10 atm
Band: Oyster stainless steel, folding clasp with extension link
Price: $13,900
Variations: various bracelets and dials

Oyster Perpetual Datejust

Reference number: 116243
Movement: automatic, Rolex Caliber 3135; ø 28.5 mm, height 6 mm; 31 jewels; 28,800 vph; glucydur balance with microstella regulating screws; COSC certified chronometer
Functions: hours, minutes, sweep seconds; date
Case: stainless steel, ø 36 mm, height 11.6 mm; yellow gold bezel set with 52 diamonds; sapphire crystal; screw-in crown; water-resistant to 10 atm
Band: Oyster stainless steel and yellow gold, folding clasp with extension link
Remarks: mother-of-pearl dial set with 10 diamonds
Price: $22,050
Variations: various bracelets and dials

Oyster Perpetual Day-Date

Reference number: 118138
Movement: automatic, Rolex Caliber 3156 (base Caliber 3135); ø 28.5 mm, height 6.45 mm; 31 jewels; 28,800 vph; glucydur balance with microstella regulating screws; COSC certified chronometer
Functions: hours, minutes, sweep seconds; date and weekday
Case: yellow gold, ø 36 mm, height 11.6 mm; sapphire crystal; screw-in crown; water-resistant to 10 atm
Band: reptile skin, folding clasp
Price: $22,150
Variations: various dials and straps

Caliber 3135

Automatic; single barrel spring, 42-hour power reserve; COSC tested chronometer
Functions: hours, minutes, sweep seconds; date
Diameter: 28.5 mm
Height: 8.05 mm
Jewels: 42
Balance: glucydur balance with microstella regulating screws
Frequency: 28,800 vph
Balance spring: Parachrom with Breguet overcoil
Shock protection: Kif

Caliber 4130

Automatic; single barrel spring, 42-hour power reserve; COSC tested chronometer
Functions: hours, minutes, subsidiary seconds; chronograph
Diameter: 30.5 mm
Height: 6.5 mm
Jewels: 44
Balance: glucydur balance with microstella regulating screws
Frequency: 28,800 vph
Balance spring: Parachrom with Breguet overcoil
Shock protection: Kif
Remarks: used in the Daytona

Caliber 3156

Automatic; single barrel spring, 42-hour power reserve; COSC tested chronometer
Functions: hours, minutes, sweep seconds; date, weekday
Diameter: 28.5 mm
Height: 6.45 mm
Jewels: 31
Balance: glucydur balance with microstella regulating screws
Frequency: 28,800 vph
Balance spring: Parachrom spring
Remarks: used in the Day-Date II

RJ WATCHES SA
11 Rue du Marché
CH-1204 Geneva
Switzerland

Tel.:
01141-22-319-29-39

Fax:
01141-22-319-29-30

E-Mail:
info@romainjerome.ch

Website:
www.romainjerome.ch

Founded:
2004

Number of employees:
approx. 15

Annual production:
3,000 watches and accessories

Distribution:
Please contact Romain Jerome headquarters in
Switzerland for any enquiries.

Most important collections/price range:
Titanic-DNA, Moon-DNA, Liberty-DNA /
from $9,000 to approx. $500,000 for highly
complicated watches

Romain Jerome

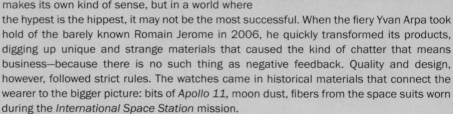

Tchaikovsky once said that he always put his best ideas into his work—and took them out again when editing. This singular approach to creativity makes its own kind of sense, but in a world where the hypest is the hippest, it may not be the most successful. When the fiery Yvan Arpa took hold of the barely known Romain Jerome in 2006, he quickly transformed its products, digging up unique and strange materials that caused the kind of chatter that means business—because there is no such thing as negative feedback. Quality and design, however, followed strict rules. The watches came in historical materials that connect the wearer to the bigger picture: bits of *Apollo 11,* moon dust, fibers from the space suits worn during the *International Space Station* mission.

Following the course laid out by Arpa was not easy for the new CEO, Manuel Emch, who took over the brand in 2010. Gradually, however, the more outrageous materials, like volcanic ash and coprolite (fossilized dino dung), and expressionistic dials disappeared. The oversize Moon Invader saw a shift toward a cooler techno design using the company's stock of lunar module shreds. The Steampunk Chrono won the "Couture Time Award for Watch Architecture" in Las Vegas in 2012. Sticking with the historic theme, Romain Jerome has also combined the Steampunk models with *Titanic's* oxidized and stabilized metals, and in sharp contrast, some verdigris scraps from the Statue of Liberty are integrated into a clever, minimalist watch. The latest talking piece is the Spacecraft, a seventies-style sci-fi time-telling object in a trapezoidal shape with a linear hour line on the side and a minute disc on top, a bit of a slap at the vintage crowd. No one is surprised to find that Emch collaborated with Eric Giroud and Jean-Marc Wiederrecht.

Liberty-DNA

Reference number: RJ.T.AU.LI.001.01
Movement: automatic, Caliber RJ001-A;
ø 30.4 mm, height 7.9 mm; 23 jewels; 28,800 vph;
42-hour power reserve
Functions: hours, minutes
Case: black PVD-coated steel; ø 46 mm, height
16 mm; antireflective sapphire crystal; flame of
liberty lighting up stars and stripes engraved on
case back; water-resistant to 3 atm
Band: brown vintage finish alligator
Remarks: bronze bezel shaped like crown; verdigris
dial with Miss Liberty DNA
Price: $14,900, limited to 125 pieces

Games-DNA —
Space Invaders Purple

Reference number: RJ.M.AU.IN.006.07
Movement: automatic; Caliber RJ001-A;
ø 30.4 mm, height 7.9 mm; 23 jewels; 28,800 vph;
42-hour power reserve
Functions: hours, minutes
Case: black PVD-coated steel; ø 46 mm; height
16 mm; antireflective sapphire crystal; case back
with *Apollo 11* parts and medallion in Moon Silver
alloy; water-resistant to 3 atm
Band: vulcanized rubber, black PVD-coated steel
folding clasp
Remarks: black 3D bead-blasted, satin-brushed
dial; lacquered Space Invaders
Price: $17,900, limited to 78 pieces

Spacecraft

Reference number: RJ.SC.AU.001.01
Movement: automatic; Caliber RJ2000-A;
54 jewels; 28,800 vph; 42-hour power reserve
Functions: hours, minutes, small seconds at 9;
30-minute chronograph counter at 3
Case: titanium with black PVD-coated titanium
elements; 50 x 44.5 mm, height 18.5 mm;
antireflective sapphire crystal; water-resistant to
3 atm
Band: black polyamide, titanium buckle
Price: $33,400, limited to 99 pieces

Titanic-DNA — Steampunk Metal Octopus

Reference number: RJ.T.AU.SP.001.01
Movement: automatic; Caliber RJ002-A2; ø 30.4 mm, height 6.6 mm; 23 jewels; 28,800 vph; 42-hour power reserve
Functions: hours, minutes, propeller-shaped small seconds at 9
Case: brushed stainless steel; ø 45 mm, height 18.8 mm; inner bezel with 60-minute divisions activated by screw-in crown at 3; screw-in crown at 9; antireflective sapphire crystal; water-resistant to 25 atm
Band: black rubber, steel folding clasp
Remarks: bezel of stabilized steel from *Titanic*; octopus design on back, suction cups on band
Price: $13,750, limited to 2,012 pieces

Steampunk Black Chrono

Reference number: RJ.T.AU.SP.002.01
Movement: automatic; Caliber RJ001-CS; ø 30.4 mm, height 6.6 mm; 39 jewels; 28,800 vph; 42-hour power reserve
Functions: hours, minutes, subsidiary seconds; chronograph, 30-minute totalizer at 3
Case: black PVD-coated steel; ø 50 mm, height 16.6 mm; antireflective sapphire crystal; water-resistant to 3 atm
Band: black rubber, steel folding clasp
Remarks: bezel of stabilized steel from *Titanic*; dial integrated into movement; bead-blasted, satin-brushed rhodium-colored bridge
Price: $18,000, limited to 2,012 pieces

Titanic Red Chrono Tourbillon

Reference number: RJ.T.TO.CH.002.01
Movement: automatic; Caliber 1450RJ; ø 30 mm, height 7.4 mm; 33 jewels; 21,600 vph; 120-hour power reserve; tourbillon
Functions: hours, minutes; chronograph counters at 2 and 10; tourbillon at 6
Case: black PVD-coated steel with red gold; ø 50 mm, height 15.9 mm; rusted steel bezel; antireflective sapphire crystal; water-resistant to 3 atm
Band: black rubber, pink gold folding clasp
Remarks: bezel in stabilized rusted steel from *Titanic*; dial integrated into movement
Price: $240,900, limited to 9 pieces

MOON-DNA — Moon Invader Speed Metal Chrono

Reference number: RJ.M.CH.IN.005.01
Movement: automatic, Caliber RJ001-CH; ø 30.4 mm, height 7.9 mm; 23 jewels; 28,800 vph; 42-hour power reserve
Functions: hours, minutes; subsidiary seconds; chronograph; 12-hour/30-minute counters at 6 and 3
Case: black PVD-coated steel; ø 46 mm; height 16 mm; screw-in crown; antireflective sapphire crystal; water-resistant to 3 atm
Band: vulcanized rubber, black PVD-coated steel folding clasp
Remarks: case back with *Apollo 11* parts, Moon Silver medallion; optimal wrist adjustment
Price: $14,900, limited to 1,969 pieces

Moon — DNA Moon Invader Speed Metal Auto

Reference number: RJ.M.AU.IN.001.01
Movement: automatic, Caliber RJ001-A; ø 30.4 mm, height 7.9 mm; 23 jewels; 28,800 vph; 42-hour power reserve
Functions: hours, minutes; subsidiary seconds
Case: black PVD-coated steel, ø 46 mm, height 16 mm; antireflective sapphire crystal; water-resistant to 3 atm
Band: black vulcanized rubber, black PVD-coated steel folding clasp
Remarks: case back with *Apollo 11* parts, Moon Silver alloy medallion; black gem-set gridwork motif; ball-and-socket joints for optimal wrist adjustment
Price: $11,500, limited to 1,969 pieces

MOON-DNA — Moon Dust Red Mood Set Chrono

Reference number: RJ.M.CH.003.02
Movement: automatic, Caliber RJ001-CH1; ø 30.4 mm, height 7.9 mm; 25 jewels; 28,800 vph; 42-hour power reserve
Functions: hours, minutes; subsidiary seconds; chronograph, 12-hour/30-minute counters at 6 and 3
Case: pink gold; ø 46 mm, height 17.2 mm; antireflective sapphire crystal; pink gold screw-in crown; 4 paws set with diamonds; carbon fiber and pink gold bezel; water-resistant to 3 atm
Band: fabric, pink gold and black steel folding clasp
Remarks: dial containing moon dust
Price: $40,300, limited to 1,969 pieces

Schaumburg Watch
Lindburgh & Benson
Kirchplatz 5 and 6
D-31737 Rinteln
Germany

Tel.:
01149-5751-923-351

E-Mail:
info@lindburgh-benson.com

Website:
www.schaumburgwatch.com

Founded:
1998

Number of employees:
7

Annual production:
not specified

Distribution:
retail

U.S. distributor:
Schaumburg Watch
About Time Luxury Group
210 Bellevue Avenue
Newport, RI 02840
401-846-0598
nicewatch@aol.com

Most important collections/price range:
mechanical wristwatches / approx. $1,500 to
$13,000

Schaumburg Watch

Frank Dilbakowski is the owner of this small watchmaking business in Rinteln, Westphalia, which has been producing very unusual, yet affordable timepieces since 1998. The name Schaumburg comes from the surrounding region. The firm has gained a reputation for high-performance timepieces for rugged sports and professional use. The chronometer line Aquamatic with water resistance to 1,000 m and the Aquatitan models, secure to 2,000 m, confirm the company's maxim that form, function, and performance are inseparable from one another. By the same token, traditional watchmaking is also high on the agenda. The Rinteln workbenches produce the plates and bridges and provide all the finishing as well (perlage, engraving, skeletonizing). Some of the bracelets, cases, and dials are even manufactured here, but the base movements come from Switzerland. The current portfolio includes such outstanding creations as a special moon phase, which, rather than simply showing a moon, has a "shadow" crossing over an immobile lunar aspect. The Bullfrog is a simpler watch with a modern dial. Thanks to the tapered case, the tall piece does not look bulky, and if you look at the profile, it *is* reminiscent of a frog.

AGM - Bullfrog Vision

Movement: automatic, SW Caliber 20a (base ETA 2824-2); ø 25.6 mm, height 4.6 mm; 25 jewels; 28,800 vph; 38-hour power reserve
Functions: hours, minutes, sweep seconds; additional 24-hour display; date
Case: titanium, ø 42 mm, height 12 mm; sapphire crystal, water-resistant to 20 atm
Band: calf leather, buckle
Price: $1,740

Triple - Blue Bridge

Movement: manually wound, SW Caliber 07.9/nano (base ETA 6498); ø 36.6 mm, height 5.9 mm; 17 jewels; 18,000 vph; blue guilloché three-quarter plate ("Schaumburg bridge"), hand-engraved balance cocks; 38-hour power reserve
Functions: hours (off-center), minutes, subsidiary seconds
Case: stainless steel, ø 42 mm, height 12 mm; sapphire crystal, transparent case back; water-resistant to 5 atm
Band: calf leather, folding clasp
Price: $3,325

Traveller

Movement: manually wound, SW Caliber 07.9 (base ETA 6498); ø 36.6 mm, height 5.9 mm; 17 jewels; 18,000 vph; guilloché three-quarter plate ("Schaumburg bridge"), hand-engraved balance cock; 38-hour power reserve
Functions: hours, minutes, subsidiary seconds; additional 12-hour display (second time zone)
Case: stainless steel, ø 42 mm, height 11 mm; sapphire crystal, transparent case back; water-resistant to 5 atm
Band: calf leather, folding clasp
Price: $2,800

Audubon's Birds of America
The National Audubon Society
Baby Elephant Folio

Now with full-color illustrations throughout,
this marvelous edition of *Audubon's Birds of
America* displays all 435 of John James Audubon's
brilliant hand-colored engravings in exquisite
reproductions taken from the original plates
of the Audubon Society's archival copy of the
rare Double Elephant Folio. Organized and
annotated by Roger Tory Peterson, America's
best-known ornithologist, and issued with the full
endorsement and cooperation of the Audubon
Society, this magnificent volume is as thorough
in scientific classification as it is beautiful. The
colorful captions in the back provide fascinating
commentaries on each featured bird.

By Roger Tory Peterson and Virginia Marie Peterson
482 full-color illustrations
694 pages · Cloth · $185.00
ISBN 978-0-7892-1135-4
E-BOOK ISBN 978-0-7892-6017-8

"A brilliant achievement."
—*The New York Times*

Published by ABBEVILLE PRESS
137 Varick Street, New York, NY 10013
1-800-ARTBOOK (in U.S. only)
Also available wherever fine books are sold
Visit us at www.abbeville.com

Seiko Holdings

Ginza, Chuo, Tokyo
Japan

Website:
www.seikowatches.com

Founded:
1881

Number of employees:
not specified

Annual production:
not specified

U.S. distributor:
Seiko Corporation of America
1111 Macarthur Boulevard
Mahwah, NJ 07430
201-529-5730
custserv@seikousa.com
www.seikousa.com

Most important collections/price range:
Grand Seiko / approx. $5,000 to $14,500; Ananta
/ approx. $2,400 to $8,500; Astron / approx.
$1,850 to $3,400; Seiko Elite (Sportura, Premier,
Velatura, Arctura) / approx. $430 to $1,500

Seiko

The Japanese watch giant is a part of the Seiko Holding Company, but as far as the development and production of its watches are concerned, the brand is fully self-sufficient. Seiko makes every variety of portable timepiece, and in its vast collection it offers mechanical watches with both manual and automatic winding, quartz watches with battery and solar power or with the brand's own mechanical "Kinetic" power generation, as well as the groundbreaking "Spring Drive" hybrid technology. This intelligent mix of mechanical energy generation and electronic regulation is reserved for Seiko's top models.

Also in the top segment of the brand is the Grand Seiko line, a group of watches that enjoys cult status among international collectors. For the Grand Seiko's fiftieth anniversary, the Tokyo-based company put together an extensive collection comprising numerous new models and, for the first time, officially offered them on the global market. These were not necessarily available at all Seiko sales points, but certainly at the more profitable ones. Today, among the new GS models are several watches with the interesting Spring Drive technology, but most new Grand Seikos are conventional, mechanical hand-wound and automatic watches.

Grand Seiko Spring Drive Chronograph

Reference number: SBGC001
Movement: manually wound, Seiko Caliber 9R86; ø 30 mm, height 7.6 mm; 50 jewels; electromagnetical Tri-synchro Regulator escapement system with sliding wheel; column wheel control of chronograph functions/vertical clutch
Functions: hours, minutes, subsidiary seconds; 12-hour display (second time zone); chronograph; date; power reserve indicator
Case: stainless steel, ø 43.5 mm, height 16.1 mm; sapphire crystal, transparent case back
Band: stainless steel, folding clasp
Price: $8,600

Grand Seiko Automatic Hi-Beat 36,000

Reference number: SBGH001
Movement: automatic, Seiko Caliber 9S85; 37 jewels; 36,000 vph; protected from magnetic fields up to 10,000 A/m, 55-hour power reserve
Functions: hours, minutes, sweep seconds; date
Case: stainless steel, ø 40 mm, height 13 mm; sapphire crystal, transparent case back; water-resistant to 10 atm
Band: stainless steel, folding clasp with safety lock
Price: $6,300
Variations: black dial $6,300

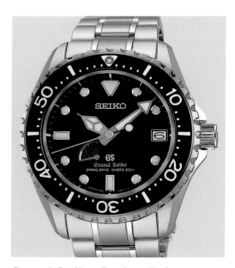

Grand Seiko Spring Drive Diver's Watch

Reference number: SBGA031
Movement: manually wound, Seiko Caliber 9R65; ø 30 mm, height 5.1 mm; 30 jewels; electromagnetical Tri-synchro Regulator escapement system with sliding wheel; 72-hour power reserve
Functions: hours, minutes, sweep seconds; date; power reserve indicator
Case: titanium, ø 44.2 mm, height 14 mm; unidirectional bezel with 60-minute divisions; sapphire crystal; screw-in crown; water-resistant to 20 atm
Band: titanium, folding clasp
Price: $7,700

Ananta Automatic Chronograph

Reference number: SRQ017J1
Movement: automatic, Seiko Caliber 8R28;
ø 28 mm, height 7.2 mm; 34 jewels; 28,800 vph;
column wheel and vertical clutch control of
chronograph; 45-hour power reserve
Functions: hours, minutes, subsidiary seconds;
chronograph; date
Case: stainless steel with titanium carbide coating,
ø 42.7 mm, height 14 mm; sapphire crystal;
transparent case back; water-resistant to 10 atm
Band: stainless steel with titanium carbide layer,
folding clasp
Remarks: dial with real Japanese lacquer
Price: $5,000, limited to 300 pieces

Ananta Spring Drive Chronograph

Reference number: SPS009J1
Movement: Seiko Caliber 5R86; ø 30 mm, height
7.6 mm; 50 jewels; electromagnetical Tri-synchro
Regulator escapement system with sliding wheel;
column wheel and vertical clutch control of
chronograph; 72-hour power reserve
Functions: hours, minutes, subsidiary seconds;
chronograph; date; second time zone (24-hour
display); power reserve indicator
Case: stainless steel with titanium carbide
coating, ø 46 mm, height 16 mm; sapphire crystal;
transparent case back; water-resistant to 10 atm
Band: reptile skin, folding clasp
Price: $6,400

Astron GPS Solar

Reference number: SAST001G
Movement: quartz, Seiko Caliber 7X52; solar energy-
saving function
Functions: hours, minutes, sweep seconds; second
time zone (24-hour indicator); date; world-time display
(GPS coordination in 39 time zones); flight mode;
signal reception indicator; power reserve indicator; DST
indicator
Case: titanium with titanium carbide layer, ø 47 mm,
height 16.5 mm; ceramic bezel; sapphire crystal;
screwed-in crown; water-resistant to 10 atm
Band: titanium with titanium carbide layer, folding clasp
Remarks: additional silicon strap
Price: $3,850, limited to 2,500 pieces

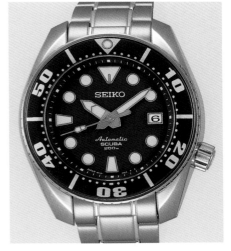

Premier Kinetic Direct Drive Moon Phase

Reference number: SRX007P1
Movement: quartz, Seiko Caliber 5D88; own energy
source from rotor-driven micro-generator, hand
winding as well; 1-month power reserve
Functions: hours, minutes, sweep seconds; date,
weekday, moon phase; power reserve indicator
Case: stainless steel, ø 41.5 mm, height 10 mm;
sapphire crystal; water-resistant to 10 atm
Band: stainless steel, folding clasp
Price: $1,395

Sportura Kinetic Perpetual

Reference number: SNP055P1
Movement: quartz, Seiko Caliber 5M85; own energy
supply from rotor-driven micro-generator; darkness
power reserve up to 6 months
Functions: hours, minutes, sweep seconds; 24-hour
display (second time zone); date
Case: stainless steel, ø 44.4 mm; sapphire crystal;
screw-in crown; water-resistant to 10 atm
Band: stainless steel, folding clasp
Price: $750

Scuba Automatic 200 m

Reference number: SBDC003
Movement: automatic, Seiko Caliber 6R15;
23 jewels; 50-hour power reserve
Functions: hours, minutes, sweep seconds; date
Case: stainless steel, ø 44 mm; unidirectional bezel
with 60-minute divisions, synthetic glass, screw-in
crown; water-resistant to 20 atm
Band: stainless steel, folding clasp
Price: $640

Sinn Spezialuhren GmbH
Im Füldchen 5-7
D-60489 Frankfurt/Main
Germany

Tel.:
01149-69-9784-14-200

Fax:
01149-69-9784-14-201

E-Mail:
info@sinn.de

Website:
www.sinn.de

Founded:
1961

Number of employees:
approx. 100

Annual production:
approx. 12,500 watches

U.S. distributor:
WatchBuys
888-333-4895
www.watchbuys.com

Most important collections/price range:
Financial District, U-Models, Diapal / from approx.
$700 to $27,500

Sinn

Pilot and flight instructor Helmut Sinn began manufacturing watches in Frankfurt because he thought the pilot's watches on the market were too expensive. The resulting combination of top quality, functionality, and a good price-performance ratio turned out to be an excellent sales argument.

Sinn Spezialuhren zu Frankfurt am Main—as this company is officially called—is for many a brand that finds its origins in technology. There is hardly another manufacturer that offers watch aficionados such a sophisticated and reasonable collection of sporty watches, many of which are conceived to take extreme pressure.

In 1994, Lothar Schmidt took over the brand, and his product developers began looking for inspiration in other industries and the sciences. They did so out of a practical technical impulse without any plan for launching a trend. "Products need to speak for themselves," Schmidt explains. That is why he continues to invest in research and development, with the aim of improving the everyday functionality of his watches. This includes application of special Sinn technology like the moisture-proof technology by which the noble gas argon is pumped into the case. Other Sinn innovations include the Diapal (a lubricant-free lever escapement), the Hydro (an oil-filled diver's watch), and Tegiment processing (for hardened steel surfaces).

The latest Sinn creation is not technological. Having noticed a lack of norms for aviator watches, Schmidt negotiated a partnership with the Aachen Technical University to create the Technischer Standard Fliegeruhren (TESTAF, or Technical Standards for Aviator Watches), which is housed at the Eurocopter headquarters. And the brand promptly manufactured several TESTAF-certified models.

103 Ti UTC TESTAF

Reference number: 103.0791
Movement: automatic, modified ETA Caliber 7750; ø 30.4 mm, height 7.9 mm; 25 jewels; 28,800 vph; shockproof and antimagnetic (DIN-norm); 42-hour power reserve
Functions: hours, minutes, subsidiary seconds; additional 12-hour display; chronograph; date
Case: pearl-blasted titanium, ø 41 mm, height 17 mm; bidirectional bezel with 60-minute divisions; sapphire crystal; transparent case back; water-resistant to 20 atm
Band: calf leather, buckle
Remarks: TESTAF certified; Ar-dehumidifying technology (protective gas)
Price: $4,200

EZM 10 TESTAF

Reference number: 950.011
Movement: automatic, Sinn Caliber SZ 01 (base ETA 7750); ø 30 mm, height 8.5 mm; 33 jewels; 28,800 vph; shockproof, antimagnetic (DIN-norm); sweep minute counter
Functions: hours, minutes, subsidiary seconds; additional 24-hour display; date
Case: tegimented/pearl-blasted titanium, ø 46.5 mm, height 15.6 mm; bidirectional bezel with 60-minute division; sapphire crystal; screw-in crown; hard-coated pushers; water-resistant to 20 atm
Band: calf leather, buckle
Remarks: TESTAF certified; Ar-dehumidifying technology (protective gas)
Price: $6,700

857 UTC TESTAF

Reference number: 857.040
Movement: automatic, ETA Caliber 2893-2; ø 25.6 mm, height 4.1 mm; 21 jewels; 28,800 vph; shockproof, antimagnetic (DIN-norm); 42-hour power reserve
Functions: hours, minutes, sweep seconds; additional 24-hour display (second time zone); date
Case: tegimented/pearl-blasted stainless steel, ø 43 mm, height 12 mm; bidirectional bezel with 60-minute division; sapphire crystal; water-resistant to 20 atm
Band: calf leather, buckle
Remarks: TESTAF certified; Ar-dehumidifying technology (protective gas)
Price: $2,850

T1 (EZM 14)

Reference number: 1014.010
Movement: automatic, SOP A10-2A (base Soprod A10); ø 25.6 mm, height 3.6 mm; 25 jewels; 28,800 vph; shockproof and antimagnetic (DIN-norm); 42-hour power reserve
Functions: hours, minutes, sweep seconds; date
Case: pearl-blasted titanium, ø 45 mm, height 12.5 mm; unidirectional bezel with 60-minute division; sapphire crystal; screw-in crown; water resistant to 100 atm
Band: rubber, folding clasp with safety lock and extension link
Remarks: EU diving certified; Ar-dehumidifying technology (protective gas)
Price: $4,350

140 A

Reference number: 140.040
Movement: automatic, Sinn Caliber SZ 01 (base ETA 7750); ø 30 mm, height 8.5 mm; 33 jewels; 28,800 vph; shockproof and antimagnetic (DIN-norm); sweep minute counter; lubricant-free escapement (Diapal)
Functions: hours, minutes, subsidiary seconds; additional 24-hour display; chronograph; date
Case: tegimented stainless steel, ø 44 mm, height 15 mm; crown-adjustable inner bezel with 60-minute divisions; sapphire crystal; screw-in crown; water-resistant to 10 atm
Band: calf leather, buckle
Remarks: Ar-dehumidifying technology
Price: $5,900; limited to 500 pieces

900 Diapal

Reference number: 900.013
Movement: automatic, Sellita Caliber SW500; ø 30 mm, height 7.9 mm; 25 jewels; 28,800 vph; shockproof and antimagnetic (DIN-norm); lubrication-free escapement (Diapal); 48-hour power reserve
Functions: hours, minutes, subsidiary seconds; additional 24-hour display; chronograph; date
Case: tegimented stainless steel, ø 44 mm, height 15.5 mm; crown-adjustable inner bezel with 60-minute division; sapphire crystal; screw-in crown; water-resistant to 20 atm
Band: stainless steel, folding clasp
Remarks: Ar-dehumidifying technology; magnetic field protection to 80,000 A/m
Price: $5,350

104 St Sa

Reference number: 104.010
Movement: automatic, Sellita Caliber SW220-1; ø 25.6 mm, height 5.05 mm; 26 jewels; 28,800 vph; shockproof and antimagnetic (DIN-norm); 38 hours power reserve
Functions: hours, minutes, sweep seconds; weekday, date
Case: stainless steel, ø 41 mm, height 11.5 mm; bidirectional bezel with 60-minute division; sapphire crystal; transparent case back; screw-in crown; water-resistant to 20 atm
Price: $1,550
Variations: with stainless steel bracelet ($1,850)

EZM 7

Reference number: 857.030
Movement: automatic, ETA Caliber 2893-2; ø 26.2 mm, height 4.1 mm; 21 jewels; 28,800 vph; shockproof and antimagnetic (DIN-norm)
Functions: hours, minutes, sweep seconds; additional 24-hour display; date
Case: tegimented stainless steel, ø 43 mm, height 12 mm; unidirectional bezel with 60-minute divisions; sapphire crystal; screw-in crown; water-resistant to 20 atm
Band: calf leather, buckle
Remarks: Ar-dehumidifying technology (protective gas); magnetic field protection to 80,000 A/m
Price: $2,900

856 UTC

Reference number: 856.010
Movement: automatic, ETA Caliber 2893-2; ø 25.6 mm, height 4.1 mm; 21 jewels; 28,800 vph; shockproof and antimagnetic (DIN-norm); 42-hour power reserve
Functions: hours, minutes, sweep seconds; additional 24-hour display; date
Case: tegimented stainless steel, ø 40 mm, height 11 mm; sapphire crystal; rubber, folding clasp
Remarks: Ar-dehumidifying technology (protective gas)
Price: $2,400
Variations: without second time zone (from $2,250); with rotating bezel (from $2,750)

917

Reference number: 917.011
Movement: automatic, ETA Caliber 7750;
ø 30.4 mm, height 7.9 mm; 25 jewels; 28,800 vph
Functions: hours, minutes, subsidiary seconds;
chronograph; weekday, date
Case: stainless steel, ø 44 mm, height 15.5 mm;
crown-adjustable inner bezel with 60-minute
divisions; sapphire crystal; transparent case back;
screw-in crown; water-resistant to 10 atm
Band: calf leather, buckle
Remarks: Ar-dehumidifying technology
Price: $3,500
Variations: with stainless steel band ($3,850); with
power reserve indicator (from $4,100)

901

Reference number: 901.010
Movement: automatic, ETA Caliber 7750; ø 30 mm,
height 7.9 mm; 25 jewels; 28,800 vph; shockproof
and antimagnetic (DIN-norm); 42-hour power
reserve
Functions: hours, minutes, subsidiary seconds;
chronograph; date
Case: tegimented stainless steel, 36.8 x 38.4 mm,
height 16.5 mm; sapphire crystal; water-resistant
to 10 atm
Band: calf leather, buckle
Remarks: slide-adjustable lugs for band length
adjustment
Price: $4,700

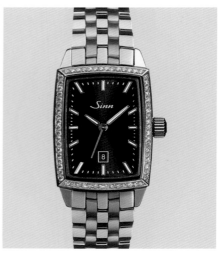

243 TW66 WG S

Reference number: 243050
Movement: automatic, ETA Caliber 2671;
ø 17.2 mm, height 4.8 mm; 25 jewels; 28,800 vph;
shockproof and antimagnetic (DIN-norm)
Functions: hours, minutes, sweep seconds; date
Case: titanium, 22.5 x 29.5 mm, height 9 mm; bezel
in white gold set with 66 brilliant-cut diamonds;
sapphire crystal; water-resistant to 10 atm
Band: titanium, double folding clasp
Price: $7,350
Variations: without diamonds (from $3,200)

6000 Rose Gold

Reference number: 6000.040
Movement: automatic, modified ETA Caliber 7750;
ø 30.4 mm, height 7.9 mm; 25 jewels; 28,800 vph;
fine finishing; 42-hour power reserve
Functions: hours, minutes, subsidiary seconds;
additional 12-hour display (second time zone);
chronograph; date
Case: rose gold, ø 38.5 mm, height 15.4 mm;
crown-adjustable inner bezel with 12-hour
divisions; sapphire crystal; transparent case back;
water-resistant to 10 atm
Band: reptile skin, buckle
Price: $16,000

6090

Reference number: 6090.010
Movement: automatic, ETA Caliber 2892-A2;
ø 25.6 mm, height 3.6 mm; 21 jewels; 28,800 vph;
shockproof and antimagnetic (DIN-norm); 42-hour
power reserve
Functions: hours, minutes, sweep seconds;
additional 12-hour display; large date
Case: stainless steel, ø 41.5 mm, height 11 mm;
crown-adjustable inner bezel with 12-hour divisions;
sapphire crystal; transparent case back; water-
resistant to 10 atm
Band: stainless steel, double folding clasp
Remarks: comes with additional calf-leather band
Price: $4,300

1746 Classic

Reference number: 1746.011
Movement: automatic, ETA Caliber 2892-A2;
ø 26.2 mm, height 3.6 mm; 21 jewels; 28,800 vph;
shockproof and antimagnetic (DIN-norm)
Functions: hours, minutes; date
Case: stainless steel, ø 42 mm, height 9.5
mm; sapphire crystal; transparent case back;
water-resistant to 10 atm
Band: calf leather, buckle
Remarks: enamel dial
Price: $2,575
Variations: as smaller 1736 Classic model
($2,350)

Peter Speake-Marin

Speake-Marin
Chemin en Baffa 2
CH-1183 Bursins
Switzerland

Tel.:
01141-21-825-5069

E-Mail:
info@speake-marin.com

Website:
www.speake-marin.com

Founded:
2002

Number of employees:
5

Annual production:
500 watches

U.S. distributor:
Martin Pulli, Inc.
4337 Main Street
Philadelphia, PA 19127
215-508-4610
martinpulli@aol.com
www.martinpulli.com

Most important collections:
HMS, Spirit Mark 2, Triad, Resilience, Serpent
Calendar, Renaissance, Marin-1, Marin-2

"*Genius* does what it must, and *talent* does what it can," said statesman Edward Bulwer-Lytton. The quote comes to mind when considering the life and career of Peter Speake-Marin. This watchmaker's watchmaker brings realism, genius, and a sense of romance to his work. As a horological innovator—he could have been a poet or adventurer—he has managed within little more than a decade to establish an outstanding reputation for originality, virtuosity, and being an outstanding colleague. His hand has contributed to such iconic pieces as the HM1 of MB&F, the Chapter One of Maîtres du Temps, and the Harry Winston Excenter Tourbillon. Born in Essex in 1968, Speake-Marin attended Hackney College, London, and WOSTEP in Switzerland before earning his first spurs restoring antique watches at a Somlo in Piccadilly. In 1996, he moved to Le Locle, Switzerland, to work with Renaud et Papi, at which point he set about making his own pieces. A dual-train tourbillon (the Foundation Watch) opened the door to the prestigious AHCI.

Speake-Marin has never stopped reflecting, creating, recreating, and questioning his pieces. He called his first independent product the Piccadilly. The case is a remarkably simple affair: a cylinder with a narrow bezel that allows the dial to express itself frankly. The Serpent Calendar saw a twisted sweep date hand in blued metal, a modern "surprise" perfectly in tune with the essentially eighteenth-century marine look of the pieces.

His Spirit Mark 2 watch is an homage to the hardy spirit of his fellow watchmakers and bears the inscription "Fight, Love & Persevere." The recession taught him something crucial: "I was a watchmaker, not an entrepreneur," he shares. "I had to become entrepreneurial to become a watchmaker again." His aim is for high horology to be better known and appreciated. With such pieces as the new Serpent Calendar (with a shorter date hand) and the brilliant Triad, the first in his Mechanical Art collection, he seems headed in the right direction.

Resilience

Movement: automatic, Speake-Marin Eros 2 Caliber; ø 30.4 mm, height 4.35 mm; 35 jewels; 28,800 vph; twin spring barrels; "topping tool" mystery winding rotor; hand-finished bridges and rotor; 120-hour power reserve
Functions: hours, minutes, sweep seconds
Case: pink gold, 3-part "Piccadilly" case, ø 38 mm, height 12 mm; sapphire crystal; transparent case back; water-resistant to 3 atm
Band: reptile skin, buckle
Price: $25,700
Variations: with 42 mm case ($30,700)

Spirit Mark 2

Movement: automatic, Caliber TT738; ø 30.4 mm, height 4.35 mm; 35 jewels; 28,800 vph; twin spring barrels; "topping tool" mystery winding rotor; hand-finished bridges and rotor; 120-hour power reserve
Functions: hours, minutes, sweep seconds
Case: stainless steel, 3-part "Piccadilly" case, ø 42 mm; height 12 mm; sapphire crystal; water-resistant to 3 atm
Band: calf leather, buckle
Remarks: domed compression back engraved with "Fight, Love & Persevere"
Price: $7,700

Triad

Movement: automatic, Speake-Marin Eros 2 Caliber; ø 30.4 mm, height 4.35 mm; 35 jewels; 28,800 vph; twin spring barrels; "topping tool" mystery winding rotor; hand-finished bridges and rotor; 120-hour power reserve
Functions: 3 hour and minute hands; second time zone (world-time display); date
Case: stainless steel, 3-part "Piccadilly" case, ø 42 mm; height 13 mm; pink gold bezel; sapphire crystal; water-resistant 3 atm
Band: reptile skin, buckle
Remarks: 3 black and 3 gilded "Triad" wheels, "topping tool" logo in pink gold on dial center
Price: $29,700, limited to 88 pieces

Stowa GmbH
Gewerbepark 16
D-75331 Engelsbrand
Germany

Tel.:
01149-7082-9306-0

Fax:
01149-7082-9306-2

E-Mail:
info@stowa.com

Website:
www.stowa.com

Founded:
1990

Number of employees:
15

Annual production:
maximum 4,000 watches

Distribution:
direct sales; please contact the company in
Germany; orders are taken by phone Monday-
Friday 9 a.m. to 5 p.m. European time

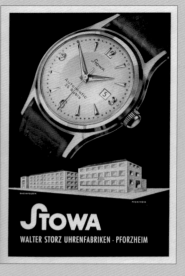

Stowa

When a watch brand organizes a museum for itself, it is usually with good reason. The German firm Stowa may not be the biggest fish in the horological pond, but it has been around for more than eighty years, and its products are well worth taking a look at as expressions of German watchmaking culture. Stowa began in Pforzheim, then moved to the little industrial town of Rheinfelden, and now operates in Engelsbrand, a "suburb" of Pforzheim. After a history as a family-owned company, today the brand is headed by Jörg Schauer, who has maintained the goal and vision of original founder Walter Storz: delivering quality watches at a reasonable price.

Stowa is one of the few German brands to have operated without interruption since the beginning of the twentieth century, albeit with a new owner as of 1990. Besides all the political upheavals, it also survived the quartz crisis of the 1970s, during which the European market was flooded with cheap watches from Asia and many traditional German watchmakers were put out of business. Storz managed to keep Stowa going, but even a quality fanatic has to pay a price during times of trouble: With huge input from his son, Werner, Storz restructured the company so that it was able to begin encasing reasonably priced quartz movements rather than being strictly an assembler of mechanical movements.

Schauer bought the brand in 1996. Spurred on by the success of his eponymous line, he also steered Stowa back toward mechanical watches. His new Stowa timepieces are for the most part interpretations of successful old models now powered by Swiss ETA movements. For the last six years, Schauer has sold Stowa watches almost exclusively online or factory-direct, keeping its retail prices more than reasonable.

Marine Chronograph

Reference number: MarineChronograph
Movement: automatic, ETA Caliber 7753; ø 30.4 mm, height 7.9 mm; 27 jewels; 28,800 vph; 42-hour power reserve
Functions: hours, minutes, subsidiary seconds; chronograph
Case: stainless steel, ø 41 mm, height 14.7 mm; sapphire crystal
Band: reptile skin, buckle
Price: $1,964
Variations: with calf leather band ($1,876); with stainless steel band ($1,964)

Chrono 1938

Reference number: StowaChronocremematt
Movement: automatic, ETA Caliber 7753; ø 30.4 mm, height 7.9 mm; 27 jewels; 28,800 vph; 42-hour power reserve
Functions: hours, minutes, subsidiary seconds; chronograph
Case: stainless steel, ø 41 mm, height 14.7 mm; sapphire crystal, transparent case back; water-resistant to 5 atm
Band: reptile skin, folding clasp
Price: $2,031
Variations: with calf leather band ($1,942); with stainless steel band ($2,031)

Flieger Chrono

Reference number: FliegerChrono
Movement: automatic, ETA Caliber 7753; ø 30.4 mm, height 7.9 mm; 27 jewels; 28,800 vph; 42-hour power reserve
Functions: hours, minutes; chronograph
Case: stainless steel, ø 41 mm, height 14.7 mm; sapphire crystal; water-resistant to 5 atm
Band: calf leather, buckle
Price: $1,920
Variations: with retro leather band ($1,876); with stainless steel bracelet ($2,009)

Flieger T01 Testaf

Reference number: FliegerT01TESTAF
Movement: automatic, ETA Caliber 2824-2;
ø 25.6 mm, height 4.6 mm; 25 jewels; 28,800 vph;
rhodium-plated, blued screws, côtes de Genève;
38-hour power reserve
Functions: hours, minutes, sweep seconds
Case: titanium, ø 45 mm, height 12.9 mm;
bidirectional bezel with aluminum inserts and
60-minute division; sapphire crystal, water-resistant
to 20 atm
Band: calf leather, buckle
Remarks: TESTAF certification
Price: $1,432
Variations: with rubber strap ($1,398)

Flieger GMT Worldwide

Reference number: FliegerGMTWorldwide
Movement: automatic, ETA Caliber A07.171;
ø 36.6 mm, height 7.9 mm; 24 jewels; 28,800 vph;
rhodium-plated, blued screws, ribbing; 48-hour
power reserve
Functions: hours, minutes, sweep seconds;
additional 24-hour display (second time zone)
Case: titanium, ø 45 mm, height 15.5 mm;
bidirectional bezel with aluminum inserts and
24-hour division; sapphire crystal, transparent case
back; water-resistant to 20 atm
Band: calf leather, buckle
Price: $1,876
Variations: with rubber strap ($1,876)

Flieger Without Logo

Reference number: FliegerohneLogo
Movement: automatic, ETA Caliber 2824-2;
ø 25.6 mm, height 4.6 mm; 25 jewels; 28,800 vph;
blued screws; handmade German silver rotor
Functions: hours, minutes, sweep seconds
Case: stainless steel, ø 40 mm, height 10.2 mm;
sapphire crystal; water-resistant to 5 atm
Band: calf leather, buckle (optionally folding clasp)
Price: $788
Variations: with reptile band ($921); with stainless
steel bracelet ($921)

Seatime Black

Reference number: SeatimeSchwarz
Movement: automatic, ETA Caliber 2824-2;
ø 25.6 mm, height 4.6 mm; 25 jewels; 28,800 vph;
38-hour power reserve
Functions: hours, minutes, sweep seconds; date
Case: stainless steel, ø 42 mm, height 13.5 mm;
unidirectional bezel with reference marker; screw-in
crown; sapphire crystal, water-resistant to 30 atm
Band: rubber, double safety folding clasp with
extension link
Price: $865
Variations: with calf leather band ($865); with
stainless steel band ($965); various bezel colors

Antea 365 A 10

Reference number: Antea365A10
Movement: automatic, Soprod Caliber A10;
ø 25.6 mm, height 3.6 mm; 25 jewels; 28,800 vph;
blued screws; 42-hour power reserve
Functions: hours, minutes, sweep seconds; date
Case: stainless steel, ø 36.5 mm, height 8.1 mm;
sapphire crystal, transparent case back; water-
resistant to 5 atm
Band: calf leather, folding clasp
Price: $921
Variations: with reptile band ($1,054); with
stainless steel bracelet ($1,015)

Marine Original

Reference number: MarineOriginalpolweissarabisch
Movement: manually wound, ETA Caliber 6498-1;
ø 36.6 mm, height 4.5 mm; 17 jewels; 18,000 vph;
screw balance; swan-neck fine adjustment; blued
screws; with côtes de Genève; 46-hour power
reserve
Functions: hours, minutes, subsidiary seconds
Case: stainless steel, ø 41 mm, height 12 mm;
sapphire crystal; water-resistant to 5 atm
Band: calf leather, buckle
Price: $1,021
Variations: with reptile band ($1,110); with
stainless steel bracelet ($1,110)

TAG Heuer
Branch of LVMH SA
6a, rue L.-J.-Chevrolet
CH-2300 La Chaux-de-Fonds
Switzerland

Tel.:
01141-32-919-8000

Fax:
01141-32-919-9000

E-Mail:
info@tagheuer.com

Website:
www.tagheuer.com

Founded:
1860

Number of employees:
approx. 1,000

Annual production:
not specified

U.S. distributor:
TAG Heuer/LVMH Watch & Jewelry USA
960 South Springfield Ave.
Springfield, NJ 07081
973-467-1890

Most important collections/price range:
TAG Heuer Formula 1, Aquaracer, Link, Carrera, Grand Carrera, Monaco / from approx. $1,000 to $20,000

TAG Heuer

Measuring speed accurately in ever greater detail has been the ultimate goal of TAG Heuer. The brand has also established numerous technical milestones. There was the first automatic chronograph caliber with a microrotor (created in 1969 in cooperation with Hamilton-Büren, Breitling, and Dubois Dépraz). Of more recent vintage is the fascinating mechanical movement V4 with its belt-driven transmission, unveiled in a limited edition for the brand's 150th anniversary. At the same time TAG Heuer released its first chronograph with an in-house movement, the caliber 1887, the basis of which was an existing chronograph movement by the Japanese company Seiko. Some of the components are made by the company itself in Switzerland, while assembly is done entirely in-house.

Lately, TAG Heuer has increased its manufacturing capacities to meet the strong and growing demand and to maintain its independence. It also serves as an extended workbench for companion brands Zenith and Hublot, also part of the LVMH Group.

TAG Heuer continues to conceive some spectacular concept watches and to break world speed records for mechanical escapements. In 2005, the outstanding Caliber 360 combined a standard movement with a 360,000 vph (50 Hz) chronograph mechanism able to measure 100ths of a second. In 2011, the Micrograph 1/100th housed a time display and measurement mounted on a single plate. Shortly after, the development department under Guy Sémon broke the 1,000th of a second barrier with the Mikrotimer Flying 1000. And in 2012, the frequency was doubled with the Mikrogirder 2000, featuring a vibrating metal strip instead of a balance wheel. The latest development is the MikrotourbillonS with a chronograph built on the dual-chain, start- and stopwatch principle. It has two escapements, each with a tourbillon. The chronograph one revolves in five seconds, driven at a record-breaking 360,000 vph, ten times that of the Zenith El Primero.

TAG Heuer Formula 1 Calibre 16

Reference number: CAU2010.BA0873
Movement: automatic, TAG Heuer Caliber 16 (base ETA 7750); ø 30.4 mm, height 7.9 mm; 25 jewels; 28,800 vph
Functions: hours, minutes, subsidiary seconds; chronograph; date
Case: stainless steel, ø 44 mm, height 15.2 mm; bezel with ceramic insert; sapphire crystal; screw-in crown; water-resistant to 20 atm
Band: stainless steel with ceramic inlays folding clasp with extension link
Price: $3,300

Aquaracer 500M Calibre 16

Reference number: CAK2110.BA0833
Movement: automatic, TAG Heuer Caliber 16 (base ETA 7750); ø 30.4 mm, height 7.9 mm; 25 jewels; 28,800 vph
Functions: hours, minutes, subsidiary seconds; chronograph; date
Case: stainless steel, ø 43 mm, height 16 mm; unidirectional bezel with ceramic inlay and 60-minute divisions; sapphire crystal; screw-in crown; automatic helium valve; water-resistant to 50 atm
Band: stainless steel, folding clasp with safety pushers
Price: $4,300

Aquaracer 500M Calibre 5

Reference number: WAK2110.BA0830
Movement: automatic, TAG Heuer Caliber 5 (base ETA 2824-2); ø 26 mm, height 4.6 mm; 25 jewels; 28,800 vph
Functions: hours, minutes, sweep seconds; date
Case: stainless steel, ø 43 mm, height 13.5 mm; unidirectional bezel with ceramic inlay and 60-minute divisions; sapphire crystal; screw-in crown; automatic helium valve; water-resistant to 50 atm
Band: stainless steel, folding clasp with safety pushers and extension links
Price: $2,900
Variations: with black-coated case ($3,300); stainless steel/yellow gold ($3,500)

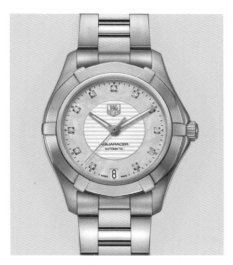

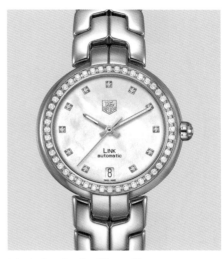

Aquaracer Calibre 5 Lady Diamonds

Reference number: WAP2351.BD0838
Movement: automatic, TAG Heuer Caliber 5 (base ETA 2824-2); ø 26 mm, height 4.6 mm; 25 jewels; 28,800 vph
Functions: hours, minutes, sweep seconds; date
Case: stainless steel, ø 34 mm, rose gold bezel; sapphire crystal; transparent case back; screw-in crown; water-resistant to 20 atm
Band: stainless steel with rose gold inlays, folding clasp with safety pushers
Remarks: dial set with 11 diamonds
Price: $5,400
Variations: without diamonds ($4,600)

Link Calibre 16

Reference number: CAT2010.BA0952
Movement: automatic, TAG Heuer Caliber 16 (base ETA 7750); ø 30.4 mm, height 7.9 mm; 25 jewels; 28,800 vph
Functions: hours, minutes, subsidiary seconds; chronograph; date
Case: stainless steel, ø 43 mm, height 16 mm; sapphire crystal; screw-in crown; water-resistant to 10 atm
Band: stainless steel, folding clasp with safety pushers
Price: $3,200
Variations: with silver dial; in bicolor version (stainless steel/rose gold) with leather band ($6,500)

Link Lady Calibre 7

Reference number: WAT2314.BA0956
Movement: automatic, TAG Heuer Caliber 7 (base Sellita SW300); ø 26.2 mm, height 5.05 mm; 25 jewels; 28,800 vph
Functions: hours, minutes, sweep seconds; date
Case: stainless steel, ø 34.5 mm, height 11 mm; bezel set with 48 diamonds; sapphire crystal; transparent case back; water-resistant to 10 atm
Band: stainless steel, double folding clasp
Remarks: dial set with 11 diamonds
Price: $7,400
Variations: without diamond bezel ($4,300); in bicolor version in stainless steel/rose gold with dial set with 11 diamonds ($6,800)

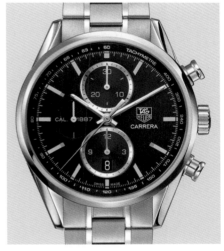

Carrera Calibre 16 Day-Date

Reference number: CV201AG.BA0725
Movement: automatic, TAG Heuer Caliber 16 (base ETA 7750); ø 30.4 mm, height 7.9 mm; 25 jewels; 28,800 vph
Functions: hours, minutes, subsidiary seconds; chronograph; weekday, date
Case: stainless steel, ø 41 mm, height 14.5 mm; aluminum bezel; sapphire crystal; water-resistant to 10 atm
Band: stainless steel, folding clasp with safety pushers
Price: $4,500
Variations: with reptile skin band ($4,500); with rubber strap ($4,500)

Carrera Calibre 1887

Reference number: CAR2A10.BA0799
Movement: automatic, TAG Heuer Caliber 1887; ø 29.3 mm, height 7.13 mm; 39 jewels; 28,800 vph
Functions: hours, minutes, subsidiary seconds; chronograph; date
Case: stainless steel, ø 43 mm, height 14.8 mm; ceramic bezel; sapphire crystal; transparent case back; water-resistant to 10 atm
Band: stainless steel, folding clasp with safety pushers
Price: $5,500
Variations: with reptile skin band ($5,500); with gray dial

Carrera Calibre 1887

Reference number: CAR2110.BA0720
Movement: automatic, TAG Heuer Caliber 1887; ø 29.3 mm, height 7.13 mm; 39 jewels; 28,800 vph
Functions: hours, minutes, subsidiary seconds; chronograph; date
Case: stainless steel, ø 41 mm, height 14.6 mm; sapphire crystal; transparent case back; water-resistant to 10 atm
Band: stainless steel, folding clasp with safety pushers
Price: $5,400
Variations: various dial colors; with reptile skin band ($5,400)

Carrera Calibre 1887

Reference number: CAR2012.FC6235
Movement: automatic, TAG Heuer Caliber 1887; ø 29.3 mm, height 7.13 mm; 39 jewels; 28,800 vph
Functions: hours, minutes, subsidiary seconds; chronograph; date
Case: stainless steel, ø 43 mm, height 14.6 mm; sapphire crystal; transparent case back; water-resistant to 10 atm
Band: reptile skin, folding clasp
Price: $6,300
Variations: with black dial; with stainless steel bracelet ($6,300)

Carrera Calibre 1887 Jack Heuer Edition

Reference number: CAR2C11.FC6327
Movement: automatic, TAG Heuer Caliber 1887; ø 29.3 mm, height 7.13 mm; 39 jewels; 28,800 vph
Functions: hours, minutes, subsidiary seconds; chronograph; date
Case: titanium, ø 45 mm, height 14.5 mm; stainless steel bezel with black titanium carbide coating; sapphire crystal; transparent case back; water-resistant to 10 atm
Band: reptile skin, folding clasp
Remarks: special edition for Carrera 50th anniversary with the so-called bullhead case with crown and pushers at upper lug
Price: $7,800

Carrera Calibre 1887 Carbon

Reference number: CAR2C90.FC6341
Movement: automatic, TAG Heuer Caliber 1887; ø 29.3 mm, height 7.13 mm; 39 jewels; 28,800 vph
Functions: hours, minutes, subsidiary seconds; chronograph; date
Case: carbon fiber, ø 45 mm, height 14.8 mm; sapphire crystal; transparent case back; water-resistant to 10 atm
Band: reptile skin, folding clasp
Remarks: so-called bullhead case with crown and pushers at upper lug
Price: $12,000

Grand Carrera Calibre 8 Grande Date GMT

Reference number: WAV5011.FC6291
Movement: automatic, TAG Heuer Caliber 8 RS (base ETA 2892-A2); ø 26.2 mm, height 3.6 mm; 21 jewels; 28,800 vph; COSC tested chronometer
Functions: hours, minutes, sweep seconds; additional 12-hour display (second time zone); large date
Case: stainless steel, ø 41 mm, height 12.7 mm; sapphire crystal; transparent case back; water-resistant to 10 atm
Band: reptile skin, folding clasp
Price: $9,500
Variations: with gray reptile skin band ($9,500); with black dial

Carrera Calibre 36 Carbon

Reference number: CAR2B10.BA0799
Movement: automatic, TAG Heuer Caliber 36 RS (base Zenith El Primero 400); ø 30 mm, height 6.6 mm; 31 jewels; 36,000 vph; mounted in shockproof cage
Functions: hours, minutes, sweep seconds; flyback chronograph; date
Case: stainless steel, ø 43 mm, height 15 mm; sapphire crystal; transparent case back; water-resistant to 10 atm
Band: stainless steel, folding clasp
Price: $7,900
Variations: with reptile skin band ($7,900); with white inner bezel; "Racing Edition" in titanium with PVD coating ($8,900)

Carrera Mikrograph 100 Limited Edition

Reference number: CAR5041.FC8178
Movement: automatic, TAG Heuer Caliber Mikrograph; ø 35.8 mm, height 7.95 mm; 62 jewels; 28,800 and 360,000 vph; 2 separate balance wheels and escapements for watch movement and chronograph display
Functions: hours, minutes, subsidiary seconds; chronograph; date
Case: rose gold, ø 43 mm, height 16 mm; sapphire crystal, transparent case back; water-resistant to 10 atm
Band: reptile skin, buckle
Price: $50,000, limited to 150 pieces

Carrera Mikropendulum 100

Reference number: CAR2B80.FC6339
Movement: automatic, Calibre Mikrograph;
ø 35.8 mm; 58 jewels; 28,800 and 360,000 vph;
"Pendulum" system (4 magnets in place of balance
spring) with separate high frequency escapement
for chronograph function; display of 1/100th
seconds; 42-hour power reserve (watch), 90-minute
(chronograph); COSC certified chronometer
Functions: hours, minutes; chronograph
Case: titanium, ø 45 mm; sapphire crystal;
transparent case back; water-resistant to 10 atm
Band: reptile skin, folding clasp
Price: on request

Carrera Mikrotourbillon S 100

Reference number: CAR5A51.FC6323
Movement: automatic, TAG Heuer Caliber
Mikrotourbillon S; ø 35.8 mm; 75 jewels; 28,800
and 360,000 vph; 2 separate balance wheels with
tourbillon; display of 1/100th seconds; 45-hour
power reserve (watch), 60-minute (chronograph)
Functions: hours, minutes; power reserve indicator;
chronograph
Case: rose gold, ø 45 mm; sand-blasted titanium
bezel; sapphire crystal; transparent case back;
water-resistant to 10 atm
Band: reptile skin, folding clasp
Price: $250,000

Grand Carrera Calibre 17 RS

Reference number: CAV511E.BFC623
Movement: automatic, TAG Heuer Caliber 17 RS
(base ETA 2894-2); ø 28.6 mm, height 6.1 mm;
37 jewels; 28,800 vph; disc display ("Rotating
System")
Functions: hours, minutes, subsidiary seconds;
chronograph; date
Case: stainless steel, ø 43 mm, height 15 mm;
sapphire crystal; transparent case back; screw-in
crown; water-resistant to 10 atm
Band: reptile skin, folding clasp
Price: $9,500
Variations: with stainless steel bracelet ($9,500);
blackened titanium ($10,500)

Monaco Calibre 12 Limited Edition Automobile Club de Monaco

Reference number: CAW211M.FC6324
Movement: automatic, TAG Heuer Caliber 12
(base Sellita SW300 with Dubois-Dépraz module);
ø 30 mm, height 7.3 mm; 59 jewels; 28,800 vph
Functions: hours, minutes, subsidiary seconds;
chronograph; date
Case: stainless steel bezel, with black titanium
carbide coating; 39 x 39 mm, height 13.5
mm; sapphire crystal; transparent case back;
water-resistant to 10 atm
Band: calf leather, folding clasp
Price: $8,200

Monaco Calibre 36 Twenty Four

Reference number: CAL5113.FC6329
Movement: automatic, TAG Heuer Caliber 36 (base
Zenith El Primero 400); ø 30 mm, height 6.6 mm;
31 jewels; 36,000 vph; mounted in shockproof cage
Functions: hours, minutes, subsidiary seconds;
chronograph; date
Case: stainless steel, 40.5 x 40.5 mm, height
18 mm; sapphire crystal; transparent case back;
water-resistant to 10 atm
Band: reptile skin, folding clasp
Price: $13,500
Variations: "Steve McQueen" edition with blue and
white dial

Monaco V4 Limited Edition

Reference number: WAW2080.FC6288
Movement: automatic, TAG Heuer Caliber V4; 36
x 36 mm; 18,000 vph; tungsten carbide linear
winding mass; 4 spring barrels; 13 miniature power
transmission belts; 39 micro ball bearings
Functions: hours, minutes, subsidiary seconds
Case: titanium coated with silicon nitride ceramic,
41 x 41 mm, height 18 mm; sapphire crystal;
transparent case back; water-resistant to 10 atm
Band: reptile skin, folding clasp
Remarks: faceted sapphire crystal
Price: $65,000, limited to 200 pieces

Temption GmbH
Raistinger Str. 46
D-71083 Herrenberg
Germany

Tel.:
01149-7032-977-954

Fax:
01149-7032-977-955

E-Mail:
ftemption@aol.com

Website:
www.temption.info

Founded:
1997

Number of employees:
4

Annual production:
700 watches

U.S. distributor:
TemptionUSA
Debby Gordon
2053 North Bridgeport Drive
Fayetteville, AR 72704
888-400-4293
temptionusa@sbcglobal.net

Most important collections/price range:
automatics (three-hand), GMT, chronographs,
and chronographs with complications / approx.
$1,900 to $4,200

Temption

Temption has been operating under the leadership of Klaus Ulbrich since 1997. Ulbrich is an engineer with special training in the construction of watches and movements, and right from the start, he intended to develop timekeepers that were modern in their aesthetics but not subject to the whims of zeitgeist. Retro watches would have no place in his collections. The design behind all Temption models is inspired more by the Bauhaus or the Japanese concept of wabi sabi. Reduction to what is absolutely necessary is the golden rule here. Beauty emerges from clarity, or in other words, less is more.

Ulbrich sketches all the watches himself. Some of the components are even made in-house, but all the pieces are assembled in the company facility in Herrenberg, a town just to the east of the Black Forest. The primary functions are always easy to read, even in low light. The company logo is discreetly included on the dial.

Ulbrich works according to a model he calls the "information pyramid." Hours and minutes are at the tip, with all other functions subordinated. To maintain this hierarchy, the dials are dark, the date windows are in the same hue, and all subdials are not framed in any way.

The Cameo rectangular model is a perfect example of Ulbrich's aesthetic ideas and his consistent technological approach: Because rectangular sapphire crystals can hardly be made water-resistant, the Cameo's crystal is chemically bonded to the case and water-resistant to 10 atm. The frame for the crystal was metalized inside to hide the bonded edge. The overall look is one of stunning simplicity and elegance.

CM05

Reference number: 16
Movement: automatic, Temption Caliber T15.1 (base ETA 2892-A2); ø 25.6 mm, height 3.6 mm; 21 jewels; 28,800 vph; 42-hour power reserve
Functions: hours, minutes, sweep seconds; date
Case: stainless steel, ø 42 mm, height 11 mm; unidirectional bezel, 12-hour division, sapphire crystal; transparent case back; screw-in crown; water-resistant to 10 atm
Band: stainless steel, double folding clasp
Price: $2,400

Cameo-B

Reference number: 14
Movement: automatic, Temption Caliber T15.1 (base ETA 2892-A2); ø 25.6 mm, height 3.6 mm; 21 jewels; 28,800 vph
Functions: hours, minutes, sweep seconds; date
Case: stainless steel, 37.4 x 40.7 mm, height 9.9 mm; sapphire crystal; transparent case back; screw-in crown; water-resistant to 10 atm
Band: calf leather, folding clasp
Price: $2,100

Chronograph CGK205

Reference number: 205
Movement: automatic, Temption Caliber T18.1 (base ETA 7751); ø 30 mm, height 7.8 mm; 25 jewels; 28,800 vph; finely decorated
Functions: hours, minutes, subsidiary seconds; additional 24-hour display; chronograph; full calendar with month, moon phase, weekday, date
Case: stainless steel, ø 43 mm, height 14 mm; bezel with tachymeter scale, sapphire crystal; transparent case back; screw-in crown and pusher, with onyx cabochons; water-resistant to 10 atm
Band: stainless steel, double folding clasp
Price: $4,000

Thomas Ninchritz

In 1520, the locksmith Peter Henlein of Nuremberg was the first craftsman in Europe who could create "portable clocks." About half a millennium later, a trip to Nuremberg is still well worth the effort for watch aficionados: In his atelier, watchmaker Thomas Ninchritz produces a small collection of fascinating wristwatches.

The core of Ninchritz's watches is the extremely robust ETA Unitas caliber—though when he adds his own well-proportioned three-quarter plate, it is hardly recognizable. The master's

meticulous work lends the classic manually wound movement a finish that does not need to shy away from comparisons even to expensive *manufacture* movements. Screw-mounted gold chatons, hand-engraved balance cocks, and swan-neck fine adjustments are among the elements that make a watch enthusiast's heart beat faster.

The creative watchmaker came up with a very interesting idea for his Vice Versa model: Using a relatively simple method, he routes the dial train of ETA Caliber 6498 (the hunter version featuring subsidiary seconds at 6 o'clock) across two transmission wheels and a long stem through to the back of the movement. There is enough room to poke it through between the spring barrel and the balance, with the hand arbors now appearing in a small dial on the gear train bridge, which Ninchritz has extended to become a true three-quarter plate decorated with a stripe pattern, engraving, and chatons secured by little blued screws. Additionally, the index is accompanied by a beautiful swan-neck spring, to ensure that no one will mistake this work of art for the "back" of the movement.

Thomas Ninchritz
Niebüller Strasse 7
D-90425 Nuremberg
Germany

Tel.:
01149-911-552-363

Fax:
01149-911-581-7622

E-Mail:
th.ninchritz@t-online.de

Website:
www.ninchritz-uhren.de

Founded:
2005

Number of employees:
1

Annual production:
not specified

Distribution:
WatchBuys
888-333-4895
www.watchbuys.com

Most important collections/price range:
Black & Diamonds, Fliegeruhr, Grande Seconde, Kathedral, Ornatis / $2,400 to $23,250

Vice Versa

Reference number: NI 2000.6
Movement: manual winding, TN Caliber 203 (base ETA 6498-1 "Unitas"); ø 36.6 mm, height 4.03 mm; 18 jewels; 18,000 vph; three-quarter plate with gold chatons; swan-neck fine adjustment; back inverted by relocating hand gears
Functions: hours, minutes (off-center), subsidiary seconds (on back)
Case: stainless steel, ø 42 mm, height 10.5 mm; sapphire crystal; transparent case back
Band: calf leather, buckle or folding clasp
Price: $5,560
Variations: rose gold ($20,500); stainless steel with bezel, back, and crown in rose gold ($10,800)

Kathedral

Reference number: NI 2000.4
Movement: manual winding, TN Caliber 200; ø 36,6 mm, height 4.03 mm; 17 jewels; 18,000 vph; three-quarter plate with screwed-in gold chatons; hand-engraved balance cock; swan-neck fine adjustment
Functions: hours, minutes, subsidiary seconds
Case: stainless steel, ø 42 mm, height 10.5 mm; sapphire crystal; transparent case back
Band: calf leather, buckle
Price: $3,470
Variations: stainless steel and gold ($8,600); yellow or rose gold ($19,600)

Grande Seconde

Reference number: NI 2000.31
Movement: manually wound, TN Caliber 200 (base ETA 6498-1); ø 36,6 mm, height 4.03 mm; 17 jewels; 18,000 vph; three-quarter plate with gold chatons; hand-engraved balance cock; swan-neck fine adjustment
Functions: hours, minutes, subsidiary seconds
Case: stainless steel, ø 42 mm, height 10.5 mm; rose gold bezel; sapphire crystal, transparent case back
Band: calf leather, buckle
Price: $8,450
Variations: yellow or rose gold ($19,600)

Tissot SA
Chemin des Tourelles, 17
CH-2400 Le Locle
Switzerland

Tel.:
01141-32-933-3111

Fax:
01141-32-933-3311

E-Mail:
info@tissot.ch

Website:
www.tissot.ch

Founded:
1853

Number of employees:
not specified

Annual production:
not specified

U.S. distributor:
Tissot
The Swatch Group (U.S.), Inc.
1200 Harbor Boulevard
Weehawken, NJ 07086
201-271-1400
www.us.tissotshop.com

Most important collection/price range:
T-Touch / from $575

Tissot

The Swiss watchmaker Tissot was founded in 1853 in the town of Le Locle in the Jura mountains. In the century that followed, it gained international recognition for its Savonnette pocket watch. And even when the wristwatch became popular in the early twentieth century, time and again Tissot managed to attract attention to its products. To this day, the

Banana Watch of 1916 and its first watches in the art deco style (1919) remain design icons of that epoch. The watchmaker has always been at the top of its technical game as well: The first antimagnetic watch (1930), the first mechanical plastic watch (Astrolon, 1971), and its touch-screen T-Touch (1999) all bear witness to Tissot's remarkable capacity for finding unusual and modern solutions.

Today, Tissot belongs to the Swatch Group and, with its wide selection of quartz and inexpensive mechanical watches, serves as the group's entry-level brand. Within this price segment, Tissot offers something special for the buyer who values traditional watchmaking, but is not of limitless financial means. The brand, which celebrated its 160th anniversary in style in 2013 with a comprehensive retrospective in Geneva, has gravitated toward the sports crowd. Tissot is timing everything from basketball to superbike racing, from ice hockey to fencing—and water sports, of course. The Sailing Touch, a watch that provides sailors with a vast array of needed information, came out in 2010. The chronograph Couturier line is outfitted with the new ETA chronograph caliber C01.211. This caliber features a number of plastic parts: another step in simplifying, and lowering the cost of, mechanical movements.

Heritage Navigator

Reference number: T078.641.16.037.00
Movement: automatic, ETA Caliber 2893-3; ø 25.6 mm, height 4.1 mm; 21 jewels; 28,800 vph; 46-hour power reserve; COSC certified chronometer
Functions: hours, minutes, sweep seconds; world-time display with 24 time zones (second time zone)
Case: stainless steel, ø 43 mm, height 9.62 mm; crown rotates inner ring with reference cities; sapphire crystal, transparent case back; water-resistant to 3 atm
Band: calf leather, folding clasp
Price: $1,650
Variations: with black dial; rose gold, limited to 333 pieces ($8,250)

T-Complication Squelette

Reference number: T070.405.16.411.00
Movement: manually wound, ETA Caliber 6497; ø 36.6 mm, height 4.5 mm; 17 jewels; 21,600 vph; skeletonized; 46 hours power reserve
Functions: hours, minutes, subsidiary seconds
Case: stainless steel, ø 43 mm, height 11.99 mm; sapphire crystal, transparent case back; water-resistant to 5 atm
Band: calf leather, folding clasp
Price: $1,950

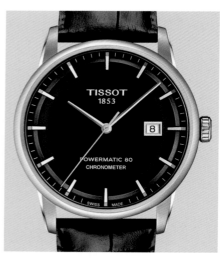

Luxury Automatic COSC Gent

Reference number: T086.408.16.051.00
Movement: automatic, Tissot Powermatic 80 (base ETA 2824-2); ø 25.6 mm, height 4.6 mm; 23 jewels; 21,600 vph; variable inertia balance; 80-hour power reserve; COSC certified chronometer
Functions: hours, minutes, sweep seconds; date
Case: stainless steel, ø 41 mm, height 9.75 mm; sapphire crystal, transparent case back; water-resistant to 5 atm
Band: calf leather, double folding clasp
Price: $1,075
Variations: various bands and cases

Bridgeport Lady Automatic

Reference number: T71.1.478.71
Movement: automatic, ETA Caliber 7750 Valjoux; ø 30 mm, height 7.9 mm; 25 jewels; 28,800 vph; 46-hour power reserve
Functions: hours, minutes, subsidiary seconds; chronograph; date
Case: stainless steel, ø 37.7 mm, height 12.62 mm; rose gold-plated bezel, crown, and pushers; sapphire crystal, transparent case back; water-resistant to 3 atm
Band: calf leather, double folding clasp
Remarks: mother-of-pearl dial
Price: $1,750
Variations: with various bands

PRS 516 Extreme Automatic

Reference number: T079.427.27.057.00
Movement: automatic, ETA Caliber C01.211; ø 30 mm, height 8.44 mm; 15 jewels; 21,600 vph; 45-hour power reserve
Functions: hours, minutes, subsidiary seconds; date; chronograph
Case: stainless steel, black PVD coating, ø 44.4 mm, height 15.73 mm; sapphire crystal, transparent case back; water-resistant to 10 atm
Band: rubber, buckle
Price: $1,450

Le Locle Small Second

Reference number: T006.428.11.038.00
Movement: automatic, ETA Caliber 2825-2; ø 25.6 mm, height 4.6 mm; 25 jewels; 28,800 vph; 42-hour power reserve
Functions: hours, minutes, subsidiary seconds; date
Case: stainless steel, ø 39.3 mm, height 11.55 mm; sapphire crystal; transparent case back; water-resistant to 3 atm
Band: stainless steel, double folding clasp
Price: $850

Couturier Small Second

Reference number: T035.428.36.051.00
Movement: automatic, ETA Caliber 2825-2; ø 25.6 mm, height 4.6 mm; 25 jewels; 28,800 vph; 42-hour power reserve
Functions: hours and minutes (off-center), subsidiary seconds; date
Case: stainless steel with rose gold-colored PVD coating, ø 39 mm, height 11.95 mm; sapphire crystal, transparent case back; water-resistant to 10 atm
Band: calf leather, double folding clasp
Price: $950

T-Race MotoGP Automatic Chronograph Limited Edition 2013

Reference number: T048.427.27.057.02
Movement: automatic, ETA Caliber C01.211; ø 30 mm, height 8.44 mm; 15 jewels; 21,600 vph; 45-hour power reserve
Functions: hours, minutes, subsidiary seconds; chronograph; date
Case: stainless steel, ø 45.3 mm, height 16.09 mm; bezel with black PVD coating; sapphire crystal, transparent case back; water-resistant to 10 atm
Band: rubber, folding clasp
Price: $1,425

T-Race Touch

Reference number: T081.420.17.057.00
Movement: quartz, ETA Caliber E49.301; multifunctional with LCD display
Functions: hours, minutes, subsidiary seconds; additional 12-hour display (second time zone), compass, tides calculator, 2 alarm functions; chronograph with 2 countdown timers; perpetual calendar with date, month, end-of-life function (EOL) of power left in battery
Case: stainless steel, ø 42.15 mm, height 13.45 mm; sapphire crystal, water-resistant to 10 atm
Band: synthetic; buckle
Price: $575

Towson Watch Co.
502 Dogwood Lane
Towson, MD 21286

Tel.:
410-823-1823

Fax:
410-823-8581

E-Mail:
towsonwatchco@aol.com

Website:
www.twcwatches.com

Founded:
2000

Number of employees:
4

Annual production:
200 watches

Distribution:
retail

Most important collections/price range:
Skipjack GMT / approx. $1,750; Mission / approx.
$2,500; Cockpit / approx. $2,300; Potomac
/ approx. $2,000; Pride II / approx. $3,900;
Choptank / $4,500; BayPilot / $2,800; custom
watches / $10,000

Towson Watch Company

"The old charm, in truth, still survives in the town, despite the frantic efforts of boosters and boomers who, in late years, have replaced all its ancient cobblestones with asphalt," commented H. L. Mencken, and much has changed in Baltimore since the days when he lived there. No doubt he would have sprayed his caustic ink at some of the more recent urban renewal projects as well, but while he did have a blind spot for horology, he would still have welcomed the Towson Watch Company, which was founded in 2000 by two men with a deep-seated passion for mechanical timepieces. After forty years repairing high-grade watches, repeaters, and chronographs and making his own tourbillons, George Thomas, a master watchmaker, met Hartwig Balke, a graduate in mechanical engineering and also a talented watchmaker, by chance.

To create something special, mechanical instruments of beauty and precision, was always each man's dream. Thomas built his first tourbillon pocket watches, now displayed at the National Watch and Clock Museum in Columbia, Pennsylvania, in 1985 when he was fifty-three years old. In 1999, Balke made his first wrist chronograph, the STS-99 Mission, for a NASA astronaut and mission specialist, and it was worn during the first space mission in the new millennium. A second watch, worn on the same mission, is also on display at the Columbia museum.

For more than ten years now, these two men's passion has gone into timepieces named for local sites and sights, like the Choptank or Potomac rivers or the old skipjack sailboats. After a few non-horological setbacks that hobbled the brand's development, Towson has announced production of a new GMT and a chronograph patterned after an airplane instrument.

Pride II

Reference number: PR250-S
Movement: automatic, ETA Caliber 2892-A2;
ø 25.6 mm, height 3.6 mm; 21 jewels; 28,800 vph;
glucydur balance; Nivarox hairspring; fine finishing
with côtes de Genève
Functions: hours, minutes, sweep seconds, date
Case: stainless steel, 39 x 44 mm, height 9.5 mm;
sapphire crystal; water resistant to 5 atm
Band: reptile skin, folding clasp
Remarks: *Pride of Baltimore II* engraved on case
back
Price: $3,850; limited to 100 pieces

Choptank

Reference number: CT250-S
Movement: automatic, ETA Caliber 7751
("Valjoux"); ø 30 mm, height 7.9 mm; 25 jewels;
28,800 vph; glucydur balance; Nivarox hairspring;
fine finishing with côtes de Genève
Functions: hours, minutes, subsidiary seconds;
24-hour display; chronograph; weekday, month,
date, and moon phase
Case: stainless steel, 40 x 44 mm, height 13.5 mm;
sapphire crystal, screwed-on back secured with 8
screws; sapphire crystal exhibition window; water-
resistant to 5 atm
Band: reptile skin, folding clasp
Price: $4,375
Variations: with stainless steel bracelet ($4,750)

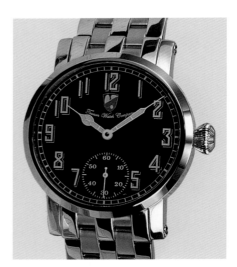

Baypilot

Reference number: BP250-B
Movement: manually wound, Soprod Unitas Caliber
6498; ø 37.2 mm, height 4.5 mm; 17 jewels;
18,000 vph; swan-neck fine adjustment; glucydur
screw balance; Nivarox hairspring; fine finishing with
côtes de Genève
Functions: hours, minutes, subsidiary seconds
Case: stainless steel, ø 42 mm, height 13.5 mm;
domed sapphire crystal; screwed-down back;
sapphire crystal exhibition window; water-resistant
to 5 atm
Band: stainless steel, double folding clasp
Price: $2,800
Variations: with leather strap ($2,450)

Montres Tudor SA
Rue François-Dussaud 3-7
Case postale 1755
CH-1211 Geneva
Switzerland

Tel.:
01141-22-302-2200

Fax:
01141-22-300-2255

E-Mail:
info@tudorwatch.com

Website:
www.tudorwatch.com

Founded:
1946

Number of employees:
not specified

Annual production:
not specified

U.S. distributor:
Tudor Watch U.S.A., LLC
665 Fifth Avenue
New York, NY 10022
212-897-9900; 212-371-0371 (fax)
www.tudorwatch.com

Most important collections/price range:
Heritage / $3,100 to $6,075; Pelagos / $4,125;
Grantour / $2,475 to $8,000; Fastrider / $3,675
to $4,925

Tudor

The Tudor brand came out of the shadow cast by its "big sister" Rolex in 2007 and worked hard to develop a personality of its own. The strategy is to focus on distinctive models that draw inspiration from the brand's rich past and to remain in the "affordable quality watch segment," which derives from its close connection with its parent company.

Rolex founder Hans Wilsdorf started Tudor in 1946 as a second brand in order to offer the legendary reliability of his watches to a broader public at a more affordable price. To this day, Tudor still benefits from the same industrial platform as Rolex, especially in the area of cases and bracelets, assembly and quality assurance, not to mention distribution and after-sales. However, the movements themselves are not in-house. They are delivered by ETA and "tudorized" according to the company's own aesthetic and technical criteria.

A new cross-marketing effort with the famous Italian motorcycle maker Ducati centers on the remarkable chronographs with red dials. This means that Tudor has been able to make deep inroads with a target group that has been almost totally ignored by most other brands, namely motorbike enthusiasts, who have been showing greater readiness than ever to pay good money to support their pastime. And so one great timepiece after another keeps emerging from the treasure trove of the brand's own historic models. Following the success of the Heritage Black Bay (modeled on a 1954 piece), Tudor has come out with a new version of the 1973 Chronograph Montecarlo, featuring blue accents.

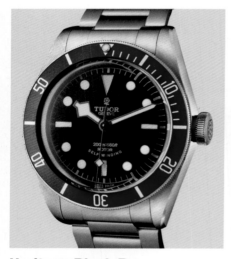

Heritage Black Bay

Reference number: 79220R
Movement: automatic, Tudor Caliber 2824
(base ETA 2892-A2); ø 25.6 mm, height 4.6 mm;
25 jewels; 28,800 vph; 38-hour power reserve
Functions: hours, minutes, sweep seconds
Case: stainless steel, ø 41 mm, height 12.95 mm;
unidirectional bezel with 60-minute divisions;
sapphire crystal; screw-in crown; water-resistant to
20 atm
Band: stainless steel, folding clasp with safety catch
Price: $3,425
Variations: with leather strap ($3,100)

Heritage Advisor

Reference number: 79620TN
Movement: automatic, Tudor Caliber 2892-901
(base ETA 2892-A2); ø 30.4 mm, height 6.3 mm;
31 jewels; 28,800 vph; additional module for
mechanical alarm
Functions: hours, minutes, sweep seconds; alarm
clock; date
Case: stainless steel, titanium, ø 42 mm, height
14 mm; sapphire crystal; water-resistant to 10 atm
Band: textile, buckle
Remarks: with optional stainless steel bracelet
Price: $6,075
Variations: with reptile skin strap ($5,850)

Heritage Chrono Blue

Reference number: 70330B
Movement: automatic, Tudor Caliber 2892 (base
ETA 2892-A2 with chronograph module); ø 30 mm,
height 6.9 mm; 55 jewels; 28,800 vph; 42-hour
power reserve
Functions: hours, minutes, subsidiary seconds;
chronograph; date
Case: stainless steel, ø 42 mm, height 13.38 mm;
bidirectional bezel with 12-hour divisions; sapphire
crystal; screw-in crown and pushers; water-resistant
to 15 atm
Band: textile, buckle
Remarks: with additional stainless steel bracelet
Price: $4,425

Pelagos

Reference number: 25500TN
Movement: automatic, Tudor Caliber 2824 (base ETA 2824-2; ø 25.6 mm, height 4.6 mm; 25 jewels; 28,800 vph; 38-hour power reserve
Functions: hours, minutes, sweep seconds; date
Case: stainless steel, titanium, ø 42 mm, height 14.25 mm; unidirectional bezel with 60-minute division; sapphire crystal; screw-in crown; water-resistant to 50 atm
Band: titanium, folding clasp with self-adjusting extension link
Remarks: with additional rubber strap
Price: $4,125

Fastrider Black Shield

Reference number: 42000CR
Movement: automatic, Tudor Caliber 7753 (base ETA 2892-A2); ø 30.4 mm, height 7.9 mm; 27 jewels; 28,800 vph; 46-hour power reserve
Functions: hours, minutes, subsidiary seconds; chronograph; date
Case: matt ceramic, ø 42 mm, height 14.48 mm; ceramic bezel with tachymeter scale; sapphire crystal; water-resistant to 15 atm
Band: rubber, buckle
Price: $4,925
Variations: with alcantara ($4,925)

Fastrider Chronograph

Reference number: 42000D
Movement: automatic, Tudor Caliber 7753 (base ETA 2892-A2); ø 30.4 mm, height 7.9 mm; 27 jewels; 28,800 vph; 46-hour power reserve
Functions: hours, minutes, subsidiary seconds; chronograph; date
Case: stainless steel, ø 42 mm, height 14.3 mm; steel bezel with tachymeter scale; sapphire crystal; water-resistant to 15 atm
Band: calf leather, folding clasp and safety catch
Remarks: comes with additional textile band
Price: $3,875

Grantour Chrono Fly-Back

Reference number: 20550N
Movement: automatic, Tudor Caliber 2892-A20 (base ETA 2892-A2); ø 30 mm, height 6.9 mm; 55 jewels; 28,800 vph; 42-hour power reserve
Functions: hours, minutes, subsidiary seconds; flyback chronograph; date
Case: stainless steel, ø 42 mm, height 12.6 mm; black lacquered bezel with 12-hour divisions; sapphire crystal; screw-in crown and lockable pushers; water-resistant to 15 atm
Band: stainless steel, folding clasp
Price: $4,725
Variations: with leather strap ($4,400)

Grantour Chrono

Reference number: 20530N
Movement: automatic, Tudor Caliber 7753 (base ETA 2892-A2); ø 30.4 mm, height 7.9 mm; 27 jewels; 28,800 vph; 46-hour power reserve
Functions: hours, minutes, subsidiary seconds; chronograph; date
Case: stainless steel, ø 42 mm, height 12.6 mm; black lacquered bezel with 12-hour divisions; sapphire crystal; screw-in crown and pushers; water-resistant to 15 atm
Band: calf leather, folding clasp
Price: $3,775
Variations: with stainless steel bracelet ($4,100)

Glamour Double Date

Reference number: 57000
Movement: automatic, Tudor Caliber 2892 (base ETA 2892-A2); ø 26 mm, height 4.6 mm; 21 jewels; 28,800 vph; 42-hour power reserve
Functions: hours, minutes, subsidiary seconds; large date
Case: stainless steel, ø 42 mm, height 12.1 mm; sapphire crystal; water-resistant to 10 atm
Band: leather, folding clasp
Price: $3,100
Variations: with stainless steel bracelet ($3,425); various dials

Tutima Uhrenfabrik GmbH
Pf. 1153
D-27770 Ganderkesee
Germany

Tel.:
01149-4221-988-320-22

Fax:
01149-4221-988-377

E-Mail:
info@tutima.de

Website:
www.tutima.de

Founded:
1957

Number of employees:
approx. 60

Annual production:
not specified

Distribution:
retail

U.S. distributor:
Tutima USA, Inc.
P.O. Box 983
Torrance, CA 90508
1-TUTIMA-1927
www.tutima.com

Most important collections/price range:
Patria, Military, Grand Classic, Classic, Yachting, FX/Valeo / approx. $1,200 to $28,500

Tutima

The name Glashütte is synonymous with watches in Germany. The area, known also for precision engineering in general, already had quite a watchmaking industry going when the outbreak of World War I closed off markets, followed by the hyperinflation of the early twenties. To rebuild the local economy, a conglomerate was created to produce finished watches under the leadership of jurist Dr. Ernst Kurtz consisting of the movement manufacturer UROFA Glashütte AG and UFAG. The top watches were given the name Tutima, derived from the Latin *tutus,* meaning whole, sound. Among the brand's most famous timepieces was a pilot's watch which set standards in terms of aesthetics and functionality.

A few days before World War II ended, Kurtz left Glashütte and founded Uhrenfabrik Kurtz in southern Germany. A young businessman and former employee of Kurtz by the name of Dieter Delecate is credited with keeping the manufacturing facilities and the name Tutima going even as the company sailed through troubled waters. In founding Tutima Uhrenfabrik GmbH in Ganderkesee, this young, resolute entrepreneur prepared the company's strategy for the coming decades.

Delecate has had the joy of seeing Tutima return to its old hometown and vertically integrated operations, meaning it is once again a genuine *manufacture.* Under the direction of renowned designer Rolf Lang, it has developed an in-house minute repeater. In 2013, Tutima proudly announced a genuine made-in-Glashütte movement (at least 50 percent must be produced in the town), Caliber 617. With characteristic restraint, the brand has placed this fine piece of engineering—with a three-quarter plate and decorated wheels—inside the new Patria, which comes with a subsidiary second display or a second time zone.

Patria

Reference number: 6600-01
Movement: manually wound, Tutima Caliber 617; ø 31 mm, height 4.78 mm; 20 jewels; 21,600 vph; screw balance with gold weight screws and Breguet spring; Glashütte three-quarter plate; winding wheels with click; gold-plated and finely finished; 65-hour power reserve
Functions: hours, minutes, subsidiary seconds
Case: rose gold, ø 43 mm, height 9.7 mm; sapphire crystal; transparent case back; water-resistant to 5 atm
Band: reptile skin, buckle
Price: $18,900

Patria Dual Time

Reference number: 6601-01
Movement: manually wound, Tutima Caliber 619; ø 31 mm, height 4.78 mm; 20 jewels; 21,600 vph; screw balance with gold weight screws; Glashütte three-quarter plate; winding wheels with click; gold-plated and finely finished; 65-hour power reserve
Functions: hours, minutes, subsidiary seconds; additional 12-hour display (second time zone);
Case: rose gold, ø 43 mm, height 9.7 mm; sapphire crystal; transparent case back; water-resistant to 5 atm
Band: reptile skin, buckle
Price: $19,900

Hommage Minute Repeater

Movement: manually wound, Caliber 800; 42 jewels; 21,600 vph; screw balance with 14 gold weight screws; Glashütte three-quarter plate; Breguet spring; winding wheels with click; finely finished by hand; 65-hour power reserve
Functions: hours, minutes, subsidiary seconds; hour, quarter-hour, and minute repeater
Case: rose gold, ø 43 mm, height 13.4 mm; sapphire crystal
Band: reptile skin, buckle
Price: on request

Saxon One Automatic

Reference number: 6120-02
Movement: automatic, Tutima Caliber 330; ø 25.6
mm, height 5.05 mm; 25 jewels; 28,800 vph;
38-hour power reserve
Functions: hours, minutes, sweep seconds;
weekday, date
Case: stainless steel, ø 42 mm, height 12.4 mm;
sapphire crystal; transparent case back; screw-in
crown; water-resistant to 20 atm
Band: stainless steel, double folding clasp
Price: $4,400
Variations: with anthracite dial

Saxon One Chronograph

Reference number: 6420-01
Movement: automatic, Tutima Caliber 521; ø 30
mm, height 7.9 mm; 25 jewels; 28,800 vph; sweep
minute counter; 46-hour power reserve
Functions: hours, minutes, subsidiary seconds;
additional 12-hour display; chronograph; date
Case: stainless steel, ø 44 mm, height 15.3 mm;
sapphire crystal; transparent case back; screw-in
crown; water-resistant to 20 atm
Band: stainless steel, double folding clasp
Price: $7,990
Variations: with silver-white dial

M2 Pioneer

Reference number: 6450-01
Movement: automatic, Tutima Caliber 521;
ø 30 mm, height 7.9 mm; 25 jewels; 28,800 vph;
sweep minute counter; 46-hour power reserve
Functions: hours, minutes, subsidiary seconds;
additional 24-hour display; chronograph; date
Case: titanium, ø 46.5 mm, height 15.85 mm;
bidirectional bezel with 60-minute divisions; sapphire
crystal; screw-in crown; water-resistant to 30 atm
Band: calf leather, buckle
Remarks: soft-iron inner case for magnetic field
protection
Price: $7,400
Variations: with titanium band ($7,900)

M2 Chronograph

Reference number: 6451-02
Movement: automatic, Tutima Caliber 521;
ø 30 mm, height 7.9 mm; 25 jewels; 28,800 vph;
sweep minute counter; 46-hour power reserve
Functions: hours, minutes, subsidiary seconds;
additional 24-hour display; chronograph; date
Case: titanium, ø 46 mm, height 15.35 mm;
sapphire crystal; screw-in crown; water-resistant to
30 atm
Band: titanium, folding clasp
Remarks: soft-iron inner case for magnetic field
protection
Price: $7,600

Grand Flieger Airport
Automatic

Reference number: 6101-01
Movement: automatic, Tutima Caliber 330;
ø 25.6 mm, height 5.05 mm; 25 jewels; 28,800
vph; 38-hour power reserve
Functions: hours, minutes, sweep seconds;
weekday, date
Case: stainless steel, ø 43 mm, height 13 mm;
bidirectional bezel with 60-minutes divisions;
sapphire crystal; transparent case back; screw-in
crown; water-resistant to 20 atm
Band: calf leather, buckle
Price: $2,650
Variations: with stainless steel bracelet ($2,950)

Grand Flieger Classic
Automatic

Reference number: 6102-01
Movement: automatic, Tutima Caliber 330;
ø 25.6 mm, height 5.05 mm; 25 jewels;
28,800 vph; 38-hour power reserve
Functions: hours, minutes, sweep seconds;
weekday, date
Case: stainless steel, ø 43 mm, height 13 mm;
bidirectional bezel with red reference marker;
sapphire crystal; transparent case back; screw-in
crown; water-resistant to 20 atm
Band: calf leather, buckle
Price: $2,650

U-Boat

Hi-tek Office srl
Via Vecchia Romana 685
I-55100 Lucca
Italy

Tel.:
01139-0583-469-288

Fax:
01139-0583-462-249

E-Mail:
info@u-boatwatch.com

Website:
www.uboatwatch.it

Founded:
2000

Number of employees:
not specified

Annual production:
not specified

U.S. distributor:
Infinity Time Group
4330 NE 2nd Ave.
Miami, FL 33137
305-573-4476
info@infinitytimegroup.com

Most important collections/price range:
Classico / $2,400 to $32,700; Flightdeck /
$3,350 to $36,500; U-42 / $6,150 to
$17,000; U-51 / $7,250 to $15,000

U-Boat

Gloss and glitz aren't Italo Fontana's thing: The Italian designer likes it matte-finished, martial, and mega-big. At least where his U-Boat watches are concerned, that is. His diver's watches have a decidedly nostalgic look, a theme that, with the success of today's Panerai watches, has just come into vogue within the past sixteen years.

In the 1940s, Italo Fontana's grandfather Ilvo had drawn plans for a naval pilot's watch. At some point, the drawings landed in the young fashion designer's hands. The sketches got Italo Fontana's inspirational juices going, and, soon after, in 2000, he opened his own watch company in his hometown of Lucca.

U-Boat watches stand out not only for their generously dimensioned cases, made, in part, with unusual materials—silver, bronze, aluminum, and titanium—but also for their striking, elaborately secured winding crowns, which have been installed on the left side of the watch so as not to dig into the back of the wearer's hand. And, like these watches' overall retro look, the special winding crown protection devices, made to keep the timepiece from being inadvertently wound, have been presented to the watch-loving public in a most steampunk fashion. Cases, dials, and hands for Fontana's creations are made in Italy; U-Boat movements hail from Switzerland.

U-51 Chimera Bronze

Reference number: 6945
Movement: automatic, Caliber ETA 7750; ø 30 mm, height 7.9 mm; 25 jewels; 28,800 vph; 42 hours power reserve
Functions: hours, minutes, subsidiary seconds; chronograph; date
Case: bronze, ø 47 mm, height 19.6 mm; sapphire crystal; crown on left with screw cap guard; water-resistant to 30 atm
Band: calf leather, buckle
Price: $9,900, limited to 300 pieces

U-42 GMT

Reference number: 6474
Movement: automatic, Caliber U-28 (base ETA 2824-2); ø 25.6 mm, height 4.1 mm; 25 jewels; 28,800 vph; 42 hours power reserve
Functions: hours, minutes, sweep seconds; second time zone (additional 24-hour display); third time zone available; date
Case: titanium, ø 53 mm; bidirectional bezel with 24-hour divisions; sapphire crystal; articulated crown cam, screwed down to case; water-resistant to 30 atm
Band: calf leather, buckle
Price: $6,850, limited to 300 pieces

U-51 Rattrapante

Reference number: 2063
Movement: automatic, Caliber "Arola" Alfred Rochat & Fils (base ETA 7750); ø 30 mm, height 8.1 mm; 28,800 vph
Functions: hours, minutes, subsidiary seconds; split-second hand chronograph; date
Case: stainless steel, ø 51 mm, height 19.6 mm; sapphire crystal; transparent case back; crown on left with screw cap guard; water-resistant to 12 atm
Band: rubber with reptile-skin inlay, buckle
Price: $15,000, limited to 100 pieces

Spirit Stones
*The Ancient Art
of the Scholar's Rock*

Photography by Jonathan M. Singer
Text by Kemin Hu
Foreword by Thomas S. Elias
216 pages · Cloth with slipcase · $95.00
ISBN 978-0-7892-1152-1

Fine Bonsai
Art & Nature

Photography by Jonathan M. Singer
Text by William N. Valavanis et al.
416 pages · Cloth with slipcase · $150.00
ISBN 978-0-7892-1112-5
Also available in a Deluxe
leather-bound edition
416 pages · Cloth with slipcase · $225.00
ISBN 978-0-7892-1116-3

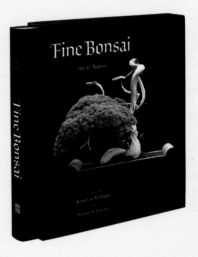

Botanica Magnifica
*Portraits of the World's
Most Extraordinary
Flowers and Plants*

Photography by Jonathan M. Singer
510 photographs in full color
354 pages · Cloth with slipcase · $135.00
ISBN 978-0-7892-1033-3

Tulipae Hortorum

A landmark collector's portfolio featuring ten
extraordinary portraits of tulips.

Specifications:
10 photographs printed on 24 × 30 in. sheets signed
and numbered by the artist.
Strictly limited to 33 sets
Presented in a clamshell box
For more information and to reserve a
portfolio, please contact Abbeville Press
at 212-366-5585 or visit www.abbeville.com.

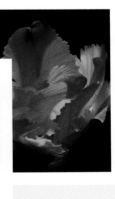

Published by ABBEVILLE PRESS
137 Varick Street, New York, NY 10013
1-800-ARTBOOK (in U.S. only)
Also available wherever fine books are sold
Visit us at www.abbeville.com

Ulysse Nardin SA
3, rue du Jardin
CH-2400 Le Locle
Switzerland

Tel.:
01141-32-930-7400

Fax:
01141-32-930-7419

Website:
www.ulysse-nardin.ch

Founded:
1846

Number of employees:
not specified

Annual production:
not specified

U.S. distributor:
Ulysse Nardin Inc.
7900 Glades Rd., Suite 200
Boca Raton, FL 33434
561-988-8600; 561-988-0123 (fax)
usa@ulysse-nardin.com

Most important collections:
Marine chronometers and diver's watches; Dual Time (also ladies' watches); complications (alarm clocks, perpetual calendar, tourbillons, minute repeaters, jacquemarts, astronomical watches)

Ulysse Nardin

At the beginning of the 1980s, following the quartz crisis that devastated the Swiss watch industry, Rolf Schnyder revived the venerable Ulysse Nardin brand, which once upon a time had a reputation for marine chronometers and precision watches. But those days were long gone when Schnyder bought what was essentially just a vague memory of a big name in the business.

Nevertheless the entrepreneur had a vision. And he had the luck to meet the multitalented Dr. Ludwig Oechslin, who realized Schnyder's vision of astronomical wristwatches in the Trilogy of Time collection. Overnight, Ulysse Nardin became a name to be reckoned with in the world of fine watchmaking. Oechslin, always an independent advisor, developed a host of innovations for Ulysse Nardin, from intelligent calendar movements to escapement systems. He was the first to use silicon and synthetic diamonds and thus gave the entire industry a great deal of food for thought. Just about every Ulysse Nardin has become famous for some spectacular technical innovation, be it the Moonstruck with its stunning moon phase accuracy or the outlandish Freak series that more or less does away with the dial.

Following Schnyder's sudden death in 2011, his wife, Chai Schnyder, was named president of the board of directors, and Patrik Hoffmann was appointed CEO. Ulysse Nardin continues exploring new paths to outstanding horology. The company has quietly focused on building new movements, a number of which were presented at Baselworld 2013, while cutting back on new models. To allow aesthetic explorations, a venture was launched with a company specializing in lithography, electroplating, and molding. Acquisition of the enameler Donzé Cadrans SA has already produced the Marine Chronometer Manufacture, powered by UN-118.

Skeleton Tourbillon Manufacture

Reference number: 1702-129
Movement: manually wound, Caliber UN-170; ø 37 mm, height 5.86 mm; 23 jewels; 18,000 vph; 1-minute tourbillon; skeletonized; twin spring barrels, 170-hour power reserve
Functions: hours, minutes
Case: rose gold, ø 44 mm, sapphire crystal; transparent case back
Band: reptile skin, buckle
Remarks: skeletonized dial
Price: $75,000
Variations: platinum ($85,000)

GMT Perpetual "El Toro"

Reference number: 329-03
Movement: automatic, Caliber UN-32, ø 31 mm, height 6.95 mm; 34 jewels; 28,800 vph; perpetual calendar mechanism (adjustable forward/backward); COSC certified chronometer
Functions: hours, minutes, subsidiary seconds; 24-hour display; perpetual calendar with large date, weekday, month, year
Case: rose gold, ø 43 mm, height 12.5 mm; ceramic bezel, 24-hour division; sapphire crystal; transparent case back
Band: reptile skin, folding clasp
Price: $69,900, limited to 500 pieces
Variations: platinum ($57,400)

Freak Diavolo

Reference number: 2080-115
Movement: manually wound, Caliber UN-208; ø 35 mm, 28 jewels; 28,800 vph; 8-day orbital flying carousel tourbillon; silicon lever escapement and hairspring; components used as hands; time adjusted with bezel, winding by turning case back; 8-day power reserve
Functions: hours, minutes, subsidiary seconds
Case: white gold, ø 45 mm, height 13.5 mm; bidirectional bezel; sapphire crystal; transparent case back
Band: reptile skin, double folding clasp
Price: $153,500
Variations: platinum ($137,000)

"Stranger" Musical Watch

Reference number: 6902-125
Movement: automatic, Caliber UN-690; ø 37 mm, height 10.06 mm; 64 jewels; 28,800 vph; silicon escapement, pallet lever and hairspring, music box on dial with visible peg disc, 10 gongs
Functions: hours and minutes (off-center), subsidiary seconds; date: music box (plays "Strangers in the Night" hourly or on demand)
Case: pink gold, ø 45 mm; sapphire crystal
Band: reptile skin, double folding clasp
Price: $112,000, limited to 99 pieces

Sonata Streamline

Reference number: 675-00
Movement: automatic, Caliber UN-67; ø 31 mm, height 6.95 mm; 109 jewels; 28,800 vph; silicon pallet lever, escape wheel, and hairspring alarm with gong settable to the minute
Functions: hours, minutes, sweep seconds; additional 24-hour display (second time zone); alarm clock; countdown display to alarm; large date
Case: titanium, ø 44 mm, height 13 mm; ceramic bezel; sapphire crystal; transparent case back; crown/pushers of rose gold
Band: reptile skin, folding clasp
Price: $35,000
Variations: with gold bezel ($46,000)

Moonstruck

Reference number: 1062-113
Movement: automatic, Caliber UN-106, ø 37.3 mm, height 8.17 mm; 42 jewels; 28,800 vph; silicon escape wheel, pallet lever, balance, and hairspring
Functions: 24 hours; moon position display, moon phase, tide display, sun position display
Case: rose gold, ø 46 mm, height 14.2 mm; ceramic bezel with date numbers; sapphire crystal; transparent case back; screw-in crown
Band: reptile skin, double folding clasp
Price: $97,500, limited to 500 pieces
Variations: platinum ($125,500)

Maxi Marine Chronometer Manufacture

Reference number: 1186-122/42
Movement: automatic, Caliber UN-118; ø 31.6 mm, height 6.45 mm; 50 jewels; 28,800 vph; "DIAMonSIL" escapement, silicon balance and hairspring; 60-hour power reserve; COSC certified chronometer
Functions: hours, minutes, subsidiary seconds; power reserve indicator; date
Case: rose gold, ø 45 mm, height 13 mm; sapphire crystal; transparent case back; screw-in crown
Band: reptile skin, double folding clasp
Price: $35,300
Variations: polished titanium ($10,400)

Maxi Marine Chronometer Manufacture

Reference number: 1183-122-3/42
Movement: automatic, Caliber UN-118; ø 31.6 mm, height 6.45 mm; 50 jewels; 28,800 vph; "DIAMonSIL" escapement, silicon balance and hairspring; 60-hour power reserve; COSC certified chronometer
Functions: hours, minutes, subsidiary seconds; power reserve indicator; date
Case: polished titanium, ø 45 mm, height 13 mm; sapphire crystal; transparent case back; screw-in crown
Band: rubber with titanium elements, folding clasp
Price: $10,300
Variations: with rose gold bezel ($37,400)

Maxi Marine Chronometer Manufacture

Reference number: 1186-126-3/63
Movement: automatic, Caliber UN-118; ø 31.6 mm, height 6.45 mm; 50 jewels; 28,800 vph; "DIAMonSIL" escapement, silicon balance and hairspring; 60-hour power reserve; COSC tested chronometer
Functions: hours, minutes, subsidiary seconds; power reserve indicator; date
Case: rose gold, ø 43 mm, height 13 mm; sapphire crystal; transparent case back; screw-in crown
Band: rubber and rose gold, folding clasp
Price: $31,800
Variations: with reptile skin band ($29,800)

Maxi Marine Chronometer Manufacture

Reference number: 1183-126-3/61
Movement: automatic, Caliber UN-118; ø 31.6 mm, height 6.45 mm; 50 jewels; 28,800 vph; "DIAMonSIL" escapement, silicon balance and hairspring; 60-hour power reserve; COSC certified chronometer
Functions: hours, minutes, subsidiary seconds; power reserve indicator; date
Case: polished titanium, ø 43 mm, height 13 mm; sapphire crystal; transparent case back; screw-in crown
Band: rubber with titanium elements, folding clasp
Price: $10,300
Variations: with reptile skin band ($10,400)

Marine Chronograph Manufacture

Reference number: 1506-150/61
Movement: automatic, Caliber UN-150; ø 31 mm, height 6.4 mm; 27 jewels; 28,800 vph; silicon escapement
Functions: hours, minutes, subsidiary seconds; chronograph; date
Case: rose gold, ø 43 mm, height 15 mm; sapphire crystal; transparent case back; screw-in crown
Band: reptile skin, double folding clasp
Price: $33,200
Variations: stainless steel ($12,900)

Marine Chronograph Manufacture

Reference number: 1503-150-3/62
Movement: automatic, Caliber UN-150; ø 31 mm, height 6.4 mm; 27 jewels; 28,800 vph; silicon escapement
Functions: hours, minutes, subsidiary seconds; chronograph; date
Case: polished titanium, ø 43 mm, height 15 mm; sapphire crystal; transparent case back; screw-in crown
Band: rubber with titanium elements, folding clasp
Price: $12,700
Variations: rose gold ($34,900)

Black Sea Chronograph

Reference number: 353-92-3C
Movement: automatic, Caliber UN-35; ø 30 mm, height 6.9 mm; 57 jewels; 28,800 vph; 42-hour power reserve
Functions: hours, minutes, subsidiary seconds; chronograph; date
Case: stainless steel with rubber coating, ø 45.8 mm, height 14.5 mm; unidirectional bezel with 60-minute divisions; sapphire crystal; transparent case back
Band: rubber with ceramic elements, folding clasp
Price: $10,500
Variations: with rose gold bezel with black elements ($24,800)

Maxi Marine Diver Black Sea

Reference number: 263-82-3C/923
Movement: automatic, Caliber UN-26; ø 25.6 mm, height 5.1 mm; 28 jewels; 28,800 vph; 42-hour power reserve; COSC certified chronometer
Functions: hours, minutes, subsidiary seconds; power reserve indicator; date
Case: stainless steel with rubber coating, ø 45.8 mm, height 14 mm; unidirectional bezel with 60-minute divisions; sapphire crystal; transparent case back; screw-in crown
Band: rubber with ceramic elements, folding clasp
Price: $8,600
Variations: with red or yellow hands and indices

Maxi Marine Diver Titanium

Reference number: 265-90-3/93
Movement: automatic, Caliber UN-26; ø 25.6 mm, height 5.1 mm; 28 jewels; 28,800 vph; 42-hour power reserve; COSC certified chronometer
Functions: hours, minutes, subsidiary seconds; power reserve indicator; date
Case: titanium, ø 45 mm, height 14 mm; unidirectional rose gold bezel with 60-minute divisions; sapphire crystal; transparent case back; screw-in crown; water-resistant to 20 atm
Band: rubber with rose gold elements, folding clasp
Price: $22,200
Variations: stainless steel ($7,800)

Executive Dual Time

Reference number: 246-00-3/42
Movement: automatic, Caliber UN-24, ø 25.6 mm, height 5.35 mm; 23 jewels; 28,800 vph
Functions: hours, minutes, subsidiary seconds; additional 24-hour display; large date
Case: stainless steel, ø 43 mm, height 12 mm; ceramic bezel; sapphire crystal; transparent case back; screw-in crown
Band: reptile skin, double folding clasp
Price: $22,200
Variations: stainless steel ($8,700)

Executive Dual Time

Reference number: 243-00/43
Movement: automatic, Caliber UN-24, ø 25.6 mm, height 5.35 mm; 23 jewels; 28,800 vph
Functions: hours, minutes, subsidiary seconds; additional 24-hour display; large date
Case: stainless steel, ø 43 mm, height 12 mm; ceramic bezel; sapphire crystal; transparent case back; screw-in crown
Band: reptile skin, double folding clasp
Price: $8,700
Variations: pink gold ($22,200)

GMT Dual Time

Reference number: 243-55/92
Movement: automatic, Caliber UN-24; ø 25.6 mm, height 5.35 mm; 23 jewels; 28,800 vph
Functions: hours, minutes, subsidiary seconds; second time zone (additional 24-hour display); large date
Case: stainless steel, ø 42 mm, height 12 mm; sapphire crystal; transparent case back; screw-in crown
Band: reptile skin, double folding clasp
Price: $7,300
Variations: rose gold with roman numerals ($22,200)

Caliber UN-118

Automatic; patented DIAMonSIL escapement; single spring barrel, power reserve approx. 60 hours
Functions: hours, minutes, subsidiary seconds; date; power reserve indicator
Diameter: 31.6 mm
Height: 6.45 mm
Jewels: 50
Balance: silicon balance with variable inertia
Frequency: 28,800 vph
Balance spring: silicon
Shock protection: Incabloc
Remarks: perlage on plate, bridges with concentric côtes de Genève ("côtes circulaires")

Caliber UN-208

Manually wound; flying 1-minute tourbillon on orbital carousel; movement is used as hands; silicon escapement and hairspring; power reserve approx. 8 days
Functions: hours, minutes, subsidiary seconds
Diameter: 35 mm
Height: 7.2 mm
Jewels: 28
Balance: silicon
Frequency: 28,800 vph
Balance spring: silicon
Remarks: winding using mobile case back, hand setting using bezel

Caliber UN-32

Automatic; single spring barrel, power reserve approx. 45 hours
Functions: hours, minutes, subsidiary seconds; 24-hour display; perpetual calendar with month, weekday, date
Diameter: 31 mm
Height: 6.95 mm
Jewels: 34
Balance: glucydur
Frequency: 28,800 vph
Remarks: perpetual calendar mechanism can be set forward or backward using a single crown; patented quick setting of second time zone

Urban Jürgensen & Sønner
P.O. Box 7170
CH-2500 Biel/Bienne 7
Switzerland

Tel.:
01141-32-365-1526

Fax:
01141-32-365-2266

E-Mail:
info@ujs-chronometry.ch

Website:
www.ujs-chronometry.ch

Founded:
1773/1980

Number of employees:
not specified

Annual production:
max. 200 watches

U.S. distributor:
John McBarron
312-643-0148
usa@ujs-chronometry.ch

Most important collections:
High-end references with in-house movements

Urban Jürgensen & Sønner

For all aficionados and collectors of fine timekeepers, the name Urban Jürgensen & Sønner is synonymous with outstanding watches. The company was founded in 1773 and has always strived for the highest rungs of the horological art. Technical perfection consistently combines with imaginative cases. A lot of attention is given to dials and hands.

Today, Urban Jürgensen & Sønner—originally a Danish firm—manufactures watches in Switzerland where a team of eight superbly qualified watchmakers do the work in three ateliers. For over a quarter century now, they have been making highly complicated unique pieces and very upmarket wristwatches in small editions of 50 to 300 pieces. The series were based mostly on *ébauches* by Frédéric Piguet. Like all keen watchmakers, those at Urban Jürgensen & Sønner have also sought to make their own movements, which would meet the highest standards of precision and reliability and not require too much servicing. In 2003, a team began collaborating with a well-known external design engineer to construct a base movement. The new UJS-P8 was conceived with both a traditional Swiss lever escapement and in a special variation featuring a pivoting chronometer escapement, available for the first time in a wristwatch. The initial watch containing the new movement was the Reference 11, which is visibly an Urban Jürgensen. It comes in platinum and rose gold cases. The Reference 11 with pivoting chronometer escapement typically has a hand-guilloché silver dial with three hands and a power reserve indicator. The latter is controlled by a newly developed and patented differential. The version with the lever escapement does not feature a power reserve indicator.

Montre Observatoire Enamel

Reference number: 11C/R/E/O
Movement: manually wound, Urban Jürgensen Caliber UJS-P8; ø 32 mm; height 5.25 mm; 25 jewels; 21,600 vph; patented chronometer escapement with a UJS pivoted detent, free-sprung large balance with hacking second; very finely finished; 2 spring barrels, 88-hour power reserve
Functions: hours, minutes, subsidiary seconds; power reserve indicator
Case: rose gold, ø 42 mm, height 12.3 mm; sapphire crystal
Band: reptile skin, buckle
Remarks: hand-painted enamel dial
Price: $80,200, limited to 20 pieces

P-8 "Platinum Noir"

Reference number: 11C Aviator
Movement: manually wound, Urban Jürgensen Caliber UJS-P8; ø 32 mm; height 5.25 mm; 25 jewels; 21,600 vph; patented chronometer escapement with a UJS pivoted detent, free-sprung large balance with hacking second; very finely finished; 2 spring barrels, 88-hour power reserve
Functions: hours, minutes, subsidiary seconds; power reserve indicator
Case: platinum, ø 42 mm, height 12.3 mm; sapphire crystal
Band: reptile skin, buckle
Remarks: hand-guilloché silver dial
Price: $62,000
Variations: rose gold ($51,300)

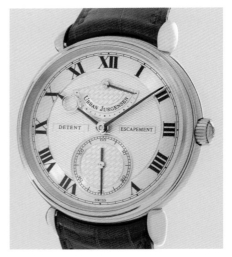

P-8

Reference number: 11C R
Movement: manually wound, Urban Jürgensen Caliber UJS-P8; ø 32 mm; height 5.25 mm; 25 jewels; 21,600 vph; patented chronometer escapement with a UJS pivoted detent, free-sprung large balance with hacking second; very finely finished; 2 spring barrels, 88-hour power reserve
Functions: hours, minutes, subsidiary seconds; power reserve indicator
Case: rose gold, ø 42 mm, height 12.3 mm; sapphire crystal
Band: reptile skin, buckle
Remarks: hand-guilloché silver dial
Price: $51,300
Variations: platinum ($62,000)

Urwerk

Felix Baumgartner and designer Martin Frei count among the living legends of innovative horology. They founded their company Urwerk in 1997 with a name that is a play on the words *Uhrwerk*, for movement, and *Urwerk*, meaning a sort of primal mechanism. Their specialty is inventing surprising time indicators featuring digital numerals that rotate like satellites and display the time in a relatively linear depiction on a small "dial" at the front of the flattened case, which could almost—but not quite—be described as oval. Their inspiration goes back to the so-called night clock of the eighteenth-century Campanus brothers, but the realization is purely *2001: A Space Odyssey*.

Among their great achievements is the Black Cobra, which displays time using cylinders and other clever ways to recoup energy for driving rather heavy components. The Torpedo is another example of high-tech watchmaking, again based on the satellite system of revolving and turning hands. These pieces remind one of the frenetic engineering that has transformed the planet since the eighteenth century, and Baumgartner and Frei still have not finished lucubrating as the current crop shows.

Urwerk SA
114, rue du Rhône
CH-1204 Geneva
Switzerland

Tel.:
01141-22-900-2027

Fax:
01141-22-900-2026

E-Mail:
info@urwerk.com

Website:
www.urwerk.com

Founded:
1995

Number of employees:
not specified

Annual production:
150 watches

U.S. distributor:
Urwerk
132 South Rodeo Drive, Fourth Floor
Beverly Hills, CA 90212
310-205-5555

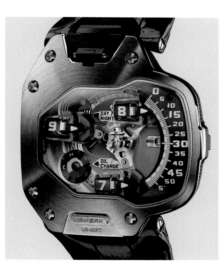

UR-110PT

Movement: automatic, Caliber UR-9.01; 46 jewels; 28,800 vph; parallel rotating hour satellites revolving on planetary gears; winding system regulated by fluid dynamics decoupling; 39-hour power reserve

Functions: hours (digital, rotating), minutes; day/night indicator; servicing indicator

Case: titanium, blackened, 47 x 51 mm, height 16 mm; platinum bezel; sapphire crystal; water-resistant to 3 atm

Band: reptile skin, buckle

Remarks: tips of 3 hour satellites indicate minutes clockwise on semicircular scale

Price: $135,000

UR-110PTH

Movement: automatic, Caliber UR-9.01; 46 jewels; 28,800 vph; parallel rotating hour satellites revolving on planetary gears; winding system regulated by fluid dynamics decoupling; 39-hour power reserve

Functions: hours (digital, rotating), minutes; day/night indicator; servicing indicator

Case: titanium with PVD coating, 47 x 51 mm, height 16 mm; platinum bezel with PVD coating; sapphire crystal; water-resistant to 3 atm

Band: reptile skin, buckle

Remarks: tips of 3 hour satellites indicate minutes clockwise on semicircular scale

Price: $140,000

UR-210 AlTiN

Movement: automatic, Caliber UR-7.10; 51 jewels; 28,800 vph; mainplate of Arcap P40; revolving hour satellites on planetary gear drive, telescopic minute hand, winding system regulated by fluid dynamics decoupling; 39-hour power reserve

Functions: hours (digital, rotating), minutes; power reserve indicator; winding efficiency indications

Case: titanium, aluminum titanium nitride (AlTiN) coating, 43.8 x 53.6 mm, height 17.8 mm; sapphire crystal; water-resistant to 3 atm

Remarks: tips of 3 hour satellites indicate minutes clockwise on semicircular scale

Price: $185,000

UTS Watches, Inc.
630 Quintana Road, Suite 194
Morro Bay, CA 93442

Tel.:
877-887-0123 or 805-528-9800

E-Mail:
info@utswatches.com

Website:
www.utswatches.com

Founded:
1999

Number of employees:
2

Annual production:
fewer than 500

Distribution:
direct sales only

Most important collections/price range:
sports and diver's watches, chronographs /
from $2,500 to $7,000

UTS

UTS, or "Uhren Technik Spinner," was the natural outgrowth of a company based in Munich and manufacturing CNC tools and machines for the watch industry. Nicolaus Spinner, a mechanical engineer and aficionado in his own right, learned the nitty-gritty of watchmaking by the age-old system of taking watches apart. From there to making robust diver's watches was just a short step. The collection has grown considerably since he started production in 1999. The watches are built mainly around ETA calibers. Some, like the new 4000M, feature a unique locking bezel using a stem, a bolt, and a ceramic ball bearing system invented by Spinner. Another specialty is the 6 mm sapphire crystal, which guarantees significant water resistance. Spinner's longtime friend and business partner, Stephen Newman, is also the owner of the UTS trademark in the United States. He has not only worked on product development, but has also contributed his own design ideas and handles sales and marketing for the small brand. A new watch released last year, the 4000M Diver, boasts an extreme depth rating even without the need for a helium escape valve and is available in a GMT version. The collection is small, but UTS has a faithful following in Germany and the United States. The key for the fan club is a unique appearance coupled with mastery of the technology. These are a pure muscle watches with no steroids.

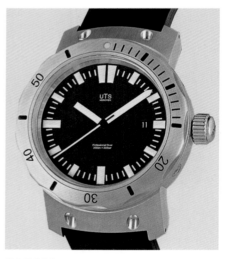

Diver 4000M

Movement: automatic, ETA Caliber 2824-2; ø 25.6 mm, height 4.6 mm; 25 jewels; 28,800 vph; 42 hours power reserve
Functions: hours, minutes, sweep seconds; date
Case: stainless steel, ø 45 mm, height 17.5 mm; bidirectional bezel with 60-minute scale; 6-mm sapphire crystal; antireflective on back; screwed-down case back; screw-in crown; locking bezel; screw-in buttons; water-resistant to 400 atm
Band: stainless steel with diver's extension folding clasp or rubber or leather strap
Price: $6,300

Diver 4000M GMT

Movement: automatic, ETA Caliber 2893-2; ø 25.6 mm, height 4.6 mm; 25 jewels; 28,800 vph; 42 hours power reserve
Functions: hours, minutes, sweep seconds; date, second time zone
Case: stainless steel, ø 45 mm, height 17.5 mm; bidirectional bezel with 60-minute scale; 6-mm sapphire crystal; antireflective on back; screwed-down case back; screw-in crown; locking bezel; screw-in buttons; water-resistant to 400 atm
Band: stainless steel with diver's extension folding clasp or rubber or leather strap
Price: $7,000

2000M

Movement: automatic, ETA Caliber 2824-2; ø 25.6 mm, height 4.6 mm; 25 jewels; 28,800 vph; 42 hours power reserve
Functions: hours, minutes, sweep seconds; date
Case: stainless steel, ø 44 mm, height 16.5 mm; unidirectional bezel with 60-minute scale; automatic helium escape valve; sapphire crystal; antireflective on back; screwed-down case back; screw-in crown; screwed-in buttons; water-resistant to 200 atm
Band: stainless steel with diver's extension folding clasp, comes with rubber leather strap
Price: $3,750

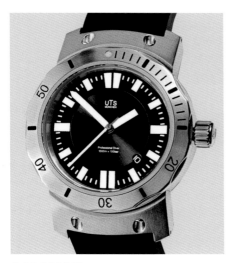

1000M V2

Movement: automatic, ETA Caliber 2824-2; ø 25.6 mm, height 4.6 mm; 25 jewels; 28,800 vph; 42 hours power reserve
Functions: hours, minutes, sweep seconds; date
Case: stainless steel, ø 43 mm, height 14 mm; unidirectional bezel with 60-minute scale; sapphire crystal; antireflective on back; screwed-down sapphire (optional) crystal case back; screw-in crown; screw-in buttons; water-resistant to 10 atm
Band: stainless steel with diver's extension folding clasp or rubber or leather strap
Price: $3,000

1000M GMT

Movement: automatic, ETA Caliber ETA 2893-2; ø 25.6 mm, height 4.1 mm; 21 jewels; 28,800 vph; 42 hours power reserve
Functions: hours, minutes, sweep seconds; second time zone; date; quickset GMT hand
Case: stainless steel, ø 43 mm, height 14 mm; unidirectional bezel with 60-minute scale; sapphire crystal; antireflective on back; screwed-down case back with optional transparent back (sapphire crystal); screw-in crown; screw-in buttons; water-resistant to 100 atm
Band: stainless steel with diver's extension folding clasp or rubber or leather strap
Price: $3,750

Adventure Automatic

Movement: automatic, ETA Valgranges Caliber A07.111; ø 36.6 mm, height 7.9 mm; 24 jewels; 28,800 vph; 46 hours power reserve
Functions: hours, minutes, sweep seconds; date
Case: stainless steel, ø 46 mm, height 15.5 mm; screw-in crown; antireflective sapphire crystal; screwed-down sapphire crystal case back; water-resistant to 50 atm
Band: rubber, buckle
Price: $4,000
Variations: leather strap; stainless steel bracelet with folding clasp and diver's extension

Adventure Automatic GMT

Movement: automatic, ETA Valgranges Caliber A07.171; ø 36.6 mm, height 7.9 mm; 24 jewels; 28,800 vph; 46 hours power reserve
Functions: hours, minutes, sweep seconds; date, second time zone
Case: stainless steel, ø 46 mm, height 15.5 mm; screw-in crown; antireflective sapphire crystal; screwed-down sapphire crystal case back; water-resistant to 50 atm
Band: rubber, buckle
Price: $4,550
Variations: leather strap; stainless steel bracelet with folding clasp and diver's extension

Chrono Diver

Movement: automatic, ETA Valjoux Caliber 7750; ø 30 mm, height 7.9 mm; 25 jewels; 28,800 vph; 45-hour power reserve
Functions: hours, minutes, subsidiary seconds; date; chronograph
Case: stainless steel, ø 46 mm, height 16.5 mm; unidirectional bezel with 60-minute scale; screw-in crown and buttons; antireflective sapphire crystal; screwed-down case back; water-resistant to 600 m
Band: stainless steel, folding clasp
Price: $5,000
Variations: leather strap

Adventure Manual Wind

Movement: manually wound, ETA Unitas Caliber 6497; ø 36.6 mm, height 5.4 mm; 18 jewels; 18,000 vph; 48 hours power reserve
Functions: hours, minutes, subsidiary seconds
Case: stainless steel, ø 46 mm, height 14 mm; screw-in crown; antireflective sapphire crystal; screwed-down sapphire crystal case back; water-resistant to 50 atm
Band: leather, buckle
Price: $3,000
Variations: rubber strap

Vacheron Constantin
Chemin du Tourbillon
CH-1228 Plan-les-Ouates
Switzerland

Tel.:
01141-22-930-2005

E-Mail:
info@vacheron-constantin.com

Website:
www.vacheron-constantin.com

Founded:
1755

Number of employees:
approx. 800

Annual production:
over 20,000 watches (estimated)

U.S. distributor:
Vacheron Constantin
Richemont North America
645 Fifth Avenue
New York, NY 10022
877-701-1755

Most important collections:
Patrimony; Malte; Quai de l'Ile; Overseas;
Historiques; Metiers d'Art

Vacheron Constantin

The origins of this oldest continuously operating watch *manufacture* can be traced back to 1755 when Jean-Marc Vacheron opened his workshop in Geneva. His highly complex watches were particularly appreciated by clients in Paris. The development of such an important outlet for horological works there had a lot to do with the emergence of a wealthy class around the powerful French court. The Revolution put an end to all the financial excesses of that market, however, and the Vacheron company suffered as well . . . until the arrival of marketing wizard François Constantin in 1819.

Fast-forward to the late twentieth century: The brand with the Maltese cross logo had lost some of its pizzazz but evolved into a tradition-conscious keeper of *haute horlogerie* under the aegis, starting in the mid-1990s, of the Vendôme Luxury Group (today's Richemont SA). In the last few years, a new collection has come to light that combines modern shapes with traditional patterns. The company has been expanding steadily. In 2013 it opened new boutiques in the United States as well as China, and it has become a leading sponsor of the New York City Ballet.

The brand's core locations are production facilities and headquarters in Plan-les-Ouates; workshops in Le Sentier in Switzerland's Jura region; and the *maison* housing a museum and boutique in the heart of Geneva's old town. Tradition has Vacheron Constantin guaranteeing customer service for all timepieces produced by the company since its founding.

Patrimony Traditionnelle "Calibre 2253"

Reference number: 88172/000R-X0001
Movement: manually wound, Caliber 2253 VC; ø 32 mm, height 9.6 mm; 30 jewels; 18,000 vph; 1-minute tourbillon; 336-hour power reserve; Geneva Seal
Functions: hours, minutes, subsidiary seconds (on tourbillon cage); equation of time display with sunrise and sunset times; perpetual calendar with date, weekday, month, leap year
Case: rose gold, ø 44 mm, height 15.71 mm; sapphire crystal; transparent case back
Band: reptile skin, double folding clasp
Price: $479,700

Patrimony Traditionnelle 14 Days Tourbillon

Reference number: 89000/000R-9655
Movement: manually wound, Caliber 2260; ø 29.9 mm, height 6.8 mm; 31 jewels; 18,000 vph; 1-minute tourbillon; 336-hour power reserve; Geneva Seal
Functions: hours, minutes, subsidiary seconds (on tourbillon cage); power reserve indicator
Case: rose gold, ø 42 mm, height 12.2 mm; sapphire crystal; transparent case back; water-resistant to 3 atm
Band: reptile skin, folding clasp
Price: $279,800

Patrimony Contemporaine Perpetual Calendar

Reference number: 43175/000R-9687
Movement: automatic, Caliber 1120 QP; ø 29.6 mm, height 4.05 mm; 36 jewels; 19,800 vph; Geneva Seal
Functions: hours, minutes; perpetual calendar with date, weekday, month, moon phase, leap year
Case: rose gold, ø 41 mm, height 8.9 mm; sapphire crystal; transparent case back; water-resistant to 3 atm
Band: reptile skin, folding clasp
Price: $79,000

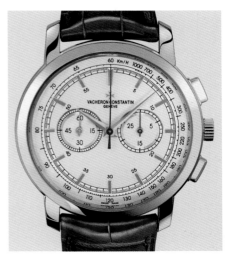

Patrimony Traditionnelle World Time

Reference number: 86060/000R-9640
Movement: automatic, Caliber 2460 WT; ø 36.6 mm, height 8.1 mm; 27 jewels; 28,800 vph
Functions: hours, minutes, sweep seconds; world-time display with 37 zones
Case: rose gold, ø 42.5 mm, height 11.5 mm; sapphire crystal; transparent case back; water-resistant to 3 atm
Band: reptile skin, folding clasp
Price: $48,900

Patrimony Contemporaine Bi-Retro Day Date

Reference number: 86020/000R-9239
Movement: automatic, Caliber 2460 R31 R7; ø 32.8 mm, height 6.75 mm; 27 jewels; 28,800 vph
Functions: hours, minutes; weekday, date
Case: rose gold, ø 42.5 mm, height 10.07 mm; sapphire crystal; transparent case back; water-resistant to 3 atm
Band: reptile skin, double folding clasp
Price: $45,900
Variations: white gold ($45,900)

Patrimony Traditionnelle Chronograph

Reference number: 47192/000R-9352
Movement: manually wound, Caliber 1141; ø 31.5 mm, height 5.6 mm; 21 jewels; 18,000 vph; column wheel control of chronograph functions; Geneva Seal
Functions: hours, minutes, subsidiary seconds; chronograph
Case: rose gold, ø 42 mm, height 10.94 mm; sapphire crystal; transparent case back; water-resistant to 3 atm reptile skin, folding clasp
Band: reptile skin, folding clasp
Price: $55,900
Variations: white gold ($55,900)

Patrimony Traditionnelle Manual Winding

Reference number: 82172/000P-9811
Movement: manually wound, Caliber 4400; ø 28.6 mm, height 2.8 mm; 21 jewels; 28,800 vph; 65 hours power reserve; Geneva Seal
Functions: hours, minutes, subsidiary seconds
Case: platinum, ø 38 mm, height 7.77 mm; sapphire crystal; transparent case back; water-resistant to 3 atm
Band: reptile skin, buckle
Price: $34,000
Variations: white gold ($19,900); pink gold ($19,900)

Patrimony Contemporaine Date Automatic

Reference number: 85180/000R-9248
Movement: automatic, Caliber 2450 VC; ø 26.2 mm, height 3.6 mm; 27 jewels; 28,800 vph; Geneva Seal
Functions: hours, minutes, sweep seconds; date
Case: rose gold, ø 40 mm, height 8.31 mm; sapphire crystal; transparent case back; water-resistant to 3 atm
Band: reptile skin, buckle
Price: $26,500
Variations: yellow gold ($26,500); white gold ($26,500)

Patrimony Traditionnelle Automatic

Reference number: 43075/000R-9737
Movement: automatic, Caliber 1120 VC; ø 28.4 mm, height 2.45 mm; 36 jewels; 28,800 vph; 40-hour power reserve; Geneva Seal
Functions: hours, minutes
Case: rose gold, ø 41 mm, height 7.26 mm; sapphire crystal; transparent case back
Band: reptile skin, buckle
Price: $31,300

Patrimony Contemporaine Gold Bracelet Small Model

Reference number: 85515/CA1R-9840
Movement: automatic, Caliber 2450 Q6/2460 SC; ø 26.2 mm, height 3.6 mm; 27 jewels; 28,800 vph; 40-hour power reserve; Geneva Seal
Functions: hours, minutes, sweep seconds; date
Case: rose gold, ø 36 mm, height 9.15 mm; bezel set with 68 diamonds; sapphire crystal; water-resistant to 3 atm
Band: rose gold, folding clasp
Price: $49,700

Malte Tourbillon

Reference number: 30130/000R-9754
Movement: manually wound, Caliber 2795; 27.37 x 29.3 mm, height 6.1 mm; 27 jewels; 18,000 vph; form movement with 1-minute tourbillon; Geneva Seal
Functions: hours, minutes, subsidiary seconds (on tourbillon cage)
Case: rose gold, 38 x 48.24 mm, height 12.73 mm; sapphire crystal; transparent case back; water-resistant to 3 atm
Band: reptile skin, folding clasp
Price: $183,900

Malte Small Seconds

Reference number: 82130/000R-9755
Movement: manually wound, Caliber 4400 AS; ø 28.6 mm, height 2.8 mm; 21 jewels; 28,800 vph; Geneva Seal
Functions: hours, minutes, subsidiary seconds
Case: rose gold, 36.7 x 47.61 mm, height 9.1 mm; sapphire crystal; water-resistant to 3 atm
Band: reptile skin, folding clasp
Price: $24,600

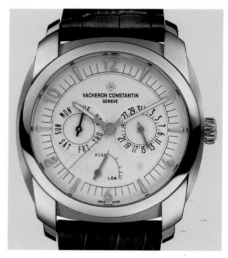

Malte Lady

Reference number: 25530/000G-9801
Movement: quartz
Functions: hours, minutes
Case: white gold, 28.3 x 38.75 mm, height 7.28 mm; bezel set with 50 diamonds; sapphire crystal
Band: satin, folding clasp
Price: $33,600
Variations: rose gold ($33,600)

Quai de l'Ile Retrograde Annual Calendar

Reference number: 86040/000R-I0P29
Movement: automatic, Caliber 2460 QRA; ø 26.2 mm, height 5.4 mm; 27 jewels; 28,800 vph; Geneva Seal
Functions: hours, minutes, subsidiary seconds; annual calendar with date, month, moon phase
Case: rose gold, 43 x 53.8 mm, height 13.5 mm; sapphire crystal; transparent case back; water-resistant to 3 atm
Band: reptile skin, folding clasp
Price: $68,000
Variations: many options for personalization

Quai de l'Ile Day Date with Power Reserve

Reference number: 85050/000D-9341
Movement: automatic, Caliber 2475 SC1; ø 26.2 mm, height 2.8 mm; 27 jewels; 28,000 vph; Geneva Seal
Functions: hours, minutes, sweep seconds; power reserve indicator; weekday, date
Case: palladium, 41 x 50.5 mm, height 12.9 mm; sapphire crystal; transparent case back; water-resistant to 3 atm
Band: reptile skin, folding clasp
Price: $49,600
Variations: many options for personalization

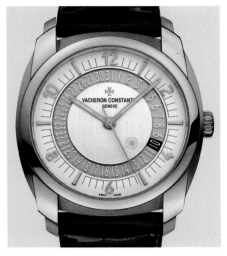

Quai de l'Ile Date Automatic

Reference number: 86050/000R-I0P29
Movement: automatic, Caliber 2460 QH;
ø 26.2 mm, height 5.7 mm; 27 jewels; 28,800 vph;
Geneva Seal
Functions: hours, minutes, sweep seconds; date
Case: rose gold, 41 x 50.5 mm, height 12.9 mm;
sapphire crystal; transparent case back; water-
resistant to 3 atm
Band: reptile skin, folding clasp
Price: $40,900
Variations: many options for personalization

Overseas Chronograph Perpetual Calendar

Reference number: 49020/000R-9753
Movement: automatic, Caliber 1136 QP; ø 28 mm,
height 7.9 mm; 37 jewels; 21,600 vph; Geneva Seal
Functions: hours, minutes, subsidiary seconds;
chronograph; perpetual calendar with date,
weekday, month, moon phase, leap year
Case: rose gold, ø 42 mm, height 12.8 mm;
sapphire crystal; screw-in crown and pusher; water-
resistant to 15 atm
Band: reptile skin, folding clasp
Price: $99,200

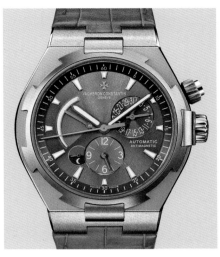

Overseas Dual Time

Reference number: 47450/000W-9511
Movement: automatic, Caliber 1222 SC; ø 26 mm,
height 4.95 mm; 34 jewels; 28,800 vph; antimagnetic
protection with soft iron cap
Functions: hours, minutes, sweep seconds;
additional 12-hour display (second time zone); day/
night indicator; power reserve indicator; date
Case: titanium, ø 42 mm, height 12.45 mm; sapphire
crystal; screw-in crown and pusher; water-resistant
to 15 atm
Band: reptile skin, folding clasp
Price: $17,900
Variations: rose gold ($44,500)

Overseas Chronograph

Reference number: 49150/B01A-9745
Movement: automatic, Caliber 1137; ø 26 mm,
height 6.6 mm; 37 jewels; 21,600 vph; Geneva Seal
Functions: hours, minutes, subsidiary seconds;
chronograph; large date
Case: stainless steel, ø 42 mm, height 12.4 mm;
sapphire crystal; screw-in crown; water-resistant to
15 atm
Band: stainless steel, folding clasp
Price: $21,500

Overseas Automatic

Reference number: 47040/000R-9666
Movement: automatic, Caliber 1226; ø 26.6 mm,
height 3.25 mm; 36 jewels; 28,800 vph; Geneva
Seal
Functions: hours, minutes, sweep seconds; date
Case: rose gold, ø 42 mm, height 9.7 mm; sapphire
crystal; water-resistant to 15 atm
Band: reptile skin, folding clasp
Price: $32,300

Historiques Ultra-Fine 1955

Reference number: 33155/000R-9588
Movement: manually wound, Caliber 1003;
ø 21.1 mm, height 1.64 mm; 18 jewels; 18,000
vph; thinnest movement produced at current time;
Geneva Seal
Functions: hours, minutes
Case: rose gold, ø 36 mm, height 4.1 mm; sapphire
crystal; transparent case back; water-resistant to
3 atm
Band: reptile skin, buckle
Price: $30,600

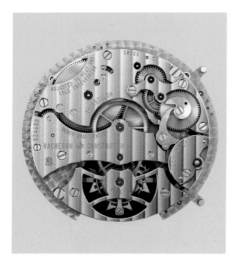

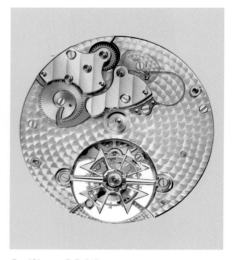

Caliber 2755

Automatic; 1-minute tourbillon; single spring barrel, 55 hours power reserve; Geneva Seal
Functions: hours, minutes, subsidiary seconds (on tourbillon cage); perpetual calendar with month, leap year, weekday, date; hour, quarter-hour, and minute repeater; power reserve indicator on case back
Diameter: 33.3 mm
Height: 7.9 mm
Jewels: 40
Balance: glucydur
Frequency: 18,000 vph
Remarks: 602 components

Caliber 2253

Automatic; 1-minute tourbillon; 4 paired spring barrels run in series, 14-day power reserve; Geneva Seal
Functions: hours, minutes, subsidiary seconds; perpetual calendar with month, leap year, weekday, date, equation of time indicator; power reserve indicator on case back
Diameter: 32.5 mm
Height: 9.6 mm
Jewels: 30
Balance: glucydur
Frequency: 18,000 vph
Remarks: limited to 10 pieces

Caliber 2260

Manually wound, 1-minute tourbillon; single spring barrel, 336 hours power reserve; Geneva Seal
Functions: hours, minutes, subsidiary seconds (on tourbillon cage)
Diameter: 29.1 mm
Height: 6.8 mm
Jewels: 31
Balance: glucydur
Frequency: 18,000 vph

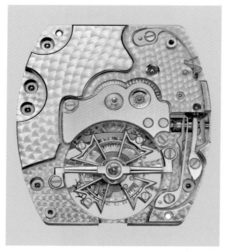

Caliber 1136/QP

Automatic; column wheel control of chronograph functions; single spring barrel, 40 hours power reserve
Functions: hours, minutes, subsidiary seconds; perpetual calendar with weekday, month, moon phase, leap year
Diameter: 28 mm
Height: 7.9 mm
Jewels: 38
Balance: glucydur
Frequency: 21,600 vph
Remarks: 228 components

Caliber 2795

Automatic; 1-minute tourbillon; single spring barrel, 45 hours power reserve; Geneva Seal
Functions: hours, minutes, subsidiary seconds (on tourbillon cage)
Measurements: 27.37 x 29.3 mm
Height: 6.1 mm
Jewels: 27
Balance: glucydur
Frequency: 18,000 vph
Remarks: tonneau-shaped

Caliber 2460 QRA

Automatic; single spring barrel, 40 hours power reserve
Functions: hours, minutes, subsidiary seconds; annual calendar with date (retrograde), month, moon phase
Diameter: 26.2 mm
Height: 5.4 mm
Jewels: 27
Balance: glucydur
Frequency: 28,800 vph

Caliber 2460 WT

Automatic; single spring barrel, 40 hours power reserve

Functions: hours, minutes, sweep seconds; second time zone (world-time display for 37 time zones); day/night indicator
Diameter: 36.6 mm
Height: 8.1 mm
Jewels: 27
Balance: glucydur
Frequency: 28,800 vph

Caliber 1120 SQ

Automatic; single spring barrel, 40 hours power reserve; Geneva Seal
Functions: hours, minutes
Diameter: 28.4 mm
Height: 2.45 mm
Jewels: 36
Balance: glucydur
Frequency: 19,800 vph
Remarks: ultra-slim construction: completely skeletonized and engraved movement

Caliber 2460 G4

Automatic; gold rotor; single spring barrel, 43 hours power reserve; Geneva Seal
Functions: disc display for hours, minutes, date, and weekday
Diameter: 25.6 mm
Height: 6.05 mm
Jewels: 27
Balance: glucydur
Frequency: 28,800 vph
Remarks: perlage on plate, beveled edges, bridges with côtes de Genève

Caliber 2460 SCC

Automatic; stop-second system; single spring barrel, 43 hours power reserve
Functions: hours, minutes, sweep seconds
Diameter: 26.2 mm
Height: 3.6 mm
Jewels: 27
Balance: glucydur
Frequency: 28,800 vph
Remarks: perlage on plate, beveled edges, bridges with côtes de Genève; polished steel parts; "Chronomètre Royal" golden rotor type

Caliber 1003

Manually wound; single spring barrel, 31 hours power reserve; Geneva Seal
Functions: hours, minutes
Diameter: 21.1 mm
Height: 1.64 mm
Jewels: 18
Balance: glucydur
Frequency: 18,000 vph
Remarks: currently thinnest movement being manufactured

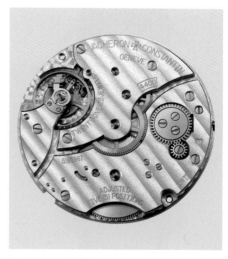

Caliber 4400

Manually wound; single spring barrel, 65 hours power reserve; Geneva Seal
Functions: hours, minutes, subsidiary seconds
Diameter: 28.5 mm
Height: 2.8 mm
Jewels: 21
Balance: glucydur
Frequency: 28,800 vph
Remarks: perlage on plate, beveled edges, bridges with côtes de Genève

Victorinox Swiss Army Watch S.A.
Chemin des Grillons 4
CH-2501 Bienne/Biel
Switzerland

Tel.:
01141-32-344-9933

Fax:
01141-32-344-9936

E-Mail:
info@victorinoxswissarmy.com

Website:
www.victorinoxswissarmy.com

Founded:
1884 / watches since 1989

Number of employees:
1,700

Annual production:
not specified

Distribution:
retail, shop systems

U.S. distributor:
Victorinox Swiss Army
7 Victoria Drive
Monroe, CT 06468
800-422-2706
www.swissarmy.com

Most important collections/price range:
Active, Classic, Professional / $325 to $3,695

Victorinox Swiss Army

This brand with the Swiss cross in its logo is a real child of the years of rapid industrial expansion in central Europe. Today, it is as much a symbol for Switzerland as cheese and chocolate are. In 1884, the brand was founded as the cutler to the Swiss army, and in the over 125 years of its existence, the practical and versatile officer's knife known as the Swiss Army Knife has become a legend, especially in what has grown to be its main market: the United States. The Victorinox concern, which is a family enterprise, owns a handful of divisions, though, whose products all epitomize the principle of functionality coupled with style.

Perfect quality, high reliability, and consistent functionality also characterize this brand's watches and its business practices as well. Faced with a massive recession, CEO Karl Elsener saw to it that redundant employees had alternative sources of income till after the storm, while he opened new markets and developed new products, such as a line of suitcases and perfumes.

Since the purchase of its American branch, Swiss Army Brands, Inc. in 2002, the Victorinox concern has gone by the name Victorinox Swiss Army and has successfully begun to transfer the proverbial versatility and robustness of the practical pocketknives to its affordable watch line. The evidence can be found in the Infantry, Airboss, and Alpnach watches, which have emerged over the past several years and established themselves in the market. The Chrono Classic cleverly converts the watch's hour and minute hands into a chronograph with 100ths of a second displayed in the large-date window.

Chrono Classic

Reference number: 241616
Movement: quartz, Soprod Caliber FM13D; hour and minute hands used for chronograph display; 1/100th second on large date display
Functions: hours, minutes, sweep seconds; chronograph; perpetual calendar with large date
Case: stainless steel with gray PVD coating, ø 41 mm, height 12 mm; sapphire crystal, water-resistant to 10 atm
Band: calf leather, folding clasp
Price: $850

Infantry Mechanical

Reference number: 241587
Movement: automatic, ETA Caliber 2824-2; ø 25.6 mm, height 4.6 mm; 25 jewels; 28,800 vph; 42-hour power reserve
Functions: hours, minutes, sweep seconds; date
Case: stainless steel, ø 40 mm, height 11 mm; sapphire crystal, water-resistant to 10 atm
Band: stainless steel, folding clasp
Price: $750
Variations: with leather strap ($695)

AirBoss Mechanical Chronograph

Reference number: 241597
Movement: automatic, ETA Caliber 7750; ø 30 mm, height 7.9 mm; 25 jewels; 28,800 vph; 42-hour power reserve
Functions: hours, minutes, subsidiary seconds; chronograph; date
Case: stainless steel, ø 42 mm, height 13.8 mm; sapphire crystal, transparent case back; water-resistant to 10 atm
Band: calf leather, folding clasp
Price: $2,195
Variations: with stainless steel bracelet ($2,295)

Vogard

In 2002, Michael Vogt founded his brand with the intention of creating the "best travel watch there is." With the Timezoner, he turned his vision into reality. Within but a few years, the brand became a specialist in the design and production of mechanical world-time wristwatches.

According to Vogt, luxury objects must satisfy both emotional and functional needs.

Accordingly, these objects must also offer real value in daily life—and they must be absolutely reliable when it comes down to the wire. Thus the time-measuring functions of the Chronozoner are simpler to operate than those of conventional chronographs thanks to a new arrangement of the control elements: The crown is positioned at 6 o'clock, while the start and stop buttons are found at 4 and 8, respectively. The Chronozoner also utilizes the ingeniously simple Vogard time zone setting mechanism: By opening a lever on the left side of the case and turning the bezel to the desired city name, the time for that destination can be read; when the lever is closed again, the watch is automatically set to the new time zone. The skeletonized 24-hour hand identifies both day and night. This system is not only exceptionally practical on trips; it can also be used to see the time in other parts of the world—for example, if the wearer wanted to make a phone call to a faraway city. The bidirectionally rotating bezel can be manipulated as much as the wearer sees fit without ever losing a second.

Vogard SA
Oberer Kanalweg 12
CH-2560 Nidau/BE
Switzerland

Tel.:
01141-32-931-9000

Fax:
01141-32-931-9003

E-Mail:
discover@vogard.com

Website:
www.vogard.com

Founded:
2002

Number of employees:
5

Annual production:
approx. 500 watches

Distribution:
Please contact the company directly.

Most important collections/price range:
Timezoner / $7,250 to $31,000; Chronozoner / $13,500 to $17,500; Datezoner / $15,000 to $19,000

Licensed Pilot

Reference number: LP 2634
Movement: automatic, Caliber Timezoner 01 (base ETA 2892-A2); ø 33 mm, height 5 mm; 21 jewels; 28,800 vph; patented bezel-activated world-time mechanism
Functions: hours, minutes, sweep seconds; world-time display; date; day/night indicator
Case: stainless steel, ø 43 mm, height 14 mm; aluminum bezel with IATA airport codes, sapphire crystal; transparent case back; lateral activation and locking lever; water-resistant to 10 atm
Band: reptile skin, double folding clasp
Remarks: cities can be chosen by customer
Price: $8,250
Variations: with rubber strap ($8,250); with stainless steel bracelet ($8,750)

Chronozoner F1 Limited Edition

Reference number: CZ F161
Movement: automatic, Caliber Chronozoner CZ 1 (base ETA 7750); ø 36 mm, height 8.7 mm; 25 jewels; 28,800 vph; bezel-activated world-time mechanism
Functions: hours, minutes, subsidiary seconds; world-time display; chronograph
Case: titanium, black carbide-coated, ø 48 mm, height 18 mm; stainless steel bezel with engraved racetracks, bidirectional time zone setting; sapphire crystal; transparent case back; activation/locking lever at side of case; water-resistant to 5 atm
Band: alcantara, double folding clasp
Remarks: city references on bezel or F1 locations
Price: $15,000, limited to 99 pieces

Datezoner Pilot

Reference number: DZP 6332
Movement: automatic, Caliber Datezoner 01 (base ETA 7750); ø 36 mm, height 8.7 mm; 25 jewels; 28,800 vph; patented bezel-activated world-time mechanism; synchronized big date and time zone
Functions: hours, minutes, subsidiary seconds; second time zone; date; day/night indicator
Case: titanium, ø 48 mm, height 18 mm; stainless steel bidirectional bezel for time zone and date; sapphire crystal; lateral activation/locking lever; transparent case back; water-resistant to 5 atm
Band: reptile skin, double folding clasp
Remarks: bezel with IATA airport codes or cities
Price: $16,500

Koliz Vostok Co. Ltd.
Naugarduko 41
LT-03227 Vilnius
Lithuania

Tel.:
011370-5-2106342

Fax:
011370-4-2130777

E-Mail:
info@vostok-europe.com

Website:
www.vostok-europe.com

Founded:
2003

Number of employees:
15

Annual production:
25,000 watches

U.S. distributor:
Vostok-Europe
Détente Distribution Group
31 Halls Hill Road
Colchester, CT 06415
1-877-4VOSTOK
www.russia2all.com

Most important collections/price range:
Anchar collection / starting at $759; Caspian Sea
Monster / starting at $799

Vostok

Shortly after the fall of the Berlin Wall, one very common sight was people—often soldiers from the formerly Soviet Russian army—selling paraphernalia in the streets or flea markets of eastern Berlin. Among the items going for pennies were watches whose dials bore insignia from the various military tiers. Vostok was one of the military outfitters, born from the Slava factory, which had been evacuated from Moscow in 1942 and had already started making products for civilians in 1943. The name appeared on dials in 1957 ("Восток" in Cyrillic). Unlike many brands in the West, however, Vostok kept on making mechanical movements throughout the quartz craze, which became a boon after the opening of Eastern Europe. It has since focused on expanding capacities and fine-tuning its movements.

The two most recent calibers are the automatic 2416 with a variety of displays and functions. The erstwhile Poljot calibers 2609 and 2619 are also being manufactured.

In 2003, the company Koliz-Vostok set up shop in Lithuania to better serve the American and European markets. The designs created in Vilnius are modeled on the bold, extroverted shapes of the sixties and seventies. Martial aspects are consciously reduced, though some of the recent models do give a nod to Soviet engineering. The Ekranoplan is named after that strange ground-effect vehicle that travels on the Caspian Sea, and the Anchar was one of the Soviet Union's fastest submarines. It's a little, harmless wave of nostalgia, and Vostok is riding it well.

Ekranoplan

Reference number: 2432.01-5454108
Movement: automatic, Vostok Caliber 2432.01 (base Vostok 2416/B); ø 24 mm, height 6.3 mm; 32 jewels; 18,000 vph; blued screws; decorated rotor; 31-hour power reserve
Functions: hours, minutes, sweep seconds; date; day/night display; 24-hour display
Case: black PVD-coated stainless steel, ø 47 mm, height 15 mm; unidirectional bezel with 60-minute divisions; mineral crystal; transparent case back; screw-in crown
Band: silicon, buckle
Price: $749

GAZ 14 Limousine

Reference number: 2426-5601058
Movement: automatic, Vostok Caliber 2426 (base Vostok 2416/B); ø 24 mm; 31 jewels; 18,000 vph; 31-hour power reserve
Functions: hours, minutes, sweep seconds; additional 24-hour display; date
Case: stainless steel, ø 43 mm, height 13.8 mm; mineral glass; transparent case back; water-resistant to 5 atm
Band: calf leather, buckle
Price: $419
Variations: with coated case

Anchar "Tritium Gas Light"

Reference number: NH35/5104144
Movement: automatic, Seiko Caliber 35A; ø 27.4 mm, height 5.32 mm; 24 jewels; 21,600 vph; 45-hour power reserve
Functions: hours, minutes, sweep seconds; date
Case: stainless steel, ø 48 mm, height 15.5 mm; unidirectional bezel with 60-minute divisions; mineral glass; screw-in crown; water-resistant to 30 atm
Band: rubber, buckle
Remarks: comes with calf-leather band
Price: $739

Vulcain

In 1858, Maurice Ditisheim opened his own, high-quality pocket watch business in La Chaux-de-Fonds. Among the timepieces he produced were chronographs, a perpetual calendar, and a minute repeater. It was not until 1894 that Ditisheim gave his wares a brand name, Vulcain. After various name changes in the late 1800s and early 1900s, the company became Vulcain & Volta in 1911, Vulcain and Studio in the 1950s, and finally, simply Vulcain.

Ditisheim saw the potential of the wristwatch early on and soon began making various models with in-house calibers. The company's major turning point came at the 1947 World's Fair, where it presented its Cricket wristwatch. The aptly named timepiece with alarm, with its double soundboard that produced a loud, cricket-like chirp, was a huge sensation. The modern Cricket line banks on retro appeal—the love affair people have

with the Western world of the 1940s and '50s, when work and money were plentiful after World War II. But Vulcain is also giving itself a face-lift under new CEO Renato Vanotti. Models like the cushion-cased, a touch gaudy, reedited Nautical Seventies are a reminder that the decade of disco wasn't too bad either. The Cloisonné series represents a bit of a break from the past, with bright enamel motifs in the middle of the dial.

Still, Vulcain's greatest claim to fame will always be that it became the unofficial brand of the U.S. Presidency—every commander in chief since Harry Truman has received his own engraved Cricket, with the exception of George W. Bush—earning the watch its nickname of "The Time Minister."

Manufacture des montres Vulcain S.A.
Chemin des Tourelles 4
CH-2400 Le Locle
Switzerland

Tel.:
01141-32-930-8010

Fax:
01141-32-930-8019

E-Mail:
info@vulcain-watches.ch

Website:
www.vulcain-watches.com

Founded:
1858

Number of employees:
20

Annual production:
5,000 watches

Distribution:
For sales information, contact Vulcain directly

Most important collections/price range:
50s Presidents / from $3,875; Aviator / from $5,525; Nautical / from $5,975; Anniversary Heart / from $7,450

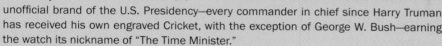

50s Presidents' Moonphase

Reference number: 580158.328L
Movement: automatic, Vulcain Caliber V-58; ø 25.6 mm; 25 jewels; 28,800 vph; rhodium-plated; blued screws, côtes de Genève; 42-hour power reserve
Functions: hours, minutes, sweep seconds; full calendar with date, weekday, month, moon phase
Case: stainless steel, ø 42 mm, height 11 mm; sapphire crystal, transparent case back; water-resistant to 5 atm
Band: reptile skin, buckle
Price: $6,675
Variations: rose gold ($23,675)

Nautical Seventies

Reference number: 100159.081L
Movement: manually wound, Vulcain Caliber V-10; ø 28 mm; 25 jewels; 18,000 vph; 42-hour power reserve
Functions: hours, minutes, sweep seconds; alarm
Case: stainless steel, ø 42 mm, height 17.6 mm; crown-adjustable inner bezel with 60-minute divisions; hesalite crystal; screw-in crown; water-resistant to 30 atm
Band: calf leather, buckle
Remarks: limited to 300 pieces
Price: $5,975

Aviator GMT Pilot

Reference number: 100108.333C/BN
Movement: manually wound, Vulcain Caliber V-10; ø 28 mm; 25 jewels; 18,000 vph; 42-hour power reserve
Functions: hours, minutes, sweep seconds; additional 24-hour display (second time zone); alarm
Case: stainless steel, ø 42 mm, height 13.4 mm; crown rotates inner ring with reference cities; sapphire crystal, water-resistant to 10 atm
Band: calf leather, buckle
Price: from $5,525

Gerhard D. Wempe KG
Steinstrasse 23
D-20095 Hamburg
Germany

Tel.:
01149-40-334-480

Fax:
01149-40-331-840

E-Mail:
info@wempe.de

Website:
www.wempe.de

Founded:
1878

Number of employees:
500 worldwide; 35 at Wempe Glashütte i/SA

Annual production:
4,000 watches

U.S. distributor:
Wempe Timepieces
700 Fifth Avenue
New York, NY 10019
212-397-9000
www.wempe.com

Most important collections/price range:
Wempe Zeitmeister / approx. $1,000 to $4,500;
Wempe Chronometerwerke / approx. $5,000 to
$95,000

Wempe

Ever since 2005, the global jewelry chain Gerhard D. Wempe KG has been putting out watches under its own name again. It was probably inevitable: Gerhard D. Wempe, who founded the company in the late nineteenth century in Oldenburg, was himself a watchmaker. And in the 1930s, the company also owned the Hamburg chronometer works that made watches for seafarers and pilots.

Today, while Wempe remains formally in Hamburg, the manufacturing is done in Glashütte—a natural, since the company has long entertained a close relationship with the Saxon hub of horology. The workshops have been set up in the former Urania observatory and a factory in the Altenburgerstrasse.

But this does mean that the coveted Swiss COSC seal of approval is not an option, since the watches are of German provenance. So Wempe built its own chronometer testing site, which operates under the German Industrial Norm (DIN 8319) with the official blessings from the Saxon and Thuringian offices for measurement and calibration and accreditation from the German Calibration Service.

The Zeitmeister collection meets all the requirements of the high art of watchmaking and, thanks to its accessible pricing, is attractive for budding collectors. As for the watches under the Wempe Chronometer logo (Chronometerwerke), these are the result of a partnership of ideas at the highest level. Both models were designed on the basis of an exclusive agreement with the Nomos watch *manufacture* in Glashütte, where they are also built.

Chronometerwerke Tonneau Tourbillon

Reference number: WG 740002
Movement: manually wound, Wempe Caliber CW 2; 22.6 x 32.6 mm, height 6.5 mm; 19 jewels; 21,600 vph; 1-minute tourbillon, Breguet balance spring, bridges with sunburst pattern, rhodium-plated, DIN certified chronometer
Functions: hours, minutes, subsidiary seconds
Case: platinum, 40.9 x 51 mm, height 13.7 mm; sapphire crystal, transparent case back
Band: reptile skin, buckle
Remarks: limited to 25 pieces
Price: $110,500

Chronometerwerke Manually Wound Tonneau Pavé

Reference number: WG 040013
Movement: manually wound, Wempe Caliber CW 1; 22.6 x 32.6 mm, height 3.6 mm; 23 jewels; 21,600 vph; 80-hour power reserve; DIN tested chronometer
Functions: hours, minutes, subsidiary seconds
Case: rose gold, 37 x 45.6 mm, height 10.2 mm; sapphire crystal, transparent case back
Band: ray skin, buckle
Remarks: mother-of-pearl dial, case set with 369 brilliants
Price: $42,800
Variations: stainless steel

Chronometerwerke Manually Wound Tonneau

Reference number: WG 040012
Movement: manually wound, Wempe Caliber CW 1; 22.6 x 32.6 mm, height 3.6 mm; 23 jewels; 21,600 vph; double spring barrel, swan-neck fine adjustment, three-quarter plate with sunburst pattern; hand-engraved balance cock, DIN certified chronometer
Functions: hours, minutes, subsidiary seconds
Case: stainless steel, 37 x 45.6 mm, height 10.2 mm; sapphire crystal, transparent case back; water-resistant to 5 atm
Band: reptile skin, buckle
Price: $6,350

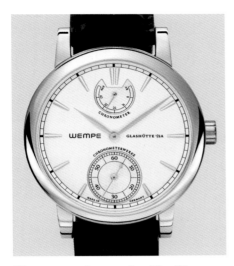

Chronometerwerke Up/Down

Reference number: WG 080001
Movement: manually wound, Wempe Caliber CW 3;
ø 32 mm, height 6.1 mm; 42 jewels; 28,800 vph;
three-quarter plate, 3 screwed-in gold chatons,
hand-engraved balance cock, Glashütte stopwork;
80-hour power reserve; DIN tested chronometer
Functions: hours, minutes, subsidiary seconds;
power reserve display
Case: stainless steel, ø 42 mm, height 12.5 mm;
sapphire crystal, transparent case back; water-
resistant to 5 atm
Band: reptile skin, buckle
Price: $8,950
Variations: yellow gold ($19,950)

Chronometerwerke Up/Down

Reference number: WG 080006
Movement: manually wound, Wempe Caliber CW 3;
ø 32 mm, height 6.1 mm; 42 jewels; 28,800 vph;
three-quarter plate, 3 screwed-in gold chatons,
hand-engraved balance cock, Glashütte stopwork;
80-hour power reserve; DIN tested chronometer
Functions: hours, minutes, subsidiary seconds;
power reserve display
Case: yellow gold, ø 43 mm, height 12.5 mm;
sapphire crystal, transparent case back; water-
resistant to 5 atm
Band: reptile skin, buckle
Price: $19,950
Variations: stainless steel ($8,500)

Chronometerwerke Up/Down

Reference number: WG 080005
Movement: manually wound, Wempe Caliber CW 3;
ø 32 mm, height 6.1 mm; 42 jewels; 28,800 vph;
three-quarter plate, 3 screwed-in gold chatons,
hand-engraved balance cock, Glashütte stopwork;
42-hour power reserve; DIN tested chronometer
Functions: hours, minutes, subsidiary seconds;
power reserve display
Case: yellow gold, ø 43 mm, height 12.5 mm;
sapphire crystal, transparent case back; water-
resistant to 5 atm
Band: reptile skin, buckle
Price: $19,950
Variations: stainless steel ($8,500)

Zeitmeister Large Date with Second Time Zone

Reference number: WM 370001
Movement: automatic, Wempe Caliber TT651.00
(base ETA 2892-A2); ø 26.2 mm, height 5.25 mm;
21 jewels; 28,800 vph; DIN certified chronometer
Functions: hours, minutes, sweep seconds;
additional 12-hour display (second time zone); large
date; month, moon phase, weekday, date
Case: stainless steel, ø 42 mm, height 13.65 mm;
sapphire crystal, water-resistant to 5 atm
Band: reptile skin, buckle
Price: $3,580

Zeitmeister Aviator Watch Chronograph

Reference number: WM 600005
Movement: automatic, ETA Caliber 7753; ø 30 mm,
height 7.9 mm; 27 jewels; 28,800 vph; 42-hour
power reserve; DIN tested chronometer
Functions: hours, minutes, subsidiary seconds;
chronograph; date
Case: stainless steel, ø 44 mm, height 16 mm;
sapphire crystal, water-resistant to 5 atm
Band: leather, buckle
Price: $3,580

Zeitmeister Aviator Watch Chronograph Ceramic

Reference number: WM 600003
Movement: automatic, ETA Caliber 7753; ø 30 mm,
height 7.9 mm; 27 jewels; 28,800 vph; DIN certified
chronometer
Functions: hours, minutes, subsidiary seconds;
chronograph; date
Case: ceramic with titanium inner case, ø 44 mm,
height 16 mm; sapphire crystal, water-resistant to
5 atm
Band: rubber, folding clasp
Price: $5,150

Zenith SA
34, rue des Billodes
CH-2400 Le Locle
Switzerland

Tel.:
01141-32-930-6262

Fax:
01141-32-930-6363

Website:
www.zenith-watches.com

Founded:
1865

Number of employees:
over 330 employees worldwide

Annual production:
not specified

U.S. distributor:
Zenith Watches
966 South Springfield Avenue
Springfield, NJ 07081
866-675-2079
contact.zenith@lvmhwatchjewelry.com

Most important collections/price range:
Academy / from $173,000; Captain / from
$5,600; El Primero / from $6,700; Heritage / from
$5,000

Zenith

The tall narrow building in Le Locle, with its closely spaced high windows to let in daylight, is a testimony to Zenith's history as a self-sufficient *manufacture* of movements and watches in the entrepreneurial spirit of the Industrial Revolution. The company, founded in 1865 by Georges Favre-Jacot as a small watch reassembly workshop, has produced and distributed every possible type of watch over seven generations, from the simple pocket watch to the most complicated calendar. But it remains primarily associated with the El Primero caliber, the first wristwatch chronograph movement boasting automatic winding and a frequency of 36,000 vph. Only a few watch manufacturers had risked such a high oscillation frequency—and none of them in association with such complexity as the integrated chronograph mechanism and the bilaterally winding rotor of the El Primero.

That the movement even celebrated its fortieth anniversary, though, was thanks to the revival of the mechanical watch. After Zenith was sold to the LVMH Group in 1999, the label was fully dusted off and modernized perhaps a little too much. Eccentric creations catapulted the dutiful watchmaker's watchmaker into the world of *haute horlogerie*.

The sharp decline of the brand's most important export markets led to a change in management just after Baselworld 2009. The new president, Jean-Frédéric Dufour, placed his trust in tradition, reason, core horological values, and a real price-performance ratio—age-old virtues of Zenith. Not surprisingly, the leader of the comeback was the El Primero–based Striking 10th. And the company has continued producing stunning pieces ever since, like the Academy Christophe Colomb, with its gyroscopic model.

El Primero Chronomaster Power Reserve

Reference number: 03.2080.4021/01.C494
Movement: automatic, Zenith Caliber 4021 "El Primero"; ø 30 mm, height 7.85 mm; 39 jewels; 36,000 vph; partially skeletonized below the regulator part; 50-hour power reserve
Functions: hours, minutes, subsidiary seconds; power reserve indicator; chronograph; moon phase
Case: stainless steel, ø 42 mm, height 14.05 mm; sapphire crystal; transparent case back; water-resistant to 10 atm
Band: reptile skin, folding clasp
Price: $9,600
Variations: with stainless steel bracelet ($10,100)

El Primero Chronomaster 1969

Reference number: 03.2040.4061/69.C496
Movement: automatic, Zenith Caliber 4061 "El Primero"; ø 30 mm, height 6.6 mm; 31 jewels; 36,000 vph; 50-hour power reserve
Functions: hours, minutes; chronograph
Case: stainless steel (special alloy), ø 42 mm, height 13 mm; sapphire crystal; transparent case back; water-resistant to 10 atm
Band: reptile skin, folding clasp
Price: $9,600
Variations: rose gold ($21,600)

El Primero Chronomaster Open Grande Date

Reference number: 03.2160.4047/01.C713
Movement: automatic, Zenith Caliber 4047 "El Primero"; ø 30.5 mm, height 9.05 mm; 32 jewels; 36,000 vph; 50-hour power reserve
Functions: hours, minutes, subsidiary seconds; chronograph; large date; display of sun and moon phases (integrated day/night indication)
Case: stainless steel, ø 45 mm, height 15.6 mm; sapphire crystal; transparent case back; water-resistant to 5 atm
Band: reptile skin, folding clasp
Price: $12,700
Variations: with black dial; rose gold ($32,000)

El Primero 36,000 VpH 1969

Reference number: 03.2040.400/69.C494
Movement: automatic, Zenith Caliber 400B
"El Primero"; ø 30 mm, height 6.6 mm; 31 jewels;
36,000 vph; 50 hours power reserve
Functions: hours, minutes, subsidiary seconds;
chronograph; date
Case: stainless steel, ø 42 mm, height 12.75 mm;
sapphire crystal; transparent case back; water-
resistant to 10 atm
Band: reptile skin, folding clasp
Price: $9,000

El Primero 36,000 VpH "Tribute to Charles Vermot"

Reference number: 03.2041.400/51.C496
Movement: automatic, Zenith Caliber 400B
"El Primero"; ø 30 mm, height 6.6 mm; 31 jewels;
36,000 vph; 50-hour power reserve
Functions: hours, minutes, subsidiary seconds;
chronograph; date
Case: stainless steel, ø 42 mm, height 12.75 mm;
sapphire crystal; transparent case back; water-
resistant to 10 atm
Band: reptile skin, folding clasp
Price: $8,500

El Primero 36,000 Vph

Reference number: 03.2040.400/21.M2040
Movement: automatic, Zenith Caliber 400B
"El Primero"; ø 30 mm, height 6.6 mm; 31 jewels;
36,000 vph; 50-hour power reserve
Functions: hours, minutes, subsidiary seconds;
chronograph; date
Case: stainless steel, ø 42 mm, height 12.75
mm; sapphire crystal; transparent case back;
water-resistant to 10 atm
Band: stainless steel, folding clasp
Price: $9,000
Variations: with reptile skin band ($8,500)

El Primero Stratos Flyback Striking 10th "Tribute to Felix Baumgartner"

Reference number: 03.2062.4057/69.M2060
Movement: automatic, Zenith Caliber 4057B
"El Primero"; ø 30 mm, height 6.6 mm; 31 jewels;
36,000 vph; foudroyante (sweep chronograph makes
revolution every 10 seconds); totalizer for 6 revolutions
minutes; 50-hour power reserve
Functions: hours, minutes, subsidiary seconds; flyback
chronograph; date
Case: stainless steel, ø 45.5 mm, height 14.1 mm; bezel
with ceramic insert; unidirectional bezel with 60-minute
divisions; water-resistant to 10 atm
Band: stainless steel, folding clasp
Price: $10,400

El Primero Stratos Flyback

Reference number: 03.2060.405/21.M2060
Movement: automatic, Zenith Caliber 405B
"El Primero"; ø 30 mm, height 6.6 mm; 31 jewels;
36,000 vph; 50-hour power reserve
Functions: hours, minutes, subsidiary seconds;
flyback chronograph; date
Case: stainless steel, ø 45.5 mm, height 14.1
mm; unidirectional bezel with ceramic inlay and
60-minute divisions; sapphire crystal; transparent
case back; water-resistant to 10 atm
Band: stainless steel, folding clasp
Price: $9,200
Variations: with rubber strap ($8,500)

El Primero Espada

Reference number: 03.2170.4650/01.M2170
Movement: automatic, Zenith Caliber 4650
"El Primero"; ø 30 mm, height 5.58 mm; 22 jewels;
36,000 vph; 50-hour power reserve
Functions: hours, minutes, sweep seconds; date
Case: stainless steel, ø 40 mm, height 11.7 mm;
sapphire crystal; transparent case back; water-
resistant to 10 atm
Band: stainless steel, folding clasp
Price: $6,700
Variations: with black dial; rose gold on bracelet
($29,100); rose gold with white MOP with baguettes
dial on strap ($22,200); rose gold with brown dial
on strap ($17,700)

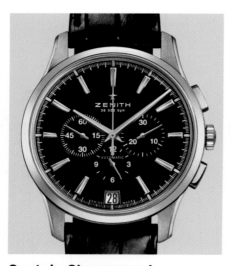

Captain Chronograph

Reference number: 03.2110.400/22.C493
Movement: automatic, Zenith Caliber 400B
"El Primero"; ø 30 mm, height 6.6 mm; 31 jewels;
36,000 vph; 50-hour power reserve
Functions: hours, minutes, subsidiary seconds;
chronograph; date
Case: stainless steel, ø 42 mm, height 12 mm;
sapphire crystal; transparent case back; water-
resistant to 5 atm
Band: reptile skin, folding clasp
Price: $8,300
Variations: rose gold ($17,800)

Captain Central Second

Reference number: 03.2020.670/22.C498
Movement: automatic, Zenith Caliber 670
"Elite"; ø 25.6 mm, height 3.47 mm; 27 jewels;
28,800 vph; 50-hour power reserve
Functions: hours, minutes, sweep seconds; date
Case: stainless steel, ø 40 mm, height 8.15 mm;
sapphire crystal; transparent case back; water-
resistant to 5 atm
Band: reptile skin, folding clasp
Price: $5,600
Variations: rose gold ($14,500); stainless steel and
rose gold ($10,600)

Captain Moonphase

Reference number: 03.2140.691/02.C498
Movement: automatic, Zenith Caliber 691
"Elite"; ø 25.6 mm, height 5.67 mm; 27 jewels;
28,800 vph; 50-hour power reserve
Functions: hours, minutes, subsidiary seconds;
moon phase
Case: stainless steel, ø 40 mm, height 8.9
mm; sapphire crystal; transparent case back;
water-resistant to 5 atm
Band: reptile skin, buckle
Price: $7,600
Variations: rose gold ($16,600)

Captain Winsor

Reference number: 18.2070.4054/02.C711
Movement: automatic, Zenith Caliber 4054
"El Primero"; ø 30 mm, height 8.3 mm; 29 jewels;
36,000 vph; 50-hour power reserve
Functions: hours, minutes, subsidiary seconds;
chronograph; full calendar with date, weekday,
month
Case: rose gold, ø 42 mm, height 13.85 mm;
sapphire crystal; transparent case back; water-
resistant to 5 atm
Band: reptile skin, buckle
Price: $22,200
Variations: stainless steel ($10,400)

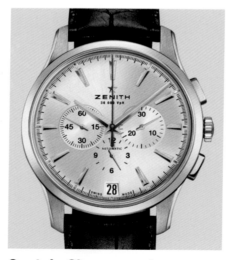

Captain Chronograph

Reference number: 03.2110.400/01.C498
Movement: automatic, Zenith Caliber 400B
"El Primero"; ø 30 mm, height 6.6 mm; 31 jewels;
36,000 vph; 50-hour power reserve
Functions: hours, minutes, subsidiary seconds;
chronograph; date
Case: stainless steel, ø 42 mm, height 12
mm; sapphire crystal; transparent case back;
water-resistant to 5 atm
Band: reptile skin, folding clasp
Price: $8,300
Variations: rose gold ($17,800)

Heritage Ultra Thin

Reference number: 03.2010.681/01.C493
Movement: automatic, Zenith Caliber 681 "Elite";
ø 25.6 mm, height 3.47 mm; 27 jewels; 28,800 vph
Functions: hours, minutes, subsidiary seconds
Case: stainless steel, ø 40 mm, height 8.3 mm;
sapphire crystal; transparent case back; water-
resistant to 5 atm
Band: reptile skin, buckle
Price: $5,300
Variations: with silver, black, or blue dial ($5,300)

Pilot Doublematic

Reference number: 03.2400.4046/21.C721
Movement: automatic, Zenith Caliber 4046
"El Primero"; ø 30 mm, height 9.05 mm; 41 jewels;
36,000 vph; 50-hour power reserve
Functions: hours, minutes; world-time display
(second time zone); alarm clock with display of
functions and power reserve; chronograph; large
date
Case: stainless steel, ø 45 mm, height 15.6 mm;
crown rotates inner bezel with reference city names;
sapphire crystal; transparent case back; water-
resistant to 5 atm
Band: reptile skin, folding clasp
Price: $14,200
Variations: rose gold ($31,900)

Pilot Big Date Special

Reference number: 03.2410.4010/21.M2410
Movement: automatic, Zenith Caliber 4010
"El Primero"; ø 30 mm, height 7.65 mm; 31 jewels;
36,000 vph; 50-hour power reserve
Functions: hours, minutes, subsidiary seconds;
chronograph; large date
Case: stainless steel, ø 42 mm, height 13.5 mm;
sapphire crystal; transparent case back; water-
resistant to 5 atm
Band: stainless steel Milanese mesh, folding clasp
Price: $7,700
Variations: with calf leather band ($7,600)

Montre d'Aeronef Type 20 GMT

Reference number: 03.2430.693/21.C723
Movement: automatic, Zenith Caliber 693 "Elite";
ø 25.6 mm, height 3.94 mm; 26 jewels; 28,800 vph;
50-hour power reserve
Functions: hours, minutes, subsidiary seconds;
additional 12-hour display (second time zone)
Case: stainless steel, ø 48 mm, height 15.8 mm;
sapphire crystal; water-resistant to 10 atm
Band: calf leather, buckle
Price: $7,900

Montre d'Aeronef Type 20 GMT "Red Baron"

Reference number: 96.2430.693/21.C703
Movement: automatic, Zenith Caliber 693
"Elite"; ø 25.6 mm, height 3.94 mm; 26 jewels;
28,800 vph; 50-hour power reserve
Functions: hours, minutes, subsidiary seconds;
additional 24-hour display (second time zone)
Case: titanium with black PVD coating, ø 48 mm,
height 15.8 mm; sapphire crystal; water-resistant
to 10 atm
Band: calf leather, buckle
Price: $8,600

Montre d'Aeronef Type 20 Annual Calendar

Reference number: 03.2430.4054/21.C721
Movement: automatic, Zenith Caliber 4054
"El Primero"; ø 30 mm, height 8.3 mm; 29 jewels;
36,000 vph; 50-hour power reserve
Functions: hours, minutes, subsidiary seconds;
chronograph; full calendar with date, weekday,
month
Case: stainless steel, ø 48 mm, height 15.8 mm;
sapphire crystal; water-resistant to 10 atm
Band: calf leather, buckle
Price: $11,000

Montre d'Aeronef Type 20

Reference number: 03.1930.681/21.C723
Movement: automatic, Zenith Caliber 681
"Elite"; ø 25.6 mm; height 3.47 mm; 27 jewels;
28,800 vph; 50-hour power reserve
Functions: hours, minutes, subsidiary seconds
Case: stainless steel, ø 40 mm, height 11.8 mm;
sapphire crystal; water-resistant to 10 atm
Band: calf leather, buckle
Price: $6,400

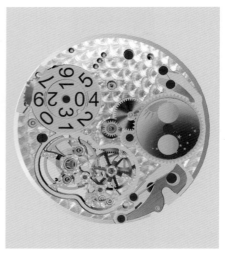

Caliber El Primero 410

Automatic; single spring barrel, 50-hour power reserve

Functions: hours, minutes, subsidiary seconds; chronograph; full calendar with date, weekday, month, moon phase
Diameter: 30 mm
Height: 6.6 mm
Jewels: 31
Balance: glucydur
Frequency: 36,000 vph
Balance spring: self-compensating flat spring
Shock protection: Kif

Caliber El Primero 4054

Automatic; single spring barrel, 50-hour power reserve

Functions: hours, minutes; chronograph; annual calendar with date, weekday, month
Diameter: 30 mm
Height: 8.3 mm
Jewels: 29
Balance: glucydur
Frequency: 36,000 vph
Balance spring: self-compensating flat spring
Shock protection: Kif

Caliber El Primero 4047

Automatic; single spring barrel, 50-hour power reserve

Functions: hours, minutes; chronograph; large date; display of sun and moon phases (integrated day/night indication)
Diameter: 30.5 mm
Height: 9.05 mm
Jewels: 41
Balance: glucydur
Frequency: 36,000 vph
Balance spring: self-compensating flat spring
Shock protection: Kif

Caliber El Primero 4057B

Automatic; single spring barrel, 50-hour power reserve

Functions: hours, minutes, subsidiary seconds; chronograph shows 1/10th of a second thanks to fast drive of chronograph hands (1 revolution every 10 seconds), totalizer for 6 revolutions; date
Diameter: 30.5 mm
Height: 6.6 mm
Jewels: 31
Balance: glucydur
Frequency: 36,000 vph
Balance spring: self-compensating flat spring
Shock protection: Kif

Caliber El Primero 400B

Automatic; single spring barrel, 50-hour power reserve

Functions: hours, minutes, subsidiary seconds; chronograph; date
Diameter: 30 mm
Height: 6.6 mm
Jewels: 31
Balance: glucydur
Frequency: 36,000 vph
Balance spring: self-compensating flat spring
Shock protection: Kif

Caliber Elite 681

Automatic; single spring barrel, 50-hour power reserve

Functions: hours, minutes, subsidiary seconds
Diameter: 25.6 mm
Height: 3.81 mm
Jewels: 27
Balance: glucydur
Frequency: 28,800 vph
Balance spring: self-compensating flat spring
Shock protection: Kif

Zeitwinkel

Timeless, simple, and sustainable—three attributes every watch manufacturer aspires to endow its creations with. Zeitwinkel models hew tightly to this perspective: The simplest of the company's offerings is a two-hand watch and the most complicated is a three-hand watch with power reserve display and large date. The dials are completely flat and marked with the company logo, a stylized "W." With their relatively heavy, steel cases designed by Jean-François Ruchonnet (TAG Heuer V4, Cabestan, among others), the watches look fairly "German," which comes as no surprise, because Zeitwinkel's founders, Ivica Maksimovic and Peter Nikolaus, hail from there.

The most valuable part of the watches is somewhat hidden, though. Behind the sapphire crystal backs tick veritable *manufacture* movements the likes of which are very rare in the business. The calibers were developed by Laurent Besse and his *artisans horlogers*, or watchmaking craftspeople. All components come courtesy of independent suppliers— Zeitwinkel balance wheels, pallets, escape wheels, and Straumann spirals, for example, are produced by Precision Engineering, a company associated with watch brand H. Moser & Cie.

In keeping with the company's ideals, you won't find any alligator in Zeitwinkel watch bands. Choices here are exclusively rubber, calfskin, or calfskin with an alligator-like pattern. "Gold cases are also taboo with us," says Nikolaus, "until we find a supplier who can guarantee that the gold comes from fair trade sources."

Zeitwinkel Montres SA
Rue Pierre-Jolissaint 35
CH-2610 Saint-Imier
Switzerland

Tel.:
01141-32-914-17-71

Fax:
01141-32-914-17-81

E-Mail:
info@zeitwinkel.ch

Website:
www.zeitwinkel.ch

Founded:
2006

Number of employees:
not specified

Annual production:
approx. 800 watches

U.S. distributor:
Tourneau
510 Madison Avenue
New York, NY 10022
212-758-5830
Also in Dallas, Costa Mesa, Las Vegas, and Denver

Most important collections/price range:
mechanical wristwatches / starting at around
$5,500

273°

Reference number: 273-43-0123
Movement: automatic, Caliber ZW0103;
ø 30.4 mm, height 8 mm; 49 jewels; 28,800 vph;
German silver three-quarter plate and bridges, côtes de Genève; beveled and polished screws and edges;
72-hour power reserve
Functions: hours, minutes, subsidiary seconds;
large date; power reserve indicator
Case: stainless steel, ø 42.5 mm, height 13.8 mm; sapphire crystal; transparent case back;
water-resistant to 5 atm
Band: calf leather, folding clasp
Price: $11,490
Variations: with black or silver dial; various strap options

188°

Reference number: 188-24-0124
Movement: automatic, Caliber ZW0102;
ø 30.4 mm, height 5.7 mm; 28 jewels; 28,800 vph;
German silver three-quarter plate and bridges; côtes de Genève, beveled and polished screws and edges;
72-hour power reserve
Functions: hours, minutes, subsidiary seconds;
date
Case: stainless steel, ø 39 mm, height 11.6 mm; sapphire crystal, transparent case back;
water-resistant to 5 atm
Band: calf leather, folding clasp
Price: $7,490
Variations: various dials and straps; 42.5 mm case

032°

Reference number: 032-31-0141
Movement: automatic, Caliber ZW0102;
ø 30.4 mm, height 5.7 mm; 30 jewels; 28,800 vph;
German silver three-quarter plate and bridges; côtes de Genève, beveled and polished screws and edges;
72-hour power reserve
Functions: hours, minutes, sweep seconds; date
Case: stainless steel, ø 42.5 mm, height 11.7 mm; sapphire crystal, transparent case back;
water-resistant to 5 atm
Band: calf leather, folding clasp
Price: $7,490
Variations: various dials and straps; 39 mm case

ETA

This Swatch Group movement manufacturer produces more than five million movements a year. And after the withdrawal of Richemont's Jaeger-LeCoultre as well as Swatch Group sisters Nouvelle Lémania and Frédéric Piguet from the business of selling movements on the free market, most watch brands can hardly help but beat down the door of this full service manufacturer.

ETA offers a broad spectrum of automatic movements in various dimensions with different functions, chronograph mechanisms in varying configurations, pocket watch classics (Calibers 6497 and 98), and manually wound calibers of days gone by (Calibers 1727 and 7001). This company truly offers everything that a manufacturer's heart could desire—not to mention the sheer variety of quartz technology from inexpensive three-hand mechanisms to highly complicated multifunctional movements and futuristic Etaquartz featuring autonomous energy creation using a rotor and generator.

The almost stereotypical accusation of ETA being "mass goods" is not justified, however, for it is a real art to manufacture filigreed micromechanical technology in consistently high quality, illustrated by the long lead times needed to develop new calibers. This is certainly one of the reasons why there have been very few movement factories in Europe that can compete with ETA, or that would want to. Since the success of Swatch—a pure ETA product—millions of Swiss francs have been invested in new development and manufacturing technologies. ETA today owns more than twenty production locales in Switzerland, France, Germany, Malaysia, and Thailand.

The world of movements is poised on the brink of a new dawn, however. In 2002, ETA's management announced it would discontinue providing half-completed component kits for reassembly and/ or embellishment to specialized workshops, and from 2010 only offer completely assembled and finished movements for sale. ETA is already somewhat of a competitor to independent reassemblers such as Soprod, Sellita, La Joux-Perret, Dubois Dépraz, and others thanks to its diversification of available calibers, which has led the rest to counter by creating their own base movements.

Caliber A07.111 Valgranges

Mechanical with automatic winding, ball bearing rotor, stop-seconds, power reserve 42 hours
Functions: hours, minutes, sweep seconds; quick-set date window at 3 o'clock
Diameter: 36.6 mm (16 3/4''')
Height: 7.9 mm
Jewels: 24
Frequency: 28,800 vph
Index system: Etachron with index correction
Related calibers: A07.161 (power reserve display)

Caliber A07.171 Valgranges

Mechanical with automatic winding, ball bearing rotor, stop-seconds, power reserve 42 hours
Functions: hours, minutes, sweep seconds; separately settable 24-hour hand (second time zone); quick-set date window at 3 o'clock
Diameter: 36.6 mm (16 3/4''')
Height: 7.9 mm
Jewels: 24
Frequency: 28,800 vph
Index system: Etachron with index correction

Caliber A07.211 Valgranges

Mechanical with automatic winding, ball bearing rotor, stop-seconds, power reserve 42 hours
Functions: hours, minutes, subsidiary seconds at 9 o'clock; chronograph (30-minute counter at 12 o'clock, 12-hour counter at 6 o'clock, sweep chronograph seconds); quick-set day and date window
Diameter: 36.6 mm (16 3/4''')
Height: 7.9 mm
Jewels: 25
Frequency: 28,800 vph
Index system: Etachron with index correction

Caliber 2660

Mechanical with manual winding, power reserve 42 hours

Functions: hours, minutes, sweep seconds
Diameter: 17.2 mm (7 3/4''')
Height: 3.5 mm
Jewels: 17
Frequency: 28,800 vph
Fine adjustment system: Etachron

Caliber 1727

Mechanical with manual winding, power reserve 50 hours

Functions: hours, minutes, subsidiary seconds at 6 o'clock
Diameter: 19.4 mm
Height: 3.5 mm
Jewels: 19
Frequency: 21,600 vph
Fine adjustment system: Etachron
Remarks: based on design of AS 1727

Caliber 7001

Mechanical with manual winding, ultra-flat, power reserve 42 hours

Functions: hours, minutes, subsidiary seconds at 6 o'clock
Diameter: 23.3 mm (10 1/2''')
Height: 2.5 mm
Jewels: 17
Frequency: 21,600 vph

Caliber 2801-2

Mechanical with manual winding, power reserve 42 hours

Functions: hours, minutes, sweep seconds
Diameter: 25.6 mm (11 1/2''')
Height: 3.35 mm
Jewels: 17
Frequency: 28,800 vph
Fine adjustment system: Etachron
Related caliber: 2804-2 (with date window and quick set)

Caliber 6497

Only a few watch fans know that ETA still manufactures two pure pocket watch movements. Caliber 6497 (the so-called Lépine version with subsidiary seconds extending from the winding stem) and Caliber 6498 (the so-called hunter with subsidiary seconds at a right angle to the winding stem) are available in two qualities: as 6497-1 and 6498-1 (rather sober, undecorated version); and 6497-2 and 6498-2 (with off-center striped decoration on bridges and cocks as well as beveled and striped crown and ratchet wheels). The photograph shows Lépine Caliber 6497-2.

Caliber 6498

Mechanical with manual winding, power reserve 38 hours

Functions: hours, minutes, subsidiary seconds
Diameter: 36.6 mm (16 3/4''')
Height: 4.5 mm
Jewels: 17
Frequency: 21,600 vph
Fine adjustment system: ETACHRON with index
Remarks: the illustration shows a finely decorated hunter version like Nuremberg-based watchmaker Thomas Ninchritz uses

Caliber 2671

Mechanical with automatic winding, ball bearing rotor, stop-seconds, power reserve 38 hours

Functions: hours, minutes, sweep seconds; quick-set date window at 3 o'clock

Diameter: 17.2 mm (7 3/4''')

Height: 4.8 mm

Jewels: 25

Frequency: 28,800 vph

Fine adjustment system: Etachron with index

Related caliber: 2678 (additional day window at 3 o'clock, height 5.35 mm)

Caliber 2681 (dial side)

Mechanical with automatic winding, ball bearing rotor, stop-seconds, power reserve 38 hours

Functions: hours, minutes, sweep seconds; quick-set date and day window at 3 o'clock

Diameter: 19.4 mm (8 3/4''')

Height: 4.8 mm

Jewels: 25

Frequency: 28,800 vph

Fine adjustment system: Etachron with index

Related caliber: 2685 (sweep date hand and moon phase 6 o'clock)

Caliber 2000

Mechanical with automatic winding, ball bearing rotor, stop-seconds, power reserve 40 hours

Functions: hours, minutes, sweep seconds; quick-set date window at 3 o'clock

Diameter: 19.4 mm (8 3/4''')

Height: 3.6 mm

Jewels: 20

Frequency: 28,800 vph

Fine adjustment system: Etachron with index

Caliber 2004

Mechanical with automatic winding, ball bearing rotor, stop-seconds, power reserve 40 hours

Functions: hours, minutes, sweep seconds; quick-set date window at 3 o'clock

Diameter: 23.3 mm (10 1/2''')

Height: 3.6 mm

Jewels: 20

Frequency: 28,800 vph

Fine adjustment system: Etachron with index

Caliber 2824-2

Mechanical with automatic winding, ball bearing rotor, stop-seconds, power reserve 38 hours

Functions: hours, minutes, sweep seconds; quick-set date window at 3 o'clock

Diameter: 25.6 mm (11 1/2''')

Height: 4.6 mm

Jewels: 25

Frequency: 28,800 vph

Fine adjustment system: Etachron with index

Related calibers: 2836-2 (additional day window at 3 o'clock, height 5.05 mm); 2826-2 (with large date, height 6.2 mm)

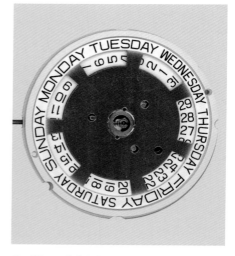

Caliber 2834-2 (dial side)

Mechanical with automatic winding, ball bearing rotor, stop-seconds, power reserve 38 hours

Functions: hours, minutes, sweep seconds; quick-set date window at 3 o'clock and day

Diameter: 29 mm (13''')

Height: 5.05 mm

Jewels: 25

Frequency: 28,800 vph

Fine adjustment system: Etachron with index

Caliber 2891-A9

Mechanical with automatic winding (base caliber ETA 2892-A2), ball bearing rotor, stop-seconds, power reserve 42 hours
Functions: hours, minutes, sweep seconds; perpetual calendar (hand displays for date, day, and month), moon phase disk, leap year indication
Diameter: 25.6 mm (11 1/2''')
Height: 5.2 mm
Jewels: 21
Frequency: 28,800 vph
Fine adjustment system: Etachron with index
Related calibers: 2890-A9 (without second hand and stop-seconds)

Caliber 2892-A2

Mechanical with automatic winding, ball bearing rotor, stop-seconds, power reserve 42 hours
Functions: hours, minutes, sweep seconds; quick-set date window at 3 o'clock
Diameter: 25.6 mm (11 1/2''')
Height: 3.6 mm
Jewels: 21
Frequency: 28,800 vph
Fine adjustment system: Etachron with index

Caliber 2893-1

Mechanical with automatic winding, ball bearing rotor, stop-seconds, power reserve 42 hours
Functions: hours, minutes, sweep seconds; quick-set date window at 3 o'clock; world time display via central disk
Diameter: 25.6 mm (11 1/2''')
Height: 4.1 mm
Jewels: 21
Frequency: 28,800 vph
Fine adjustment system: Etachron with index
Related calibers: 2893-2 (24-hour hand; second time zone instead of world time disk); 2893-3 (only world time disk without date window)

Caliber 2895-1

Mechanical with automatic winding, ball bearing rotor, stop-seconds, power reserve 42 hours
Functions: hours, minutes, subsidiary seconds at 6 o'clock; quick-set date window at 3 o'clock; world time display via central disk
Diameter: 25.6 mm (11 1/2''')
Height: 4.35 mm
Jewels: 30
Frequency: 28,800 vph
Fine adjustment system: Etachron with index

Caliber 2896 (dial side)

Mechanical with automatic winding, ball bearing rotor, stop-seconds, power reserve 42 hours
Functions: hours, minutes, sweep seconds; power reserve display at 3 o'clock
Diameter: 25.6 mm (11 1/2''')
Height: 4.85 mm
Jewels: 21
Frequency: 28,800 vph
Fine adjustment system: Etachron with index

Caliber 2897

Mechanical with automatic winding, ball bearing rotor, stop-seconds, power reserve 42 hours
Functions: hours, minutes, sweep seconds; power reserve display at 7 o'clock
Diameter: 25.6 mm (11 1/2''')
Height: 4.85 mm
Jewels: 21
Frequency: 28,800 vph
Fine adjustment system: Etachron with index

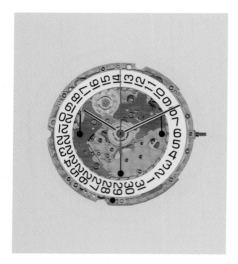

Caliber 2094

Mechanical with automatic winding, ball bearing rotor, stop-seconds, power reserve 40 hours
Functions: hours, minutes, subsidiary seconds at 9 o'clock; chronograph (30-minute counter at 3 o'clock, 12-hour counter at 6 o'clock, sweep chronograph seconds); date window at 3 o'clock
Diameter: 23.3 mm (10 1/2''')
Height: 5.5 mm
Jewels: 33
Frequency: 28,800 vph
Fine adjustment system: Etachron with index

Caliber 2894-2

Mechanical with automatic winding, ball bearing rotor, stop-seconds, power reserve 42 hours
Functions: hours, minutes, subsidiary seconds at 3 o'clock; chronograph (30-minute counter at 9 o'clock, 12-hour counter at 6 o'clock, sweep chronograph seconds); quick-set date window at 4 o'clock
Diameter: 28.6 mm (12 1/2''')
Height: 6.1 mm
Jewels: 37
Frequency: 28,800 vph
Fine adjustment system: Etachron with index
Related caliber: 2894 S2 (skeletonized)

Caliber 7750

Mechanical with automatic winding, ball bearing rotor, stop-seconds, power reserve 42 hours
Functions: hours, minutes, subsidiary seconds at 9 o'clock; chronograph (30-minute counter at 12 o'clock, 12-hour counter at 6 o'clock, sweep chronograph seconds); quick-set date and day window at 3 o'clock
Diameter: 30 mm (13 1/4''')
Height: 7.9 mm
Jewels: 25
Frequency: 28,800 vph
Fine adjustment system: Etachron with index
Related caliber: 7753 (tricompax arrangement of counters)

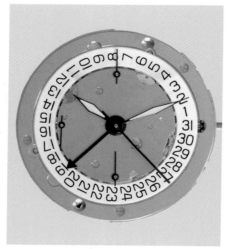

Caliber 7751 (dial side)

Based on chronograph Caliber 7750, Caliber 7751 differs in having 24-hour hand, moon phase indication, sweep date hand, and windows for day and month placed prominently below the 12. All calendar functions, including moon phase, can be quick set.

Caliber 7754 (dial side)

Mechanical with automatic winding, ball bearing rotor, stop-seconds, power reserve 42 hours
Functions: hours, minutes, subsidiary seconds at 9 o'clock; chronograph (30-minute counter at 12 o'clock, 12-hour counter at 6 o'clock, sweep chronograph seconds); quick-set date window at 3 o'clock; settable sweep 24-hour hand (second time zone)
Diameter: 30 mm (13 1/4''')
Height: 7.9 mm
Jewels: 25
Frequency: 28,800 vph
Fine adjustment system: Etachron with index

Caliber 7765

Mechanical with manual winding, stop-seconds, power reserve 42 hours
Functions: hours, minutes, subsidiary seconds at 9 o'clock; chronograph (30-minute counter at 12 o'clock, sweep chronograph seconds); quick-set date window at 3 o'clock; settable sweep 24-hour hand (second time zone)
Diameter: 30 mm (13 1/4''')
Height: 6.35 mm
Jewels: 17
Frequency: 28,800 vph
Fine adjustment system: Etachron with index
Related caliber: 7760 (with additional 12-hour counter at 6 o'clock and day window at 3)

[P R I M E D]

Mk II FULCRUM

In our continuing pursuit of perfection we are pleased
to introduce the new Mk II Fulcrum. The successor to
the Mk II LRRP, the Fulcrum features a new case with
vintage-styled high-domed sapphire crystal, our new
Lume-brik dial markers, and antimagnetic shielding
(80,000 A/m). Each timepiece is driven by a high-grade
Swiss Made automatic movement and hand assembled
and tested in the USA.

Sellita

Sellita, founded in 1950 by Pierre Grandjean in La Chaux-de-Fonds, is one of the biggest reassemblers and embellishers in the mechanical watch industry. On average, Sellita embellishes and finishes about one million automatic and hand-wound movements annually—a figure that represents about 25 percent of Switzerland's mechanical movement production according to Miguel García, Sellita's president.

Reassembly can be defined as the assembly and regulation of components to make a functioning movement. This is the type of work that ETA loved to give to outside companies back in the day in order to concentrate on manufacturing complete quartz movements and individual components for them.

Reassembly workshops like Sellita refine and embellish components purchased from ETA according to their customers' wishes and can even successfully fulfill smaller orders made by the company's estimated 350 clients.

When ETA announced that it would only sell *ébauches* to companies outside the Swatch Group until the end of 2010, García, who has owned Sellita since 2003, reacted immediately, deciding that his company should develop its own products.

García planned and implemented a new line of movements based

on the dimensions of the most popular ETA calibers, whose patents had expired. Having expanded within a new factory on the outskirts of La Chaux-de-Fonds with 3,500 square meters of space, Sellita offers a number of movements—such as SW 200, which corresponds in all of its important dimensions to ETA Caliber 2824, and Caliber SW 300, equivalent to ETA Caliber 2892. Another expansion project began as a joint venture with Mühle Glashütte: Gurofa in Glashütte currently makes some components for Calibers SW 220 and 240.

Caliber SW 200

Mechanical lever movement with automatic winding, ball bearing rotor, stop-seconds, power reserve 38 hours

Functions: hours, minutes, sweep seconds, date window with quick-set function

Diameter: 25.6 mm (11 1/2'''); **Height:** 4.60 mm

Jewels: 26; **Frequency:** 28,800 vph

Fine adjustment system: eccentric screw

Balance: nickel-plated for standard movement, glucydur on request

Balance spring: Nivaflex II for standard movements, Nivaflex on request

Shock protection: Novodiac

Remarks: base plate and rotor with perlage

Caliber SW 220

Mechanical lever movement with automatic winding, ball bearing rotor, stop-seconds, power reserve 38 hours

Functions: hours, minutes, sweep seconds, day/date window with quick-set function

Diameter: 25.6 mm (11 1/2'''); **Height:** 5.05 mm

Jewels: 26; **Frequency:** 28,800 vph

Fine adjustment system: eccentric screw

Balance: nickel-plated for standard movement, glucydur on request

Balance spring: Nivaflex II for standard movements, Nivaflex on request

Shock protection: Novodiac

Remarks: base plate and rotor with perlage

Caliber SW 300

Mechanical lever movement with automatic winding, ball bearing rotor, stop-seconds, power reserve 42 hours

Functions: hours, minutes, sweep seconds, date window with quick-set function

Diameter: 25.6 mm (11 1/2'''); **Height:** 3.60 mm

Jewels: 25; **Frequency:** 28,800 vph

Fine adjustment system: eccentric screw

Balance: nickel-plated for standard movement, glucydur on request

Balance spring: Nivaflex II for standard movements, Nivaflex on request

Shock protection: Novodiac

Soprod

Soprod, at home in Reussilles, Switzerland, has made a name for itself in the era of the mechanical renaissance by reassembling mechanical movements from ETA *ebauches*. Now the company also manufactures interesting display and function modules that can be added to a standard ETA caliber. Power reserve displays, dial train modifications for subsidiary seconds and regulators, calendar modules, and many other variations have given numerous small watch brands the possibility of adding value to their collections with somewhat more exclusive dials, thus setting themselves apart from other manufacturers.

ETA's announcement of no longer offering individual components or *ébauche* kits for reassembly after 2010 has thus hit Soprod especially hard.

In 2005, this company was purchased by a group of Swiss investors —and so came into direct contact with SFT (quartz movements) and Indtec (micromechanics and component production) in Sion, which also belonged to the same concern and already had automatic and chronograph movements developed to the serial production stage.

The Peace Mark Group, headquartered in Hong Kong, purchased all three companies in 2007 and began adding capacity, especially to the reassembly departments. At the same time, business with universally usable automatic calibers in the popular eleven-and-a-half-line format (such as ETA 2824 and 2892) is slated for expansion.

Surprisingly, at the end of 2008, the Festina Lotus Group, whose president also owns the H5 Group (Perrelet, Le Roy), formerly a minority shareholder, acquired Soprod's entire capital stock. Thus, Festina and the other companies belonging to that group have now also received a new platform base for Swiss-made mechanical watches. Soprod will continue to supply third-party brands.

Caliber A10

Mechanical with automatic winding, stop-seconds, regulated in 4 positions, power reserve 42 hours
Functions: hours, minutes, sweep seconds, date window with quick-set function
Diameter: 25.6 mm (11 1/2''')
Height: 3.60 mm
Jewels: 25
Frequency: 28,800 vph
Fine adjustment system: index system with pinion
Balance spring: flat hairspring
Shock protection: Incabloc
Remarks: base plate available with various fine finishings

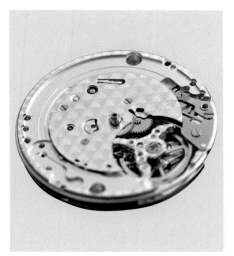

Caliber A10 Visible Balance

Mechanical with automatic winding, stop-seconds, regulated in 4 positions, power reserve 42 hours
Functions: hours, minutes, sweep seconds
Diameter: 25.6 mm (11 1/2''')
Height: 3.60 mm
Jewels: 25
Frequency: 28,800 vph
Fine adjustment system: index system with pinion
Balance spring: flat hairspring
Shock protection: Incabloc
Remarks: cutaway in base plate to make balance visible, base plate available with various fine finishings

Caliber A10 Red Gold

Mechanical with automatic winding, stop-seconds, regulated in 4 positions, power reserve 42 hours
Functions: hours, minutes, sweep seconds, date window with quick-set function
Diameter: 25.6 mm (11 1/2''')
Height: 3.60 mm
Jewels: 25
Frequency: 28,800 vph
Fine adjustment system: index system with pinion
Balance spring: flat hairspring
Shock protection: Incabloc
Remarks: red gold, base plate available with perlage, côtes de Genève or côtes circulaire; bridges with côtes de Genève

Concepto

The Concepto Watch Factory, founded in 2006 in La Chaux-de-Fonds, is the successor to the family-run company Jaquet SA, which changed its name to La Joux-Perret a little while ago and then moved to a different location on the other side of the hub of watchmaking. In 2008, Valérien Jaquet, son of the company founder Pierre Jaquet, began systematically building up a modern movement and watch component factory on an empty floor of the building. Today, the Concepto Watch Factory employs eighty people in various departments, such as Development/Prototyping, Decoparts (partial manufacturing using lathes, machining, or wire erosion), Artisia (production of movements and complications in large series), as well as Optimo (escapements).

In addition to the standard family of calibers, the C2000 (based on the Valjoux), and the vintage chronograph movement C7000 (the evolution of the Venus Caliber), the company's product portfolio includes various tourbillon movements (Caliber C8000) and several modules for adding onto ETA movements (Caliber C1000). A brand-new caliber series, the C3000, features a retrograde calendar and seconds, a power reserve indicator, and a chronograph. The C4000 chronograph caliber with automatic winding is currently in pre-series testing.

These movements are designed according to the requirements of about forty customers and at times heavily modified. Complicated movements are assembled entirely, while others are sold as kits for assembly by the watchmakers. Annual production is somewhere between 30,000 and 40,000 units, with additional hundreds of thousands of components made for contract manufacturing.

Caliber 2000

Automatic; column wheel control of chronograph functions; single spring barrel, 48-hour power reserve
Functions: hours, minutes, subsidiary seconds; chronograph; date
Diameter: 30.4 mm; **Height:** 8.4 mm
Jewels: 27
Balance: screw balance
Frequency: 28,800 vph
Balance spring: flat hairspring
Shock protection: Incabloc
Remarks: plate and bridges with perlage or côtes de Genève, polished steel parts and screw heads

Caliber 8000

Manually wound; 1-minute tourbillon; single spring barrel, 72-hour power reserve
Functions: hours, minutes
Diameter: 32.6 mm
Height: 5.7 mm
Jewels: 19
Balance: screw balance
Frequency: 21,600 vph
Balance spring: flat hairspring
Remarks: extensive personalization options for finishing, fittings, and functions

Caliber 8050

Automatic; 1-minute tourbillon; bidirectional off-center winding rotor; single spring barrel, 72-hour power reserve
Functions: hours, minutes
Diameter: 32.6 mm
Height: 7.9 mm
Jewels: 19
Balance: screw balance
Frequency: 21,600 vph
Balance spring: flat hairspring
Remarks: extensive personalization options for finishing, fittings, and functions

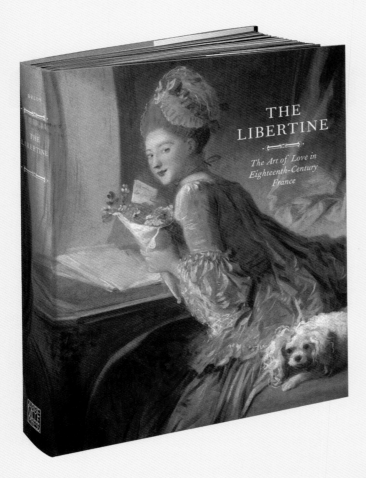

"A delicious fête galante, from a century that equated the feeling of love with an amazing freedom."—*L'Express*

"The game of seduction, the sly glances, the sweet love notes, denuded shoulders, and other pleasures of love are illustrated by works of a refined sensuality by Watteau, Boucher, Greuze, and other poets of the fête galante."—*Le Figaro Magazine*

"The eighteenth century seems to flirt everywhere: in salons, boudoirs, forests; on screens, earthenware, and fans; and the bodies are posed at the reader's disposal. Delectable."—*Le Monde*

"This work is a masterpiece."—*Point De Vue*

The Libertine
The Art of Love in Eighteenth-Century France

A lavishly presented tasting menu of excerpts from eighteenth-century libertine literature, expertly paired with delectable period artworks.

This sumptuous volume re-creates the milieu of the libertine in all its lively decadence, bringing together more than eighty brief selections from eighteenth-century French literature, grouped into eight broad themes—including tales of seduction, fantasies of exotic lands, and the discoveries of youth—and introduced by an eminent French scholar.

Edited by Michel Delon
Foreword by Marilyn Yalom
400 full-color illustrations
496 pages · 9⅝ × 12¼ in.
Cloth · $150.00
ISBN 978-0-7892-1147-7

Published by ABBEVILLE PRESS
137 Varick Street, New York, NY 10013
1-800-ARTBOOK (in U.S. only)
Also available wherever fine books are sold
Visit us at www.abbeville.com

Watch Your Watch

Changing dates can cause trouble.

Mechanical watches are not only by and large more expensive and complex than quartzes, they are also a little high-maintenance, as it were. The mechanism within does need servicing occasionally—perhaps a touch of oil and an adjustment. Worse yet, the complexity of all those wheels and pinions engaged in reproducing the galaxy means that a user will occasionally do something perfectly harmless like wind his or her watch up only to find everything grinding to a halt. Here are some tips for dealing with these mechanical beauties for new watch owners and reminders for the old hands.

1. Date changes

Do not change the date manually (via the crown or pusher) on any mechanical watch—whether manual wind or automatic—when the time indicated on the dial reads between 10 and 2 o'clock. Although some better watches are protected against this horological quirk, most mechanical watches with a date indicator are engaged in the process of automatically changing the date between the hours of 10 p.m. and 2 a.m. Intervening with a forced manual change while the automatic date shift is engaged can damage the movement. Of course, you can make the

adjustment between 10 a.m. and 2 p.m. in most cases—but this is just not a good habit to get into. When in doubt, roll the time past 12 o'clock and look for an automatic date change before you set the time and date. The Ulysse Nardin brand is notable, among a very few others, for in-house mechanical movements immune to this effect.

2. Chronograph use

On a simple chronograph start and stop are almost always the same button. Normally located above the crown, the start/stop actuator can be pressed at will to initiate and end the interval timing. The reset button, normally below the crown, is only used for resetting the chronograph to zero, but only when the chronograph is stopped—never while engaged. Only a "flyback" chronograph allows safe resetting to zero while running. With the chronograph engaged, you simply hit the reset button and all the chronograph indicators (seconds, minutes, and hours) snap back to zero and the chronograph begins to accumulate the interval time once again. In the early days of air travel this was a valuable complication as pilots would reset their chronographs when taking on a new heading—without having to fumble about with a three-step procedure with gloved hands.

Nota bene: Don't actuate or reset your chronograph while your watch is submerged—even if you have one of those that are built for such usage, like Omega, IWC, and a few other brands. Feel free to hit the buttons before submersion and jump in and swim while they run; just don't push anything while in the water.

3. Changing time backward

Don't adjust the time on your watch in a counterclockwise direction—especially if the watch has calendar functions. A few watches can tolerate the abuse, but it's better to avoid the possibility of damage altogether. Change the dates as needed (remembering the 10 and 2 rule above).

4. Shocks

Almost all modern watches are equipped with some level of shock protection. Best practices for the Swiss brands allow for a three-foot fall onto a hard wood surface. But if your watch is running poorly—or even worse has stopped entirely after an impact—do not shake, wind, or bang it again to get it running; take it to an expert for service as you may do even more damage. Sports like tennis, squash, or golf can have a deleterious effect on your watch, including flattening the pivots, overbanking, or even bending or breaking a pivot.

5. Overwinding

Most modern watches are fitted with a mechanism that allows the mainspring to slide inside the barrel—or stops it completely once the spring is fully wound—for protection against overwinding. The best advice here is just don't force

Bovet's barrier to pressing the wrong pusher

Panerai makes sure you think before touching the crown.

it. Over the years a winding crown may start to get "stickier" and more difficult to turn even when unwound. That's a sure sign it is due for service.

6. Jacuzzi temperature

Don't jump into the Jacuzzi—or even a steaming hot shower—with your watch on. Better-built watches with a deeper water-resistance rating typically have no problem with this scenario. However, take a 3 or 5 atm water-resistant watch into the Jacuzzi, and there's a chance the different rates of expansion and contraction of the metals and sapphire or mineral crystals may allow moisture into the case.

7. Screw that crown down (and those pushers)!

Always check and double-check to ensure a watch fitted with a screwed-down crown is closed tightly. Screwed-down pushers for a chronograph—or any other functions—deserve the same attention. This one oversight has cost quite a few owners their watches. If a screwed-down crown is not secured, water will likely get into the case and start oxidizing the metal. In time, the problem can destroy the watch.

8. Magnetism

If your watch is acting up, running faster or slower, it may have become magnetized. This can happen if you leave your timepiece near a computer, cell phone, or some other electronic device. Many service points have a so-called degausser to take care of the problem. A number of brands also make watches with a soft iron core to deflect magnetic fields, though this might not work with the stronger ones.

9. Tribology

Keeping a mechanical timepiece hidden away in a box for extended lengths of time is not the best way to care for it. Even if you don't wear a watch every day, it is a good idea to run your watch at regular intervals to keep its lubricating oils and greases viscous. Think about a can of house paint: Keep it stirred and it stays liquid almost indefinitely; leave it still for too long and a skin develops. On a smaller level the same thing can happen to the lubricants inside a mechanical watch.

10. Service

Most mechanical watches call for a three- to five-year service cycle for cleaning, oiling, and maintenance. Some mechanical watches can run twice that long and have functioned within acceptable parameters, but if you're not going to have your watch serviced at regular intervals, you do take the chance of having timing issues. Always have your watch serviced by qualified watchmaker (see box), not at the kiosk in the local mall. The best you can expect there is a quick battery change.

Do it yourself at your own risk.

Gary Girdvainis is the founder of Isochron Media Llc., publishers of WristWatch *and* AboutTime *magazines*

Glossary

ANNUAL CALENDAR

The automatic allowances for the different lengths of each month of a year in the calendar module of a watch. This type of watch usually shows the month and date, and sometimes the day of the week (like this one by Patek Philippe) and the phases of the moon.

ANTIMAGNETIC

Magnetic fields found in common everyday places affect mechanical movements, hence the use of anti- or non-magnetic components in the movement. Some companies encase movements in antimagnetic cores such as Sinn's Model 756, the Duograph, shown here.

ANTIREFLECTION

A film created by steaming the crystal to eliminate light reflection and improve legibility. Antireflection functions best when applied to both sides of the crystal, but because it scratches, some manufacturers prefer to have it only on the interior of the crystal. It is mainly used on synthetic sapphire crystals. Dubey & Schaldenbrand applies antireflection on both sides for all of the company's wristwatches such as this Aquadyn model.

AUTOMATIC WINDING

A rotating weight set into motion by moving the wrist winds the spring barrel via the gear train of a mechanical watch movement. Automatic winding was invented during the pocket watch era in 1770, but the breakthrough automatic winding movement via rotor began with the ball bearing Eterna-Matic in the late 1940s. Today we speak of unidirectional winding and bidirectionally winding rotors, depending on the type of gear train used. Shown is IWC's automatic Caliber 50611.

BALANCE

The beating heart of a mechanical watch movement is the balance. Fed by the energy of the mainspring, a tirelessly oscillating little wheel, just a few millimeters in diameter and possessing a spiral-shaped balance spring, sets the rhythm for the escape wheel and pallets with its vibration frequency. Today the balance is usually made of one piece of antimagnetic glucydur, an alloy that expands very little when exposed to heat.

BAR OR COCK

A metal plate fastened to the base plate at one point, leaving room for a gear wheel or pinion. The balance is usually attached to a bar called the balance cock. Glashütte tradition dictates that the balance cock be decoratively engraved by hand like this one by Glashütte Original.

BEVELING

To uniformly file down the sharp edges of a plate, bridge, or bar and give it a high polish. The process is also called *anglage*. Edges are usually beveled at a 45° angle. As the picture shows, this is painstaking work that needs the skilled hands and eyes of an experienced watchmaker or *angleur*.

BRIDGE

A metal plate fastened to the base plate at two points leaving room for a gear wheel or pinion. This vintage Favre-Leuba movement illustrates the point with three individual bridges.

CALIBER

A term, similar to type or model, that refers to different watch movements. Pictured here is Heuer's Caliber 11, the legendary automatic chronograph caliber from 1969. This movement was a coproduction jointly researched and developed for four years by Heuer-Leonidas, Breitling, and Hamilton-Büren. Each company gave the movement a different name after serial production began.

CERAMIC

An inorganic, nonmetallic material formed by the action of heat and practically unscratchable. Pioneered by Rado, ceramic is a high-tech material generally made from aluminum and zirconia oxide. Today, it is used generally for cases and bezels and now comes in many colors.

CARBON FIBER

A very light, tough composite material, carbon fiber is composed of filaments comprised of several thousand seven-micron carbon fibers held together by resin. The arrangement of the filaments determines the quality of a component, making each unique. Carbon fiber is currently being used for dials, cases, and even movement components.

CHAMPLEVÉ

A dial decoration technique, whereby the metal is engraved, filled with enamel, and baked as in this cockatoo on a Cartier Tortue, enhanced with mother-of-pearl slivers.

CHRONOGRAPH

From the Greek *chronos* (time) and *graphein* (to write). Originally a chronograph literally wrote, inscribing the time elapsed on a piece of paper with the help of a pencil attached kind of hand. Today this term is used for watches that show not only the time of day, but also certain time intervals via independent hands that may be started or stopped at will. Stopwatches differ from chronographs because they do not show the time of day. This exploded illustration shows the complexity of a Breitling chronograph.

CHRONOMETER

Literally, "measurer of time." As the term is used today, a chronometer denotes an especially accurate watch (one with a deviation of no more than 5 seconds a day for mechanical movements). Chronometers are usually supplied with an official certificate from an independent testing office such as the COSC. The largest producer of chronometers in 2008 was Rolex with 769,850 officially certified movements. Chopard came in sixth with more than 22,000 certified L.U.C. mechanisms like the 4.96 in the Pro One model shown here.

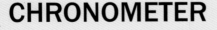

COLUMN WHEEL

The component used to control chronograph functions within a true chronograph movement. The presence of a column wheel indicates that the chronograph is fully integrated into the movement. In the modern era, modules are generally used that are attached to a base caliber movement. This particular column wheel is made of blued steel.

CONSTANT FORCE MECHANISM

Sometimes called a constant force escapement, it isn't really: in most cases this mechanism is "simply" an initial tension spring. It is also known in English by part of its French name, the *remontoir*, which actually means "winding mechanism." This mechanism regulates and portions the energy that is passed on through the escapement, making the rate as even and precise as possible. Shown here is the constant force escapement from A. Lange & Söhne's Lange 31—a mechanism that gets as close to its name as possible.

COSC

The Contrôle Officiel Suisse de Chronomètrage, the official Swiss testing office for chronometers. The COSC is the world's largest issuer of so-called chronometer certificates, which are only otherwise given out individually by certain observatories (such as the one in Neuchâtel, Switzerland). For a fee, the COSC tests the rate of movements that have been adjusted by watchmakers. These are usually mechanical movements, but the office also tests some high-precision quartz movements. Those that meet the specifications for being a chronometer are awarded an official certificate as shown here.

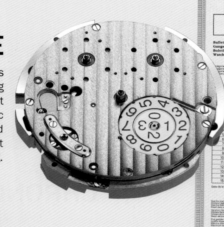

CÔTES DE GENÈVE

Also called *vagues de Genève* and Geneva stripes. This is a traditional Swiss surface decoration comprising an even pattern of parallel stripes, applied to flat movement components with a quickly rotating plastic or wooden peg. Glashütte watchmakers have devised their own version of *côtes de Genève* that is applied at a slightly different angle called Glashütte ribbing.

CROWN

The crown is used to wind and set a watch. A few simple turns of the crown will get an automatic movement started, while a manually wound watch is completely wound by the crown. The crown is also used for the setting of various functions, almost always including at least the hours, minutes, seconds, and date. A screwed-down crown like the one on the TAG Heuer Aquagraph pictured here can be tightened to prevent water entering the case or any mishaps while performing extreme sports such as diving.

EQUATION OF TIME

The mean time that we use to keep track of the passing of the day (24 hours evenly divided into minutes and seconds) is not equal to true solar time. The equation of time is a complication devised to show the difference between the mean time shown on one's wristwatch and the time the sun dictates. The Équation Marchante by Blancpain very legibly indicates this difference via the golden sun-tipped hand that also rotates around the dial in a manner known to watch connoisseurs as *marchant*. Other wristwatch models such as the Boreas by Martin Braun display the difference on an extra scale on the dial.

ESCAPEMENT

The combination of the balance, balance spring, pallets, and escape wheel, a subgroup which divides the impulses coming from the spring barrel into small, accurately portioned doses. It guarantees that the gear train runs smoothly and efficiently. The pictured escapement is one newly invented by Parmigiani containing pallet stones of varying color, though they are generally red synthetic rubies. Here one of them is a colorless sapphire or corundum, the same geological material that ruby is made of.

FLINQUÉ

A dial decoration in which a guilloché design is given a coat of enamel, softening the pattern and creating special effects, as shown here on a unique Bovet.

FLYBACK CHRONOGRAPH

A chronograph with a special dial train switch that makes the immediate reuse of the chronograph movement possible after resetting the hands. It was developed for special timekeeping duties such as those found in aviation, which require the measurement of time intervals in quick succession. A flyback may also be called a *retour en vol*. An elegant example of this type of chronograph is Corum's Classical Flyback Large Date shown here.

GEAR TRAIN

A mechanical watch's gear train transmits energy from the mainspring to the escapement. The gear train comprises the minute wheel, the third wheel, the fourth wheel, and the escape wheel.

GLUCYDUR

Glucydur is a functional alloy of copper, beryllium, and iron that has been used to make balances in watches since the 1930s. Its hardness and stability allow watchmakers to use balances that were poised at the factory and no longer required adjustment screws.

GUILLOCHÉ

A surface decoration usually applied to the dial and the rotor using a grooving tool with a sharp tip, such as a rose engine, to cut an even pattern onto a level surface. The exact adjustment of the tool for each new path is controlled by a device similar to a pantograph, and the movement of the tool can be controlled either manually or mechanically. Real *guillochis* (the correct term used by a master of guilloché) are very intricate and expensive to produce, which is why most dials decorated in this fashion are produced by stamping machines. Breguet is one of the very few companies to use real guilloché on every one of its dials.

INDEX

A regulating mechanism found on the balance cock and used by the watchmaker to adjust the movement's rate. The index changes the effective length of the balance spring, thus making it move more quickly or slowly. This is the standard index found on an ETA Valjoux 7750.

JEWEL

To minimize friction, the hardened steel tips of a movement's rotating gear wheels (called pinions) are lodged in synthetic rubies (fashioned as polished stones with a hole) and lubricated with a very thin layer of special oil. These synthetic rubies are produced in exactly the same way as sapphire crystal using the same material. During the pocket watch era, real rubies with hand-drilled holes were still used, but because of the high costs involved, they were only used in movements with especially quickly rotating gears. The jewel shown here on a bridge from A. Lange & Söhne's Double Split is additionally embedded in a gold chaton secured with three blued screws.

LIGA

The word LIGA is actually a German acronym that stands for lithography (*Lithografie*), electroplating (*Galvanisierung*), and plastic molding (*Abformung*). It is a lithographic process exposed by UV or X-ray light that literally "grows" perfect micro components made of nickel, nickel-phosphorus, or 23.5-karat gold atom by atom in a plating bath. The components need no finishing or trimming after manufacture.

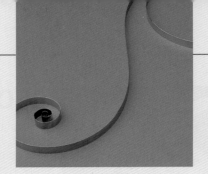

LUMINOUS SUBSTANCE

Tritium paint is a slightly radioactive substance that replaced radium as luminous coating for hands, numerals, and hour markers on watch dials. Watches bearing tritium must be marked as such, with the letter T on the dial near 6 o'clock. It has now for the most part been replaced by nonradioactive materials such as Superluminova. Traser technology (as seen on these Ball timepieces) uses tritium gas enclosed in tiny silicate glass tubes coated on the inside with a phosphorescing substance. The luminescence is constant and will hold around twenty-five years.

MAINSPRING

The mainspring, located in the spring barrel, stores energy when tensioned and passes it on to the escapement via the gear train as the tension relaxes. Today, mainsprings are generally made of Nivaflex, an alloy invented by Swiss engineer Max Straumann at the beginning of the 1950s. This alloy basically comprises iron, nickel, chrome, cobalt, and beryllium.

MINUTE REPEATER

A striking mechanism with hammers and gongs for acoustically signaling the hours, quarter hours, and minutes elapsed since noon or midnight. The wearer pushes a slide, which winds the spring. Normally a repeater uses two different gongs to signal hours (low tone), quarter hours (high and low tones in succession), and minutes (high tone). Some watches have three gongs, called a carillon. The Chronoswiss Répétition à Quarts is a prominent repeating introduction of recent years.

PERPETUAL CALENDAR

The calendar module for this type of timepiece automatically makes allowances for the different lengths of each month as well as leap years until the next secular year, which will occur in 2100. A perpetual calendar usually shows the date, month, and four-year cycle, and may show the day of the week and moon phase as well, as does this one introduced by George J von Burg at Baselworld 2005. Perpetual calendars need much skill to complete.

PERLAGE

Surface decoration comprising an even pattern of partially overlapping dots, applied with a quickly rotating plastic or wooden peg. (Here on the plates of Frédérique Constant's *manufacture* Caliber FC 910-1.

PLATE

A metal platform having several tiers for the gear train. The base plate of a movement usually incorporates the dial and carries the bearings for the primary pinions of the "first floor" of a gear train. The gear wheels are made complete by tightly fitting screwed-in bridges and bars on the back side of the plate. A specialty of the so-called Glashütte school, as opposed to the Swiss school, is the reverse completion of a movement not via different bridges and bars, but rather with a three-quarter plate. Glashütte Original's Caliber 65 (shown) displays a beautifully decorated three-quarter plate.

POWER RESERVE DISPLAY

A mechanical watch contains only a certain amount of power reserve. A fully wound modern automatic watch usually possesses between 36 and 42 hours of energy before it needs to be wound again. The power reserve display keeps the wearer informed about how much energy his or her watch still has in reserve, a function that is especially practical on manually wound watches with several days of possible reserve. The Nomos Tangente Power Reserve pictured here represents an especially creative way to illustrate the state of the mainspring's tension. On some German watches the power reserve is also displayed with the words "auf" and "ab."

PULSOMETER

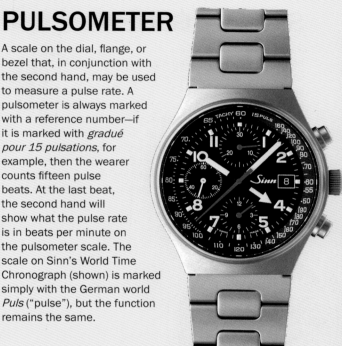

A scale on the dial, flange, or bezel that, in conjunction with the second hand, may be used to measure a pulse rate. A pulsometer is always marked with a reference number—if it is marked with *gradué pour 15 pulsations*, for example, then the wearer counts fifteen pulse beats. At the last beat, the second hand will show what the pulse rate is in beats per minute on the pulsometer scale. The scale on Sinn's World Time Chronograph (shown) is marked simply with the German world *Puls* ("pulse"), but the function remains the same.

QUALITÉ FLEURIER

This certification of quality was established by Chopard, Parmigiani Fleurier, Vaucher, and Bovet Fleurier in 2004. Watches bearing the seal must fulfill five criteria, including COSC certification, passing several tests for robustness and precision, top-notch finishing, and being 100 percent Swiss made (except for the raw materials). The seal appears here on the dial of the Parmigiani Fleurier Tonda 39.

RETROGRADE DISPLAY

A retrograde display shows the time linearly instead of circularly. The hand continues along an arc until it reaches the end of its scale, at which precise moment it jumps back to the beginning instantaneously. This Nienaber model not only shows the minutes in retrograde form, it is also a regulator display.

ROTOR

The rotor is the component that keeps an automatic watch wound. The kinetic motion of this part, which contains a heavy metal weight around its outer edge, winds the mainspring. It can either wind unilaterally or bilaterally (to one or both sides) depending on the caliber. The rotor from this Temption timepiece belongs to an ETA Valjoux 7750.

SCREW BALANCE

Before the invention of the perfectly weighted balance using a smooth ring, balances were fitted with weighted screws to get the exact impetus desired. Today a screw balance is a subtle sign of quality in a movement due to its costly construction and assembly utilizing minuscule weighted screws.

SAPPHIRE CRYSTAL

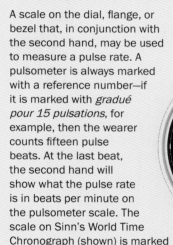

Synthetic sapphire crystal is known to gemologists as aluminum oxide (Al_2O_3) or corundum. It can be colorless (corundum), red (ruby), blue (sapphire), or green (emerald). It is virtually scratchproof; only a diamond is harder. The innovative Royal Blue Tourbillon by Ulysse Nardin pictured here not only features sapphire crystals on the front and back of the watch, but also actual plates made of both colorless and blue corundum within the movement.

SEAL OF GENEVA

Since 1886 the official seal of this canton has been awarded to Genevan watch *manufactures* who must follow a defined set of high-quality criteria that include the following: polished jewel bed drillings, jewels with olive drillings, polished winding wheels, quality balances and balance springs, steel levers and springs with beveling of 45 degrees and *côtes de Genève* decoration, and polished stems and pinions. The list was updated in 2012 to include the entire watch and newer components. Testing is done on the finished piece. The Seal consists of two, one on the movement, one on the case. The pictured seal was awarded to Vacheron Constantin, a traditional Genevan *manufacture*.

SILICIUM/SILICON

Silicon is an element relatively new to mechanical watches. It is currently being used in the manufacture of precision escapements. Ulysse Nardin's Freak has lubrication-free silicon wheels, and Breguet has successfully used flat silicon balance springs.

SKELETONIZATION

The technique of cutting a movement's components down to their weight-bearing basic substance. This is generally done by hand in painstaking hours of microscopic work with a mini handheld saw, though machines can skeletonize parts to a certain degree, such as the version of the Valjoux 7750 that was created for Chronoswiss's Opus and Pathos models. This tourbillon created by Christophe Schaffo is additionally—and masterfully—hand-engraved.

SONNERIE

A variety of minute repeater that—like a tower clock—sounds the time not at the will of the wearer, but rather automatically (*en passant*) every hour (*petite sonnerie*) or quarter hour (*grande sonnerie*). Gérald Genta designed the most complicated sonnerie back in the early nineties. Shown is a recent model from the front and back.

SPLIT-SECONDS CHRONOGRAPH

Also known in the watch industry by its French name, the *rattrapante* (exploded view at left). A watch with two second hands, one of which can be blocked with a special dial train lever to indicate an intermediate time while the other continues to run. When released, the split-seconds hand jumps ahead to the position of the other second hand. The PTC by Porsche Design illustrates this nicely.

SPRING BARREL

The spring barrel contains the mainspring. It turns freely on an arbor, pulled along by the toothed wheel generally doubling as its lid. This wheel interacts with the first pinion of the movement's gear train. Some movements contain two or more spring barrels for added power reserve.

SWAN-NECK FINE ADJUSTMENT

A regulating instrument used by the watchmaker to adjust the movement's rate in place of an index. The swan neck is especially prevalent in fine Swiss and Glashütte watchmaking (here Lang & Heyne's Moritz model). Mühle Glashütte has varied the theme with its woodpecker's neck.

TACHYMETER

A scale on the dial, flange, or bezel of a chronograph that, in conjunction with the second hand, gives the speed of a moving object. A tachymeter takes a value determined in less than a minute and converts it into miles or kilometers per hour. For example, a wearer could measure the time it takes a car to pass between two mile markers on the highway. When the car passes the marker, the second hand will be pointing to the car's speed in miles per hour on the tachymetric scale.

TOURBILLON

A technical device invented by Abraham-Louis Breguet in 1801 to compensate for the influence of gravity on the balance of a pocket watch. The entire escapement is mounted on an epicyclic train in a "cage" and rotated completely on its axis over regular periods of time. This superb horological highlight is seen as a sign of technological know-how in the modern era. Harry Winston's Histoire de Tourbillon 4 is a spectacular example.

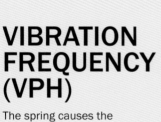

VIBRATION FREQUENCY (VPH)

The spring causes the balance to oscillate at a certain frequency measured in hertz (Hz) or vibrations per hour (vph). Most of today's wristwatches tick at 28,800 vph (4 Hz) or 21,600 vph (3 Hz). Less usual is 18,000 vph (2.5 Hz). Zenith's El Primero was the first serial movement to beat at 36,000 vph (5 Hz), and the Breguet Type XXII runs at 72,000 vph.

WATER RESISTANCE

Water resistance is an important feature of any timepiece and is usually measured in increments of one atmosphere (atm or bar, equal to 10 meters of water pressure) or meters and is often noted on the dial or case back. Watches resistant to 100 meters are best for swimming and snorkeling. Timepieces resistant to 200 meters are good for scuba diving. To deep-sea dive there are various professional timepieces available for use in depths of 200 meters or more. The Hydromax by Bell & Ross (shown) is water-resistant to a record 11,000 meters.

Copyright © 2013 HEEL Verlag GmbH, Königswinter, Germany

English-language translation copyright © 2013 Abbeville Press,
137 Varick Street, New York, NY 10013

Editor-in-Chief: Peter Braun
Editor: Marton Radkai
Copy Editor: Ashley Benning
Layout: Muser Medien GmbH
Composition: Paul Aljian

For more information about advertising, please contact:
Gary Girdvainis
Isochron Media, LLC
25 Gay Bower Road, Monroe, CT 06468
Tel. 203-485-6276, garygeorgeg@gmail.com

For more information about book sales, please contact:
Abbeville Press, 137 Varick Street, New York, NY 10013, 1-800-Artbook, or www.abbeville.com.

ISBN 978-0-7892-1148-4

Sixteenth edition
10 9 8 7 6 5 4 3 2 1

Library of Congress Cataloging-in-Publication Data available upon request.

For bulk and premium sales and for text adoption procedures, write to Customer Service Manager,
Abbeville Press, 137 Varick Street, New York, NY 10013 or call 1-800-Artbook.

Visit Abbeville Press online at www.abbeville.com.

ISBN 978-0-7892-1148-4   U.S. $37.50
EAN
9 780789 211484   53750